DREAM CAR

DREAM CAR

Malcolm Bricklin's Fantastic SV1 and the End of Industrial Modernity

DIMITRY ANASTAKIS

UNIVERSITY OF TORONTO PRESS
Toronto Buffalo London

Toronto Buffalo London
utorontopress.com
Printed in the USA

ISBN 978-1-4875-5581-8 (cloth) ISBN 978-1-4875-5585-6 (EPUB)
ISBN 978-1-4875-5582-5 (paper) ISBN 978-1-4875-5583-2 (PDF)

Library and Archives Canada Cataloguing in Publication

Title: Dream car : Malcolm Bricklin's fantastic SV1 and the end of industrial modernity / Dimitry Anastakis.
Names: Anastakis, Dimitry, 1970– author.
Description: Includes bibliographical references and index.
Identifiers: Canadiana (print) 20230573045 | Canadiana (ebook) 2023057307X | ISBN 9781487555818 (cloth) | ISBN 9781487555825 (paper) | ISBN 9781487555856 (EPUB) | ISBN 9781487555832 (PDF)
Subjects: LCSH: Bricklin, Malcolm. | LCSH: Bricklin automobile. | LCSH: Automobile industry and trade – Social aspects. | LCSH: Automobile industry and trade – History – 20th century.
Classification: LCC TL215.B59 A53 2024 | DDC 338.7/629222097151 – dc23

Cover design: EmDash Design
Cover image: Malcom Bricklin posing in front of a Bricklin automobile.
Photo from the cover of *Maclean's* magazine, 17 November 1975.
Courtesy of *Maclean's* magazine.

We wish to acknowledge the land on which the University of Toronto Press operates. This land is the traditional territory of the Wendat, the Anishnaabeg, the Haudenosaunee, the Métis, and the Mississaugas of the Credit First Nation.

This book has been published with the help of a grant from the Federation for the Humanities and Social Sciences, through the Awards to Scholarly Publications Program, using funds provided by the Social Sciences and Humanities Research Council of Canada.

University of Toronto Press acknowledges the financial support of the Government of Canada, the Canada Council for the Arts, and the Ontario Arts Council, an agency of the Government of Ontario, for its publishing activities.

Canada Council for the Arts | Conseil des Arts du Canada

ONTARIO ARTS COUNCIL
CONSEIL DES ARTS DE L'ONTARIO
an Ontario government agency
un organisme du gouvernement de l'Ontario

Funded by the Government of Canada | Financé par le gouvernement du Canada | Canada

Contents

Preface

To start, a few notes about this book.

First, on automobile music.

From the moment Henry Ford's famous Model T, the "Tin Lizzie," appeared in the 1910s and began to reorder society, spread industrial modernity, and reshape global consciousness, the automobile has been the subject or object of thousands of songs, from ditties to ballads, anthems, protests, and laments.[1] There is, effectively and understandably, a car song for virtually every human occasion, situation, or emotion. Car music provides the soundtrack of modernity.

Many of the book's chapters include titles of car songs of the era, songs about the Bricklin car itself, or songs from the funky 2010 musical play based on the Bricklin incident, *The Bricklin: An Automotive Fantasy*. The *Dream Car* playlist can be found, sampled, and enjoyed on YouTube Music: https://bit.ly/49MQusc.

Second, on reading the book.

Dream Car uses a car from the Seventies, the Bricklin Safety Vehicle-1, to explain the evolution of the automobile and its impact across North America's twentieth and twenty-first centuries and on ideas about the future, technology, entrepreneurship, risk, safety, showmanship, politics, sex, gender, business, the state, and the industry's birth, decline, and rebirth. Following the prologue and introduction, the book has a narrative, argumentative, and biographical arc that unfolds chronologically and successively.

But *Dream Car*'s seven chapters have also been structured and written in a way that allows them to be read in any order, determined by whichever theme the reader finds most interesting. In combining the music and the manner in which *Dream Car* is written, the book can be read or listened to as a kind of choose-your-own-adventure story or podcast.

Finally, a note on terminology.

In Bricklin firm documents and press releases, the car was called “the Bricklin Safety Vehicle-1,” “the Bricklin,” and either “SV-1” or “SV1,” the latter of which is used throughout the book for consistency.

Playlist

1. "O' the Bricklin," Charlie Russell, from *Bricklin and Other Sound Investments*, 1975
2. "Born to Run," Bruce Springsteen, from *Born to Run*, 1975
3. "Drive My Car," The Beatles, from *Rubber Soul*, 1965
4. "I'm Changing My Name to Chrysler," Tom Paxton, from *The Paxton Report*, 1980
5. "Cars," Gary Numan, from *Cars*, 1979
6. "High Risk Venture," from *The Bricklin: An Automotive Fantasy* (original cast recording), Allen Cole and Paul Ledoux, 2010
7. "Fame," David Bowie, from *Young Americans*, 1975
8. "The Entertainer," Scott Joplin (1905), from *The Sting* (soundtrack), Marvin Hamlisch, 1973
9. "Little Red Corvette," Prince and the Revolution, from *1999*, 1982
10. "Paradise by the Dashboard Light," Meatloaf, from *Bat Out of Hell*, 1977
11. "Lord, Mr. Ford," Jerry Reed, from *Lord, Mr. Ford*, 1973
12. "Spark Plugs," from *The Bricklin: An Automotive Fantasy* (original cast recording), Allen Cole and Paul Ledoux, 2010
13. "My Hometown," Bruce Springsteen, from *Born in the USA*, 1984
14. "A Hell of a Ride," from *The Bricklin: An Automotive Fantasy* (original cast recording), Allen Cole and Paul Ledoux, 2010
15. "Highway to Hell," AC/DC, from *Highway to Hell*, 1979

Bonus Track 1. "The Time Warp," Susan Sarandon, Barry Bostwick, Richard O'Brien, from *The Rocky Horror Picture Show* (original film soundtrack), 1975
Bonus Track 2. "New York, New York," Frank Sinatra, from *Trilogy: Past Present Future*, 1980
Bonus Track 3. "Fast Car," Tracy Chapman, from *Tracy Chapman*, 1988

PROLOGUE

On Stage, the Four Seasons Restaurant, New York City, 25 June 1974: Malcolm Bricklin, Richard Hatfield, and Their Fantastic Car

***Dream Car* Song 1: "O' the Bricklin," Charlie Russell, 1975**

In 1974, Malcolm Bricklin became famous.

In what was the glorious and notorious apex of an entrepreneurial career that spanned more than half a century, in that year Bricklin gained a type of popular cultural celebrity that could be achieved only in America, and recognition that could be conferred upon him only by America's most important twentieth-century business, the automobile industry. A modern-day "automotive P.T. Barnum," as journalists later dubbed him, Bricklin attained the kind of fame that most people can only imagine and never truly understand, the kind of notoriety that lingers for decades, long after the actual moment of celebrity has passed.[1]

The source of Bricklin's fame was the launch of his car, the Safety Vehicle-1 (SV1) – "the Bricklin," as it came to be known. In debuting his daring, sexy, sporty, but flawed dream car, Bricklin, a consummate salesman, spent a frenzied year gallivanting across North America in a binge of promotion – and self-promotion – that went down in the annals of business history as one of the greatest eruptions of entrepreneurial hubris that the automobile industry had ever seen. Bricklin's gambit was, in retrospect, a spectacularly risky move, given the historically titanic egos that had created America's largest and most important industrial and consumer sector. Moreover, launching a new car and a new car company in the early

1970s – an era of automotive oligopoly and innovational atrophy, one also beset by a host of economic, political, regulatory, technological, and public relations challenges in the auto industry – was not for the faint of heart.

Yet Malcolm Bricklin seemed equal to the task. Young, handsome, charismatic, and confident, Bricklin cemented his place in North America's public consciousness by doing what he knew best: selling himself and selling people on his dream car. In 1974, Bricklin and his SV1 seemed to be everywhere, all at once. There was Malcolm on *The Today Show* or *The Tonight Show* with Johnny Carson, talking about the car. There he was in Las Vegas at a sneak preview of the SV1, hobnobbing with movie star Paul Newman and racing icon Bobby Unser. There he was at his ranch in Arizona, being flown in a helicopter to FasTrack International Raceway near Phoenix for some spins around the track in his car. The SV1's creator was featured in *Time*, *Playboy*, *People*, and just about every other magazine and periodical in between. The business press, especially the automotive press, could not get enough of Bricklin, who was heralded as a swashbuckling throwback to an era of devil-may-care auto entrepreneurs and quickly likened to a latter-day Louis Chevrolet, Walter Chrysler, or Preston Tucker.

The Bricklin car itself, with its sleek profile, futuristic reinforced plastic (fiberglass) body, spectacular gull-wing doors, and unique emphasis on safety, made its own numerous appearances on television, from popular gameshows like *The Price Is Right* and *Let's Make a Deal* to hit sitcoms such as *Chico and the Man*, North America's third-highest rated show in 1974. The car appeared in dozens of magazines and on the covers of auto industry bibles *Car and Driver* and *Road & Track*, heralded as a legitimate competitor to General Motors' iconic Chevrolet Corvette.[2]

It was a bacchanal of automotive promotion, a whirlwind of fame and potential fortune.

And why shouldn't Bricklin and his car be famous? After all, Bricklin, the man, seemed to be a living example of that quintessential mid-twentieth-century American dream: the self-made automotive entrepreneur, pulling himself up by his own bootstraps, a modern-day Henry Ford, re-imagining what the American sports car – the pinnacle of American manufacturing and America's image in the world – could be. On the face of it, cowboy-persona-embracing Bricklin and his car exemplified the entrepreneurial ideals of individual initiative, innovation, and business daring that Ford himself had made into traits that were as American as apple pie.

Inevitably, despite the flurry of excitement generated by the SV1's launch, more than a few doubts were cast Bricklin's way. This was unsurprising, given the enormity of the task. Amazingly, no American had successfully launched a completely new car company and put a vehicle into production since the 1940s.[3] But Bricklin seemed to have all the necessary chutzpa, and his origin story fit the bill. Hadn't he become a millionaire by the age of twenty-five in the mid-1960s by opening a chain of successful hardware stores? Hadn't he had the pioneering and profitable foresight in 1968 to bring the first Subaru cars to America from Japan, just a few years before launching his SV1? Young, stylish, charismatic Bricklin seemed to perfectly fit the idealized mould of a self-made auto mogul on the rise.

Yes, it seemed believable that Malcolm Bricklin and his new car were up to the task of challenging Detroit's Corvettes, Mustangs, Chargers, and Challengers, not to mention the wave of Japanese Datsun 240s or Toyota Celicas that were invading the booming 1970s US sports car market. Moreover, Bricklin was doing it the American way, by following in the footsteps of the great American automotive entrepreneurs, innovators, promoters, and managers who had preceded him. He was building a car company that might be the equal, if not in size but certainly in its structure and ambition, to the Big Three of General Motors (GM), Ford, and Chrysler. At the same time, Bricklin was willing to break dramatically from many of Detroit's long-established practices to achieve his dream. This was no boring Detroit organization man, but a risk-taking, fast-talking, genuine entrepreneur.

Or so it seemed, in 1974.

In June of that year, in the midst of his cross-continental promotional blitz, Bricklin officially launched the SV1, the "World's First Production Safety Vehicle," at a glitzy event at New York's famed Four Seasons restaurant. It was the perfect setting. The Four Seasons was housed on the ground floor of architect Mies van der Rohe's 1958 edifice of modernity, the Seagram Building, a gleaming epitome of American big business, internationalism, and postwar prosperity. It mattered little that the Four Seasons restaurant was by then coming to be seen as somewhat past its prime; Bricklin himself shined brilliantly as the height of early-1970s masculine style, clad in his bell-bottomed "safari suit and open-necked casual shirt revealing a two-strand necklace of Indian beads." Ever the showman, Bricklin made a flashy attempt to imprint the car with a "B" branding iron. The imprinting failed, perhaps a symbolic portending of the car's future.[4]

Standing near Bricklin, watching these theatrical proceedings, was another equally flamboyant promoter of the dream of the SV1, Richard Hatfield, a young Canadian politician, little known in America. "Disco Dick" was the "mod" bachelor premier of New Brunswick, and his government had taken a majority stake in Bricklin's car manufacturing operation, directly supporting the venture with millions of tax dollars, factory buildings, and the province's good name. In backing the Bricklin, Hatfield was taking a tremendous risk that his small, economically stultified province could use the SV1's production to vault itself into a future of automobile-fuelled industrial modernity, one that had shaped and made prosperous the luckiest, smartest, and most technologically innovative regions of North America and the world.

On stage together, basking in the glow of their fantastic car and their shared dream of automotive success and prosperity, it was Bricklin's and, to a lesser degree, Hatfield's defining, shining, moment. That moment would not last, though its meaning, like Malcolm Bricklin's automotive fame, and Richard Hatfield's political legacy, would linger for decades to come.

Figure P.1. Richard Hatfield, Malcolm Bricklin, and their dream car, New York City, June 1974.

INTRODUCTION

Industrial Modernity, Bricklin, and Industrial Postmodernity

***Dream Car* Song 2: "Born to Run," Bruce Springsteen, 1975**

The story of Malcolm Bricklin and his car explains how automobility made and unmade industrial modernity.

The Bricklin – as a fanciful, mostly forgotten curio of automobile lore, a tall tale, a melodrama, a microhistory, a case study, a warning from the past, a prophecy, or however one might wish to look at it – sits, in chronology and meaning, at the breakpoint of a century and a half of automobile modernity, automobility. Automobility, from its beginnings in the late nineteenth century to the early 1970s and the Bricklin's emergence, transformed industrialization into industrial modernity. Then, in the half century that followed and flowed from the Bricklin's 1974 launch and ultimate failure just two years later, automobility was refashioned as industrial postmodernity. The Bricklin, both as an event and an artefact, signalled a passage between these distinctive historical eras and differing economic and social systems; its rise and demise also marked a transitional moment when fundamental aspects of society – technology, entrepreneurship, risk, safety, fame, politics, sex, business, and the state – underwent transformations both profound and subtle.

As a signpost, symbol, and technological talisman of change between these two eras – the industrial modern and the industrial postmodern[1] – the Bricklin SV1 is a most fitting representative of that economic, political, social, and environmental singularity of our time, the gasoline-powered automobile. After all, the car is, arguably, the key animating cause and consequence of how we understand the one and half centuries of North American history from the 1890s to the 2020s: automobile, industrial, modernity – automobility.

Immediately, an incredulous reader will rightfully ask the obvious question: How can the story of an obscure, early-1970s car company located in, of all places, New Brunswick, Canada, and one that Richard Hatfield himself called an "impossible dream"[2] as it ignominiously collapsed into a $25 million bankruptcy in 1975, explain these momentous economic, political, and social changes in North America? How, really, can Malcolm Bricklin and the story of his (in)famous car be used to explain industrial modernity and the shift to industrial postmodernity?

The Bricklin episode can act as a cipher for these tectonic changes for three key reasons. First, since the automobile and its central place in North American society was a defining feature and main agent of industrial modernity and its transformation across the twentieth and twenty-first centuries – the "great god CAR," as one scholar called it – I would argue that an automobile, in this case, the Bricklin, can serve as an ideal vehicle for understanding these changes.[3] And while it is indeed true that the SV1 only barely made it into production, that Bricklin manufactured fewer than three thousand vehicles, and that the company lasted but three years, it is also true that Bricklin was the only new American automotive firm that successfully managed to build and sell cars in North America between the 1940s and the 2008 launch of Tesla's production Roadster.[4] The automobile and its industry were lynchpins of twentieth-century North American industrial modernity; because the Bricklin was the only viable automotive venture to emerge and survive, however briefly, during the seven-decades that spanned that era, the saga of the SV1 is, almost as much by design if not by default, among automotive modernity's most revealing and historically useful episodes.[5]

Second, and just as importantly, while the Bricklin may retain its status as the most legendary unknown car of the twentieth century, the company's brief existence coincided almost exactly with one of the most intense and transformational periods in recent North American and global history. Events in the early 1970s, as many histories and historians have shown, announced the end of North America's and Western Europe's *trente glorieuses*, and, in turn, a dramatic shift in economic, cultural, political, and social values. The changes were many – some quiet, but others quite loud. The United States reaching peak conventional oil production in 1970. The collapse of the postwar international financial order, which was predicated on

Figure I.1. Bricklin promotional image, 1973.

the Bretton Woods system, and the disruptive 1971 American "shoku" to the international economy. The impact of the 1973 Organization of Petroleum Exporting Countries' (OPEC) oil embargo. The 1973 US Supreme Court decision in *Roe v. Wade*. The 1974 resignation of disgraced President Richard Nixon. Rampant inflation and the imposition of wage and price controls. And the rapid emergence of economic dislocation, stagflation, and deindustrialization. "Astute observers," wrote journalist David Halberstam, "would mark that particular time, mid-1973, as the last moment of the old order in the industrialized world." What followed was, in the words of scholar David Harvey, a "sea change in cultural as well as in political-economic practices since around 1972." All these events were part of the Bricklin's immediate landscape and deeply shaped the car, its company, and its legacy. The Bricklin's meteoric rise and demise can both reflect and act as a representation of the seemingly sudden end of American postwar economic hegemony and of the volatile domestic political and cultural issues that further exacerbated the material changes felt by ordinary people in this period, in both the United States and Canada.[6]

Finally, although the company and its output were small, the Bricklin is a uniquely North American story, one whose impact spanned the length and breadth of the continent and reflected both the permeability of borders and their continuing persistence. Malcolm Bricklin was an American self-styled alpha male who was born in Philadelphia, grew up in Florida, fancied himself an Arizonan, and came to a small, pastoral province in Canada led by a flamboyant young premier to build his cars, which were to be sold exclusively to dealers and customers in the United States. With offices in Detroit, New York, Scottsdale, Arizona, and Saint John, New Brunswick, the Bricklin company was itself a disjointed amalgam of multiple, cross-border divisions, imitative of the Big Three in scope, if not scale. The firm's structure was consciously designed to take advantage of governments and workers in Canada, to connect with consumers, bankers, and important auto industry nodes in the United States, and to exploit media outlets across the continent.

Furthermore, Bricklin was also the first (and only) vehicle company in history specifically designed to fully exploit the recently integrated cross-border Canada-US auto sector, created by the 1965 Automotive Products Trade Agreement between the two countries, the auto pact. By the early 1970s, the border-erasing auto pact, North America's first real tariff-free trade zone, and the precursor to all later continental integration, was in full bloom. Detroit's multinational auto industry was, of course, already operating in Canada through its branch plant subsidiaries. But it was the first sector to fully embrace cross-border North American *duty-free* trade and operational integration, and Bricklin was the first new auto producer to actively attempt to take advantage of the continentalizing agreement following its creation by the Big Three and the US and Canadian governments.[7]

Bricklin's continental presence was also helped by the fact that, despite some significant differences in Sixties politics and culture, Americans and Canadians had gained a postwar cultural and consumptive experience that was very similar, at least for many white, middle-class, English-speaking people on either side of the border.[8] By the time Bricklin launched his car and became famous, North Americans had together already experienced decades of deeply shared intergenerational automobility. This cross-border connectivity was particularly strong for the baby boom generation, the giant demographic cohort of potential customers that Bricklin had targeted for the new "safety sports car" category he had created with the SV1. In 1969, historian Arthur Lower had written that "Henry Ford was a figure who could hardly have been other than American. Canada did not provide a stage for such as he."[9] Unusually, Malcolm Bricklin became an automotive-inspired celebrity in America for something he had done mostly in Canada. Bricklin was pioneering continentalism at its finest.

Thus, far from simply representing a failed company, a triviality in the history of car making, a minor government-backed venture gone awry, or, worse yet, the punchline of a joke, the Bricklin story epitomizes a transformational moment in society, reflecting a multitude of economic, political, and cultural shifts across many facets of North American life.

Like all histories, this is a book about change. Change is, of course, the only constant, and the question of change over time is one of the fundamental elements of how we understand history. But, when trying to understand the shift from industrial modernity to industrial postmodernity, what is being addressed, exactly, and what do these terms mean, precisely? When assessing the Bricklin and its place in this moment of change in the 1970s, how can these broader changes be conceptualized and understood through the prism of *this* car in particular? What was the context *before* Bricklin, and how were things different *after* Bricklin? What, exactly, changed, and how is the Bricklin a representation of these changes? Just as importantly, which aspects of society that underlay the changes revealed by the Bricklin remained the same during this period of transformation, and why?

Bricklin's role in the great tremors that had been building to eruption by the early 1970s reflected a kaleidoscope of changes across a host of different timescales, established societal structures, people's lived experiences and actions, and their everyday behaviours, practices, and beliefs. The Bricklin can be used to decipher some of the era's key changes, from the tangible and the material to the ideological and the intellectual and to the famous and the ordinary. This is because, at the centre of so many of these changes, was the automobile and its industry, the two elements of automobility that profoundly impacted *everyone* in North America in the twentieth century, whether they realized it or not.

Thus, the starting point must be the idea of modernity itself, and its concomitant, automotive industrial modernity. Defining "modernity" is something of a mug's game, a futile intellectual pursuit with more starting points, descriptions, and interpretations than can practically be imagined.[10] Though the onset of modernity was a long process – one that spans centuries, in some scholars' views – the late nineteenth and early twentieth century brought a seismic acceleration of transformations to human society most often defined as "modernity," "the lived experience of unremitting change," according to Ian McKay.[11] The historian Keith Walden has catalogued these changes:

> Cities grew inexorably; powerful new business organizations announced their presence with high-rise office towers and sprawling factories; bureaucratic centralization and regulation became more pronounced; migrations from distant parts of the globe snowballed; medical breakthroughs abounded; scientific discoveries spawned startling new theories; and bicycles, automobiles, dry-process photographs, halftones, movies, tractors, electric lights, typewriters, telephones, and other marvels of technological sophistication appeared with dizzying regularity.[12]

A central contention of this book is that the 150 years or so from the 1880s to the 2020s were marked by what could be called "automobile industrial modernity," an all-encompassing phenomenon that the mobility scholar Gijs Mom called in its initial phase "Atlantic automobilism" and that the sociologist John Urry referred to ultimately as a global "'system' of automobility." Urry saw automobility as a totalizing concept with six components: "the quintessential *manufactured object*"; "the major item of *individual consumption*"; "an extraordinarily powerful *complex*" spanning the economy and social interlinkages; "the predominant global form of 'quasi-private' *mobility*"; the "dominant *culture* that sustains major discourses of what constitutes the good life"; and the "single most important cause of *environmental resource-use*."[13] Automobile industrial modernity, then, was nothing less than an almost complete recreation of society by the car and its use. It encompassed the car's essential impact on the underlying structures that gave the automobile such universal pre-eminence: social interaction, capitalism, oil geopolitics, and the planet's cultural, political, environmental, and built landscapes. All this is what Henry Ford meant when he boasted that "I invented the modern age." Even in his titanic arrogance, Ford was not entirely wrong.[14]

More precisely, this book contends that automotive industrial modernity in North America evolved across three phases. The first phase was the rapid adoption followed by the ubiquitous use of the automobile from the early 1900s to the 1970s, which, through Ford's Model T and his second industrial revolution, created *industrial modernity*, often referred to as Fordism. This techno-societal system, based on the automobile and its impact, including its business practices, industrial processes, and especially its internal combustion engine, reached a zenith in the 1950s and 1960s, a second subperiod that can be called *high industrial modernity*.[15] Then, starting in the 1970s, and owing to the economic and social changes outlined in this book – many of which were also a consequence of the production and use of the automobile and can be seen through the story of Bricklin and his SV1 – North America entered a third period, *industrial postmodernity*.[16]

Importantly, industrial postmodernity was an erosion of Fordist practices and structures and was characterized by the onset of flexible accumulation, a third industrial revolution, an emerging neoliberalism, and the beginnings of the fourth industrial revolution. Just as significantly, the end of industrial modernity did not mean the end of the automobile's reign, though it did, after the 1960s, see the car and many of its externalities as problems to be solved.[17] Indeed, in the industrial postmodern 2010s and 2020s, entrepreneurs and state actors alike sought to solve the problems caused by the automobile and its fossil-fuel-based propulsion ecosystem – the literal engine of industrial modernity – by decarbonizing the car and launching the electric vehicle revolution, exemplified by Tesla's Elon Musk and his symbolically named Model 3. In their efforts to reclaim the car's place in the American dream, these entrepreneurs and state actors were very careful not to alter the car's fundamental design or to constrain the convenience and personal freedom that the car had bestowed on people since automobility's emergence.[18]

This three-phase periodization of automobile modernity consciously adopts the terminology utilized by anthropologist James C. Scott, whose seminal work focuses on twentieth-century state planners' attempts to tame and control nature with giant structures and expertise, but whose "seeing like a state" schemes often resulted in unintended consequences.[19] Automobile industrial modernity was, in many ways, the purest distillation of Scott's high modernism: in the period between 1900 and the 1960s, state planners reacted to the emergence of the car by unquestioningly refashioning virtually all of North America's human and built landscape to accommodate the automobile, including massive highway- and road-building projects, the reconstruction of cities and towns, and the emergence of car-oriented suburbs and exurbs.[20]

Significantly, collective state power aimed at facilitating this reshaping of the human and natural landscape to implement automotive industrial modernity also reflected the fact that the automobile was essentially a system of mobility that remade society's relationship to nature on an *individual* level. This system was initiated mostly by private capital instead of public power, though the process was certainly helped by the latter. After all, what was the privately owned automobile if not humanity's ultimate, individualistic effort to overcome nature itself, each person doing so from the comfort of their own vehicle? The car was the greatest symbol and most widespread instrument of humans' individual conquest of the landscape, and of time and distance, too, as most North Americans happily and willingly chose to see the world "like a car." They did so as drivers, passengers, pedestrians, and ultimately as an entire population whose existence was deeply shaped by automobility.[21] Meanwhile, the collective impact of the automobile and its industry – of having *a whole society* "seeing like a car" – meant the literal conquest and ultimate defeat of nature, with graver consequences than Henry Ford or any other of gasoline-powered motordom's earliest advocates could have ever imagined.[22]

Spurred on by automobile-intoxicated individuals, firms, and states, all of whom *desired* the car and its industry, this broad historical progression – industrial modernity to high industrial modernity to industrial postmodernity – was facilitated by shifting *technological and productive systems.* In the 1910s, Ford and his awesome production processes had spectacularly driven mass manufacturing (and consumption) to the pinnacle of the economy and society, the Model T loudly proclaiming the symbolic end of the first industrial revolution and the beginning of the second. In the 1970s, the SV1's launch also represented a signal milestone, one that marked the overlapping transition between the second and third industrial revolutions, and the symbolic moment of Fordism's partial passing: the SV1 marked both the height and the end of industrial modernity.[23]

But, unlike Ford, Bricklin and the story of his car serve only to illustrate the beginning of a postmodern era of challenge for North American manufacturing, and especially automotive manufacturing. In the 1970s, Fordist car making was almost knocked from its pedestal by the forces of globalization, automation, financialization, and digitization – cumulatively, processes of deindustrialization. Fordism was forced to evolve: it was transformed and, starting in the 1970s and in the wake of the Bricklin's demise, was made leaner and even more ruthlessly efficient by robotics and new production processes and labour relations. If the Model T was the big bang of the second industrial revolution and industrial modernity, the SV1 was its whimper. Nevertheless, as only a new car and automobile company could, Bricklin also symbolized the start of something new, the beginnings of a lean deindustrialization that ultimately reflected a decarbonized, electrified, and digitized postindustrial modernity.[24]

The technological and production transition from the second to the third industrial revolutions that the Bricklin signified was also a shift in *economic and social systems.* Automobile-demarcated industrial modernity reached its futuristic, technologically optimistic peak in the 1950s and 1960s, during the middle of the Cold War. Not coincidentally, this period of high industrial modernity overlapped with the zenith of postwar North American Keynesianism, an economic system of which a key cause and progenitor was 1930s automobile industrialism. But, in the midst of the economic disruptions of the 1970s, Keynesianism also came under duress, its ideas quickly coming to be seen as economically and intellectually

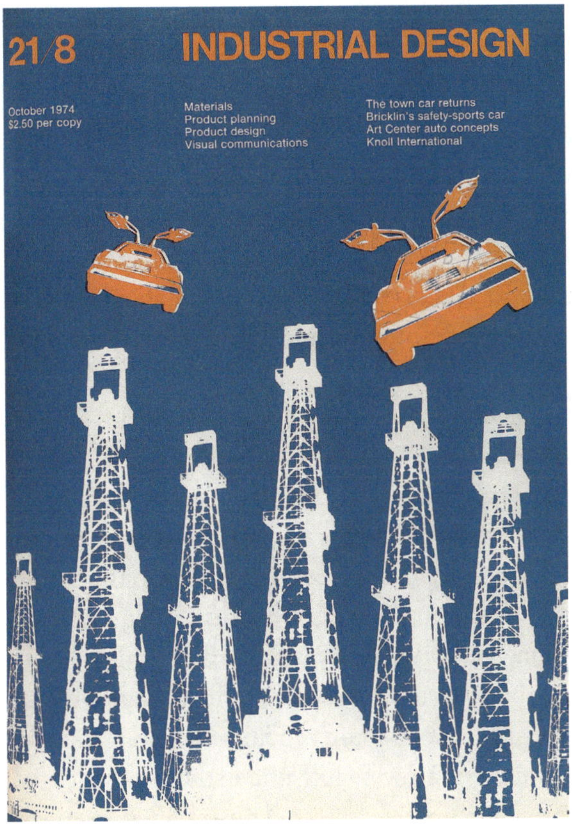

Figure I.2. Industrial modernity's transitional moment: futuristic, gull-winged SV1s fly above oil wells on the cover of *Industrial Design* magazine, October 1974.

bankrupt. Instead of the macroeconomic and policy interventions of (relatively) Big Government that had shaped industrial modernity since the Great Depression, starting in the 1970s, individualism, free-market fundamentalism, free trade, low wages, and other microeconomic remedies became a pernicious new orthodoxy. For the prophets of microeconomic theory who advocated lessening the state's role in society, the spectacular failure of Bricklin, a government-owned company, and the resultant decades-long political stench offered irrefutable evidence confirming the ills of statist intervention in the economy. A new, industrial postmodern, *neoliberal* economic order could be seen rising from the ashes of the Bricklin, one that also reshaped politics and culture.

These shifts – from the industrial to the industrial postmodern, from the second to the third industrial revolutions, and from liberal to Keynesian to neoliberal economic political and social systems – were all, in turn, instigated and shaped by individual actors and entities within a capitalist, liberal democratic society, including firms, unions, and the state. Standing above all others, entrepreneurs (business) and politicians (the state) were the crucial protagonists in this dynamic. They played the greatest roles in shaping the working and consumer choices of individuals and communities, the success or failure of firms, the visible or invisible hand of markets, the influence of labour and the power of unions, and the relative strength or weakness of governments in regulating all these variables. More than any other actors within automobile industrial modernity's realm, entrepreneurs/firms and politicians/government determined the scale and scope of economic, technological, social, and political change. Entrepreneurs initiated and brought about creative destruction; politicians reacted to creative destruction and, at times, were its helpmate, its hindrance, or its remedy.[25]

In their careers and life stories, Malcolm Bricklin and Richard Hatfield, both as individuals and in their joint effort with the SV1, are exemplars of this dynamic. Their biographies can act as guides to the changing nature of entrepreneurship and politics during this transitional moment. Their stories can also provide a deeper insight into the shifting structural balance of power between corporations, unions, and the state, as these entities shaped and were shaped by the tremendous upheavals of the era, and by society's changing values and views about these entities.

Ultimately, it is here, at this most basic level – in revealing the changes in attitudes, perceptions, beliefs, and *ideas* – that the Bricklin provides the most utility in understanding this liminal moment and era. How people understood and engaged with matters as disparate as entrepreneurship, risk, safety, fame, politics, sex, gender, business, the state, and the direction of society as it shifted in behaviours large and small, can best be revealed by "seeing like a car" – in this case, the Bricklin SV1, and the two dreamers, an entrepreneur and a politician, who launched the vehicle.

After all, it was largely the car, writ large, that created the fundamental nature and characteristics of North American society between the early 1900s and today, one whose essence was its automobile industrial modernity.

Along with change, this book is also about memory and how the past is remembered. The memory of things and events like the Bricklin, and *how* things and events like the Bricklin are remembered in the public consciousness, reflects both the context of the moment and how that moment can be obscured or shaped to fit the past within a particular narrative.[26] In the automotive world, the Bricklin is remembered as a quixotic promotional adventure, a failed but noble effort that gave showman Malcolm Bricklin enough credibility as an entrepreneur to keep him in the automotive game for decades thereafter. In the academic literature, the

Figure I.3. Gull-winged, not-so-distant cousins: a DMC DeLorean (left) and a Bricklin SV1.

SV1 project is remembered largely as a condemnatory example of the failure of state enterprise; in this view, the Bricklin was a ludicrous adventure destined to fail from the outset, and an unrealistic attempt to change a path of dependency for a province and its people. In popular memory, the most common way in which the Bricklin story appears in the public consciousness is through the media, where it is almost universally understood as a failure, a flop, the punchline.[27]

In retrospect, it is easy to scoff at the notion of the Bricklin as a success. Given the challenges Bricklin and Hatfield faced in launching a "safety sports car" in the early 1970s, the very idea of the SV1 seems absurd, a dream doomed to inevitable failure. Correspondingly, time has not been kind to the Bricklin. When remembered in the pop cultural consciousness, it is as a shorthand for Seventies' excesses, a type of postmodern, post-embargo Edsel, an obvious road sign that marks a decade of decline.[28] Books such as *How to Brickle: The New Brunswick Funny Book* (1977) made a mockery of the car and the whole episode, as did songs like country music disc-jockey and erstwhile performer Charlie Russell's "The Bricklin," from his 1975 album, *The Bricklin and Other Sound Investments*.[29] The Bricklin SV1 regularly appears on lists of the worst cars of all time, and the commentary attached to the vehicle is usually brutal in its assessment.[30] So unserious and whimsical is the notion of the Bricklin that a musical, *The Bricklin: An Automotive Fantasy*

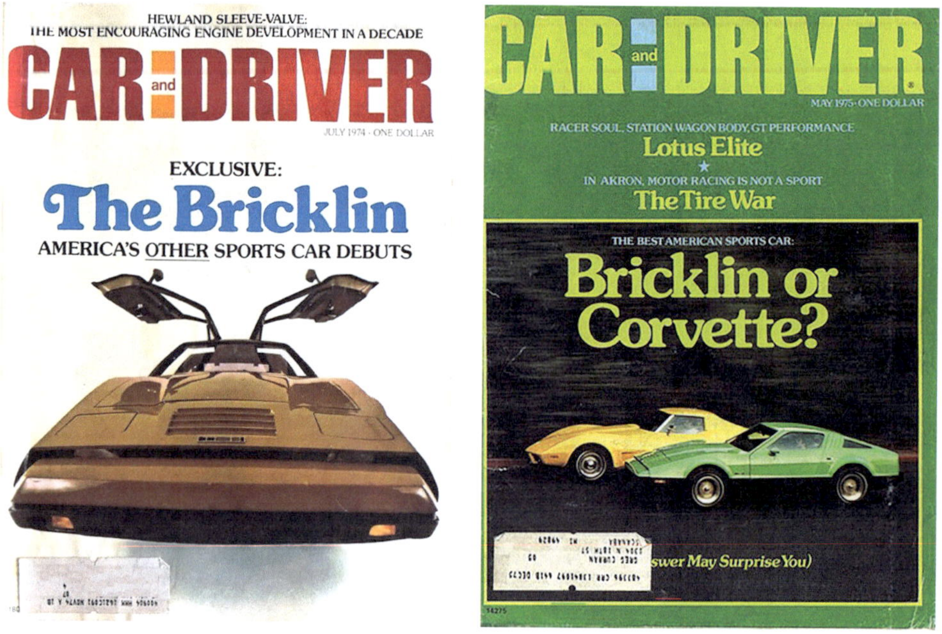

Figure I.4. The Bricklin, *Car and Driver*, 1974 (left) and 1975 (right).

(ironically, supported by a $2 million government grant) successfully premiered in New Brunswick in 2010.[31] The SV1 has become, like its gull-winged doppelgänger and spiritual successor the DeLorean Motor Company's 1981–3 DMC DeLorean (made famous by the *Back to the Future* films), something of a cultural joke.[32]

Yet, initially, this was not the case. The SV1 was not considered a joke when Bricklin and Hatfield held their glitzy 1974 launch in New York City. With Broadway crooner Sammy Cahn singing "The Most Beautiful Car in the World" (substituting "car" for "girl") as an added touch of publicity, the car received largely favourable reviews. "The naked truth" about the Bricklin, proclaimed *Autoweek*, was that it was "a real, viable and honest motorcar that is going to sell well and make several thousand people happy."[33] The Bricklin's rakish appearance and the innovative promise of making a virtue out of safety – an issue increasingly on the minds of American consumers – generated genuine optimism about its potential and an incredible amount of positive media attention.[34] And why not? A scant ten years earlier, another rakish sports car, the 1965 Ford Mustang, had also been launched in New York at the futuristic 1964 World's Fair by another dynamic young auto entrepreneur, Lee Iacocca. By the end of 1965, Ford had sold nearly two million Mustangs, an astoundingly successful debut. From Malcolm Bricklin's perspective, the two cars had quite a bit in common, including an attempt to create a new subcategory of sports car, stylish looks, fantastic promotion, and a booming target market.[35]

Captured by its appearance and its innovative safety and performance potential, contemporary observers in the auto industry were indeed enthusiastic about the SV1. *Car and Driver*'s May 1975 cover story trumpeted, "The Best American Sportscar: Bricklin or Corvette? (The Answer May Surprise You)." The magazine pronounced that Bricklin had "finally produced a tangible threat to the Corvette. Skeptics be damned; the Bricklin lives." The two cars came off "amazingly close … On paper, they're almost interchangeable – with the Corvette enjoying a small performance edge."[36] *Road & Track* declared that "from what we have seen of the car so far we have to think that the future of the Bricklin is a bright one, but only time and sales will tell."[37] As late as September 1975, *Mechanix Illustrated* published "We Test the Amazing Bricklin," an article that overlooked the car's persistent quality problems and enthused that "we look for the '76 and '77 models to show even better craftsmanship and design development."[38]

This enthusiasm spilled over to the car-buying public, which also seemed keen on the Bricklin. Even as the company foundered during that fall of 1975, whatever SV1s were being bolted and glued together in New Brunswick were sold before they even shipped. In fact, every single Bricklin ever produced had a buyer, and even in receivership the company had a backlog of orders for the car from its over three hundred dealers, which Malcolm Bricklin publicly stated to be 46,000 vehicles.[39] The Bricklin was, initially, mostly a success, at least from a sales and marketing perspective.

But this is not how the Bricklin is remembered. Yet thinking about the Bricklin differently reveals another way of understanding its importance. Instead of being mocked solely as an unrealistic venture or inevitable failure, the Bricklin should be recognized as a legitimate attempt that may not have succeeded, but from which much can be learned. Bricklin was not simply an example of mismanagement, or corporate collapse, or a failure of state enterprise, but a signpost that reflected profound industrial, business, and social changes in North American society. These included a much broader ideological, political, and economic turning away from Keynes, and a shift in the *willingness* – though not necessarily the ability – of the state to intervene in the economy. The Bricklin failed not solely because it had poor management and poor production processes, or because it was an attempt to do something no one had successfully pulled off for half a century; it failed because of a lack of gumption by a provincial government that did not understand the cost of the modern auto industry, and it ultimately succumbed to the emerging belief that there should be a lessening in the power and place of the state in the economy. The death of the Bricklin should be remembered as an important step in neoliberalism's emergence in the 1970s, but it should also be remembered in terms of *how* it became damning evidence in neoliberalism's quest to kill the very notion of state enterprise in North America.

Good activist history points to the paths not taken and the noble paths attempted, and, ultimately, to how the unknown paths stumbled upon were eventually taken. Historians, and especially business historians, have come to terms with the importance of failure as a way to illuminate different paths and have come to realize that understanding failure is as important as recognizing how entrepreneurs, businesses, and, yes, even states, paved their ways to success.[40] Exploring the failure of the Bricklin and how this dream may have turned out differently can be far richer and more informative than producing yet another hagiography of a business success story. In that sense, Bricklin and his SV1 are a perfect example of the utility of failure and how its memory can help reimagine the pathways of the past and the possibilities of the future.

As the Safety Vehicle-1 itself was, and is, a material artefact of modernity, *Dream Car* is grounded in the business-driven narrative of a motor vehicle company, one that was also a project of state enterprise. At its core, this is a book about a firm: General Vehicle Incorporated (GVI) was the parent company of Bricklin Vehicle Corporation (BVC) and the Canadian subsidiary that built the SV1, Bricklin Canada Ltd. (BCL). In Bricklin's complicated structure, Malcolm Bricklin himself (and the banks) owned GVI and BVC, but New Brunswick owned a majority share in BCL, the production arm of the venture, and where almost all the money for GVI came from.

Along with entrepreneurs, the modern firm is, of course, among the basic elements of how business history is understood and studied, especially when drawing on the mid-twentieth-century managerial- and corporation-focused historical framework of Alfred D. Chandler that profoundly shaped the field. Institutions and markets, which are also central to the present story, have also deeply shaped the practice of business history. The Chandlerian, firm-focused, managerial revolution has been a bedrock of American and global business history since the 1960s; GVI, an automotive firm that aspired to that centrally managed, multidivisional form – the basis of so much of Chandler's research and interpretation – provides a useful case study of the evolving scale, structure, and scope of the American corporation.[41]

Indeed, as the study of a firm and its rise and demise, *Dream Car* might have easily been solely conceptualized and written as a standard, firm-focused case,

Figure I.5. Dreamers: Bricklin and Hatfield, 1974.

useful in any business school assessment of management, strategy, and marketing. The Bricklin story could also have been written as a classic treatment of business-government relations, also a keystone of the study of enterprise in the capitalist system, and one with an especially important emphasis in Canada, where state enterprise – what the economic historian H.G.J. Aitken called "defensive expansionism" – remained much more central to economic development than in the United States.[42] Further, as an example of a failed attempt at a regional development scheme, the Bricklin speaks to an economic industrial policy strategy that has played a central role in Canadian economic history, particularly in the mid-twentieth century.[43]

Methodologically, *Dream Car* is also grounded in the narrative biographical treatment of its main protagonists, Bricklin and Hatfield. Dissimilar, yet sharing many traits, these two men became forever famously entwined in each other's legacies, following their brief but intense three years together during the Bricklin incident. Biography is a time-honoured genre in history, especially in business history, which is so often focused upon individual entrepreneurs and their impact. Some of the most compelling and informative biographical studies of business leaders, and their business practices and accomplishments, have been essential to understanding the evolution of business and entrepreneurship.[44] The same long-standing biographical approach obviously holds true for politicians and policymakers, whose influence on the economy and business has also been tremendous.[45]

Dream Car utilizes methodological elements of both a firm-focused case study and a biographical approach, while addressing the layers of analysis of change outlined above. But it does so by moving beyond a traditional corporate history of a firm's evolution, or a simple, straightforward business or political biography of two individuals. Instead, it weaves the narrative of the Bricklin firm and the biographies of its two main protagonists into a broader analysis of eras, systems, institutions, and values. As a result, elements of Bricklin's and Hatfield's complex personalities appear at different times throughout the book, and the book's fragmented approach to the biographical narrative of the two men reflects the varying facets of each man's personality. Malcolm Bricklin was, simultaneously, the entrepreneur, innovator, showman, cowboy, playboy, dealmaker, and survivor. Richard Hatfield was, concurrently, the politician, performer, industrial proselytizer, dream-weaver, collector, bachelor, statesman, drug user, and survivor. These biographical fragments also serve to reveal many of the changes that basic values – those associated with risk, fame, sex, business, and politics – were undergoing during the transformative moment that the Bricklin represented in this period.

Change, memory, modernities, succeeding industrial revolutions, evolving economic systems, shifting attitudes and values, and corporate and biographical explorations are major themes of *Dream Car*, and all are woven into the book's chapters to reveal the landscape of automobility as seen from behind the wheel of a Bricklin SV1.

To achieve this, every chapter does three things. First, as their titles (and subtitles) indicate, each chapter's theme(s) examine how automobility – the automobile and its industry – impacted and shaped disparate aspects of society from the late nineteenth century to the early twenty-first. Second, at some point, each chapter (save for chapter 2) narrates a part of the story of Malcolm Bricklin and his SV1 from its late 1960s start to the 1980s, by which time the car's tale was firmly ensconced in automotive industry lore. Finally, each chapter's theme is viewed from the perspective of the Bricklin SV1 (and, in some chapters, its two main instigators); seeing the world from the view of this car in particular reveals fundamental changes in some of North American society's most powerful ideas and foundational realities, as automobility shaped industrial modernity and shifted towards industrial postmodernity starting in the 1970s. Some of these elements and themes reappear across many of the chapters, unfolding a longer tale of their evolution and meaning.

The book's chapters can be read sequentially or in any order. *Dream Car* is an open road, and each reader's roadmap can be (re)arranged to take the path they find most interesting. Certainly, a drive straight through the book would be the story's most direct route. But readers can also steer along a more winding, scenic tour, gazing through the windshield of their SV1 at important features of North America's changing twentieth- and twenty-first-century auto-scape. In this way, *Dream Car*'s structure encourages readers to pick and choose their own stops along some of automobility's most important sites of cause and consequence, spanning a range of historical, political, business, economic, social, and cultural ideas, issues, and experiences, mapped to their interests. Doing so can provide a moment of contemplation about each reader's own choice of curated journey: why they decided to drive in *that* direction, in particular, or why they did not. Readers might also slow down to consider – in a world where automobility's speed often moves modern society along ever faster – what is lost if not all roads are taken.[46] In an SV1, navigational self-awareness can be as revelatory as the destinations visited.

Importantly, *Dream Car*'s open road does not map every area of automobility's sprawling, impossibly vast landscape, nor every aspect of the Bricklin story. Automobility and its role in settler colonialism is not considered. Neither oil geopolitics nor media concentration is addressed, despite the presence of the industrialist Irvings and their relationship to the province (and Hatfield). Work and labour and the impact of the Bricklin's events on New Brunswick's working people are only briefly discussed. Intersectional issues of language and of race (in a bilingual yet increasingly multicultural province) are not considered. Nor are some important aspects of automobility's role in politics or impact on the environment, or details of Hatfield's long political life in a changing province. While technology is a main theme of the book, many important aspects of technologies, including the digitization and computerization of the third industrial revolution of the 1960s–80s, do not play a role. This is not because all these issues (and many others) are insignificant, but the nature of the Bricklin story – of *this* car, its industry, its creators, and its place and time – spoke most unswervingly to the themes and issues visited in the book's seven chapters.

Chapter 1 starts not in the past, but with the idea of the Future (Technology), and of modernity. It sets the stage by first providing a contextual landscape of the Sixties' optimistic technological zeitgeist, revealing how industrial modernity emerged in its highest form in the postwar promise of a space age, jet age, robotic, plastic future, one personified by its greatest technological talisman, the automobile.

Malcolm Bricklin's SV1, dreamily conceptualized at the height of this moment and realized as a prototype in 1973, perfectly encapsulated the spirit of high industrial modernity's technological futurism in its design, features, and materials.

Next, this chapter shows how the dream of the future was seen in the economic and cultural impact of automobility, and of Fordism, and the way that governments from across the globe sought to capture the promise of car-fuelled prosperity, usually through different forms of state-supported enterprise. The quest for industrial modernity also happened in Canada, in the Maritimes, and in hardscrabble New Brunswick, a province dominated by resource extraction and the imperious oil man K.C. Irving. The chapter ends with the start of Bricklin's New Brunswick story and how Malcolm Bricklin and his fantastic idea of the futuristic SV1 drew in and captivated a young premier and his economically underdeveloped province. Troublingly, just as Bricklin and Hatfield embarked on their quest for the future, industrial modernity faced its own crisis, as the economic and political shocks of the early 1970s profoundly disrupted the postwar system that automobility had largely created.

Chapter 2 arrives at the idea of the Entrepreneur (Archetype) as the main instigator of automobile industrial modernity. It introduces the metaphor of the pantheon of four entrepreneurial archetypes – innovators, promoters, managers, and saviours – that can be applied to the men who created the car and its industry and, in doing so, shaped American business forever. Next, by telling a mini-tale of one of the greatest business icons of all time, auto executive Lee Iacocca, the chapter connects these archetypes to the notion of an entrepreneurial lifecycle. Iacocca's career both exemplified the four archetypes and accentuated some important changes in the evolving nature of automotive entrepreneurship in this period. In this chapter, his career is compared and contrasted with that of another upstart, his contemporary and fellow auto entrepreneur Malcolm Bricklin. Bricklin's own entrepreneurial record as an innovator, promoter, manager, and saviour is further examined across four of the book's subsequent chapters, adding additional perspectives and layers to the overall analysis.

The third chapter stops to look at the Risk (Safety) dynamic that the Bricklin as a car and Bricklin Canada as a venture embodied in their role as a representation of the evolving postwar automobile and its industry. At the micro level, the automobile changed the way ordinary people and policymakers saw risk and how, starting in the 1960s, they reacted to the destructive impact of cars by embracing a regime that imposed safety for drivers and passengers and began to limit cars' harmful consequences and to regulate vehicles. Simultaneously, and somewhat paradoxically, at the macro level, as government shifted its policies towards less economically statist approaches, a geographically unmoored and increasingly financialized North American auto industry shifted from a foundation of stability and prosperity to a much riskier proposition, one where corporate decision-making could threaten the collective economic well-being of entire towns and regions.

Designed and marketed as a "safety car," the SV1 underscored Bricklin's effort to become a Henry Ford–like innovator (the first entrepreneurial archetype) in an industry that was, by the 1970s, slow to change and, simultaneously, quickly being changed by public sentiment, shifting economic geographies, offshore competition, evolving trade regimes, and government regulation. For his part, Hatfield's willingness to take a chance on the car and its namesake reflected the increasing riskiness that auto manufacturing represented in a world being buffeted and transformed by economic upheaval. Nonetheless, Hatfield and most New Brunswickers were willing to risk much, not simply because of all the material benefits that a successful auto industry promised, but as a way to prove themselves to a country and a continent that had little faith in their ability to achieve industrial modernity.

Chapter 4 takes an extended, two-part biographical tour with Bricklin, the Showman, and Hatfield (the Politician) that explores the nature of fame, performative entrepreneurship, politics, and entertainment across the twentieth century. In Malcolm Bricklin's case, his career as a promoter (a second entrepreneurial archetype) is considered as a seven-act show. Promotion emerges as *the* constituent aspect of Bricklin's personality, one that explains his unusual success over time, and why he is considered the P.T. Barnum of the automotive world. For Hatfield, the dream-weaving politician with a Houdini-like ability to escape scandal, his own five-part electoral melodrama illustrates his political rise, longevity, and defeat. Drawn together by their shared dream to make the SV1 a triumph, both men's stories reflect the influence of media and celebrity on a North America obsessed with success, whether real or perceived, and the allure of fame. The two protagonists' tales also provide a way to explore the shifting meanings and manners of performative business and politics, and whether – as so many people accused them of doing so – they were simply running a multimillion-dollar confidence/electoral trick on the taxpayers/voters of New Brunswick.

Dream Car's fifth chapter detours from the entrepreneurially driven thematic sub-narrative to explore the question of automobility and Sex (Gender), including as a central element of the SV1 and its maker's character. Motor vehicles completely reordered sexuality and gender relations and identities and, with the postwar introduction of the sports car, turbocharged the automobile's connection to sex and created muscle-car masculinity. The SV1, whose sexiness was a core element of its identity, is used to illustrate the profound impact of the car on intimacy, gender, and ideas of sexuality over time, but also to show how the personal biographies of each of the main protagonists reveal important aspects of the ongoing sexual revolution. Bricklin, a swaggering near-caricature of heteronormative '70s sexuality, and Hatfield, the closeted gay politician who dealt with issues of sexual identity, LGBTQ rights, abortion, privacy, and the media, are perfect representations of persistent patriarchal structures *and* changing attitudes during a period of profound sexual upheaval.

Chapter 6 takes a drive through the Business of cars and centres the story of the Bricklin firm within the automobile manufacturing industry's dramatic upheavals of the Seventies. This two-part chapter reflects, first, on *why* cars were built and shows that the philosophy behind the auto business was changing across the twentieth century, as emerging ideas about managers' and firms' roles in the sector (and the broader economy) shifted in an increasingly financialized business world.

The second part of the chapter provides a business case study of the Bricklin firm, GVI, and its subsidiaries. Looking at the firm's structure, management, production, labour, and government relations offers lessons about the shifting nature of the automobile industry and the dynamics of how and where cars were built, and who built them, in this transitional period. Bricklin's operations reflected a giant industry in flux, as it bridged Fordist and industrially postmodern manufacturing worlds with difficulty. But Bricklin and GVI's interactions with New Brunswick also signalled an important moment in the state's changing role in business-government relations, from the evolving economic geography of the North American auto sector to the impact of subsidies and direct state ownership. All were central elements of the Bricklin tale and were – and are – part of the broader story of industrial modernity's transition towards an increasingly neoliberal political and economic landscape. The chapter finishes by assessing Bricklin's abilities as a twentieth-century businessman and manager (a third archetype).

The seventh chapter, "Demise (Rebirth)," brings the Bricklin journey to an end, though not to the conclusion of the Bricklin tale. It begins by narrating three entwined stories of demise. First, an exploration of GVI and Bricklin's receivership and bankruptcy highlights Bricklin's role as a saviour and marks the fourth, and last, stage of his entrepreneurial lifecycle. Second, the chapter examines the subsequent denouncement of Bricklin's failure as a symbol of state intervention, but also as an early example of an emerging post-embargo, lean deindustrialization, one that ultimately impacted hundreds of thousand of people. And third, the story moves to the scandalous and rather sad end to Richard Hatfield's journey.

The chapter finishes with three stories of Rebirth, each reflecting the ongoing legacy of Bricklin and his car: the many efforts to revive the firm, and the SV1's lasting impact as an artefact of material automobile culture; the Bricklin's unique automotive legacy, both through its connection to the famous DeLorean DMC and Bricklin's impact on a host of industry practices; and, finally, Bricklin's connections to Elon Musk and their shared similarities in the context of the newest age of industrial postmodern automobile entrepreneurship.

The conclusion reflects on several questions. First, in the end, could the SV1 have worked? Second, what can be learned from "seeing like a SV1"? Third, what can the Bricklin episode tell us about the themes raised in each chapter? Finally, what does the Bricklin story mean more broadly in explaining the shift from industrial modernity to industrial postmodernity? In answering these questions, the conclusion places Malcolm Bricklin and the SV1 within the arc of automobile modernity's next great revolution, a decarbonized, digitized, and fundamental reimagination of the car, one sparked by Tesla's Musk and a new generation of innovative entrepreneurs beginning in the 2010s.

The epilogue takes readers to the Tesla Factory in Fremont, California, which, since 2010, has been the site of the first *successful* mass automobile manufacturing firm in North America since the 1940s, and what it and its Model 3 can tell us about Malcolm Bricklin and the end of industrial modernity.

Before departing, a few words about dreams, and cars.

This book is called *Dream Car* because, from its very beginning, throughout its brief yet fantastical existence and in the decades after the car and its company had failed, the idea of the Bricklin was regularly portrayed and *seen* as a dream. From its most ardent supporters and advocates, to the journalists who covered the story, and to the cynics and critics who dismissed or condemned it, almost anyone who was part of the venture or opined on the Bricklin invariably came to connect the SV1 to the idea of a dream, either as a potentially magical success or as a nightmare of folly and waste. Wherever Bricklin or his car went, the word "dream" followed, even long after the last of the approximately 2,900 SV1s had been rolled out of Bricklin Canada's rudimentary yet innovative Saint John, New Brunswick, plant in the autumn of 1975.[47]

As with so many other things, portraying the SV1 as a dream was, of course, a perfect representation of that unquenchable American individual desire for earthly success, freedom, power, fame, and fortune, "the American dream," and, perhaps, the most powerful version of that dream. Since the first decade of the 1900s, the automobile, and everything it stood for, was and remains a central, essential component of how the American dream has been defined, and the two have often been conflated. In 1931, when the writer James Truslow Adams popularized the term in his book *The Epic of America*, he explicitly recognized how, by the 1930s, the material success of automobility and industrial modernity – Fordism – had become foundational to any notion of an American dream, though he demanded more. "The American Dream," in Adams's hopeful analysis, "is not a dream *of motor cars and high wages merely*, but a dream of a social order in which each man and each woman shall be able to attain to the fullest state of which they are innately capable and recognized by others for what they are."[48]

Despite Adams's admonitions, since automobility and industrial modernity's advent, no material object and its impact have come anywhere near to the automobile and its industry in being so closely identified with the notion of the American dream of worldly success. Although he expressed distaste for the "vulgarity" of Big Three offerings, the influential French-American designer Raymond Loewy pronounced in 1935 that "the American automobile has changed the habits of every member of modern society." Moreover, "in the past fifty years," Loewy continued, the automobile "has become the symbol, all over the world, of American industrial genius and enterprise. It has become so potent a force that it is very nearly the symbol of American thought and morals to people who don't know us. It is more than an object to be sold for money. The automobile is an American cultural symbol." A year after Loewy's missive, General Motors' chief designer, Harley Earl, was feted by the *New York Times* as America's "dreamer-in-chief."[49] The conflation of cars as American dreams persisted for decades. In 1980, historian Charles L. Sanford plainly asserted that, since automobility's arrival, the car had become "the chief carrier of the American Dream of freedom and plenitude."[50]

There was considerable truth in those grandiose sentiments. Automobility made real a previously unimaginable level of personal mobility and freedom. It allowed the dream of good wages, secure employment, home ownership, and a middle-class existence to come to life for countless North Americans (though, pointedly, not all), especially during those three prosperous postwar decades of high industrial modernity. Automobility – industrial modernity – was an idea that proved that the grandest dreams of the most ambitious people – from a Henry Ford to an Elon Musk – to reshape the world could come true. The auto sector, as historian Pamela Walker Laird has remarked, had "attracted entrepreneurs eager to pioneer in developing and producing the single most important manufactured status symbol available to consumers in the past one hundred years."[51] And for politicians and planners, the dream of an auto industry was the national or provincial dream of prosperity, wealth, respect, and industrial might. All these dreams were shaped by

Detroit's dream weavers, who made it their business to connect automobility and its business to the American dream in the minds of consumers and workers, and people and politicians, all around the world.[52]

So powerful was the dream of the car that automobility shaped and created much of the modern world as ordinary people understood it. Henry Ford's world. Automobility not only uprooted and remade society, it reconstructed individual identity. As Keith Walden and others have argued, perhaps the two most important elements of cultural modernity after 1900 were mobility (speed) and anonymity, and the automobile was essential to both. With automobility came the opportunity to quickly access multiple social environments where one was essentially unknown.[53] As cars overwhelmed cities, towns, growing suburbs, and the spaces that connected them, anonymity-though-mobility was often embraced by individuals who could be, in effect, different people according to their situation and in their different, distanced places. Driving to church on Sunday, they could be one kind of person; on Monday morning at work, they could be another kind; and on Friday night, at Studio 54 or the gay bar in a different town, they could be yet another. Automobile anonymity allowed people, and especially the modern men who were its main instigators and beneficiaries, to destabilize their identities in creative ways and to reshape images of themselves.[54]

That destabilization was, to some degree, unsettling. So, too, was being an anonymous individual mechanically roaming across mass, industrial, consumerist North American society, one whose chief currency and largest industries were capitalist-fuelled technology, especially motor cars, and their use. Once the car had liberated individualities from their local moorings, how could people project meaningful identities to the thousands of strangers who surrounded them? Ironically, the car, the very cause of these problems, also offered solutions. Automobility conferred identity through the very act of ownership and use of a motor vehicle (or, less commonly, not), one that signalled the degree of each person's embrace of modernity and the nature of their interaction with car-dominated society. *If* one drove, *what* one drove, and *where* one drove were fundamental aspects of modern identity. Moreover, the twentieth-century hierarchy of brands and models that had been created by GM, Ford, and Chrysler – the differing denominations of that particular and most important currency of technology, the automobile – allowed individuals to peg themselves and conform to highly specific social strata, which further solidified both their self-identities and their social identities.[55]

If the car made its new landscapes and environments accessible for anonymous individuals, drivers also *projected* an image onto that asphalt roadscape and to its denizens through their choice of vehicle (or lack thereof): arriving, unknown, in a luxurious Cadillac or Lincoln meant something very different than arriving in an economical Chevy or Ford, or yet again, in a flashy Bricklin SV1. The driver of the car, who presumably was its owner, was projecting information about themselves and what they valued, or at least *an image* of themselves and their values, one bound up in ideals about what their particular type or brand of car was seen by society to represent – from organization men in their establishment Buicks, to contemporized cowboys in their Mustang or other "pony" cars, to "soccer moms" in their utilitarian minivans. And since everyone in society *knew* or could easily intuit what each car signified – wealth, class, family status, age, and self-actualizations about speed, style, utility, sexuality, or safety – individual people's self-proclaimed identities became very much tied up in the cars they drove. Of course, the image created by a person's choice of car might obscure their actual lived realities, or who they really were. But at the very least, it did say something fundamental about who or what they may have *aspired* to be seen as. And for those individuals who did not possess a motor car, that fact was acutely fundamental to the way they existed in modern society; it was equally true of nations (or provinces) that did not possess an automobile industry and yet desired the wealth and status that manufacturing cars created.

This, too, was part of the dream of the Bricklin. Standing on stage together at the Four Seasons restaurant in June 1974, Bricklin and Hatfield and their car represented nothing less than the promise of the future, of prosperity. If the futuristic, sexy, sporty yet safe Bricklin SV1 was a success, it would provide a similar image creation and projection for the people who purchased and drove the cars, the ambitious promoter who had envisioned and launched the vehicle, the determined premier who had tied his province's reputation and treasury to the venture, and the people of that province who were building the car. The dream of the Bricklin was the dream of industrial modernity: to prosperously, perpetually, create oneself anew individually and collectively through technological mobility, exemplified by the automobile.

Unfortunately, for all those who shared this dream, the realities of the 1970s meant that taking a chance on the Bricklin also meant that, if the SV1 failed, they risked being revealed as something much less than the image that they had hoped to project. For an entrepreneur like Malcolm Bricklin and a politician like Richard Hatfield, chasing that dream was worth the risk. If Bricklin could solve the puzzle of industrial modernity and make the project work, if thousands of SV1s could be miraculously conjured into existence from his imagination and become the tangible, physical manifestation of worldly success, the sexy car would be the vehicle to make both men triumphant beyond their wildest ambitions – embodiments of the American dream.

In the twentieth and twenty-first centuries, the automobile and its business sat squarely at the intersection of North Americans' most cherished dreams, but also of their sharpest, most materially grounded realities. In 1974, the futuristic Safety Vehicle-1 was about to collide head-on with society's growing automobile-induced problems and its quickly changing economic, political, and cultural landscape. Little could Bricklin and Hatfield realize, then, what the venture and its demise would reveal about the end of industrial modernity, and the beginnings of the industrial postmodern.

CHAPTER ONE

The Future (Technology)

***Dream Car* Song 3: "Drive My Car," The Beatles, 1965**

The 1960s was the decade of the future. Despite the grim, global Cold War conflicts and domestic upheavals across the planet, in North America and Europe the Sixties were also a period of optimism, youthful exuberance, growth, and unprecedented technological change. Just as importantly, at least in the West, there was a genuine general belief that technology was on an inevitable progressive trajectory, one that would save humanity from its worst excesses. From the space race to the jet age, from robotics to plastics, society, especially Western society, seemed to be on the verge of achieving a futuristic world of convenience and prosperity through modern technologies.[1]

In North America, this faith in technology was widespread and meshed perfectly with the attitudes of the baby boomers, a generation that had grown up in an age of apparently never-ending, futuristic, consumptive, technological progress. In retrospect, the prevalence and permeation of the future in popular culture – from the postwar boom in science-fiction writing and films to Fantastic Four comics and Jetson cartoons – reflected not a generation's quixotic or unrealistic dreams but, rather, their practical and achievable aspirations. Technology had made the jet age a commonplace reality, had put a man on the moon, had supposedly solved the global food crisis, and had seemingly provided every household in North America with the latest leisure and labour-saving gizmos and gadgets.[2] Techno-dreams could come true, after all.

Of course, lurking in the background of this futuristic facade was the truth that not everyone in North American society had access to the wonders of technology. Gendered, racialized, class, and regional technological divides and material and social inequalities continued largely unabated, despite the 1960s American wars on poverty or Canadian just societies. It was also undeniably true that an unshakeable pessimism about the Cold War, nuclear annihilation, and overpopulation continued to stalk the landscape; these concerns were both causes and consequences of this great postwar technological leap forward. Moreover, the early warnings of environmental degradation, first sounded by scientists such as Rachel Carson in her 1964 book *Silent Spring* or on television shows such as the Canadian Broadcasting Corporation's *The Nature of Things* (debuting in 1960), were becoming increasingly difficult to ignore, as North America's air, water, and land were unmistakably being polluted by humans and the consequences of their technologies – and one technology, in particular.

Unsurprisingly, then, dystopian films and neo-Malthusian predictions of doom were just as much a part of the Sixties cultural landscape as was Stanley Kubrick's fantastically futuristic 1969 opus, *2001: A Space Odyssey*. Parts of that film that celebrated the wonders of technology were an antidote to Kubrick's masterful 1964 Cold War critique, *Dr. Strangelove or: How I Learned to Stop Worrying and Love the Bomb*. Yet, despite these gnawing realities, many people in North America remained positive about the potential of technology to solve their problems: they placed their faith in technology; technology was the future, and the future was to be found in technology.[3]

In the midst of this technological zeitgeist, Malcolm Bricklin, a true believer in the power and potential of the future, and of technology, launched his audacious car project. Conceptualized as a prototype in 1972, the first production Bricklin SV1 appeared in September 1974, just two years after the final moon landing, at a moment when the impact of the economic disruptions of the early 1970s had not yet transmorphed into a justification for the corrosive neoliberalism that eventually came to define the era.[4] Appearing when it did, the SV1, its creator, and its ethos perfectly encapsulated both the period's optimism about technology and, also, the grudging but growing realization that the sky-high expectations of the 1960s were about to crash into the gritty political and economic realities of the dour 1970s. This sports car, with its futuristic look, futuristic skin, and futuristic gull-wing doors was, nonetheless, also sold as a "safety vehicle," one that boasted, in a post–Ralph Nader automotive world, a roll cage and crash-worthy bumpers.

The deepest appeal of the idea of the Bricklin was that it was a testament to the possible, to the potential of the new, the untested, and the bold – a testament to the future. That such a car could be built in New Brunswick, perhaps Canada's least economically advanced province, was not an ironic incident; it was, in fact, almost an inevitable outcome, given its premier's unrelenting desire to change his, and his province's, own trajectory. Richard Hatfield was quite sure that building cars, and especially cars as fantastic as the Bricklin SV1, was New Brunswick's technological ticket to the future, and to industrial modernity. All he had to do was to convince his fellow New Brunswickers that his dream, and Malcolm Bricklin's dream, was their dream too.

At a moment when the future seemed within grasp, when it beckoned so easily, so tantalizingly, and so provocatively, the launch of the Bricklin SV1 was more than the dream of a car – it was a technology that could be driven towards a prosperous, new, and modern reality for a promoter, a premier, a province, and its people. In 1973, at the start of the venture, little did these dreamers realize that Bricklin's fantastical enterprise would eventually come to represent so much more.

Part I. The Promise of the Future: The Technological Currency of High Industrial Modernity

The promise of the future seemed to be everywhere in the 1950s and 1960s, the high point of automobility and industrial modernity. In style and substance, modernist art and architecture, industrial design, everyday technology, the space race, air travel, the innovative use of plastics, and a multitude of other futuristic advances and attitudes, the period reflected a pulsating, underlying sense of optimism that thrummed just below an otherwise conflicted political and social landscape. After 1945, high industrial modernity's futurism was fuelled by the global economic and technological domination of the United States and that country's immense wealth. America's prosperity unquestionably spilled over into Canada, which benefited from the close economic, cultural, and linguistic ties to its southern neighbour. While Canada's tight Cold War alliance with the United States sometimes chafed, Canadians by and large reaped the rewards of the world's longest undefended border, massive American foreign investment in their country, and, above all else, their easy access to American technological advances and America's unparalleled production of popular culture.[5]

The common currency of high industrial modernity was the mass consumption of technology, and the technologies of mass consumption. From fast food to labour-saving devices to music to movies to television to travel, America's new, futuristic technologies, its styles, and its products dominated North America's cultural milieu, and, albeit to a lesser extent, the rest of the Western world's too. While not all North Americans partook in this futuristic technological and consumptive binge, many could, and did. On both sides of the border, a white, middle-class, postwar generation was born into a society whose touchstones were wealth and technology – the first generation in history to grow up in a world where automobiles, telephones, televisions, radios, record players, cameras, airplanes, washing machines, vacuums, and a never-ending list of magical technological advances appeared to be commonplace, convenient, and relatively accessible. The long-imagined future of technological dominion over everyday life seemed at last to be within human reach, or at least within the grasp of a significant segment of the baby boom generation, the largest demographic cohort in North American history until the millennials.[6]

The space age, a fixture of the period's collective consciousness, undoubtedly powered much of the postwar fascination with the future, and understandably so. The dizzying pace of progressively more astounding space feats, the gripping space race between the United States and the Soviet Union, and the seemingly limitless potential for exploration meant that, despite its brooding Cold War complications, the space age inaugurated by Sputnik's 1957 launch shaped much of North America's postwar discourse about technology and the future.[7] North Americans from all generations – but especially young people – were captivated and enthralled by the United States' determination to win the space race and the increasingly daring space programs launched by the National Aeronautics and Space Administration (NASA), from the Mercury to the Gemini to the Apollo missions, which landed a human on the moon in 1969. Canadians could even make a claim on the exploits of the American space program, as so many Canadian aeronautic engineering refugees from the cancelled Avro Arrow supersonic jet program of the 1950s – Canada's own stillborn, and still greatest, technological quest to capture the future – served as NASA employees, helping to usher a generation of American astronauts into space.[8]

By the Sixties, the space age seemed to be everywhere. On radio, in newspapers and magazines, and especially on the new and now easily accessible technology of television (itself, outside of the automobile, perhaps the greatest harbinger of postwar futurism), space and its discourse seeped into the everyday, shaping popular culture, fashion, design, literature, and language. The space race, and its futuristic design cues, shaped much of postwar culture: from musical acts like Bill Haley & His Comets, to the boom in futuristic "sci-fi" writing from authors such as Isaac Asimov, Ursula K. LeGuin, Frank Herbert, and a host of others, to ground-breaking television shows like *Star Trek* (premiering in 1966), to space-age appliances, and, of course, in the shape and design of high-tech transportation vehicles.[9]

While ordinary humans could only gawk from a distance at the exploits of a Shepard, a Glenn, or a Gagarin, the futurism of high industrial modernity was felt more tangibly and immediately in forms of travel made possible in the jet age. Popular cartoon character George Jetson and his family, including a robotic dog, Astro, were emblematic of the widespread faith in new technologies that promised speed, convenience, and space-age-like expectations for near-instant, comfortable, and futuristic travel. The increasing use of jet engines for commercial air travel, starting in 1958 with the introduction of the Boeing 707 and Douglas DC-8 jetliners, meant that a growing number of ordinary (though mostly wealthy) North America travellers became enthusiastic jet-age participants.[10] American domination of the technology of air travel, the overseeing role that American policymakers and airlines played in opening international routes, and the preponderance of power that accompanied American command of the skies were key components ensuring that the postwar period would be, in the famous 1941 phrase of Henry Luce, the publisher of *Time* and *Life*, "the American Century." American dominance, according to historian Jenifer Van Vleck, reflected nothing less than a jet-fuelled "empire of air."[11]

As it expanded in the 1950s and 1960s, the American empire of the air was an immediately futuristic expression of American power and supremacy, "when sleek Boeing jets, soaring airport architecture, and glamorous stewardesses embodied the confidence and optimism of the ascendant American Century."[12] From the time-collapsing and geography-bending speed of air travel to modernistic airports – architect Luis Vidal's "cathedrals of the twenty-first century" – and to the technology of the planes themselves, air travel became a potent symbol of futurism in the years after 1950. As with so much in the postwar period, by the 1970s this expansive and hubristic jet-age view of travel ultimately foundered on the practical and physical limitations of air travel, the decline of American power after 1971 in both relative and real terms, and the global economic malaise that gripped the West. In Canada, a belief in the virtually unlimited promise of the jet age had led to a massive over-building or over-planning of airports in places like Montreal and Toronto.[13] But in the period before the mid-1970s, the optimism of the jet age and its futurism infused North America's discourse, in movies, cartoons, and cars, and in the the very notion of postwar American internationalism.

If the space race and the jet age were futuristic flights of fancy that sent human imaginations skyward, the beginnings of the robot age in the immediate postwar years seemed closer to science fiction than to fact. Industrial robotics, a core component of the third and fourth industrial revolutions, had its beginnings during the height of the second, the peak of American postwar high industrial capitalism and Keynesianism, in the 1950s and 1960s. After all, Fordism, the greatest expression of the second industrial revolution, was effectively a form of rudimentary automation, with its assembly line and use of machinery. Henry Ford had pioneered assembly line automation, but the paternalistic Ford saw the use of machines primarily as something humans did to increase their productivity, not as something to replace workers. The genius of Fordism was marshalling machines to work with humans, and in utilizing vertical and horizontal integration to further increase economies of scale and speed. In the 1960s, however, manufacturing began to change; automation included not only increased dependency on machines and progressively more efficient use of the assembly line to advance even more effective production processes but also witnessed the beginnings of the wholesale use of robotics in manufacturing.[14]

The fanciful idea of robots as humans' helpmates in society had been a staple of science fiction since the 1920s following the introduction of the word "robot" in the Czech writer Karel Čapek's 1920 play, *Rossum's Universal Robots*. Even then, entrepreneurs and inventors were working on how to put robotics to practical use, especially in manufacturing. By the 1950s, American inventor George Devol (1912–2011), along with the "father of robotics," Joseph Engelberger (1925–2015), developed the first robotic assembly machines, which they patented and put into assembly work in 1961.

That year, the world's first industrial robot, called Unimate, was introduced onto a General Motors assembly line at the company's Fisher Guide Plant (opened in 1938) in Trenton, New Jersey. Weighing two tons and with a seven-foot wingspan, Unimate's arm transported burning-hot die-castings from an assembly line and then welded these parts onto auto bodies, sparking manufacturing's, and humanity's, robotics revolution. In 1966, Unimate appeared on Johnny Carson's *Tonight Show*, where it hit a golf ball and poured a drink. This futuristic sensation gave millions of awed late-night viewers a glimpse of the potential of robots, and a sneak peak at an industrial postmodern future.[15]

Devol and Engleberger's success with Unimate led to the founding of the first industrial robotics company in the world, Unimation ("universal automation," coined by Devol's wife, Evelyn Jahelka). Soon enough, Unimation was selling robotic arms to Kawasaki in Japan, to Ford and Chrysler, and to other manufacturing companies, specializing in assembly line jobs that were dangerous for humans. In 1969, GM used Unimation robots to double the output of its Lordstown, Ohio assembly complex (opened in 1966). By the early 1970s, Unimation was the largest robotics

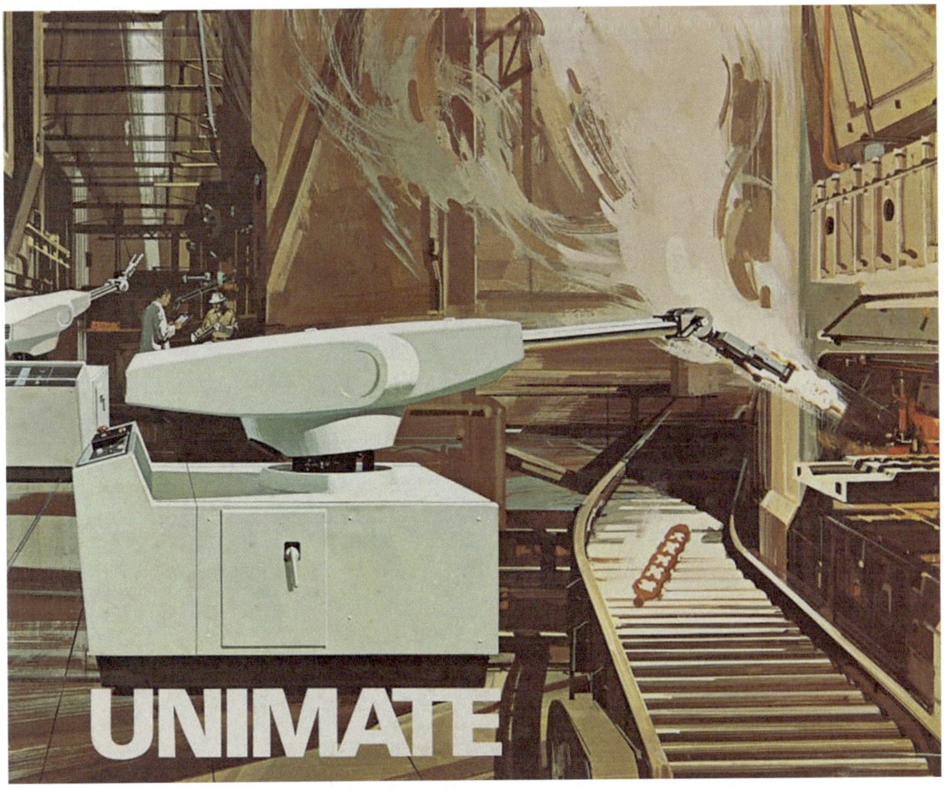

Figure 1.1. Unimate, promotional artwork, 1960s.

manufacturer in the world and, while the Asimov-inspired notion of humanoid robots was still more fiction than reality (Devol, who was Asimov's contemporary, didn't even like science fiction), industrial robots had become an essential part of the manufacturing landscape, especially, and unsurprisingly, in the automotive sector. Notably, Japan became Unimation's largest export market, and by the 1980s was the world's leading robotic economy, led by the country's booming auto companies.[16]

Since the technologies associated with the space race and jet age were out of reach for most ordinary people, and robotics were matters of specialized high technology for use in industry, nothing materially epitomized the everyday postwar faith in a technological future more than plastic. Various plastics had been invented prior to the Second World War, including the first fully synthetic plastic Bakelite, the "material of a thousand uses." Invented in 1909 by Leo Baekeland (1863–1944), dubbed "the father of plastics" in 1940 by *Time* magazine, Bakelite helped to usher in plastic's material revolution.[17] By 1937, the Society of the Plastics Industry had

Figure 1.2. Unimate at work on an auto assembly line, 1960s.

been founded, and, during the war, plastic production grew tremendously, as major corporations such as Du Pont and Dow Chemicals developed and introduced dozens of new plastic products for the war effort. After the war, plastic quickly moved from a primarily industrial use to a consumer one, with an infinite multitude of consumer products.[18]

It may seem difficult to believe now but, in the early 1950s, there was very little plastic in everyday society, though it was coming, and coming fast: Columbia Records produced the first full vinyl album in 1949, the same year that the first Tupperware party was held; the first polyester fabric, Dacron, appeared the next year; the first Ziploc bag was zipped in 1954; the first hula hooped in 1958; Barbie was born in 1959, Lego and cellophane in 1960, and GI Joe in 1964; plastic grocery bags and all-plastic chairs (the Chair Universale 4867) in 1965; the first plastic sports safety car, the Bricklin SV1, in 1974; and the first plastic Coke and Pepsi bottles in 1978. The first plastic, publicly available cell phone, a Motorola, did not appear until 1983. Clearly, along with electricity and the automobile, plastic has become the most ubiquitous, useful, destructive, and never-ending legacy of high industrial modernity and of humanity's impact upon the planet. Yet plastic, like the automobile, was and is much different in its effect than electricity (or electricity's children, computing, digitization, and the Internet), in that it has had a material, visible, and profoundly physical impact upon everyday life and the planet's environment.

But in the 1960s, plastic had optimistically come to be seen as the future's material of choice and the epitome of postwar modernity, heralded as a miracle product for the ages. In director Mike Nichols's seminal 1967 film, *The Graduate*, Dustin Hoffman's protagonist, Benjamin Braddock, is told that "there's a great future in plastics. Think about it. Will you think about it?" In Kubrick's *2001*, the vehicles, space suits, and everyday items are sheathed in spectacularly vibrant, surrealistically colourful plastic. Within a decade of these iconic films, plastic had indeed become a major industry and an accepted and heralded wonder material of modernity in North American society. The Plastics Hall of Fame was founded in 1972 by *Modern Plastics Magazine* (est. 1925) and the Society of the Plastics Industry. By then, plastic had become so wondrously – and disastrously – commonplace that, like the automobile itself, it was almost impossible to imagine a world without it. As the science writer and historian of plastic Susan Freinkel has argued,

> We were prepared, in our infatuation, to believe only the very best of our partner in modernity. Plastics heralded a new era of material freedom, liberation from nature's stinginess. In the plastic age, raw materials would not be in short supply or constrained by their innate properties, such as the rigidity of wood or the reactivity of metal. Synthetics could substitute for, or even precisely imitate, scarce and precious materials. Plastic, admirers predicted, would deliver us into a cleaner, brighter world in which all would enjoy a "universal state of democratic luxury."[19]

Of course, the realities of plastic, like so much else of industrial modernity's promise, had already started to be questioned by the time Malcolm Bricklin decided to utilize this "partner in modernity" to encase his safety sports car. Still, the fact that plastic could be so easily and directly connected to automobile modernity though the SV1 was completely logical: the plastics industry was effectively a spinoff of the petroleum industry, which was itself intimately tied to the automobile industry. Moreover, the auto industry itself came to be one of plastic's greatest users, with plastic wholly integrated into cars' design and production by the 1970s and 1980s.

After all, if plastic was the wonder material of the future, the automobile itself was the epitome of modernity, as well as its fantastic future.

Part II. The Automobile of the Future: Design, Technology, Newness, and the Futuristic Bricklin SV1

The automobile has been the embodiment of the futurism of industrial modernity since the first self-propelled vehicles trundled down cobblestoned streets in Europe or dusty Midwestern roads in America in the late nineteenth century. As a technology, the car represented nothing less than humankind's greatest leap forward: to drive a car was to unshackle the bonds of time and space and to declare victory over geography, topography, distance, and nature itself. Cars meant freedom through technology. Though the basic outlines of the automobile have remained unchanged for more than a century – four rubber, air-inflated tires for wheels; the same elementary chassis and structure; the timeless and utterly functional steering wheel – each new generation of builder, designer, driver, and passenger understood automobiles as an expression of their own freedom and their own technological faith in the future. Even after the 1960s, when attitudes towards the automobile began to sour, owing to their destructive human, environmental, and economic impact, cars retained an intense connection with futurism. Today, they continue to maintain a firm hold on the public imagination as the solution to the very problems that the internal combustion engine–powered automobile had itself done so much to cause.[20]

But before automobiles came to be seen as a problem, they were the most potent everyday symbol of the postwar period's optimistic futurism. Connecting the future and the automobile was not simply an emotional or intellectual response to the technological or psychological possibilities of what the car represented; it was a foundational aspect of motordom's corporate strategy and a mainstay of the industry's persona.[21] Detroit's unrelenting focus on newness, on heralding its next ingenious technological breakthrough, and on the notion of never-ending advances in car design had, as early as the 1920s, become the central feature of the industry's identity. That was the decade that General Motors' Alfred P. Sloan inaugurated the strategy of planned obsolescence by providing annual model changes. In doing so, Sloan vanquished Henry Ford's notion that the utilitarianism of the Model T, an

Figure 1.3. GM's first "dream car": the 1938 Buick Y-Job.

unstylish, relatively unchanging car for the people, should prevail.[22] In 1927, Ford grudgingly admitted defeat and embraced the idea of unremitting newness by ending Model T production after nearly two decades, when he launched the Model A, in 1928. After that, the annual model change became the driving, relentless cadence of the industry, the economic pulse of North American society.[23]

Even during the Great Depression of the gritty 1930s, when industrial capitalism was at its lowest ebb, the idea of connecting cars and the future was actively cemented in the car-buying public's mind by Detroit and its powerful marketing allies on Madison Avenue. Between designs and advertising copy that explicitly emphasized futuristic streamlining (the 1934 Chrysler Airflow) and the latest moderne and art deco styling, features, and sleek profiles (the 1936–7 Cord 810 and 812), newness became the defining element of the automobile, with every new year or model release promising a look into the future. Automobile futurism was further turbocharged with the 1938 introduction of the first concept car, the "Y-Job," created by the legendary chief of GM's Art and Design section, Harley Earl (1893–1969). Hired in 1927 as the first stylist at an American auto firm, the imperious Earl wanted the Y-Job, a fantastically stylish one-off car based on a Buick (that he eventually kept for himself) to be "the car of the future."[24] The Y-Job was first exhibited at the 1939 World's Fair, where, coincidentally, an elderly Leo Baekeland was also visiting. The Y-Job was the first of a never-ending series of concept cars that helped to stamp the idea of automotive, futuristic, newness onto the minds of millions of consumers. Earl christened his concept vehicles "dream cars," a fitting moniker for these conveyances to the future.

Fantastically futuristic concepts like the Y-Job were displayed at World's Fairs, but they mainly appeared at the high temples of industrial modernity: automobile shows. The first modern auto show was held at Madison Square Garden in New York City in 1900, an event that was sponsored by the Automobile Club of America and attracted ten thousand spectators.[25] Along with the auto displays at World's Fairs and firm-specific events such as GM's Motorama (first held in 1949 as "Transportation Unlimited" at New York's Waldorf Astoria hotel), auto shows became a form of exhibition that came to define the industry's efforts to make an explicit linkage between the automobile and futurism. Ford's new Model A reportedly drew a million spectators to the 1928 New York Auto Show; during the 1935 edition of the show, the new Cord 810 was first displayed, causing a sensation.[26]

After the war and the return to civilian production by the Big Three in 1945, this persistently futuristic tempo accelerated, and the automobile came to be the single greatest expression of high industrial modernity, especially in design. Earl introduced tail fins in the 1948 Cadillac, setting off a dramatic race among the Big Three over the latest styling fads and increasingly larger cars as the 1950s wore on, with ever-growing bumpers, bright colours, gadgety accessories, and shiny chrome everywhere – a "jukebox on wheels," as the design guru Raymond Loewy witheringly complained in 1955.[27] Nonetheless, Virgil Exner, Chrysler's designer (and a former employee of Loewy's), developed a "forward look," emphasizing tailfins and aerodynamics, another automotive nod to aeronautics and futuristic design.[28] Yet, despite the prominence of aeronautical or space technologies as an element of car design, following the end of the Second World War, the Big Three focused mostly on style over technical advances (though there were a few of those, too).[29]

Figure 1.4. "A Thrilling Trip to Tomorrow": auto futurism at GM Motorama, 1956.

Figure 1.5. GM's Harley Earl with a Firebird III, 1958.

By the 1960s, futuristic technology was everywhere. And in a world before the advent of personal computing, mobile phones, or the Internet, the automobile retained its status as the most desired and tangible contrivance of futuristic technology in ordinary people's lives. Planned obsolescence, the mobility of the car, and, of course, the fact that people got into cars – a physical act that transformed them from mere humans to wizards on their magic carpets of technological mobility – meant that, for most people, the automobile remained at the apex of futurism's technological reality. Cars took their design cues from the technological currents of the period, and they became the embodiment of industrial modernity.

The link between the space age and the automobile and its industry in the 1950s and 1960s was especially strong. Cars were named after astronomical phenomenon (as a small sample: the Pontiac Star Chief, 1954; Ford Galaxie, 1958; Mercury Comet, 1960; Chevy Nova, 1961; Toyota Celica, 1970), were designed to "look like rockets," and were advertised like spaceships (see figures 1.5 and 1.6). Alan Shepard, who, in 1961, became the first American to be launched into space, was given a 1962 Corvette as a gift upon his return to Earth. After that, as a thank you for their daring feats, every American astronaut based at Cape Canaveral received discount leases that, until 1971, allowed them to drive the latest Corvettes.[30] With

Figure 1.6. Automotive flights of fancy: 1956 Oldsmobile "Golden Rocket" concept.

this gesture, Detroit consciously connected itself to the exploits of America's space program and its extraordinary astronauts. It also helped that the Big Three were active participants in the space race, with Chrysler, for example, building Saturn S-1 rockets that boosted satellites and the first two Apollo missions into space. Chrysler even developed a few turbine-powered cars that took on the look of a rocket.[31]

Unsurprisingly, along with its space-age pedigree, high industrial automobility was also infused by the jet age. As it had with space, Detroit made a point of connecting its products with the technological romance of flight – albeit in an earthbound form. In 1951, Earl created a prototype Buick Le Sabre, styled and named after the US Air Force's F-86 Le Sabre fighter jet, which set in motion more than a decade of jet-themed auto styling, including the 1961 Oldsmobile Starfire (the F-94) and the 1965 Ford Mustang (a horse, but also a fighter plane, the P-51). The GM Firebirds I, II, and III, designed by Earl and showcased at the company's 1953, 1956, and 1959 Motorama shows, were essentially planes on wheels, technological flights of fancy that reflected Detroit's adoration of jet-age technology and its unceasing attempt to connect their cars to the freedom of flight.[32] By the early 1970s, jets, like space and the newness and possibility of technology, had been firmly established, both in practice and promotion, as fundamental aspects of the automobile industry.

The Bricklin Safety Vehicle-1 was the culmination of all these facets of industrial modernity's futurism. While still at Subaru of America, a firm he had co-founded in 1968 and led until 1972, Malcolm Bricklin had envisioned building a new sports car, one that blended the style and design cues of flight and space with the revolution in materials innovation and Americans' new-found desire for safety. The safety aspect had also been inspired, in part, by his time at Subaru: after *Consumer Reports*' scathing 1970 review of his Subaru 360, which it classified as "hazardous," Bricklin had the idea of "FasTrack," a chain of retail tracks where customers could race modified – and now crashworthy – Subarus. Bricklin engaged Bruce Meyers, creator of the famous 1960s dune buggy, to customize the cars, installing ultra-strong frames that were, effectively, roll cages. This design included plastic bodies for the vehicles, which gave Bricklin an idea about using acrylics (then commonly used for bathroom fixtures) as a way to make what he thought could be low-cost, coloured body panels, perfect for a sports car. Though the FasTrack plan flopped, Meyers's innovative safety designs eventually led Bricklin to the idea of a production "safety sports car" – what would become the SV1. In 1971, he set out to make the idea of a futuristic and sexy but safe sports car a reality. After convincing a few key people of the soundness of his fantastical notion, "the whole thing just sort of snowballed." By the end of the year, Bricklin had a concept ready to go.[33]

Envisioned as spectacularly modern in profile, look, and materials, the SV1 was designed by Herb Grasse (1945–2010), a fabled car stylist who would leave a tremendous mark on the history of global auto design. Grasse's four-decade career produced a portfolio as varied, expansive, and futuristic as that of any of Harley Earl's disciples, and perhaps even of Earl himself. Bricklin contracted Grasse not long after the latter's 1968 graduation from the Art Center College of Design in California. During his eclectic career, Grasse, a self-described "corporate screwball," worked for Chrysler, where he helped to design the first-generation Challenger (1970–4), and at

Figure 1.7. Subaru FasTrack Car.

Ford, where he worked on the XD Ford Falcon, the original Ford Laser, and the Ford Telstar. He was also appointed lead designer for Ford Asia-Pacific and then for Nissan Australia. A gregarious and creative free-thinker, Grasse often freelanced on the side, designing vehicles for the US military and developing concept cars, including for movie and television studios. In 1966, he designed the famous Batmobile for the television series *Batman* (1966–8), starring Adam West. Based on a Lincoln Futura (an unsurprising name for a car of that era) and built by customizer George Barris, the vehicle was a cultural phenomenon and an icon of Sixties automotive fantasy.[34]

But Grasse's crowning achievement was undoubtedly the SV1. Sparked by Bricklin's inspiration to build a new production "safety sports car" that fulfilled his futuristic vision, Grasse jumped at the opportunity when Bricklin contacted him at his Romulus, Michigan, studio in August 1972. The SV1 project, the first new American sports car in a generation, was "the chance of a lifetime." Building on an earlier "gray car" concept model (later called the "Grey Ghost") developed by another Bricklin associate, Marshall Hobart, and with a model hand-constructed by legendary custom car designer Dick Dean, by the end of 1972 Grasse had finalized what the SV1 would look like, with a design that was sweeping, rakish, and dramatic.[35]

Figure 1.8. Herb Grasse's Bricklin SV1 concepts and renderings.

Initially, Bricklin personally bankrolled Grasse's designs and the project's development with money he'd made from Subaru, setting up a group that included a number of former Big Three manufacturing men in a facility in Livonia, outside Detroit. Using Grasse's design, a clay model was crafted in less than three months – startlingly fast in comparison to the minimum of nine months that Detroit usually took to make their models. Then, amazingly, the first hand-built Bricklin SV1 was completed in 1973 in just eighty-three days, mostly utilizing a variety of off-the-shelf parts from American Motors Corporations and the Big Three. By that point, Bricklin had raised enough financing to hire Grasse and many of his team to his firm, General Vehicle Incorporated, and the dream was one step closer to reality.[36] Malcolm had a prototype, one that he could and would use to sell his dream car far and wide.

The SV1's design was shaped by four key futuristic elements: its sleek shape and profile (which included "pop-up" car lights, first introduced on the Y-Job, and

Figure 1.9. From concept to clay to prototype in record time: Bricklin development, 1973.

notoriously difficult to manufacture well); gull-wing doors; a plastic skin; and innovative safety features. When the car debuted publicly, it was uniformly praised for its forward-looking style in reviews and commentaries, particularly in the automotive press. The SV1's "sculpted" plastic panelling shaped the fresh design, which stood out, even among sports cars of the era. Grasse was recognized for his design and was named 1974 Industrial Designer of the Year in Product Design by *Industrial Design* magazine; futuristic Bricklins towering over oil rigs graced the cover of the magazine's annual automobile issue (see figure I.2). Grasse was also given the "Orange Door" award for Best Transportation Design by the Society of Art Center Alumni.[37]

Although the SV1's sleek lines were eye-catching, it was the inventive gull-wing doors that gave the car its most distinctive design feature. They reflected not just an audacious embrace of technological futurism, but also Americans' postwar obsession with air and space – they were, after all, *winged*, and therefore evocative of flight. And while they may have originally been driven by hydraulics, the doors' operation – called the "Electro Hydraulic System" in the SV1 owner's manual – clearly harkened back to Unimate's fantastic, futuristic, robotic arm. As *Car and Driver* enthused,"roll this set of gold wings into a shopping centre parking lot and it's as though a flying saucer had landed. An occasional bystander may recount memories of the legendary Mercedes 300SL, but for your average American, the Bricklin is a far out form of transportation."[38]

Nearly four decades after the demise of the SV1, Malcolm Bricklin excitedly recalled the genesis of the idea for the car's doors. "I remember it perfectly," he said. "It was a Christmas morning in the early 1970s, and my kids were watching a show called *Space: 1999*. They had these fantastic space-doors that opened up, and I thought – that would be perfect for a car."[39] Bricklin's recollection of the show was imprecise, as *Space: 1999*, with Martin Landau and Barbara Bain, did not premiere on American television until 1975, not long after the Bricklin had been launched. But the show's place in his memory reflects the powerful influence that the space age had on dreamers like himself and so many other North Americans at the time. Ultimately, the gull-wing doors became the car's most memorable feature, but also one of its most problematic.

The third futuristic feature of the SV1 was its use of plastic and especially its fibreglass skin. Plastic had been used in cars before, either as experimental materials or, by the 1970s, in some car parts. In 1941, Henry Ford had famously built a car with plastic panels made from soybeans. Chevy engineers had sheathed the first Corvette (1953) with a fibreglass skin, while Studebaker's "halo" Avanti (1962–3) also featured a fibreglass body, though that didn't save the brand. Renault had started to use plastic bumpers in 1971 for the Renault 5 (designed by Michel Boué). And some plastic was being used in car interiors, though industrial use of plastics had not yet become a standard in mainstream automotive applications.[40]

Plastic was a central feature of the Bricklin, and most of the Bricklin's body was moulded from that material. By being the first manufacturer to solely use fibreglass for a car's exterior panels, Bricklin fully embraced plastic as a defining element of the SV1 and pioneered the idea of a mass-produced plastic-panelled car, something that would not become an industry standard for decades. "If the Bricklin really is the car of the future, as its makers claim," opined *Automotive News*, "then sometime in the future we can expect cars which are at least 40 percent plastic." As *Industrial Design* magazine noted in its October 1974 feature on the Bricklin, the car's skin, a "vacuum-formed acrylic bonded to FRP [fibreglass reinforced plastic]" was "impregnated with safety or high intensity colors to a depth of .04 inches," far deeper than any of Detroit's paint finishes. The skin was "formed of space-age acrylic reinforced with fibre glass, a combination which is many times stronger than steel or fibre glass alone," Bricklin's own promotional copy declared.[41] Clearly, a leap into the future.

Plastic featured prominently in the car's interior too. Instead of fabric upholstery, "naugahyde (vinyl-coated fabric) is used throughout the interior including the bucket seats which are covered with a breathable suede version." Other elements of the SV1's "cockpit," as reviewers called the cabin, were also plastic, with moulded panels and a "crash pad made of Royalite 70 over urethane foam – an established automotive practice."[42] All of these innovative uses of plastics, on the inside and outside of the car, helped to cement the SV1's pioneering status as the epitome of modern materials usage. At the 1975 meeting of the Society of Plastics Industry, held in Washington, DC, Bricklin and the SV1 won the Transportation Award.[43]

The car's emphasis on safety was the fourth key aspect of its futurism. Advertising and promotion for the SV1 stressed that safety was a fundamental characteristic of the car's futuristic appeal. In the Bricklin's marketing materials and in interviews Malcolm gave to media, the car's safety features were blended into the SV1's futuristc vibe. The company's tag line was:

> The Bricklin Safety Vehicle:
> You'll think it's ahead of its time.
> We think it's about time.

When it appeared on the cover of *Motor Trend* magazine in July 1974, the SV1 was heralded as "America's newest safety vehicle."

Futurism, no less than the SV1's safeness or its sexiness, was Bricklin's brand. When the car was introduced as a prize on the popular television game show *Let's Make a Deal*, host Monty Hall proclaimed the Bricklin as "America's newest sports car … the car of tomorrow today!"[44] After its launch, the SV1 garnered numerous awards and recognition, both for its safety *and* its futurism: Bricklin and his car were honoured by the future-oriented Ontario Science Centre (opened in 1969, and including a prominent display on space vehicles) in Toronto for exemplifying what one member of the board of trustees said was "the philosophy of the centre." The SV1 was also, unusually, even featured at the Consumer Electronics Show (founded in 1967) in Chicago, a hotbed of new, innovative technologies not normally associated with automobiles – at least, not until the twenty-first century.[45] In a 1974 special issue of the *Journal of Popular Culture* devoted to the automobile, editor David E. Neuman opined that the Bricklin represented "both an experiment and a tested formula" and that the venture was "important to the future of the industry."[46]

In the spring of 1973, before all the accolades, publicity, and automotive fame, Bricklin only had a pitch and a prototype of his futuristic SV1. Actually manufacturing the car was still in the future, though he was sure he could do it. After all, he had already managed to build a prototype of his innovative, sexy, safe sports car. But he still needed to create a company, secure the financing for his new venture, and, most importantly, find someone, somewhere, to build his dream car. Little did he know that there was an equally ambitious young politician out there who shared Bricklin's futuristic dream – or, at least, the dream of industrial modernity for his hardscrabble province.

Part III. The Quest for the Future: The Lure of Automobile, Industrial, Modernity

In retrospect, it is easy to see how car making in the postwar period retained an allure that so powerfully gripped the imaginations of politicians, planners, and state-builders across the planet. Despite the immense difficulty that automobile manufacturing represented, it was, for some, nearly impossible to avoid being drawn, like moths to light, to the idea of building cars – and building the future. New Brunswick was not exceptional in this case – in fact, in its quest to build the Bricklin and an auto industry, the province simply reflected long-standing impulses that had been present since the beginning of the twentieth century as the impact of cars and their industry spread rapidly across North America and the world, along with the tremendous change and prosperity they generated.

This attraction arose from the intimate connection between the automobile and freedom, the future, and the very notion of modernity. The car was a technology that changed conceptions of time, place, work, leisure, space, and home; the social impact of the car was tremendous, reshaping and remaking aspects of everyday life by imposing itself upon city design, home-building, travel, the environment, and even the rituals of birth, marriage, and death, to name but a few.[47] Equally modernistic was the automotive industry, which produced the vehicles. The industry that had created modern, magical, mobility – personified by Henry Ford and Fordism – was the exemplar of the second industrial revolution, mass production, efficiency, scale, and wealth creation. Ford had successfully achieved his vision of a new future through his automobile and his mass-manufacturing processes by, quite literally, destroying the past, a fact of which he was acutely cognizant.[48]

Fordism became a worldwide phenomenon, one that described a number of causes and consequences of this new form of mass industrialization. Fordism described the mass production, standardization, and scale of the moving assembly line and the hugeness of Ford's vast industrial factories, notably, the gigantic River Rouge plant in Detroit. It also described (along with the work of F.W. Taylor – "Taylorism") the scientific management of labour and the idea of paying workers well enough so that they could purchase the products they built, epitomized by the famous "five-dollar day." Fordism also referred to the paternalistic, corporate welfare approach Henry and his Sociological Department had visited upon his tens of thousands of workers. Consequently, Fordism had also led to the creation of large-scale, cross-border industrial unions, such as North America's most powerful twentieth-century labour organization, the United Auto Workers (UAW), in 1935. Self-made Henry Ford, his cars, and his system ushered in an economic and social revolution, and he became fantastically famous and one of the wealthiest men on the planet (a billionaire by 1925).[49]

Most obviously, this revolution could be seen in the automobile industry's tremendous impact on North America's economy and society by the 1920s and 1930s. Utilizing vertical and horizontal integration to build his machines on a scale never before seen by humankind, Ford had sold fifteen million Model Ts by 1927, and soon much of the world was on wheels – or wanted to be. Henry's first international subsidiary, Ford Canada, working from its own "modern" facilities in Windsor, Ontario, built and sold hundreds of thousands of cars to far-flung locales as distant as Malaysia, Australia, and South Africa. Along with Ford, other giant companies such as General Motors utilized a new class of professional managers to create modern finance, franchising, advertising, marketing, branding, and sales and distribution networks. The effect of these sprawling, bureaucratic corporations

Figure 1.10. Diego Rivera's masterpiece of industrial modernity, *Detroit Industry*, 1932–3.

was no less than a remaking of the market and the birth of entirely new notions of consumption and production.[50]

So pervasive was the automobile and its industry's imprint as an instrument of modernity that Fordism became ubiquitous not only in everyday life and the economy, but also in artistic expression. In literature, F. Scott Fitzgerald made the car a central aspect of his seminal 1925 novel of the American dream, *The Great Gatsby*, and other American and European authors also placed the automobile at the centre of the modern experience and of what it meant to embrace modernity.[51] In art, Diego Rivera's 1932–3 industrial murals depicting auto assembly, which are in the Detroit Institute of Arts, became famous both as expressions of industrial modernity and critiques of the life-changing impact of the car and the processes that created it.[52] In his film *Modern Times* (1936), Charlie Chaplin both mocked and immortalized Ford's moving assembly line and its reduction of humanity into faceless automation.[53]

But automobile industrial modernity was more than a state of being, more than a consequence for individuals and communities, and more than a form of artistic expression. It was also an aspirational goal for nations, governments, and their politicians. In countries around the world, "automania" became the order of the day during the interwar period, and especially after 1945 (not forgetting the pivotal role that the auto industry itself had played during the war). Across the planet, car production was coveted as the paragon of a modern industrial economy and as a ticket to prosperity for states around the world.

In Latin America as early as the 1920s and 1930s, for example, Brazilians took a chance on a massive Ford rubber-growing operation while simultaneously mandating local auto production to achieve a modern economy. The car and its industry, according to the historian Joel Wolfe, created for Brazilians "hope for an eventual industrial transformation of society," one that "mirrored what Brazilians perceived to be the experiences of workers in the United States … driven by an established mythology about the ways automobility would transform the nation and its poor."[54] By the 1940s, Mexicans also saw the development of an auto sector as an essential element of the "dream of modernity" and actively pursued their own industry to build a better future.[55]

Yet the greatest global examples of industrial modernity's impact on a country's economic ascendency came in the postwar period, from Europe and Asia. There were three spectacular cases of how an automobile industry could modernize a nation's economy, its citizens' prosperity, its international standing, and its political and historical narratives: (West) Germany, Japan, and (South) Korea. These countries' embrace of industrial modernity, and their success in reshaping their futures and achieving economic supremacy through their often state-supported automotive firms and industries, acted as a clarion call to every politician, policymaker, entrepreneur, and dreamer who aspired to achieve the same economic security, status, and wealth for their own nation, region, or province – or for themselves.

In a region devastated by the Second World War, West Germany's economic miracle is famously known as the *Wirtschaftswunder*. Embracing a version of Keynesian postwar capitalism, West Germany's relatively rapid rebuilding of its automobile industry was the major engine of the country's postwar resurrection.[56] Volkswagen (VW, est. 1937) was reconstituted from the ashes of war in 1948 as a state-owned firm, jointly controlled by the West German federal government and the Lower Saxony state government, with labour representation on its board of governors – a structure that spread the company's prosperity across Germany as a national champion. The firm became a leading symbol of German reconstruction through its Type 1, the "Beetle," first built for the Nazis in 1938 and revived after the war as a low-cost, dependable mass car, a direct successor to the Model T. The Bug, as it came to be known, was a huge hit in Germany in the 1950s and, starting in the 1960s, in the rest of the world as well.[57]

Other auto companies that drove West Germany's economic miracle included the Bayerische Motoren Werke (Bavarian Motor Works – BMW, est. 1916), which had pulled itself from the rubble of the 1940s by first manufacturing motorcycles, then returning to the production of cars in the 1950s and 1960s. Daimler/Mercedes-Benz (est. 1926, building on the work of Benz Patent-Motorwagen (est. 1886) and Daimler Motoren-Gesellschaft (est. 1901)), now known globally for its luxury vehicles, launched its own postwar recovery by focusing on diesel trucks, which it sold to the government and its military. This fuelled the company's turnaround, its return to high-end production, and eventually its international expansion. By 1955, barely a decade after the war, Mercedes and West Germany signalled their full recovery and conquest of industrial modernity with the unveiling of the fantastic 300SL coupé sports car. A tribute to the country's miraculous turnaround, the car boasted, among other features, a "birdcage" reinforced frame and its amazingly innovative gull-wing doors – two innovations that eventually were incorporated into the Bricklin.[58]

Not to be outdone, on the other side of the planet, Japan experienced its own automotive-driven postwar economic miracle. As in Germany, state-supported automotive champions rebuilt from the ashes of war, reconstructing both the Japanese economy and the country's global image. Toyota was a centrepiece of this recovery. Founded in 1934, Toyota originally made looms for cloth production but decided to get into the auto business. After the war, Toyota returned to auto production, but by 1950 the firm was on the verge of bankruptcy, having produced only about three hundred vehicles that year. Then, the Korean War intervened. The occupying US military placed an order for five thousand trucks; soon after, working closely with its *keiretsu* network of companies and suppliers, banks, and the Japanese government, Toyota launched a major expansion and quickly became one of Japan's leading manufacturers. By the mid-1950s, Toyota started exporting vehicles to countries such as Australia. Helped by tariffs at home, low wages, an innovative Toyota production system (TPS), and a domestic market whose consumers did not buy foreign cars, Toyota expanded quickly in the 1960s, and by the 1970s had become a major exporter to the United States and other countries around the world. The Corolla became the biggest-selling car of all time, with more than forty million sold, while the sporty Celica landed in North America in 1974, Bricklin's first year of production.[59]

Along with Toyota, another major Japanese producer spurring the country's economic turnaround was Honda, founded in 1948. Honda, like BMW, was initially an engine company that made motorcycles and had, by 1959, become the world's largest producer of two-wheeled vehicles. After Honda started building cars in the 1960s, it became a huge success in the American market, and by the 1970s had established itself as an automotive powerhouse. Japan's postwar economic miracle was achieved by becoming a successful manufacturer and exporter of automobiles; the ascendency of firms such as Toyota, Honda, and Nissan (est. 1933; known in the United States as Datsun until 1981) earned Japan a rank in the "first world" of "modern" economies.[60]

South Korea, another postwar US dependency, embarked on its own massive modernization campaign in the 1960s, first focusing on industries such as steel and heavy manufacturing, building infrastructure including highways and ports, and developing export markets. Then, as with Germany and Japan, South Korea focused on autos and consumer electronics, utilizing its government-supported *chaebol* family-controlled conglomerates. By the 1970s and the 1980s, South Korea's economy was booming: the country's expansion was referred to as the "Miracle on the Han River," akin to the "Miracle on the Rhine River" in Germany, both of which were helped along with significant state intervention.[61]

Hyundai Motor Company, established in 1967 as a spinoff of an earlier construction and engineering firm, epitomized South Korea's transition to industrial modernity. The very name Hyundai comes from the Korean word 現代 (hanja form), which means "modernity." The company launched its first, inexpensive car, the Pony, in 1975, Bricklin's final year of production, and thereafter Hyundai followed the Japanese model of slowly expanding its product line and developing its quality, while also focusing on markets outside of South Korea. Eventually, by the mid-1980s, the Pony was the top-selling car in Canada, and the company had even established a North American plant in Quebec, although it closed in the early 1990s.[62]

Clearly, by the early 1970s, the idea of car making as the gateway to industrial modernity, prosperity, and the future was not new. Even in the Soviet Union, car production was seen as the epitome of state planning and a goal of industrial accomplishment, one that was meant to rival the Americans, though it often fell somewhat short.[63] Industrial modernity, and the status it conferred, was a worldwide goal of state politicians, planners, and ordinary people as well. In North America in the 1960s, even the spreading backlash against automobiles – starting with the growing unease about safety and emissions – did not dissuade planners and politicians from seeking auto production as a panacea for their economic ills and a way to grab the future. Most obviously, in 1965, Canada had tied its economic fate to the American auto industry with the enactment of the auto pact, though its benefits were concentrated almost solely in Ontario and Quebec.[64]

For a province such as New Brunswick, with a long history of slow and uneven economic growth based on resource extraction, and with high levels of unemployment and outmigration, the idea of having an auto industry, particularly one based upon the futuristic SV1, was enthralling. Despite the tremendous cost and difficulty of creating (and keeping) an auto industry, supporters deemed it was worth the risk. This was especially true of the idea's main provincial advocate, Premier Richard Hatfield. In a sense, in pursuing a dream of industrial modernity through automobile production, Hatfield was simply following in the footsteps of a long line of industrial development promoters across the globe, in Canada, and even in his own regional backyard.

Its advocates hoped that the Bricklin car, and all it represented, would be the brass ring that the province was looking for to create its own, modern, industrial miracle, this time on the Saint John River.

Part IV. Maritime Industrial Modernity and the Bricklin

The futurism of the postwar period did not come to New Brunswick the same way it came to other parts of North America or the world. As one of Canada's oldest colonial settlements (French – Acadians – first, in 1604, then the British, who expelled the French in the 1750s), the province remained a relatively conservative and deeply religious place, even in the face of the dramatic changes sweeping North America in the 1960s. Most ordinary New Brunswickers kept both feet firmly planted in their province's deep, traditional soil, despite important modernizing governmental efforts. Even in the early 1970s, most New Brunswickers would have been hard pressed to see themselves in the glittering space-age architectural icons built at Montreal's Expo '67 (even if there was an excellent Atlantic provinces pavilion), Toronto's futuristic CN Tower (under construction starting in 1973), the emerging technological hubs in sunny, affluent California, or even in the myriad trickle-down advances in plastics, computing, or robotics that were changing everyday existence. In 1973, one did not normally think of the future (or technology) when one thought about New Brunswick.

Which is not to say that New Brunswickers had not embraced modernity, for they had. In art, literature, architecture, and a host of other pursuits, the province was a relative hotbed of postwar modernist activity: New Brunswick visual artists were leaders in creating a Canadian modernist aesthetic; Fredericton's 1967 Centennial Building was an imposing example of the Internationalist style; the province's writers at the *Fiddlehead* journal (est. 1945) invigorated provincial poetry and prose; and a modernizing Acadian community voiced its culture and language forcefully.[65] In the period before the 1970s, wrote scholar John Laroux, New Brunswick "realized some of its greatest achievements in art, design, architecture, fine craft, and infrastructure during a time where so much seemed to matter, and so much was modern."[66]

A prime example of New Brunswick's modernist embrace, one that also reflected the glory of the province's most successful entrepreneurs (and politicians), was Fredericton's futuristic Lord Beaverbrook Gallery (est. 1959), directly across from the provincial legislature. Built by his lordship the 1st Baron Beaverbrook, Max Aitken (1879–1964), the newspaperman, financier, cement monopolist, and British politician, the gallery boasted a tremendous modern art collection, a gift to his

Figure 1.11. Salvador Dali, *Saint James the Great*, 1957, Lord Beaverbrook Gallery.

province. Surrealist Salvador Dali's towering *Santiago El Grande* (*Saint James the Great*, 1957) and two godlike 1949 and 1958 portraits of Sir James Dunn (1874–1956), Aitken's friend and another New Brunswick self-made financier, steel magnate, and industrialist, were highlights of the collection.[67]

Despite these vivid instances of cultural and artistic modernity, New Brunswick changed slowly, as the whirlwind of technology, style, and attitude shaped the Sixties zeitgeist. In 1971, the province's 634,000 people were scattered across a small corner of Atlantic Canada, with a capital, Fredericton (pop. 20,000), its largest city, Saint John (about 100,000), and a few smaller centres, including Moncton (55,000), interspersed among the province's ruggedly beautiful forests and river valleys. The populace was linguistically divided, with a two-thirds majority of anglophone Protestants, a one-third minority of French-speaking, Roman Catholic Acadians in the northeast part of the province, and a few thousand Indigenous peoples representing fifteen, mostly Mi'kmaq, First Nations. In the early 1970s, the province's population was relatively young, as befitted the era's baby boom; yet many of these young New Brunswickers also left the province, in search of better opportunities elsewhere.[68]

Figure 1.12. Florenceville, New Brunswick, 1956: cars, covered bridges, Irving Oil gas stations.

This outmigration was, in part, because, economically, New Brunswick remained overwhelmingly rural and agricultural, a province whose livelihood was still based mostly on extractive, staples industries. In an earlier age of wind and wooden sailing ships, New Brunswick had been a "timber colony"; postwar, forestry was still among its most important industries. Along with wood, and pulp and paper, the province's physical and economic landscape was dominated by farms, mostly potato farms, like the one that Richard Hatfield had grown up in the tiny, but appropriately named village of Hartland (about 800 people), on the Saint John River not far from the border with Maine.[69]

Yet New Brunswick's economy was not based solely on timber and taters. Certainly, there was some heavy industry and manufacturing, and a growing service sector in the province. But by the 1970s, much of this activity was utterly dominated by yet another successful New Brunswicker, and perhaps the most powerful of all: Kenneth Colin Irving (1899–1992), known as K.C. Considered among Canada's greatest businessmen of the twentieth century, Irving was born in Bouctouche, a tiny hamlet on the province's isolated French-speaking Acadian coast where his father, J.D. Irving, ran the local sawmill.[70] A natural entrepreneur with an opportunistic knack for figuring out the next big thing (or, the next big thing he could make money from), as a young man, K.C. first gained a foothold in business in the early 1920s selling, unsurprisingly, Ford Model Ts. Realizing that the automobile revolution was dependant on gasoline and its easy access and distribution, Irving established his first gas station, Primrose Oil, in 1924, and then a second one in nearby Shediac in 1925. Massive growth in the use of autos, even in rural New Brunswick, meant that, by the end of the decade, Irving, who eventually made his base in Saint John, had caught the booming gasoline business at just the right time. In 1929, he founded K.C. Irving Gas and Oil Ltd., and despite the Depression, Irving did well as a beneficiary of the internal combustion engine's ascendence.[71]

Gas stations were just the start for K.C. During and after the war, he expanded his petroleum holdings beyond service stations to include refineries and also developed pulp and paper, construction, food processing, real estate, and a host of other businesses, all of which came to be conglomerated as the Irving Group of Companies. Saint John, Irving's base, became the site of the massive Irving Refinery, which opened in 1960 and became one of the largest employers in the province. By the 1970s, K.C., then in his early seventies, was one of Canada's wealthiest people, and New Brunswick was unquestionably his fiefdom, as the imperious industrialist and his three sons, James, Arthur, and John (nicknamed – as if a testament to the power of the automobile and its lifeblood – Oily, Greasy, and Gassy) dominated the province's economic landscape, and increasingly its public square, too.[72]

Along with the family's industrial enterprises and real estate, K.C. owned all the English-language newspapers, radio stations, and television stations. He had essentially become New Brunswick's own version of Orson Welles's *Citizen Kane*. Despite all the family's influence, all their wealth and holdings, all the firms that they had founded and nurtured, the province remained, by the time Malcolm Bricklin showed up there in 1973, very much as it had been before the war: mostly dependent upon resource extraction and the Irvings. The Irving clan's near-feudalistic extractive control of the province's economy did little to connect New Brunswick to the burgeoning North American technological or cultural revolutions that had fostered such faith in the future.[73]

Nevertheless, long before Bricklin appeared, New Brunswick, and the Maritime provinces more generally, had actively sought to achieve industrial modernity through public means. There had been, by the early 1970s, many regional examples of attempts to "modernize" and to become "industrial." These two notions are not automatically connected. Industrial development, as an element of regional economic development, does not necessarily mean modernity. The efforts to revive the coal and steel industry in Nova Scotia, for instance, or the expansion of resource-extractive industries were attempts at economic development but not necessarily industrial modernization, which, during industrial modernity, was most associated with manufacturing and technological change. Both types of schemes have been present in the Maritimes: wholesaling, power development, mining, and the manufacture of consumer goods have all been examined as examples of Maritime or Atlantic Canadian efforts to grasp the brass ring of industrial and economic development and modernity.[74]

An example can be seen in neighbouring Nova Scotia's efforts to build a viable high-technology sector in the province. In the postwar period, Nova Scotia attempted to establish – primarily through government support such as loans and grants – a number of infant advanced technology sectors and firms. Industries as diverse as radios and heavy water were started with significant government investment, and a few were successful. New Brunswick's reformist Liberal government had launched its own industrial development initiatives, which attempted to develop a higher industrial and technological profile for the province, such as the Westmoreland Chemical Park, opened in 1965, in Dorchester.[75]

The automobile industry held out a much more tantalizing embrace of technology, capital, mass production, and – importantly – employment, than any of these previous attempts. Even in the 1970s, automobile production was very much the epitome of industrial maturity, and the wages, spin-offs, and scale of a car plant had a potential that enticed politicians in many jurisdictions to encourage automotive investment. In Nova Scotia, the provincial and federal governments provided incentives and tariff breaks for Sweden's Volvo to set up the company's first foreign plant, in 1963. Volvo's relatively rudimentary facility in Halifax became North America's first offshore "transplant" operation, and it was already well into production by the time Bricklin announced his New Brunswick venture. By the mid-1960s, Nova Scotia's economic development minister (and later premier), George Smith, proudly drove a Halifax-built Volvo as his "main car"; Hatfield would famously use an SV1 during the 1974 New Brunswick election. In 1973, Volvo's Canadian operation turned out over 10,000 vehicles, and the facility lasted until 1998. Nova Scotia also supported and was home to Canadian Motor Industries (CMI), another simple assembly plant in Cape Breton, which, starting in 1967, bolted together cheap, partially assembled Isuzus and Toyotas. Though the federal government gave Toyota tariff relief on its imports to Canada based on its Cape Breton output, Toyota shuttered the plant in 1975 after assembling about 9,000 vehicles, including about 1,300

Corollas. The province had also welcomed a Michelin tire plant, in 1971, providing it with government support.[76]

All these efforts were a testament to the seemingly irresistible draw of auto production as the most direct route to industrial modernity, and they illustrated the willingness of governments – both provincial and federal – in the 1960s to offer significant incentives, subsidies, facilities, and direct ownership stakes to foreign auto firms to set up shop in their jurisdictions. Importantly, however, the operations of Volvo, Toyota, and Michelin differed from Bricklin in that Nova Scotia was supporting established firms that produced vehicles and products that already had a market (though not necessarily a huge one), while Bricklin was a classic startup and was offering a very different kind of vehicle (even if there was a potentially large market for the SV1). Unlike Bricklin, all the firms that Nova Scotia had attracted to its shores had their own long-standing manufacturing experience, significant technological know-how, and home-country managerial expertise and sources of funding. Even so, Volvo and Toyota faced difficulties.[77]

Although the Maritimes were a relative beehive of automotive activity in the postwar period, New Brunswick was, in fact, not Malcolm Bricklin's first choice of location for his venture. Drawn by the seeming willingness of Canadians and their governments to invest in auto companies, and how his new, yet-to-be incorporated company might benefit from the continental features of the auto pact, Bricklin visited with federal government officials in Ottawa in the spring of 1973 for guidance as to where he might find a willing provincial partner for his project. Federal officials first connected Bricklin with the Quebec government. But Quebec's economic development money was already earmarked for a number of other projects. Moreover, Quebec already had its own auto industry, with a GM plant in Sainte-Thérèse (which opened in 1966 to meet auto pact obligations) and a few parts outfits. Since 1965, Quebec had also financially supported a Renault venture at a plant in Saint-Bruno-de-Montarville. After years of losing money, the facility had been shuttered in January 1973, making it the most likely place for Bricklin to build his cars in the province. Bricklin even toured the Renault plant but later said that he was dissuaded by the uncertain labour situation in Quebec.[78]

If some newspaper outlets later criticized Quebec for "missing their chance" with the Bricklin venture, it would have required a leap of faith for the Quebec government. The province was simply unwilling to take such a huge risk. According to Quebec's minister of industry and commerce, Guy Saint-Pierre, Bricklin wanted the province to invest $7.6 million in the venture,[79] yet Quebec would get only a third of the company's shares: "If the business went well, they would make a fortune, and, if it failed, we would take all the blows," grumbled Saint-Pierre. For his part, Bricklin later claimed that, while Quebec got "more than a passing glance," his firm went elsewhere because it was "impossible to get through the red tape."[80]

Luckily for Malcolm Bricklin, just across the provincial border from Quebec, a young, flamboyant, charming premier was looking for something to spark his province. Somebody named Leon Stern, an accountant or lawyer in Montreal who knew one of Bricklin's associates in New York, knew someone in New Brunswick and connected himself, Malcolm, and the Bricklin people with the province's development agency, the Multiplex Corporation. Bricklin later said that Hatfield "got in touch and said, 'come to New Brunswick,'" to which he replied "what, are you crazy?"[81] However the connection happened, Multiplex, a federal-provincial economic development agency established in 1971, was on the lookout for promising new ventures that might boost the province. Bricklin's pitch for the SV1 and a plant producing twelve thousand cars a year was passed along to people in Multiplex, who were very keen on the idea of building cars in an empty paintbrush factory in Saint John. They passed Bricklin's plan to someone in the provincial government.[82]

Simultaneously, Bricklin's proposal was eagerly presented by Multiplex to officials of what sounded like the perfect bureaucratic destination for a proposal like this: the Atlantic Division of the Government of Canada's Department of Regional Economic Expansion (DREE) (Industrial Incentives Division). In April 1973, a Multiplex official presented Bricklin's plan to a DREE official as an idea that "deserves your attention and full support."[83] Ottawa bureaucrats, however, were hesitant to put money behind what might become a high-profile venture, especially at a particularly prickly moment in Canada-US relations. The federal government was in the midst of delicate, ongoing negotiations with an American government deeply frustrated by the auto pact's "uneven" operation, one that tilted Big Three jobs and production towards Canada.[84] Ottawa bureaucrats kept a distance from Bricklin, but they did make it clear that any new automobile venture in Canada that was designed to take advantage of the cross-border auto pact had to have, to start, some kind of Canadian majority ownership.

With an ambitious goal to start production in September 1973, and the implicit threat that the venture might settle elsewhere, Bricklin had an audience with Hatfield in May. Bricklin later admitted that he knew nothing about the province and that, when he arrived in Fredericton in the spring of 1973, the city was recovering from a terrible flood. In Bricklin's retelling, the two men met in Fredericton at the Lord Beaverbrook Hotel, where Hatfield lived during his first few years as premier. Bricklin thought the premier's suite a "cardboard ghetto" but liked Hatfield immediately and found him "charming, intelligent and sophisticated." According to Bricklin, he gave the premier his pitch and showed him a movie he had made of the prototype. In response, Hatfield told him again that he should "come to New Brunswick" and that "we can get money from the federal government." It made perfect sense, in the premier's view: "Nobody knows New Brunswick. Everybody thinks we're fishermen. It will attract high visibility. It will promote the province."[85] With that meeting, Bricklin's dream became Hatfield's, too: the premier was quickly captivated by the idea of building futuristic, flashy cars in his otherwise economically dreary province. The two men struck a deal.

In June 1973, Hatfield – accompanied by Bricklin, coolly sporting sunglasses – announced at a press conference at the Admiral Beatty Hotel in Saint John that, in exchange for 51 per cent of his share of Bricklin Canada Ltd., the new manufacturing arm of the General Vehicle Incorporated (parent of the Bricklin Vehicle Corporation), Bricklin and the province had an agreement to build cars in New Brunswick, backed by $4.5 million in money and loan guarantees from provincial coffers to get started. Eventually, the venture also secured a $3 million loan from the federal government. Bricklin estimated that the plant would initially cost about $16 million, though he probably started with about $10 million. Hatfield boasted to reporters that the entirety of the first year's planned production of twelve thousand vehicles was presold and that the company fully expected to qualify eventually for auto pact status, allowing the car to enter the US market duty-free (and the company to purchase parts from across the continent, too).[86] Bricklin had successfully sold himself – and his yet-to-be officially unveiled car – to the New Brunswick government and its public. The car itself would not be revealed for another year, and the SV1 would not go into production until the fall of 1974.

When it came to Hatfield's and New Brunswick's decision to pursue the Bricklin, it was easy to see the attraction of the car's high profile and its potential to draw attention to the province, along with the jobs and prosperity that automotive manufacturing promised. The sexy, sporty Bricklin SV1 was different from the resource extraction or the heavy industries that had characterized the New Brunswick economy and business scene through the twentieth century. Hatfield himself felt as much, stating at one point that "what sets the [Bricklin] apart from an investment, in the expansion of a port or a chemical complex, is the publicity that attaches to the manufacture of a new automobile by a new automobile company. It has a high visibility, it attracts wide attention and speculative comment."[87]

Moreover, building a car was different, required different skill sets, and reflected a commitment to precision, complexity, and innovation that simply did not exist in those other, older sectors of the economy: it was the epitome of industrial modernity. Manufacturing cars could forever bury the idea of New Brunswickers as "hewers of wood and drawers of water," and they could join the ranks of all those other "modern," successful nations and regions that built autos. In addition, the Bricklin itself was perceived as being a step above most cars being produced in the 1970s; after all, in its marketing (if not its production reality), it was sold as a high-tech car, one with the latest advances in plastics, engineering, and safety features.[88]

Not only was the SV1 innovative, but it was spectacularly stylish too. This made it even more attractive to a politician like Hatfield, who was keen to use Bricklin's car as a dramatic showcase for the province's innovative potential. As Hatfield admitted in a 1985 *Maclean's* magazine interview, "It's not that I was ever very much interested in cars. It was the sheer sculptured beauty of the Bricklin, with its doors like a gull's wing: the idea that something so revolutionary could be made here, in New Brunswick."[89] The SV1 was, in the view of some in the provincial press corps, "the most modern and sophisticated product ever produced in the history of New Brunswick."[90]

The process of building the Bricklin was different too. For all the problems and criticism that cars and their industry were beginning to experience by the early 1970s, the automobile assembly line was still held aloft as the pinnacle of industrial modernity. Successfully building cars would put New Brunswick on the map in a way that no other industry or product could. The province's economic growth deputy minister, Harry Nason, put it this way:

> We have been referred to as the unknown Maritime Province, so the whole matter of assembly line production in New Brunswick with a New Brunswick work force is very much open to question. We do heavy industrial things here. We build ships, we build snow-blowers in Bathurst, but these are custom jobs, and the discipline that is required in a labour force where the line moves every few minutes and you have exactly so many minutes to do a quality job on a certain thing, is very different.[91]

This discourse, to be able to conquer Fordism and to exhibit an ability to create things on the same scale as a Detroit, Toyota City, or Oshawa, reflected an allure of the assembly line that still deeply drew in politicians and planners and dreamers, such as Hatfield and his government.

Yet the Bricklin was more than just a matter of achieving industrial modernity to benefit the province and its people; it also provided an opportunity for New Brunswick, and Hatfield, to get back at the naysayers. Hatfield could point to the

Figure 1.13. Hatfield and Bricklin in their assembly plant, August 1974.

SV1's futurism, and his province's ability to build the car, as a way of sticking it to the Ottawa bureaucrats and businessmen in Toronto and Montreal who, in his eyes, had for so long looked down on New Brunswick and its people. Behind the scenes, in Hatfield's initial talks with his federal counterparts in Ottawa, these officials had proven very difficult in terms of providing support for Bricklin, either through regional development loans or (more importantly) granting the company status under the auto pact. The latter would have helped the firm considerably by giving it duty-free importation rights to the United States from New Brunswick if it qualified as an accredited "Canadian" firm by building enough cars.[92]

Getting auto pact status was a very important consideration for a company explicitly designed to exploit the continental treaty by planning to build all its cars in Canada and to sell all of them to the US market (ironically, a Canadian sales network was never even established). In New Brunswick's dealings with the federal government over loans, Ottawa had rejected Bricklin's first application and provided financing for the firm only after the entrepreneur put some more of his own money into the project. When it came to auto pact status, one of the terms that Ottawa insisted on – in keeping with the economic nationalism of the time (the interventionist Foreign Investment Review Agency had been created in 1973) – was that Bricklin's Canadian branch must be a Canadian-owned operation. This insistance was what prompted the provincial government to take a majority share in the firm; it would likely not have done so if the federal government had not made Canadian ownership a requirement for auto pact consideration. Nobody else was willing to put up the money for such a risky venture.[93]

Bricklin was more than just an industrial development scheme, and the unwillingness of Ottawa to grant the company status under the auto pact or additional economic development loans (Ottawa was unwilling to sink any more than its initial $3 million investment into the company) simply strengthened Hatfield's commitment. According to one scholar, Hatfield "saw the response to the Bricklin proposal as another instance in which the economic development of his province was being hindered by the excessive conservatism of a federal government dominated by central Canadian interests."[94] Indeed, though one of the original reasons that drew Bricklin to come to Canada had been the idea of taking advantage of the continentalizing auto pact, Ottawa never did grant the firm official status under the agreement.

Nonetheless, Hatfield was undeterred in his dream of achieving industrial modernity and of a new future for his province. At the carnival-like opening of the Saint John plant in August 1974, the premier boldly declared to the assembled crowd that the Bricklin's "success will be our success." "We have come this far," Hatfield challenged the cynics, "despite the pessimism of some politicians and the scepticism of self-appointed experts." After all, in the premier's view, the people of his province were, "not just building a car. We're building a better New Brunswick. If it were produced in Ontario or Quebec, there would be more optimism. *We are not supposed to have dreams*. This ceremony proves they are wrong."[95]

Later, as the costs mounted and critics called for the province to disclose everything about the venture, Hatfield remained defiant, especially towards those from outside his province whom he saw as scuttling the effort. Hatfield admitted that "we cannot guarantee the success of any venture," but, he exclaimed, "the government cannot leave the economic development of New Brunswick to the mercies of the Canadian banks, the Toronto boardrooms or the federal bureaucracy."[96] Hatfield

Figure 1.14. On stage again, with Bricklin behind the podium, Saint John plant opening, August 1974.

was committed to the project, his plant-opening speech a paean to New Brunswick, to the futuristic potential of the SV1, and to industrial modernity.

Such sentiments must have been music to Malcolm Bricklin's ears. Richard Hatfield, his New Brunswick government, and the province's people had all become full partners in his endeavour, even those who were wary of this showy American businessman and his fast-talking ways. Hatfield's words showed just how committed he and his government (if not all citizens in his province) were to the SV1. For those two men, and the people who believed in them, the dream of the Bricklin was fully engaged with the future, even if all around them there were signs that things were changing dramatically, and that the seemingly never-ending prosperity of the postwar period, one that the automobile had done so much to create, was beginning to unravel. Bricklin himself tried to avoid some of these changes or to precipitate countervailing measures: his company was meant to take advantage of the new free trade in autos that had been created in North America by the auto pact; he wanted to use government resources to support his endeavour as a way to offset some of the massive cost of making cars; he innovatively designed his car to exploit the desire for safety but also tried to include the latest technologies and design features; and he used all of his promotional wiles to convince quite a few people that his idea of the SV1 promised a great future for all.

Yet building Bricklin's car at precisely this moment, when the futurism that underpinned the idea of the SV1 itself was quickly falling away, was an incredibly risky venture. In the mid-1970s, in a disruptive world of oil shocks, regulatory disruption, and brutal competition, such a test, to convince enough people that he could bring his fanciful prototype successfully to production, would require all the entrepreneurial skills that Malcolm Bricklin could muster. But, as an heir to that great generation of automotive pioneers, the men who had made the industry and had, in the words of Henry Ford, "created the modern age," Bricklin was more than ready to damn the risks and stake his claim to the future, as only an automobile entrepreneur could.

CHAPTER TWO

Entrepreneur (Archetype)

In May 1936, the *New Yorker* writer E.B. White penned "Farewell My Lovely," a tribute to Henry Ford's miraculous Model T, if not to its world-changing inventor:

> The last Model T was built in 1927, and the car is fading from what scholars call the American scene – which is an understatement, because to a few million people who grew up with it, the old Ford practically was the American scene.
>
> It was the miracle that God had wrought.
>
> And it was patently the sort of thing that could only happen once.
>
> Mechanically uncanny, it was like nothing that had ever come to the world before. Flourishing industries rose and fell with it. As a vehicle, it was hard working, commonplace, heroic; and it often seemed to transmit those qualities to the person who rode in it.[1]

Malcolm Bricklin was an entrepreneur. But Bricklin was not just any kind of entrepreneur, he was an *automobile* entrepreneur, the quintessence, the *homo erectus*, of the species.

Of course, the automotive industry did not birth entrepreneurship or modern capitalism – textiles, railways, steel, and meatpacking were its initial progenitors. Yet capitalism's essential idea of the singular, genius innovator and visionary, the iconoclastic promoter, and the all-knowing manager ultimately came to be distilled and personified in the self-made automotive entrepreneur, the male *American* automotive entrepreneur. Within industrial modernity's realm, there has been no more dynamic individual actor than the famous, successful, society-changing, economy-transforming automotive entrepreneur – save, perhaps, for the ambitious politician. Understanding the nature of the automotive entrepreneur reveals not only their influence in producing fundamental representations of entrepreneurship within an economy and society influenced profoundly by automobility, but also their role in shaping an entrepreneurial lifecycle in the business of cars and other large, mature industries. Entrepreneurship is an essential component in explaining Malcolm Bricklin's place in the arc of industrial modernity's rise, decline, and rebirth.

Certainly, there had been swashbuckling entrepreneurs and innovators before the motor car. Cornelius Vanderbilt (1794–1877) revolutionized transportation, first in steamships, then, more impactfully, in railways in the mid-nineteenth century, and became fantastically wealthy in the process. Thomas Edison (1847–1931) became America's greatest inventor, with a host of society-changing technological discoveries starting in the 1860s and 1870s. In the 1880s and 1890s, Andrew Carnegie (1835–1919) utilized new technologies and economies of scale to build the steel industry into America's industrial foundry. By 1900, John D. Rockefeller (1839–1937) had famously applied vertical and horizontal integration to create the Standard Oil trust, the largest and most powerful firm in the United States. Thomas J. Watson's (1874–1956) transformation of International Business Machines (IBM) by the 1920s into one of America's greatest businesses both predated and overlapped with the emergence of the automotive industry. These notable examples illustrate that the concept of the entrepreneur was itself entwined with the late nineteenth- and early twentieth-century emergence of modern capitalism, large-scale production and consumption, and, ultimately, industrial modernity.[2]

Despite such examples predating the car, it is with good reason that the automotive industry has been called "capitalism's favorite child," "the industry of industries," and "the world's leading business activity since the 1920s," while the automobile itself has been called "the signature product of the twentieth century" and "the preeminent machine of the modern world."[3] The concept of the society-changing innovator, and the creative destruction that results from their genius, emerged with Joseph Schumpeter's idea of the importance of the entrepreneur in the business cycle in the 1930s and 1940s, when the impact and legacy of that first, greatest generation of automotive pioneers was at its peak. Ransom E. Olds, David Dunbar Buick, Henry Leland (Cadillac's founder), the Dodge Brothers (John and Horace), Henry Ford, Billy Durant, Alfred Sloan, Walter Chrysler, and their cohort were all still alive or within living memory when Schumpeter's profoundly influential books, *The Theory of Economic Development* and *Capitalism, Socialism and Democracy*, were published in 1934 and 1943, respectively. Looming over Schumpeter's entrepreneurial innovators, whose creative destruction had sparked such profound change, were the automotive giants who had built the very landscape of modern American capitalism.[4]

Malcolm Bricklin and all entrepreneurs, but especially automotive entrepreneurs, toiled in the long shadows of these titans, and few could equal their greatness. Amazingly, between 1946, when Preston Tucker launched his ill-fated Torpedo, which did not make it into full-scale production, and 2008, when Elon Musk effectively took control of Tesla and started that company on its paradigm-shifting path to success, Malcolm Bricklin was the *only* independent entrepreneur to successfully design, launch, and bring to production a new automobile in North America, even if his firm had ultimately failed.[5] Successfully starting a new car company to launch a brand-new car, the ultimate entrepreneurial act, was a rare and extraordinarily difficult thing to accomplish, a "miracle that God had wrought," as E.B. White characterized it.

Motorization and the embrace of mass automobility had, after all, been perhaps the most profound and widespread technological, economic, political, and social transformation in North American history.[6] Indeed, in the four decades between 1890 and 1930, and particularly in the 1920s, when cars swept across North America, virtually every aspect of society was reinvented by humans' interaction with the automobile. That "roar" of 1920s was the loud, unavoidable cacophony of the car and its impact. Cities were dramatically rebuilt, and behaviours were radically modified to accommodate the millions of autos that, seemingly, had suddenly appeared on every street in North America. The state itself became far more socially invasive through licensing, policing, and road building, as governments expanded immensely to serve the car and its needs. The meaning of time and distance shifted, as the finally realized dream of true personal mobility meant virtually unlimited travel, unencumbered by regimented schedules or fixed routes, even for many *ordinary* people. Courtship and romance were utterly reshaped as age-old notions of privacy and intimacy were completely ripped from their pre-automobile moorings for every level of society. Rural and small-town people, who still constituted the majority of North America's population, were no longer as isolated, as farm families were able to connect to towns, markets, and broader communities with a newfound ease that had eluded previous generations. Small towns, and every geographical, liminal space in between, now required road signage, as spreading motor travellers commercialized and commodified local landscapes.[7] Along with this whirlwind of change came roadside culture: gas stations, motels, parking lots, parking garages, and eventually strip malls, highways, suburbs, and an almost completely automotive-oriented built environment – the modern carscape as we know it came into being.[8]

But no aspect of life was changed as much by the automobile as was the business world, whence sprang the car itself and its industry. Like a thunderbolt emanating from Detroit, cars – their production, consumption, financing, selling, distribution, and maintenance, not to mention the impact of automobiles and the auto business on popular culture, from music and literature to art and photography, and eventually from radio and television to the digital world – launched one of the greatest revolutions in business, ever.[9] By the end of the 1920s, with the emergence of the Big Three and automobility's sheer ubiquity, work, production, consumption, franchising, marketing, advertising, credit, and the very notion of a hierarchy of branding for different classes became inescapable aspects of the economy and of society. So, too, did the idea of the "new model" and planned obsolescence, which remains a fundamental element of consumption (think of phones or computers or clothing).[10] The world, argued Roland Marchand in his seminal work *Advertising the American Dream: Making Way for Modernity, 1920–1940*, was "now moving at a pace set by the automobile."[11] Cars became a symbol, both of humanity's ongoing drive for technologically fuelled continuous improvement and also of disposability and people's destructive disregard for their environment.[12] For both good and ill, cars' profound impact on business spread to virtually every other aspect of life. If "the chief business of the American people is business," as President Calvin Coolidge famously opined in 1925, at the height of the first great automotive boom, then the business of cars became the *sine qua non* of modern society, its essence.

Emerging from this maelstrom of breathtaking change was the automobile entrepreneur, an avatar of the creative destruction wrought by humankind's most pivotal technology.[13] Automobile industrial modernity had, in fact, bequeathed *four* great archetypes, whose enduring representations continue to shape American business consciousness and society's popular understanding of entrepreneurship, fame, and business success: the innovator, the promoter, the manager, and the saviour.

Part I. The Pantheon of Automotive Entrepreneurs: Innovators, Promoters, Managers, and Saviours

Entrepreneurship, and the idea of the entrepreneur, has shaped the epistemology of business and the study of business and its administration since the early twentieth-century onset of industrial modernity. It is no coincidence that entrepreneur as a category of scholarly inquiry and in the popular imagination emerged forcefully in the wake of the auto industry's ascendence in North American life. Edwin Francis

Gay, the founding dean of Harvard Business School, appointed in 1908 and a historian by trade, was originally from Detroit, the heart of the auto industry and of early twentieth-century entrepreneurship, the "capital of the twenty-first century."[14] Gay oversaw the creation of the case study method at Harvard, which, by the 1920s – motordom's most transformative decade – was pouring out hundreds of such cases a year, many of them exploring entrepreneurship.[15] By then, entrepreneurship studies were a foundational aspect of any understanding of the brave new world created by the emergence of modern business (quite a bit of which had been midwifed into existence by the auto industry). By the 1960s, Hugh Aitken's *Explorations in Enterprise* (1965) testified to the wide range of approaches to the study of entrepreneurship, varieties of which abounded.[16] More recently, entrepreneurship has become a renewed focus of historians, including an exploration of differing metaphors for how it is conceptualized.[17]

The pantheon metaphor offered here utilizes an amalgam of entrepreneurial approaches to present another way of thinking about entrepreneurship, one seen through the lens of automobility, by demarcating four entrepreneurial types across a lifecycle of firms in mature industries. The Schumpeterian entrepreneurial innovator is, necessarily, the first and greatest automotive archetype, one whose profile and *modus operandi* is seared into the collective consciousness of capitalist society: it is the innovator's disruptive inventiveness and matchless timing that sparks a wave of creative destruction that reorders business and society and, in the process, usually makes the innovator phenomenally wealthy and powerful.[18] The successful innovator has been a fundamental element of virtually all definitions of entrepreneurship. Of course, there are important caveats to this well-known formulation. Not all innovative entrepreneurs are successful, though their stories can nonetheless be profitably read to tell us much about the changing nature of their businesses, and of society too. Moreover, as business historian Daniel Wadhwani has argued, the entrepreneur's actions (and success) are shaped as much by the (often equally disruptive) societal circumstances they face: there is a two-way relationship between entrepreneurs and society, one profoundly influenced by timing and by luck.[19] Auto entrepreneurs were, and remain, exemplars of this dynamic.

Unquestionably, Henry Ford rightly towers over American business history as the greatest example of the innovator. Born on a farm in Springwells Township, Michigan, in 1863 as the eldest son of an Irish immigrant father and a Michigander mother, Ford remains the quintessential ideal of the self-made inventor and entrepreneur. A tinkerer with little formal education who grew up in post–Civil War rural America, Ford was obsessed with the idea of the self-propelled *auto*mobile as the stepping stone towards a wealthier, more egalitarian democracy and society.

Figure 2.1. Henry Ford, the Innovator, 1921.

Young Henry dreamed Herculean dreams, and he was especially committed to the fantastic notion of mass automobility – making personal mobility easy, affordable, and accessible to as many people as possible.

Ford spent much of his early life trying to build a car and a car company that would make inexpensive but dependable autos so that all types of people – not just rich people – could enjoy the countless benefits of motoring. Eventually, Ford created the most important car in history, the Model T, in 1908. The Model T was inexpensive and reliable, powered by a cheap and plentiful fuel source, and, unlike other cars of its day, easy to fix. The Tin Lizzie truly was a car for the people.[20]

Building a car for the people required incredible ingenuity and amazing innovations in production, design, and product development. The processes Ford oversaw to make his dream a reality epitomized the second industrial revolution and ushered in Fordism. Of course, innovators other than Ford, and firms and products outside of the auto industry, could stake a claim to shaping industrial modernity. Among these are the aforementioned business innovators Vanderbilt, Edison, Carnegie, Rockefeller, and Watson; sectoral advances in railways, steel, meatpacking, and consumer products like sewing machines and bicycles; technological inventions, from Charles Goodyear's vulcanization of rubber to Alexander Graham Bell's development of telephony; the railway-fuelled growth of national markets and distribution and communications networks; and even maturing financial markets and instruments and new corporate structures.[21]

But Ford's innovations, and the innovations he oversaw, not only reordered production and consumption, but created mass industrial and consumptive society on a scale unimaginable in 1903, when he, stung by two earlier failures, launched his third automotive venture in Detroit. The city was then still the heart of the Midwestern carriage trade and was already the embryonic hub of automobile innovation, the automotive Silicon Valley of its day.[22] Ford's contemporaries, auto pioneers such as Leland, the Duryea brothers, Chrysler, Olds, and Charles Kettering, among others, also achieved the status of innovators – visionary leaders who made brilliant technological or production innovations and, in doing so, also reshaped the American business landscape.[23] What differentiated Henry Ford from these other innovators was his drive, his belief that his automobiles had the potential to alter the world in ways that even he himself could not envision, and the tremendous success and impact of his innovative production processes and his sturdy, dependable, amazing little car.[24]

Despite his unquestioned innovator status, Ford cannot claim sole authorship of the myriad developments he oversaw that created industrial modernity as we know it. But he did have an eye for talent, and a relentlessness that inspired others to achieve his vision. Charles Sorensen, Ford's production manager for four decades, was actually the man behind what many consider Ford's greatest contribution, the moving assembly line, powered by the magneto flywheel and pioneered at Ford's Highland Park plant in 1913.[25] Less clear is where the idea to use lightweight and durable Vanadium steel came from. Ford claimed to have seen it in the smoking wreckage of a 1906 Palm Beach, Florida, auto race and decided then and there that it needed to be used in his Model T.[26] However it came about, Ford Motor's use of this steel, probably suggested by a well-read Ford engineer, completely revolutionized auto production.[27] Ford was not even the first to vertically or horizontally integrate his operations on a grand scale, though his integration led to one of the greatest sites of industrial enterprise ever constructed, the gargantuan River Rouge plant in Dearborn, started in 1917, opened in 1920, and completed in 1927.[28]

Nonetheless, Ford was, without question, the greatest single innovator the automotive industry had ever seen, and, by the 1920s, his titanic successes had made him a global icon of modernity. Heralded as a hero of equality, efficiency, and futurism, Ford was feted across the planet, from Brazil to Australia, and from Germany to the Soviet Union. Aldous Huxley's *Brave New World* (1932) envisioned a whole civilization that worshipped "Our Ford," while other works, such as Upton Sinclair's *The Flivver King* (1937) critiqued Ford, his company, and his impact. Songs

Figure 2.2. William Crapo Durant, the Promoter, c. 1915–20.

romanticized the Tin Lizzie and signalled the far-reaching social changes it brought about.[29] Ford's fame, wealth, and power led him to quixotic quests for world peace, social engineering, and political influence. Unfortunately, among other faults, he also embraced anti-Semitism and anti-union thuggery that profoundly challenged his impact and legacy notwithstanding his radical five-dollar day. Despite these failings, Henry Ford is, to this day, regularly cited as among the greatest American entrepreneurs of all time, if not the greatest.[30]

The second entrepreneurial archetype bequeathed by the automotive industry to modern capitalism is that of the promoter. The promoter is the visionary salesman, the man (and men were the initial imprint in all these archetypes) who can convince people of the greatness of an *idea*. Once a great innovation had emerged, it still often requires promotion. Though he invented the image of the inventor–folk hero who modernizes the world (and was good at media self-promotion and "a pioneer in public relations"), folksy Ford was himself no charismatic salesman – he paid little attention to sales and marketing in the first decade of the Model T, as the car simply sold itself.[31] But other firms, such as the emergent General Motors, initially were built and grew as much through combination, promotion, and marketing as they did through technological, production, or organizational innovation.

The first and perhaps greatest automotive promoter and salesman was the flamboyant William Crapo Durant. Little known today, Durant's spectacular career has been examined in works with names such as *The Dream Maker* and "The Fabulous Billy Durant," as two of the few scholarly treatments of this mercurial man are titled.[32]

Billy Durant and his promotional exploits in the earliest years of the auto industry are legendary. He has also become the stuff of legend by having his story mostly forgotten, lost to the mists of time. Born two years before Henry Ford into relative privilege (his father was elected governor of Michigan in 1864), Durant was a classic hustling salesman and on-the-edge risk-taker. He worked his way from cigars to insurance to bicycles to carriages and eventually to cars, taking control of Flint, Michigan's Buick car company, then the largest vehicle producer in America, in 1904. Durant's promotional moxie eventually led him to use Buick to create General Motors, a firm that became the world's largest industrial enterprise for most of the twentieth century.

Unlike Henry Ford, few in the general public today know the name Durant, a deeply ironic outcome in an industry where the preponderance of automotive marques are named after their founders – Benz, Daimler, Toyota, Honda, Dodge, Chrysler, Ferrari, Porsche, Bricklin, DeLorean, and so many others, including GM brands like Buick, Oldsmobile, and Chevrolet. These ubiquitous nameplates are a reflection of the unique power and status of the automotive entrepreneur in the capitalist world.[33] Yet no car company still exists that bears Durant's name, even though, at one point, Billy had launched a short-lived and ill-fated Durant Motors.[34] Other, also largely forgotten promoters in this period included Benjamin Briscoe, who crossed paths with Billy, but did not make the same lasting impact on the industry.[35] Later, there would be still other memorable salesmen and promoters, such as Preston Tucker in the 1940s, Malcolm Bricklin in the 1970s, John DeLorean and Lee Iacocca in the 1980s, and, of course, Elon Musk in the 2010s.[36]

But none could hold a candle to Billy, promoter extraordinaire. In 1908, the same year that Ford launched the Model T, Durant started to build GM through a mix of savvy stock promotion, an aggressive and sometimes illogical acquisition strategy, and an unfailing belief that bigger was better, and that the car was, indeed, the future of mobility. Between 1908 and 1911, he acquired ten different car companies (including Buick, Cadillac, Oakland, Carter, Elmore, Ewing, Marquette, and Ranier), two truck manufacturers (Rapid and Reliance), and a series of parts makers (including Champion spark plugs), mostly with little cash down. Durant's gamble was to create a combination that he hoped would provide the economies of scale to make his fledgling auto firm viable and would also hit on the winning technologies, models, and styles that car-hungry consumers did not yet even know they wanted in the early days of North America's automobile-buying frenzy. Twice he tried to buy Ford's operations, but Henry's demand for upfront cash was too rich for Billy.[37]

Starting in 1911, in a dizzying series of acquisitions, costly mistakes, corporate chicanery, and hubris, Durant lost GM, regained it (by using Chevrolet to engineer a reverse take-over of the firm), and lost it again, finally being forced out in 1920 by bankers from J.P. Morgan and the Du Pont family, who had gained control of the sprawling agglomeration. Along the way, in 1918, Durant had convinced Canadian Sam McLaughlin of Oshawa, Ontario, owner of the largest Canadian automobile producer, to sell to GM, creating GM Canada. (Ford of Canada had been created in 1904 when Gordon McGregor of Windsor's Walkerville Wagon Works went to Detroit to strike a deal with Henry Ford.)

Undaunted, Billy quickly started another combination, Durant Motors, to compete with GM, though he eventually lost that, too, during the Great Depression. But before being forced out of GM, Durant had created yet another combination, United Motors, this time in parts. In doing so, Durant in 1916 purchased the Hyatt Ball Bearing Company (est. 1892, Harrison, NJ) and thus inherited a youngish manager by the name of Alfred P. Sloan. Durant also bought the Dayton Engineering Laboratories Company (Delco) in 1918, which brought Charles Kettering and the electric starter into the GM family.[38] The two men, one a manager, the other an innovator, would prove essential to GM's success in the 1920s and beyond.[39]

Clearly, Durant the promoter was no inventor, and not much of a manager, and he could not save himself from his own hubristic promotional excesses. As Alfred Chandler concluded in *The Visible Hand: The Managerial Revolution in American Business*, in which he used GM as "an appropriate final case study in the history of the rise of modern business enterprise in the United States," Durant, "an entrepreneur of imperial ambitions ... had little interest in the processes and needs of management." Even his successor, Sloan, viewed Durant's "master salesman's optimism unchecked by facts" as "downright disturbing." Ultimately, Durant's promotional ambitions cost him everything. He died in 1947, the same year that Henry Ford passed away, but, unlike Ford, whose death sparked national and international headlines, Durant died bankrupt and largely forgotten. His last endeavour was running a restaurant and bowling alley in his hometown of Flint, a sad end to the story of the greatest entrepreneurial promoter in automotive history.[40]

Durant's demise and Sloan's ascendence to the top of the GM hierarchy signalled the emergence of the third great archetype that the automobile industry bequeathed to American business: the entrepreneurial manager. Innovation and

Figure 2.3. Alfred P. Sloan, the Manager, 1937.

promotion had produced giant corporations that required expert managers – a new breed of non-owners and non-promoters who shepherded these immense entities towards ever greater heights of success and domination. Automotive leaders such as Sloan and Walter Chrysler (who was both an innovator and a first-class manager) and, later, Henry Ford II stabilized the early sector and created and utilized a centrally overseen, multidivisional model of business organization to effectively manage the size and scale necessitated by the immense difficulty and risk in the automobile-manufacturing industry.[41] The manager remains the most indelible and enduring entrepreneurial archetype arising from automobile industrial modernity.

Alfred Sloan stands alone as the greatest example of the entrepreneurial manager and "company man." Between the 1920s and 1950s, he took Durant's unwieldly GM, transformed it into a multidivisional, multi-tiered model of centralized organizational efficiency and production and applied his marketing genius to it, making the auto industry the cornerstone of twentieth-century consumerism and advertising.[42] Meanwhile, in the late 1940s, a young Henry Ford II, the founder's grandson (known as "the Deuce"), salvaged the family firm from the jaws of demise in the wake of the company's near collapse during the Second World War, and, over a nearly four-decade reign, rebuilt his grandfather's empire into a colossus.[43] Ford II did so by replicating in the 1940s and 1950s Sloan's successes at GM in form and function, and structure and scope, to resuscitate his ailing behemoth (he kept a GM organizational chart on his office wall for four decades).[44] Thus, Sloan and Ford II personified a class of entrepreneurial managers who led the auto sector to the pinnacle of American and world industrial domination for much of the twentieth century.

Even more than the innovator or promoter, the legacy of the entrepreneurial manager, *the* iconic form of business leader within the large-scale twentieth-century American corporation, created the image of the prototypical businessman, the organization man, and the modern corporate executive. This idea of the entrepreneurial manager – and their skill in managing and leading the large-scale business enterprise in creative and innovative ways to push the vast enterprise forward while fastidiously watching the bottom line – was cemented in the public's consciousness by Sloan and GM's dominating mid-century performance. The idea was further entrenched by the 1956 decision of Henry Ford II and the Ford Foundation to make a spectacular initial public offering (IPO) of 22 per cent of the company, which valued Ford Motor at an astounding $3.2 billion. The IPO allowed 350,000 people to buy a share of America's most famous auto firm and a literal piece of the American dream. Amazingly, one of the world's greatest industrial enterprises had been wholly owned by the family (from 1919) and its charitable arm (from 1936) before what became the largest IPO in American history to that point.[45] In the postwar period, and industrial modernity's and postwar capitalism's zenith, Sloan and Ford II, and their organizational successors, epitomized the quintessential, buttoned-down yet ruthless chief executive, a shrewd accountant, builder, and profit maker: the idealized manager.

The entrepreneurial manager was contemporaneously venerated by three wildly successful auto-centred books that effectively established the mid-century canon of business writing and the centrality of the manager in overseeing the corporate ship of state. The first of these was, of course, management guru Peter Drucker's 1946 *Concept of the Corporation*, which lionized GM but emphasized, above all else, the merger of structure and manager to explain the modern firm's success. The second was historian Alfred D. Chandler's 1962 pathbreaking *Strategy and Structure: Chapters in the History of the American Industrial Enterprise*, which utilized GM (among others) to establish the organizational turn in business history and create its own historiographical subfield. The third book was Alfred Sloan's own seminal 1964 publication, *My Years with General Motors*, a book that did more than any other in history to deify the visible hand of the all-knowing manager, and whose writing boasts its own fascinating story.[46]

By the 1960s, the notion of the omnipotent manager had become ubiquitous as a central trope of successful business. The hagiography around Henry Ford II's post-war hiring of the "Whiz Kids" – management geniuses who helped the Deuce turn around a floundering Ford Motor Company – was a prominent example of this. So, too, were the legion of stories, books, movies, and television shows that glorified (and sometimes critiqued) the "organization man" and his quest to bravely traverse the bureaucratic corporate world, always striving for the top of the ladder as the epitome of postwar manliness, order, and business savvy.[47] Entrepreneurial managers' power lay not in their ability to create new businesses, but rather in building and conquering the large-scale multidivisional corporation, putting their stamp on it, shaping it, and inevitably pushing it in a direction that ensured its continued success. By the 1970s, that success had come to be defined, above all else, by a firm's profitability.

Legendary automobile business managers who followed in Sloan's footsteps included GM's Charles Wilson and Thomas Aquinas Murphy, Ford's Ernest Breech and Arjay Miller, and, as will be discussed below, Chrysler's Lee Iacocca. All these managers had climbed the corporate hierarchy to effectively lead gigantic firms to even greater heights of power and profitability, extending their companies' influence across North America and the world. Even in the twenty-first century, automotive industry managers have emulated the titans of yesteryear – leaders such as Chrysler/Fiat's Sergio Marchionne, Nissan/Renault's Carlos Ghosn (before his fall), and GM's Mary Barra, the first woman to lead a major automotive assembler. Tesla's Elon Musk was able to move beyond his roles as innovator and promoter and proved his managerial prowess by taking what was effectively a niche, exotic electric sports car company in the 2010s and turning it into a full-fledged electric vehicle (EV) mass manufacturer in the early 2020s.[48]

Finally, the auto sector can claim the provenance of the fourth great entrepreneurial archetype: the saviour. The saviour is the daring visionary who rescues the failing firm and turns it around through sheer entrepreneurial force of will, ingenuity, and creativity, often combining their skills as an innovator, promoter, and manager to do so. In reviving Ford Motor from the brink of disaster at the end of the Second World War, Henry Ford II became the prototype of the saviour, few of whose aspirants have achieved legitimate success.[49] Indeed, in the annals of automotive history, only Lido (Lee) Iacocca was able to surpass the Deuce, becoming a living automotive legend by rescuing Chrysler from near-certain bankruptcy in the late 1970s and early 1980s during that firm's first great bailout. He was the greatest in a series of post-1970s "saviors" who became famous for cost cutting, downsizing,

Figure 2.4. Lee Iacocca, the Savior, 1970s.

and managing decline to make a "comeback." Iacocca truly made the saviour archetype his own.

Perhaps just as important, Iacocca's successful evolution across the four archetypes, from innovator to promoter, manager, and saviour, also provides a template of what might be called the "automotive entrepreneurship lifecycle." The automotive entrepreneurship lifecycle illustrates not only how Iacocca came to exemplify the four entrepreneurial archetypes during his remarkable career while working at Ford, and then at Chrysler during that company's turnaround, but also how Chrysler's painful and somewhat miraculous survival itself reflected an important transition in the shift from industrial modernity to industrial postmodernity. Moreover, Iacocca's fascinating career and his role in Chrysler's near demise can be used as a point of contrast with Malcolm Bricklin's own place in the pantheon of automotive archetypes and to better understand his company's rise and fall, and its broader meaning.

***Dream Car* Song 4: "I'm Changing My Name to Chrysler," Tom Paxton, 1979**

Part II. Lee Iacocca and the Automotive Entrepreneurship Lifecycle

In mature, large-scale industries such as the automotive sector, the entrepreneurial roles of innovator, promoter, manager, and saviour have acted as sometimes distinct but often overlapping and sequential roles, as firms progressed from innovation and creation to growth, maturity, and stability, and then to decline, recreation, and renewed growth. This lifecycle may best be understood as a continuum of these varying and intersecting entrepreneurial archetypes. The lifecycle is a well-established approach in business studies, though more so for explaining firm performance and strategy than entrepreneurship.[50] If the first part of the pantheon metaphor presents an approach to understanding varieties of entrepreneurship, the lifecycle bridges entrepreneurship with business cycles, in this case by looking at modern business through the lens of automobility.

Cleary, quite a few of the first generation of auto pioneers held multiple entrepreneurial roles across the trajectory of their firm(s). Yet Lee Iacocca excelled in all four archetypal roles, and thus his story exemplifies the automotive entrepreneurial lifecycle. Iacocca's journey can provide a comparison to Bricklin's own career and can be used to illuminate important aspects of twentieth-century American automotive entrepreneurship, the evolution of large-scale automotive enterprises, and Iacocca's own role in these dynamics. Iacocca's tale also overlaps with many of the challenges and opportunities that Bricklin contemporaneously faced within the auto sector, and many of the broader economic and societal disruptions of the era.

Like Henry Ford, Lee Iacocca's business prowess made him unquestionably famous – his 2007 book, *Where Have All the Leaders Gone?* reassures readers that (before Donald Trump) he was "the most widely recognized business executive of all time." Iacocca graced *Time* magazine's cover thrice and could boast three *New York Times* bestsellers. In the 1980s, an already famous Iacocca became a cultural icon, instantly recognized by millions. He was heralded as a possible presidential candidate. Motivational speakers held seminars entitled "Lessons from the Great Leaders: From Hannibal to Iacocca." Theses and scholarly articles explored Iacocca as "an American western mythical hero" or placed him at the centre of investigations with titles such as "Entrepreneurial Masculinity: Re-tooling the Self-Made Man." He was a television celebrity, appearing in Chrysler commercials and on an episode of the stylish 1980s cop show *Miami Vice*. There even was a children's play written about his amazing Horatio Alger story.[51]

From the 1970s to the early 2000s, ordinary North Americans not only knew who Lee Iacocca was, they also knew *why* he was so famous. He was, as the dust jacket from one of his books stated, "a self-made man … [who] saved the Chrysler

Corporation from financial ruin [and] masterminded the creation of the minivan." Iacocca seemed to combine Henry Ford's innovative vision, Billy Durant's promotional street smarts, and Alfred Sloan's managerial genius. Yet he also had the distinction of accomplishing something that none of those others ever did – he almost single-handedly *saved* a giant American auto firm from certain death. Even Elon Musk, undoubtedly a first-class innovator, promoter, and sometimes effective manager, has yet to save a car company from death, though he may at some point. Iacocca could rightly be declared among the greatest American automotive entrepreneurs of all time, a business leader for the ages.

Before reaching these lofty heights, Iacocca had risen from humble beginnings. Born in 1924, the son of Italian immigrants, Iacocca grew up in small-town Pennsylvania, where he distinguished himself academically before heading off to Lehigh University and then Princeton to study as an engineer. Upon completing his schooling in 1946, he immediately joined the Ford Motor Company, but soon switched from engineering to sales, where he excelled in the mid-1950s, quickly moving up the company ladder to become general manager of the Ford Division itself in 1960.[52] From that point, Iacocca would make his name in automotive history.

As an innovator, Iacocca can lay claim to not one, but two society-changing innovations in the auto industry. Iacocca followed in the footsteps of the "Whiz Kids" to carve out his own legendary status at Ford with his mythical creation and marketing of the Mustang in 1964. In developing and launching the Mustang, Iacocca created a whole new, lucrative, subcategory of sports car, the "pony car." Not a total speedster like the Corvette, or necessarily a big, brawny, muscle car like the 1964 Pontiac GTO, the Mustang was a solid but sensibly powered, very attractive, near-muscle roadster. In the fall of 1964, the stylish and sexy Mustang hit a sweet spot of baby boom–driven, youthful American exuberance. The Mustang was immediately a huge success and has since become one of Ford's best-known and most profitable nameplates, second only to the iconic F-150 truck. The car even hatched its own subcategory of Big Three pony doppelgängers, all chasing baby boomer sports car enthusiasts, the demographic that Bricklin would also target.[53]

Iacocca's second, game-changing innovation was his shepherding of a new type of vehicle, the "minivan," to launch in 1983 for the 1984 model year, after he had saved Chrysler from collapse (more on that in a moment). On its own, the minivan innovation puts Iacocca at the top of the automotive entrepreneurship hierarchy. Here, again, Iacocca tapped into new consumer and demographic patterns to reconceptualize who used cars and how they were used. The minivan redefined the family-oriented people (and stuff) mover, and it is almost impossible to think of the term "suburbs" and not think of that vehicle. When the Chrysler minivan

Figure 2.5. Lee Iacocca on the cover of *Time*, 1964 (top left), 1983 (top right), and 1985 (bottom).

launched, it was an immediate success, and, over the course of its existence, the company has sold more than fifteen million of the vehicles – more than the Model T. The 1984 Plymouth Voyager and Dodge Caravan essentially created a new class of vehicle – one that, for more than a generation, was among the auto sector's most profitable and important segments. Since the 1980s, there is probably not a single neighbourhood in North America that has not seen the backside of more than one or two (thousand) minivans.[54] Those two game-changing vehicles, the Mustang and the minivan, were brought to fruition very much by Iacocca, even though others were pivotal to their success.[55]

Clearly, Iacocca was an auto visionary and an innovator. Yet it was his salvation of the foundering Chrysler Corporation between 1979 and 1981, and the company's spectacular revival by the mid-1980s, that secured his place in the pantheon of automotive entrepreneurship as a manager, promoter, and – ultimately – a saviour. By briefly looking at Iacocca's role in the Chrysler bailout, it becomes clear how the four archetypes of automotive entrepreneurship were a natural evolution across the different stages of Chrysler's lifecycle as a company and how each type of entrepreneurship played a role in Iacocca's salvaging and revitalization of the firm, though in a lessened, if still profitable, form.

First, some background. In the mid-1970s, around the time that Bricklin was launching his SV1, and despite some years of record-breaking profits, the North American auto industry was in a precarious state. Some of this was not Detroit's fault: the Ralph Nader–inspired wave of safety regulation had knocked the Big Three backwards, as had the 1973 OPEC embargo and further governmental demands for better emissions control and fuel efficiency, embodied by the 1975 US *Clean Air Act.*[56] Offshore competition had increased (and improved) dramatically, too. But the Big Three, and especially Chrysler, had also authored much of their own misfortune. Though it had a long-standing reputation for engineering excellence, a legacy of being Walter Chrysler's company, Chrysler was too dependent on "gas guzzlers" for profits and had not paid enough attention to safety or fuel efficiency. Critics also pointed to Chrysler's ill-advised foreign ventures, and chair John Riccardo's decision to cull the engineering, styling, and marketing departments to trim costs, prompting one Chrysler executive to remark that the "only engineers around [here] were working on government regulations."[57]

By the end of the decade, Chrysler, America's tenth-largest firm by revenues, was in trouble. At a dramatic 1979 Detroit press conference, Riccardo admitted that the company was bleeding red ink. Chrysler owed $4 billion, nearly 10 per cent of all US corporate debt. Eighty thousand unsold vehicles worth over $700 million sat on dealer lots.[58] Chrysler's $1.2 billion loss in 1979 was the largest recorded in US corporate history. The company's impending demise was – prior to the Great Recession bailouts in 2008–9 – the largest in history and, for many, its crisis represented *prima facie* evidence of the end of American postwar economic hegemony and of the emerging and quickly accelerating deindustrialization of North America. [59]

Enter Lee Iacocca. After his string of successes at Ford, Iacocca had become president of the company in 1970, serving until his infamous firing by Henry Ford II in 1978. The Deuce might have been a genius manager and saviour in revitalizing and building Ford into a behemoth in the late 1940s and 1950s, but in 1978, his managerial acumen seemed to fail him. In asserting his birthright ownership, Ford II dismissed Iacocca with the pithy statement that he "didn't want strong guys around."[60] Iacocca was quickly hired as Chrysler president in 1979, tasked with turning around the faltering company. In retrospect, it was a match made in heaven:

serendipitously, Iacocca's very name was an acronym for his role at the company: "**I** **A**m **C**hairman **O**f **C**hrysler **C**orporation **A**merica." Iacocca took four key steps in the period between 1979 and 1982 that saved Chrysler but that also signalled a transformational shift, pushing North America's auto industry, its business practices, and its economy further along a path towards an industrial postmodern society.

First, Iacocca used his managerial bullhorn, his promotional skills, and Chrysler's dire situation to convince the vast number of individuals, groups, and stakeholders affected by the crisis (and the general public) that saving the company *his* way was the best and only option for Chrysler. In doing so, Iacocca innovatively utilized a form of "brink management." This contrasted with the traditional approach to "crisis management" in the sense that this was not a question of a product recall, or a calamitous outside event, or sabotage that had adversely affected the company, all of which are well-known in the annals of crisis management.[61] Iacocca's task was different: to achieve management goals, he needed to keep the company afloat, all the while emphasizing the organization's precarious situation of being on the "brink."

Iacocca required little help in publicizing Chrysler's situation. Headlines screamed that, if Chrysler failed in 1980, an estimated 400,000 workers would lose their jobs and that Detroit's unemployment rate would jump from 8.7 per cent to between 16 and 19 per cent. The US economy itself would lose $30 billion of commercial production, or 1.5 per cent of America's entire gross national product. Welfare costs would increase by $1.5 billion a year, while $500 million in Chrysler tax revenues would disappear. At a time when America's trade balance was already in sharp deficit, a Chrysler failure would add a further $1.5 billion to the shortfall.[62]

These dire warnings essentially became Iacocca's talking points to the nation. Everywhere he went, Iacocca walked the tightrope of emphasizing the trouble the corporation was in (which required government help and concessions) and, at the same time, maintaining that the situation was not irrecoverable. Testifying before Congress, he stated that he was speaking for over two million Americans "who would be severely impacted by the failure of this company."[63] Long before the term "too big to fail" had become commonplace, Iacocca was making that exact case to justify public and government support for Chrysler's survival.

Second, by asking for government aid, Iacocca broke the traditional Detroit automotive manager mould by challenging the historical role of the Big Three and the automotive industry as the avatars of postwar capitalism. In 1979 and 1980, Iacocca had to convince politicians that the notion of government help through loan guarantees was necessary, and not necessarily un-American. Iacocca recalled that, during the debate over Chrysler's fate "everybody was beating on us. Everybody saying, 'How dare you violate the altar of free enterprise and ask for a loan guarantee?'"

But, Iacocca argued, "we did not take taxpayer money. We had a guarantee, but for fifty years [the government has] guaranteed."[64]

Unsurprisingly, many observers both within the auto industry and beyond viewed this stance as anathema. From the Business Roundtable to commentators as disparate as Ralph Nader and Milton Friedman, Iacocca was skewered for what critics saw as an unconvincing conversion to state intervention. This attitude was best summed up by GM chair Thomas Murphy in 1979: "I do not think," Murphy sniffed about the prospect of government assistance for Chrysler, "that is in accordance with what made this country great."[65] Iacocca was shifting the discourse around the role of the state in supporting the automotive industry, something that Bricklin had also already attempted to do in New Brunswick years earlier. In Chrysler's, and Bricklin's, wake, consistent government funding to support the auto sector became standard practice in the North American political economy of the automobile industry after the 1980s, continuing until today.

Third, beyond government, Iacocca successfully managed and negotiated the myriad networks of management, suppliers, and banks within the Chrysler constellation to position the company to be able to take advantage of the government loan package. Many suppliers initially balked at the concessions demanded by the company, though they all eventually agreed after Iacocca's cajoling. Perhaps most miraculously, Iacocca convinced all of the company's 442 lending institutions to agree to the plan so that Chrysler could collect on the loan guarantees.[66] This was also important from a continental perspective, as Iacocca also needed the support of Canadian governments, unions, and banks, which reflected the increasingly integrated nature of the North American auto sector, a fact that Bricklin himself had, earlier, assiduously sought to exploit.

More difficult, however, was Iacocca's decision to fire thousands of managers and salaried staff and to close a number of plants, cutting the number of blue-collar Chrysler workers dramatically. Given the shape that the firm was in, union leadership was mostly grudgingly onside and agreed to concessions to keep the company going, but not without acrimony. Moreover, the Canadian part of the international United Auto Workers effectively split from the union because of the bailout concessions. Ultimately, Iacocca laid off tens of thousands of assembly line workers, and in January 1980, the famous Dodge Brothers' "Main" plant, opened in 1911 in Hamtramck, Michigan, the symbolic heart of Walter Chrysler's company, was shuttered; it was demolished the next year.[67] Despite government support, the Chrysler layoffs and closures accelerated and gave a permanence to the deindustrialization that was already starting to be seen in much of America's industrial heartland.

Fourth, and finally, Iacocca made a conscious decision to utilize his promotional skills as a salesperson to create a marketing and communications strategy that made him the central actor in Chrysler's turnaround strategy. Iacocca the salesman levelled not only with the politicians about Chrysler and its problems; he also levelled with all of Chrysler's employees and stakeholders about what needed to be done to save the company. As Iacocca tells it, "when Chrysler was fighting for its life, I went to every single plant so I could speak directly to the workers. I thanked them for hanging in there during those hard times, and I asked them to join me in restoring the company to greatness. There were a lot of cheers and some boos, but I got them involved."[68]

Along with communicating to the company's workers, Iacocca took a step that was perhaps most pivotal in the Chrysler turnaround story. He levelled with the American people and, in doing so, became the company's very public face. This promotional effort started small, with Iacocca at the height of the crisis signing full-page newspaper and magazine "open letters" to the American people. The ads attempted to debunk the "myth" of Chrysler's "gas guzzlers" and to be honest about Chrysler's situation.[69] Then came the commercials, which utilized Iacocca's marketing skills and natural charisma to make him perhaps the most recognizable CEO/spokesperson in business history to that point ("If you can find a better car, buy it!"). Perhaps more than anything else in the Chrysler saga, Iacocca's skills as a promoter (both to Congress and the American people) not only reshaped the discourse surrounding the company, but also made the man a star.[70] Iacocca had yet again transformed his image: at Ford he had been an innovator, then a quintessential company man; he had morphed these skills to become the promotional personification of Chrysler, and then its undisputed managerial mastermind. Iacocca's odyssey across the entrepreneurial lifecycle from innovator to promoter, and then to manger made him the industry's greatest saviour.

When President Jimmy Carter finally announced the bailout package in 1980, he stated that it was necessary "to avoid the loss of hundreds of thousands of American jobs among automobile workers and to keep a highly competitive automobile industry in our country."[71] The bailout plan passed by Congress provided $1.5 billion in loan guarantees. But it also required the company to secure another $1.43 billion in private financing, and further concessions from banks and suppliers. The plan also mandated $462.5 million in concessions from the company's unionized employees, another $125 million from salaried workers, and exemptions from clean air standards, allowing Chrysler to meet the new requirements two years later than originally expected.[72] To the immense relief of over 100,000 Chrysler workers (a decline from nearly 200,000 in the mid-1970s), President Carter signed the bill into law in January 1980.

The turnaround in Chrysler's fortunes came swiftly and stunningly. In July 1981 – just two years after Riccardo's dire press conference – Iacocca announced a profit for the second quarter. Though a meagre $11.6 million (versus $3 billion in 1979–81 losses), these earnings were followed by a virtual tidal wave of income, and in 1983 Chrysler paid off its federally guaranteed loans an astounding seven years ahead of schedule.[73] Chrysler's startling recovery did, indeed, seem to be a miracle, and there was no doubt who had been the miracle worker behind the turnaround.[74] By the mid-1980s, in the wake of Chrysler's revival, Iacocca was heralded as a genius manager. Observers called the Chrysler recovery Iacocca's "little miracle."[75] Books and papers were written heralding the Iacocca management technique, and business leaders, teachers, and millions of average Americans learned, read, wrote, and taught about Iacocca's management and Chrysler's miracle recovery.[76]

Beyond all the hagiography, Chrysler's greatest operational innovation during Iacocca's time was to shift more of its assembly north to Canada, where costs were lower and productivity and quality were higher.[77] In this way, Iacocca was accelerating a trend begun with the integration of the North American auto industry following the 1965 Canada-US auto pact – a feature of the auto pact that Malcolm Bricklin had already taken to its logical extreme by building his car solely in Canada for sale solely in the United States. Though there may have been a "New Chrysler," there was not a fundamentally new Chrysler way of running operations. Only in the late 1990s and early 2000s did Chrysler, along with the other Big Three, belatedly embrace Japanese-style lean production and flex manufacturing, the most significant shift in North American auto production in decades.[78]

Iacocca's other managerial moves at Chrysler included restructuring most of the company's multinational organization. And he purchased the dying American Motors Corporation (AMC) in 1987, with its lucrative Jeep nameplate. While these two moves were not necessarily any stroke of genius – unlike Durant's consolidation/combination vision of the 1910s and 1920s, or Henry Ford II's complete reorganization of his grandfather's foundering company from 1945 to 1949 – they, particularly the AMC acquisition, did have an hugely important and long-lasting impact on Chrysler's fortunes. Jeep eventually became among the most important and profitable nameplates of Stellantis, the sprawling global automotive entity created in 2021 with the merger of the Italian firm Fiat, the American icon Chrysler (which had previously paired up in 2014), and French automaker Peugeot Société Anonyme (PSA).[79]

Ultimately, then, Iacocca became the greatest example of the last automotive archetype, the saviour. Ford II had been an earlier iteration of this archetype, but Iacocca truly made the role his own. Iacocca's identification with the automotive saviour archetype has been so powerful that it has transcended business boundaries. In the decades since the Chrysler bailout, there have been numerous other government bailouts and amazing turnarounds in mature industries, including in the auto industry itself, notably in 2008–10.[80] But none have created a star in the way that the Chrysler crisis and bailout created the legend of Iacocca, the saviour. More-recent aspirants to the saviour archetype are Ford's former CEO Alan Mulally, as he revitalized the company in the early 2000s, and Nissan-Renault's turnaround master, Carlos Ghosn, whose own spectacular accomplishments (and, thereafter, his equally spectacular personal decline) are second only to Iacocca's successes. Of course, it remains to be seen where Elon Musk will end up in the pantheon of automotive entrepreneurs.

Part III. Malcolm Bricklin as Automotive Entrepreneur

Across his remarkable half-century career as an automotive entrepreneur, did Malcolm Bricklin distinguish himself as an innovator, promoter, manager, or saviour? And how does he compare with the giants of the American automotive story, if at all, and particularly with Lee Iacocca, whose own career overlapped with Bricklin's and also coincided with the transition from industrial modernity to industrial postmodernity? Is it even fair to compare the two, given their wildly different legacies? Indeed, why should Malcolm Bricklin, who failed with the Bricklin, be compared to any (successful) auto entrepreneur?

Comparing Bricklin's and Iacocca's entrepreneurial careers is a legitimate exercise, to a degree. I would contend that, while the legacies of Bricklin and Iacocca are virtually at opposite ends on any scale of success, scope, and impact on the broader auto industry, there are some common points, given their shared industry and contemporaneous careers, and some similar issues that confronted them, the analysis of which can shed light on the entrepreneurial archetypes and lifecycle and illuminate wider trends in the auto sector and in American business. It is first important to acknowledge an obvious difference: while Bricklin's SV1 venture was a rarity as a true automotive startup, Iacocca's accomplishments were in the service of Ford and then Chrysler, two of the Big Three – established, giant enterprises that faced the automobile industry's challenges in the 1960s, 1970s and 1980s from a much different perspective, even if the circumstances were similar. Despite this difference, however, a comparison of the two men is useful in three ways.

First, Iacocca's career is obviously a broader reflection of the difficulties faced by mature industries in this period, and his story can provide insight into the automotive entrepreneurial lifecycle in a way that Bricklin's fragmented and uneven career cannot. But Bricklin's ventures, especially but not only the attempt to create a new car and car category with the SV1, illuminate just how difficult it had become by the 1970s to succeed in this oligopolistic, mature, established sector. If anything, comparing the two further illustrates the dramatic changes that were occurring in the industry and broader economy – Iacocca from the perspective of established firms that exemplified large postwar American business, and Bricklin from the perspective of a startup that underscores the changing dynamics of the postwar auto sector.

Second, while Iacocca's career has been judged as a resoundingly successful one, Bricklin's record is – to be charitable – uneven. Contrasting Iacocca's successes with the Bricklin venture provides an insight into business failure, a theme that has become a renewed focus of business historians.[81] Examining *how* Bricklin was able to get so far, just how difficult it was for him to launch a new car company in the 1970s, and *why* he ultimately failed provides an opportunity to understand the utility of failure and what it can teach about the changing nature of entrepreneurship, the changing economic and societal dynamics of this period, and the broader challenges American business was grappling with during an era of industrial decline and a shift towards industrial postmodernity. The folly and failure of Bricklin and his firm, both in their historical reality and as they retrospectively came to be perceived, are just as useful as Iacocca's achievements and accomplishments in helping us understand American business evolution and the broader societal shifts in this period.

Finally, a synopsis of Iacocca's career as an innovator, manager, promoter, and saviour provides an additional layer of analysis in understanding entrepreneurship, Malcolm Bricklin's career as an auto entrepreneur, and the Bricklin company's place in postwar North American history. Demonstrating how Iacocca was able to achieve his status as an exemplar of the four automotive entrepreneurial archetypes provides a basis for exploring Bricklin's own attempts, whether he made them consciously or not, to achieve entrepreneurial immortality. Thus, Bricklin's efforts to be an entrepreneurial innovator, promotor, manager, and saviour provide four additional stops along the SV1's open road to understanding his career: his place as a safety innovator and broader questions about Risk; his promotional abilities as a Showman; his effectiveness as the manager of a Business; and his efforts to save his company as it faced its Demise.

Ultimately, Bricklin was far more successful as a promoter than an innovator, manager, or saviour. Even the SV1's technological innovations, while genuine accomplishments to establish safety as a feature of the car, were almost as much the product of promotion as they were legitimate advances that impacted the broader

Figure 2.6. Malcolm Bricklin, automotive entrepreneur, Las Vegas, 1974.

industry. In that, Bricklin presaged Iacocca, who, just a few years after the Bricklin fiasco, became even more famous than he had been at Ford, largely because of his ability to sell himself, his company's cars, and the notion of a Chrysler bailout to the public and the government. The scale, scope, and success of Bricklin's and Iacocca's tales contrast starkly, yet their stories are not so different: Iacocca sold government and the public on the idea of bailing out a company, after it had gone bankrupt, and became famous for doing so; Bricklin sold government and the public on the idea of buying into an auto company that eventually became bankrupt, and he became infamous for doing so. In the end, they were both promoters and salesman – one ultimately successful by every measure of the American dream; the other, not quite so much, try though he did.

There is a great irony in Bricklin's initial success in selling himself as an automotive entrepreneurial archetype. He needed to be a larger-than-life character and fit the narrative of the quintessential auto entrepreneur in order to make the idea of the SV1 believable to his stakeholders and the public – and, initially, he largely succeeded. In September 1975, *Road & Track*, one of the auto industry's mainstream publications, romanticized this very notion:

> Bricklin the man comes across as a very self assured, perhaps even cocky, individual. And "individual" is an apt description of Bricklin, both the man and his car. From his dress (Levi's, cowboy hat, open-neck shirt with strands of Indian jewelry), to his office in Scottsdale, Arizona (furnished in a ghost-town motif complete with 19th century saddles for barstools, a live cactus garden and rattlesnakes – skinned, thankfully), he's the antithesis of the typical white shirt ultraconservative Detroit auto executive.[82]

The lore of a successful startup auto tycoon called for an independent-minded, flamboyant, yet folksy, outside-the-box individualist anti-suit: a technological genius and innovator, or a brilliant promoter – a Henry Ford or a Billy Durant. Bricklin valiantly tried to make himself a postwar Ford-type innovator with safety (and styling). His innovative and promotional abilities were enough to convince people to get his car company started, but his managerial reality was nowhere near what was needed to actually make it work.

No, Bricklin was much more successful as a promoter, a salesman. And, like Durant, he understood that, when it came down to it, he really wasn't much more than a promoter. Like Durant, he too had a checkered past and a volatile relationship to the companies that he started. In the summer of 1975, when he was forced to resign from the presidency of Bricklin, he admitted that managing a car company was "not a strong point" for him, though, it was "common knowledge" that he had "promoting ability," which is what he would concentrate on going forward.[83]

Unfortunately for Bricklin, the auto industry had matured and changed dramatically, and there was little chance for an innovator or a promoter to make it in an oligopolistic automotive world run on a massive scale. However, one automotive archetypal image did persist. Bricklin's image may have been "the antithesis of the typical white shirt ultraconservative Detroit auto executive," but the reality of the 1970s auto industry called for exactly that white-shirted organization man. Only the third automotive archetype – the patrician, stern ultra-manager, with his finger always on the finances – could flourish in the postwar, multidivisional, bureaucratic auto industry. But Malcolm Bricklin was no Alfred Sloan, and the automotive world had become one almost entirely made up of Sloans, though that, too, was changing. For all his innovations and promotional abilities, what made Iacocca really famous in the auto sector was his *managerial* salvation of Chrysler, one that required a powerful performance to convince the American government, banks, workers, and consumers to finance the company. Not until Elon Musk would another auto entrepreneur successfully challenge Iacocca as an innovator, promoter, and manager, surpassing him by spectacularly breaking through with the startup creation of a society-changing, successful auto firm, and only then because advances in electric batteries and a host of other technologies and advances by the early 2000s allowed him to do so.

Therein lay the paradox of the postwar auto industry. History dictated that individual hubris, genius, and recklessness were required to make a new car company work, and Bricklin played that role so well that he became the industry's consummate showman, a postwar Billy Durant. But, after 1945, the modern American auto industry was, in reality, gradually more averse to hubris, genius, and recklessness. By the early 1970s, Detroit remained rigidly oligopolistic, was increasingly financialized, and sought profits above all else. The managers who ran the industry were the antithesis of Bricklin. The company man – a Sloan, a Wilson, a Smith, a Deuce, and even an Iacocca – now reigned supreme.

People still identified cars with their legendary, vibrant, innovative founders, even in 1974. But by then, the actual leaders of the Big Three were all finance men. Would the public have been interested in a new car company whose "vision" was supplied by an accountant? Probably not. Could a lawyer who had climbed the corporate ladder inspire the passion and emotion in the car-buying public to make them *want* a car in the old-fashioned way? Not likely. Bricklin, as the iconoclastic innovator and promoter, fulfilled his role well when it came *starting* a car company, but by the 1970s that role was not especially useful when it came to *running* a car company. Except in the rarest and most unusual of circumstances – an Iacocca or a DeLorean, and, later, a Musk – the corporate manager had effectively vanquished the other strains of automotive entrepreneur forever. When it came to Detroit and its Big Three, the postwar business of cars was now all about business – it was much more about revenues and profits and oligopolistic practices, and less about cars themselves. Detroit had done its best to eradicate risk from the car-making business.

Building a *new* car and starting a *new* car company from scratch, on the other hand, was a titanically complicated and tremendously expensive entrepreneurial venture. As *Road Test* magazine remarked in August 1974, just as the SV1 was about to go into production,

> *if* production gets off the ground with no major snags so that the cars reach the showrooms, *if* they sell well, and *if* they give reliable service, then the car has a fighting chance. It's conceivable that the car could be an artistic success and yet fail if the biggest *if* of them all isn't satisfied: *if* it can be sold at an attractive price at a profit.

> As Bricklin well knows by now, the stakes are high. You either win big or lose big in this business.[84]

Like the cocky and confident auto entrepreneurs of yore, Bricklin was undoubtedly aware of the stakes – of the strong possibility of public and costly failure, but also of the potential riches, fame, and power that beckoned if he were successful. Malcolm was willing to take that bet and prove that his plastic, sexy, safety car was worth the risk.

CHAPTER THREE

Risk (Safety)

***Dream Car* Song 5: "Cars," Gary Numan, 1979**

Risk, and understanding risk, is an inherent feature of society and a central aspect of human identity as people navigate through their lives. The idea of risk – the very notion of danger – the threat of injury or death, and the multitudinous ways that humans seek to mitigate these threats permeate and profoundly shape our social order. From the infinite number of decisions people make every day as individuals, parents, family members, workers, managers, teachers – the limitless variety of roles in which risk must be judged – to the broader decisions that firms, governments, institutions, or any organized body makes as it operates in society and collectively makes choices, risk is one of the fundamental characteristics of human interaction, and of civilization itself.[1]

The appearance of the automobile and its industry at the start of the twentieth century fundamentally changed the nature of risk in society and how risk is understood. The car itself reshaped individual and collective risk in innumerable ways, both obvious and subtle. To be sure, after the car had established itself as industrial modernity's greatest cause and condition, disease, injury, accident, and death continued to stalk the human landscape, just as it had since time immemorial. But the car, by virtue of its sheer preponderance in everyday life, unquestionably redefined automobile-demarcated risk as a key determinant of how modernity is understood, and thus became a focal point of the nature of risk in modern society. Risk of all types – physical and psychological, individual and familial, legal economic and social, and environmental – became intimately intertwined with humanity's production, use, consumption, and disposal of automobiles.[2]

By the 1960s, the most immediate risk and hazard posed by the automobile – physical injury through motor vehicle accidents – began to be reassessed, given the appalling number of traffic fatalities and injuries on the roads, a horrific figure that had been growing every year since the end of the Second World War. As more and more North American families became one- and often two-car households, and the total number of miles travelled by automobile grew almost unimaginably large, so too did the number of automobile-related deaths.[3] For much of automobility's reign, the industry and its supporters had sought to ensure that the car *itself* was not seen as the main reason for the horrendous carnage on the roads; instead, they pointed to human – driver – error as the root cause of those tens of thousands of annual deaths and often gruesome injuries, while the automobile, the fount of industrial modernity, was seen as largely blameless.

Yet, starting in 1965, the safety revolution inspired by Ralph Nader transformed people's view of the place of the automobile in society, and of how the car should, and could, be regulated to be made safer. Coincidentally, just as this transition to a new understanding of what constituted acceptable automobile-demarcated personal physical risk (and safety) in society was happening, another, equally profound, transformation was beginning to occur. At the very moment that public sentiment had determined that unsafe cars were a *risk* no longer acceptable for *individuals* – thus requiring legislation, regulation, and consumer protection – the auto industry itself began to lose its role as a guarantor of *collective* economic *safety*, one that had shaped its relationship with citizens since the 1940s. Just as Nader was hitting his stride in convincing the state to protect individuals (that is, consumers) from uncaring, giant firms, these same firms started to become unmoored from the predictable Fordist processes, relatively stable labour relations, and secure national boundaries that had, for the most part, shaped their existence. These changes put at risk the security of the very economic system that the auto sector had done so much to create in North America. Both these trends – the shift from personal automobile risk to safety, and from collective automotive industry economic safety to risk – could be seen in the changes reshaping the post-1965 automobile industry, of which the Bricklin story was, and is, a microcosm.

Indeed, by the early 1970s, when Malcolm Bricklin showed up in New Brunswick with his plan to build a car, it was becoming clear that, beyond personal safety, the automobile's emergence as a mass phenomenon had come to be recognized as one that also carried immense collective economic risks. From a macroeconomic standpoint, the broader consequences of gaining, having, or – worst of all – losing an auto industry also carried the risks of gaining, having, or losing gigantic commercial opportunities, massive investments, or – again, worst of all – potentially thousands of well-paying, blue- and white-collar jobs, in other words, all the material benefits of the dream of industrial modernity that nations across the globe had sought.

Thus, the personal risk that the automobile represented for ordinary drivers and consumers in terms of their individual safety had a corollary for governments, politicians, and their economies: the increasing risk that auto companies' behaviours and the evolution of the auto industry itself could have for the collective. Beginning in the 1970s, a decision made in the corporate boardrooms of these giant enterprises, often in Detroit or Dearborn, could mean prosperity or despair for workers and families, and for entire communities, towns, cities, and regions across North America. Capital mobility, and the risk that whole manufacturing industries could now be quickly shifted to different nations, resulting in deindustrialization and rust, became a grave and growing threat, as Chrysler's near demise would show.[4]

Somewhat paradoxically, then, just when it was becoming safer for individuals to get into a car, the auto industry itself was becoming a much riskier proposition. Both aspects of this paradox came into focus in the 1970s, and the latter, especially, reflected the dramatic changes happening to a society that had, for more than half a century, been built on the relatively stable economic bedrock of automobile industrial modernity.

Appearing precisely at this contradictory breakpoint, Malcolm Bricklin, his car, and his company perfectly encapsulated the quickly changing risk-safety dynamic, both in terms of Nader's automobile safety revolution for individual drivers *and* in terms of the increased economic risk that car companies and their actions represented to the collective's well-being and its future. Bricklin's car was, after all, the *Safety* Vehicle-1, predicated on the idea that individual consumers were keenly aware of the societal shift towards safety – not to mention auto manufacturers' newly imposed requirement to enhance it. Yet Malcolm Bricklin's car company, and especially its Canadian manufacturing branch, represented a veritable Greek tragedy of tremendously costly economic risk, one that foretold not only the harsh, new, volatile realities of the 1970s auto industry and the broader economy, but also an emerging ideology that itself would profoundly reshape society, as well as notions of individual and collective risk: neoliberalism.

Part I. Changing the Nature of Risk in Postwar Society: Ralph Nader and the Automobile Safety Revolution

A result of the onset of mass automobility at the start of the twentieth century was that motor vehicle accidents became a leading cause of death and a threat to young and old alike. Such a threat required never-ending vigilance on the part of individuals. Eventually, after much death and bitter debate about the role of the automobile in society, especially during the car's first few decades, it became clear that the ever-present threat of automobile death, which lurked around every corner, was one that people had, by and large, determined that they were willing to accept. As a result, from 1900 onwards, cities, towns, and the countryside spaces in between were almost completely rebuilt around the car, especially in North America, where automobility had its first and fullest embrace. Because of cars' preponderant role in society, the scale of their use, and their dangerous complexity, mitigating motor vehicles' risk (and hazard) required the complete reordering of society's built environment, its legal frameworks, and its state structures. This reordering also applied to ordinary people's everyday behaviours. Of course, this was inherently the case for drivers and passengers. But, just as importantly, it was true for *everyone* in a society impacted by the automobile, particularly vulnerable pedestrians – effectively, the entire population, and for all their active lives.[5]

As with risk, society's understanding and conceptualization of *death* was also profoundly changed by the arrival of the car. Before automobile modernity, death, and the threat of sudden, unexpected death, was commonplace and simply part of everyday life for people of all ages; there was little notion of such a thing as "tragic" or "accidental" death, save for those associated with some large-scale, unexpected disasters. Society was a dangerous place. After 1945, however, unexpected death became rarer and rarer. Advances in modern medicine, vaccinations, the health and welfare benefits associated with prosperity, workplace safety campaigns, and expert advice all helped to make most indoor spaces safer and made sudden death much less common.[6] Life in North America as a whole became progressively less dangerous – save for on its city streets, highways, and country roads, and, outside of disease, automobile "accidents" became society's leading cause of premature death, especially for children.[7] For more than half a century – from the Model T's introduction in 1908 until the early 1970s – death from automobile accidents increased every year in North America.[8] After the coming of the car, the tragic words "they were in an accident" could mean but one thing.

Nonetheless, over time, North Americans had largely come to accept the calculated risk of automobile death in exchange for all the benefits that the car had bestowed on them. Part of this acceptance was, unquestionably, a collective recognition that the automobile had become an incontrovertible fact of modernity, a theism that North American society was inconceivable without the economic, political, social, and cultural gains that those magical machines of personal mobility had granted. After all, hadn't the auto industry, the "arsenal of democracy," won the war? Hadn't Detroit's Big Three made postwar prosperity possible and created North America's middle class?

Perhaps most importantly, the postwar narrative surrounding the roadside carnage that did occur was one that placed the blame for any accidents squarely on *individual* drivers. High automobile modernity's theism also proselytized that, for all the death that it caused, the car itself was not at fault. As John B. Rae, the dean of American automobile historians and one of the founders of technology history, wrote in 1965 (the same year Ralph Nader published *Unsafe at Any Speed*), any criticism about the car "exemplified man's propensity to blame his technology rather than himself for whatever evil consequences it might produce." If a car was used for the wrong purposes, or resulted in unhappy outcomes, argued Rae, "the fault was with the users." In any event, the destruction caused by cars was, in Rae's view, balanced by motordom's benefits: "to offset the carnage on the highways was the fact that medical assistance, for illness as well as for accidents, could get to where it was needed far more rapidly than in the days of the horse and buggy."[9]

Society was willing to tolerate the level of automobile traffic deaths (in the United States, a horrific postwar peak of 54,589 fatalities in 1972, just slightly less then the total number of US soldiers lost in the entire Vietnam War) because it was willing to accept the risks that car travel represented. The risk could be rationalized largely because an ordinary individual's chance of auto death was, statistically speaking, still relatively low. Moreover, because, for the most part, cars killed individuals in single accidents, most people did not see the collective impact of automotive death, focusing only on personal tragedies. And even if they did look beyond the individual accident, they were conditioned to see driver error as the cause. This approach, according to the historian Peter Norton, reflected a mid-century era of "control," the second of Norton's thoughtfully conceptualized "four paradigms" of traffic safety across the twentieth century. This was the era from the 1930s to the 1960s, when traffic experts and engineers targeted human behaviour or poorly designed roadways as the main causes of auto death. It was the highway-building era of high modernity.[10]

And yet, despite the admonitions of Rae and the traffic experts, by the 1960s, things were changing. People began to question cars' profound reshaping of society and the risk associated with motor vehicle use in a manner they had not done since the 1920s. The impetus wasn't just car accidents: a new stage of consciousness about the automobile and its impact was emerging in the wake of not only the calamitous death on North America's streets and highways but also the unchecked sprawl of automobility's concrete infrastructure and the damaging environmental and health consequences of the car's undeniable externalities.[11] A variety of remedies were offered as antidotes to the automobile's diverse, destructive influence upon society. Clean-air advocates forced legislation and new technologies to curb the automobile's poisonous effluent. Anti-highway activists mobilized to stop freeway construction and urban demolition. Beautification experts, including presidential spouse Lady Bird Johnson, sought to clean up a visually polluted landscape of highway signs run amok and the "junkers" that a half-century of car abandonment had left along the continent's roadsides and in its "junkyards," themselves a phenomenon of automobility. Even the US Justice Department sought to curb the power of the Big Three, especially General Motors, for the risk their corporate size posed to competition and consumer choice.[12] All of these reactions emerged in tandem with a broader Sixties progressive activism that challenged many of the structures of industrial modernity, but especially its foundation, the car and its industry.[13]

Perhaps the most immediate impact on ordinary people that emerged from society's awakening to the problems of the automobile came in the form of Ralph Nader's safety revolution, one that focused on "crashworthiness." Nader's actions forever changed the course of the automobile industry, consumerism, and North Americans' views of the automobile itself. Most importantly, Nader played a key role in reframing the car, its industry, and government, forcing a move away from the witting acquiescence of personal automobile risk and towards an acceptance of state regulation in the service of safety for individual consumers and, ultimately, modern society itself. While these shifts may have happened without Nader, his actions accelerated a societal change that had immense ramifications for how individuals interacted with each other, with corporations, with the state, and with the very notions of risk in society. Because of Nader, the essence of *caveat emptor* was reconceptualized, as the notion of unquestioningly accepting an almost completely unregulated auto sector – the world's biggest industry, producing the world's most important and dangerous product – would seem, after the 1960s and in retrospect, utterly preposterous.[14]

Ralph Nader's meteoric rise to prominence in the mid-1960s as a safety crusader and Detroit's nemesis is a well-known tale. Born in 1934 in Winstead, Connecticut, to Lebanese immigrants, Nader put himself through Princeton University and Harvard Law School in the 1950s, and by the early 1960s had come to the attention of Senator Abraham A. Ribicoff (D-Connecticut). As an unpaid consultant for Ribicoff's 1965 inquiry into the federal role in traffic safety, Nader became the point person for the senator's investigations into safety in the auto industry and on America's roads, a subject on which the young lawyer happened to be writing a book.[15] That book, *Unsafe at Any Speed: The Designed-in Dangers of the American Automobile*, cemented Nader's place in consumer and automotive history. A muckraking exposé on a par with Ida Tarbell's trustbusting *The History of the Standard Oil Company* (1904) or Upton Sinclair's revelatory 1906 novel about the meatpacking industry, *The Jungle*, Nader's graphic, gripping manifesto took the public by storm. The book revealed how a seemingly indifferent General Motors Corporation disregarded easily rectified design flaws in its cars, callously leaving drivers and passengers at risk. An almost completely unregulated Detroit was sent into shock as Nader's exposé generated headlines and a public relations nightmare that not only uncovered the Big Three's shoddy design decisions but also brought into question their authority – not to mention their ethics and morality.[16]

Nader's book was a brutal portrayal of the *unnecessary* risk imposed on drivers and passengers by Detroit as the Big Three seemed to prioritize styling over safety and (as was quickly inferred) profits over people. In 1965, when *Unsafe at Any Speed* was published, GM's Harley Earl was still lionized as a legendary designer who had made tail fins cool, had stretched the average American car to an astounding length (the 1974 Cadillac Fleetwood was twenty-one feet long), and had done more than just about any other American to shape the image of the automobile, the symbol of mid-century American modernity. In 1965, the automobile was still very much America's greatest product and industry, and the deepest wellspring of its "free world" global economic and cultural hegemony.

Nader, and *Unsafe at Any Speed*, completely exploded that image. From Nader's very first sentence – "For over half a century the automobile has brought death, injury, and the most inestimable sorrow and deprivation to millions of people" – the book's pages were filled with horrifying stories and images of how America's cars were poorly designed, unnecessarily over-styled, and downright dangerous. Nader's book purported to show that Chevrolet's small, unusually shaped, rear-engine, and cheap 1961–3 Corvair (the name a portmanteau of Chevy brands Corvette and Bel Air) flipped over at high speeds, a consequence of poor product design and mechanical flaws. Just as bad, Nader's book contained a kaleidoscope of carnage, full of grotesque tales of impalements, injuries, and even decapitation, all courtesy of the Big Three's unwillingness to utilize safer designs in their cars. Nader revealed that, on impact, Detroit's poorly designed car interiors resulted in a "second collision," in which a driver not wearing a seat belt could literally be skewered by a non-collapsible steering column, while the passengers could be diced like ground

Figure 3.1. Nader's target: General Motors' Corvair de luxe 700, in a 1960 advertisement.

beef across sharp, protruding dashboards designed with chrome and cutting-edge aesthetics but with little regard for crashworthiness. While the industry had developed shatterproof glass, seat belts, restraints, and collapsible steering columns, and could easily redesign its interiors for much less lethal outcomes in crashes, Detroit claimed that costs, consumer preference, and driver error were the real reasons for all the death resulting from accidents.[17]

In a postwar era of hitherto unquestioned American corporate power, the thirty-one-year-old Nader's book clearly encapsulated the anti-authority, "don't trust anyone over thirty," counter-establishment outlook that had become a staple of 1960s

Figure 3.2. Detroit's nemesis: Ralph Nader testifying before Congress, 1966.

cultural questioning. GM, for its part, embarrassed itself further with a smear campaign aimed at Nader that completely backfired, resulting in a public relations debacle when Nader sued the company. In 1966, Nader was called to testify before Congress by Ribicoff, as were executives from General Motors. The GM suits did not perform well under the congressional klieg lights. With the hearings, decades of industry arrogance and insularity, compounded by an obstinate belief that the modern automobile corporation was the height of American and global business, were punctured by Nader's work and the committee's pointed accusations, for which Detroit's executives had little response.[18] Humiliated, GM's leadership was forced to personally apologize to Nader and to pay him damages.[19]

Nader used the $425,000 award from GM's humbling to start the Center for Auto Safety, and he eventually joined the staff of *Consumer Reports* (*CR*), the world's oldest and most influential consumer advocacy magazine, founded in 1936 as part of the Consumers Union non-profit organization. The consumer rights revolution had its champion, and its first and greatest foe was the almighty auto sector and the personal physical risk that the industry represented. As consumer historian Lizabeth Cohen has argued, "by embracing for his flagship cause the product most integral to the success of the Consumers' Republic" – the automobile – Nader's investigations

Figure 3.3. Ralph Nader, in Bricklin-esque colours, illustrating *Time*'s cover story "The Consumer Revolt," 12 December 1969.

were "just the spark that [was] needed to turn a hundred small consumer fires into a major conflagration for greater legislative and regulator protection."[20]

In 1966, President Lyndon Johnson, sparked by Nader and awakened to the shifts in popular sentiment – not to mention the ever-increasing impact of America's ongoing automotive carnage – decried the "slaughter on our highways" and announced in his State of the Union address support for congressional action on safety. Soon thereafter, Congress passed the Highway Safety Act and the National Traffic and Motor Vehicle Safety Act, which led to the creation in 1970 of the the National Highway Transportation and Safety Administration (NHTSA), a direct consequence of Nader's pioneering safety and consumer protection efforts. As an agency of the new Department of Transportation, which became operational in 1967, the NHTSA emerged from Johnson's Great Society initiatives, and it reflected a progressive and practical response to the problems of automobile risk. Nader had established beyond a shadow of a doubt that Detroit needed to be regulated – if not for its own sake, then certainly for the sake of millions of (North) American drivers, who might not realize that the cars that they were driving may not have been designed with safety as the primary consideration.

Despite Nader's headline-grabbing takedowns of the Corvair and GM, safety regulation was a slow-moving process. When Bricklin got into the safety game, the NHTSA was still developing the expertise necessary to test cars and to establish the regulatory framework for safety recalls.[21] As an emerging government entity that was still finding its way, the agency depended on the voluntary participation of the Big Three, a public that was transitioning towards a new, personal risk–averse culture, and a legal landscape that still needed to catch up to the regulatory rules being constructed in Washington, almost out of whole cloth.[22] Nonetheless, by 1972, when *Unsafe at Any Speed* was republished with a new introduction detailing the tremendous changes that had occurred since 1965, Nader had become a household name in America, and automobile safety (and regulation) had been established as a fundamental aspect of the auto business, whether Detroit liked it or not.[23]

Into this dynamic stepped Malcolm Bricklin, with his idea for a new car, one meant to ride the burgeoning safety wave to success – with all the sportiness, stylishness, and sexiness that he could muster.

Part II. Mitigating Personal Automobile Risk: The SV1 as a Safety Sports Car, and Malcolm Bricklin as an Innovator

It is something of an irony that Malcolm Bricklin's vision for the SV1 was of a vehicle that had safety at its core and as its greatest virtue and selling feature. The "world's first safety vehicle," as Bricklin liked to proclaim it, was being promoted by the man who had made his most recent get-rich-quick fortune importing Fuji Heavy Industries' Subaru 360 into the United States from Japan. With a partner, Bricklin had founded Subaru of America in 1968 to distribute what was then the least expensive car sold in America – and one of the least safe. At $1,297, the 360 was advertised as a 960-pound "bubble" car, effectively a motorcycle with the shell of a mini-car. It sported a four gear, twenty-five-horsepower engine and that took its brave drivers a leisurely 37.5 seconds to reach fifty miles per hour.[24]

Unfortunately for Bricklin, in April 1969, *Consumer Reports* published a devastating review of the 360. Riding a crest of popularity following the Nader/GM disclosures, America's most prominent consumer rights magazine found that its 360 test car (the model conveniently weighted in at seven pounds under the thousand-pound threshold required to meet federal safety standards) was "unacceptably hazardous." *CR*'s review coldly stated that the 360's front bumpers were "virtually useless against anything more formidable than a watermelon" and that "it was a pleasure to squirm out of the Subaru, slam the door and walk away." The magazine's final assessment was that the car was "not acceptable." Bricklin's Subaru venture quickly turned into a public relations fiasco, though, as he later liked to point out, he still made money from the deal.[25]

Bricklin learned his lesson. An emphasis on safety could be a real innovation in a marketplace that embraced Nader's philosophy and the bloodless officiousness of *Consumer Reports*, but still wanted the flare of a sports car. Safety was becoming a big thing, and so were sports cars, as the market numbers showed. Nader's regulatory revolution provided Bricklin – who, like any good entrepreneur, was always on the lookout for his next big innovative idea – with an opening. In the automotive world of 1973, pairing "safety" with "sports car" to create a new crossover category, the safety vehicle (SV), was about as improbable as combining "sports" with "utility" and "vehicle," though the latter eventually became the most successful crossover category of all time, the SUV. The SV1, a "safety sports car," was Bricklin's first genuine innovation (outside of importing cheap foreign cars), and if it caught on, it might just launch him along a path to automotive entrepreneurial greatness.

But it was a tough sell, one that would require all Bricklin's wiles and promotional chutzpa. History had shown that becoming a Ford-like innovator was an extraordinarily difficult achievement – a "miracle that God had wrought." Henry Ford, after all, had been most famous for his revolutionary *technological* changes, changes with a capital (model) T. Technological innovations – advances either in the vehicles themselves (say, for example, the self-starting motor or crash-proof glass) or in the production processes (the moving assembly line, just-in-time production techniques) – require a different type of entrepreneurialism than promotional or managerial innovations. Yet technology is key to both the reality and the image of the innovator. Henry Ford's career happened to coincide with dramatic technological advances in machining, metallurgy, and materials, many of which he took advantage of, and some of which he also helped to propel, as did so many others in that first generation of automotive pioneers.[26] Elon Musk is the best twenty-first-century analogue to Ford, as his automotive career luckily coincided with advances in digitization, electric battery technology, and innovative materials, all of which he embraced.

For his part, Bricklin had neither Ford's nor Musk's technological timing. If an entrepreneur is only as successful as favourable societal circumstances allow, Bricklin's appearance as an innovator came at an inauspicious moment. Unfortunately for him, Bricklin's automotive career coincided with a period in the American auto industry where technological change was more incremental than the dramatic shifts that had taken place in the period between 1890 and 1930, or would again between 1990 and 2020.[27] Many significant innovations did occur in the sector during the late 1960s and early 1970s (sometimes as a consequence of regulatory demands), particularly around emissions control (catalytic converters, for example), fuel efficiency (advances in engines, such as turbochargers), and safety (windshield wipers, seat belts, airbags, anti-lock brakes), many of them originating from outside North America. In Detroit, the Big Three remained committed to the fossil fuel–burning internal combustion engine and to a corporate philosophy that was increasingly driven more by profitability than by innovation. The American auto industry, one detailed sectoral analysis reported in 1971, "can be described as a technologically stagnant industry in terms of its product. Cars are not fundamentally different from what they were in 1946; very little new technology has been instigated by the industry."[28] Moreover, some of the most significant developments in electric battery technology, telematics (electronics within the automobile) or light-weight materials (like plastic) were, in 1973, still in their infancy, as Bricklin would soon realize.

Even without a genuinely great technological breakthrough (though he was trying, with the use of plastic), Bricklin's focus on safety as the car's hook was a brilliant approach. Safety, with a dash of technology, would be Bricklin's innovation. In the increasingly safety-conscious early 1970s, this approach immediately gave him credibility as someone who was serious about innovation and technology. With the SV1, safety was more than just an important marketing consideration. The disruptive impact of Nader's exposé had traumatized the industry, and safety was becoming a major concern for consumers, one that also fit well with Americans' quickly shifting tastes in the marketplace. For car buyers, the early 1970s was a period akin to the immediate postwar years, when the war had disrupted Big Three production and opened the market for established and new "independent" marques, such as Nash and Studebaker, or Kaiser and Tucker, who were offering something different than what was found in Big Three showrooms.[29]

And, just as had happened during the early postwar period (and would happen again in the 2010s and 2020s), opportunities abounded in the early 1970s for innovative auto companies – and entrepreneurs – who could take advantage of the changing landscape. This was especially true in the wake of all the new safety, emissions, and fuel-economy regulations. And foreign car companies were at the forefront of such innovation. One needed only to look as far as the upstart, opportunistic success of Japan's Honda Civic, whose humble exterior hid the company's "technological triumph": the compound vortex controlled combustion (CVCC) engine, a motor that could meet 1970 Clean Air Act standards without an expensive catalytic converter.

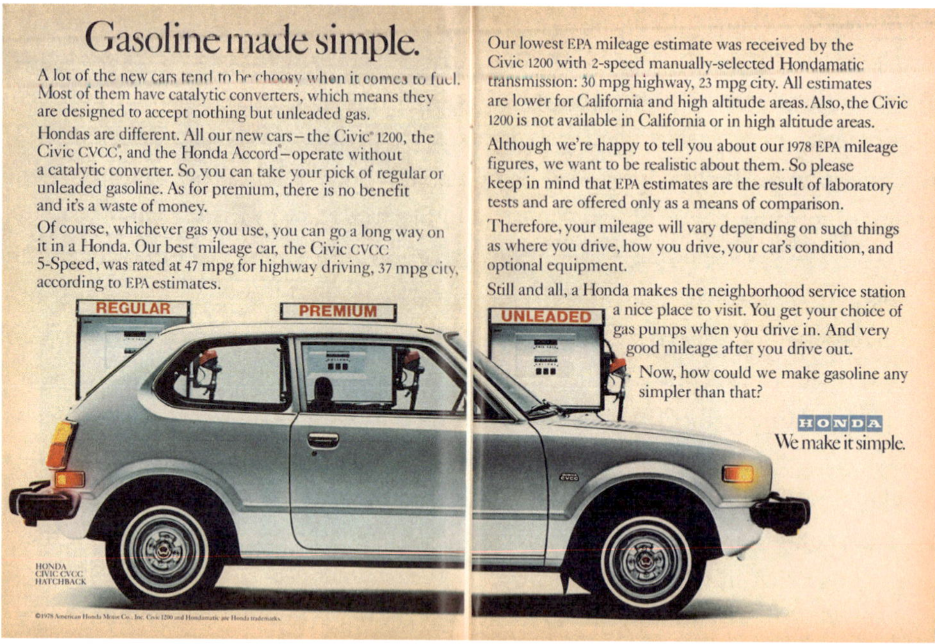

Figure 3.4. Advertisement for a 1978 Civic, the game-changing Honda.

The first-generation Civic, not much bigger than a Subaru 360, debuted in 1972, just four years after Bricklin had brought his first Subarus to America, and a year before he launched the SV1. By 1975, when Honda introduced the CVCC version, the company was selling ten thousand Civics a month in the American market.[30] Boasting high fuel efficiency and front-wheel drive, the Civic was perfect for the post–oil embargo automotive landscape, and its arrival marked an important moment in the Japanese import wave of the 1970s and 1980s. With his Civic, Soichiro Honda, the "Japanese Henry Ford," as *People* called him, looked like a genius when it came fuel economy and emissions regulation.[31]

Bricklin was trying to do something similar with safety. In merging safety with sports cars, he had hit on an innovation that could allow him to promote a narrative and image of futuristic automobile techno-social invention, one that would last a career. Indeed, Bricklin's efforts at innovation with the SV1 – the emphasis on its advanced safety features, the gull-wing doors, the fiberglass bodies with no welding – really did echo a Henry Ford's or a Walter Chrysler's efforts at technological innovation, and really did reflect a genuine effort to advance the technology of automobile safety, if not its acceptance.

In the past, safety had not been an easy sell for the Big Three to American consumers. Ford pioneered some early crash testing in 1955 and launched a Lifeguard

Design package to improve its cars' interior safety, but seat belts remained optional.[32] In 1971, one auto executive lamented that "we tried for years to persuade people to take seat belts as an option. All we asked was that they pay for them. They wouldn't, by and large."[33] A year later, Lee Iacocca declared that "safety doesn't' sell."[34] And despite Nader's revelations and the emergence of a whole new set of safety standards overseen by the NHTSA, quite a few American car buyers were still reluctant to fully embrace safety as a distinguishing feature of their cars (Volvo drivers remained a vocal but very small minority). Meanwhile, Detroit itself was fighting costly regulations almost every step of the way, with GM having put pressure on Ford to drop its safety emphasis.[35] And even as Bricklin was promoting various safety facets of his sports car (Bricklin's glossy brochure explained the SV1's lack of cigarette lighter by saying, "we don't think smoking while driving is safe and we don't want you dropping a hot cigarette in your lap and driving our beautiful car into a tree"), Americans were busy rejecting seat-belt ignition interlock regulators, which in 1973 had provoked a tremendous backlash.[36]

Undeterred, Bricklin was determined to make safety a defining element of his car. This included, Bricklin claimed to the *New York Times*, "features now only talked about by the major automakers."[37] That was true. Most significantly, the SV1 boasted a perimeter box or "birdcage" that gave four sides of protection in the case of a crash, more than anything being offered by the Detroit Three. Bolted to the car's frame, the cage "completely encircle[d] the occupants in protective steel" that the company claimed was "four times as strong as the steel being utilized" in Detroit's comparable vehicles.[38] (As noted earlier, another notable sports car that famously boasted a reinforced birdcage frame was the gull-winged 1954–7 Mercedes Benz 300SL.) The SV1 also had a rollbar, which was decidedly not standard for Big Three vehicles, or even sports cars. Further, the fuel tank and the engine were enclosed separately from the passenger compartments, a safety feature that reflected concerns about exploding fuel tanks – as had infamously been the case with the 1973 Ford Pinto. The SV1's interior was thus protected, and it further included an "instrument panel … fully padded" for additional safety, removing the worst possibilities of a "second crash" within the car, which Nader had so gruesomely described.[39]

Beyond the impressive chassis, there were other safety features built into car, not the least of which were its bumpers. Bumpers had been a legislative and judicial hot potato in the late 1960s and early 1970s. In 1971, the NHTSA had passed regulations requiring that bumpers be standardized in height and able to withstand a five-mile-per-hour crash. In 1973, it extended the regulations to rear bumpers as well. Compared to other cars, the SV1's bumpers were unusually prominent, "incorporating Delco shock-absorber units bolted to the frame plus an outer layer

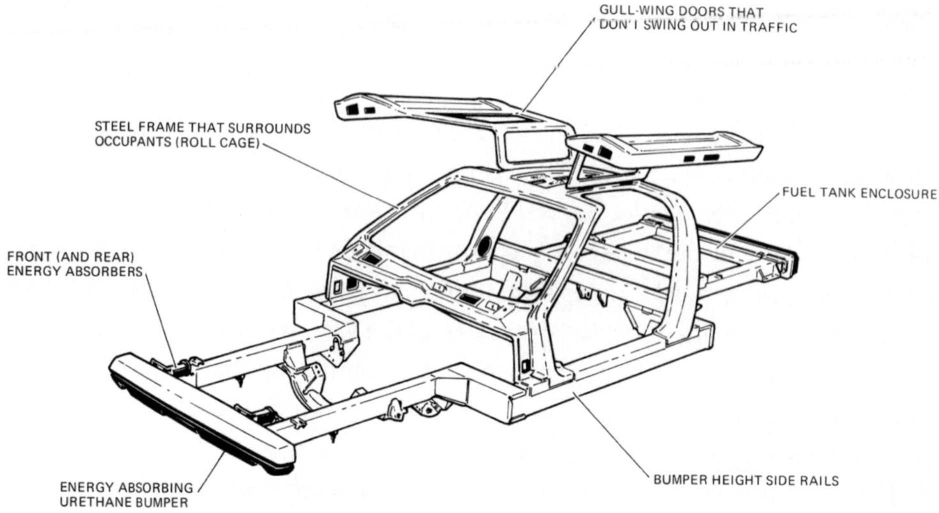

BRICKLIN SAFETY FRAME AND ROLL CAGE

BRICKLIN SAFETY FRAME

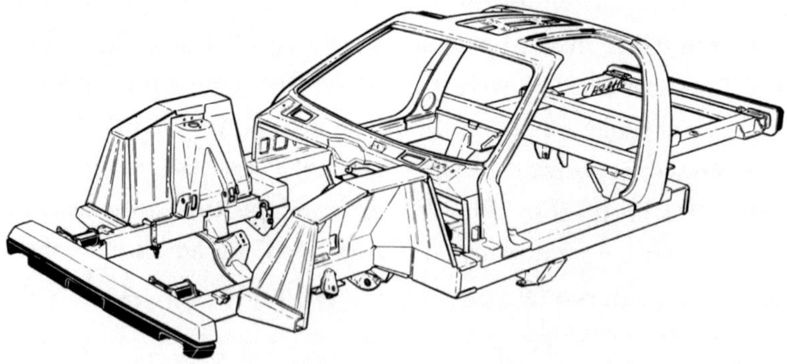

Bricklin safety frame including: "Bird Cage" roll bar passenger compartment unit., perimeter box steel frame and energy absorbing front and rear bumper system.

Figure 3.5. Bricklin safety specs.

Figure 3.6. Bricklin advertising: marketing safety, and plastic, as a virtue.

of urethane over a steel backed bumper bar." The company's prospectus claimed that they "exceed government specs" and that both the front and back bumpers would be able to withstand a crash of up to ten miles per hour – twice the federal standard. This aspect of the SV1 was featured in the car's promotional materials; by highlighting better-than-regulation bumpers, Bricklin was taking advantage of a high-profile issue that safety-conscious consumers were likely aware of.[40]

The safety theme even permeated the performance and aesthetics of the vehicle. The SV1 boasted a "fast braking system" and "a short turning radius of 34-feet" according to Bricklin.[41] Moreover, the car's fantastic-looking gull-wing doors were pitched as having a mild safety functionality in that they lessened the risk of being swung out into oncoming traffic. An eight-inch-wide black strip was painted along the bottom of the doors and fenders, supposedly to make the car appear lower and to hide stone chips and assorted road grime. Keeping with the safety theme, the names of the SV1's five exterior shades were prefixed with the word "safety" – "Safety Green," Safety Red," "Safety White," "Safety Orange," and the very Seventies "Safety Suntan."[42] The Bricklin's shiny, colourful, plastic cladding certainly made the cars stand out, especially when compared to Detroit's standard palette.

With this kind of savvy promotion, it wasn't surprising that the automotive and business media lapped up the safety angle. When the SV1 debuted in 1974, the reviews were good, and the notion of Bricklin as an innovator, and the idea of the car as something innovative and new, was repeatedly emphasized in the mainstream and automotive press. *Car and Driver*, for example, enthused that "safety is the most marketable attraction" of the SV1.[43] In a 1975 article with a photo that featured a cowboy-booted Bricklin straddling his car, the *Washington Post* labelled him an "inventor" and quoted him as offering sage words: "This car is safer, but everything is relative. I don't mean you don't get dead, but you're safer."[44]

And the hype was at least partly true: the car often outperformed other well-known nameplates on some important safety metrics. In 1972, Bricklin had an SV1 prototype crash tested against a Chevrolet and a Volkswagen by an organization called California Automotive Research. While its competitors sustained considerable damage in ten- and fifteen-miles-per-hour crashes (in the case of the VW, making the car "not driveable"), the Bricklin "sustained no cosmetic damage and the vehicle was in satisfactory driveable condition."[45] When the NHTSA released its assessment of 1976 vehicle performance, the Bricklin was rated as being in the top echelon of cars in terms of acceleration and passing ability, tied with the Chevrolet Corvette in second place to the front-running Jaguar XJ, and tops in the braking performance, beating out the Renault 5 and the Corvette.[46]

These results were supported by the testimonials of actual Bricklin drivers who had experienced real-world incidents that proved the vehicle's safety bona fides. Prospective SV1 buyer Ronald C. Makowski had been taken for an SV1 test drive by Latrobe, Pennsylvania, Bricklin dealer Jon Scalzitti when another car suddenly pulled in front of them. Though they avoided the vehicle, "the Bricklin spun across the highway, struck a cement drainage culvert and flipped over on its side." Despite this, Makowski and Scalzitti "crawled out of the vehicle and walked away without a scratch. It was truly unbelievable." Makowski was convinced that "we would have either been killed or severely injured in most any other vehicle," and he could not say enough about "the remarkable safety features" of the Bricklin. Irving S. Soble wrote to Bricklin in June 1975 to "thank him with all my heart for saving several lives," including that of his best friend. The two men had been driving Soble's Bricklin, Vehicle Identification Number (VIN) 713, when they were involved in a head-on

Figure 3.7. Plastic as innovation: displaying SV1 panels, 1974.

collision. While the other car's passengers were hospitalized, the Bricklin's occupants "walked away with nary a scratch." The Bricklin, he enthused, had "performed flawlessly."[47]

The SV1's safety innovations allowed Bricklin to pitch to potential investors that his sports car had "a marketing differentiation of safety features" that would "have a greater impact on consumer acceptance than any other recent [automotive] innovation." Bricklin claimed that the car surpassed federal safety standards and that its "birdcage" structure could easily withstand even major impacts. Overall, as an early Bricklin investment prospectus confidently stated, "it is the combination of the frame, bumper impact absorption units and Plexiglass DR body that provide the safety features on the Bricklin."[48] A later promotional brochure for a potential Bricklin operation in Mexico included the boast that "the Bricklin is considered to be the safest mass-produced car in the world today."[49]

Along with safety, a selling feature of the SV1 was its durability. The plastic body shell was a "vacuum formed acrylic sheet formed into panels and reinforced with an inner layer of fiberglass" and was "impervious to the elements." The body was then bolted onto a steel frame that could be "easily detached for quick repairs, if necessary." Because of the space-age process, the brochure declared, "you'll notice the perfection with which all the body panels fit." The vibrant fiberglass skin itself was "impregnated" with colour to a depth of .3 inches, much deeper than the paint finish on Detroit's cars, meaning that chips and scratches could be sanded out, without the car having to be repainted. Since the SV1 had no outside chrome, and its bumpers were designed to withstand an impact at ten miles per hour, it was much less likely than other cars on the road to be dinged and dented. As a result of these innovations, in 1975 the Bricklin was awarded top prize in the Transportation Division of the Society of the Plastics Industry at their thirtieth annual conference.[50]

With the SV1, Malcolm Bricklin had successfully carved out a small space for himself in the early 1970s automotive world as a safety innovator, given some of the genuinely innovative features of his car. Athough the venture failed rather spectacularly, the car's notorious demise did not deter Bricklin from continuing to search for that elusive entrée into the world of the recognized automotive entrepreneur, especially as an innovator. Indeed, in that pursuit, the credibility of technological innovation continued to draw Bricklin back, again and again, to the futuristic potential of automobiles. He doggedly sought the legitimacy that technological innovation would bestow upon him, privileging it above the other archetypes that attached themselves to the automotive entrepreneur, even above the one area in which he was genuinely and unquestionably successful – promotion. In this pursuit – and in between his many other, mostly promotional, ventures – Bricklin was persistent, sometimes prescient, and always striving.

Thus, it is unsurprising that, not too long after the demise of the New Brunswick venture, Bricklin resurfaced in Arizona, in 1976, back with a fresh attempt to make a name for himself as a technological innovator. His first project after the SV1 was the development of a new type of rotary engine. Instead of safety, this time the innovation was fuel economy, another major concern for the industry in the 1970s, one spurred by the OPEC embargo. The "rotary vee" engine, Bricklin claimed in a press release, would provide "exceptional fuel economy, is also lighter weight, more efficient and [has] a less complex power plant than the engines presently being used." Moreover, the engine also promised to be "less expensive to manufacture, easier to maintain and more flexible in application." Given his track record, and the lingering wreckage of the SV1, Bricklin's idea was met with scepticism: *Maclean's* magazine scoffed that Bricklin's latest innovation was "a new invention that will … uhhh … revolutionize the transportation industry … Déjà-vu?"[51] Though a few prototypes of the engine were built, it never came to fruition, owing to technical and financial problems. The project was "eventually discontinued."[52]

From the 1990s through to the early 2000s, Bricklin continually sought to grasp the brass ring of technological innovation. In the '90s, he tried electric bikes. In the early 2000s, he announced that he had developed an engine modification system that would tremendously boost fuel economy. With a device designed to be added to cars coming off a production line, Bricklin claimed that he and his team of engineers had created a hydrolysis system to extract hydrogen from water and add it to the fuel mix, which would "immediately improve the mileage by 100 per cent." Ever the technological optimist, Bricklin promised that "now we have it" and that "very shortly we'll be putting it on some General Motors and Chrysler products that we can sell while we develop it to the next stage – which is one day, you'll be able to drive a vehicle using the hydrogen that comes out of the water 100 per cent." This was to be done through his firm Visionary Vehicles, which planned to get into plug-in hydrogen vehicles and take advantage of the willingness of President Barack Obama's administration to use government funds to push the sector towards more fuel-efficient and innovative new powertrains and vehicles.[53]

That didn't work out, either, as Bricklin was likely a couple of decades ahead of his time when it came to the use of hydrogen. But he didn't stop trying to innovate. In the mid-2010s, his company developed the 3EV, a three-wheeled, electric-powered, two-passenger, enclosed car. This time, the innovation was cheap electric mobility – a kind of Subaru 360 for the twenty-first-century EV age, but one that Bricklin and his firm had designed. Bricklin aimed to achieve some sort of technological innovation, this time by taking advantage of the EV revolution to claim his stake in the next automotive bonanza. Enough people believed in it to give him, and the EV3, something of a chance.[54]

Bricklin's record as a technological innovator retained a currency that he returned to time and again throughout his career to recharge his credibility. At the time of the SV1, safety was a genuinely innovative idea, and, even if the vehicle wasn't a success, it put him on the map. That was enough to fuel his other promotional ideas, a category of innovation all on their own. Prior to that, however, Bricklin's idea of a safety sports car was good enough to convince people to take a chance on his car company in 1973. That decision, and everything that happened to Bricklin thereafter, reflected the rapidly changing nature of the postwar auto industry and the newfound riskiness that it represented to the collective. In this case, the risk was collectively to the people of the province of New Brunswick, who, after all, were the ones who were taking a calculated risk by giving their money to Bricklin (and their votes to Richard Hatfield).

But why not? The investment was about the auto industry, the dream of industrial modernity.

***Dream Car* Song 6: "High Risk Venture," Allen Cole and Paul Ledoux, 2010**

Part III. The Changing Nature of Safety in Postwar Society: From Fordist Economic Security to Fragmentation and Risk in the 1970s

In the first three decades after the Second World War, the auto industry represented about the safest economic bet in America. Once the wartime Big Three and the rest of American manufacturing had won the war and then completed their transition back to civilian production by the late 1940s, the immense size and stability of Detroit's giant corporations, their sheer industrial impact, and the mass employment they provided meant that the (North) American auto sector became the bulwark of postwar prosperity and of economic security. In the 1950s and 1960s, the manufacturing and automotive sectors made up about a quarter of the American economy – then the world's biggest. Between the 1940s and the 1970s, General Motors, Ford, and Chrysler dominated the sector, with over 90 per cent market share in the United States and Canada; a few small "independents" and a smattering of imports shared the rest. Each Big Thee firm also controlled sprawling international empires, though Chrysler's overseas operations were not as well developed as GM's and Ford's multinational enterprises (MNEs).

Led by General Motors, the largest industrial multinational in the world, the Big Three were usually among the American corporations with the highest revenues in the postwar period, often vying with their soulmates in the oil industry for top honours. In 1960, GM led all American corporations, with revenues of $11.2 billion, besting Exxon (Standard Oil of New Jersey) at $8 billion, followed by Ford's $5.3 billion; Chrysler ranked ninth, with a mere $2.6 billion in revenue. In 1970, the same companies held the top three positions again, with GM at a staggering $24 billion, Ford again just behind Exxon at $14 billion, and Chrysler improving to sixth place, with $7 billion. For context, the Canadian government's entire 1970 budget was $16 billion (at that point, the two countries' currencies traded at almost par.).

But the auto sector didn't simply boast immense revenues; it was also a sure thing when it came to piling up enormous and steady profits. Prosperity, and oligopoly, meant predictable, safe returns. Between 1955 and 1970, GM's income totalled an astounding $21 billion, and the firm never came close to losing money.[55] "It would be hard to argue," wrote one economic analyst in 1971, "that an investment in General Motors or Ford was a very risky proposition."[56]

Equally secure were the auto manufacturing strongholds across North America. Since the era of Henry Ford, Billy Durant, and Colonel Sam McLaughlin, auto assembly had largely been geographically concentrated in the American Midwest and Southern Ontario (the "Golden Horseshoe"), but, by the prosperous 1960s, the Big Three (and the few remaining independents) operated plants, parts facilities, distribution centres, and marketing and sales operations in every state and province on the continent. GM, for instance, opened new plants in places as far flung as Fremont, California (1964), Sainte-Thérèse, Quebec (1966), and Lordstown, Ohio (1966). Between 1960 and 1970, the auto sector built an astounding 110 million cars across hundreds of North American assembly and parts facilities. In 1970, the year that the United States reached peak conventional oil production, the US and Canadian industries combined to produce 10 million cars, an astonishing figure, even for an average year's output.[57]

Meanwhile, all the secondary and tertiary industries that supported these assembly plants with steel, glass, rubber, and fabrics, along with a host of other sectors (not to mention the oil industry itself), formed a constellation of industrial might and economic stability, geographically concentrated around the Great Lakes, that further underpinned the continental economy. During this period, the height of Fordism, the notion that "one in every seven jobs" in America was tied to the sprawling auto sector became something of an economic axiom, one that was, by and large, true: from the more than two million workers in assembly and parts facilities to the thousands of auto dealerships that every small town in America depended on (usually as their largest employer); from the armies of mechanics, aftermarket parts makers, advertisers, lenders, gas station attendants, auto insurers and agents, highway and road construction crews, motel workers, and innumerable drive-in employees of all stripes to, well, anyone else who depended in one way or another on the automobile and its production for their livelihoods.[58]

These millions of automotive jobs meant prosperity. In the 1950s and 1960s, the auto industry essentially created the North American middle class.[59] While Detroit's white-collar salaried workers epitomized the postwar, corporate organization man, the Big Three's mass of blue-collar, hourly, assembly-line employees sat at the apex of wages, benefits, and job security for ordinary working people. Their union, the United Auto Workers, founded in 1935, was the continent's largest and most important industrial union and had, by the 1960s, done more than any other institution to force the Big Three to share their immense wealth with their workers and thus spread automotive prosperity more evenly across society. Following the UAW's recognition during the New Deal era and the war, and especially once the 1950 "treaty of Detroit" and 1955 negotiations had established pattern collective bargaining (with the UAW achieving the same basic contract across their entire Big Three membership), the long-sought dream of economic security for millions of ordinary families had become a reality.[60] Because of the auto industry, and the New Deal policies it underpinned, for the first time in history a plurality of (North) Americans were experiencing relative economic security and *safety*.

As the anchor of this new era of economic stability, prosperity, and growth, the auto sector became the subject of numerous scholarly studies, all designed to explain the success of the postwar economy. The focus on these giant enterprises and their impact was epitomized by the work of the Canadian-American Harvard economist and public servant John Kenneth Galbraith. In his troika of influential books, *American Capitalism: The Concept of Countervailing Power* (1952), *The Affluent Society* (1958), and *The New Industrial State* (1967), Galbraith detailed the possibilities and problems inherent in the American economic system, with a special focus on the role of giant corporations, oligopoly, and industrial power. Historian Alfred D. Chandler's work had largely lionized the structure, scale, and scope of giant American corporations like GM; Galbraith's *The New Industrial State*, coming as it did towards the end of the Sixties, provided an especially salient, if implicit, critique of the auto sector, one centred on the industry's size, anti-competitive behaviour, dependence on technology, and (ironically) aversion to risk.[61]

Yet by the early 1970s, fractures were beginning to appear in this edifice of industrial might. Some of these cracks were the result of the slow but inevitable evolution of the American auto sector's industrial processes: a Fordist model that had only incrementally changed since Henry's time was beginning to creak under the weight of three decades of postwar path dependency. The production techniques and labour relations that had established American industrial hegemony were beginning to atrophy, as plants, managers, and workers aged and became set in their ways. Old, often still successful, habits became difficult to break. Decades of steady profits, stable market shares, and growing revenues – the fruits of oligopoly – bred complacency. Complacency bred tiredness and rigidity. America's most dynamic and technologically important industry, once the safest economic bet of all, was becoming, especially after 1970, less of a sure thing. Risk was beginning to creep into an industry whose long-established structures and practices were starting to change, even if these changes were only slowly coming into focus by the time Bricklin launched his SV1.

Not all the problems that were beginning to appear in the American auto sector arose from old age alone; some disruption was being wrought by new technologies and methods. By the early 1970s, industrial robots had moved from being prototypes of futurism to full-blown partners in production. In 1966, Unimate, the robotic (hydraulic) arm, was still a late-night television curio when the first production model was installed at GM's Linden, New Jersey, plant, to transfer blistering hot aluminium door handles along the assembly process. But by 1972, robots in the auto industry were a small but important cog in an emerging third industrial revolution. Inaugurating North American manufacturing's shift to robotics, GM had made its Lordstown facility a centrepiece of this new technology, installing hundreds of Unimate robotic arms to speed production and reduce (human) labour costs. At the same time, GM's vast, bloated empire also continued to operate facilities that were – in industrial years – verging on decrepit. More cracks in the Fordist model started to appear.[62]

The Big Three's early adoption of robots as the first machines to begin replacing humans at work became the latest flashpoint between Detroit and its erstwhile partner and oft-adversary in the industry, labour. The relationship between the UAW (a cross-border union with locals in the US and Canada) and the companies had always been based on mutual loathing and conflict, going back to the bitter and sometimes bloody battles over union recognition in the 1930s and 1940s, on both sides of the border.[63] By the 1960s, the UAW and the Big Three had settled into their own long cold war, punctuated by hot strikes every so often but exhibiting a general trend towards better wages and benefits for workers in the industry. In 1970, during one of the longest and bitterest postwar strikes – sixty-seven days at GM – the union achieved one of its greatest victories, the accomplishment of "30 and out," or retirement and a pension after thirty years' service for workers. It was a high point for the labour movement. By the early 1970s, even this predictable UAW–Big Three pattern was beginning to fray. With advancing robotics, new production techniques, restructuring, and closures, deindustrialization had started to take its toll, and union power was eroded.[64]

The challenges facing the American auto industry were not only about production changes and labour problems. Another emerging risk was the competition from newfangled offshore vehicles, whose firms encapsulated their own countries' postwar dreams of industrial modernity. Following its quiet introduction to the US market in 1949 (total sales: 2), the German-made, small, cheap, unusually shaped, rear-engine Volkswagen Beetle took America by storm in the 1960s. Spurred by one of the greatest ad campaigns ever conceived (Doyle Dane Bernbach's 1959 "Think Small" ads), the Bug was another example of the counterculture, anti-establishment ethos personified by Ralph Nader. Buying a VW Beetle was the classic Sixties act of rebellion by baby boomers against their parent's generation, many of whom worked at one of those one-in-seven jobs connected to the American auto industry, many of whom had fought against the Germans and the Japanese in the war, and all of whom proudly bought and drove American-made vehicles. Beetle sales peaked at 400,000 in 1968, stealing a surprising 4 per cent of the US market, about half of the foreign cars sold in America that year.[65] Even if this was a relative trickle, VW's undeniable accomplishment of profitably breaking into the giant American marketplace with the Beetle had been noticed. GM's own problematic Corvair had, in fact, been envisioned as an American-made, small, cheap, rear-engine response to the German interloper. The Beetle's success had also undoubtedly helped spark Malcolm Bricklin's own decision to import the Japanese-made, small, cheap, unusually shaped, rear-engine Subaru 360, also in 1968. The Bug's relative triumph (and GM's deepening troubles with the Corvair, and with Nader) portended disruption and a dramatically changed landscape in the 1970s when it came to cars imported from outside the US, including offshore. Bricklin undoubtedly understood this: his Subaru venture eventually flourished in the American market, as did so many Japanese makers.

Foreign cars were the direct consequence of another looming issue in the auto sector, one that foreshadowed other, emerging risks for the broader postwar economy: the role of multinational enterprises. American firms, and especially auto firms, had been leaders in spreading their business products and practices across the globe since the nineteenth century. But by the late 1960s, the wider issue of MNEs and their actions at home and abroad – both the idea of American-owned corporations shifting investment and production to foreign locales, and the newfound competition from multinationals based in countries like Japan or Germany – was becoming a major focus of scholarly, critical study, and a political issue, too. In 1971, as part of his New Economic Policy (NEP) "shoku" that ended gold convertibility and much of the postwar Bretton Woods international monetary system, Richard Nixon imposed a 10 per cent surcharge on imports. Designed to stem the flow of goods coming into the US from abroad – most of them made by foreign multinational firms, which obviously included automobiles – the NEP measures were met with international displeasure, and foreign protests illustrated just how important MNEs had become to global trade and to the auto industry.[66]

A boom in academic output that investigated the role of MNEs, foreign direct investment, and the relations between these giant enterprises and their "home" and "host" countries (or, in the new lingo of the day, "markets") emerged over the course of the decade, and by the early 1970s increasingly shifted towards a more critical tone. Seminal works such as historian Mira Wilkins's and Ford biographer Frank Ernest Hill's relatively benign *American Business Abroad: Ford on Six Continents* (1964) gave way to sharper assessments such as economist Charles P. Kindleberger's *American Business Abroad: Six Lectures on Direct Investment* (1969) and political scientist Raymond Vernon's *Sovereignty at Bay: The Multinational Spread of US Enterprises* (1971). In Canada, the issue of American MNEs' influence became an existential *cause célèbre* for economic nationalists, exemplified by sociologist Kari Levitt's pathbreaking and headline-grabbing 1970 work deploring Canadian economic (and political) "dependency" on America, *Silent Surrender: The Multinational Corporation in Canada.*[67]

By 1974, when Wilkins completed her massive two-volume treatment of MNEs, *The Emergence of Multinational Enterprise: American Business Abroad from the Colonial Era to 1914* and *The Maturing of Multinational Enterprise: American Business Abroad from 1914 to 1970*, a new academic subfield had fully emerged, one that recognized the importance of MNEs and the economic challenge they represented, both at home and abroad. Unlike Galbraith's work, which focused primarily on the problems of size and oligopolistic tendencies of US corporations at home, these scholars were concerned with the power represented by American and foreign MNEs in their global operations in terms of *where* they produced their goods, sent their technologies, generated their profits, and, more importantly, employed their workers. Many Americans were particularly worried about the potential problem of US MNEs shifting industrial production and investment away from the United States towards their wholly owned foreign operations to take advantage of lower labour costs, something that already seemed to be happening in some industries and in companies such as technology manufacturing firm RCA.[68]

Ultimately, fears of the "runaway plant" augured a phenomenon that would become all too familiar later in the 1970s – deindustrialization. Labour leaders had been warning of, and warring against, runaway plants for decades, mostly as factories moved elsewhere within the United States to avoid unions, often from North to South (though not yet in the auto sector). But now, around the time that Bricklin was visiting New Brunswick, looking to establish his own, *foreign*, low-wage auto plant, the issue had become acute, as industrial facilities were starting to desert the United States entirely. Writing in a 1973 special issue of *Foreign Policy* dedicated to labour and multinationals, journalist and union activist Gus Tyler warned of the risks posed by MNEs and their willingness to embrace such mobility. In Tyler's view, experience showed that "the runaway did not necessarily run away: he could continue his business here while removing some or all of his manufacture elsewhere. That's how many unions had their first unhappy introduction to the multinational corporation."[69] Full-fledged, foreign-fostered deindustrialization in America was yet to appear, but one could hear its rumble getting closer.

Obviously, the Big Three had always had their foreign multinational operations, but those overseas branch plants usually produced cars only for local markets, and almost never for export back to the United States. In the 1950s and 1960s, Americans built, on average, about 95 per cent of the cars that they bought. Quality concerns about foreign-made vehicles, America's particular sizes and styles (tail fins!), and tariffs on autos and parts usually prevented foreign imports (the 1908 Payne-Aldrich tariff taxed autos at 45 per cent, though it was reduced over time; the 25 per cent tax on trucks that the Johnson administration established in 1964 remains). Similarly, the US auto industry had not yet embraced Mexico as a locale for assembly production, a development that would not occur in earnest until the 1980s and 1990s. In any event, despite the inroads of the Beetle and a few other foreign vehicles, the idea of cars being "made in America" still meant something to the vast majority of American consumers in the 1960s; as late as 1965, less than 6 per cent of US car sales were of imports.[70]

Unbeknownst to virtually all Americans, the multinational corporations that made up the United States auto industry had, in the 1960s, already started to embrace the idea of selling Americans cars from runaway foreign plants, but in somewhat of a backdoor manner – that is, from Canada. Indeed, during the decade, for American consumers, "made in America" became, to a significant degree, "made in *North* America."

The 1960s northward shift had started with one of the last remaining independents, Studebaker. Founded in 1852, and once the world's largest maker of horse-drawn wagons, Indiana-based Studebaker had expanded into autos in 1902 and steadfastly kept its car business alive despite an unsustainably meagre 3 per cent market share by the early 1960s. In 1963, facing certain demise if something drastic was not done, Studebaker closed its struggling South Bend manufacturing facility and transferred all its remaining assembly operations to the firm's branch plant in Hamilton, Ontario, which had been established in 1948. The plan was to keep the business going by taking advantage of a Canadian government tariff manipulation scheme that effectively gave a tax rebate to boost production north of the border and encourage exports southward. For three years, every one of the approximately 25,000 Studebaker Cruisers, Daytonas, and Commanders sold in the United States was no longer being made in the good ol' US of A, but in Canada. Studebaker customers either didn't know or didn't care, and if the company could use a federal government program and cheaper Canadian labour to survive a little longer, so be it. Even though Studebaker's Hamilton facility shut down in 1966, leaving 700 people out of work, the experiment had proved that Americans would buy Canadian-built cars.[71]

The real chance for the American Big Three to make a shift to foreign production came in 1965. That year, following heated negotiations between the two countries and the manufacturers, Prime Minister Lester Pearson and President Johnson signed the auto pact, the genesis of all modern free trade in North America. This continentalizing, managed trade agreement, pushed by the Canadian government, Henry Ford II, his allies in the Big Three, and even the UAW, allowed the auto companies to send cars and parts across the Canada-US border without paying tariffs, and thus to fully integrate their Canadian facilities *into* their US operations. Prior to this, tariff walls had resulted in separate industries on either side of the border; Canadian miniature branch plants of the Big Three produced the same cars as across the border, but in much smaller batches.[72]

The auto pact meant that the Big Three could use their Canadian facilities to build for the entire North American market, instead of only for Canada, thus making *all* their operations even more efficient on a continental basis. With cheaper Canadian labour costs and the promise of even greater economies of scale, the Big Three stood to rationalize and improve their operations dramatically, and to increase their profitability. In exchange, they had to continue to build as many cars and trucks as they sold in Canada, invest an extra $260 million into their Canadian plants by 1968, and thereafter ensure that their cars contained a certain percentage of North American content. After 1965, Canadian plants became the sole or significant source for a slew of Big Three cars sold in the United States, including, among others, GM's Chevy Impala (Oshawa, Ontario, 1965–84, and Sainte-Thérèse, Quebec, 1967–72), the Ford LTD (Oakville, Ontario, 1972–82), and the Chrysler Cordoba (Windsor, Ontario, 1975–83).[73]

Unsurprisingly, under the auto pact regime, Canadian production boomed, as did Canadian Big Three jobs and plants, while the Canadian trade deficit with the United States shrank. In 1963, before the auto pact, out of the 632,000 vehicles built in Canada, a grand total of 921 were exported to the United States. In 1973, with the auto pact in full bloom, Canada built 1,589,000 vehicles and exported *1,092,000* of them to the United States.[74] (That year, the United States had the second-best year in car sales ever (1988 holds the record), with over 11 million sold.) Starting in the 1970s, about one in every ten cars sold in the United States was built north of the border. Made in (North) America, indeed.

Equally unsurprisingly, quite a few Americans were outraged by this development, especially politicians from the states that seemed to be feeling this northward production shift most acutely. From 1965 until the early 1970s, lawmakers such as Senators Vance Hartke (D-Indiana) and Al Gore Sr. (D-Tennessee) led a vociferous campaign against the auto pact, but to no avail. With the Big Three's support, the agreement sailed through Congress in 1966 and withstood congressional attempts to annul the treaty in the early 1970s. Auto pact abrogation had, initially, been included in the Nixon administration's 1971 list of economic shocks. But the agreement had avoided its demise only because administration officials realized the utter disruption and chaos that *de*integration of the Big Three's continentally oriented production and supply chains would cause if the agreement were undone.[75] This notion became a recurring theme in North American trade history, notably during the negotiations over the 2020 US-Mexico-Canada Trade Agreement.

The auto industry had been continentalized, and it was clear to many Americans that the auto pact presented yet another risk to the sector's stability, one that could threaten whole communities, states, and regions. Given that Detroit wasn't yet moving production *offshore*, and the fact that the Canadian companies were US-owned branch plants staffed by UAW workers, Big Three decisions to shift American production to "runaway" Canadian locations did not raise the same level of alarm that the slowly building wave of German or Japanese imports did. But the effect was the same: after 1965, production decisions, and *where* cars were built, were no longer framed along national lines. By the early 1970s, Malcolm Bricklin recognized that the auto pact was an opportunity that his operation could exploit, and he did so to the fullest extent.

Of course, as always, the biggest risk that one could take in the auto sector remained attempting to launch a brand new car into the marketplace. In the postwar period, the research, production, and marketing costs of introducing a new automobile were astronomical. The first challenge was the creative complications of researching and designing a vehicle, which sometimes took years to solve. The second was the technological complexity of production, assembly, and distribution: as just one example, the average car contains thousands of parts, often sourced from hundreds of different outside suppliers. Third, marketing and advertising decisions had to be made, and who knew what kind of campaign would resonate with consumers? These challenges, compounded by the basic task of making a vehicle that would work, and work safely, meant that building a new car was an incredibly difficult venture. In 1971, economist Lawrence J. White estimated that even a modest attempt to create a new firm, one that produced 200,000 vehicles a year (the lowest viable output Smith calculated), would "require $300 million and carry high long-run risks."[76]

Even if a car were successfully designed, produced, and brought to market, a new firm had to build enough vehicles, well enough, and fast enough, to at least break even in order to stay in business. Moreover, it was no sure thing that the public would like the new car, or that they would purchase enough of the vehicles to cover the enormous costs of building them in the first place, let alone enough to make money.[77] If the launch of a new car was successful, as it was for Lee Iacocca with the 1965 Ford Mustang, the rewards could be enormous. But if a car launch failed, it would be incredibly costly and threaten the very viability of an auto firm.

Automakers had always been acutely aware of this risk, an existential aspect of the industry's institutional memory. After all, more than 500 automobile startups had gone bankrupt by the 1920s, leaving only the Big Three and a few others. Even GM had faced a brush with mortality, with the failure of Charles Kettering's 1923 Chevrolet Series-C Copper Cooled car (original estimated output, 50,000; actual output before it nearly destroyed GM, 725). A more recent, unavoidable, example of the risk that a new car entailed was the 1958 Ford Edsel, called "the most colossal, stupendous and legendary blunder in the history of American marketing."[78] Ford spent an estimated $250 million to build and market the car (over $2 billion in twenty-first-century dollars), which, Ford historian Douglas Brinkley concluded, "was not well received by the public, failing to find even a fraction of the customers necessary to make it a break-even proposition." It had been the first time that a Big Three firm had attempted to offer a new brand since 1938.[79]

Any way one looked at it, launching a new vehicle was a tremendous risk, even for established auto makers like GM and Ford, who had the know-how, production processes, and capital to absorb the costs, and the risk. Launching *a new car company* and with only one vehicle to offer consumers made an already colossal bet even riskier: it seemed nothing less than reckless abandon – a dream that could quickly turn into a nightmare. This risk explained, in part, why the American auto sector existed and functioned in the way that it did by the 1960s, as a risk-averse, cost-conscious, and essentially three-firm oligopoly. It also explained why no one since the 1940s had successfully managed to launch a new vehicle produced by a new car company.

As for all those new car brands that were starting to appear in the US auto market – the Volkswagens, Toyotas, Hondas, and Volvos – they inevitably had something in common: they were being launched by very large enterprises that had significant government support of some sort or another, which was meant to mitigate the incredibly costly risk that every one of these automobile ventures represented. The postwar German and Japanese economies had benefited from government contracts and a flood of American government money to restart their auto sectors. Moreover, the Germans had a heavy dose of state ownership in *Volks*wagen (the *people's* car, after all), and the Beetle itself had been a statist leftover of the Nazi era. For their part, Japanese firms had significant support from their Ministry of International Trade and Industry and their government-approved *keiretsu*. The Americans didn't have direct government support or ownership, though they had invented the Fordist economies of scale and production processes to create the mass market car in the first place, and they had consolidated their industry down to a bare minimum of three main competitors (and a few "independents") in order to survive and to prosper.

By then, the Big Three's oligopolistic structure, the astronomical cost of building a new model of vehicle, let alone a completely new type of car, and Detroit's collusive tactics made launching a *new*, independent car venture a decidedly dicey proposition. If one added the growing onslaught of (state-supported) foreign competition that was starting to challenge the Big Three at home, and the wave of safety regulations sparked by Nader, not to mention Washington's demands for better emissions and fuel economy beginning in the 1970s, starting a new car company was a spectacularly risky idea, one that required substantial resources, financial and otherwise.

Perhaps most of all, it required an extraordinary amount of faith in the possible.

Part IV. Mitigating Collective Economic Risk: The Safety Car and Bricklin Canada as an Act of Faith

In the postwar era, automobility's immense impact on notions of individual and collective risk and safety – whether the personal and environmental harm of automobiles, or the economic threat represented by a culturally, geographically, and technologically changing auto industry – began to shift. And yet, even as the horrendous toll from automobile accidents mounted and the economic dislocation of a quickly transforming auto sector became clearer, it was also true that risk (and safety) remained not only a personal danger or material hazard, per se, but also a calculation and a way of perceiving the world. Whether or not ordinary North Americans were thinking about the lived consequences of roll cages, bumpers, and seat belts or about the economic viability of producing an entirely new car, they were unquestionably involved in consciously embracing the gamble of risk and of willingly relinquishing their fates to matters of faith and trust, and of dreams.[80]

In the early 1970s, as these sometimes contradictory and often challenging impulses played themselves out, subtly and sharply, across society's collective consciousness and its material reality, the Bricklin venture appeared at just the right moment to become a perfect encapsulation of these dynamics. As a vehicle, the SV1 itself embodied North Americans' emerging concerns about their relationship to automobiles on a personal, intimate level. Meanwhile, the Bricklin firm, and the unquestionable financial danger it represented, sat at the intersection of the broader, disruptive economic changes that portended an increasingly perilous society.

Against this daunting backdrop, Malcolm Bricklin had convinced Richard Hatfield to help him make his dream car a reality. Before meeting Bricklin, Hatfield was not unaware of the risks he was taking, and he voiced scepticism about the power of firms in the economy and the trustworthiness of unsolicited

Figure 3.8. Malcolm Bricklin at the launch of his risky safety car, 6 August 1974.

economic development proposals.[81] Once the deal had been agreed to, however, Hatfield changed his tune, dazzled by the potential of the car and the tantalizing possibility of economic (and political) success that it held out. Even in the early 1970s, as the harsh realities of a new economic landscape were quickly becoming apparent with each shock, crisis, or upheaval, the immense risk of an automobile venture was something that could be mitigated with faith and belief. Paul Creaghan, Hatfield's economic growth minister, agreed: "I agree it is a high risk venture for the province … From the beginning it was a high risk venture," but "if successful it can mean a great deal to this province."[82] Hatfield was not unaware of these risks, but proclaimed at the August 1974 ceremony marking Job 1, the first SV1 to roll off the Saint John assembly line, that "I hope and believe the Bricklin car will now become a symbol of what New Brunswick and its people can do, an example of the risks we must run, the patience we must show, the faith we must keep if we are to become a province of economic opportunity and diversity."[83]

The dream of industrial modernity that Bricklin represented was a risk that required faith, and faith in the future, which Hatfield and his colleagues had in no short supply. Risk reflected the nature of business and entrepreneurialism that was also such a feature of modernity, and increasingly so in a rapidly changing 1970s auto sector, as well as the broader economy. Creaghan told New Brunswickers in

1974 that "now is the time to have faith" in the Bricklin. This prompted one waggish citizen to reply that, "indeed, for the well being of this province, all we can do is have faith, though many experts in the field do not, and are impatiently awaiting the first disaster … Seeing it is our 'pennies' involved, Mr. Creaghan, we must indeed have faith in it."[84] Similarly, the *Moncton Times* opined that a key to the success of the Bricklin was that there must be "*confidence* here where it is being brought to life." The *Times* continued:

> The pooh-poohing of the project to date seems to indicate that there are some New Brunswickers who almost want to see Bricklin fail … The road ahead of the Bricklin is not an easy one to travel, but the route can be eased somewhat if confidence is exhibited in the project in this province, by all parties and by the public as a whole. After all, if it is sniped at and criticized here where it is being built how can one expect dealers and would-be purchasers to have confidence at the other end of the line?[85]

At the car's glitzy New York launch in June 1974, Hatfield sounded more like a revivalist preacher than a hard-nosed politician: "Evidence of faith, they say, is evidence of things not seen." Hatfield had, he admitted, "invested a lot of faith in this car. When I say that I've invested a lot of personal faith in this car, that's what I mean from the point of view of my political career because if it all goes bust, as a lot of people have said it would, everybody would say I was a damn fool." But he was still hopeful: "I still think you've got to try, and you've got to believe, and you've got to try new things. Some may go under and some of them may succeed. But nothing will happen unless you try something."[86]

Hatfield, ever the romantic, likened the risk that Bricklin represented to the great nation-building ventures of the past. In 1970 and 1971, Canadian author Pierre Berton had published *The National Dream* and *The Last Spike*, his bestselling histories of the construction of the Canadian Pacific Railway across Canada. The Bricklin, in Hatfield's view, was analogous. The car was a calculated risk, one that reflected the particularities of its time but also the timeless desire of a politician looking to improve their people's lot. At industrial modernity's last moment, Hatfield declared that "it's time that someone in Canada took a chance." Bricklin required a gamble, a leap of faith: "We Canadians are very conservative. The last time we took a real risk, it was on a Canadian Pacific Railway – and it worked!"[87]

Now Hatfield, and Bricklin, had only to convince the people of New Brunswick that the risk was worth it. It would take all the promotional skills, political charm, and showmanship they could muster. For both men, it would be the performance of a lifetime.

CHAPTER FOUR

Showman (Politician)

***Dream Car* Song 7: "Fame," David Bowie, 1975**

Let the show begin.

In North America's industrially modern twentieth century, the fame of business and politics was usually somewhat different from that of the regular celebrity of movie and television stars, athletes, or artists. The former was, and is, necessarily built on a foundation of credibility, one frequently earned by some tangible achievement, like launching or leading a successful business or winning an election. The latter is similar, but regular artistic or sporting celebrity is often a consequence of a singular or ongoing performance in the cultural space – the fame of the entertainment industry. Which is not to say that business leaders or politicians are not performative in their endeavours. On the contrary. Often they are greater actors than the stars of screen and stage; in some famous cases, they are entrepreneurs, politicians, *and* Hollywood stars. Performative fame remains the common, transmutable, currency of the realms within which each act.[1]

For entrepreneurs in the twentieth century, the grandest stage of all was the motor vehicle industry. The car business made many of the most famous and innovative businessmen of all time – the Fords, Sloans, Chryslers, and Iacoccas; the Toyodas and Hondas; the Benzs, Porsches, DeLoreans, and Musks. As the Tinseltown of the business world, the auto sector commanded the most attention and promised the most spectacular material rewards.[2] Malcolm Bricklin, in his own pursuit of those potentially immense riches, became one of the industry's most legendary promoters and raconteurs, the "P.T. Barnum of the automotive world," as the *New York Times* anointed him in 2005.[3] And, indeed, over the course of his long career, Bricklin came to understand that, to sell his increasingly risky and expensive dream(s), he had to convincingly play the role of the successful automobile *promotional* entrepreneur. This required a combination of hustling salesmanship, headline-grabbing publicity, outrageous performances, and at least B-list-celebrity-level fame.

He was, in other words, a showman.

That's what made Malcolm Bricklin tick. Bricklin "goes nonstop" Academy award–winning documentarian Morgan Spurlock declared in 2009: "He's testosterone unleashed, a brilliant negotiator and an incredible character." By 2013, *Rolling Stone* had also identified Bricklin's performative method, describing him as "brash, bombastic, and pathologically prone to betting the farm on pie-in-the-sky automotive endeavors." In 2017, *Autoweek* said that Bricklin had "a mind that works like a machine gun," while *Automotive News* publisher Keith Crain described him as "one of those toy clowns that when you punch it, it bounces right back up."[4] Bricklin became famous because, both prior to meeting Richard Hatfield and forever thereafter, he played a starring role as the iconoclastic risk-taker, a latter-day Billy Durant and a preamble to Elon Musk – a cowboy.

For politicians, their most heralded postwar performances had been for turning their states into modern, industrial economies. *Time* magazine awarded its Man of the Year to German chancellors Konrad Adenauer (in 1953) and Willy Brandt (in 1970) for overseeing their country's economic miracle. Japanese prime ministers Shigeru Yoshida and Yasuhiro Nakasone became political legends for their postwar stewardship of Japan's transition to industrial modernity. Both nations were included in what was originally the G5, the group of the most economically powerful countries convened by Richard Nixon in the wake of the 1973 OPEC embargo and the economic crises of the early 1970s (Canada didn't join until 1976).

Meanwhile, boyish Canadian politician Richard Hatfield was already a minor local political celebrity by the time Bricklin came to New Brunswick in 1973 – or at least as famous as one can be as the premier of a small, rural, bilingual province in the Maritimes. But there was also no doubt that *because* of those high-stakes years during the Bricklin venture, Hatfield tasted (North) American fame in a manner that few Canadian politicians have. For the charismatic, celebrity-seeking Hatfield, Bricklin was a risk he was willing to bet quite a bit of his political capital on.

Irresistibly drawn to each other's automotive-fuelled ambitions, Bricklin and Hatfield stood together on that New York stage in June 1974, each playing his role.

Unfortunately for the two men, whatever fame and fortune that the Bricklin SV1 granted, it also took away. For Malcolm, the episode reflected not just the spectacular failure of his dream to build a car; his career trajectory thereafter starkly demonstrated just how far financialization had seeped into the postwar American economy, and into the auto industry itself. Similarly, because of the car, Hatfield may have gained national and international recognition for himself and his province, but the Bricklin's failure showed how politicians in the 1970s (and thereafter) could become so easily intoxicated and then laid low by the potential riches and real risks conferred by the auto industry. Moreover, the incident also illustrated how an elected official like Hatfield found ways to escape accountability for the consequences of his actions, even if he never completely outran the Bricklin's notorious legacy.

More immediately, as the car's 1975 demise generated headlines across the continent, the Bricklin's dangerously enticing alchemy transformed fame and celebrity into notoriety, mockery, and suspicion. Even during the car's most optimistic moments, when the pregnancy of possibility was in its fullest bloom, observers, advocates, and critics alike nonetheless questioned each man's motives: Was oft-sued, fast-talking promoter Malcolm Bricklin a swindler and typical American grifter, who in 1973 had swooped in like a snake-oil salesman to take advantage of the rubes in a desperate province, all just to get rich? Was flamboyant yet folksy, smooth-talking Richard Hatfield the caricature of the ruthless pol, who in 1974 had promised an industrial utopia on the banks of the Saint John River, all to connive New Brunswickers into believing in his own version of Malcolm's fantasy, just to get elected?

Had the dream of the Bricklin just been a show, a fantastic *performance* by the two men?

Had it all just been a con?

And, if so, who, exactly, had been conned?

Part I. "Brenda, … from Now on, We Don't Pay Cash for Anything": Malcolm Bricklin as Promoter – A One-Man Show in Seven Acts

Malcolm Bricklin "was born to hustle."

So wrote the journalist Michael Enright in his November 1975 *Maclean's* cover story, "Wheeler-Dealer: How Mr. Bricklin Got His Dream Car and Mr. Hatfield Got the Bill," a few months after Bricklin's collapse. Enright's essay was a penetrating portrait of the young entrepreneur. Bricklin, according to Enright, saw himself as "a man whose job is to push, promote, hype, juice, goose, inflate, mesmerize and sell, baby, sell." Of course, this unquenchable impulse to sell, baby, sell, was tempered by the reality that, as Bricklin so succinctly put it, "you can sell anything once: to sell it twice, you have to prove you have something to sell." And, well, as Bricklin told Enright, "If you need to sell twice, you might as well sell thousands of times," which was why he had "picked cars."[5]

Born to hustle, indeed. In Philadelphia, on 9 March 1939, to parents Albert and Gertrude. Albert managed a fur store in Philly, but when Malcolm was ten, he moved the family to central Florida so he could run a construction supply operation in booming Orlando (Disney would start building there in the 1960s). Bricklin graduated from William R. Boone High School in 1956, once having been mentioned in the *Orlando Sentinel* for being on the publicity committee of the annual Twirp Twirl dance. Accepted at the University of Florida in Gainsville, Bricklin mostly "majored in time and space," as he remembered it, though he also found time to join the Pi Lambda Phi fraternity and become sales manager for both the University of Florida *Alligator* and the freshman *F Book*. After two years at Florida, nineteen-year-old Mal dropped out and, in 1958, opened his own building supply store, Cranis-Bricklin Inc., with his father's old partner, Jack Cranis, Jr. In 1959, Bricklin married Brenda Hochman of Miami, and he settled into a comfortable yet mundane central Florida suburban existence: "I had a nice little sports car, not new but nice. I didn't owe a single penny and I was very proud of that, okay?"[6]

But Bricklin wanted something more from life, and he came to the realization that there were ways to, effectively, get something for almost nothing. In a 1975 interview, Bricklin told the story of his eureka moment, one that perhaps explains much of his career, and quite a bit of the financialization of the postwar American economy, too: "So, one day," he recalled,

> I walk into the bank where I had my savings account and just for the hell of it, I say, "I'd like to take out a small loan."
>
> The loan manager says, "We can't make you a loan, Mr. Bricklin. You don't have any credit."
>
> "What do you mean I don't have any credit?" I say. "I don't owe anybody a cent. Besides which, I have more money in my savings account that I want to borrow."
>
> "Sorry, the only way you can get a loan is to establish credit."
>
> "You mean if I already owe somebody money I can get a loan, but if I don't owe anybody anything, I can't?"
>
> "That's right Mr. Bricklin."
>
> So, I go home, get the car, take it back to the bank and let them finance it. Then I take the finance papers to the loan manager of the same bank and say, "OK, I owe money, can I get a loan now?"

Figure 4.1. Malcolm Bricklin, c. 1974.

"Absolutely," he says.

I get the loan, go home, and say "Brenda, open a charge account in every store in Orlando.

"From now on, we don't pay cash for anything."[7]

This moment marked the starting point of a succession of business promotions by a serial entrepreneur that would become increasingly complicated, would usually be financed either through franchise fees or borrowed money, and would usually end in ignominy, sometimes for Malcolm, and almost always for his business partners. Just as importantly, it also marked the beginning of how he financed, marketed, and produced what became the performance of a lifetime: The Malcolm Bricklin Show of Fantastic Promotions.

Act I. The Franchising Way: Handyman Hardware Stores
Orlando, Florida, 1960–4

In the early 1960s, Malcolm Bricklin was a twentysomething finding his entrepreneurial way. His first act as a businessman didn't land him far from the family tree: his father had most recently been in hardware, so that's where Malcolm started. Aiming to cash in on the growing home-improvement wave of the baby boom era, Bricklin established the first of what became a chain of late-night hardware outlets called Handyman, open seven days a week. As with every Bricklin venture going forward, Handyman asked its potential investors to take a chance on an "outside-the-box" idea pushed by an enthusiastic promoter who had some experience in the field and talked a good game yet didn't bring a lot of his own money to the arrangement.

Bricklin's deal was largely a franchising play: he'd sell Handyman franchises to various investors by showing them how well the outlets were doing in Orlando, where he had signed up about a dozen of the "colorful A-framed" stores. For a $15,000 fee, franchisees would get Handyman merchandising and signage, and would also get access to a centrally located distribution centre for Handyman supplies. By the early 1960s, Bricklin (and his father) had sold a number of franchises to businessmen across the country. Bricklin had hustled himself into franchising, with a sideline in real estate, a business model that had become incredibly successful in postwar America, exemplified by the evolution of McDonald's, which began in California in 1955.[8]

Bricklin's first Handyman investor, W. Quealy Walker, owner of the Dixie Paint & Varnish firm of Brunswick, Georgia, agreed to sink $300,000 into the Handyman chain, mortgaging his family business to do so. But Bricklin's idea didn't work out exactly as promised. The stores didn't do that well, and it turned out there was no real value in the Handyman name, or the late-night, seven-days-a-week business model. In 1965, Handyman franchisees in California, Florida, and New York sued Bricklin for over $2 million, claiming he'd misled them. After complicated legal proceedings in Florida and California, the courts ruled against Bricklin, but the company declared bankruptcy in Orlando before the judgment could be enforced. Bricklin himself had already bailed from Handyman, in 1964.[9] Despite the ruling, and the bankruptcy (the first he was associated with), Bricklin maintained that he had *sold* the chain for a million bucks, framing himself as a young business genius and planting the seeds of credibility for future ventures. Bricklin also later asserted that, because of his business acumen, "149 Handyman franchises" had been established across the country (in reality, it was closer to sixteen).[10]

W. Quealy Walker, Jr., the son of Bricklin's first Handyman investor, vehemently disputed this characterization, saying that Dixie Paint & Varnish never paid Bricklin any money to get Malcolm out of the business. "It was really a bad deal," said Jr. "Bricklin disappeared with the money and my dad was left holding the bag." By the mid-1960s, according to New Brunswick journalists H.A. Fredericks and Allan Chambers, who wrote a book about the Bricklin incident, "Bricklin's name was on half a dozen lawsuits."[11] Nonetheless, Malcolm could claim that he had launched a successful business and become a millionaire by the time he was twenty-five. Wasn't that the American dream?

In any event, by then, Bricklin had hustled off to his next act.

Act II. Living la Dolce Vita: Italian Motor Scooters
Philadelphia, Milan, and New York City, 1965–8

In 1965, Bricklin headed back north to his hometown, looking for his next venture. He set up a one-man consulting firm, Universal Marketing Inc., with himself as president. Before long, a relative of Bricklin's got him in touch with one David Rosen, who was in the vending machine business. Rosen was heading to Italy to check into the possibility of distributing the "Cine Box," a kind of early music-video-on-demand "visual jukebox" manufactured by the Milanese firm Innocenti. Bricklin, ever on the lookout for new business opportunities and some adventure, came along for the trip.[12]

By the mid-1960s, Italy had become a cultural force in Europe and North America, fuelled by film, fashion, and food. And, like Germany and Japan, Italy's vehicle sector had been an integral aspect of this postwar recovery, one that had been kickstarted by motorized scooters, especially the Vespa. First introduced in 1946 by inventor Enrico Piaggio and made famous in films like *Roman Holiday* (1953), Vespa was by 1960 selling two million of the little motorcycles annually.[13] Another postwar Italian scooter, Innocenti's Lambretta, which debuted in 1947, had also had some success in the marketplace.

The Cine Box didn't work out (Bricklin discovered that about the only videos available to play on the machines were short pornographic films), but during the Italian trip he did manage to convince Innocenti to allow him to become their exclusive US distribution agent. It just so happened that Innocenti had about 25,000 unsold Lambrettas sitting in a Long Island warehouse. If Innocenti gave him a salary and an expense account, Malcolm would sell the scooters, and they'd all make money.[14] Such a deal took Malcolm one step further along capitalism's value chain, and it also allowed him to leave behind the legal unpleasantness of the hardware business. Soon, Bricklin was selling Lambrettas out of a Rolls Royce that came courtesy of his Innocenti expense account. He successfully sold all the scooters, including a few thousand to the New York City Police Department for its Central Park patrols.[15] Eventually, the scooter business led Bricklin to Rabbit scooters, made by Fuji of Japan. Bricklin figured that Rabbits could be sold into the American market even more profitably than the Italian jobs. Off to Japan he jetted.

Figure 4.2. Lambretta scooters, New York City, 1970s.

Act III. "Cheap and Ugly Does It": Subaru 360 Bubble Cars

Tokyo, Philadelphia, and Arizona, 1967–71

Landing in bustling Tokyo in 1967 to do a deal for Rabbitt scooters, Bricklin discovered that Fuji Heavy Industries Ltd. (est. 1953) also manufactured inexpensive minicars. At a time when cheap Beetles were selling like hotcakes, Fuji's Subaru 360 "bubble car" might be Bricklin's ticket to the grandest entrepreneurial (and technological) stage of all, cars. In the 1960s, the Japanese were slowly starting to penetrate the US marketplace, and Bricklin thought the inexpensive little vehicle could sell in the growing, low-end import segment of the market dominated by the VW Beetle. However, the Japanese were not entirely keen on the idea, and new government automobile safety regulations, courtesy of Ralph Nader, posed a problem. Luckily, Bricklin discovered that the regulations applied only to cars with "over 1,000 pounds curb weight," and that the 360 checked in at about 960 pounds. Bricklin had found a loophole that provided a doozy of an opportunity to import and sell cheap Japanese cars in America "with virtual impunity." After some cajoling, he soon had a deal with Fuji and, along with partner Harvey Lamm (whose family was in the furniture business), created Philadelphia-based Subaru of America in 1968. Lamm put in $25,000; Bricklin, $50,000. Fuji required them to purchase two thousand vehicles in the first year and a thousand cars a year thereafter to sell into the American market. It was one of the first Japanese-American auto deals of its kind, and Bricklin and Lamm figured that they could make about $660 per vehicle, retailing at $1,297 a car, about $500 cheaper than the Beetle.[16]

Now, Bricklin just had to sell the cars. He wouldn't retail the cars directly, even though he and Lamm had an import deal with Fuji – the innovation here was to be a distributor, selling regional franchises to independent dealers, to thus "avoid the consumer marketplace altogether," creating a kind of multi-level distribution organizational structure. Like franchising, legal pyramid schemes (called direct sales) had come into their own as a popular business and sales technique in post-war America, one that in some instances generated immense success (for example, Amway, created in Michigan in 1959). Direct sales represented yet another example of the increasing financialization of the economy and of the emphasis on hustling salesmanship. The technique peaked in the 1970s, "not in spite of the economic recession but because of it."[17]

Then there was the advertising for the 360. Even during a decade of memorable, unorthodox import advertising (Volkswagen's "Think Small" was particularly catchy), Bricklin's Subaru campaign stood out: "Cheap and Ugly Does It" proclaimed the 360's cheeky, groovy ads ("Happy Talk from Subaru"). "They said we couldn't use the word cheap," Bricklin proclaimed like a carnival barker, "but we are using it." Upping the rhetorical ante, he also declared that the 360 was "just as ugly as any other little car on the road today." Since the 360 looked like the Bug, had better milage, and was considerably cheaper, the car initially caught on. By early 1969, Bricklin was selling about a thousand 360s a month. Bricklin and Lamm signed up dozens of franchisees, and they cashed in by selling three hundred thousand shares of the company on the Philadelphia stock exchange. Bricklin's Subaru of America Inc. was the first and "only publicly owned importing firm in America," *Automotive News* noted.[18]

Times were good, and Bricklin was flush. Quickly, the firm procured a yacht and started using private jets. Bricklin and Lamm set themselves up in an opulent headquarters, a ten-storey "circular building of Japanese motif" designed by Malcolm's brother-in-law on an eight-acre site in New Jersey that included a helipad. The building was a "Wizard-of-Oz put on," topped only by Bricklin's fantastic space-age office: his desk had high-tech built-in phones and seven television sets. He hired his mother, Gertrude, as bookkeeper and hatched plans for a series of extravagant Subaru training centres.[19] With the Subaru venture, Bricklin had made it big.

Then, disaster struck – a devastating April 1969 *Consumer Reports* review of the 360. The review, coupled with Nader's denunciation ("983 pounds of collapsible Japanese lantern"), ultimately cemented the vehicle's status as "the worst car ever sold in America."[20] Sales completely collapsed. By mid-1969, Bricklin had imported

Figure 4.3. "Cheap and ugly does it": Subaru 360 ad, 1969.

about six thousand 360s, half of which now sat rusting, unsold, on shipping docks. With worthless inventories and Malcolm's profligate spending, Subaru of America soon had a negative cash flow of $750,000. Worse, the public relations disaster of the 360 (not to mention an ethics scandal involving a friendly Pennsylvania legislator who was moonlighting as a Subaru director) threatened to sink Subaru of America forever. The company was in trouble, even as Malcolm reassured nervous dealers that "the consumer forgets quickly" and that "attitudes change fast."[21] Undaunted, Bricklin doubled down by pressuring Fuji to allow him to sell a better model, the Subaru FF-1 Star, but the Japanese company refused. The impasse was resolved only when new investors took control of the firm and Tokyo effectively forced Bricklin out, though not without difficulty. According to one story, from business author Randall Rothenberg's 1994 book *Where the Suckers Moon: The Life and Death of an Advertising Campaign*, towards the end, Bricklin and Lamm managed to delay the inevitable by devising a dramatic tactic to "get rid of unwanted visitors" who nosily came calling at the Subaru headquarters:

> Confronted by a disagreeable guest, Mal would excuse himself, pick up his phone and call Harvey. They'd start arguing. At a prearranged signal, Harvey would slam down the phone, rush in and continue the argument in person. Malcolm would then pull a gun from his drawer and shoot his partner. The guest – auditor, supplier, whoever – would flee, never to learn that the pistol was filled with blanks.[22]

As part of his complicated Subaru buyout, Bricklin got about a thousand 360s and the rights to FasTrack, a racetrack enterprise where Bricklin could recycle the unsellable minicars as go-karts. That venture ended in acrimony as well, with reports that his investors sued him for "misappropriation of funds."[23]

Nonetheless, with the Subaru promotion, Bricklin had truly made a name for himself in the automobile business. In 1973, Subaru of America sold 38,000 vehicles, and Bricklin's undeniable prescience in bringing Japanese cars to America at the beginning of the 1970s Asian import wave gave him a credibility, and fame, that he would bank on, again and again, in the years to come.

Act IV (Main). Dream Car: Malcolm Bricklin's Fantastic Safety Vehicle-1

Saint John, New Brunswick, Scottsdale, Arizona, etc., 1971–5

The greatest example of Bricklin's promotional moxie was, without a doubt, his launch of the SV1. By then a seasoned impresario, Bricklin began in 1971 to tease the industry and the public with snippets about his rumoured vehicle, building suspense like a circus ringmaster. It began with leaks in the press, as reporters started to "hear things" about a mysterious "safety sports car" with gull-wing doors. Soon there were "reports" of parts orders, and further breathless accounts of millions of dollars in financing from some "very respected lending institutions." Then, "just when it appeared that the whole thing was a 'sting,'" a photo of the vehicle was leaked.[24] Despite the 360 debacle, Bricklin's continued connection to Subaru provided gravitas and opened doors, since he was, according to the press, "still a major shareholder." By then, the Japanese brand with its six-star logo (it was the sixth of Fuji's divisions) was coming to be seen as a success.[25]

In 1972, Bricklin had used some of his own Subaru money to design and build an SV1 prototype. Even though it was nowhere near a production model, Bricklin had publicity photos taken of the vehicle and created a short movie about the car, which he could use for his pitch. His Subaru reputation, the prototype, and the movie allowed Bricklin to convince banks, such as the First Pennsylvania Banking and Trust Company, to lend him money (he pledged his Subaru shares as collateral). Most importantly, he now had something tangible enough to allow him to start signing up dealers. For a deposit of $8,800, new Bricklin dealers would get the rights to sell the car and to start taking their own deposits from prospective SV1 buyers. Additionally, dealers got the rights to Bricklin signage, tools, and parts for their franchise. Malcolm also used the film in his pitches to other potential investors, including Hatfield.[26]

In 1973, Bricklin hired the public relations firm Rogers & Cowan (est. 1950, Beverly Hills, California) and the ad agency Lois, Holland, Callaway (est. 1968, New York City). Together, the two firms began an all-out promotional blitz that saw Bricklin and his car launched into the public's consciousness. There were dozens of print and broadcast media appearances by Bricklin and the SV1, numerous SV1 product placements, and a very significant national ad campaign (though mostly targeted in the Northeast, where Bricklin had his most established network of potential dealers).[27]

With an ad budget of $300 a vehicle – Detroit usually budgeted $50–60 a car – Bricklin was spending an immense amount of money on promotion. According to adman George Lois, his firm's Bricklin campaign was going to generate "so much excitement." Lois announced that Bricklin's innovative ads would, in fact, be "more like posters." Lois had first gained advertising fame as a member of Doyle Dane Bernbach (which created the "Think Small" campaign for VW), and he boasted a long and interesting Madison Avenue career. He was later criticized for exaggerating his role in some famous campaigns, but, with the SV1, Lois reassuringly stated that "you don't have to yell." Moreover, since so many of the cars were "already presold" to waiting customers (according to Mal), it was "almost embarrassing to do advertising for it."[28]

That summer, teasing ads aimed at potential dealers across the eastern United States began appearing in their mailboxes: "For the past few months, you might have heard some enticing tidbits of information about an exceptional new automobile called the Bricklin, a car which has been under development for the past three years" (really, two). Now was their chance to get in on the first ever "safety sports car" from America's newest auto company, but they had to act quickly, since the Bricklin was soon "going into production," and many dealers had already signed up. The Bricklin firm, officially and impressively called General Vehicle Incorporated,

Figure 4.4. An SV1 under guard, Las Vegas preview, February 1974.

was still seeking “well-capitalized, well-established dealers” that the firm could start “appointing” as Bricklin franchisees.[29]

In February 1974, Bricklin showed the SV1 prototype to prospective dealers at a well-attended “exclusive” event at the Riviera Hotel in Las Vegas, coinciding with the annual meeting of the National Automobile Dealers Association. Bricklin dramatically blanketed his event with high security, including rifle-toting law enforcement officers and metal detectors to catch any cameras, ensuring there were no unauthorized leaks of the car’s image to undermine its mystique. He also had actor Paul Newman and racing star Bobby Unser hang around the car, signing autographs and lending credibility, and thus helping to generate more potential dealer agreements. The Vegas event cost Bricklin $10,000, but he signed up 112 dealers; by mid-summer, he had lined up over 200 dealerships to sell the cars. “The showing was a ‘real show,’” G.S. Wheatley, the New Brunswick government official tasked with overseeing the project, reported from the field, though “part of the reason for it was to keep the tempo up to keep the financiers confident.”[30]

Whenever Malcolm met with potential dealers, he always gave them the spectacular Bricklin brochures produced by Lois, Holland, Callway. Utilizing the SV1’s five vibrant colours, the glossy pamphlets blazed with bright, futuristic possibility

Figure 4.5. Malcolm Bricklin with Paul Newman and Bobby Unser, Las Vegas preview, February 1974.

as it explained the features of the innovatively safe, sporty, and *sexy* car. Titillating prospective dealers and buyers, it promised that "there's more to Bricklin than sexy doors." The copy captured the essence of the car and, presumably, the man. "Dealers," wrote Fredericks and Chambers, "would pay for franchises on the strength of his brochures" alone.[31] Little did they know that "the good looking red car" photographed for the brochure "was only a shell of hand made body parts, plexiglass windows and windshield, no interior trim, and no roll-up windows."[32] By February 1975, Bricklin told a *Washington Post* reporter that he had 50,000 orders for the car through his dealers, with deposits, and that the firm had received 5,000 applications from interested dealers.[33]

The publicity for the car was so successful that, by the fall of 1974, it had "reached staggering proportions," according to *Motor Trend*.[34] There were hundreds of articles about Bricklin and the SV1 in automobile and industry trade publications, national and local newspapers, and mainstream magazines sold at grocery store checkouts. *People* magazine featured the "millionaire Malcolm Bricklin" and "his

Figure 4.6. Bricklin promotional moment: cowboy Bricklin with Senator Barry Goldwater, c. 1975.

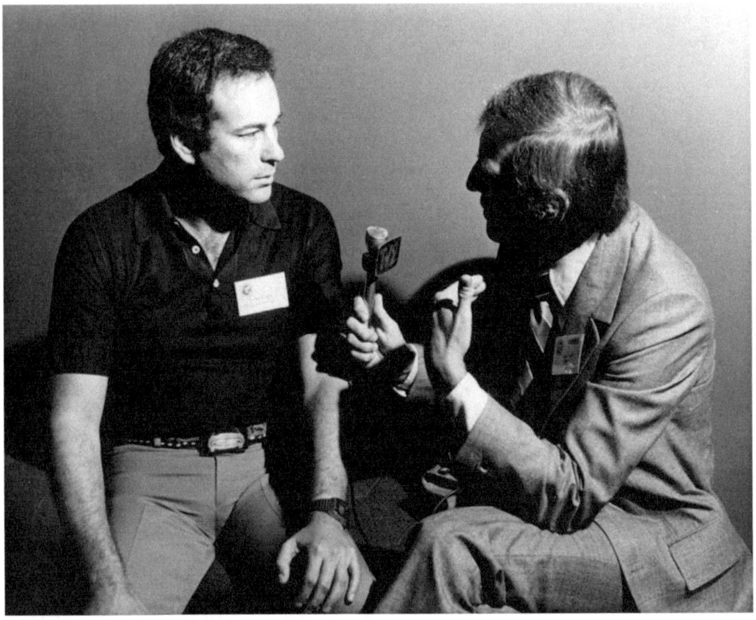

Figure 4.7. Bricklin with *Auto News*'s Wally Scott, c. 1975.

Figure 4.8. A Bricklin as the pace car, and on display, at the Arizona 150/Bricklin 150, 1974.

magic car"; *Time* called him the "Don Quixote of Detroit"; and *Business Week* declared that "a promoter cranks up a new car."[35] Bricklin appeared on dozens of television talk shows and newscasts across the continent, often in front of millions of people, from *The Mike Douglas Show* (co-hosted by Roger Moore) to NBC's *Today*. Malcolm and his SV1 were featured on national television game shows (*To Tell the Truth*, *The Price Is Right*), dramas (*Switch*, *McCoy*), and sitcoms (*Chico and the Man*), also in front of millions of potential consumers. Bricklin even drove a pace car in the Bricklin 150 race he sponsored in Phoenix, Arizona, which was shown on ABC's *Wide World of Sports* and attended by luminaries such as Senator Barry Goldwater and King Faisal of Saudi Arabia. The car made dozens of promotional appearances across North America, from the Canadian National Exhibition to Santa Claus parades, and was used to promote products as diverse as Gatorade and DuPont wax finishes. Bricklin spent much of his time jetting to auto shows in Los Angeles, San Francisco, Chicago, New York, and Toronto. He loved to tell the story of how, once, when rushing through the Chicago airport, dressed in his cowboy attire, a child pointed and yelled out "Mommy, there goes the Marlboro Man!"[36]

Figure 4.9. The reveal: the SV1 under wraps, New York City, June 1974.

Figure 4.10. Albert Bricklin, Malcom's father, with a branding iron, standing with Richard Hatfield, New York City, June 1974.

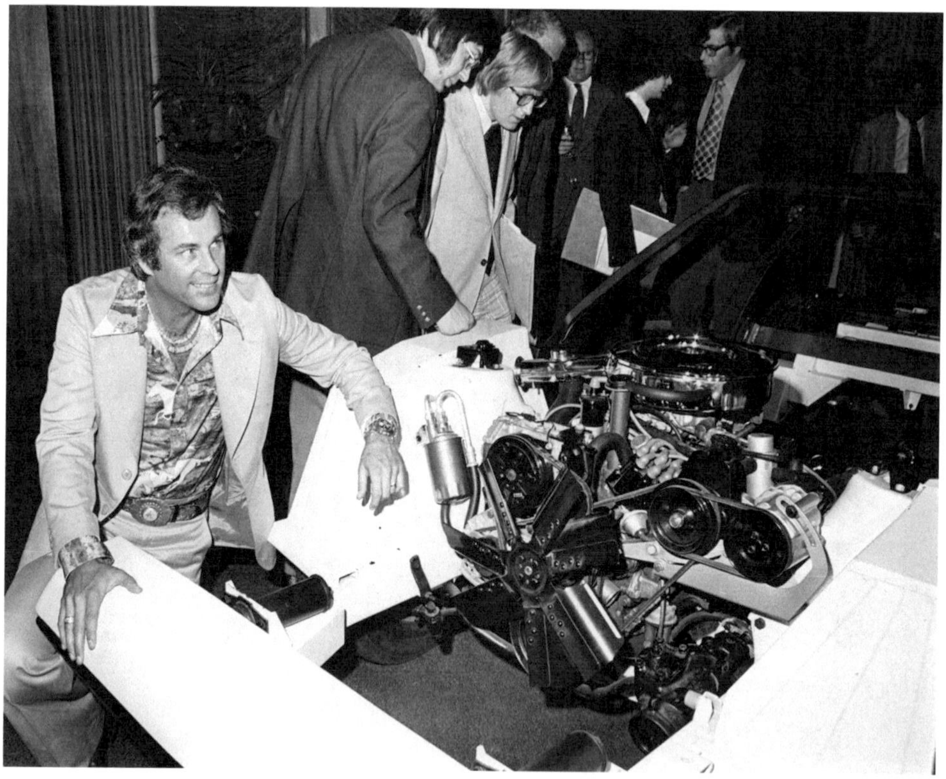

Figure 4.11. The personification of a Seventies, stylish, nonconformist auto entrepreneur.

Promoting the car required travel, dozens of media interviews, and hobnobbing with movie stars, race-car drivers, models, and politicians.

Malcolm revelled in the promotional attention, and in the performance. His starring role in automotive promotional showmanship and the resulting fame drew on his most natural and best entrepreneurial self. And it was during the SV1 years that Bricklin fully took on the cowboy persona, moving to Arizona, wearing cowboy gear, and playing up his western image. He seemed to suit the role well, with his natural charisma and confidence. Of course, not all the press Bricklin received was fawning, as some mainstream publications like the *Wall Street Journal* cast a more jaundiced eye towards the colourful promoter from, ahem, Philadelphia. A November 1974 *Motor Trend* article, "Adventures along the 'Yellow Bricklin Road'" (written as a *Wizard of Oz*–inspired parable, naturally), concluded that whether or not Malcolm "can build, market and sell his sports car remains to be seen." Nonetheless, even in their scepticism, many journalistic assessments still held out hope that Malcolm could pull it off – in Bricklin, the American dream remained alive and well.[37]

Figure 4.12. At the Tavern on the Green, Central Park.

The Bricklin promotional blitz reached a crescendo at the splashy June 1974 launch event in New York. The Four Seasons ballroom, rented at a rumored cost of $50,000 (actual $25,000), was packed with about one thousand "specially invited" guests, including press, Bricklin employees and hangers-on, potential dealers, and – having just jetted in the day before – the swinging, single, premier of New Brunswick, Richard Hatfield, with a crate of fresh Atlantic salmon (Hatfield had to drive to Bangor, Maine, first, as there were no direct flights to New York from New Brunswick). The program: cocktails and buffet at 11:30 a.m.; unveiling of the car at 12:30 (with Sammy Cahn singing); press conference. The five bars did a brisk business, and the numerous models hired for the occasion milled about the car and the mostly male guests. Bricklin's family was part of the show. Albert took a key role in helping his son attempt to brand the car by being the one to press the hot iron poker into the white vehicle as Malcolm dramatically exclaimed "I name this car 'Bricklin'!" ("Don't worry, it will get buffed out"). Meanwhile, Malcolm's young sons Craig and Kevin were busily handing out press kits, embossed in suede patterns matching the car's interior.[38] Malcolm threw a good party.

In actuality, the glitzy event was a bit of smoke and mirrors, and it had taken Malcolm quite a bit of moxie to pull it off. The crowd did not know that the night before, Bricklin had realized that the cars would not fit through the glass doors to the ballroom. In a mad rush, he had the cars drained of fluids, tilted on a spit, and then squeezed through the doors, barely avoiding an expensive Picasso tapestry. Nor did the crowd know that the cars on display were hand-built prototypes, not production vehicles. Fredericks and Chambers later claimed in their 1977 book, *Bricklin*, that "one of the cars at the ceremony lacked a radiator," while the signature gull-wing doors of the "Safety Orange" SV1 on the main stage "were wired to a generator under the platform to ensure that they would open and close all day." In reality, the SV1's greatest selling features, the innovative doors and fiberglass bodies, were already causing severe engineering and production problems in Livonia and New Brunswick. And while Bricklin's gleaming cars looked fantastic, he would have to admit, if you were to ask him, that the firm was not yet ready for production. "The first two cars should come off the line in the next couple of days," he'd reassure you. "Maybe not this Friday," but "certainly by the following Friday" (actually, not until September).[39] It was a little bit of razzle-dazzle salesmanship, Malcolm Bricklin style.

So were some of Bricklin's other promotional gimmicks, which he unveiled over the course of the venture. For example, Bricklin liked to demonstrate at events how difficult the SV1's plastic body was to dent by "whacking the hood with a big hammer." Lois, Holland, Callaway even shot a commercial based on the stunt, one of a series of ten, though the commercials were never released (with orders pouring in after the New York launch's success, Bricklin felt that there was no need to do additional advertising and cancelled the "$3 million campaign"). As another gimmick, in December 1974, Bricklin announced that he would be leasing five SV1s to the Scottsdale, Arizona, Police Department, for $1 a year.[40] Meanwhile, Gertrude Bricklin, known as "Mother Bricklin," was styled director of customer relations. The Bricklin promotional materials described her as having a "broad educational background, including a degree in human relations and 'graduate work completed in the East, West, and all over.'" She always answered the 1-800 phone number on the back of every "Bricklin Owner" card that came along with each SV1's "birth certificate," and her holiday cards cheerfully read "Wishing you

Figure 4.13. The show must go on: an SV1 tilted on a spit to get it into the Four Seasons. Note the very clean, fully assembled undercarriage.

a VERY bright New Year, May All Your Dreams Come True."[41] Bricklin had excellent customer service.

With the SV1, Bricklin emerged fully as a promoter and a showman par excellence. Nevertheless, the company ended up as Bricklin's second, though much more spectacular, bankruptcy. Yet, just as with his Subaru promotion, he had done something real, something that no one had achieved in decades. Bricklin had actually managed to build an auto company and, even more amazingly, had managed to mass manufacture and sell three thousand cars, thus forever carving his name into American auto industry lore. Indeed, even after Bricklin had declared bankruptcy in 1975, the currency of his now-famous name was something that not only still had value but likely had been enhanced by the incident: as the bankruptcy judge stated, "the bankrupt has licensed his name in the past but said license has been cancelled. He claims the right to use his name as a personal attribute not subject to the use or sale by the bankruptcy trustee."[42] Bricklin's name had become his

Figure 4.14. SV1s in action as police vehicles, Scottsdale, Arizona, 1975.

brand, which had value because of his visionary abilities, despite his multiple bankruptcies. (Sound familiar?) That fact gave him enough auto-sector credibility – and fame – to keep the Malcolm Bricklin production going for decades.

Act V. The World's (Second) Worst Car: Renewed Promotion and Other Ventures

New York and Kragujevac, Serbia, 1984–92

In the mid-80s, Bricklin hit upon one of his most famous ventures. Burned by his experience *building* cars, he realized that his true talent was in promoting import cars, and the distribution deals attached. Bricklin's first big success had been his 1960s Subaru deal, and he went back to his roots: importing cheap cars to America. By the 1980s, Americans had developed an insatiable appetite for inexpensive foreign vehicles, without much concern about their origin. A scant three decades after the Second World War, US consumers were snapping up compact German and Japanese cars by the millions from their erstwhile foes while Detroit languished.[43] This was exactly Malcolm's game; something old, something new.

At the time, the United States may have been deep in the Reaganite phase of its Cold War with the Soviet Union, but that didn't stop Bricklin from betting on a cheap, small, Eastern-bloc, Yugoslavian-made car: the Yugo 45. Bricklin had been importing Italian Fiats through his firm International Automotive Importers when he saw a Yugo in London and was entranced. Back in the States, he discovered that a Californian already had a deal for five thousand cars a year with the Yugo's builder, Serbian firm Crvena Zastava (est. 1853, for canons; 1955, for cars). In 1984, Bricklin bought out the Californian and started Yugo America Inc., with himself as chair and CEO and owner of 51 per cent of the firm. Eventually, former (and future) diplomat Lawrence Eagleburger joined Yugo's board at Henry Kissinger's personal suggestion, according to Bricklin.[44] Yet again, Malcolm was back; yet again, he was importing a car into the United States; and yet again, he was dealing with government officials who were chasing the dream of automotive industrial modernity riches, though this time they were communists.

Compared to most of the 1980s import car market, the Yugo was a piece of junk. Initially, it had no air conditioner, no power steering, no automatic transmission, no airbags, and no … well, the list went on. Yugos broke down a lot (*Consumer Reports* said it was better to just buy a used car instead), had terrible mileage (worst in its class) and horrible emissions (seriously, what could one expect from Soviet Europe?), and they weren't really all that safe (ranking dead last – thanks, Nader). As Bricklin later admitted, even though he pushed Crvena Zastava to boost the manufacturing quality and had also spent his own money to improve the vehicle, it was "a 20-year-old Fiat [built] in a 50-year-old factory."[45] But it was *very* cheap. Bricklin priced the Yugo at $3,995, by far the cheapest car sold in the United States. Canada's cheapest car, the $5,000 Hyundai Pony, which had debuted in 1983, was that country's top-selling vehicle in 1985 and 1986.[46]

Amazingly, something similar to the Pony story in Canada happened with the Yugo in the United States. Before long, "there were lines at dealerships ten deep," wrote Jason Vuic in *The Yugo: The Rise and Fall of the Worst Car in History* (despite his book's title, Vuic actually considered the Subaru 360 a worse vehicle). Between 1985 and 1992, Bricklin sold, astoundingly, approximately 150,000 Yugos, and the car became one of the fastest-selling imports of all time. At the height of "Yugomania," Bricklin (called a "brilliant marketer" by industry guru Brock Yates) was making $2 million a month importing one of the worst vehicles ever produced, anywhere.[47] There was even talk of importing the cheap Malaysian Proton, too.

Then, a familiar pattern set in. Buoyed by the good times, Bricklin bought a $2.3 million Colorado ranch and turned to living an elaborate, expensive, cowboy lifestyle. When Yugo Inc. needed another $20 million to survive (it had to get a new

Figure 4.15. A latter-day Model T or Bug? Advertising the Yugo, 1980s.

product), the company found new investors, but in exchange Bricklin had to go: the word was that "Malcolm Bricklin is a terrific promoter … But he has to come to grips with the fact that he is an ideas guy, not an operations guy." For his part, according to Bricklin, he got out after a chilling meeting with Serbian nationalist Slobodan Milosevic at an event in Yugoslavia prior to the Balkans War – a meeting that, decades later, still made the hairs on Malcolm's arm stand up. In the end, Bricklin made at least $7 million (and likely more) for walking away.[48] Plus, he got to keep the thirty-two Yugos he had parked in Colorado.

Again, like so often before, just as he was leaving, everything started to fall apart. Sales dried up completely. Yugo had no new product to offer. The cars on the road were falling apart. Dealers were angry. In 1989, Yugo went bankrupt.

Shortly thereafter, so did Bricklin, after being sued by Yugo dealers for $17.5 million. Yet again, Bricklin's venture ended in lawsuits and acrimony. But he'd done well off the deal, even though in 1991 he had to sell the the Bricklin Ranch to Henry Kravis of hedge fund KKR fame, for $5.5 million. While newspapers at the time reported that much of that money went to pay debts, Bricklin later disputed this.[49] No matter: despite the fallout, Malcolm had, with the Yugo, again proven his entrepreneurial abilities and delivered yet another notable performance in his long promotional career.

In the early 1990s, Bricklin got some distance from Yugo by attempting to reimagine the way used cars were sold. In 1991, he announced plans to open a chain of "auto ranches" that would sell "remanufactured" cars. The purported $60 million endeavour, designed to market vehicles "with Disney-land-like hoopla," was yet another of Bricklin's outside-the-box ideas. "What we have here," he declared with his usual unshakeable confidence, "is the beginning of an earthquake in the automobile business." The remark prompted one wag to sarcastically reply, "Anybody feel the earth move?"[50] The answer was a resounding no, and, this time, the promotion didn't work out at all.

Act VI. One Step Ahead of the Future: Selling Electrified Bicycles
Burbank, California, 1995–7

In the mid-90s, Bricklin was back to tech: electrified bikes. By then, electric vehicles seemed to be just around the corner, as technological advances had accelerated the effectiveness of batteries and shrunk their size. In 1996, General Motors' EV1 would famously give North Americans an early glimpse at a decarbonized future. Bricklin, ever the visionary, had seen the potential of electrification, too. In 1995, three decades before electric bikes became common (and three decades after his Italian and Japanese scooter ventures), Bricklin launched the Electric Bicycle Co., located in sunny, television-soaked Burbank, California, to sell his EV Warrior electrified bike.[51]

Again, Bricklin was a little ahead in his timing. The bicycles, running on two 12-volt batteries, were to be manufactured in partnership with Japanese electronics giant Sanyo. EV Warriors came in three models, which retailed from $1,200 to $2,000, and were to be sold nationwide through selected car dealerships (Bricklin's partners, yet again; by 1996, over a hundred had signed up). As always, Bricklin held highly publicized launch events, this time in Portland, Oregon, as well as Las Vegas (a Bricklin favourite), and he forged a partnership with Malcolm Currie, a former CEO of Hughes Aircraft and former US defence department undersecretary.

Figure 4.16. Malcolm Bricklin with his electric electric bikes in the California sunbelt, 1996: only slightly before their time.

Investors included St. Louis Rams owner Georgia Frontiere and author Sidney Sheldon. Lee Iacocca had his own electric bike idea (EV Global Motors), but Malcolm beat him to the market (and, later, claimed to have shown Lee the EV ropes during a visit to Iacocca's Beverly Hills mansion). Consumers, however, were not quite ready to go to an auto dealership to buy the bikes or to pay that much for them (Honda scooters were only slightly more expensive). By 1997, the venture had gone bankrupt, "costing investors millions." "For the third time in 20 years," reported the *Los Angeles Times*, "Malcolm Bricklin was either ahead of his time, over the top, or out of his element."[52]

Act VII. The Entrepreneur Strikes Back: Importing Chinese Vehicles

Wuhu, China, and New York City, 2002–9

Bricklin's greatest entrepreneurial act after the SV1 was likely his ill-fated, headline-grabbing, and well-documented deal in the first decade of this century to bring Chinese-built cars to the American market. Initially, he had simply been looking to import another cheap vehicle into North America. In 2002, he embarked on a years-long global tour to find a viable product, factory, or partner, jetting from Poland to Romania to the former Yugoslavia to England to India, and finally to China, where he landed on the doorstep of the Chery Automobile Company (est. 1997, Wuhu, Anhui Province), then the eighth-largest automaker in the People's Republic. Chery, which sounded a lot like "Chevy," had gained some notoriety after being sued in 2003 by GM for copying one of its Korean-built small cars, the Daewoo Maitz, which looked a lot like a Chery QQ (the suit was settled).

Bricklin's plan for achieving his dream of importing Chinese-made cars – one that brashly echoed many of his past escapades, but on a larger scale – was to create a new firm, not immodestly called Visionary Vehicles Incorporated, to connect American dealers to Chery, which would supply the cars. Bricklin was betting that he could be the first to crack the American market with made-in-China vehicles. But first he had to convince the Chinese. During his initial 2005 meeting with Chery's senior management at their glittering Wuhu headquarters, Bricklin – never known for taking the traditional approach – startled his would-be partners by stripping down to his bare chest mid-way through his pitch, claiming that he would give them the shirt off his back if that's what it took for them to truly know him. As *Inc.* magazine described the scene,

> "The word I hear about doing business in China is relationship," declared Bricklin, his face flushed. He then ratcheted down his red silk tie and punctuated his next words by unbuttoning his once-dry white shirt:
>
> "The way I see it, [pop]
> we have two choices. [pop]
> We can either take our time [pop]
> and get to know each other. [pop]
> Or, we can get naked!"

The shirt-ripping, button-popping incident, and much of the venture, was chronicled by Malcolm's documentarian son, Johnathan, for the 2007 film about his father, *The Entrepreneur*. Bricklin's business was always a family affair, and Jonathan's cameras were present for every step of the deal as it evolved, shooting over 1,500 hours of material for the documentary.[53]

Yet again, however, it seemed as if Bricklin was a step ahead of his time. While the Japanese, Koreans, and Europeans had all had success in the US market – in the case of the Japanese, Bricklin himself had helped pave the way with Subaru – bringing Chinese-made cars to America was a completely different kettle of fish. In the early 2000s, the US market was already saturated with foreign product. Just as importantly, while China had joined the World Trade Organization in 2003 and its economy functioned in a nominally capitalist fashion, it was still a communist, authoritarian, regime, as perhaps most dramatically illustrated by the protests in Tiananmen Square, Beijing, in 1989. Although the Chinese economy was booming, doing business in China was not the same as it was elsewhere, especially when it came to cars. For decades, foreign manufacturers had been forced into stringent joint ventures with Chinese firms, many of which were state-owned. At the same time, China was an emerging rival superpower, not a defeated adversary, as the Japanese and Germans had been when their products had swept into America. China provoked different reactions in the US automobile marketplace from consumers: if getting a deal with the Chinese was no easy matter, convincing Americans to buy Chinese cars, in 2006, might prove even more challenging.[54]

After some serious wrangling, Bricklin got his deal. The plan was to offer five Chery-made models – a small sedan, an SUV, a mid-size sedan, a sporty car, and a crossover – all designed by Italy's well-known Bertoni and Pininfarina firms (with whom Bricklin had worked in the past). But the deal was contingent. In exchange for the right to import 250,000 Chery cars into the United States starting in 2007 (and 25,000 into Canada), Bricklin had to secure $200 million in financing and establish a dealer network. As was typical with a Bricklin car business, individual auto dealers would pay to get the rights to sell the cars, this time for $2 million each. Bricklin managed to get just under a hundred dealers signed up, a sizeable figure. Things looked good.

But then momentum seemed to stall. Perhaps the price was too high, or Americans were cool to the idea of Chinese cars. Needing more financing, Bricklin sought out high-profile partners and angel investors, and was quite successful in doing so. The impressive list included shipping mogul Per Arneberg, US representative to the United Nations William J. vanden Heuvel, and Maurice Strong, the Canadian industrialist and former UN undersecretary general. Strong was even tapped as chair of Visionary's technology and environmental advisory board. At one point, George Soros was involved, and had put millions in escrow, while the venerable Allen & Co. investment firm was hired to structure the deal.[55]

Yet, after much drama, Bricklin's Chinese venture collapsed. It soon became clear that Chery really wanted a joint venture and much more control than Bricklin was willing to cede, to them or anyone else involved in the deal. Word out of China was that "Chery executives grew uncomfortable with Bricklin's supersalesman style." Moreover, the cars "never met US standards," and Chery eventually reneged, "leaving Bricklin to face angry dealers."[56] For Portland, Oregon's Ron Tonkin, who owned seventeen dealerships and had "lost several hundred thousand dollars" on previous Bricklin's ventures, it was clear that "Malcolm should have been a carnival promoter."[57]

But that was only one side of the story. Bricklin, with the backing of many of his dealers, launched lawsuits across three different continents over the failed agreement, including at Chery, for $26 million on the initial investment and $1.1 billion in projected lost earnings.[58] Chery, it was alleged, had been making additional deals behind Malcolm's back, including with a former Visionary Vehicles employee (eventually, Chery did cut a deal with Chrysler, but it was later rescinded). By 2007, Visionary Vehicles, by then no longer exclusively dealing with Chery, had announced plans to produce electric vehicles at three facilities in the United States. Twenty-nine dealer groups were signed up, with a target of selling cars by 2009.[59] Eventually, however, this too fell apart. In the wreckage of the Chery debacle, Bricklin "got zero" from the lawsuits, as he lamented, despite decisions in his favour against a former employee.[60]

Chery was the only business deal Bricklin said he ever regretted, though *The Entrepreneur* did get good reviews and extensively toured the film circuit. The *Washington Post* called the film "a hidden gem of a documentary." It wrote of Bricklin: "Profane, irascible, combative and gloriously indefatigable, Malcolm is an utterly mesmerizing leading man, the kind of alternately charismatic and offensive character viewers will gladly follow."[61] If Bricklin had succeeded with the Chinese, it might have made the documentary a huge hit.

Like so many other of his entrepreneurial ventures, Malcolm's Chery deal had *almost* worked out. If it had hit, Bricklin would have changed the North American industry by being the first American firm to import Chinese-made cars, just as he had done in 1968 with Japanese-made Subarus. Yet again, Malcolm had been ahead of his time: within two decades, Tesla (founded by Martin Eberhard and Marc Tarpenning in 2003, in San Carlos, California) would begin exporting to Canada Model Ys directly from its Shanghai Gigafactory (the world's most efficient plant), the first time Chinese-made cars were imported into North America. Tesla's Chinese competitor, the BYD Auto Company (est. 2003 in Xi'an, Shaanxi Province), the world's leading EV manufacturer in 2023, had not yet announced plans to do the same but was exporting to Europe. (As yet another reminder of automobility's power of dreams, BYD stands for "Build Your Dreams.")[62]

By the early 2020s, Visionary, renamed V Cars LLC, was based out of New York City and Boca Raton, Florida. It was engaged in a number of promotional business projects, including an electric car, the Bricklin 3EV. The innovative car's tagline was "Redefining the Price of Fabulous."

~ Intermission ~

Dream Car Song 8: "The Entertainer," Scott Joplin (1905), Marvin Hamlisch, 1973

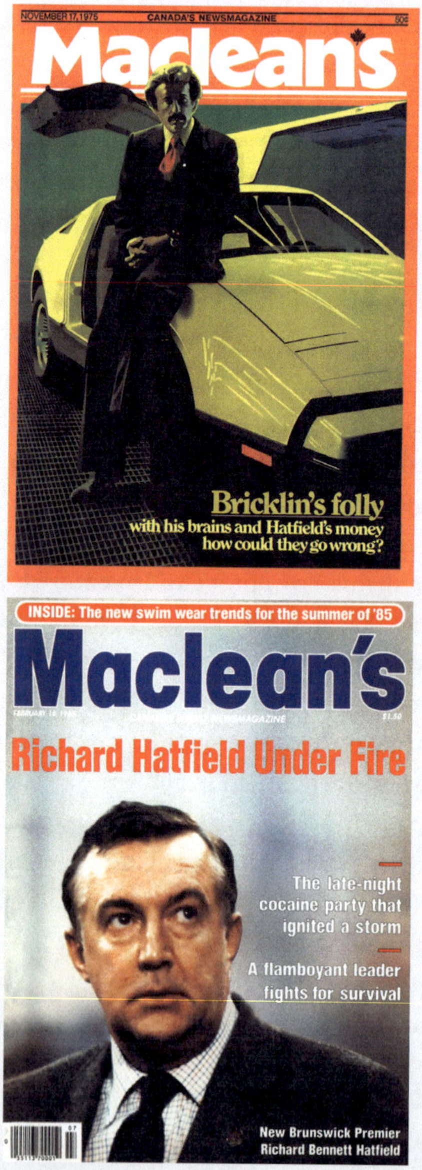

Figure 4.17. Cover stories, *Maclean's* magazine, 1975 (top) and 1985 (bottom).

Part II. "You Gotta Believe": Richard Hatfield as Politician – A Melodrama in Five Elections

If Malcolm Bricklin was born to hustle, Richard Hatfield was born to charm.

And what a charmer he was, wrote Sandra Gwyn in a 1979 *Saturday Night* piece, "Hanging Out with Hatfield: The Happiest Premier, If Not the Best." Hatfield was "one of those flamboyant, quixotic, compulsively interesting figures who flit in and out of" Anthony Powell's *A Dance to the Music of Time*.[63] Another fawning assessment claimed that being in Hatfield's presence "reminds one of what the court of Louis XIV must have been like – aristocratic hauteur, cold steely intellect, and a soft handshake."[64] Much of Hatfield's charm came from his deeply rooted connection to New Brunswick and its people. He was one of them, but also, whatever his faults, what they might aspire to be. He was homespun and rural, yet a cosmopolitan globe-trotter. Studiously, eligibly handsome, yet he remained unusually unattached, leading a fun "bachelor life." A hard-nosed, conservative politician who lived in a modest house, yet loved art and theatre and had a rag doll collection. A local guy, yet a big name in national politics.[65]

It mattered not that, in 1979, Hatfield had spent 165 days outside his province, jetting on a government-leased plane to party hotspots from New York to Montreal to Marrakech, earning himself the nickname "Disco Dick." Conservative guru Dalton Camp retorted that "Richard was elected to govern New Brunswick – no one said he had to *live* there." Chosen four times by his people and in office for a record seventeen years, being New Brunswick's premier was Richard Hatfield's role of a lifetime. It's what made him tick. As he told a reporter in 1985, "I cannot make a distinction between what I do in the interest of my person and my responsibilities as premier. I am always premier of the province."[66] *L'etat, c'est moi.*

Richard Bennett Hatfield was born in 1931 in rural, anglophone, Protestant, bible-belt New Brunswick. His hometown was the village of Hartland, which boasted the world's longest covered bridge, on the picturesque Saint John River (named Wolastoq, "bountiful," in Maliseet-Passamaquoddy). The youngest of five children, born into the family businesses of politics and potatoes, Richard had been named after the sitting Conservative prime minister, R.B. Bennett. His father, Heber, was a successful potato farmer, mayor, and Progressive Conservative member of Parliament (federal) for the riding of Victoria-Carleton (1940–52). Richard and his sisters grew up close to the corridors of power in Ottawa: future prime minister John Diefenbaker himself once threatened to whip the impetuous youngster if Heber didn't discipline him. Graduating from Acadia University in 1952 and Dalhousie law school in 1956, Richard was naturally drawn to politics, and after

Figure 4.18. Young and debonair, Richard Hatfield at a luncheon in the Dorchester building on Park Lane in London, 22 November 1972.

the family potato operation was sold in the mid-1960s to Humpty Dumpty Snack Foods, he devoted himself to the vocation full time. In 1961, he won the Carleton (provincial) riding, and he gained the provincial Progressive Conservative (PC) leadership in 1969. It was the start of an unprecedented, if chequered, political performance that would last more than three decades across five provincial elections and might be entitled "Richard Hatfield's Theatre of Fun and Escapist Politics."

26 October 1970 – "We Don't Intend to Be Conned": Richard Hatfield, 42 Seats; Louis Robichaud, 26 Seats

In 1970, thirty-nine-year-old Dick Hatfield knocked off a giant, P'tit-Louis, as Liberal premier Louis Robichaud (1925–2005) was known. Ten years earlier, Robichaud, the first Acadian to be elected premier, had revolutionized New Brunswick by transforming French-English relations and modernizing the province's educational, social, and economic policies through his Equal Opportunity programs. But after a decade of Liberal rule, Robichaud was exhausted. Hatfield, the shinier and newer option (and very pro-bilingual), pledged to provide better and smarter government: "I give you my word, and my word is good." Called New

Brunswick's first "cool," "mod premier," "Hatfield swept into office with a sizeable mandate, including support from the Acadian community, on the age-old slogan of 'We need a change.'"[67]

Soon into his first government, Hatfield's flamboyant personality and unorthodox ways started to emerge. He lived alone in a suite in the Lord Beaverbrook Hotel in Fredericton. He spent hours at the modernist Beaverbrook Art Gallery (est. 1959) across from the legislature, staring at the collection's magnificent Salvador Dali and other paintings. He travelled extensively to international capitals and exotic places in the Middle East and Africa, often in a government-leased plane. He loved artists, musicians, and actors, and regularly attended Theatre New Brunswick, also near the legislature (nothing is ever far away in Fredericton). Hatfield never missed a premiere and often invited cast and crew back to his place for boozy, late-night parties.[68] Self-confident, and with a flair for the dramatic, in 1972 he boasted that "I think I can become the Kennedy of New Brunswick, maybe even the Maritimes."[69]

Reporters loved him. He had a larger-than-life persona, and was a late-night partier, a recontour, and a political junkie – in other words, a lot like them. Allan Fotheringham, the curmudgeonly *Maclean's* back-page columnist, took a particular shine to the New Brunswicker. Admiring Hatfield's style and élan, he once took the premier to Ottawa's parliamentary press gallery dinner as his "date." As Fotheringham recalled, Hatfield had "escaped the covered bridge for the delights of Morocco and Manhattan." New Brunswickers, he wrote, "were long transfixed with secret envy/admiration for his jet-set style before longevity and careless excess turned them off."[70]

When the young premier was in Fredericton, he sometimes faced questions about government support for business, then all the rage in Atlantic Canada. In 1971, he pledged that he would steer clear of any risky business ventures that came looking for provincial money. "The trouble," Hatfield sermonized, was that "our governments haven't always realized the price they were paying. It's easy to see now where they were wrong, but then hindsight is always wiser than foresight. Anyway, that day is past," Hatfield confidently declared. "We don't intend to be conned."[71]

18 November 1974 – The Bricklin Election: Richard Hatfield, 33 Seats; Robert Higgins, 25 Seats

Despite his prior proclamations, by mid-1973 Hatfield was all in on Malcolm Bricklin and his idea of building the SV1 in New Brunswick with government money. Though some observers in the province had responsed with scepticism to Bricklin's appearance, Hatfield's economic growth minister, Paul Creaghan, reassured New Brunswickers that "Malcolm Bricklin is squeaky clean." Moreover, when it came to Bricklin's background, "we've checked. I don't just mean he doesn't have any court actions or financial problems. I mean he's Simon-pure all the way."

"Everything he says," Creaghan confidently declared, "is 100%."[72]

One hundred per cent simon-pure, indeed. When Hatfield faced the electorate for the second time, in November 1974, just four months after the New York launch of the Bricklin, he decided to make the car the campaign's central issue and was driven across the province in a borrowed "Safety-Orange" SV1. Meanwhile, his party's television ads prominently featured the car and Bricklin's assembly line, which had finally started up in September.[73] With his dreams of what the SV1 could do for the province, the press reported, Hatfield "captured the imagination of a province of Ford and Chevrolet drivers by touring its winding highways" in the car. At campaign events and rallies, and in news stories, Hatfield, Bricklin, and the car were ever-present. The sleek, bright, sexy Bricklin stuck out dramatically from all the other cars on the road, truly "unlike anything most New Brunswickers had ever seen." The idea of building the space-age SV1 in New Brunswick became more than a simple subtext to the campaign: there was an explicit understanding that a Hatfield mandate meant the province's continued support for the venture. If ever there was an electoral campaign built around the futuristic allure and potential of the auto industry in postwar North America, this was it. And if Malcolm Bricklin was an automotive P.T. Barnum, Hatfield was a revivalist preacher, weaving his own rhetorical dream to part New Brunswickers from their votes. "I am proud of the Bricklin," Hatfield declared at one campaign stop, "because it is a symbol of what can be accomplished in this province and what is being accomplished." For his campaign slogan, Hatfield chose "You gotta believe."[74]

Initially, even Hatfield's opponents hedged their criticism of the car, given the Bricklin's innovative (and economic) potential. Though new Liberal Opposition leader Robert Higgins remained "a bit on the sceptical side," he "sincerely" hoped it would work, and he understood what the car could mean: "I don't want to be the guy that turns down the Wright brothers."[75] Others were not so enamoured, and one critic later mockingly called Hatfield's SV1 the "Great Pumpkin out of Cinderella."[76] But by the campaign's end, Hatfield had convinced enough New Brunswickers to take a chance on his, and Bricklin's, dream. He believed in it, and so should they.

For Hatfield, the Bricklin election was a memorable performance. In *Maclean's*, Fotheringham intuited that the "affable" premier was playing a part. At the end of a campaign press conference, Fotheringham remembered, journalists left "in a smelly bus for the inevitable cocktail reception across town," while

Figure 4.19. The 1974 "Bricklin campaign."

> Hatfield zoomed off in the dishy Bricklin plastic car before the nation's press. Several blocks later, at a red light, we passed him – the dream car had broken down and collapsed beneath him. As we hooted out the windows at him, he grinned and took it – he could always laugh at himself, a gift possessed by too few politicians.[77]

Later, Hatfield cheekily admitted that "if you're going to have a politically embarrassing failure, it should be something you have a lot of fun with." Besides which, he said, "it got me on the *Today Show*. I was almost interviewed by Barbara Walters." Such a comment, another *Maclean's* journalist wrote, was "typical of a man who clearly enjoyed his reputation for flamboyance and who said repeatedly that he believed politics should be fun."[78] Hatfield made politics entertaining.

Once the election was over – giving Hatfield a reduced majority – sharper questions started to be raised about the veracity of the Bricklin operation and how much taxpayer money Hatfield was giving the firm. In the legislature, Saint John Harbour representative John Turnbull pursued the matter "hatchet in hand," even as Hatfield and his cabinet continued to support the project and its soaring costs.

Figure 4.20. In his element: Hatfield driving an SV1 at the Bathurst, NB, Festival Parade, July 1975.

Hatfield's *new* minister of economic growth, Lawrence Garvie, became the government's main defender; his rare Bricklin reports to the legislature were delivered with the "stoic absence of emotion" akin to "a newscaster documenting casualties in a distant war."[79] In the summer of 1975, after relentless demands for more disclosure on the Bricklin firm's operations as the government's expenditures mounted, Garvie announced that no such revelation would be made, "in the interests of avoiding hurting the company in the marketplace." The response, according to one report, was "shocked silence, even among supporters who had clung to the belief that Bricklin was on the level." Opposition members fumed "Too much!" and that "this time Hatfield has really gone too far!" Demands were made for the premier's resignation. Nonetheless, Hatfield refused to discuss details of the project and gaslit his opponents, accusing them of "harming development in New Brunswick by saying we can't do things here."[80]

A few months later, after Hatfield's September decision to put Bricklin into receivership, the accusations of skullduggery came fast and furious. In the legislature, the Liberal Opposition accused Hatfield of being Bricklin's dupe and demanded to see the government's records on the project. One member, Andrew Robichaud, declared to Hatfield that "I believe Malcolm Bricklin was a crook. I believe that you dealt with a crook ... You got conned pretty badly, and now you are paying for it." Opposition leader Robert Higgins's accusations were equally damning, and he even presented his own evidence of Bricklin's duplicity. "How much investigating did the government do?" he accusingly demanded. Then, he dramatically revealed that

> I phoned some lawyers down through New Jersey, New York, California, and Florida to get some background on Malcolm Bricklin. One of the first questions I asked one of the lawyers was:
>
> "What do you know about Malcolm Bricklin?"
>
> He said, "Oh my God, is his daddy, Albert, involved with him?" That was his initial reaction.
>
> I said, "Yes, he is president."
>
> He said, "You have got to be kidding. What is Malcolm?"
>
> I answered, "He is chairman of the board."
>
> He said, "Oh my God, whatever you do, don't give them any money."
>
> I said, "They are giving them money."[81]

As the legislature erupted, Higgins delivered his summation: "This is why we want to see the documents." Both inside the legislature and outside of it (where he could be sued for libel), Higgins was adamant: "I called him a con man."[82] By then, the Liberal Opposition were braying for Hatfield's resignation, while a few of the province's newspapers called for a royal commission of inquiry. But the premier wouldn't budge.[83] Despite the condemnation, a defiant Hatfield refused to turn over any documents, stonewalled all enquiries, and minimized the subject as much as possible.[84] The Bricklin venture failed in the fall of 1975, at which point the premier declared that no public disclosure of the firm's finances would be forthcoming, because "Bricklin is a private company and it is entitled to the privileges of a private company."[85]

Hatfield had three years before the next election. Perhaps it was enough time for New Brunswickers to forgive, or even forget.

23 October 1978 – High-Wire Act:
Richard Hatfield (PC), 30 Seats; Joseph Daigle (Lib.), 28 Seats

By the third time that Richard Hatfield faced the electorate, the tenor had changed. In the wake of Bricklin's demise, he'd lost some credibility with his fellow New Brunswickers. Although the episode seemed to be somewhat in the rearview mirror,

Figure 4.21. "My Record Speaks for Itself," cartoon by Josh Beutel, *Telegraph-Journal*, 1978.

Hatfield nonetheless spent years attempting to minimize the taint of the debacle, which seemed to follow him. Now, instead of a revivalist preacher, Hatfield's was more a high-wire act. He spent much of his energies avoiding the insinuation that he (and the province) had been swindled by a smooth American operator, a view that had gained quite a bit of traction with New Brunswickers. Along with the waves of negative editorial opinion on the matter, *How to Brickle: The New Brunswick Funny Book* appeared in bookstores in the province in October 1977. With a folksy introduction written by management consultant H.A. Fredericks under the pseudonym Still Pickens and "Dedicated to the taxpayers of New Brunswick … and Canada," for "at least 30 million reasons," *How to Brickle* lampooned Hatfield and his band of hapless government officials as Bricklin's suckers. Chock-full of mocking, captioned photos, the book, which was followed with a 1978 sequel, *Bricklemanship: The New Brunswick Grief Book*, included a "Special Coupon for Charlie Russell's Hit Record."[86] Those two books, of course, followed Fredericks and Chambers's condemnatory 1977 exposé, *Bricklin*.

In his defence, Hatfield made the case that the SV1 had been a valiant effort that did not work out, despite being a good product in a good market. Hatfield mostly blamed outside forces or bad management for conspiring to take the company down – it certainly was not the fault of noble New Brunswick workers, or the

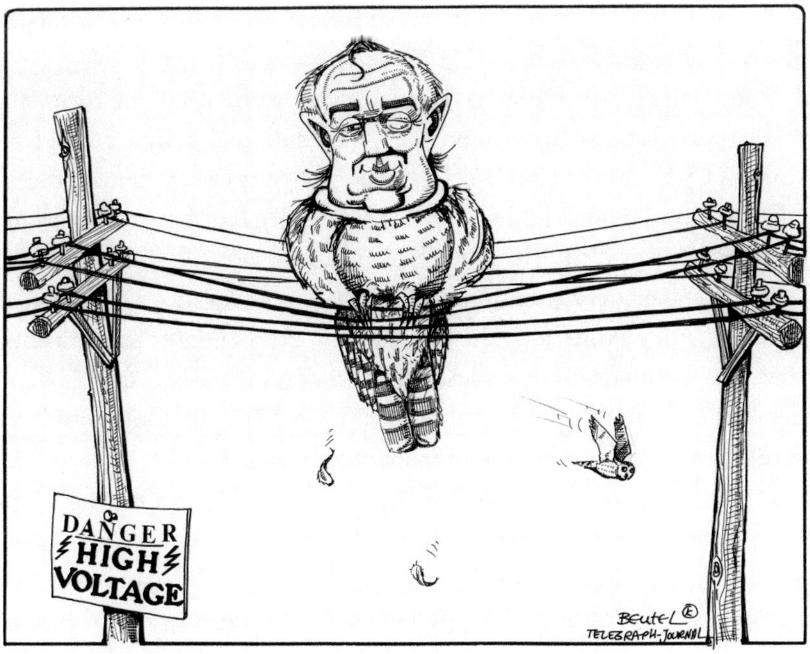

Figure 4.22. "The Hatfield High-Wire Act," cartoon by Josh Beutel, *Telegraph-Journal*, 8 April 1986.

government itself. In Hatfield's view, the Bricklin didn't fail; it had been failed by an uncaring federal government, and a businessman who was a better promoter than manager. Besides which, Hatfield maintained that, as premier, he had little to do with Bricklin's day-to-day matters: "I'm not a detail man," he told Sandra Gwyn in 1979. "I don't like sitting around planning things out." Gwyn herself went easy on Hatfield, blaming the Bricklin fiasco on his "lack of attention" and "an excess of romanticism."[87]

Unfortunately for the premier, that same lack of attention, plus "a lordy I-don't-want-to-know-about-that-kind-of-thing attitude," had resulted in other major political and spending scandals.[88] One involved a Tory kickback scheme that landed Hatfield and his government in court. Another was the massive construction cost overrun of the Point Lepreau nuclear plant (another modernization scheme). Budgeted in 1972 at $466 million, construction costs had ballooned to $895 million by 1979. The multiple scandals led one journalist to write that, for Hatfield, "dancing along a political high wire is nothing new."[89] In the legislature, the press reported, the Liberals were "hammering away" at the nuclear plant while, down the street, the kickback trial was continuing, and "Hatfield himself had been subpoenaed to testify." Meanwhile, "in a nearby parking lot, an orange Bricklin sports car sat mouldering in the sweltering heat – a relic of Hatfield's most spectacular industrial failure."[90] Things looked bad.

Luckily for Hatfield, his pursuers overreached. His main Liberal tormentors on the Bricklin, party leader Higgins and MLA Turnbull, had both accused Hatfield's government of political interference into the police investigation of the alleged kickback schemes. Higgins had stated unequivocally that he would resign if his allegations were disproved. Turnbull, the most tenacious and effective Bricklin critic, had also staked his reputation on the kickback accusations. When a January 1978 judicial inquiry exonerated the government, both Higgins and Turnbull tendered their resignations within minutes of the report's release. Hatfield had caught a major break – his most vocal legislative critics on Bricklin, honourable men of their word, were miraculously and permanently vanquished.[91]

By the time of the provincial election in October 1978, Hatfield had benefited immensely from the departures of Turnbull and Higgins; with their resignations, Bricklin had largely "faded from the spotlight."[92] Though allegations of the government's corruption connected to the kickback scheme reappeared in the early 1980s, Hatfield never faced direct accountability on that issue, or, for that matter, on Bricklin.[93] Indeed, the 1978 Tory campaign "was so beautifully orchestrated and choreographed" that there was "a real danger" that voters would "lose all perspective of the premier's actual record," as one editorial lamented.[94]

In any event, by the late 1970s, much of the province's political oxygen was being sucked up by the period's federal-provincial constitutional politics, during which Hatfield cut himself a reputation as an elder statesman and national figure of French-English reconciliation. In Gwyn's view, before the election of the separatist Parti Québécois in 1976, "Hatfield had intruded on the national consciousness hardly at all," save for being "quirky and unconventional" and having "lost a bundle on the Bricklin." But, by October 1978, Hatfield had managed to transform himself into a national spokesperson for federalism and bilingualism and to hold onto power, two seats ahead of the provincial Liberals.[95] A local boy who had made it big on the national stage, Hatfield had, amazingly, escaped direct accountability for the Brickliln, yet again.

12 October 1982 – Still Holding On: Richard Hatfield (PC), 39 Seats; Doug Young (Lib.), 18 Seats; George Little (NDP), 1 Seat

When Hatfield miraculously emerged with a fourth electoral win in 1982, despite being beset by a poor economy and a long, growing list of ongoing scandals, *Maclean's* declared him "a political survivor, a phoenix who has risen from so many political ash heaps that his staying power may be his best known feature across

Figure 4.23. "The Phoenix Riseth," almost like a Dali painting, cartoon by Josh Beutel, *Telegraph-Journal*, 2 February 1985.

the country." The scandals, including the Bricklin debacle and Hatfield's frequent foreign excursions, "brought furious denunciations but never defeat." Exasperated, Doug Young, the fourth Liberal leader to lose to Hatfield, declared the man "an artist at survival."[96]

But Hatfield's magical ability to escape the political traps he had created for himself was ebbing. Most of his government's scandals had been that – government scandals. After 1982, Hatfield's increasingly erratic and scandalous personal behaviour would become the issue that finally toppled him from power.

13 October 1987 – The End:
Richard Hatfield (PC), 0 Seats; Frank McKenna (Lib), 58 Seats

By the end of the 1987 campaign, Hatfield's magic touch with the voters was completely gone, his fame turned to notoriety. He faced rejection, even from his own constituents: at meet-and-greets, they avoided the premier, refusing to even talk to or interact with the man from Hartland. Though Hatfield remained stoic, it was

Figure 4.24. "The Emperor's New Clothes," cartoon by Josh Beutel, *Telegraph-Journal*, 9 February 1985.

clear that the people of New Brunswick had turned on him. Hatfield's luck, his ability to overcome controversy, and his knack for avoiding direct scrutiny had finally run out. Despite some genuine policy successes, including his work in bridging the linguistic divide in the province, and his important role during the constitutional wars of the 1970s and 1980s, Hatfield's showy lifestyle had finally caught up to him. The electoral wipeout of the Progressive Conservatives – the loss of every single one of the province's constituencies, including Hatfield's own, to Frank McKenna's Liberals – went far beyond fatigue with a leader or a government that had been in office for seventeen years. It was a complete and utter repudiation by ordinary New Brunswickers of Hatfield's behaviour and excesses, one that marked the sad demise of what had been an unprecedented political career.

Part III. Was It All Just a Con? Showmen, Politicians, Tricksters, and Conmen: Bricklin, Hatfield, and the People of New Brunswick, Canada

Malcolm Bricklin was a showman, a promoter, an entrepreneur, a salesman, and a hustler. Richard Hatfield was a politician, a performer, a preacher, a salesman, and a charmer.

The act of convincing enough people that one's idea, product, or proposition will succeed and make their individual or collective worlds better – "the pitch" – is a fundamental aspect of discourse in a liberal democracy, both in capitalism and politics. The pitch is the essence of the deal: once agreed upon, it is the basis of trust between people.[97] But, as promoters and politicians seek to win over that audience and finally seal the deal, and gain people's confidence, sometimes that fine line between the promotional idea and the political promise – between what is possible on the one hand, and what is realistic, on the other – can become blurred. For those whose money or votes or confidence is being sought, the outcome of the deal may sometimes make it feel as though the pitch was based on a false premise, that they have been taken advantage of, that they have been swindled. In the case of Malcolm Bricklin and Richard Hatfield, their roles in the Bricklin event can be used to explore some of the shifting meanings and manners of performative business and politics, and whether – as so many people accused them of doing so – they were simply running a multi-million-dollar electoral confidence trick, a grift, on the citizens of New Brunswick.

Now, there have always been charlatans and con artists, and the showman, the ringmaster, the pitchman, the fortune-teller, the snake-oil salesman, the hustler, the humbug, the grifter, the fraudster, the man behind the curtain is a long-standing character in (North) America, one much studied, celebrated, cursed, and venerated. The trickster is, of course, one of the fundamental tropes of folklore and of North American Indigenous oral culture. The trickster is a teacher of lessons and morals and often appears in different guises – the trickster can be a villain, a fool, or an intelligent schemer, but is always a performer.[98]

As the *modern* con artist materialized across the eighteenth and nineteenth centuries to take advantage of the abundant opportunities that accompanied industrialization, urbanization, and capitalism – what historian Karen Halttunen describes as the "era of the confidence man" – he or, less often, she became a prominent and persistent fixture in everyday society. Usually self-made, the industrious showman/promoter/conman also represented the democratization of fame, the increasing influence of media, and the concurrent ascendency of middle-class amusement. In 1835, the "age of showmanship" was famously inaugurated with fabulist Phineas T. Barnum's (1810–91) first highly publicized act: a hoax in which he exhibited his recently purchased slave, Joice Heth, the alleged 161-year-old former nurse of President George Washington (in actuality, she was closer to eighty).[99] By the late nineteenth century, Barnum's legendary showmanship and willingness to part "a fool and his money" made him the most successful of a long line of showmen and tricksters, all of whom created for themselves personas (and often realities) of worldly success through performance. Though Barnum admitted that his name had, as he said, "long been associated with 'humbug,'" he nonetheless became tremendously famous and wealthy, and his innovations created fundamental aspects of modern American popular culture and showmanship, of entertainment.[100]

The Barnum-like figure and the conman also became a staple in literature and fiction, and of performance and entertainment. Seminal nineteenth-century literary works in the genre include *The Confidence-Man: His Masquerade* (1857) by Herman Melville, Mark Twain's *Adventures of Huckleberry Finn* (1884), and Frank L. Baum's *The Wonderful Wizard of Oz* (1900) and its many sequels. The last, whose title character was revealed as a Barnum-inspired political "humbug," became one of the most popular tales in American literature, adapted into numerous plays and films, including the 1939 classic with Judy Garland. Later, interwar novels like F. Scott Fitzgerald's car-centric *The Great Gatsby* (1925) made Jay Gatsby famous as the questionably *nouveau riche* mystery man pursuing his American dream. In the postwar period, *The Music Man*, a story "as American as apple pie" of conman Harold Hill, who dupes a rural community into buying musical instruments, became hugely successful as a play (1957) and film (1962).[101]

These few fictional examples were only slightly less believable than their real-world counterparts. Across nineteenth- and twentieth-century North American society, the performative, Barnum-like, Wizard of Oz showman/confidence figure became famous, his exploits often blurring the distinction between politicians, preachers, and entertainers. Again, only a few examples suffice: New York's nineteenth century Tammany Hall machine politician, "Boss" William Tweed (1823–78); Louisiana's mesmerizing "Kingfish," Huey P. Long (1893–1935); Canadian-American radio priest Father Charles Coughlin (1891–1979); Alberta's "funny money" preacher/politician "Bible Bill" Aberhart (1878–1943); Elvis Presley's promoter/manger, "Colonel" Tom Parker (1909–97); televangelist Billy Graham (1918–2018). All were charismatic promoters, shrewd operators, masters at media manipulation, and (un)scrupulous image makers who blurred the line between entertainment, politics, and/or religion.[102]

Obviously, this performative liminality included and overlapped with the world of business. After all, Barnum, the original showman, had gained tremendous fame by successfully blending his entertainment humbug with his skills as a promotional salesman, as an *entrepreneur* – a businessman. From the mid-nineteenth century onwards, as salesmanship flourished and became increasingly professionalized, there remained across the growing world of business classes of men whose performative promotion ranged from the legitimate to the outright deceptive. As Edward Balleisen writes in *Fraud: An American History from Barnum to Madoff*,

> From the American Revolution onward, the country's lionization of entrepreneurial freedom has given aid and comfort to the perpetrators of duplicitous business schemes. Enterprising risk takers have enjoyed leeway from the arbiters of social norms, the makers of socioeconomic policy, and the practical operation of law, even when enthusiasm encouraged shading the truth or cutting legal corners.[103]

From Horatio Alger's stories of self-made men, to Dale Carnegie's gospel of self-help, to unsavoury small-time boiler-room stock promoters, and to full-fledged Ponzi-schemers, the world was full of salesmen, and, even as they became increasingly professionalized, there remained a fine line between a legitimate pitch and a confidence trick. The distinctions between business leaders, promoters, pitchmen, salesmen, and conmen became progressively blurred as North American society became increasingly materialistic, financialized, and celebrity-obsessed over the course of the twentieth century, especially after the 1970s.[104]

By the time hustling young Malcolm Bricklin and charming young Richard Hatfield embarked on their fantastic car venture, North American society and popular culture were awash with conmen. In December 1973, *The Sting*, a film about two handsome, young, *heroic* 1930s Chicago con artists, starring Robert Redford and Paul Newman, was released. Coincidentally, Newman had appeared at Bricklin's Las Vegas SV1 event in February 1974, where he also played a pitchman, just a few weeks before *The Sting* won the Academy Award for best picture.[105] The year 1973 also saw the publication of Neil Harris's *Humbug: The Art of P.T. Barnum*, yet another study of the man and his tremendous influence upon American society.[106] Given these contexts, it is wholly unsurprising that, as Malcolm Bricklin's own career unfolded before, during, and especially after the SV1, he became so easily and closely identified with Barnum, an omnipresent figure with whom Bricklin made "a pretty respectable comparison," as his son Jonathan once acknowledged.[107]

So, was the Safety Vehicle-1 just a Barnum-like con, perpetrated by Malcolm Bricklin?

By the early 1970s, Bricklin had intuitively recognized that the spectacularly risky and hubristic act of launching a car company wasn't by itself enough to penetrate North America's popular, oligopolistic, car-consuming consciousness. Bricklin also had to *perform* the role of the entrepreneurial automobile promoter in a way that would make his fantastic, dreamy project believable. When Bricklin magically appeared in New Brunswick to dazzle Hatfield and his province, he seemed to epitomize swaggering American entrepreneurial success. "The promoter," as the *Financial Post* described Bricklin in the wake of the SV1's demise in 1975, "seemed to have property all over the place, was well connected, backed by the right bank, [and] had a couple of million to spend on the project." For Hatfield, Bricklin's apparent track record spelled success. He was, above all, "believable" and looked like "a real life Horatio Alger."[108] As Hatfield himself once stated,

> The most important thing is to make a gut determination, and that is the only way you can make it. You know, is this man, who says he wants to come to your province, and wants to invest, and has this proposal, *is he a con artist, or is he really an entrepreneur*? I made the decision that Malcolm Bricklin was an entrepreneur.[109]

Figure 4.25. Mal, Dick, their car, and those gull-wing doors, c. 1975.

That fine line between the conman and the entrepreneur was sometimes hard to distinguish, as Hatfield himself could attest.

Unquestionably, Malcolm Bricklin was most successful as the promoter, that second great automotive entrepreneurial archetype. That's because he was a natural salesman, a hustler, an incarnation of the Fabulous Billy Durant. In January 1975, the *Saint John Telegraph Journal*, a paper that had intimately followed the Bricklin story, pegged him perfectly: Bricklin was "a dreamer, a promoter, and an entrepreneur." The adjectives kept flowing: Bricklin was "imaginative, confident, cocky." Moreover, he "just plunge[s] ahead" and "doesn't believe in looking back."[110] Indeed, twice-bankrupt Durant would have been proud of Bricklin's accomplishment in selling himself, and the dream of his car, to North Americans, to the New Brunswick government, and to the province's people.

Bricklin's pitch was a particular, performative, entrepreneurial narrative. As Malcolm told it, he exemplified the rugged, determined individualist, the quintessential American rags-to-riches story. His success with Subaru (which was doing

Figure 4.26. A credible profile: Hatfield and Bricklin with Harvey Lamm, Subaru America CEO from 1971 to 1990, c. 1975.

well by 1975) proved that he was a self-made auto man, as Chrysler, Durant, and Ford had been (and, later, Musk would be), and gave him credibility and confidence. And like Ford (and, again, Musk), Bricklin was brash, opinionated, contradictory, and always in the spotlight. According to one 1976 postmortem, there were "many Malcolm Bricklins." There was "Bricklin the hustler," "Bricklin the promoter," "Bricklin the 36-year-old wheeler-dealer who claimed his 'textbook was the seat of his pants.'" And, like all those entrepreneurial promoters before him, Bricklin created an aura of material success about himself that gave him credibility in the eyes of his audience: "Everything about him spelled success. The background, the self-confidence, the lifestyle," and, most of all, the "highly credible stories he told." Bricklin was a "believable, truthful, yet outspoken guy." Despite some scepticism, the media nonetheless "turned the tall lanky businessman" from Philadelphia and Phoenix into an "instant celebrity."[111]

Essential to this performance was the frontier, cowboy image. Though Henry Ford had ushered in the age of modernity with his Model T, he had emphasized his plainspoken Midwestern roots and cultivated a pastoral pre-automotive ideal in his company and its workers.[112] Bricklin embraced the pre-car cowboy image as completely as he could.[113] Bricklin the showman played the outlaw, the anti-organization man, the iconoclastic cowboy on a quixotic quest, the "Don Quixote of Detroit," as *Time* magazine called him. In 1974, he was popping up everywhere, including on late-night television talk shows and in magazines like *People* and *Playboy* – places where respectable, button-down auto executives had rarely if ever been featured.[114] Even his costume was different: as *Time* noted, he "wears studded denims and bedecks himself with silver-and-turquoise jewellery."[115] There had been flamboyant car promoters and auto executives before but, in the 1970s, none like Malcolm Bricklin.

Yet Bricklin's performance, and its result, also represented a shift. He was an automobile entrepreneur in the 1970s, at a moment when the organization man at large corporations (especially auto companies) was still king. But the organization man was himself in the process of being transformed into the "transaction man," as Nicholas Lemann has convincingly argued. The transaction man, according to Lemann, was someone "who works in a job that is literally transactional," as business became much more financialized, less about building things, and more about making money.[116] Ultimately, Bricklin symbolized a turn towards what might be called "performative financialization" in the auto industry. In his own quest to save Chrysler, Lee Iacocca had mastered performative financialization, a skill that became an increasingly important aspect of postwar "charismatic business leadership," as the Harvard business historian Richard Tedlow called it.[117]

Performative financialization was the promotional, entrepreneurial ability to convince people of certain things by creating a particular image and telling a particular story, one often based on the real (and perceived) fame, success, and wealth that the automobile industry represented. By the 1970s, it seemed as though the whole economy was being financialized, with a huge increase in complicated financial instruments like derivatives and leveraged buyouts, the growth of franchising, multi-level marketing and pyramid schemes, and the boom in real estate speculation. *And* it was seemingly becoming even more performative across politics, too – witness Hatfield, Ronald Reagan, Arnold Schwarzenegger, and so many others. But it was also true that the automobile and its industry remained closely associated and identified with the American dream, even as the industry became more financialized. Bricklin was very much a man of his moment, representing so many facets of these emerging trends.

Despite his chequered past, his many spectacular and public failures, and his sometimes questionable reputation, Bricklin's long auto sector involvement and his success at performative financialization had, decades after the SV1, given him a form of respectability in the industry, and the imprimatur of an *eminence grise*. It mattered little that Bricklin was labelled an "impresario-huckster" by *Motor Trend* or that *Fortune* remarked that, "to some, he is at best a promoter and at worst a charlatan."[118] In 2005, Bricklin was invited to address the Society of Automotive Analysts on "the future of the automotive industry." The flattering biographical sketch in the program characterized his past episodes as successes, reflecting a willingness to overlook some of the more unsavoury outcomes of his ventures:

> In 1968, Bricklin founded Subaru of America, Inc., now a leading importer of Japanese cars with US sales of more than 187,000 vehicles. During the 1970s, he founded Bricklin Motors and produced the world's first "safety sports car," which was well designed, easy to drive, and decades ahead of its time in terms of driver safety. In the 1980s, he formed Yugo America, Inc. With 160,000 vehicles sold during its launch phase, the Yugo quickly became the fastest selling European import in automotive history. Today, Bricklin has returned to the roots of his success: Asian automobile imports.[119]

That year, Bricklin was the subject of a glowing article in *Inc.* magazine, "Would You Buy a Chinese Car from This Man?" (subhead: "Malcolm Bricklin is on a quest to revolutionize the auto industry at 14,845 words per hour").[120] In 2007, the same year that Tesla launched its Roadster, Bricklin was a guest columnist in the *Financial Times*, dispensing sage advice about the future of the auto industry with a byline "Chief Executive of Visionary Vehicles."[121] In 2009, when he launched, at age seventy, yet another venture (this time to get into hydrogen plug-ins), it was clear that he had "lost none of his ability to think big, talk fast or take chances." His "dream, his pitch, what he asks you to believe in now, is that he will take an affordable, powerful car straight off the production line, modify it and create a car that gets 100 miles per gallon." He was also described as "a millionaire who brought the sturdy Subaru (a success) and the boxy Yugo (a dud, but he made money)" to the United States.[122] By then, Bricklin had become not just the P.T. Barnum of the automotive world but a representative figure in the shift to the industrial postmodern. He was the showman, always looking to the future, one money-making deal at a time, in a new, financialized, American business landscape. Some of his promotional gambits worked, some didn't, but, with Bricklin, people knew what they were getting into.

So, had Malcolm Bricklin conned New Brunswick and its premier? Without question, Hatfield and his government, despite their protestations to the contrary, did not vet Bricklin as thoroughly as they should have. Bringing a car like the SV1 to production was a task that was beyond Bricklin's managerial capabilities, no matter how hard he tried, or appeared to be trying. But if it was a con, it was a tremendously elaborate one, given the fact that Bricklin had actually launched the vehicle, produced nearly three thousand of them, had *almost* succeeded with the venture, and had ended up in personal bankruptcy. As *Motor Trend* reported in 1974 after visiting Bricklin's busy research and development centre in Livonia, "even a hardened cynic would have trouble dismissing the seriousness of the project."[123]

Those who had watched Bricklin closely during the SV1 episode weren't convinced that he wasn't genuine. In April 1975, C.E. Sawyer, a management consultant hired to assess the project by New Brunswick, told economic minister Harry Nason that "I have reached a conclusion that the 'web' we see is 'not orderly enough' to be a deliberate and calculated deception. If Malcolm Bricklin has misled anyone, he has surely misled himself more."[124] Nevertheless, as Hatfield's biographer, Richard Starr, later wrote, "reduced to its basic elements, the Bricklin story is an all too familiar one: fast talking promoter comes from away and fleeces the job hungry locals." Hatfield, Starr concludes, "was certainly familiar with the script and should have been immune to the siren songs of people like Malcolm Bricklin who peddle economic development to the poor regions like so much snake oil."[125]

Whatever one's view (and quite a few New Brunswickers, along with Starr, firmly believed it was indeed a con), the SV1, from Bricklin's perspective, had been a costly entrepreneurial lesson: that he should never again attempt to actually *build* the cars he was selling. If Bricklin had learned anything, it was that he was a natural at selling cars, ahead of his time when it came to being an automotive technological innovator, and definitely not cut out to manage a car-*manufacturing* company. Despite everything that happened and all the accusations, the New Brunswick venture had been only the most notable promotion in a long, performative career. In retrospect, that career, especially after the 1970s, reflected the increasingly blurred and shifting lines between entrepreneurship, business, politics, and celebrity, and between what was promised, what could be achieved, and what was realistic.

Then there was Richard Hatfield. Had the premier conned the people of New Brunswick, just to get re-elected? For Hatfield, it's clear that he genuinely believed that the innovative potential of the SV1 could launch his province towards a future of automobile industrial modernity, like it had in other places, even if, eventually, he could no longer justify the project's ever-escalating costs and had to end the venture. But, as the 1974 election showed, selling the Bricklin was also simply another fun part of the job of premier, of selling himself and selling his province (in his view, one and the same), all of which required its own politics of performance. Alex MacFarlane, Hatfield's long-time campaign co-ordinator, recalled that

> Richard's fascination with the Bricklin belied any lack of interest in cars and things mechanical. He talked about it incessantly, bragging about its safety features; he showed it off to his friends, drove it in parades and, unfortunately, in an election campaign. He repeatedly tested the brakes with sudden stops just short of the stone walls of the Legislature building and generally treated the Bricklin as his pride and joy … For Richard, the Bricklin was a symbol and a toy that just happened to be a car.[126]

It was also part of a show. In 1975, a ride in a Bricklin SV1 with Hatfield was the "grand item" at a charity auction held at Theatre New Brunswick.[127] Even after the Bricklin's demise, the *Woodstock Bugle* reported in 1976 that Hatfield and Charlie Russell had "co-starred in a production" in front of four thousand people at a Fredericton hockey arena: "the premier drove a Bricklin around the ice as part of a skit" while Russell sang his hit song, "The Bricklin." Afterwards, Russell presented Hatfield with a "autographed copy of his record, and said the Premier told him he appreciated it very much."[128]

As a young man at university, Hatfield had taken part in some campus plays and had been in an amateur dramatics group.[129] In 1981, he remarked that his acting experience "was extremely valuable." In fact, in Hatfield's view, "it would benefit every politician to have a bit of theatre training." Acting was "one reason Ronald Reagan will do well in the White House. Too many politicians get caught up using big words to impress, but don't know how to project *feelings*."[130] Like so many of the charismatic politicians, promoters, businessmen, and entertainers that had shaped industrial modernity and politics, Richard Hatfield understood the necessity of projecting and performing belief *with feeling*. The politics of performance was foundational not only to Hatfield's role with the Bricklin but also to a career that became a case study in public perception, accountability, and identity, including his sexual identity.

Had Bricklin and Hatfield conned each other? Perhaps. It is a difficult question to answer, given that both men clearly believed in the project, despite its longshot odds for success and the fantastical pitch required to convince New Brunswickers of the SV1's viability. In retrospect, Bricklin said of Hatfield that "he tied himself to the car, and the car tied itself to him. And we worked together, and we were stuck together, for both good and bad. And, unfortunately, it was to the bad."[131] Two decades before the Bricklin, John Kenneth Galbraith, that prolific twentieth-century economist and public servant, had published *The Great Crash, 1929*, his study of the causes and consequences of the Great Depression. In the book, Galbraith explored how the depression economy shaped "that most interesting of crimes," embezzlement. In his analysis, Galbraith coined the term "the bezzle," which he defined as "the magic interval when a confidence trickster knows he has the money he has appropriated but the victim does not yet understand that he has lost it," and might not for months or even years. In the meantime, Galbraith wrote, the mark "enjoys a net increase in 'psychic wealth.'"[132] As economist John Kay later remarked, "the joy of the bezzle is that two people – each ignorant of the other's existence and role – can enjoy the same wealth." The bezzle is an imperfect analogy for Bricklin and Hatfield, given that each was keenly aware of each other's role in the Bricklin show, but perhaps comes closest to how their relationship might be understood.

Finally, and most importantly, had the people of New Brunswick been conned? As with so many aspects of North America's shared culture, the trope of the conman in American history has its own Canadian derivative, one that New Brunswickers were keenly sensitive to – the fear of the *American* grifter who comes across the border to bilk the unsophisticated provincial locals. Suspicion of smooth-talking Yankees stretches back through Canadian history, triggered by eighteen- and nineteenth-century invasions, political and economic little-brother touchiness, and ordinary Canadians' never-ending envy of their wealthier and worldlier American cousins. Even during the mid-twentieth-century era of Cold War continental commonality and consumerism, Canadians retained a healthy worry about US political, economic, and cultural domination.[133] Hence, the Canadian government's requirement that Bricklin Canada Ltd. have majority Canadian ownership.

By the Sixties, Canadian distrust towards the United States was widespread in many areas of the two countries' interacctions. Ironically, from the perspective of the Bricklin, one of Canadians' key concerns in the postwar period was about the amount of US foreign direct investment and ownership in their economy. By the early 1970s, Canadian economic nationalists decried their "silent surrender" to the imperialism of US multinational enterprises, called for a "third way" that moved Canadian trade dependence away from the United States, and had even instituted new measures such as the 1972 Foreign Investment Review Agency (FIRA), aimed at controlling the level of US ownership in Canadian firms.[134]

Politically, the administrations of Lester Pearson and Pierre Trudeau were known as much for their sharp disagreements with the US government and their presidential counterparts as they were for significant advances in bringing the two countries closer together. While Pearson and Lyndon Johnson successfully realized the integrationist auto pact, the Texan, a legendary deal-maker, had famously exploded at the Canadian leader's mild criticism of US bombing in Vietnam. Nixon and Trudeau managed cordial public relations, but that did not stop Nixon from referring to Trudeau in private as "that asshole" and unilaterally imposing economic shocks on its closest trading partner, including the near abrogation of the auto pact itself, in 1971.[135]

Culturally, many Canadian baby boomers vocally protested the war in Vietnam and condemned American social disruption; "American Woman," the number 1 Billboard hit from Winnipeg band the Guess Who, declared to Americans that "I don't need your war machines / I don't need your ghetto scenes," and made it clear that Canadians were aware of the temptations that Americans offered: "Colored lights can hypnotize / Sparkle someone else's eyes." While American draft resisters were welcomed, their remained a deep suspicion towards promise-making Americans coming across the border. Filmmaker Sandy Wilson's memories of her smooth-talking American cousin's arrival in 1950s rural British Columbia in a fancy sports car reflected this long-standing anxiety and became the basis of her 1985 film, *My American Cousin*.

Thus, by the time Bricklin arrived in Fredericton, "like a snake-oil salesman at a county fair," many Canadians had become deeply wary of their American cousins, despite Canada's undeniably close cultural and technological connection to the United States.[136] This wariness undoubtedly added to some New Brunswickers' fear of being conned. After all, Bricklin talked a big game. At the opening of the Saint John plant in August 1974, despite not yet being in production, Bricklin had told the assembled throng "We didn't just build a car, we built a magnificent car that will be acclaimed around the world, that we'll all be proud of, and me especially to have my name on the back of that car." Throughout the Bricklin venture, Malcolm delivered "smooth" speeches at service clubs, conventions, political events, and anywhere he could find an audience to charm. Like an automotive Harold Hill, the conman from *The Music Man*, Bricklin struck a populist note with of the SV1: "That's our car out there," he might as well have sung. "Yours and mine."[137]

Certainly, if one listened to the accusations levelled in the legislature or read the condemnatory newspaper editorials, it was equally clear that many New Brunswickers felt that Bricklin had indeed conned the province, and Hatfield, too, if he wasn't in on it. Yet, even as the Bricklin firm teetered on the brink of failure in 1975, just as many New Brunswickers argued that the project had been worth all the trouble, and that Hatfield (and Bricklin) should be given the benefit of the doubt. One anonymous "Bricklin Booster" wrote to the *Saint John Times Globe* that "it's high time someone had a few good words for both the Premier and the Bricklin project." Bricklin Booster even included a poem, "The Opposition," written by

Leora Foster of North Lake Parish, just a little south of Hartland. The somewhat unevenly written poem optimistically declared that

The promises [Hatfield] made us
He fulfilled them every one,
And if they give him half a chance
The new ones will be done.
And if you are so worried
About our Province dear
Just put your shoulder to the wheel
And help him with this deal.
By telling all the people
About this nifty car
And how it is a bargain
That will take you far.
And even buy a car or two
And then you'll see the Bricklin
Roll off the assembly line.

Ultimately, in the years to come, New Brunswickers such as Bricklin Booster may or may not have felt that they had been conned. But there was no question that, in the early 1970s, many thought that it was worth taking such a risky chance "with this deal." After all, as Bricklin Booster declared, "no matter what anyone says," Malcolm Bricklin, Richard Hatfield, and their SV1 had "made Saint John the most publicized city in North America these days."[138] In a world awash in the shifting meanings of and ideas about showmanship, publicity, and celebrity, perhaps this was all that mattered. If the Bricklin incident wasn't a con on New Brunswickers, at the very least it was a tell, one that revealed much about the changing nature of, and increasingly blurry relationship between, fame, entrepreneurship, and politics in twentieth-century North America.

CHAPTER FIVE

Sex (Gender)

Dream Car Song 9: "Little Red Corvette," Prince and the Revolution, 1982

Tin *Lizzie*. The car that first and forever reshaped sex was famously gendered female.

Cars and sex are inextricable; automobile industrial modernity begat sexual and gender modernity. Long before the contraceptive pill reshaped sex starting in the 1960s, the automobile had already launched its own sexual revolution. Even by the early 1900s, cars' utter disruption of society – of work, leisure, time, space, and virtually every aspect of human interaction – had also totally upended the dynamics of relationships and the practicalities of sexual intercourse. Inevitably, as the automobile redefined romantic relationships and sexual activity, the car also reshaped, yet simultaneously reaffirmed, conceptualizations of gender. By the Jazz Age, as a vehicle for courtship and marriage, a site for sex (both as a liminal space and a location facilitator), a status-signifying mark of gender (and class and racial) identity, and a sexualized object itself, the automobile had already become the Gatsby-esque symbol of a roaring decade of sexual notoriety, female liberation, and flappers. Just as the Model T had been anthropomorphized female, the Jordan Motor Car Company's 1923 Playboy was a car "built for her," as the famous ad declared, "somewhere west of Laramie" – and everywhere else, too, it seemed. Jordan Motors failed in 1931, but, over time, the connection it had made between the idea of the *playboy* and the automobile only grew.

Figure 5.1. "Somewhere West of Laramie": an ad for the Playboy, manufactured by the Jordan Motor Car Company (Cleveland, Ohio), *Saturday Evening Post*, 23 June 1923.

The interwar years' earth-moving automobile-induced changes with respect to dating, courtship, marriage, sex, and gender were paused only slightly by the immense disruptions of the Great Depression and the Second World War. After the war, as the baby boomers blossomed into teenagers and young adults – the first generation in history to take the automobile for granted as a fundamental part of everyday life – dating, sex, and gender became utterly impossible to disentangle from cars. Simply put, automobiles turbocharged almost every aspect of sexual activity and sexual identity.

Then, with the launch of GM's Chevy Corvette in 1953, the same year that Hugh Hefner's *Playboy* magazine debuted, the subspecies of the American "sports car" emerged as the mass-market embodiment of postwar sexuality and muscle-car masculinity, and of high industrial modernity, too. Soon, other all-American expressions of virility and libido followed the Corvette out of Detroit, as Ford and Chrysler launched their own muscle machines. Aimed at the young, male, baby boom market, with an explicit appeal to sexuality, these sporty and rugged "pony" and "muscle" cars became an indelible part of North American society and its cultural landscape at the height of the Sixties counterculture. By the early 1970s, the Big Three were selling 200,000 vehicles annually in this profitable category. Japanese carmakers soon launched their own attempts to gain a part of the lucrative, testosterone-driven sports car market, including the Datsun 240Z (1969), the Toyota Celica (1971), and, eventually, the Mazda RX-7 (1978).[1] Sex didn't just happen in cars, it *sold* them, too – especially to a cohort of males who saw themselves as driven, single, vibrant men in a rapidly changing sexual world.

Exploding across North America's popular imagination in 1974, Malcolm Bricklin's SV1 sportscar was among the last, purest expressions of sexualized automobility, mid-century masculinity, industrial modernity, and corporate strategy, though with some notable twists. In its design and marketing, the Bricklin's sexy look and perceived sexual power was accentuated, even more than most typical sports cars of the period, but with the added virtue of being sold as the world's first "safety vehicle." More fundamentally, the SV1's circumstances – its bold launching as the first mass-market sports car by an independent American automobile firm since the Second World War – made it unique. The timing of the Bricklin's appearance, in the wake of the sexual revolution and its reverberations, promoted by Seventies-vintage machismo sex symbol Malcolm Bricklin, and with the backing of New Brunswick's flamboyant, controversial, and closeted premier, Richard Hatfield, revealed much more than the routine unveiling of yet another sports car.

Indeed, the appearance at that moment of the Bricklin car signalled profound changes in the sexual and gender norms of postwar North America: the sexuality of cars themselves; the Seventies idea of the male "sex symbol"; the shifting relationships between men and women; and the evolution of issues such as homosexuality, LGBTQ rights, and abortion following the sexual revolution. Bricklin and Hatfield, the car's creators and promoters, sat at an intersection of sexual and cultural change, yet one that still reflected white, male, heterosexual privilege, and dominance of the car industry, business, politics, and much of the rest of society. As an avatar of patriarchy and heteronormativity, Malcolm Bricklin may have loved the fact that, when viewed from above, with the doors open, the SV1 "looked like a cock and balls."[2] But, that crude phallic symbolism obscured the deeper meanings of what the Bricklin SV1 and its story represented when it came to the remarkable changes that the automobile had wrought for twentieth-century sexuality and all its complications.

Part I. Automobile Sexual Modernity: Cars, Courtship, Marriage, Sex, and Gender

The creative destruction unleashed by Henry Ford's Model T spawned a second industrial revolution and profoundly reshaped North American society forever. At the start of the Roaring Twenties – that loud decade of phones, talkies, radios, speakeasies, the Charleston, the stock market crash, and, above all, the automobile – Ford's giant Detroit factories were already banging out a million Model Ts a year. By 1928, when Henry reluctantly replaced the Model T with the new Model A, more than fifteen million Tin Lizzies had been built. The Model T's transformational impact is well known: by providing "wheels for the world," as the historian Douglas Brinkley has written, Ford, his cars, and his processes – Fordism – remade the North American economic, social, cultural, and physical landscape, and virtually every aspect of human interaction.[3]

The Model T also forever transformed courtship, marriage, sex, and gender. Before the car, courtship in North America's largely rural, agriculturally dominated society was parentally controlled, formal, and usually slow-paced. Courtship itself was the product of local kinship and community networks, familial relations, and financial considerations, not to mention religious, racial, ethnic, and class constraints, and was usually a process of chaperoned couples getting to know one another on the slow journey to marriage. In keeping with the family dynamics that had structured settler-rural agricultural economies for centuries, arranged marriages, and the idea of marriage as an economic contract, was the norm. Romantic love existed, of course, but for most young men and women in rural North America before 1900, relationships and marriage were matters that were closely managed and overseen by parents, and they were most often deeply formal and structured events.[4]

The car significantly changed these practices, playing a key role in reshaping courtship. In cities, even as early as the 1910s, "calling" – the practice of young men visiting with young women to sit and hold respectable conversations in parlours, under the watchful eye of chaperoning parents – was quickly transformed by the automobile. If a single man came to a young woman's home in a car, she expected to go out on a "date," a word that first appeared in 1914 in the *Ladies' Home Journal*, according to the historian Beth Bailey.[5] With the rapid adoption of automobiles in rural areas and smaller centres, changes to courtship marked by the informality of dating spread quickly, fuelled by the car's magical powers of mobility. Localism was no more, as the car extended courtship from the "five-mile radius of the horse and buggy to ten, twenty, and fifty miles or more."[6] This was certainly true among young, white, and more affluent people in both rural and urban areas, though initially less so for economically, politically, or racially marginalized groups that, for a host of reasons, had less access to automobiles.[7]

In the 1920s, the car's impact on relationships accelerated dramatically, driven by the sheer number of vehicles in North America by the end of the decade. Ford and his Model T had democratized automobility to a degree unimaginable. By 1929, Americans were the greatest users of automobiles on the planet, with an astounding twenty-six million vehicles on the road, a car for every five Americans, as the United States truly become what historian Cotten Seiler has called a "republic of drivers." Canada, a less wealthy country than its southern neighbour, nonetheless benefited from its branch plant proximity and became the nation with the second-highest incidence of car ownership by 1929, with 1.2 million vehicles, or one for every ten Canadians.[8]

With so many automobiles suddenly appearing in North American society, marriage was also quickly transformed by the car, as automobility became a central element not only of marriage proposals but also of the modern, motorized, wedding ritual. From the first wedding featuring a car (a Daimler, in 1903) to wealthy Gilded Age displays of automobile splendour and to ordinary people dangling cans from the backs of their Model Ts, cars became a standard, expected, and often necessary rite of marriage across the twentieth century, and to this day. Additionally, driveable honeymoon destinations became a major segment of North American automobile tourism, especially during the interwar period, as motor hotels, "motels" (another auto-accessible sanctuary for intimacy), proliferated across the continent and became a part of the everyday landscape.[9]

Automobility's transformation of courtship and marriage was equalled by its profound impact on sexual behaviour. By the interwar period, the relationship between sex and the automobile was fully consummated. Across North America, by allowing time and space to be privatized and made easily accessible, the Model T facilitated sexual activity and liberation, for everyone. The story of Len Keith and "Cub" Coates, two gay men in rural New Brunswick whose long relationship, which started in the 1910s, was deeply shaped by automobility, was a testament to the reach of the car's immense social and geographic impact on intimacy and relationships.[10]

Figure 5.2. Cover of sheet music for "Take Me on a Buick Honeymoon," 1922.

While the notion of a car as an object that was sexy or had "sex appeal" was well-established, when the industry rapidly switched to mostly "closed" bodies by the mid-1920s, cars themselves became private spaces, a movable refuge that could both shield young couples from prying eyes and transport them to ever-more secluded spaces.[11] In *Only Yesterday*, his 1931 bestselling book chronicling the 1920s, Frederick Lewis Allen wrote that the automobile "offered flaming youth two things not previously available with the horse and buggy: anonymity and privacy … an almost universally available means of escaping temporarily from the supervision of parents and chaperons, or from the influence of neighborhood opinion." Another innovation seemingly designed to make the car a vehicle for youthful indiscretion was the "rumble seat," a cozy space for two at the back of a roadster, perfect for a romantic rendezvous.[12]

Figure 5.3. Rumble seat, 1930.

These developments alarmed many (North) Americans, who saw the car's power of sexual liberation as a threat to social order – a "devil's wagon." An Atlanta judge declared in 1921 that many of his cases were the result of "too much automobile and too little parental control. It is not too much to ask the parents to throw in the clutch and put on the brakes or our entire civilization will take one last joy ride to destruction."[13] A 1922 *Chicago Journal* article condemned the "unrestricted use of the automobile" as a "demoralizing influence," and opined that "parents who allow boys to take high school girls joy riding are doing much to break down the moral standards of the community." In *Middletown: A Study of Modern American Culture* (1929), the famous examination of small-town American life, including the impact of the car in shaping that life, Helen Merrell Lynd and Robert S. Lynd quoted a juvenile court judge who declared that the automobile had become a "house of prostitution on wheels." Of the thirty sex crimes cases that annually came before that court (in Muncie, Indiana), two-thirds were committed in an automobile. Meanwhile, in early 1920s California, law enforcement officials complained that all their resources were being utilized to police "night riders" and "coupe lovers" who parked "on darkstreets" or "along country boulevards" to "douse their lights to indulge in orgies." It was rumoured that Henry Ford himself had shortened the seat in the Model T to deter couples from indulging their "indecent urges."[14] Even as depression and war placed economic and military constraints on automobile usage and production that temporarily slowed the car's societal domination, the automobile retained its place as a sanctuary for intimacy.[15]

After the war, pent-up car sexuality exploded. Despite the era's overarching sexual conservatism, in the 1950s and early 1960s sex and cars were further coupled together, both in practice and in the public's mind, through ordinary experience, books, magazines, advertising, movies, and celebrity culture. Teenage baby boomers were only the foremost of a succession of postwar generations whose initial sexual experience was frequently in a car, and whose cultural understanding of cars often intersected with intimacy and sex, usually of the premarital variety. For the generation of Americans who turned fifteen between 1954 and 1963, an astounding 82 per cent had had premarital sex; for those who turned fifteen after 1964, the figure was at least 91 per cent. "Parking," the act of "petting" (or more) in parked vehicles, became such an unavoidable aspect of postwar teenage life that it created a moral panic, inspired slasher films, and reaffirmed the car's centrality in human sexual interactions of all kinds. From lovers' lanes to secluded suburban parking lots to drive-in theatres, which "almost seemed to have been created for sex in cars," the automobile relentlessly accelerated sexual activity. In 1956, Fats Domino found his thrill on Blueberry Hill, as did so many other (North) Americans, presumably with the help of a car. Two decades later, Meatloaf was singing about "paradise by the dashboard light."[16]

At the same time, novels, books, and magazines often connected cars to the adventure of America's open road, and to sex, too. Vladimir Nabokov's *Lolita* (1955) and beat writer Jack Kerouac's *On the Road* (1957) were explicit in their scandalous depictions of cars and fornication.[17] Tom Wolfe's 1963 racy New Journalism series about custom cars and youth culture for *Esquire* magazine (published as a book, *The Kandy-Kolored Tangerine-Flake Streamline Baby*, in 1965) included the lines "I don't have to dwell on the point that cars mean more to these kids than architecture did in Europe's great formal century, say 1750 to 1850. [Cars] are freedom, style, *sex*, power, motion, color – everything is right there." Specialized car magazines also proliferated, further bonding in the public's mind the connection between cars, freedom, and youthful exuberance. *Motor Trend* (1949), *Road & Track* (1948), *Sports Car Illustrated* (1955, becoming *Car and Driver* in 1960), and *Sports Car Graphic* (1961) infused car coverage with undertones of freedom, success, possession, and youth, "along with two other pervasive themes, sex and power."[18]

Automobile advertising itself played on the sexuality of automobiles, though initially Detroit was relatively subtle, and traditional, in its approach. Despite the

Jordan Motor Car Company's titillating interwar ad copy emphasizing "the enjoyment of something besides mere transportation" and the feel of a "personal, individual intimate car," the Big Three's advertising did not immediately exploit the sexualized subtext that their products offered (though gender tropes abounded in auto advertising, as discussed below).[19] But in the postwar period, Detroit's approach was starting to change. Harley Earl had overseen the liberal use of bullet-shaped chrome guards on the front of GM cars, called "Dagmar" bumpers, after a Hollywood starlet known for her conical bra cups. Earl's successor at GM from 1958 to 1977, the equally legendary designer Bill Mitchell (1912–88), believed that, "unlike a gas range, a car has sex." Auto stylists in the 1950s and early 1960s, argued David Gartman in his book *Auto Opium: A Social History of American Automobile Design*, "sought to make cars look sexy by unconsciously drawing on the cultural association of sex and leisure created by Fordism."[20] Detroit's explicit sexualization in automobile advertising would eventually arrive, starting in the mid-1960s.

Meanwhile, many of the era's biggest movie and music celebrities – its sex symbols – especially its young male stars, were powerfully identified with cars. Heartthrob James Dean became famous for the car-oriented film *Rebel without a Cause* (1955), following his death from an auto accident just before the film's release. Elvis Presley, "the virtuoso of hootchy-kootchy" as the *New York Times* called him in 1956 amid the moral panic caused by his intensely sexualized performances, famously flaunted his connection to automobiles. This included Presley's own outrageously expensive and expansive (for the time) car collection (especially his Cadillacs) and his many film roles that featured cars or cast him as a race car driver (*Spinout* in 1963, *Viva Las Vegas* in 1964, and *Speedway* in 1968). He also had some racy car-oriented songs (notably, "No Room to Rhumba in a Sports Car," 1963). And, of course, there were the never-ending series of screaming incidents that included cars and women, almost always accompanied by a media frenzy. Cars played no small part in Elvis's fame, and his sexual power.[21]

Thus, by the mid-1960s, sexual interaction and cars had become synonymous, especially when it came to sporty and stylish cars. Convertibles, whose postwar popularity peaked in 1973 at 6.4 per cent of American sales, represented much more than a simple form of motorized coveyance. To one young driver, they were nothing less than "sex, romance, wind in your hair – hey, man, it's the American dream."[22] From California "hot rods" to the Beach Boys' "Little Deuce Coupe" (1963) to plays and films like *Grease* (1971) and George Lucas's paean to cruising, *American Graffiti* (1973), the cultural popularity and influence of sexualized, exuberant cars, and the sex occurring in them, were pervasive. As if to emphasize the collision of sexuality and cars (and safety concerns) that had been building in the

Sixties, in 1973 J.G. Ballard published his controversial novel *Crash*. The "first pornographic novel about technology," as he called it, the book's sexually promiscuous characters fetishize automobile crashes, a dystopia triggered by Ballard's concern about "the spectres of sinister technologies and the dreams that money can buy."[23]

That same year, Malcolm Bricklin launched the world's first sexualized safety sports car.

The automobile's impact on gender was as profound as it was on sex. The car's influence on conceptions of male and female identity, and notions of femininity and masculinity, remains among the most central and contested intersections of technology and gender. Indeed, the car has had a foundational effect on what it means to be "modern," or a "man" or a "woman," and what those words came to signify across the twentieth century. Incredibly, and as if to confirm its utterly ubiquitous and pervasive influence in shaping automobility's impact, not until the 1980s did scholars begin to investigate the car's society-shaping role with respect to gender. One of the first analyses was Charles Sanford's "'Woman's Place' in American Car Culture," in a 1980 special issue of the *Michigan Quarterly Review* devoted to the car's impact on society.[24] The automobile's gendered uses, its gendered identifications and representations, and its effect on conceptions of masculinity and femininity are – whether recognized or not – central touchstones for how modern human interaction *and* identity are understood.[25]

Since the outset of automobility in the 1880s, the car has been seen as a "man's technology." Automobile invention, production, and use were public activities involving technology, tinkering, and business, and car enthusiasm and adoption were, initially, mostly the domain of men. The motor car, as the historian Margaret Walsh has noted, "was perceived to be a piece of masculine machinery which was difficult and dirty to drive and was beyond the capability and fastidiousness of women to operate." Yet, women's changing place in society could be gauged, to a large degree, by their relationship to and use of automobiles. After 1910, once it was clear that the automobile was to be a vehicle for the masses, the notion of excluding women from driving cars was never seriously entertained in North America (with some important exceptions), and women's ownership or use of cars was a significant element of equality and independence, and modernity. Early automobile innovations, such as electric cars or the self-starting engine, which were sometimes targeted towards white, middle-class female car consumers, reflected both Progressive-era sensibilities and the obviousness to automakers of the inadvisability of discounting

Figure 5.4. Women as automobiles and automobile adornment.

half their potential car-buying customers (men bought electrics just as often as women). Even if they were a minority of drivers, women were full participants in the automobile age almost from its genesis, and the car was an essential aspect of the struggle for female equality during the first-wave feminist movement.[26]

By the 1920s, automobile use had profoundly reshaped women's role in society, especially for young, single women. In 1909, twenty-two-year-old Alice Ramsey became the first woman to drive across America, while Emily Post's 1922 *Etiquette in Society, in Business, in Politics, and at Home* told young women that it was perfectly acceptable for them to drive, even alone.[27] Mass automobility's emancipatory quickening saw the emergence of the modern "It girl," the flapper. Fitzgerald's *Gatsby* featured Jordan Baker, the liberated, auto-driving golfer whose name was derived from two cars marketed to women, the Jordan Playboy and the Baker Electric.[28] Ned Jordan, whose company built the Playboy, may have declared his vehicle "a car for a man's man," but it was also for "a girl who loves the out-of-doors."[29] Famous feminist drivers of the era included writers Edith Wharton and Gertrude Stein. Transgressive figures such as car-driving, rum-running Albertan fugitive Filumena (Florence) Lassandro (who was executed in 1923) or car-driving, bank-robbing Texan fugitive Bonnie Parker of Barrow gang fame (who was killed in a police shoot-out in 1934) represented gender-shifting rebellion. Both cases were later immortalized on stage and in film.[30]

Yet the nature of women's interactions with the automobile also imposed traditional roles upon them, commodified them, and reinforced their objectification.[31] As Walsh explains, "the Victorian cultural norm, the 'cult of domesticity,' may have been challenged both by gaining the suffrage and by technological improvements," such as the car, "but it still remained widely held." During the 1920s, auto advertising continued to infantilize women, depicting them as car models, from the "Limousine" to the "Country Roundabout Model." What was a male-dominated automobile manufacturing and advertising industry, argued American studies scholar Laura Behling, "created the ideal woman by reinforcing the same traditional sex and gender roles that much of society feared had been irretrievably lost *en route* to women's enfranchisement."[32] Moreover, women often found that the car's liberating aspects were accompanied by vulnerability and the ever-present threat that male domination of driving represented. Cars could as easily be a site of danger as a ride to freedom. The wartime and early postwar period witnessed the car's continued paradoxical impact on women's role, with "Rosie the Riveter" working in Detroit's munitions factories just as effectively as a man yet with most women forced "homeward bound" once those assembly lines returned to automotive manufacture, and mostly back to men.[33]

By the 1950s, however, it was undeniable that, while women's car usage and consumption were increasingly conceptualized through traditional gendered roles such as suburban homemaker and caregiver, millions of women worked outside the home, purchased cars, and drove – and not just to purchase groceries or ferry children. By 1970, women constituted 43 per cent of America's drivers and 37 per cent of its work force, with similar figures for Canada. Nonetheless, women's place in the auto world was circumscribed, as it remained a largely male domain into the early 1970s, even as postwar feminism created new, if often gendered, roles for women in work and mobility technologies. And despite their undeniable place as automobile consumers in the marketplace, women were "not taken seriously for the most part in the designing or marketing of cars by Detroit or offshore carmakers," as *Chatelaine*, Canada's "women's magazine," remarked as late as 1986. When women appeared in auto ads, it was most often still as adornment.[34] Long after the Model T, automobiles remained gendered female. Industrial psychologist Ernest Dichter's 1940s studies for Chrysler, showing that "the typical American male looked upon the convertible as his mistress and the saloon as his model wife," influenced decades of Detroit's advertising and reasserted automobiles' objectification of women.[35]

Given all this, its not surprising that the onset of high industrial modernity was inaugurated by the arrival of the sports car, a material expression that reflected male domination of industry, business, technology, and conceptions of gender, too. It is also equally unsurprising that the muscle car and, eventually, the sexy safety sports car emerged just as the norms of the postwar period were being challenged by dramatic changes in sexual identity and practice. In some ways, Malcolm Bricklin and the SV1 were a logical outcome of a revolution that had been building for a quite some time.

***Dream Car* Song 10: "Paradise by the Dashboard Light," Meatloaf, 1977**

Part II. Sex Symbol: Sixties Sports- and Muscle-Car Masculinity and the Sexual Revolution

Perhaps it was a legacy of Henry Ford's utilitarian influence on Americans' car-buying habits, but before the 1953 introduction of the Chevrolet Corvette, sports cars were relatively rare and exotic for the North American driving public. Racing cars had been a mainstay of American motoring since the frenzy of cross-country rallies in the 1890s and Henry Ford's 1901 publicity-generating race. Louis Chevrolet became famous as a race-car driver in the 1910s and as the namesake of Billy Durant's lynchpin 1911 auto firm in his creation of General Motors. By the 1920s, high-performance and luxury vehicles such as Jay Gatsby's Rolls Royce and the exclusive Bugatti and Bentley marques had also carved out a place for foreign vehicles as signifiers of wealth and privilege. Mass-market motoring in America, as personified by Ford's utilitarian Model T, and even Sloan's ladder of a car for every purse and purpose, did not yet include American sports cars, and that did not change during the depression and war years. Up until the 1950s, British and European makes dominated the relatively small North American market for roadsters.

After the Second World War, American prosperity and technological prowess opened the door for a new category of vehicle, one that reflected the futuristic and confident jet-age values of high industrial modernity: the American sports car. Despite the enormous size of the postwar car-buying market, the idea of the sports car was embraced only tentatively at first. One of the last independent car firms, the Nash-Kelvinator Corporation (founded as Nash Motors Company in 1916 and merging with Hudson in 1954 to create American Motors Corporation), can rightfully claim the first sports car, with the launch of the stylish 1951 Nash-Healey, though only about five hundred were built over four model years.[36] Chevrolet's famous reveal of a prototype Corvette at the 1952 Motorama display in New York City sparked a huge amount of interest in the car, and GM's subsequent decision to go into production was a milestone towards the mass-market sports car, the "dream car of many fifties youth." The Corvette was different than customized hot rods or foreign roadsters. For white, middle-class (North) American men – its primary creators and consumers – the colourful, plastic-coated Corvette conflated vibrant, youthful, exuberance and status-affirming material success. A powerful new car category had been established; with the 'Vette, Chevrolet had taken "the mass-American view of success and put it on wheels."[37] It was the car given to astronauts, a symbol of American masculinity.

Corvette sales immediately skyrocketed, primarily because of its sumptuous look and racy appeal. "The sports car was sexy," wrote historian David Gartman, "because it was impractical for work and tailored to the realm of leisure extravagance and waste."[38] Ford's introduction of its two-seater Thunderbird in 1955 began what eventually became a torrent of increasingly more sexy, powerful, and muscularly designed sports cars from Detroit: Ford's Mustang (1964); Pontiac's GTO (1964) and Firebird (1967); Chevrolet's Camaro (1967); Plymouth's Road Runner (1968); and Chrysler's Charger (1966) and Challenger (1970).[39] The undeniable sexual power of these vehicles thrummed from beneath their hoods, expressions of mid-century, high-modern industrial masculinity.

In 1961, at the start of this muscle-car era and just as the earliest of the baby boomers came of driving age, pharmaceutical firm Meyers introduced the first female oral contraceptive. Two years later, Betty Friedan published *The Feminine Mystique*. As the sexual revolution unfolded, sports and muscle cars became something like a (male) corollary to the (female) pill: both exploded in the public consciousness in the early 1960s; both became touchstones of the sexual revolution; and each reflected different aspects of a deeply patriarchal society. After all, sports cars were designed and marketed by and sold to men. The contraceptive pill was also designed and marketed by men, but obviously sold to women. While the pill ostensibly was a form of (female) birth control, it facilitated (male) promiscuity, and both sports cars and the pill could be seen ultimately as assertions of masculinity. The pill was about having sex and sexual liberation, an expression of a driven, male libido that allowed testosterone-inspired fantasies of risk-free sex to come true.[40] Even as the pill liberated women, the "new teenage 'auto culture,'" writes Walsh, "looked backwards rather than forwards in terms of gender equality."[41] Between the pill and Detroit's emphasis on the sexualized power of their sporty, muscular vehicles, what emerged was nothing less than a high-octane sports- and muscle-car masculinity, the peak of automobile sexual modernity.

This was new, and it was a change from how masculinity had predominantly been shaped by the car in the 1950s. Certainly there had been avowedly car cultures centred on male youth before and after the war, especially for racing and customizing.[42] But sports cars, and especially muscle cars, emerged to signal a broader, more mainstream acceptance of car-fuelled masculinity. If anything, in the first two postwar decades, automobile manliness had asserted itself mostly in the guise of responsibility, power, and control. Most men of that wartime generation responsibly drove aspiring sedans that could be found, usually, at the brand midpoint of the Big Three's price ladders, maybe a family-friendly Buick or a boring Ford. The early postwar, responsible, modern driver was also a trope shaped by Detroit, who wished to keep the focus for motor vehicle accidents on individual drivers, most of whom were men.[43]

The change could be seen in how these increasingly sexualized cars were marketed by the Big Three. Predictably, by the mid-1960s, sports and muscle cars' advertising epitomized the adage "sex sells." Advertisements focused on sleek, powerful vehicles and made explicit their connections to sexuality. The television commercial for the 1970 Dodge Charger 500, for example, set the scene, with nerdy Elliot in his brand new Charger, parked at the beach with his plain girlfriend Charlotte, about to make a wedding proposal. Yet the pure sexual energy generated by Elliot's vehicle prompts their conversation to be interrupted:

> Elliot: We've been going together for three years now.
> Charlotte: Four.
> Elliot: Will … will you be my, my –
> Charlotte: Yea – [knock, knock, knock]
> Elliot: Oh my! [rolls down window]
> Bikini-Clad Girl 1: Gorgeous car … What is it?
> Elliot: It's the new charge dodger – uh, Dodge Charger 500.
> Girl 1: Dynamite …
> Bikini-Clad Girl 2: What's that?
> Elliot: That's the optional Hurst shifter.
> Charlotte: Elliot?
> Girl 2: Hey, where are the headlights?
> Elliot: They're hidden, where the bumper loops around the grill.
> [Girl 2 pushes Charlotte out of car, seductively slides into seat]

Girl 2: Hey, [are] these new highback seats?
Elliot: Yeah, [more confidently] see how *nice* they fit?
Girl 1: My name's *Sheila*. What's yours?
Charlotte: ELLIOT?!
Girl 1: That's a *cute* name. Bet it really rides smooth, huh, El? [Girl 1 enters car]
Elliot: Why don't we find out? [car pulls away, leaving Charlotte alone on beach]
Charlotte: ELLLIOTTT!!
Beautiful Narrator: The Dodge Charger 500. If you can cope with a whole new image, you could be Dodge material.[44]

Detroit's print ads also used highly suggestive images and wordplay in their copy (see figure 5.5). Sports and muscle cars appeared on television shows, as prizes on game shows, and at car shows, where beautiful female models framed and caressed the latest models on display.[45]

There was also product placement in movies and television. American *muscle, w*hether Corvettes, Mustangs, Barracudas, or GTOs – the last designed by GM wonderkid John Z. DeLorean – was promoted by rugged, macho movie stars like Steve McQueen in films like *Bullitt* (1968), with its spectacular chase scene. The Seventies marked the heyday of muscle-car movies, with car-oriented films such as *The French Connection* (1971, which won the Academy Award for best picture), *The Gumball Rally* (1976), *Corvette Summer* (1978), and *Cannonball Run* (1981) filling theatres. Massively popular television shows such as *Starsky and Hutch* (1975–9), *The Rockford Files* (1974–80), and *Charlie's Angels* (1976–81, featuring the three sexy agents sharing a Ford Mustang Cobra II) all prominently featured American muscle cars as a major elements of the show. Racing itself became a major expression of American sports entertainment and masculinity in the postwar period, with the growth and popularity of stock-car and open-wheel series and major races such as the Indianapolis 500 and the Daytona 500.[46]

But nothing aroused sports-car sexuality and muscle-car masculinity better than *Playboy*. In 1953, the same year that the Corvette was unveiled, Chicagoan Hugh Hefner (1926–2017) published his debut issue of *Playboy*, featuring Hollywood sex symbol Marilyn Monroe. A modern man's magazine, with an emphasis on nudity, sex, politics, music, fashion, and fiction, *Playboy* also regularly and enthusiastically showcased sexy, sporty automobiles. After all, Hefner had named the publication itself after the defunct Playboy Automobile Company (Buffalo, NY; 1947–51; ninety-seven cars produced), and the magazine regularly connected his vision of what constituted vibrant, modern masculinity to content that emphasized the manliness of sports and muscle cars (for example, "The Complete Sports Car Stable," 1957;

Figure 5.5. Sex sells: advertising sportscar sexuality and muscle car masculinity – the 1966 Ford Mustang (top left) and the 1969 Dodge Charger (top right and bottom).

"*Playboy*'s Sportscar Jacket," 1960). One 1974 reflection in the magazine on the Pontiac GTO included the proclamation that "buying a GTO is like getting two inches added to your cock." Advertisements in *Playboy* were heavy on alcohol, tobacco, gadgets (especially music equipment), and, of course, automobiles, particularly sporty European makes and sexy roadsters.[47]

Hefner himself boasted a legendary car collection, including a gull-winged Mercedes 300SL, often ostentatiously displayed at his *Playboy* mansions across the country. *Playboy* "Bunnies" who became "Playmates of the Year" received a pink-tinted vehicle – the first a Mustang, in 1965. According to Elizabeth Fraterrigo's *Playboy and the Making of the Good Life in Modern America*, cars, technology, and mobility were central to Hefner's vision of the playboy, who "traveled both for business and pleasure" and was no "downtrodden, Willy Loman–like traveling salesman, but a jet-setting, debonair businessman flitting from city to city in high style."[48] *Playboy* reached a peak circulation in November 1972, with 7.2 million copies sold. And in September 1974, Malcolm Bricklin and his car appeared in a glossy article in the magazine entitled "Safety Fast," one that declared that, "sleek, sexy and overprotective, the Bricklin is trying to gull-wing its way into America's heart."[49]

Part III. Sex Machine, Playboy, Cowboy: The SV1, Malcolm Bricklin, and Muscle-Car Modernity's Climax

In 1974, (North) American muscle car modernity reached a notable peak with the Safety Vehicle-1 and its promoter. As much as Bricklin had sought to fashion himself in the image of a futuristic innovator with the SV1's safety angle, he also consciously promoted his car and himself as symbols of Seventies heteronormative masculine sexuality. Doing so reflected a performative promotional persona for Bricklin and a sales strategy for the car that was based on an important strain of postwar masculinity, but also a white, straight, male reaction to the sexual revolution. All this could be seen in the SV1's design, how it was advertised, how it was perceived and the reactions it generated.

The car's sexual power was something in which Bricklin took especial joy. The SV1 was, in his eyes, a sex symbol in and of itself, its design and shape meant to stir sexual reactions. From the very start of the car project, one thing that Bricklin had known for certain was that he wanted to make a car "that was sexy, and that sex appeal was going to be the primary selling point."[50] Bricklin played up the SV1's sexuality and masculinity in the car's advertising and promotion. The firm's sleek promotional brochures were full of suggestive language, stating that the car had

Figure 5.6. Muscle-car masculinity on display: Josette Cowan and Paul Newman, Las Vegas, 1974 (left); Bricklin eruption, c. 1974 (right).

"beauty that's more than skin deep. Aesthetically, the car speaks for itself." The cabin of the SV1 was its "cockpit," the "acrylic body panels" were "color impregnated," and the Bricklin's muscular "351 cubic inch V8 engine with a two barrel carburetor" gave the car "performance as exciting as it looks."[51] As one memorable Bricklin tagline stated, "Sooner or later, you're going to drive a Bricklin, which might prove to be the first great sexual experience of your lifetime."

The brochures also included an image of the Bricklin car strategically photographed in front of a geyser eruption, leaving little to the potential buyer's imagination (see figure 5.6). At the Las Vegas and New York events, Bricklin ensured that beautiful models were on stage with the SV1 and mingled in the crowd. In Vegas, Paul Newman and Bobby Unser provided an extra injection of automobile masculinity. Even at the press conference after the firm was put into receivership, sex permeated the presentation. Canadian journalist Michael Enright described "the Girl" who accompanied Bricklin to the event as "beautiful and sexy and wholesome, but above all wholesome." Bricklin's "companion," Enright dutifully reported, "has a pound of sand-drift hair that falls just right, framing what is, quite simply a perfect face," and her "body is everything a body ought to be." Then, there was the car, itself: "The Bricklin, like the Girl, is beautiful and sexy and above all wholesome. The little man's dream car, the gull-winged beauty that was supposed to take your Chevy inclinations and turn them inside out."[52]

If, as Bricklin once boasted to a reporter, the SV1 "was built to have sex appeal," it seemed to have worked. Harold Nason, Hatfield's deputy minister of economic growth after 1975, was frank in his assessment of the car's sexual power: "There is no question about it," the normally reserved Harold told reporters. "From day one, the car had a certain sex appeal."[53] Hatfield, also clearly captured by the look of the car, waxed more romantically about the Bricklin's effect on him. As he admitted in a 1985 interview, "it's not that I was ever very much interested in cars. It was the sheer sculptured beauty of the Bricklin, with its doors like gull's wings: the idea that something so revolutionary could be made here, in New Brunswick." The sexy SV1 was "the most modern and sophisticated product ever produced in the history of New Brunswick."[54]

The SV1's sexual magnetism was highlighted in press reviews of the car. *Car and Driver*, which featured the SV1 on its July 1974 cover, wrote, "hit the road with a Bricklin and women fall hopelessly in love from two lanes away." Circling competitors would have to admit that "this new kid on the block has lowered their cars sex appeal by a hefty notch." The SV1's ability to "radiate such excitement is so vigorous" that Bricklin could not hope to "satisfy all [his] cash customers."[55] Another *Car and Driver* review declared that the doors were "the Pure Sex element in the selling equation," while Bricklin himself declared, "Those doors are *sex*. They're what turn people on."[56] Indeed, *Road & Track*'s initial Bricklin review might have been mixed, but the magazine had to admit that the SV1 "simply turns on the man in the street." This view was echoed by Bricklin, who enthusiastically told the magazine that the car was for "the guy who wants a beautiful car but doesn't know a fuckin' thing about cars … the guy who'll go into debt up to his ears for that one dream – the car of his dreams." Bricklin and his car weren't featured on *Playboy*'s cover, but Hefner's magazine did pronounce that "the Bricklin has a gutsy don't-tread-on-me look about it – somewhere between a Datsun 240Z and a Maserati Ghibli, with Mercedes 300SL–like wings thrown in for good measure." Sumptuously photographed across a two-page spread, the car "displayed body lines," according to *Playboy*, that were an "aesthetic delight."[57] Even the stolid *Atlantic Advocate* acknowledged that the car had "a strong male image and the locker-room boys would line up to buy it."[58]

The young, male buyers of Bricklin's target market were just as sexually captivated with the SV1, according to Malcolm. "I used to get letters from young guys who owned the Bricklin," he claimed. "'Dear Mr. Bricklin, thank you so much for building this car. I never got laid before I bought a Bricklin.'" In Bricklin's view, this

Figure 5.7. An early promotional image for the Bricklin, c. 1973.

alchemy "was a big deal to a lot of people."[59] He liked to recall a particular evening in New York City:

> We were in New York, and the car had been launched. It was December of 1974 or 1975. I was with someone, and we decided to walk through the Park. It was the dead of night and the dead of winter; we got through the park, and when we got onto the street, believe it or not there was a Bricklin stopped at the lights. I had to go the car – knocked on the window and asked the owner how he liked his car; he said he loved it. I explained to the car's occupants, which included a young woman, that I was Malcolm Bricklin – and then we started walking away. Even though it was snowing, the girl in the car chased me down in the snow and gave me her underwear with her phone number on it.[60]

Clearly, in Bricklin's view, if the car was meant to have undeniable sex appeal as an expression of muscle-car masculinity, so too, was the man. Just as his car reflected important postwar trends in the connections between sex, gender, and cars, Bricklin perfectly encapsulated aspects of this era of sexual change. When he and his car exploded on the North American public consciousness in 1974, Bricklin

Figure 5.8. Miss Saint John with an SV1, 1974.

was only thirty-five years old. Not only did his entrepreneurial cowboy persona fit the innovator and promoter archetypes, but his virile, rugged image also perfectly personified Sixties muscle-car masculinity and the emerging post-counterculture sexuality of the Seventies. As Enright described him, Bricklin's dress was "managerial hip, tight cutesybum pants, print sports shirt, boots and a Bricklin belt buckle with the gull-winged car embossed in hammered silver." The man "exudes confidence, Mark Spitz good looks all in place."[61] When Hatfield won the 1974 election on his promise of a Bricklin-fuelled better future, Malcolm was also there to celebrate, "decked out in Western-style garb, the epitome of the *Playboy* male."[62] Bricklin knew exactly who the target market for his sexy car was: "He's me," as he confidently told *Road & Track* in 1975.[63]

Bricklin's sexy image was both a genuine reflection of his age, attitude, and era, and, at the same time, carefully constructed. Good looking, tall, young, tanned, and stylish, and often sporting a robust, dark mustache, Bricklin exuded a musky, Burt

Figure 5.9. Malcolm, the sexy cowboy.

Reynolds–like cowboy sexuality, one that was often commented upon. Reynolds, the American actor, had gained iconic sex symbol status following his April 1972 nude appearance as the first-ever male centrefold for *Cosmopolitan* magazine, an event considered a milestone in the sexual revolution.[64] Reynolds went on to dominate movie screens in the 1970s with sports car–themed films such as *Smokey and the Bandit* (1977), taking on a macho, muscle-car cowboy persona, and wearing a Stetson as he drove a 1977 Pontiac Firebird Trans-Am, with a T-bar roof. A few years earlier, Bricklin had projected a very similar image. As two New Brunswick journalists later remarked, "slim in his tight jeans, wide cowboy belt and unbuttoned shirt, Bricklin," the "promoter from Arizona," "was the epitome of the Seventies male."[65]

Bricklin, of course, was originally from Philadelphia, and his Arizona cowboy persona was largely an affectation. Not long after the Bricklin venture started,

Figure 5.10. Playboy, cowboy, muscle-car dreams: Bricklin in Phoenix, 1974 (left); Burt Reynolds in *Smoky and the Bandit*, 1977 (right).

Malcolm and his family moved to Phoenix, where he rented an office in the tallest building in the city (the Camelback Tower, built in 1972), which he decked out in a western motif. Malcolm would sit on a saddle-topped stool, dressed in cowboy gear from head to toe, holding court with media as he directed the Bricklin enterprise (a picture of this scene made it into *People* magazine). J.A. Fredericks remarked that, at the start of the venture, Bricklin transformed himself "almost immediately" into "the model of a western cowboy."[66] Bricklin "had flair, and he worked it," said Herb Grasse. "He worked it really good."[67] And just like Burt Reynolds, SV1-era Malcolm Bricklin became so identified with the macho cowboy image that his character in the 2010 musical *The Bricklin: An Automotive Fantasy* wears a Stetson, belt buckle, and cowboy boots during the performance.

Bricklin's cowboy image harkened back to and was, in part, an inheritance from the original advertisements for the Playboy created by Ned Jordan. Appearing in the *Saturday Evening Post* between 1918 and 1926, the Playboy campaign, according to the advertising historian Roland Marchand, "revolutionize[d] car advertising copy and change[d] the public's perception of the car forever." It's no wonder that Bricklin picked Jordan's cowboy/playboy image; the car driver as untamed cowboy on the open road has reappeared many times since, in television, film, and song, and has been a staple of popular culture and car advertising for a century. Jordan's was the original, "emotional, rhetorical, irresistibly flattering" conflation of a cowboy West with untamed sexuality and the power of the automobile, and it was aimed directly at women, too.[68] Jordan's Playboy ad copy was the poetry of automobile sexual modernity:[69]

> SOMEWHERE west of Laramie there's a bronco-busting, Steer-roping girl who knows what I'm talking about.
>
> She can tell what a sassy pony, that's a cross between greased lightning and the place where it hits, can do with eleven hundred pounds of steel and action when he's going high, wide, and handsome.
>
> The truth is – the Playboy was built for her.

Whether he conflated the playboy and the cowboy consciously or subconsciously to forge his image of Seventies muscle-car masculinity, Bricklin was undoubtedly also a reflection of the rapidly changing sexual and gendered landscape in which he found himself. The Bricklin's appearance in the early 1970s – at the height of most boomers' teenage sports car–buying exuberances – came at a moment when the longer-term impacts of the sexual revolution were coming into view. Canada's 1969 omnibus bill loosened laws on divorce, homosexuality, and abortion. "There's no place for the state in the bedrooms of the nation," said Pierre Trudeau, the legislation's champion, amending a phrase from a *Globe and Mail* editorial.[70]

In the early 1970s, when Bricklin started selling his car, the place of women in society in both the United States and Canada was shifting quickly, as they fought to expand their legal and political rights. In 1970, Canada's Royal Commission on the Status of Women issued its seminal report outlining the many areas in work and law where women remained unequal, and it presented 167 recommendations to rectify these inequalities. In the United States, in 1971 and 1972, the two chambers of Congress passed the Equal Rights Amendment following a decades-long campaign to entrench American women's legal and political equality, though it never achieved state ratification. In 1973, the *Roe v. Wade* decision by the US Supreme Court legalized abortion access.[71] Nonetheless, despite all of these advances, equality was still an aspirational goal for many women, and North American society (and automobile industrial modernity) remained deeply heteronormative, patriarchal, and often misogynistic.

Figure 5.11. Jordan Motors ad for the Playboy, 1926.

For avowedly heterosexual men like cowboy Malcolm Bricklin, who believed that a sexy car was the playboy's ticket to accessible and easy risk-free sex, their sexual revolution had an unambiguous and lasting legacy, one that spilled into the 1970s. As the counterculture faded and the youngest baby-boomers moved into their thirties, what remained for many was a "me generation" landscape of sexual liberation, singles bars, "wife-swapping," and exploding divorce rates. Films like *Bob and Carol and Ted and Alice* (1969) chronicled this new post-pill, post-protest, post-university reality for the baby boomers. Books such as Christopher Lasch's *The Culture of Narcissism* (1979) and Barbara Ehrenreich's *The Hearts of*

Men: American Dreams and the Flight from Commitment (1983) sought to determine the new era's sociological and psychological causes and consequences.[72]

If postwar male heteronormative automobility had reached a peak in the muscle-car masculinity of the Seventies with the SV1, its very slow decline after the Bricklin venture's end attested to patriarchy's continued sway over society. Was Malcolm Bricklin a reflection of patriarchy? Undoubtedly. He was the fecund head of a sprawling family, one that included six sons from four different partners (all of Bricklin's ex-spouses remained on good terms with him), but one that also reflected his view of the importance of family. Was Bricklin a symbol of the male reaction to the sexual revolution or a sexist because he sold his sexy vehicle as a way for young men to "get laid," or because he thought the SV1 looked like a "cock and balls" from above? No doubt, he was a product of his times.

Yet, interestingly, after the SV1, Malcolm never again focused explicitly on sex as a way to sell any of his future ventures. This was because, by the mid-1970s, the changes sparked by the sexual revolution were working in tandem with some of the other economic and policy upheavals of the era to reshape the car, its uses, and its industry yet again. The safety, fuel economy, and emissions revolutions caused by Nader, OPEC, and the green movement significantly reined in the era of muscle car-masculinity, and it also signalled an end to the untamed power of industrial modernity's postwar peak. Design and engineering regulatory changes meant that cars were required to be smaller and lighter and were built even more with safety and fuel economy in mind. Frankly, cars became less sexy in their styling and design. The tame, if not completely dull, second-generation 1974 Mustang, with its improved fuel economy and reduced emissions, was a far cry from its more powerful earlier iterations. Muscle cars such as the Plymouth Barracuda, Dodge Challenger, and AMC Javelin were all discontinued by the mid-1970s. Corvette sales reached their peak in 1979 (at 53,807). Overall, by the beginning of the 1980s, sports cars became a smaller category of vehicle sales, pushed out by new categories like Iacocca's minivan. This also reflected the evolving demographics of the baby boom generation, as they started to have their own families.

All these changes signalled a noticeable softening in muscle-car masculinity after the SV1 and some weakening in the explicit sexuality of cars. As early as September 1973, *Fortune* magazine declared that "the auto industry has lost its masculinity." By 1980, historian David Lewis wrote that, "just as the golden age of the auto is receding, so the salad days of sex and cars are on the wane." Even drive-ins, those dens of automobile-fuelled sex iniquity, were "fading into yesteryear." Sex didn't sell quite as well anymore; in fact, some found explicitly linking cars to sexuality offensive.[73] Nonetheless, even if, in the 1980s and 1990s, Detroit no longer trafficked so regularly and unabashedly in the sex-machine business, the sexualization and gender identification of cars (and, increasingly after the 1970s, of pickup trucks), the objectification of women, and their neglect as consumers, continued in the automobile industry long after Bricklin's sexy car had started to fade into obscurity.[74] If Malcolm Bricklin and the SV1 were Seventies symbols of how notions of sex and masculinity were changing, they also showed just how much society remained wedded to continuing conceptions of sexuality and gender.

Then there was Richard Hatfield. Although he had embraced Bricklin's muscle-car masculinity in his effort to industrially modernize his province, and the two men were both young, confident, attractive, and dynamic, they could not have been more different, sexually speaking. One was the consummate hetero alpha-male with many spouses and children; the other, the closeted gay man who remained a bachelor all his life. Yet, in each their own way, Bricklin and Hatfield were symbols of different facets of the sexual revolution, both of its sprawling impact and its limits in a post-1970 world.

Part IV. Sex and the Single Premier: Richard Hatfield and the Other Sexual Revolution

"Disco Dick" Hatfield was an unusual man in the 1970s. Good looking, successful, and quite the man about town, in the hedonistic, swinging world that had emerged in the wake of the sexual revolution, Hatfield remained a bachelor and, publicly, something of a sexual anachronism. For Malcolm Bricklin, a self-styled ladies' man, Hatfield's seeming lack of female companionship was a matter of keen interest and curiosity, given the premier's single status, celebrity, and sociability – traits that clearly drew them together. According to the automotive entrepreneur, about a year into the Bricklin venture, the two men were vacationing together in Acapulco: "I asked him, 'Mr. Premier, how come I never see you with women, a man such as yourself?' The premier told me that he was gay, but that it wasn't a problem for him as he was too busy anyways. But that it was a difficult time to be a gay man in politics."[75] Now, Bricklin himself is definitely a salesman, a showman, and sometimes even something of a fabulist, but there is really no reason for him to fabricate stories about Hatfield, or what the premier might have said on this matter.

Regardless, it is undoubtedly true that Richard Hatfield's own sexual identity stands in stark contrast with that of Malcolm Bricklin, especially within the context of the sexual revolution. That Hatfield was the premier of a very conservative province across two decades of tumultuous social change around sexuality, privacy, and politics can provide an even more illuminating window into the changing realities of sexual politics emerging in New Brunswick, Canada, and North America in the 1970s and 1980s. As one scholar of gay Fredericton has written, "discussion of Hatfield is nigh inevitable in casual conversation of queer history in New Brunswick," given his prominent place.[76] Even as he embraced the SV1 and Bricklin's vision of muscle-car masculinity, the evolving politics around Hatfield's own bachelorhood, his sexual identity, and his government's conservative policies towards LGBTQ rights and abortion reveal much about the dramatic changes wrought by the sexual revolution but also the continued resistance to these changes. Though Hatfield's sexual history is only indirectly related to the story of the SV1, it is an essential aspect of his biography, and his political career, too.

By the time he became premier in 1970 at the age of thirty-eight (he was only about seven years older than Bricklin), Hatfield was already well known as a bachelor. Initially, voters and observers did not find anything unusual in this. After all, in 1968, a cool, mod, *forty-seven*-year-old bachelor, Pierre Trudeau, had just been elected prime minister of Canada. Nonetheless, early on, there were a few questions raised on the hustings and in the legislature about Hatfield's domestic arrangements and when he would "settle down." In his first few years in office, Hatfield was still living in his mother's home, and then in the Lord Beaverbrook Hotel in Fredericton. Eventually, he bought a modest house within walking distance of the legislature, and near his beloved Saint John River, at 7 Elmcroft Place, a home that became the site of all sorts of nocturnal socializing. Despite this gesture towards domesticity, the question of Hatfield's bachelor status was again raised in 1972, following Trudeau's own marriage, given the fact that the premier, now in his early forties, remained single and unattached.[77]

But Hatfield exhibited no public interest in marriage, or even dating, for that matter. Indeed, at times he was even publicly disdainful of the idea of the traditional family, once telling a reporter that "the nuclear family – one wife, two kids and one dog – looks nice on Christmas cards, but they pay an awful price."[78] Such a sentiment was truly unorthodox for a politician and an illustration of Hatfield's willingness to embrace his bachelorhood and revel in his unconventional marital status. Certainly, it was for a politician from a small, rural, conservative province that was generally united (Protestant and Catholic alike) in holding traditional views on marriage. As Norm Atkins, the Conservative senator, bagman, and campaign strategist, remarked after Hatfield's death, his "political and personal persona were absolutely the same.

Figure 5.12. Hatfield monkeying around with Stompin' Tom Connors.

Often in politics today, people are critical of politicians who create one impression of themselves in public but are in fact quite different in private." Atkins believed that "for Richard Hatfield there was no contradiction. There were some who viewed that essentially as eccentricity. There were others who found the mold so different from the traditional politician that they did not quite know how to handle it."[79]

While he may not have dated publicly, this is not to say that Hatfield did not enjoy a healthy social life; in fact, the contrary is true. Hatfield was the life of the party in New Brunswick and just about anywhere else he went. By the time the Bricklin rolled around, Hatfield had gained a reputation as an incredibly social animal. Disco Dick enjoyed the single life, jetting to exotic locales and dancing at Studio 54, the glitzy New York City night club that became the hottest spot of the Seventies scene. The club hosted rock stars, artists, actors, models, and other luminaries, including a by-then-separated Margaret Trudeau and an aspiring New York realtor by the name of Donald J. Trump.[80] In New York, Hatfield often attended the legendary parties thrown by Truman Capote, the openly homosexual doyen of the New York literary scene. Like Hatfield, Capote was referred to as flamboyant and lived a life of excess and eccentricity. Like Capote, Hatfield was a social butterfly, a gregarious host, and a well-known dancer, drinker, and raconteur, inviting all types

Figure 5.13. Poet Arlen Nowlan, Johnny Cash, June Carter Cash, Hatfield, and Claudine Nowlan, May 1975, Lord Beaverbrook Rink, Saint John.

of people to his own late-night, and sometimes all-night, parties at Elmcroft Place. In fact, his partying behaviour in the 1980s helps explain his demise.

Yet, through all his social visibility, there was little evidence of interest in women: indeed, Hatfield was never publicly tied to a particular woman.[81] Speculation about his bachelor status came mostly from out-of-province media enquiring about his personal life. For most of his time in office, local and provincial media left his private life private, a journalistic approach that was something of a remnant of a bygone era.[82] After Hatfield died, the *Globe and Mail* journalist Michael Valpy remarked that "gregariousness defined him: gregariousness about everything except his private life, which [was] enveloped in a silence willingly respected by the many journalists who were his acquaintances and chroniclers."[83] The *Maclean's* columnist Allan Fotheringham asked Sandra Gwyn, who had written a laudatory 1979 profile of Hatfield in *Saturday Night* magazine, why she hadn't mentioned the fact that, out of all of Canada's ten premiers, only Hatfield remained unmarried well into his forties. Gwyn was, in Fotheringham's view "quite stunned: it simply had never occurred to her to mention the fact." "Even unconsciously," Fotheringham admitted, "we protected him – when he didn't need it."[84]

Notwithstanding their self-imposed circumspection, there were, in fact, constant references in the press to Hatfield as "colourful" or "eccentric," but most often, the word used to describe him was "flamboyant." Journalist Nancy Southam's book of testimonials on Hatfield stated that "his style had more than a touch of flamboyance." Sandra Gwyn also thought of Hatfield as being "flamboyant." On the cover of *Maclean's*, he was referred to as "a flamboyant leader." A 1985 profile in the *Chicago Tribune* described him as "a flamboyant, eccentric, and controversial figure with a penchant for modern art, rock and roll, and New York night life – so much so that critics have nicknamed him 'Disco Dick.'" The *Trib* also noted that the fifty-three-year-old bachelor had a doll collection "in which he takes great pride."[85] Charlie Russell's hit record, "The Bricklin," included the lines, "Now the Premier he's not married / He's a sporty kind of guy."

By then, rumours about Hatfield's sexuality were becoming more openly discussed. Often, hints and whispers about Hatfield took on mildly euphemistic turns of phrase. As early as Hatfield's first electoral campaigns in the 1960s, opponents such as Charlie Van Horne had publicly branded him as a "mother's boy."[86] During the 1978 provincial election, Liberal leader Joseph Daigle called Hatfield a "faded pansy," a remark that, according to his biographer, "played right into Hatfield's efforts to portray himself as the subject of unfair attacks from the opposition."[87] When the election results were tallied, the accusations had not seemed to have dented Hatfield's popularity, and he won a third term as premier. In 1981, *Chatelaine* referred to him as a "bon vivant" and commented on how he dressed, noting that he wore "a well cut black velvet dinner jacket with satin colour" to the legislative assembly's opening ball or "a pale blue Miami Beach outfit" to address a demonstration of striking Maritime fisherman. "Despite all the 1970 fanfare about 'New Brunswick's eligible bachelor,'" the article speculated, there was no question of his ever marrying: Hatfield "brushed aside questions with the assertion, 'I'm married to politics.'"[88]

Until the early 1980s, Hatfield was able to either ignore the insinuations about his sexuality or turn them against his opponents as unscrupulous attacks on his character. In the view of Gerald Regan, former premier of Nova Scotia, while Hatfield faced criticism "from those who favoured more traditional behaviour," Richard "was totally unconcerned about such reactions. He felt that if was doing his job of governing the province to the best of his ability, his personal life was nobody's business but his own."[89] New Brunswick author (and later senator) David Adams Richards felt that, in Hatfield, New Brunswickers had accepted "an original man in a traditional role … for seventeen years, most of the time with more love than hatred, more trust than mistrust. And the relationship was, looking back, a kind of

Figure 5.14. Richard Hatfield, n.d.

mutual celebration."[90] Most voters probably agreed, returning Hatfield for a fourth term, despite the growing whispers about his personal life. Their attitudes changed dramatically when the premier's sexuality and eccentricities were overshadowed by more alarming behaviours, especially around his alleged drug use and over-the-top social life.

Richard Hatfield's private persona – so much of which was already on full display during his controversial life – was fully revealed after he died in 1990. Within a year, Cormier and Michaud published *Richard Hatfield: Un dernier train pour Hartland* (translated into English a year later as *Richard Hatfield: Power and Disobedience*), which directly broached Hatfield's sexuality. The authors interviewed Hatfield a year after his 1987 defeat and raised the issue: "An individual's sexual orientation does not interest us at all, Mr. Hatfield, but in your case, it does seem necessary to bring up the matter because it was an issue during the election campaign." Hatfield refused to reply. "After a few moments of silence, we tried again." Eventually, Hatfield responded, discussing the whisper campaigns about his homosexuality, saying that "it never bothered me. I have a very generous respect for the people."[91]

Four years after he died, during the 1994 inquiry led by Justice Horace Krever into the contamination of the Canadian blood supply in the 1980s that had resulted in thousands of Canadians being infected with Hepatitis C and HIV, Hatfield was, in effect, outed. At the inquiry's Fredericton stop in July 1994, inquiry counsel

Douglas Elliott asked Hank Williams of the group Fredericton Lesbians and Gays "Was Richard Hatfield a homosexual?" Williams responded that "to the best of knowledge I believe he was." Elliott also stated matter of factly during the inquiry that "when we got to New Brunswick I was well aware of the sexual orientation of Mr. Hatfield. I knew people who had sex with him. It was well known in New Brunswick."[92] There was little press reaction to the event, with sparse headline coverage and only a few comments in the media to "let Hatfield rest in peace."[93]

While these statements were not corroborated by any individual who came forward publicly at any time to claim that he had had a relationship with the premier, no one has ever claimed that Hatfield was not a homosexual, either. As in his interview with Cormier and Michaud, Hatfield never directly refuted the accusation. By the 2010s, Hatfield's sexuality seemed to have become common knowledge. For example, *Globe and Mail* columnist Gary Mason remarked in a piece about the sexual orientation of political leaders that there "has been at least one gay premier in Canada, although New Brunswick's Richard Hatfield remained in the closet throughout his career."[94] Even during those numerous early 1980s scandals that led to his downfall, and that brought intense press scrutiny, Hatfield remained closeted.

Obviously, Hatfield's sexual identity must be considered within the context of an emerging North American LGBTQ rights movement, a key aspect of the sexual revolution that directly overlapped with this time in office. The 1970s marked a pivotal moment in the battle over recognition of the LGBTQ community in Canada and North America more broadly, particularly in the wake of a number of events that had occurred during the 1960s. One high-profile mid-1960s case involved Everett George Klippert, a mechanic in the Northwest Territories. During a 1965 arson investigation, Klippert (who had nothing to do with the case) told police that he was gay, was charged with "gross indecency," and put in prison. Branded a "dangerous offender," which meant an indefinite prison sentence, Klippert unsuccessfully appealed to the Supreme Court of Canada. Eventually, the reaction to Klippert's case convinced many Canadians that their laws concerning homosexuality were outdated. Coupled with liberalizing legal changes in 1967 in the United Kingdom, the Klippert case helped to spur Trudeau's own liberalizing reforms in 1969.[95]

In 1969, another seminal event in the LGBTQ fight for equality took place in New York City: the police raid on Greenwich Village's Stonewall Inn galvanized the gay rights movement. Stonewall generated headlines across the continent and empowered gays and lesbians to stand up to police harassment and discrimination. As a result, starting in the 1970s, new organizations and leaders, and activism including pride parades across North America, spurred the gay rights movement forward.[96] In the midst of these movements, openly gay municipal leader Harvey Milk (1930–78) was elected to the San Francisco board of supervisors in 1977. Assassinated by a disgruntled fellow councillor, Milk became a symbol of gay rights and the ongoing challenges faced by homosexuals, who continued to face police harassment, discrimination, and violence. In 1981, Toronto police launched "Operation Soap," raided four bathhouses, and arrested three hundred men for being in a "bawdy house." The arrests and harsh tactics sparked mass protests and outrage over police behaviour. Over time, the bathhouse raids became symbolic for the gay community across Canada and were the start of protests that eventually morphed into Toronto's Gay Pride Parade.

Richard Hatfield would have been acutely aware of all these events.

Despite his "mod" reputation as a "non-traditional man in a traditional role," and notwithstanding his national status, Hatfield was no trailblazer when it came to gay rights, and conservative New Brunswick was, unsurprisingly, not a national leader on the issue. As a largely rural, extraction-based, and deeply religious province, New Brunswick did not acknowledge the issue of gay rights in the same way that Ontario, Quebec, and British Columbia – with their larger, more diverse populations and bigger cities – did. Those provinces acted as magnets for LGBTQ communities and activism.[97] Even in comparison to the Prairie provinces, Atlantic Canada, and especially New Brunswick, came to the gay rights movement sometimes later and less visibly.[98] Fredericton Lesbians and Gays (FLAG) was founded in 1979, and the city saw the opening of its first gay bar in 1985.[99] The province's first pride parade was not held until 2000, in Moncton. Fredericton, the capital, and where Hatfield lived such a flamboyant life, did not hold its first parade until 2010.

The province's lack of interest contrasts with elsewhere in Canada, where, in response to the demands of LGBTQ activists, many provinces and the federal government began in the 1970s to grapple with the impact of outdated laws, prejudice, and discriminatory policies towards gays and lesbians. While changes were not always effective and approaches were uneven, human rights codes and laws were slowly created to prohibit workplace discrimination and outright harassment. Municipal governments passed laws prohibiting discrimination in hiring based on sexual orientation in the mid-1970s. In 1977, Quebec did so on a provincial basis. Ontario revised its Human Rights Code in 1986 to include sexual orientation. Over the nearly two decades that coincided with Hatfield's time in office, Canadians witnessed a sea change in attitudes towards sexual orientation, with a slow but growing acceptance of the LGBTQ community.[100] By 1986, legal scholar Philip Girard could state that the "general principle that one's sexual orientation does not justify discrimination in the private or public sphere seems to have become well-established in Canadian public opinion."[101]

In New Brunswick, the province's Human Rights Commission, created to oversee the 1967 Human Rights Act, added a number of areas of discrimination to its purview in the 1970s and 1980s: "sex" was added in 1971, but "sexual orientation" was not added until 1992, after Hatfield's time in office.[102] Understandably, given the complicated history of the English-speaking and Acadian communities in the province, the focus of much of the discussion of rights in New Brunswick during Hatfield's premiership was language. Despite the societal and legal changes related to LGBTQ issues across Canada and in North America more generally, and despite his own sexual orientation – or perhaps because of it – Hatfield's government did little with respect to LGBTQ rights, and New Brunswick remained a very conservative province during his premiership.

This conservatism could be seen in one high-profile issue related to the gay community: AIDS and, in the Canadian context, the tainted blood scandal of the 1980s, which had resulted from blood transfusion recipients contracting a disease that had initially been associated largely with homosexual men. Though he had, essentially, been outed by the Krever Commission, more significant was the insinuation that Hatfield, because of his sexual orientation, had done little to address the issue of AIDS and how it was impacting both blood transfusion recipients and the gay community in the 1980s. As Douglas Elliott stated following his testimony at the inquiry, "in this case, I'm sorry to say, one of the reasons for the lack of pro-active approach [from Mr. Hatfield in and out of office] was not [overt] homophobia, it was because he didn't want to be thought of as deviant. It was fear of exposure. Yet knowing his progressive approach on other issues, if he'd been heterosexual, I'm sure he would have been more active."[103] Another, scholarly, assessment was that "Hatfield had weathered years of speculation about his sexual orientation; his desire to downplay those rumours was seen as an obstacle to lobbying the Hatfield government on behalf of gays and lesbians."[104] Though this point is debatable, and New Brunswick was probably not really out of line with the response of other governments in Canada on the issue, it is clear that Hatfield did little to address directly the tainted blood scandal – or, for that matter, other LGBTQ issues – during his time in office.

Another issue associated with the sexual revolution that emerged during Hatfield's time in office, and one in which he was more directly involved, was abortion. Despite

Trudeau's 1969 changes to the law, which allowed very limited access to abortion, the procedure was not available on demand, nor could it be provided outside of a hospital. The Abortion Caravan, a high-profile protest movement in 1970 that galvanized attention for the liberalization of the law, reflected the efforts of feminist activists in the Vancouver Women's Caucus and elsewhere to push the issue onto the national stage.[105] Many Canadian women were forced to leave the country to procure abortions; in many cases, since the practice was still illegal outside of hospitals, it was dangerous.[106] The Royal Commission on the Status of Women had made accessible abortion on demand one of its key recommendations. Meanwhile, in the United States, *Roe v. Wade* had legalized abortion, sparking social and culture conflict and helping revitalize the New Right as a political movement.

Dr. Henry Morgentaler (1923–2013) became a key figure in the battle for Canadian abortion rights. Establishing abortion clinics in Montreal and Toronto, Morgentaler directly challenged the laws that made procuring or providing an abortion a crime. Morgentaler's fight eventually found its way to the Supreme Court of Canada. In a famous 1988 case, *R. v. Morgentaler*, the court found that, for a variety of reasons (there were three separate decisions in favour and one dissent), the criminalization of abortion did infringe women's rights under the 1982 Charter of Rights and Freedoms, and that the law limiting abortion was unconstitutional and thus invalid. In 1990, the government of Brian Mulroney attempted, unsuccessfully, to pass new legislation regulating abortion.[107]

When it come to abortion, Hatfield was as inactive as he was on LGBTQ rights, or, at least, did little to challenge the conservative orthodoxy that prevailed in the province regarding the issue. While this is not surprising, given his political orientation, it is clear the Hatfield's policies regarding abortion were more conservative than most of those in the rest of Canada. During Morgentaler's legal fight in the 1980s to establish abortion clinics and overturn prohibitions on the procedure, Hatfield's government responded by passing Bill 92, "An Act to Amend an Act Respecting the New Brunswick Medical Society and the College of Physicians and Surgeons of New Brunswick" (1985), making it illegal for abortions to be performed outside of hospitals.

At that time, out of New Brunswick's three dozen hospitals, only four provided abortion services, making the procedure relatively difficult to procure; in 1984, only 267 abortions were performed in a province with a population of over 700,000, making New Brunswick's rate of abortions considerably lower than elsewhere in Canada. Although Bill 92 was eventually found unconstitutional in 1994, during the 1980s Hatfield increasingly embraced an anti-abortion position, a reflection of the province's regionalism and its cultural and religious personality – and clearly a contrast with Hatfield's own "non-traditional" persona. As the abortion question became increasingly polarized in New Brunswick during his last years in office, Hatfield acceded to the pressure applied by anti-abortion activists to keep New Brunswick one of Canada's least hospitable places for the procedure.[108]

What explains Richard Hatfield's unusual sexual revolution story and his conservative, seemingly contradictory positions on sexuality, LGBTQ rights, and abortion, given his own sexual orientation and his career as an unconventional politician who clearly often marched to the beat of his own drum?

Like Bricklin, Hatfield was a man of his times. His status as Canada's "bachelor" premier, one that only nominally concealed his sexuality, reflected the competing tensions among his multiple identities and roles. On the one hand, he plainly enjoyed the increasingly liberated, swinging '70s social and sexual culture that allowed him to flit across North America and the globe as New Brunswick's *enfant terrible*, hobnobbing with both the straight and gay glitterati of the disco scene but also getting the province's name out there (just so long as *he* wasn't out). The Bricklin SV1 had been a perfect vehicle for that persona, one that could only add to his profile.

On the other hand, Hatfield was a conservative, male politician from straight-laced New Brunswick, one who actively encouraged heteronormative muscle-car masculinity as an economic, electoral, and image-making ideal for his province and his own political prospects. He clearly basked in the limelight, but, in a world where business could have a tremendous impact on politics – Richard Hatfield's vocation and the purpose of his being – he had to take care of the province's commerce, which meant dealing with the economy and development, and, ultimately, with business.

Of course, doing so wasn't easy. In the 1970s, business itself was changing. This was especially true of the prominent business in which he found himself, the business of making automobiles – with his business partner, Malcolm Bricklin.

CHAPTER SIX

Business (The State)

***Dream Car* Song 11: "Lord, Mr. Ford," Jerry Reed, 1973**

In the 1970s, the business of manufacturing and selling cars fundamentally changed. And because the automobile manufacturing sector was the core of American enterprise and the largest component of the North American economy, the changes that occurred in the auto industry mirrored a wider and deeper, more essential transformation of American business itself and in how the broader economy and society functioned.

Some of these changes were seemingly abrupt and obvious, such as the three-crested wave of safety, fuel-economy, and emissions regulations that had quite literally reshaped the way cars looked, how they were built, and how they operated.[1] Another equally transformative indicator of just how quickly and permanently the North American car market was changing was the tsunami of foreign cars, mostly Japanese, that had begun to crash upon North America's shores starting in the early 1970s, snapped up by eager consumers content to upend a half-century of car-buying habits. Even more dramatically, and as a direct consequence of these seismic developments, the shocking near demise of Chrysler at the end of the decade, and the uneven financial results and deteriorating market shares of General Motors and Ford, was the clearest sign that it was no longer business as usual in the North American auto sector.[2]

But there were other equally important, yet less easily perceptible, shifts that reflected deeper, underlying transformations in *why* automobiles were being built at all, in *how* they were manufactured, in *who* manufactured them, and *where* in North America they were manufactured.

Henry Ford had been obsessed with putting the world on wheels. So too, was Billy Durant, the Dodge Brothers, Walter Chrysler, Charles Kettering, and so many of the other pioneers of the early industry. To be sure, those first few generations of automotive giants wanted to make as much money as the next fellow, and their pursuit of profits undoubtedly played a central role in their obsession. But it is also true that they were just as fixated on their products and production processes – and the broader goal of mass automobility – as they were on their profits. Even as Henry's era gave way to leaders such as Alfred Sloan, Henry Ford II, and Lee Iacocca, the mission of *making cars* was still Detroit's primary business.

Yet, by the 1960s, the thinking behind building and selling cars had started to change. Over the course of the Big Three's long reign as the apogee of American business, entrepreneurial automotive innovators and promoters had become managers. Managers had become organization men. And organization men, whose only aim and sole criteria of success was to make the corporation profitable, had come to dominate car companies. By the time Bricklin arrived on the scene in 1974, automobile businesses were organizations that were no longer in the control of auto men, but of men for whom producing or even selling cars was not their primary calling. Malcolm Bricklin's dream may have been to become a Horatio Alger–like success story of entrepreneurship – to secure his spot in the pantheon of automotive greatness with his sexy yet safe sports car. But in order to do so, Bricklin had to navigate the expectations and realities of what the quintessential automotive business leader had become by the 1970s and, just as importantly, what the auto business itself was becoming.

Unfortunately for Bricklin, when he started his car company in 1973, the idea of making innovative *things* like the SV1 was in the process of being sacrificed on the altar of a religious revival in American business: a singular focus on *profit* or, in the language of the day, "shareholder value." The "American system" of manufacturing, as historian David Hounshell called it, and of manufacturing in an American way – how American industry had asserted itself in the world since the late nineteenth century and had subsequently transformed itself with the advent of the car and the "ethos of mass production" – had given way to a new philosophy.[3] In 1921, Alfred Sloan had made the case that "the primary object of the corporation … [is] to make money, *not just to make motor cars*."[4] In the 1970s, this aphorism had seemingly been more starkly reformulated by GM executive Thomas Aquinas Murphy, who was credited with the apocryphal statement that "General Motors is not in the business of making cars. It is in the business of making money."[5]

Spurred on by this philosophical shift in why cars were built, equally fundamental transformations were starting to take place by the early 1970s in the how, who, and where of the automobile business. These quickly evolving aspects of auto manufacturing were likely less apparent to ordinary car-buyers than were the millions of Hondas, Toyotas, and Subarus suddenly appearing on North America's sprawling roads and highways, but they were just as profound. The industry's long-standing Fordist practices were being challenged by increasing automation, robotics, and, most importantly, a much more efficient and responsive Toyota production system. At the same time, the gleam of the US auto industry was showing its first signs of rust, as producers increasingly looked beyond America's manufacturing clusters, and the country's borders, to make their cars (and as consumers bought more and more foreign cars). Increasingly, auto work was deliberately being shifted to lower-paid or non-unionized workers, and production and geographical disruptions roiled the industry.[6]

If the auto business itself was changing in the 1970s, so too was the government's role, especially in how it related to and impacted the automobile industry. Paradoxically, over the course of this transformative decade, the state's place in auto-sector change simultaneously grew and shrunk. On the one hand, state action directed towards the industry reflected a more aggressive willingness by government to interfere in the internal functioning of the auto business and its market. The state did so by imposing all those new regulatory burdens on the automakers with respect to safety, emissions, and fuel economy. Also for the first time, governments started to utilize financial incentives to influence the investment location decisions of the manufacturers. The state also, ultimately, intervened directly in the fate of auto companies deemed too big, or too important to their economies, to be left to the dictates of the market, either through direct ownership (Bricklin) or government bailouts (Chrysler).[7]

On the other hand, governments had concurrently receded in their influence by surrendering to the auto companies some of the most powerful sovereign and economic tools at their disposal. In ratifying the 1965 auto pact, the US and Canadian governments had, in exchange for promises of greater efficiency and increased employment on a continental basis, willingly erased their own national borders, relinquishing the tariffs that they had imposed for decades on the manufacturers' products. Because of the treaty's continentalizing impact, the Big Three had truly become untethered from the restraints imposed by national boundaries and, after 1965, could roam across the Canada-US border, unencumbered by any national interest. Now, corporate economic self-interest would be maximally pursued, regardless of political geography.[8] To recoin a phrase, after the auto pact's passage, what was good for General Motors was no longer necessarily good for the United States.

In launching his new car venture precisely in 1973, and embarking on production in 1974, Malcolm Bricklin and General Vehicle Incorporated (GVI) encapsulated all these issues and their paradoxes: it revealed where the postwar American car business had been; where it stood in the 1970s as it dealt with these dramatic changes; and where it was headed to in a post-Fordist, increasingly globalized world. By examining GVI as a case study of a firm undergoing change, it becomes clear that, in its structure and its management practices, Bricklin's company – despite its small size and limited output – remained beholden to mid-twentieth-century Big Three expectations of what a successful automobile manufacturing firm looked like and how it should operate. Yet Bricklin's circumstances, as a one-vehicle start-up launched at an incredibly challenging moment of change for the industry, also forced the firm to utilize unorthodox and often innovative "outside-the-box" production practices and techniques in its attempt to succeed. When it came to its labour and governmental relations, from GVI's border-hopping structure and its unconventional production processes to its unusual partnership with government (at least for a North American firm), Bricklin did things differently. As a result, GVI anticipated and pursued many strategies and sectoral trends that would become standard practices in the industry after the 1970s.

In this sense, in manufacturing the SV1 in the way that he did, Malcolm Bricklin's managerial actions made him, his company, and his car anachronisms in automobile industrial modernity's present, but also a precursor to its postmodern future. If, in the 1970s, the business of cars, America's business, was undergoing transformations both obvious and intrinsic, Malcolm Bricklin, in his role as president and chairman of General Vehicle Incorporated – as the archetypal *manager* of an automobile manufacturing firm – was a uniquely telling indicator of just how profound these changes were.

Part I. Why – The Philosophy of Cars: From Entrepreneurs to Organization Men; From Products to Profits

Since the dawn of the horseless age, making money had, of course, always been a core motivating aspect of the motor car industry and its original entrepreneurs. But profitability alone was not the sole inspiration driving those pioneers, nor was it necessarily so for their mid-century successors. Because of automobility's society-changing impact, there had always been other reasons for making cars, beyond simply making money. Some were noble, some were paternalistic, some were practical, and some were not rooted in money at all.

Henry Ford, the greatest automotive entrepreneur of all, had as his abiding objective the democratization of mobility for ordinary people. For all his shortcomings (and there were many), Ford's vision of the social utility of mass automobility transcended the profit motive and even aspired to what he would have considered to be a greater, collective, good. Coming, as he did, from a farming background in Michigan, Ford saw his inexpensive, mass-produced Model T primarily as a way by which to improve ordinary people's lives. His magical car did so by connecting communities, transcending the time and distance to markets and towns, and easing the burdens of rural loneliness. Ford's thrifty, democratizing ways were most apparent in his relentless drive to push the price of the Model T ever downward, with the goal that every American (and whomever else) could afford one of his dependable little cars.[9]

Certainly, as the creed of nineteenth-century liberalism dictated, Ford saw himself as the main beneficiary of his innovative ideas. But he also wanted to share his wealth, as so many successful paternalists did. Ford understood that the mass automobility he had wrought could generate wealth and spread prosperity, and that profits were not the primary goal of the Model T. Instead, the purpose of the Tin Lizzie was, according to Ford, "to give employment, and send out the car where people can use it . . . and *incidentally* to make money." As if to emphasize the point, Ford, one of the greatest capitalist figures of all time, declared that "business is a service, not a bonanza."[10]

Ford's belief in principles over profits was sincere. Many key episodes in his career were shaped by his democratizing and populist virtues, even if they ultimately also helped his bottom line, or were later obscured by his increasing bitterness and isolation. Ford's pivotal, if sometimes forgotten, 1911 courtroom victory over the Selden patent freed all auto manufacturers from an early attempt to monopolize the industry. His introduction, in 1914, of the five-dollar day, which tripled his workers' wages and was decried by Wall Street as a socialist plot, remains among the most studied and controversial episodes in labour history. The five-dollar day-made Fordist consumption possible, generated a global, fawning fame for the man and his firm, and helped spark the Great Migration.[11] In his 1919 courtroom feud with the Dodge brothers, who owned 10 per cent of Ford's company and wanted their share of its spectacular profits, Henry fought for the right to *not* pay dividends but, instead, to plough the money back into the Rouge Plant to make Ford Motor

Figure 6.1. "A Giant Who Works for You," Ford Motor ad, 1924.

even more efficient, as a service to the people, "a giant who works for you." Even leaving aside Ford Motor's actions during the wars, Henry held the conviction that the great business of car making was as much for other ends as it was for making money.[12]

Ford's democratizing notion of a utilitarian "everyman" car was ultimately defeated in the 1920s by Alfred Sloan's branded price ladder of "a car for every purse and purpose." Yet Sloan himself also understood that the auto sector, and especially GM, could, and should, claim a grander purpose beyond simply making money. For his part, Sloan emphasized the importance of bringing order and efficiency to markets, of finding a way to keep the industry going during the challenging interwar period, of transitioning the giant sector towards the war effort (and then back again to manufacturing automobiles), and of attempting to perfect the corporate form. At the same time, GM also worked to propagate the gospel of automobility, which meant spreading modern American ideals about capitalism and consumption to the rest of the world.[13] Obviously, all these motives were profit-driving, yet Sloan's legacy, like Ford's, consists of more than simply increasing shareholder returns.[14]

Even in the 1950s, at the height of the Big Three's dominance, the industry's leaders remained committed to more than simple profit-taking. In 1953, GM president Charles E. Wilson was nominated to become US defence secretary. Wilson, who had worked at GM since 1912, was being questioned in Congress about potential conflicts of interest, given his long-standing service to the firm (and his shares in the company, which he sold before joining government). During the hearing, Wilson was infamously misquoted as stating that "what's good for General Motors is good for the United States." This misreported declaration quickly became a shorthand for corporate arrogance and avarice. Yet the actual transcript of Wilson's testimony before the Senate Armed Services Committee tells a different story:

> Q: Sen. Robert C. Hendrickson, Republican of New Jersey: Well now, I'm interested to know whether if a situation did arise where you had to make a decision which was extremely adverse to the interests of your stock and General Motors corporation or any of these other companies, or extremely adverse to the company, in the interests of the United States government, could you make that decision?
>
> A: Charles E. Wilson: Yes, sir. I could. I cannot conceive of one because for years I thought what was good for our country was good for General Motors, and vice versa. The difference did not exist.
>
> Our company is too big. It goes with the welfare of the country. Our contribution to the nation is considerable.[15]

Wilson was undeniably misquoted, even if one questioned whether GM's "contribution to the nation" was considerable, or not.[16]

When Henry Ford II took over his grandfather's ailing company in 1945 after returning from military service, "the Deuce's" own abiding goal was to save the family firm. The Ford Motor Company was not simply an automobile manufacturer bent on making money, it was the most potent instigator of American industrial modernity. Before the Second World War, Ford and its products had remade American society. During the war, Ford's Willow Run operation had churned out an astounding nine thousand B-24 bombers, helping to turn the tide in the Allies' favour and establishing American air supremacy. After the company's postwar revival, Ford became a symbol of prosperity and increasing economic equality, helping to create North America's middle class, at least for a large swath of the population. The massive 1956 Ford IPO was heralded as a way to share the company's success and wealth with ordinary Americans. Clearly, for much of the twentieth century, the business of making cars was more than simply about making money, even if those other considerations were sometimes difficult to discern, given the sector's astonishing postwar profits.

By the 1960s, a renewed debate was emerging about the overarching purpose of the auto industry and its broader impact upon society. Times had changed. The Nader revelations about GM had brought into sharp relief difficult questions about the sector's social utility, with tectonic implications for the industry. If Detroit was willing to sacrifice safety (and everything else good and noble it supposedly stood for) for the sake of profits, as Nader had charged, then the Big Three had lost whatever residue of Fordist societal benefit they could collectively point to. Ultimately, *Unsafe at Any Speed* was nothing less than a damning accusation that the auto industry – the wartime arsenal of democracy and the main agent of twentieth-century mobility, prosperity, and social change – had become a temple of irresponsible greed.

Nader's activist example sparked an unprecedented shareholder insurgency movement aimed at forcing corporations, and GM in particular, to take greater social responsibility for their activities. In 1970, a group of young lawyers (indirectly connected to Nader) formed the Campaign to Make General Motors Responsible, known as Campaign GM. Having purchased twelve shares in the company (out of 285 million outstanding common stocks), Campaign GM demanded that the world's largest and most profitable corporation focus its vast power on the problems for which it considered GM responsible, from safety issues and pollution to racial inequities to the firm's position on public transit. These "corporate guerilla fighters," as one journalist dubbed them, were supported by Maine senator Edmund Muskie, who accused GM of shirking its responsibility to address pollution. Only the most prominent of a host of shareholder revolts that emerged in the period, Campaign GM generated headlines and marked a signal moment in the growing discourse over the role of the corporation in society, one that provoked a sharp debate and contest about the profits, purpose, and impact of corporations – especially auto corporations.[17]

In fact, no less a figure than Milton Friedman, that rising luminary of market fundamentalism, recognized the threat posed by the GM insurrection, and its potential implications. In a seminal 1970 opinion piece published in the *New York*

Times Magazine, "The Social Responsibility of Business Is to Increase Its Profits," Friedman defiantly declared that the only duty of the corporation was to make money, and, in so doing, he launched the "shareholder value" counterrevolution in business.[18] Friedman's 3,000-word article, one of his most cited, celebrated, and condemned pieces, and "a staple" in introductory business ethics courses, became a signpost in the emerging neoliberal economic reaction to what he and his disciples saw as an attack on corporate prerogatives and the very essence and purpose of the modern firm. On the fiftieth anniversary of its publication, the *New York Times* referred to Friedman's article as "a free-market manifesto that changed the world." Tellingly, the 1970 "crusade" against GM (as Friedman called it) was the sole example of shareholder activism cited in the entire article.[19]

GM's own response to the shareholder revolt was equally strident. Though Campaign GM did manage to get a few of its proxy proposals onto the agenda at the company's 1970 and 1971 annual meetings, the insurgency was squelched. GM vociferously rebutted Campaign GM's accusations and cajoled institutional investors to support management. Major shareholders, including the Carnegie, Ford, and Rockefeller Foundations and multiple university endowments, either abstained or echoed Friedman's mantra as their reasons to vote the proposals down. In the end, Campaign GM never received more than 3 per cent of the shareholders' votes. But in GM's 1971 annual report, the company did list the measures it was taking to meet environmental and social concerns, though it reiterated that "it should be emphasized that our activities directed towards our national social objectives are possible only because GM has been able to earn the profit necessary to meet its traditional obligations." Nonetheless, according to one contemporary analyst, a "feeling prevailed that the campaign had made a significant contribution to corporate life, and that things would not be quite the same as before."[20]

Just as importantly, the campaign's defeat also reflected the fact that, at this point in the firm's evolution, GM's corporate culture (and its organizational structure) had shifted perceptibly. By the early 1970s, many of GM's original and even succeeding generations of auto men had moved on. Charles Kettering had died in 1958; Sloan in 1966. Engineering chief Ed Cole left GM in 1974. Corvette boss Zora Arkus-Duntov retired in 1975. John Z. DeLorean had left GM in a huff in 1973, complaining that "creativity, innovation and foresight" were being "neglected for short-term profit."[21] Financial men were almost in complete control of the executive positions and especially the overseeing committees that dictated the giant firm's direction.[22] Indeed, in 1974, Thomas Aquinas Murphy, an accountant by trade and a GM finance veteran, became the giant firm's leader. Just three years before, Murphy had admitted that "despite spending 32 years in the automobile business, I suddenly realized I didn't know the first thing about an automobile, let alone the mechanics of meeting a production schedule."[23] The ideal corporate organization man, Murphy is best remembered as the GM CEO credited with the infamous reappraisal of Sloan's statement about the primary purpose of the General Motors Corporation.[24]

In Dearborn, Henry Ford II echoed GM's stern reaction, claiming, in 1972, that profits had *always* been the defining mission of his company, despite his grandfather's quaint populist views. "I believe," the Deuce declared, echoing Friedman, "that the social responsibility of the corporation today is fundamentally the same as it has always been: to earn profits for shareholders by serving consumer wants with maximum efficiency." He did add, however, and perhaps in deference to his grandfather's belief that business was a service, not a bonanza, that this was "not the whole matter, but it is the heart of the matter."[25]

All these developments – the Campaign GM proxy battle, Friedman's seminal response, and corporate Detroit's hardening attitudes towards its role in society – reflected a philosophical transition reshaping the auto business, and American business more broadly: the accelerating financialization of the economy. By the early 1970s, the financialization of the American economy was already well on its way.[26] The auto industry's central place in this shift – and *why* the philosophy of making cars had changed – was as much about Detroit leadership's changing values as it was about the production processes, offshore competition, and shifting consumer attitudes that were buffeting the industry and challenging its profitability. At its core, the changes stemmed from quickly evolving managerial ideas about the importance of making things, and of making money.[27]

By the end of the tumultuous decade, two particularly incisive books recognized just how profound this change had been. In 1983, Seymour Melman, the antiwar academic and shrewd observer of American capitalism, published *Profits without Production*, a scathing denunciation of the transformation occurring in American business, and especially the role of corporate managers in instigating that change. By the 1960s, Melman contended, at a time when the American intelligentsia was "seized with dreams of the post-industrial society," the "new ideal type" of manager had become "the financier-strategist, the shrewd, nimble operator who combined disparate firms into conglomerates that maximized the short-term profit-taking opportunities afforded by tax laws, securities transfers, the milking of production assets and other financial legerdemain." In this world, Melman observed, "the optimum condition is profit without any production."[28]

While Melman acknowledged that other tactics – including the "large-scale export of finance capital," the "accompanying failure to invest and reinvest in US based production," and the growth of offshore and low-wage locales for business – were also driving the shift to financialization, he laid most of the blame at the feet of a particular breed of executive manager. "The money making manager," Melman accusingly wrote, is "conditioned to maximize the 'bottom line' short term balance sheet, period." In his hands, "the quarterly report becomes primary evidence of good management, and any projection beyond one year is long-range planning." The Big Three came in for a particularly scathing critique: "The US automobile industry is more than an industrial colossus: it has long been a central feature of America's self image. Detroit made of mass production an American and then a worldwide force." This had changed. "If the United States no longer excels at rolling cars off the assembly line," Melman despaired, "what was left?"[29]

Three years later, journalist David Halberstam published *The Reckoning: A Challenge to America's Greatness*, a massive, 752-page examination of the post-1973 decline of the American auto sector. Focusing on a comparison of Ford and Nissan to explain the dramatically changing fortunes of the US and Japanese auto industries, Halberstam's weighty tome was particularly withering towards the new American corporate ethos, wherein "the actual making of goods had become a burden." In Halberstam's view, "management had become bloated," and "few of the men running industrial companies had spent very much time in the pit, working in factories, learning the process of manufacturing." One reviewer of Halberstam's book wrote that it was "old news" that "Henry Ford the First made money so that he could make cars," but that, by the 1970s, "the men who rule his company and others of great size are more inclined to make cars so that they can make money."[30]

Malcolm Bricklin decided to launch his new car venture at a time when the philosophy behind building cars was undergoing a subtle yet important transformation. His own reasons for creating the SV1 unquestionably included making money, but Bricklin, like the auto entrepreneurs of the past, had additional motives. In focusing on safety, Bricklin aimed to establish himself as a genuine automotive innovator, moving the industry towards a better (and potentially profitable) new direction. And by making his safety vehicle a sexy sports car, he clearly had other, less material motivations for building the SV1.

Yes, Bricklin clearly wanted to make money, just as Henry Ford had. But like Ford, Bricklin also saw car-making as having other purposes too. Unfortunately for Bricklin, his car appeared at precisely the moment when the auto business and its leaders were busy jettisoning any such notions as incompatible with their industry's bottom line. Bricklin, almost blissfully unaware of these developments, started his company by – logically – mimicking many of the modern structures and practices of the Big Three. After all, that was how American companies manufactured cars and made money. Of course, given the limitations of his firm, when it came to building his SV1, he also had to do things differently.

***Dream Car* Song 12: "Spark Plugs," Allen Cole and Paul Ledoux, 2010**

Part II. How, Who, and Where – A Case Study in Building a Dream: Bricklin, Managing Auto Firms, and Making Cars in the Postwar Period

Finally.

After all that futuristic innovation with safety, all that promotion and showmanship and sex, it was finally time for Bricklin to get down to the business of building the Safety Vehicle-1. As *Motor Trend* magazine plaintively wondered when production began to ramp up at the company's Saint John assembly facility, "Malcolm Bricklin has proven he can build one car. Now, the question is: can he build *thousands* of cars?"[31]

In the summer of 1974, Bricklin had on hand five custom-built SV1s, effectively prototypes, that he'd used for promoting the car at various events, including the June launch in New York, and for some testing.[32] Even if he didn't quite recognize just how difficult building the car would be, Bricklin did realize that jumping from a few prototypes to mass producing thousands of SV1s could not be accomplished in exactly the same way that the Big Three manufactured their cars, even as he mostly followed in their footsteps. Those giant corporations had well-developed organizational and managerial structures, huge pools of capital, decades of institutional industrial knowledge, massive facilities, established networks of parts suppliers, complex manufacturing processes, hundreds of thousands of workers, and – most importantly – the levels of vertical and horizontal integration necessary to economically build an entire car, from start to finish.[33]

All of those elements were absolutely essential for car-making. By the 1970s, the sheer complexity and cost of building cars had become tremendously challenging. Designing, sourcing, machining, testing, transporting, and assembling engines, transmissions, chassis, bodies, electronics, upholstery, paint, windshields, and innumerable parts and materials, not to mention the regulatory requirements to make cars safer, less polluting, and more fuel-efficient, meant that successfully producing a mass-manufactured car from scratch was, as Bricklin quickly came to realize, something of a miracle. Since the 1920s, the business of building cars had become the purview of only a few giant corporations for a very simple reason: it was incredibly difficult to manufacture motor vehicles without an army of engineers, machinists, assembly-line workers, custodians, managers, lawyers, accountants, marketers, and salespeople. Even by the 1940s and 1950s, any notion of a Horatio Alger–like tale of an individual single-handedly coaxing a new car into existence was just that, a tale – almost a legend.

In the post–Second World War period, there had, in fact, been only two serious attempts to launch a new American car company. Both had occurred in the late 1940s, when the war's disruption opened opportunities to new manufacturers outside of the Big Three (and for the tiny handful of independents that remained). One was the Kaiser-Frazer Corporation. Wartime shipbuilder Henry J. Kaiser started his car company in 1946, manufacturing a number of vehicles, including the famous Jeep, the "**G**eneral **P**urpose" military vehicle, for civilian use. But he ceased production in 1953 after spending $50 million, unable to keep up with the tremendous expenditures demanded by the industry. (The Jeep brand continued to exist under the Willys name, was bought by American Motors in 1970, and was subsequently acquired by Chrysler in 1987.) The other attempt was the legendary 1948 Tucker Torpedo, but Preston Tucker never managed to get to the assembly stage: he produced a batch of only forty-seven vehicles, after spending $40 million.[34] As the first American start-up attempt to mass manufacture a new vehicle in nearly three decades, Bricklin's venture was not for the faint of heart.

If the innovative and promotional entrepreneurial archetypes bequeathed by the automobile industry help to explain why Bricklin was initially successful in his dream to develop and sell the idea of the SV1, then the nature of the postwar automotive industry within which the Bricklin company found itself can shed much light on his managerial abilities in leading an automobile manufacturing firm and, ultimately, on his failure. Furthermore, outlining a biographical case study of the Bricklin firm reveals that in five key aspects – its structure, management/personnel, manufacturing, labour, and government relations – GVI and its subsidiaries simultaneously reflected many facets of automobility's high industrial corporate and Fordist legacies, its transitional and challenging 1970s, and its rapidly emerging industrial postmodern future.

1. Structure: GVI (Delaware), Parent Corporation of Bricklin Vehicle Corporation (Scottsdale) and Bricklin Canada Ltd. (Saint John)

At the core of the automobile business was the multidivisional corporate structure (the m-division), the edifice that Durant had initiated almost by accident and that Sloan had come closest to perfecting. The m-division was largely pioneered by and

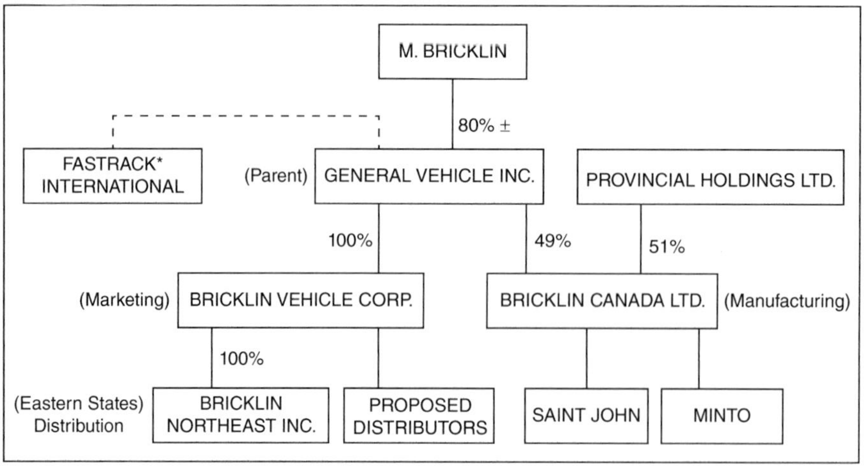

Figure 6.2. The m-division comes to Bricklin, 1973.

reached its modern zenith in the auto industry. It is, to this day, a residual cornerstone of how the industry's main players operate. Logically, then, in 1973, when Malcolm Bricklin created General Vehicle Incorporated (the name itself an echo of General Motors Corporation), he copied the multidivisional configuration that had been the basis of the industry for half a century. Based on its organizational chart, GVI did indeed look like a miniature replica of one of the Big Three, with their sprawling, multiple divisions. However, in attempting to mimic the modern automotive corporate structure, a startup like Bricklin's lacked the scale or scope of a typical auto giant. As the result, the company took the m-division format to such an extreme as to make a mockery of it.[35]

Even for such a small-scale auto operation, Bricklin had an incredibly decentralized organization, with offices and branches all over North America. GVI, the parent, was incorporated in 1971 in Delaware (where, Fredericks and Chambers caustically noted, corporate regulations were "so lax that companies . . . are not even required to file annual returns").[36] Like the Big Three, GVI had a finance office in New York City, where all the finance men were. The company's design, technology, and parts-purchasing centre (about 120 people) was in Livonia, Michigan, where all the auto men were. The sales, service, and distribution operations for the company (with about thirty employees) were based out of Whippany, New Jersey, which was ideal for the Eastern Seaboard market and Bricklin's contacts in the dealer world. Unusually for an auto firm, the parent company's head office, which employed fifteen people, was in Scottsdale, Arizona, where Bricklin lived. There was no actual reason for the Arizona headquarters beyond Bricklin's cowboy affectation

Figure 6.3. Bricklin operations: Livonia, MI (engineering) (above) and Whippany, NJ (sales, service) (below).

(though the company had its research and development office in Phoenix, with eight Bricklin employees).[37]

From Scottsdale, Bricklin also controlled Bricklin Vehicle Corporation (BVC), the American marketing and sales subsidiary of GVI. Through BVC, Bricklin established US regional distribution subsidiaries, which sold the cars to dealers, including Bricklin Northeast Inc., Bricklin Midwest Inc., and Bricklin South Inc. (Bricklin Southwest Inc., was coming). This part of the operation was similar to the kind of distribution network he had set up at Subaru. BVC bought SV1s at wholesale prices (originally, $5,400; eventually, $7,200) and imported the cars from its Canadian production sister-subsidiary division, Bricklin Canada Ltd. (BCL, est. 1973). BCL, which made the cars, was majority-owned by the New Brunswick government (initially the province owned 51 per cent of the company; by December 1975, it owned 67 per cent). Like any good Big Three executive, Bricklin himself had to visit all these sites on a regular basis. He spent one week a month in New Brunswick, one week in Livonia, and the rest on the road selling the vehicle and visiting dealers, which he often did with a company-chartered plane (he also used a helicopter to shuttle from his Scottsdale office to the firm's Arizona test facility).[38] In an earlier age, Sloan had used a customized rail car to visit GM's far-flung operations, especially its dealers.[39]

Despite its clear, traditional, m-division organizational chart, GVI's real-world operation was decidedly messy. To start, Bricklin never made it entirely clear what exactly the relationship was between GVI and BVC. The former was ostensibly the "parent" company of BVC, but the two were very close, so close, in fact, that it was difficult to see any separation between them, with Bricklin running both. Then there was GVI's relationship with BCL: the "divisions" may have, on paper, looked like divisions at Ford or GM, but they did not operate as such, at least not for accounting purposes. This muddiness came in handy for Bricklin in keeping New Brunswick officials in the dark, especially when they wanted a clearer idea of who was running things and what was going on with their money at BCL.[40]

Indeed, less than a year into the operation, the New Brunswick official tasked with keeping a close watch on BCL and the project's progress (the government had a majority ownership, after all) could barely hide his frustration at this organizational opaqueness. G. Stephen Wheatley, the secretary-treasurer of Provincial Holdings Ltd. (and a named shareholder himself), told his government superiors that "we must continue to place emphasis on accomplishing the concept of BCL as a separate entity." It was "only through such a policy," he observed, "that the best interests of BCL shareholders" could be "properly safeguarded."[41] As for GVI itself, Wheatley recognized, even from the outset, that there were "serious deficiencies in the organizational structure as it relates to a clear understanding of authority and responsibility." Accounting functions were underdeveloped, and management efficiencies required significant improvement. Government frustration grew at Bricklin's inability or unwillingness to listen to his partner's advice.[42]

It's fair to ask why Hatfield or anyone in his government didn't vet GVI more thoroughly, particulary with respect to its organizational and structural dysfunction and Bricklin's own (lack of) management fundamentals. Structurally, Malcolm was, in his view and the view of his backers, building a first-rank auto company, one that was going to take on the "majors." Major auto companies had multiple divisions and offices scattered across North America. Major auto companies also had arcane and impenetrable financials, though, in Bricklin's case, this was less a consequence of complexity than of competence or obfuscation. For those both inside and outside Bricklin's corporation, the way GVI was being run made perfect sense. It was Bricklin's version of the auto industry's corporate template, which he was doing his best to follow.

When it came to GVI's senior leadership, the company's investors – namely, New Brunswick and the banks, whose money had mostly been guaranteed by the government – assumed that Bricklin and his associates knew what they were doing. After all, he had seemingly done *very* well with Subaru, which was thriving by 1974. Moreover, Malcolm, who could cast a wonderful spell of performative financialization, looked and played the part of the auto executive extraordinarily well – at least that of the entrepreneurial promoter (all the newspapers and magazines said so). At the same time, GVI's other directors included executives from well-known entities like Diners Club and the Holiday Inn, bankers, lawyers, and the former importer of Fiat cars to America.[43] All of this was convincing, particularly the company's initial prospectus, which confidently stated that "Mr. Bricklin has had considerable experience with manufacturing and marketing of transportation vehicles."[44] The latter may have been true, but the former was a work in progress, as the SV1 was Bricklin's first attempt to manufacture anything, let alone cars.

But it was enough for Hatfield and his government to put their faith in Bricklin. In 1974, at the start of production, economic growth minister Paul Creaghan did his best to reassure legislative sceptics and the public that Bricklin and his leadership team were hiring good people in senior management roles. "I am impressed by the type of people this company has been able to attract," he said, pointing to the testimonial of Jack Hennesey, a former assistant plant manager and twenty-four-year veteran at Ford of Canada, who was hired to run BCL in Saint John. Hennesey, a Canadian who looked like a trustworthy old industry hand, told Creaghan that he "would not be there if it [the venture] wasn't feasible."[45] Moreover, according to Creaghan, Malcolm Bricklin *had* been checked out, and he was 100 per cent simon-pure.

2. Management/Personnel (Including Distribution/Sales): GVI, BVC, BCL

In terms of senior personnel, Bricklin certainly did hire some experienced auto people, especially in the development stage and at the beginning of production at BCL. The initial roster of Bricklin executives and managers seemed to read like a who's who of Detroit mid-level auto management, "an impressive management team," according to *Autoweek and Competition Press*.[46] GVI boasted, "without question and without exception," according to New Brunswick deputy minister of economic growth Harry Nason, "completely professional automobile experts." Senior officers included a number of men with significant auto business experience: Jack Reese, former head of Renault's and Mercedes's American sales operations; George B. Rahman and Douglas Bernhardt, who spent twenty-two and twenty-five years, respectively, with late-1940s disruptor Kaiser Jeep and then with Chrysler; and Richard C. Vollmer, who worked with Chrysler for ten years, including a production stint in Argentina.[47] Bricklin recruited Terry Tanner from Ford to be GVI's chief engineering manager, a job Tanner said his wife thought he was crazy to take. But for someone "used to working as a cog in an assembly line," Tanner found Bricklin's dream "to build a stupid car" irresistible.[48]

But the reality was that neither Bricklin nor his father, Albert (also a GVI executive), had any real experience in auto manufacturing, though they did have a business background and quite a record in promotion. The family had started in hardware, and most of Malcolm's expertise was in franchising and distribution deals. Even the Subaru venture had been an innovative distribution arrangement with the Japanese and had nothing to do with designing or building a vehicle. This kind of nonconformity was fine for making some import money, or even starting a car company that was a sales operation (Durant had started his sales career in cigars), but not so much for managing a firm that was actually trying to mass produce motor vehicles (see, again, Durant).

Relatively soon after SV1 production began, Bricklin recognized that he did not quite have the ability or experience to run a car company and that it was necessary to bring someone else in. At one point, he nearly struck a deal to hire John Z. DeLorean as GVI company president, for an astronomical $1.6 million salary. As the young, brash General Motors engineer who had famously launched the 1964 Pontiac GTO, become GM's VP, and then dramatically quit in January 1973, DeLorean was perfect for the Bricklin firm's image. Unfortunately, he called Bricklin back to say that the $1.6 million figure he had agreed to was *after* taxes. The real problem, Bricklin later admitted, was more about "whose name was on the back of the car."[49] Succumbing to the tenor of the times, in January 1975 Bricklin ultimately settled on a financial person, a money man, to become president of both

GVI and BCL (Bricklin was chair). Ralph Henry happened to be a former senior vice-president of the First Pennsylvania Bank, the outfit that had lent Bricklin $3 million.[50] Nonetheless, the government's outside assessors felt that "on the basis of his past record and reputation there was every expectation" that Henry "would prove to be highly qualified and an ideal person to play the role of the first senior business executive to join the project."[51]

But within a few months, questions started to be raised concerning Henry's "proficiency" and competence. In May 1975, he was booted as president of GVI by Bricklin, who, "rather in the form and scenario of a comic opera," fired Henry, then "forgave him," and then replaced him with his father.[52] For his part, even before becoming president of GVI, Albert Bricklin had already become an overweening presence at the firm. BCL's first president, Jean de Villers, who had worked at Renault, resigned in 1973 because of what he described as Albert's constant interference in company affairs, as had a number of the original automotive staff who had initially been drawn to Bricklin's vision. At one point, Bricklin had to put down a "near-rebellion" in Livonia over the engineering staff's unhappiness at the operation of the firm. Jack Hennesey left in August 1974, just as production was starting. Albert was "why the executives kept leaving," according to H.A. Fredericks.[53]

Albert was not the only familial hiring. By the time the company had run its course, Bricklin had also hired his mother, sister, brother-in-law, uncle, and girlfriend into GVI or BCL positions, with generous salaries.[54] If Bricklin's hires weren't family members, they were his associates, even in the Canadian part of the operation. Not until the spring of 1975, nearly two years after the initial Bricklin agreement with the province, did New Brunswick gain control of BCL's board of directors and start to push Malcolm to cut GVI's bloated salaries and expenses.[55] One journalist dryly noted that "money that should have gone to engineering was diverted to sybaritic lifestyles and flackery."[56]

Yet, in all this, Bricklin was simply following some of the great traditions of twentieth-century automotive management. Nepotism and cronyism were not surprising in a car company. After all, the great man himself, Henry Ford, had indulged his cronies to the point of having his security thug, Harry Bennett, essentially run the massive firm in the 1930s and 1940s.[57] Grandson Henry Ford II, who booted Bennett, had taken over after his father, Edsel, passed away in 1941. The Deuce had been running the family firm for nearly three decades by the time Bricklin started his company. This was what happened in family firms, especially family auto firms: Fords ran Ford, Toyodas ran Toyota, Agnellis ran Fiat, Chungs ran Hyundai, Quandts ran BMW, and so on, even today. It is not surprising that GVI, as a family firm, would be run by Bricklins, even if the manufacturing arm of the company was owned by the

New Brunswick government. As Bricklin himself once put it, "I love nepotism. My friends and family are smarter than most people and they certainly care more."[58]

Along with all his family and friends in the company, Bricklin also had a special relationship with the network of Bricklin dealers he had recruited as president of BVC. This made sense, as Bricklin was primarily a salesman, an *automobile dealer*. He was, in a way, one of them.

In twentieth-century North America, the word "dealer," and especially "dealership" could, like the word "accident," mean but one thing – the product itself needed no mention. Automobile dealers remain the purest distillation of the archetypical automotive promoter, always hustling, one car at a time. They were an American invention that, by the 1920s, had completely reshaped the economic landscape of North America, one Main Street at a time. Dealers, and dealerships, were everywhere, even in remote places like Bouctouche, New Brunswick, where a young K.C. Irving was toiling away selling Model Ts, one of over nine thousand Ford dealers by 1923.[59] Automobile dealers were the greatest modern salesmen, the embodiment of franchising, the biggest advertisers, and, in North America, often the largest single employer in a town. The modern art of the deal, many sales techniques, and basic questions of trust in the marketplace were established to a large degree by ordinary people's interactions with automobile salesmen in automotive dealerships.[60]

Unsurprisingly, Bricklin loved dealers and their dealerships almost as much as he loved deals. By 1975, he had signed up over three hundred dealers across eighteen US states, each of whom paid between $5,000 and $8,860 in franchise fees.[61] Taking Bricklin dealers on tours, showering them with favours, visiting with them, holding dealer events, and having his mother as his effective head of customer relations were all in Bricklin's wheelhouse. Sales matters, connecting with people, and schmoozing dealers came easily to Bricklin and were areas where his promotional abilities allowed him to excel.

In building the firm's organizational structure and personnel and its dealer network, Bricklin could largely follow the template laid down by the Big Three and depend upon his own abilities, such as they were. Managing an automotive firm that would actually manufacture a car in mass quantity was something else entirely, as Bricklin would soon discover.

3. Manufacturing: BCL, Saint John, Overall Manufacturing Operations/Production Process

Over the course of its two-year-long existence as a manufacturing operation, from June 1973 until September 1975, BCL's production processes were an anachronism of inherited Fordist practices mixed with some undeniably innovative nods towards a future of leaner manufacturing. On the one hand, BCL's facilities and production techniques in some ways echoed Henry Ford's Highland Park factory (1910–27) more than his gigantic and much more efficient Rouge Plant (1919–). Designed by architect Albert Kahn, "suffused with technology," and known as the Crystal Palace, Highland Park "blurred the line between man and machine" as the famous machine-age site of the first moving assembly line.[62] But as a functioning factory, it was hampered by being a multistorey building, one that experienced some difficult industrial mass manufacturing birth pangs in the 1910s. For his part, Bricklin ended up having his own production inefficiently spread over two buildings. Moreover, with inexperienced workers, only a few experienced managers, and no institutional memory of production, Bricklin and BCL were very much "learning by doing" when it came to assembly, as had Ford and his workers. Finally, BCL's economies of scale and some of its techniques were rather rudimentary in comparison to the massive factories of the high industrial period (carpeting in the SV1, for example, was hand-sewn).[63] Nonetheless, despite these distinctions, Bricklin's system unavoidably followed many Fordist production principles, including the assembly line.

On the other hand, Bricklin's modest circumstances meant that he simply couldn't achieve the level of production that was expected of a fully developed modern auto manufacturer. He had to make do. He had to innovate in his production processes. It just so happened that Bricklin was developing his traditional-yet-unorthodox SV1 production methods at a moment of significant change in the industry. By the early 1970s, the Fordist system was being profoundly challenged and changed by increasing automation, robotics, and, above all, competition from the emerging Toyota production system (TPS).

A revolutionary production and management philosophy and approach, the TPS had been developed by Toyota founder Eiji Toyoda (1913–2013) and industrial engineer Taiichi Ohno (1912–90) between 1948 and 1975. In the early 1950s, Toyoda had visited Ford's massive River Rouge plant, and while he was awed by the scale of the operation, he saw it as wasteful, too.[64] To improve on Fordism, the "Toyota Way" aimed to eliminate waste (*muda*) and to make manufacturing function as a system of continuous improvement (*kaizen*). It did so by emphasizing just-in-time (JIT) delivery of parts, reduced inventories (*kanban*), flexible manufacturing, modularization of components for subassembly, employment empowerment, and, above all, a focus on quality. By the 1970s, the success of the TPS, as Womack, Jones, and Roos chronicled in their seminal book, *The Machine That Changed the World*, had created lean manufacturing, an essential element of the third industrial revolution's emergence.[65]

Appearing at this pivotal moment in industrial modernity's transitional evolution, Bricklin developed his own method of lean production, one that reflected both manufacturing's Fordist legacy and its post-Fordist future. The SV1's glossy sales brochure declared as much:

> The Bricklin combines innovative technology with tried and proven components. We also had a basic advantage in that we started from scratch and didn't need to scrap existing assembly lines or expensive production equipment. Additionally, our production facilities have been designed to be flexible enough to allow us to constantly incorporate additional safety features into the cars as they are developed.[66]

BCL's transitional production model could be seen in two key approaches. First, Bricklin's slimmed-down process emphasized an early form of modularization and just-in-time delivery. "From the manufacturing man's point of view," declared BCL operations manager Albert Reynar in June 1975, building the SV1 was "a dream."[67] Reynar, a former AMC International director of manufacturing and Detroit veteran steeped in Fordist techniques, was heralding Bricklin's simplified production compared to other carmakers. Since BCL manufactured only the SV1's roll cage/frame at Saint John and its body panels in a sister plant in Minto, offered no options on the vehicle (only the choice of "safety color"), and purchased the majority of its parts and major components (including its engine) from outside suppliers, BCL had a relatively efficient assembly process, one heavily dependent on significant outsourcing and subassembly. Moreover, instead of having to source the normal 10,000–15,000 parts for a car, Bricklin needed only 1,700 for the SV1.

This kind of modularization – in Bricklin's case, outsourcing the assembly of almost all major subcomponents – made building SV1s a much leaner process.[68] First pioneered in early Detroit, modularity in production (MIP) would again come to be embraced by the industry in the 1980s and 1990s, another element of the post-Fordist production revolution.[69] Because of this approach, with its heavy reliance on outside parts, components, and subassemblies, Bricklin, in terms of assembly, more resembled a partial or complete knock-down (PKD, CKD) operation than a traditional assembly operation. Automotive PKD operations had been pioneered by Henry Ford, who shipped mostly completed Model Ts from Dearborn (and Windsor) to a constellation of satellite plants across North America and the world for final assembly, for both tariff and production reasons. In the postwar period, the Big Three had mostly moved away from the practice as they built up their international operations. But in the 1960s and early 1970s, offshore firms such as Volvo, Toyota, and Isuzu had utilized similar PKD techniques for their beachhead transplant operations in Halifax and Cape Breton in Nova Scotia.[70]

Along with emphasizing MIP and utilizing PKD, Bricklin's operation was also extremely dependent on the secure supply and timely delivery of parts and components from the Big Three, his erstwhile competitors in the sports car field. Bricklin paired his hybrid MIP/PKD process with a rudimentary form of JIT, similar to what Toyota had been developing in Japan since the 1950s. As a foundational element of the TPS, JIT would prove extraordinarily successful in reshaping production, inventory, and distribution practices in the automotive and a host of other industries starting in the 1960s (for example, Walmart, founded in Arkansas in 1962), though later for the Big Three.[71]

Second, there was Bricklin's decision to use plastic for the SV1's skin. For Bricklin, the fiberglass formed body panelling was not just an embrace of new age materials to dazzle car buyers. The rationale for attaching plastic onto his cars was much more fundamentally economic and practical. When it came to production, using plastic was much easier and cheaper than following the traditional approach to two foundational aspects of car-making: stamping and painting. Using gigantic, expensive presses to stamp steel exterior panels or full body parts, which were then welded to a car's chassis – the industry standard since the 1920s – was one of the most technically challenging aspects of automotive manufacturing.[72] And stamping body parts was well beyond the capabilities of a startup operation like BCL. Instead, by almost completely cutting stamping and welding out of the production process, Bricklin significantly lessened the cost and complexity of manufacturing the SV1, both in terms of the Saint John plant's set up and the car's actual assembly.

Moreover, if the SV1 used prefabricated coloured plastic panels, Bricklin car bodies would not need to be painted. Car painting, and a paint shop required for such a task – "the most elaborate and costly part of the final assembly plant," in the words of automotive geographer James M. Rubenstein – was another technological bridge too far to cross for Bricklin and his modest production capabilities. The advent of painted car bodies had been, in the early days of the auto industry, one of the most technically difficult problems to overcome for manufacturers. Henry Ford's celebrated, though unconfirmed, statement that customers could have "a Model T in any color they want, as long as it's black" was a testament to the complications and cost of the process. By using modernity's helpmate, plastic, to sheath his car, Bricklin not only avoided the challenges of stamping and painting, but also made a virtue from a vice, as had Ford.[73]

When "a jubilant" Malcolm Bricklin drove the first "Safety Suntan"–coloured SV1 down the ramp of the Saint John assembly plant in August 1974 to the cheers of the assembled crowd, few realized that the vehicle marked a pivotal moment in the transition in how cars were built and in the broader story of automobility.[74] Because of the particularities of the Bricklin operation's size and the timing of its appearance, the firm's production method bridged elements and practices of both the industry's Fordist heritage and its lean future. Operationally, when it came to manufacturing the SV1, this duality could be seen, first, in the company's facilities; second, in Bricklin's parts procurement; and third, in the assembly processes of Bricklin's firm.

3(A). PRODUCTION FACILITIES: BCL, SAINT JOHN (GRANDVIEW INDUSTRIAL PARK) AND MINTO (MINTO INDUSTRIAL PARK)

The most complicated aspect of an auto business is its factory. BCL's plants were in east Saint John, not far from the Saint John River, and in Minto, about 150 kilometres north (a couple hours driving time). Fredericton, where BCL's government owners sat, was in between. The main Saint John facility was the former T.S. Simms paintbrush plant in Grandview Industrial Park. Opened in 1971 at a cost of $2.5 million, Simms had vacated the 120,000-square-foot facility owing to a slowdown in its business. Multiplex, the government investment agency, had identified Simms as a good potential location for a manufacturing firm, and its availability had been an instigating factor in connecting Bricklin with New Brunswick. The plant was new; was close to the recently built-up New Brunswick Route 1, the CN railway lines, and the port; and was in New Brunswick's largest city (pop., 1973: ~100,000), which had a long history of industry and working-class life and could attract many potential workers.[75] The city was also where Irving was headquartered and had its largest operations, including its main oil refinery. The Saint John facility, on a large, fenced lot, housed the main vehicle assembly line, the frame and door subassembly areas, and the administrative offices.

BCL spent $8.8 million to get Saint John and Minto up and running, including $1.2 million on manufacturing processes (designing and engineering the two plant layouts), $1.9 million on production equipment, $2.7 million on vendor and plant tooling, and another $350,000 on "facilities improvements."[76] Additionally, although Bricklin had originally leased the Saint John facility from Simms, the government purchased the building on behalf of BCL in November 1974 for $1 million, to "permit uninterrupted operations" of the Bricklin assembly line (by then, Bricklin wasn't making lease payments).[77]

The two plants epitomized both Bricklin's Fordist inheritances and his innovative ideas. On the one hand, a former paint brush plant was not designed for automotive manufacture or well-suited for the endeavour. By the 1970s, the industry had decentralized its operations and almost exclusively developed its plants on "greenfield" sites, building massive, specially designed facilities from the ground up, which explained their tremendous expense.[78] Saint John may have *looked* like

Figure 6.4. Bricklin Canada Ltd. factory, Saint John.

a good facility, but as Terry Tanner, Bricklin's first head of manufacturing found when he arrived at the plant, it was "a basic boom factory, with a snow-load roof, with nine holes in the floor." Moreover, for a modern factory man like Tanner, the SV1's assembly line conveyor had been set up "in the wrong location in the plant," an "unbelievable" mistake. He realized that the "decision was made by people in management who couldn't spell car and had no concept of what they were doing. They didn't have any idea." And, to make matters worse, "they were family."[79]

On the other hand, out in Minto, the firm was doing something truly innovative at the body panelling facility. Early on, Bricklin had realized that he needed a separate space to produce the SV1's coloured fiberglass skins, and BCL acquired a 43,000-square-foot former cement business building in the Minto Industrial Park, the closest suitable option. Even if the plant was small, Minto's specialized plastics equipment and processes were "extremely new and in many cases innovative to the automobile industry," since BCL was the first firm attempting the technology.[80] But, overall, compared to other auto plants in North America, and certainly in Japan and Germany, BCL's facilities were very basic and lacked some of the newest features that were changing the industry (robotic arms, for instance).

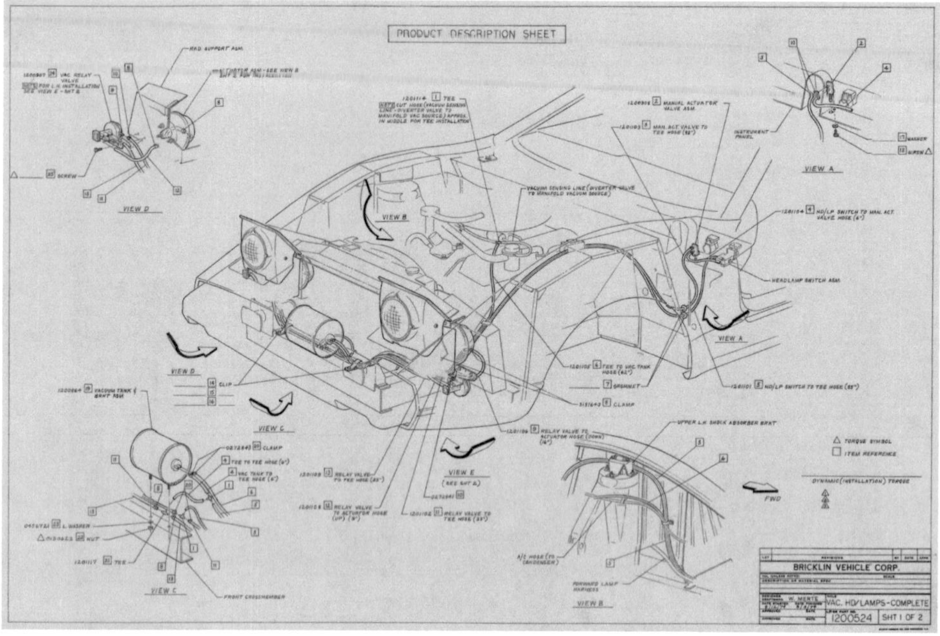

Figure 6.5. Bricklin Vehicle Corporation headlamp assembly, 1974.

3(B). PARTS PROCUREMENT AND SOURCING: GVI, BCL

Parts procurement and supply chain management are essential elements of automobile manufacturing, and the complexity of sourcing the thousands of parts required for a motor vehicle's assembly remains one of the most demanding logistical aspects of building a car. Bricklin followed traditional Big Three supply practices by sourcing most of the parts of the SV1 from other original equipment manufacturers (OEMs), but it also presented an unusual situation in that BCL itself machined only a small number of the vehicle's approximately 1,700 parts, notably its plastic parts and frames. Since Bricklin was such a small startup, it had to procure virtually all of its parts "off the shelf" from existing manufacturers. And not just individual parts: Bricklin was sourcing whole components. GVI contracted with AMC to supply about 7,000 units of chassis components, including the car's suspension and brakes, while the power steering was from GM, and the transmission from Chrysler.[81] The pop-up headlight assembly illustrated the complicated range of parts required, virtually all of which were sourced from other manufacturers.

Much of the car was modularized in this way, something that *Road & Track* recognized in 1975. "The fact is," the magazine wrote, the firm "probably couldn't have got the Bricklin into production" if they hadn't used this method.[82] In an earlier age, the modular approach had been common. Oshawa's "Colonel" Sam and his McLaughlin Motor Car Company (est. 1907; GM Canada after 1918) had imported Bruick engines for his McLaughlin-Buicks, before selling out to his friend Billy Durant.[83] Likewise, in its first two decades, GM itself had sourced whole bodies from the Fisher Body Corporation (est. 1908). Even after becoming part-owned by GM in 1919, Fisher still sold bodies to multiple Detroit manufacturers, and it did so until GM took full control in 1925, in a well-known case of vertical integration.[84] Bricklin's approach was the reverse of "body by Fisher" – in-housing the SV1's body and frame (hence, the promotional emphasis on those aspects of the car) and outsourcing the rest of the vehicle.

Then, of course, there was the SV1's engine. The internal combustion engine (ICE), the heart of any motor car, was often its greatest selling feature and had been the secret to Henry Ford's success with his Model T. Because of Henry's (and a few others') engineering innovations, the use of the mass-produced ICE exploded after 1900, helped by a massive, already existing petroleum infrastructure (facilitated, in large part, by Standard Oil, established in New York City in 1870), favourable tax policies, and the simple fact that the Tin Lizzie's game-changing four-cylinder, gas-powered planetary engine had enough power and torque to conquer North America's poor roads and rugged topography.[85]

But the SV1 had no engine of its own. Building an engine was simply too technically daunting for a company like Bricklin's. Because of the cost and complexity, only Detroit and a few small specialist outfits could manufacture engines. So, in a throwback to Detroit's early days (and an unknowing nod to the industry's future), Bricklin decided to buy the SV1's engine from his Big Three-plus-AMC competition. He first contracted with American Motors for a thousand 360-cubic-inch 200-horsepower, V8 engines, with four-speed manual or three-speed automatic transmissions, both from Chrysler. For the 1975 model year, Bricklin switched to the Ford 351, two-barrel, 175-hp engine made in Windsor, Ontario, paired with a Ford three-speed transmission, made in Cincinnati. Along with being an "off-the-shelf" option, the Ford engine had the added benefit of an emissions output below US federal requirements and thus did not require the SV1 to have a catalytic converter.[86] In an automotive world being forced to adapt quickly to the increasingly stringent emissions regime imposed by Washington, this was a significant cost savings. The Windsor engine also had the benefit of adding substantially to the car's Canadian content, a stipulation from Ottawa for any consideration to allow the company membership in the auto pact.

Successfully procuring engines had not been easy for Malcolm. Bricklin very publicly stated that, in 1974, AMC attempted to back out of their original deal,

Figure 6.6. Working on an SV1 engine, Saint John factory.

saying that, since its V8 was so popular among customers, they simply couldn't spare any. Incensed, Bricklin demanded a meeting, at which he threatened to go to Washington and bang the drum of anti-trust – "that big AMC was trying to crush his little company for no reason."[87] Bricklin had previously raised such concerns in 1973, telling *Road & Track* that "many in Detroit believe" that, if he succeeded, it would be "the best thing that could happen to squash government talk of breaking up the 'monopolistic' Big Three."[88] According to Bricklin, AMC ultimately relented, but stingily sold him only a thousand units.

The same thing happened after he reached a deal with Ford for engines. As Bricklin tells the story, he was on his way to Acapulco with Hatfield sometime in late 1973 or early 1974 when a Ford official reached him by phone (while he was in the United VIP lounge) to inform him that the company didn't want Ford engines in the SV1, since "the liability was not worth it." Bricklin frantically called everyone he knew at Ford and, when he finally got in touch with someone, apparently again threatened to go to Washington to "make their lives miserable." Soon after,

Figure 6.7. Engines and parts warehousing, Saint John factory.

he had a visit from Ford's Hal Sperlich, Lee Iacocca's right-hand man (the Deuce hadn't yet fired Iacocca). Intimating that Detroit was spooked by his accusations of anti-competitive behaviour, Bricklin said Sperlich "showed up" one day in Livonia, expressed an interest in the car, and eventually cut a deal with BCL to allow the firm to procure Windsor-built 351 engines for the SV1.[89]

Beyond engines, BCL faced parts procurement problems throughout much of its existence. Bricklin complained that, as a startup, sourcing parts was more expensive for him and that Detroit's "arrogance," proved that they were determined to fix it so "no one else will ever build a car."[90] Big Three suppliers demanded cash up front from BCL for their parts, or on a tighter thirty- or sixty-day schedule than for firms that already had established relationships with Detroit and had ninety-day windows. This was a grave imposition on a car company that was designed to be far more dependent upon JIT than much of the assembly industry (which largely sourced parts from in-house subsidiaries) and that, as a startup, had limited cash.

A good part of BCL's difficulties stemmed from challenges in managing its supply chain properly, with a problematic dependence on often unreliable single-source vendors. In November 1974, Bricklin admitted that the company had problems "because it's the first time we've done this, the first time we had to coordinate this." With so much of a dependence upon US-sourced parts being "shipped by truck and train ... crossing at many points along the border," the firm faced "delays all up and down the border." [91] While it's clear that Bricklin and GVI were not able to achieve sufficient competency when it came to parts procurement, this issue provided another illustration of just how quickly the recently integrated North American auto industry was coming to depend on cross-border supply chains, a practice that would only increase in the years to come.

Parts delays became so bad, according to Fredericks and Chambers, that BCL comptroller Ian Watson spent evenings waiting at the Saint John airport, "hoping that a late-night flight would bring parts, often bought at retail prices, that were needed for production the next day."[92] By November 1974, BCL parts shortages were already causing "severe financial difficulties due in large measure of the inability of the company to reach a level of production that would be self-sustaining." The parts shortages were also "related to funds shortages," even though, by October 1974, the company had already spent over $3 million on production parts.[93] Parts procurement, owing either to poor supply networks or lack of funds to purchase parts, was a constant, debilitating issue throughout the firm's operation.

3(C). ASSEMBLY: BCL, SAINT JOHN AND MINTO

In the fall of 1974, once all the safety and emissions testing had been completed, most of the equipment had been installed in the two facilities, the main conveyor and production processes had been laid out, and the firm had managed to ensure at least a sporadic parts supply, BCL was operational and ready to assemble the SV1. Assembling enough cars fast enough (and well enough) to meet demand (and to become profitable) was the most difficult task that Bricklin and his firm faced, the *sine qua non* of the entire enterprise. Bricklin had promised a first-year production of 12,000 vehicles, or 1,000 a *month* (about 50 cars a day), ramping up to 50,000 annually by year three of the operation, and 100,000 by year four.[94]

By the 1970s, the scale of a typical automotive assembly operation had become a hallmark of industrial modernity. In 1971, economist Lawrence J. White published his deeply researched PhD thesis as *The Automobile Industry since 1945*, which stated that "the optimum size plant" of a modern auto factory was designed to build "55–65 cars *an hour* (that is, 180–220,000 cars a year on two-shift operations)," or often up to 1,000 cars a day.[95] Plants traditionally suspended production in July and August to retool the production lines for the new model year, which started in September. Understandably, given the logistical and production complexities of this kind of scale, even Big Three assembly plants, which could count on decades of institutional and practical knowledge in mass manufacturing, often took some time to ramp up to that level of production.

For instance, in 1966, Ford Motor started construction of a $65 million greenfield facility in St. Thomas, Ontario, to build new small and medium-sized cars. Ford's decision to construct a new assembly plant stemmed, in large part, from its desire to meet production requirements under the auto pact and thus to maximize the benefits of North American integration (just as Bricklin was trying to do in his own, truncated way).[96] Following the launch of Job 1, a Ford Falcon station wagon, between December 1967 and February 1969, St. Thomas produced 108,832 Falcons as a one-shift, 1,200-worker, single-car assembly operation – about 2,000 vehicles a week, a modest output for a Big Three plant, but one that satisfied a good portion of the North American demand for the Falcon. After 1969, the plant retooled and moved to a two-shift operation, building 63 Ford Mavericks an *hour*, or about 1,050 cars a day, and was assembling nearly 150,000 vehicles annually by 1975, the vast majority of which went to the United States.[97]

Following the startup of production in August 1974, BCL's assembly of SV1s began only very slowly and never came close to achieving Bricklin's production target of 12,000 vehicles a year, which was lowered over the course of the venture more than once. In Saint John, production engineers faced "technical problems, political hassles, and marginal funding" right from the outset, reported *Automation: The Production Engineering Magazine*, in its June 1975 in-depth article, "Building the Bricklin – A Sports Car Is Born." Manufacturing the Bricklin was an "uphill battle against one crisis after another."[98]

In particular, significant difficulties emerged with the subassembly of the body, which was a "unique challenge for production engineering" because of the difficulties of fitting the gull-wing doors properly. At the same time, the forty-station assembly line slowed to a crawl as Bricklin's engineers tried to figure out how to get the hydraulically powered doors to open and close properly (or at all), to speed up their closure (Bricklin timed it at eight seconds, far too long if it was raining), and to get the windows in the doors to work (a problem DeLorean also had with his car). On top of that, there were shortages of the specialized parts required for the doors. As Bricklin later recalled, on the manufacturing side, "99 percent of the problems were getting the doors and windows to work right."[99]

The dependence on full subassemblies caused significant production problems, especially when there was a component switch, as with the engine. Switching from

Figure 6.8. Assembling SV1 frames, Saint John.

the AMC V8 to the Ford Windsor in 1975 may have boosted Canadian content for the firm and meant that the new engine could meet Washington's emissions regulations, but the change wreaked havoc on production. According to *Automation*, switching engines "created a number of problems," with "differences in engine and transmission mounts, drive shaft connections, plumbing and wiring, etc., all required changes on the assembly line."[100] The new Ford engine also needed its own significant process to "dress" the engine, including installing the transmission, power steering, pump, alternator, smog pump, and other accessories. Meanwhile, on the body and frame assembly, the most significant in-house Bricklin aspect of the SV1's manufacture, the firm had difficulties fitting the trim, and the line needed "50 to 100 jigs and fixtures" along the line.[101] All these changes caused difficulties, slowed production, and increased costs tremendously.

Similarly, up in Minto, where Bricklin was genuinely trying something new with the body panels, production was also proving very difficult. "The acrylic plastic body concept," Morris Adams, another former Detroit veteran, told *Automation*,

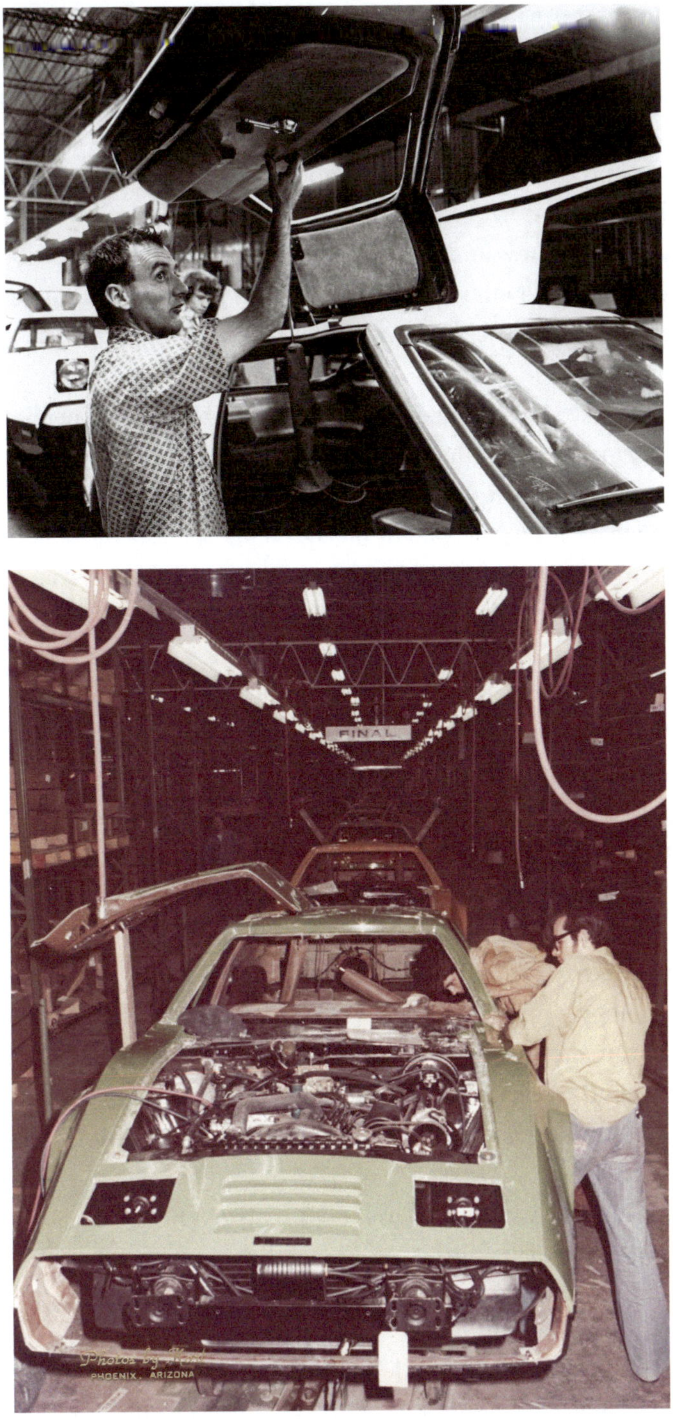

Figure 6.9. Working on the gull-wing doors (above); assembly, Saint John (below).

was "the main reason why I came in with Bricklin." But the innovative concept, he admitted, "offered many challenges." It was very complicated. Rohm and Hass (Philadelphia) supplied the raw acrylic pallets; Atlas Plastics (St. Louis, Missouri) did "the extrusion work" on the acrylic; EMC Corp. (Fort Worth, Texas) was providing the dies and presses (seven of them by August 1974) for the acrylic body panels, but the vacuum-forming, poured-acrylic process to make the twenty-three panels for each car was new and untested (it had been used to make fiberglass bathtubs) and was very challenging to work out.[102] Terry Tanner described the process, using the example of the Bricklin hood panel:

> Bricklin hoods, like all of the body parts, are acrylic bonded to fiberglass, and the acrylic is a memory plastic which was a flat sheet of material that was heated and vacuum-formed over a male die to become a hood. After vacuum forming, the material was put into a female mold and the fiberglass was applied. The mold was closed, and 150 tons of pressure was applied for 15 minutes. The result was your hood.[103]

But because of the trial and error required to get the panels right, and "evaluating the different resins and overcoming the learning curve for cold-pressing," it took significant effort and time to reach an "acceptable level" in quality, and expensive scrappage rates were very high.[104] Meanwhile, it was reported that Bricklin had switched suppliers for matching moulds to save money, and the less expensive version caused temperature issues that added to the problems.[105]

Even more challenging was figuring out how to adhere the panels to each other, and to the car, "a major headache" according to one Bricklin engineer. Malcolm Bricklin hadn't realized when he decided on acrylic and fiberglass for the car that the "technology simply was not there" yet. When a member of the province's Research and Productivity Council visited Minto and asked Albert Bricklin how he could be sure that the plastic panels had bonded to the frame, Albert replied that his method was to "hit the wing with a sledgehammer. If it holds, then the acrylic has bonded."

For some of its processes, Minto maintained two shifts, with about a hundred workers each. When they had finished enough body parts, the units were sent by truck to Saint John. There, the SV1s were often assembled based on the order of the colour runs produced by Minto.[106]

Despite all these difficulties, by the end of 1974, BCL had produced 770 1974 SV1s (with AMC engines) working on a one-shift basis, and Saint John had started building 1975 models. Even if Bricklin proudly called the Saint John operation "a real assembly line," production was slow going, as BCL managers, engineers, and

Figure 6.10. Body-panel making in Minto, NB: battery boxes.

workers struggled to fix the production problems presented by the car, and to speed the process along. By then, even though outside assessors felt that "the situation in the plant has unquestionably improved in terms of production and quality," the firm was producing only about sixteen vehicles a day, and quality issues persisted, as "only one unit on average passed inspection." With parts shortages, stoppages on the line, and problems with the various subassemblies, many of Bricklin's approximately 450 assembly-line and production workers in Saint John were often left standing, waiting for work.[107]

After a January–February 1975 shutdown to retool for production for the 1975 model year (with the Ford engine), the plant had increased production by June 1975 to around 20 vehicles a day, representing a ceiling of about 5,200 vehicles a year. With slow if steady output finally underway, and having reached the production milestone of 2,000 vehicles, Bricklin in July told audiences in New Brunswick that, with back orders of 40,000 cars to fill, the company was in good shape. Press scepticism towards the venture had also declined somewhat, and the two or three

Figure 6.11. Body-panel making in Minto. NB: door moulds.

critical weekly editorials that had dogged Bricklin had "largely disappeared."[108] By September 1975, when the plant was shuttered, BCL had begun manufacturing the 1976 models (about 76 were completed). In total, BCL produced 2,900 SV1s, averaging about 22 vehicles a day.[109]

In June 1975, *Automation* had declared that Bricklin had "come a long way" and that "the accomplishment" of manufacturing SV1s "deserved applause."[110] Behind the scenes, however, government officials complained that Bricklin had "vastly overstated production capability and understated fund requirements," and that BCL would never reach the company's break-even production level of thirty cars a day.[111] But, for a brief shining moment, despite all the production, financial, and quality problems, Bricklin had accomplished something that no one had done in three decades, and that no one would achieve again for another three decades. He had built a car, and despite his managerial shortcomings and the immense challenge of the task, had successfully manufactured thousands of them – or at least a few thousand.

Figure 6.12. Bricklin's Saint John production facility. Note the orange hood on the green car (third in line).

4. *Labour: BCL*

If the engine is the heart of any car, then workers are the heart of any car company. And at the heart of the Bricklin venture, at least from Richard Hatfield's perspective, was the most alluring of all of industrial modernity's potential riches: relatively high-paying automobile jobs. Employment (and publicity) was what Hatfield and New Brunswick were paying for.

Of course, from Malcolm's perspective, coming to New Brunswick was also about jobs. But in his case, he was looking for the lowest-paid automobile workers he could find, at least in comparison to all the other places in North America where cars were being built. New Brunswick fit the bill, with one of Canada's highest unemployment rates (especially for young people) and significant outmigration, a problem all across the Maritimes. *Goin' Down the Road* (1970), Don Shebib's famous realist film about two young Cape Breton, Nova Scotia, buddies who drive their 1960 Chevy

Impala "down the road" to the industrial riches of Toronto, perfectly encapsulated this employment dynamic (and some aspects of automobile modernity, too).

So, while Bricklin did need to offer good wages in order to hire workers for his automotive assembly plant, his rates would be less than those paid to autoworkers in Oshawa, Windsor, or Detroit, given that BCL was located in rural New Brunswick, far from Ontario's Golden Horseshoe or the American industrial Midwest. Early on, Clifford N. Taylor, Bricklin's Saint John personnel and administration manager, enquired about wage rates for his potential employees. While government officials admitted that workers at BCL's operations shared some similarities with Volvo's Nova Scotia transplant operation (est. 1963), "the lack of previous experience in the automobile assembly industry in New Brunswick makes it rather difficult to establish any valid comparisons." However, they also suggested that, if the Bricklin plants were "clean, warm and well lighted," this could "contribute to an employee accepting slightly less per hour than if he had to work in opposite conditions." In the end, in a province dominated by the Irvings and resource extraction, Bricklin's wage rates were set at $4.50 an hour, slightly lower than comparable labourers at the Irving oil refinery in Saint John (built 1960; UAW contract, 1963).[112] The UAW did come to represent BCL workers, but the union agreed to wage rates significantly less than those paid to Big Three union members in central Canada and less than the Volvo workers in neighbouring Nova Scotia.[113]

In the summer of 1974, BCL hired the initial cohort of workers for both the plants. According to one Bricklin plant manager, many were "kids" whose "average age is about 22 or 23." Mostly men from across the province, though there were quite a few young women, as well, especially in Minto, where the labour force was "extensively made up of female workers on the trim area and the press area." There, Judy Bartlett, who worked installing headlights, was twenty-five; Frank Richard, a maintenance foreman, was twenty-six. Most were baby boomers who matched well with the car and its Seventies vibe: young, vibrant, and eager to take a risk on the colourful SV1s they were building. By June 1975, the Saint John plant had about 350 workers; eventually about 500 would work there, and another 200 or so in Minto, thought the numbers fluctuated.[114]

Few had worked on anything like an automobile assembly line. Since "virtually none had any experience in or even conception of a car plant," according to *Automation,* "the most serious problem was in training people to do their jobs to an acceptable level of quality."[115] BCL did manage to receive a federal training grant, but training and productivity were works in progress throughout 1974 and into 1975, according to the government's point man on the scene, Stephen Wheatley.[116] One Bricklin insider admitted to the press that "assembly lines are incredibly

Figure 6.13. Young workers at the Bricklin plant in Saint John.

complex . . . You've got to show these workers how to do it . . . It gets very complicated."[117] For Judy Bartlett, whose task required about twelve minutes per vehicle, the production of only twenty vehicles a day "left her with considerable time to observe events" and wait around.[118]

With all those young people working at Bricklin, life on the line and in the plant was fairly social, even if production was slow and assembly line work was physically challenging and mentally exhausting. Whether it was in Livonia or Saint John, Bricklin himself was a constant presence, inspiring employees with his dream. "Malcolm could motivate a rock," Terry Tanner later recalled. This could be seen especially in the early development of the vehicle. Most new cars take seven years to get built: the Bricklin came together in seven months.[119] The *Brickline*, an employee newsletter (the name was later used for the Bricklin owners' magazine), was full of updates and announcements from the various company sites, including social events, staff marriages and births, and all manner of news about the firm. In June 1975, Bricklin held an open house at the plant, which drew 13,000 people, in part to show off the facilities to Saint John's citizens but also to attract new personnel. There were reports that Bricklin had a very high attrition rate, with, "at one point, as many as ten workers a day" quitting the plant.[120]

While turnover was a major problem, other labour issues existed as well. Though Bricklin claimed to welcome the union, in January 1975 he faced a two-day wildcat strike by 250 workers, sparked by the firing of employees who refused to remove snow from Bricklins parked in the plant's lot.[121] At the time, the plant morale "was almost negligible," according to union leaders, but Bricklin later claimed to have walked out to the workers and talked with them, asking them, "what is going on?" and convinced them to end the action. Another labour problem was what Bricklin saw as a "very liberal" unemployment benefit scheme that was designed for New Brunswick's seasonal work culture, which allowed workers to go on unemployment benefits after ten weeks of work. Bricklin claimed to be having a worker turnover of 80 per cent every ninety days or so because of the policy.[122]

The plant's workers, and their union representation, reflected BCL's Fordist heritage, but they also pointed to some emerging North American labour trends that were coming clear in the 1970s. With offshore competition in autos, steel, tires, and a host of other manufacturing sectors, the early signs of an emerging, globalized, leaner industrial postmodernity were starting to appear. At BCL, there was little sign of the robotics and digitization that had begun in the 1960s and would reshape the automotive and broader manufacturing production process so profoundly. At the same time, the Bricklin facilities revealed only a few hints of the kinds of productivity improvements and team building along a *kaizen* model that would transform industrial work in the 1990s and beyond. BCL did witness the creation of "Pride" and "Quality" teams designed to boost quality by reducing the cost of defects, repairs, and replacements to their lowest economical level.[123] The firm also attempted to utilize a "computer simulation model" in the spring of 1975 to estimate the impact of increased production on cashflow, though its impact was uncertain.[124]

But the most important factor that shaped BCL's labour force was its location. In choosing New Brunswick, Bricklin had very much anticipated how, starting in the 1980s, Japanese and European transplant operations, and the Big Three themselves, would shift their workforces away from traditional union areas in an effort to lower their costs, often with the support of local governments. Those changes were very much a matter of business-government relations. As with so many other aspects of his business, Bricklin's interactions with the New Brunswick government foretold significant changes with respect to the state's role in the automotive sector, changes that would profoundly reshape North America's industrial and economic landscape in the years to come.

5. Government Relations: GVI, BVC, BCL

If, in its structure, personnel, and production practices, Bricklin may have largely, though often poorly, mimicked the modern American auto firm in its organization and business, the company nonetheless also anticipated key developments in how the state would interact with the auto sector after the 1970s. The labour issue was only one element of the business-state equation when it came to GVI and Bricklin's relations with Hatfield and his government. Two other aspects fundamentally shaped Bricklin's government relations (GR) with the province: first, New Brunswick's willingness to offer direct investment incentives (subsidies) to the firm; and second, its (state) ownership of BCL.[125] After Bricklin, shifting labour geographies, subsidies, and state ownership would profoundly shape North American auto industry–government relations.

Seeking low wages in rural or non-union regions was only part of the changing dynamics of North America's automotive geography. Bricklin anticipated this shift by seeking out the "best" production opportunities he could, which meant taking advantage of an economically depressed rural region – in this case, New Brunswick. The province had a persistent unemployment problem, and the arrival of Bricklin was seen as a genuine measure to alleviate this joblessness. In opting to locate in the province, Bricklin was prescient. What came to drive much of the locational change underpinning deindustrialization (beyond the closures caused by competition and TPS restructuring) was the willingness of auto manufacturers to decentralize production by seeking out low-wage, non-traditional locations for their plants just as Bricklin had done with New Brunswick in 1973.

By the 1980s, a host of car firms would build plants outside of the urban or suburban auto-manufacturing clusters in the American Midwest and southern Ontario that had dominated the economic geography of the industry. Instead of Detroit, Dearborn, Windsor, or Oshawa, new plants were increasingly shifted to exurban or rural locales. The Japanese came to North America in part to avoid increasingly protectionist measures and as a hedge against a strengthening yen, but also to take advantage of lower wages (or, at least, to avoid the union) by establishing plants in areas distanced from UAW strongholds. Honda established its first major facility in Marysville, Ohio, in 1979. Nissan went to Smyrna, Tennessee, in 1983. Toyota, Japan's industry leader, came in 1988 to Georgetown, Kentucky (though it had established a joint operation with GM in California in 1984). Honda and Toyota also built complementary facilities in Ontario, but in small-town communities far from the Big Three operations in that province (Honda in Alliston in 1986; Toyota in Cambridge in 1988). In neither the United States nor Canada did any of the Japanese plants have UAW representation. Starting in the 1980s, GM established new operations in rural areas in southern locales such as Spring Hill, Tennessee (Saturn, 1985). Saturn, like BCL, also featured a modified union contract – one that, instead of low wages, emphasized Japanese-style management-worker collaboration.[126]

A second major aspect of Bricklin's relations with the New Brunswick government was the direct subsidies it received from Hatfield's government, an essential part of the shifting political economy of the auto sector. Including the initial financial promises made by Hatfield to encourage GVI to "come to New Brunswick," Bricklin had, by the fall of 1975, received $25 million from the province through direct funding, loans, loan guarantees, and the purchase of its Saint John plant. In taking direct subsidies from the New Brunswick government, GVI was one of the first auto companies in the postwar period whose production location decision was a direct consequence of government incentives (and, notably, *not* because of government tariff barriers but, rather, because of their erasure).[127] Bricklin also received an incentive subsidy from the federal government in the form of a $3 million loan guarantee. Bricklin had first gone to Ottawa in the spring of 1973 as he searched for a potential state partner, and the feds had pushed him off to the provinces. Though there was a promise of federal assistance for the project, the loan guarantee was not confirmed until May 1974.[128]

Of course, New Brunswick (or Canada) was not the only subsidy game in town. Incentives might be offered by any aspiring government seeking the potential benefits of auto production, that dream of industrial modernity. In early 1975, Bricklin announced that he had developed plans for a Mexican operation, which would build cars for the US southwestern market. Whether or not this was a legitimate effort to build a plant or another bit of performative financialization, Bricklin understood that negotiating with Mexico (or, at least, claiming to do so) could help him leverage more support out of an increasingly sceptical New Brunswick government (even as the Mexican project's prospectus claimed an SV1 backlog worth $250 million). When Bricklin started to hint that he was planning the Mexican operation, and reports began to circulate that the Mexican government had offered him an investment incentive of $20 million to locate a plant there, the implication was clear. Bricklin had another suitor, and Malcolm could be seen as playing his newfound Mexican friends off of his old Canadian patrons, always looking for a better deal.[129]

Though GVI folded before the Mexican issue came to a head, the firm's Mexican gambit points to another significant way in which Bricklin anticipated the evolution of the auto industry: the incentive competition between nations, states, provinces, and regions for automotive investment. The Bricklin episode was the first example of a powerful new dynamic that, along with the search for lower wage areas, was reshaping the state and its relations to the North American auto sector. In his *Capital beyond Borders: States and Firms in the Auto Industry, 1960–94*, Kenneth Thomas called the situation that emerged in North America starting in the 1970s vis-à-vis automotive investment a classic prisoner's dilemma. The creation of the auto pact, an agreement that eradicated automotive tariff barriers in North America, unleashed a torrent of investment incentive battles between states and provinces as they sought to gain the benefits of auto investment, especially jobs. In this new era of capital mobility, incentives became "a way of life in the automobile industry," as auto firms became adept at playing provinces and states off against one another for investment (and sometimes using the threat of moving to Mexico, as Bricklin did). The battle over auto investment incentives was classic game theory: governments should give up incentives because it weakened them financially, but they could not do so unless every other government did. Thus, in order to protect themselves, states reluctantly continued to offer incentives, making all governments competing for the investment weaker in the face of auto capital.[130]

Bricklin's Mexican manoeuvre was only the tip of the iceberg. In 1978, Ford Motor, reflecting the new incentive-driven economic geography of the integrated North American automobile sector, announced that it would build a new engine plant in either Lima, Ohio, or Essex, Ontario, depending on the amount of state subsidy offered to the company by the plant's subnational suitors. After a very high-profile, costly battle for both governments, Ontario "won" the $535 million investment, at a cost of $68 million in government incentives, about 13 per cent of the investment, or $26,000 a job.[131] The decision sparked howls of outrage from Ohio and prompted US government officials to complain to the Canadian government that something needed to be done about investment incentives. Nothing was accomplished, however, and locational bidding became the new norm, as did the increasing financial and community benefit (and risk) of automotive investment decisions. A new exurban plant investment leveraged by a subsidizing government often represented a closure elsewhere. By 1985, GM, Volkswagen, Chrysler, Toyota, Honda, and Nissan had all taken advantage of government incentive wars to build new plants across North America. Moreover, eventually, all of the Big Three also established new facilities in Mexico, often with state support. In fact, since the 1980s, there has effectively not been a single major automobile facility in North America that has not been constructed without some form of direct or indirect government investment incentive, with billions of taxpayer dollars committed to auto firms.[132]

After Bricklin's demise in the mid-1970s, government incentives became a major aspect of automotive investment decision-making and a major irritant between Canada and the United States, and between state and provincial governments, as well. The package of incentives and subsidies that Bricklin ultimately received from New Brunswick was only the first indication of a paradigm shift in North American auto investment, one that would permanently reshape the industry's relation to government, and to the state itself. Most obviously, Bricklin was at the forefront of this shift towards the unleashed mobility of automotive capital starting in the 1970s, particularly as American auto production began to decline during and after the Chrysler bailout and restructuring, and the industry accelerated the shift away from its Midwestern heartland.

Finally, the Bricklin effort was unique in that it was the first significant start-up effort to build a car in North America since the 1940s, and one that moved to a rural location to take advantage of direct government assistance. But GVI was also unique in that BCL, its manufacturing arm, was a *government-owned* auto company – the first (North) American, government-owned auto company, though not the last. There is a long history of state intervention in Canada, including many examples of outright government ownership in strategic or technologically sensitive firms and sectors, and of direct support for industrial enterprise.[133] Yet New Brunswick's effective ownership of the Bricklin operation was one of the first examples of state ownership of such a high-profile *automotive* firm, and one that was, essentially, a foreign venture.[134]

Bricklin emerged as a state-owned auto company because of a number of factors. At the outset, Bricklin was keen to get a Canadian federal government development loan, and to get Canadian approval to become a member of the auto pact, allowing it cross-border duty-free privileges. The latter was a very important consideration for a company that planned to build all of its cars in Canada, and to sell all of them in the United States. In GVI's dealings with the federal government over the loan, Ottawa rejected Bricklin's first application, and gave Bricklin the money only after he put more of his own financing into the project. When it came to auto pact status, one of the terms that Ottawa set out was that Bricklin had to be a Canadian-owned operation. This was what prompted the provincial government to take a 51 per cent equity share in Bricklin, as there were no other suitors for such a high-risk venture.[135] Hatfield would likely not have done so if the federal government had not made Canadian ownership of BCL a requirement for auto pact consideration.[136]

Bricklin's two-thirds government ownership by the time the company was placed into receivership was also a consequence of GVI's precarious financial position and the reality of the industry in the 1970s. Few institutions were willing to lend money to a start-up car company, which, in the post-embargo, post-regulatory environment, was a very dicey proposition. From the start, Bricklin's status as a new entry in the auto market, and the newness of its approach and product, left Bricklin's accountants "unable to evaluate the reasonableness of the assumptions relating to unit volume and selling prices," since the product did not yet exist, and all of the company's plans were based on assumption. Accordingly, accounting firm

Touche Ross & Co. could not "give assurance that the project results would actually be attained."[137] Another financial assessment in June 1975 from GVI's accountants indicated that "the company's continuance as a going concern" was dependent on its ability "obtain additional financing." The government eventually acceded to this reality, and Hatfield gave Bricklin more money.[138] For all its good press, Bricklin was still an auto company looking for financing in a period when the industry was in turmoil. Government was its last and only hope.

Indeed, Bricklin was government-owned because the premier of the province felt that he had no choice but to support the firm this way. Hatfield had thrown his and his province's lot in with Bricklin, and it had become a matter of provincial pride, however illogical that seemed. Even as it became clear the Bricklin was not up to the task of managing an automobile firm, and that the cost of New Brunswick's involvement was spiraling out of control, Hatfield remained defiant about what the company meant to his province. "Without the involvement of the provincial government," he declared in December 1974, after giving Bricklin another $2.5 million, "there will be no sustained economic development in New Brunswick except for the tasks these remote institutions [the central Canadian banks and the federal government] think us capable of and suitable for."[139] For a place like New Brunswick in the 1970s, government ownership was the price of starting an auto industry, the cost of the ticket to a mature industrial economy.

This view of the necessity of government support, and even ownership, of the auto sector, which may have looked provincial and pathetic in 1975, looked prescient by 1980, with Iacocca's bailout, and again in 2009. When the US, Canadian, and Ontario governments nationalized General (Government) Motors and Chrysler as the two firms collapsed into bankruptcy during the Great Recession of 2009, they did so for many of the same reasons that Hatfield had articulated as to why New Brunswick owned Bricklin. The lack of private financing, the need to protect and maintain a strategic industry and technology, the imperative of keeping thousands of people employed, and the desire to ensure economic stability and growth were all cited by government officials, including President Barack Obama.[140] In the end, in terms of its interactions with the state, and the state's response, Bricklin's relations with the government were not so different from how the rest of the auto industry in North America would come to operate.

GVI as Case Study: Malcolm Bricklin as Manager

Colliding with Malcolm Bricklin's, Richard Hatfield's, and New Brunswick's dream of the SV1 was the daunting reality of the car business in the postwar world.

Building cars was, and is, arguably the most complicated and challenging task that humans undertake on a mass scale and in a manner that has a tremendous impact on so much of humanity. The auto industry has also been, for much of modern capitalism's existence, the most competitive and costly industry on the planet, with the most employees, greatest capital demands, and most complicated and longest supply chains across its vast constellation of influence. As early as December 1973, Bricklin employees admitted that "now we know why it takes GM three years to bring out a car."[141]

Studying General Vehicle Incorporated's corporate existence and operations as a case study in business history provides three interesting lessons. First, understanding the administrative, technological, logistical, and human challenges GVI and BCL faced in manufacturing the SV1 reveals the changing nature, organization, and structure of auto firms by the early 1970s. At the outset, examining Bricklin's corporate structure and operations allows an understanding of how the industry was conceptualized by a new entrant. At the same time, analysing the firm's operational performance illuminates significant changes in the broader evolution that automobile manufacturing was undergoing in the 1970s as it transitioned from its Fordist foundations to its much leaner future. Even through its failure, Bricklin provides insights into how the company anticipated new developments and trends in the auto industry that would become important features of the North American sector. In stepping back to look at Bricklin in the broader context of the postwar auto sector, it becomes clear that the company's experience was not so anomalous. GVI and its subsidiaries shared significant traits with the established auto companies and predicted some of their key strategies after 1975. GVI also anticipated some of the operational methods of the foreign manufacturers whose cars and "transplants" were starting to appear in the industry.

Second, the corporate history of GVI and its subsidiaries provides an opportunity to assess Bricklin's performance in relation to the third entrepreneurial archetype, the manager. Whether or not Malcolm Bricklin really believed he could build the car – and all indications are that, initially, he thought he could, as did many others – he had neither enough management or manufacturing production expertise nor the necessary financial backing to pull off building a quality vehicle (despite his promotional abilities). Even if Bricklin exhibited real innovation with the SV1 in terms of its technology (plastic, safety), and with BCL in terms of its production processes (his MIP/JIT/PKD hybrid), this wasn't enough. Managing an auto company had less to do with innovation conceptualizations, or performative financialization, for that matter, and more to do with actual production execution – a

Figure 6.14. Completed and still being assembled Bricklin SV1s, Saint John.

manager needed not just reasons *why* to build a car but also the skills associated with *how* to manufacture thousands of automobiles.

By 1975, Bricklin had come to realize that he had taken on more than he was capable of, and that the sheer immensity of building a car, even if it was not completely from scratch, was beyond anything could imagine. "I thought it would be simple," Bricklin confessed in May 1974 to the *Automotive News*, and again in February 1975 to the *Washington Post*, "but it isn't." The way that he had envisioned his slimmed-down operation convinced Bricklin that he'd be "making and selling cars in a year" and that the venture would take an investment of "maybe two or three million." But, by then, he was all in: "Well, it's taken three-and-a-half years and I'm in debt for thirty million. We won't go broke I'm sure of that, but if we did, how would I pay it off? The dollar down and the dollar a week."[142]

Nonetheless – and here he echoed Hatfield – in Malcolm's view, it was still worth trying. "If we realize the difficulties of things before we attempted them," Bricklin philosophized, we "will never do anything."[143] Years later, Bricklin recognized that "I absolutely was [in] over my head" and that he had "no idea what [he] was doing."[144] In 1985, industry guru J.D. Power (of the eponymous J.D. Power Awards) summarized Bricklin's management abilities perfectly: "Bricklin's a creative promoter and comes up with new opportunities, but [he] has problems with operating and executing the ventures he's created."[145] Another study of the incident rendered a much harsher judgment on Bricklin's abilities: "his decisions had an improvised and erratic nature . . . Bricklin was behaving pathologically."[146]

A third lesson we can glean from GVI is that, notwithstanding his managerial shortcomings, the complications Bricklin and his firm faced – the dramatic changes in the business of making cars, the challenging circumstances of the 1970s, the need to innovate to launch and survive, and the shifting role of the state – directly conflicted with the idealized image of what a successful twentieth-century car company and its leadership looked and acted like, and they made managing a brand-new auto firm a titanically difficult task. Bricklin's failure can, in part, be explained by the changing expectations of what it took to be an executive of a postwar automobile firm. His short tenure as the president of GVI symbolized the transition from iconoclastic entrepreneur to dour "numbers man" that had happened in America's leading businesses, the auto sector. Straddling these worlds, Bricklin may have been, from the perspective of rapidly changing auto sector, a bad manager, but he also was a perceptive one. He and his company bore witness to – and, just as importantly – foretold many of the new strategies and tactics that became standard operating procedure in the auto sector by the end of the decade.

Like the paradox of a newly assertive regulatory state that simultaneously surrendered some of its most interventionist national economic tools, Malcolm Bricklin faced an entrepreneurial conundrum. In order to successfully *launch* an automobile company in the postwar automotive world, he had to create an image that harkened back to the auto industry's past. He had to credibly sell himself as a latter-day, larger-than-life, swashbuckling technological innovator and promoter – to convincingly become a reborn, postwar version of a Henry Ford, or at least a Billy Durant.

But, in order to successfully *manage* an automobile manufacturing company in the 1970s, one that aped the postwar form and function of the Big Three (especially as the new philosophy of cars and the new production practices transformed the industry), Bricklin had to be the archetypal buttoned-down, by-the-numbers manager – a white-collar Sloan, a Deuce, a Thomas Aquinas Murphy, or their less famous successors and subordinates.[147] Yet for Bricklin, becoming an idealized organization man, with all the postwar managerial expectations of what it took to make an auto company successful, was a difficult task. Bridging the preconceptions of the past with the possibilities of the future while overcoming the problems of the present required old-school approaches combined with newfangled ideas and unorthodox strategies. Bricklin's willingness to mimic the organizational structure and operational traditions of the Big Three, but to also embrace new production ideas and emerging notions of automotive economic geography, reflected both his limitations as a manager and his prescience in trying to make his company work.

In the end, though, in his attempt to solve the puzzle of industrial modernity, Bricklin's sometimes far-seeing new approaches did not matter as much as did his old-school managerial limitations. Even if Bricklin continued to believe that his dream car was achievable, Richard Hatfield, his partner in the venture, no longer did, or at least he did not think that spending New Brunswick's money to successfully manufacture the SV1 was worth the political cost. Soon enough, Bricklin's, and Hatfield's, dream of the Safety Vehicle-1 would crash, head-on, into this unforgiving reality.

CHAPTER SEVEN

Demise (Rebirth)

***Dream Car* Song 13: "My Hometown," Bruce Springsteen, 1984**

The early 1970s were a moment of societal fracture – the sudden end of three decades of economic prosperity and technological optimism. Until the '70s, postwar North American life had been one of booms. Baby booms. Economic booms. Sonic booms. Technological booms. The automobile, and its sprawling, booming industry, had done much to create the modern society into which Malcolm Bricklin and Richard Hatfield in May 1973 agreed to launch the SV1, a shining symbol of their faith in a future of industrial modernity.

Less than six months later, in October 1973, OPEC announced the cartel's stunning oil embargo. By cutting off the lifeblood of North America's, Europe's, and Japan's economies in response to the West's support of Israel during the Arab-Israeli Yom Kippur War – the oil that fuelled automobility and all that it entailed – OPEC triggered the greatest earthquake that industrial modernity had yet experienced, heralding and setting in motion a new era of aftershocks. Oil shocks. Economic shocks. Nixon shocks. Inflation shocks. Watergate shocks. Unemployment shocks.

Given its high-risk nature, the collapse of the Bricklin was not necessarily a shock for all those who were involved in the venture. Nor was it for those who had opined on whether or not Bricklin could succeed, even with Hatfield's seemingly abrupt decision in September 1975 to cut off the enterprise. In the end, for all its hope, all its promise, all its futuristic potential, General Vehicle Incorporated was an infamously spectacular failure as a car company. So, even if the venture's sudden end had not entirely surprised the people of New Brunswick, the SV1s meteoric rise and demise had undoubtedly jolted their province. But the Bricklin's failure also revealed deeper, underlying changes that reverberated well beyond GVI's bankruptcy, the shuttering of BCL's New Brunswick factories, and the unemployment that accompanied the firm's dissolution. In fact, the venture's aftershocks initiated three overlapping narratives of demise. Each reflects important aspects of Malcolm Bricklin's career, of the Bricklin venture's place in the broader evolution of North America's political economy, and of Richard Hatfield's fate.

First, GVI's failure illustrates not only Malcolm Bricklin's shortcomings as the manager of an automobile manufacturing firm but also his inability to save his company. In September 1975, when it became clear that GVI was simply not making enough money, wasn't building cars fast enough, continued to have production and quality problems, and needed far more financing to overcome these problems, New Brunswick put an ultimatum to Bricklin the man and Bricklin the firm. The government told Malcolm that, in order to get continued support, he needed to fix the firm's problems and find more outside money. When he instead produced a fantastical recapitalization proposal that asked for millions more from the province, Bricklin's proposal was deemed unrealistic and unacceptable.[1] In the middle of a BCL board meeting, Hatfield dramatically arrived to tell Malcolm and the Bricklin directors that no more money would be forthcoming, throwing the firm into receivership and eventually bankruptcy.[2] The company was done, and Bricklin's – and Hatfield's – dreams dashed. Unlike Lee Iacocca just a few years later, Malcolm Bricklin could not save his firm, and this narrative of demise completed the archetypal arc of his entrepreneurial career.

The end of the Bricklin also signified a second unfolding story of demise, one that represented two signal moments in the broader, evolving political economy of North America, one ideological, the other material. The firm's headline-grabbing collapse, and especially its direct government ownership, became *prima facie* evidence in the popular and academic commentaries swirling about in the early 1970s over the increasingly contested question of state intervention in the economy. Because of its high profile and notoriety, Bricklin's demise contributed a small but important shift in that discussion, which that saw the denouncement of the SV1 as a costly example of the folly of statism, and thus indirectly as a condemnation of Keynesianism, even as it portended a future of government bailouts and subsidies in the sector.

Simultaneously, the human and material consequences of the Bricklin operation's rapid rise, demise, and economic fallout for New Brunswick made it a microcosm of North American deindustrialization, an emerging real-world phenomenon that came to reshape so many communities from the 1970s to the early 2000s. The layoffs, plant closures, and financial impact of Bricklin's demise represent a prologue to a declinist narrative that became a fundamental, corrosive current of the continent's post-1973 political, economic, and cultural history, particularly in the auto industry. Yet the plant's closure also symbolized the beginnings of an emerging, leaner deindustrialization, which ultimately pointed to an industrial postmodern society more fully realized by the 2010s and 2020s.

Finally, the end of the SV1 also marked the beginning of the slow demise of Richard Hatfield's political career. To be sure, the Bricklin venture was not what ultimately broke Hatfield's connection to the people of his province, given New Brunswickers' willingness to forgive their unorthodox premier for trying something as daring as the Bricklin, and his ability to escape direct electoral or political accountability for the costly venture. But Hatfield's swaggering support for the car, and especially his legendary 1974 campaign, marked the peak of his confident, flamboyant, premiership, and his "politics of fun." After Bricklin, things were different. The sad story of Hatfield's downfall was another important facet of Bricklin's narrative of demise, even if it may not have been a direct cause.

And yet, despite these overlapping narratives of demise, elements of the Bricklin venture stubbornly persisted, and its legacies revealed glimpses of a new future, a rebirth. Malcolm Bricklin's firm may not have been salvaged, but its spirit lived on, as did the SV1 itself. As with the Bricklin's demise, these narratives of rebirth emerged across three interconnected stories. First, the idea of rebirth could be seen in the fact that the notion of a revival of the SV1 itself died hard. The Bricklin's appealing aesthetic and design, its penetration into the consciousness of North America's consumers and auto industry, and the reality that the car had in fact made it into production, prompted multiple inquiries as to whether or not the firm could be resuscitated. Some of these proposals were serious, and seriously considered. As late as 1987 the New Brunswick government was still responding to queries from interested parties about restarting production of the car, long after all the machinery had been auctioned off, the plants turned over to other ventures, and the SV1's schematics deposited in the provincial archives.[3] At the same time, with nearly three thousand SV1s actually built, the SV1 was a tangible artefact of the Bricklin dream, sustained by the determination of loyal Bricklin aficionados and enthusiasts who proudly kept the flame of the vehicle alive, decades after its demise, and despite its ignominious end.

Second, the SV1's ongoing influence could be seen in the prescience of many of Bricklin's stylistic and production innovations, processes, and strategies, long after manufacture ended in Saint John. Most obvious were the uncanny parallels between the SV1 and its spiritual successor, John Z. DeLorean's DMC, which also famously chased the dream of a sexy, gull-winged sportscar. But it wasn't just the DeLorean: in the 1980s and after, vestiges of the Bricklin could be seen across the North American auto sector in a variety of vehicles, firms, and methods. This legacy of the Bricklin was profound, yet it has been much less remarked upon. From the SV1's design cues, its emphasis on safety, and its innovative technologies, to the firm's production processes, its approach to labour, its government relations, and its hybrid ownership, Bricklin and his venture foresaw and foreshadowed important developments in the auto sector and the broader economy, and in its politics, and, again, pointed to the lean deindustrialization of the early twenty-first century.

Finally, rebirth could be seen in Malcolm Bricklin's own symbolic role as an entrepreneurial bridge across that shift from industrial modernity's Fordist legacy to its postmodern future. In his attempts at innovation, but especially his promotional abilities and flair, Bricklin in some ways presaged the entrepreneurial archetype and performance taken on by Elon Musk, who was key in creating the electrified, digitized, and robotic fourth industrial revolution. Ultimately, for all its spectacular failure, the Bricklin also represented a transitional moment towards automobility's twenty-first-century renewal.

Demise, Part I. Saviour? Bricklin, Receivership, and Bankruptcy

In the end, it wasn't financialization but a lack of financing that led to Bricklin's demise. Malcolm may have been in over his head when it came to running an automobile manufacturing firm, but his greatest managerial error was his initial, tremendous underestimation of the immense cost of launching and producing his vehicle. Hatfield, for his part, should have known better, too.

In the spring of 1973, Bricklin's opening pitch to Hatfield was that he could launch the whole venture for \$16 million. Yet by the summer of 1974, Bricklin had raised probably only about \$10 million, \$4.5 million from New Brunswick (through loan guarantees with the First Pennsylvania Bank and the Bank of Montreal), \$1 million in equity from New Brunswick's Provincial Holdings Ltd. (PHL), and an additional \$3 million loan guarantee from the federal government's Department of Regional Economic Expansion (DREE). As part of the deal, Bricklin had also pledged the design and development rights for the car to the Canadian manufacturing arm. Those were worth, by "mutual agreement," \$1 million and probably cost \$2 million to develop. Plus, there was whatever Bricklin himself brought to the venture.[4]

While this might have seemed like a significant amount of startup money, what Bricklin had promised Hatfield was simply not realistic. But neither he, nor the province, truly understood this. Compared to the last effort to launch a new company, Bricklin was massively underfunded. Kaiser-Frazer's 1940s failure had shown that "if the price in the auto industry [for entry] was $300 million in 1945," three decades later "it was infinitely higher." By the late 1970s, one Detroit expert estimated that "$2 billion was conservative" when it came to launching a new car company.[5] Unsurprisingly, even before BCL's July 1974 startup, Bricklin had burned through his initial financing, and, with no additional outside capital, he went back to New Brunswick for more money.[6] It was only the first of a succession of ever-increasing requests.

By October, during the provincial election, New Brunswick officials complained that they were already on "a 'money on demand' basis" with Bricklin.[7] In response, the government quietly granted BCL a shareholder's loan of $2 million. In return, Bricklin promised New Brunswick a $25 royalty on the first 40,000 cars shipped and $50 on the next 180,000 vehicles produced (and 200,000 shares of GVI at one cent per share), a somewhat fantastical arrangement, given the production difficulties BCL was by then facing.[8] (Bricklin had already pledged SV1 royalties as collateral for additional loans from the First Pennsylvania Bank, as well.) By then, the New Brunswick government's direct financial "involvement" had reached at least $6.5 million.

The next month, following Hatfield's victory, New Brunswick purchased Bricklin's factory for him. Because GVI was hundreds of thousands of dollars behind in payments on the leased Saint John plant, the government paid off owner T.E. Simms for $1.6 million. In addition, Bricklin needed an immediate cash infusion of $500,000 to keep the firm liquid. He also told government officials that he'd need at least $3.5 million more in the medium term to keep production going. With GVI generating little revenue and no additional outside funding coming from Malcolm or anyone else, New Brunswick had little choice but to accede to Bricklin's requests. In return, the province pushed its ownership of BCL to 67.5 per cent and received promises for additional royalties (another $6.25 per car for the first 40,000 deliveries, and another $12.50 on the next 180,000), plus another 200,000 shares of GVI, at one cent each.[9]

By December, less than six months into production and with problems and costs mounting, Hatfield faced a rising chorus of criticism. The Opposition renewed its demands for information about Bricklin's status and just how much taxpayer money was being poured into the operation. Upon returning from yet another vacation outside the country, Hatfield held a Fredericton news conference, at which he voiced continued confidence in the SV1, despite the outrage that resulted when it was revealed that New Brunswick had provided Bricklin even more funding. Instead, Hatfield aimed the bulk of his remarks at Ottawa, criticizing the federal government's unwillingness to properly support the project, in his view.[10] By then, the province's commitment to Bricklin had reached $15.4 million.[11]

In January 1975, despite the additional funds, GVI's financial situation worsened. New Brunswick was forced to give Bricklin a loan of $7.5 million, a decision that was, according to Hatfield, "based on its continued confidence in the Company and project, on the contribution that Company is making to the provincial economy, and its potential for encouraging further economic development."[12] In March, a confidential government report indicated that the total financial commitment to Bricklin had grown to $23.5 million, most of which was provided or guaranteed by the New Brunswick government.[13]

Still, Bricklin needed more. In late August, Malcolm asked for an additional $1.2 million to source major drive-train components for BCL's September production of the '76 models and for working capital to keep the company going. On 15 September, Hatfield announced an additional grant of $1.2 million in guaranteed letters of credit, justified by what he called an "additional erosion of working capital resulting from continuing start up problems."[14] In cabinet deliberations, economic growth minister Lawrence Garvie made the case that the new funding would allow BCL to "have sufficient funds to carry it through to a breakeven position," although Bricklin still faced a plethora of problems. "As a result," Garvie warned his cabinet colleagues, "there is still a risk associated with this venture, and there is no certainty to the success of the recommended investment."[15] When Bricklin laid off workers to retool, Hatfield faced outraged questions from reporters and the Opposition.

Finally, to protect New Brunswick's financial investment in the project, the government gave Malcolm an ultimatum for that September. The accounting firm of Clarkson Gordon, hired to assess the project, had reported to Garvie that there was no end in sight for the losses or for the demands for more financing.[16] Far too late to make a difference, Garvie stipulated that any additional government money was contingent on the presentation of a "satisfactory operating plan" to be submitted by Bricklin for the firm's board meeting later that month. Unfortunately for Bricklin, by then he faced an intractable situation. No matter what kind of plan he submitted, BCL's production issues and the resulting poor quality of the vehicles would continue to bedevil SV1 output, unless he expended even more money to fix the problems. But Bricklin's continued inability to solve the puzzle of mass manufacturing

Figure 7.1. Hatfield in trouble, *Edmonton Journal*, 30 September 1975.

Figure 7.2. Bricklin in trouble, *L'Evangeline*, 13 December 1975.

a quality vehicle, despite all the money the government had already given BCL, undermined any claim to managerial competence on his part and further eroded Hatfield's confidence in him and the firm.

Of course, the SV1's poor production and quality problems were only the most visible aspect of the difficulties Bricklin had gotten himself into. In the spring of 1975, as complaints from dealers and customers about quality issues mounted, Bricklin's staff had begun meeting on a weekly basis to identify all of the manufacturing and engineering difficulties. The list was long and daunting. The finish on the door jams was inadequate. The rear hatch did not fit properly. The acrylic finish faded on some cars, especially the "Safety Green" SV1s. The door panels on either side of the car were different sizes, and they did not fit properly on some vehicles. The "pop up" lights often did not pop up, or only one would do so ("giving its beleaguered owner a wry and knowing wink," according to one later assessment), and there were serious electrical problems with the vehicle.[17]

Perhaps most damaging, the vaunted gull-wing doors – Bricklin's signature feature – continued to cause serious problems, often even after SV1s had been delivered to dealers. The doors weighed too much (eighty pounds), their hydraulics froze up (sometimes the doors suddenly fell), and they sucked up too much battery power (especially if both doors were opened at the same time). If the car's battery did die, SV1 drivers would be trapped inside, forced to crawl out of the car's narrow back hatch to escape. Eventually, most Bricklin owners switched from hydraulics to an air pump mechanism developed by an engineer in Texas. Frustratingly, the doors leaked, too. Though Bricklin had told his staff that "we must engineer a car that does not leak," the door hinge area was a "disaster." The back hatch's problems with water were just as bad: a test ride during a heavy rain resulted in a flexing that caused "almost a pumping of water into the car."[18]

Fixing all these problems pushed the price of producing each vehicle ever higher. As Bricklin engineering veteran Tom Monroe remembered, servicing the door problems "in the field devoured any profits that may have been made, and the water leak problem didn't get fully solved, either."[19] With all the parts and assembly issues, the first 800 SV1s had each cost about $16,000 to manufacture, and, even by the fall of 1975, every vehicle coming off the line cost around $13,000. Based on the wholesale price, BCL was losing $6,000 for each car it manufactured.[20]

Meanwhile, any push for increased production was accompanied by a "marked deterioration in vehicle quality." In both the Minto and Saint John operations, dozens of production problems had an impact on quality, from the manufacturing of the fiberglass bodies to the production and installation of the doors to the final assembly of the vehicles. When a Bricklin finally left "the line," such that it was, there was still work to be done. As one government observer dryly noted in May 1975, every unit produced "requires at least 20 hours of repair work before it is passed for shipment to dealers."[21] There were also a number of SV1 recalls in 1975, which didn't help the safety image of the vehicle.[22] By then, it had become clear that, even in the best of circumstances, BCL had a production ceiling of about five thousand very costly, problematic vehicles a year.

Simply put, even if there was a market for the SV1, and even if BCL produced enough vehicles to meet demand, if the cars were not up to snuff, dealers wouldn't sell them, and poor-product quality would eventually kill the market, no matter the promotional pizzazz. In June 1975, GVI president, Ralph Henry, admitted to the BCL board that it was "now essential from a marketing standpoint to bring the quality of the cars to a higher level." By September, the impact of quality on sales seemed undeniable. The most alarming evidence was the fact that, of the 2,050 BCL-manufactured SV1s sold (wholesale) to dealers, only 753 had been bought at retail by final customers. This 25 per cent sales rate was, in very large part, a consequence of "negative dealer reactions to the quality of the vehicle."[23] The situation prompted Malcolm to write an open letter to Bricklin dealers in August 1975 pledging to improve quality.[24]

Just as problematically, Bricklin had had to raise the car's price from $7,490 for the '74 SV1s to $9,780 for the '75s, owing to the "escalating cost of parts and production."[25] The '76s were listed at $9,995, plus shipping, for a manufacturer's suggested retail price (MSRP) of $10,744.[26] Even in a period of dramatically rising inflation, the increase was extreme, and an SV1 at that MSRP cost more than a Corvette. Bricklin's dealers were, understandably, waiting for better product, which Malcolm was having tremendous difficulty delivering.[27] As a result, Bricklin Vehicle Corporation, the sales division that Malcolm ran, owed $1.8 million to BCL, the manufacturing division where the government money came from. Even if demand for the SV1 continued, if the quality problems weren't solved, Malcolm's vaunted ability to sell the vehicles might prove more ephemeral than claimed. Yet, as consultant G.E. Sawyer reported to the government, at "no point has management previously reported this extremely depressing situation in retail sales."[28] Unless Malcolm fixed all these problems and (or) found more money to do so, the government would pull the plug. But he was quickly losing credibility: as Sawyer complained in August of 1975, "the time is rapidly being reached when the Board needs to consider whether the credibility of Malcolm Bricklin is more important than their own credibility."[29]

The Bricklin drama reached its culmination on a rainy Wednesday, 24 September 1975. With the future of the firm at stake, Malcolm and the BCL board met at the Saint John Holiday Inn (switched from Keddy's Motor Inn to try to fool reporters).

All of the Bricklin directors were there. Bricklin had submitted a plan in response to Garvie's ultimatum, one that spectacularly overvalued GVI at $100 million, asked for another $10 million in government money, and whimsically proclaimed an anticipated level of production of 6,300 cars a year. Malcolm also asked for raises for GVI employees and access to a company plane to "increase efficiency." But the plan reported no new outside funding.[30] By then, the government was in to Bricklin for at least $23 million, $30 for each New Brunswick taxpayer.[31] In the middle of the meeting, Hatfield, along with Garvie, who had pushed the premier to finally end the episode, dramatically appeared to announce that, with no viable plan and no new outside funding, the firm was being placed in receivership. As the minutes of the meeting bloodlessly noted, "After discussion concerning the financing and future of the company … [a] motion duly moved, seconded and unanimously carried … that the directors and management of the company would cooperate fully with the appointment" of a receiver, with only Bricklin voting "nay." On his way out, Hatfield again attempted to elude reporters by sneaking through a kitchen entrance. For his part, asked years later about the meeting, Bricklin claimed to have little memory of the event.[32]

But he was out, and even if the SV1 or BCL or GVI somehow miraculously escaped receivership, Malcolm would not be involved. Two days after ending the venture, Hatfield sombrely told reporters, "I want to say that we still have confidence in the car. Unfortunately, however, there is a limit beyond which it would not be prudent for a government to risk further funds on the basis of such confidence.

That point has now been reached.[33]

A few days later, Bricklin pled his case before a national CBC television audience. The interview, on Paul Soles's *Take 30* show, was part of Bricklin's campaign to save GVI (and himself) from bankruptcy. Bricklin's ploy amounted to little more than a public relations effort in which he argued that New Brunswick should continue funding the project because it had actually *been* working, that GVI simply needed more money, and that saving the SV1 was a matter of provincial or even national pride. But, in attempting the archetypical role of saviour, Bricklin faced a much different dynamic than would Iacocca a few years later: Bricklin had less credibility and fewer options than did the Chrysler boss, and he faced a dramatically different outcome.

On *Take 30*, a candid, casually dressed Bricklin told Soles that he had sunk $2 million into the project, owed millions in "other assets," and would lose "approximately

$10 million," all told. Arizona bankruptcy proceedings, Bricklin joked, would "let me keep five milk cows and two dray horses."[34] What could he have done better, asked Soles? He could have been "smarter," Bricklin acknowledged, but he defended what had been achieved: the company had seven hundred very loyal employees, every Bricklin built was sold, and there was a great demand for the car, especially in Canada, where they had not yet become available. But ultimately, Malcolm admitted, they simply "needed more money."

Why didn't they go public instead of depending on government money? Well, Bricklin replied, if they had gone public, everything that they had done would be viewed through the lens of "fraud," since "there is a tendency whenever you go after public money for an idea, the word fraud comes up ... The only way that this could go public was to show a profit for three or four years, only then should the public have been allowed in." Malcolm wasn't completely incorrect, but he did not disclose to viewers that he had unsuccessfully floated the idea of a public offering to the BCL board.[35]

Were the Big Three "inhibiting" his success? A good question. Bricklin felt that, while they weren't going out of their way to stop him, the Big Three's "arrogance" meant that they had made his parts purchasing difficult.

Bricklin was convinced, however, that despite the receivership, all indicators pointed to the real possibility that the project could be saved and that the car "would be successful." There was still great interest in the vehicle, he declared, and the company had not yet tapped into the lucrative western US market, or even Canada, for that matter. The UAW was committed to the project and had generated a petition with 18,000 signatures to keep the Bricklin going. Even the firm's receivers, "who were not usually the most optimistic of people, felt comfortably that there was a way to save the project," according to Malcolm. Bricklin made the case that a revival would actually boost the car's profile and chances: "Crazy as it sounds, I really feel that the Canadian people really want this to succeed."[36]

Bricklin's flailing salvage campaign continued into October. In confidential discussions with New Brunswick officials, Bricklin told them that he "would not say anything negative about the province" but also warned them that he owned the Bricklin name and had backers who were willing to put money into a Detroit manufacturing operation, and that "the government was dreaming if it thought it could compete with him." But he also admitted that restarting production would require $25 million and that he actually needed the government in order to make anything happen. New Brunswick officials were not moved.[37]

Back in Toronto, Bricklin held a dramatic press conference, declaring that the "continuation" of the SV1 "was in the hands of the Canadian people" and that if

"Canada no longer supports the Bricklin project," he would build a plant in the United States.[38] Afterwards, Bricklin was interviewed by the *Financial Post* in a Chinatown restaurant, accompanied by a "lady friend." He remained adamant: "Dammit, I am not going to let them kill my sportscar. I'll get the money somehow … I only need $20 million to stay in operation." Yet Bricklin also seemed disconnected to the realities facing his situation: "Say, who's the new federal minister of trade? Is he the best one to see? No, I think maybe the Prime Minister … Might as well go to the top."[39] Elsewhere, he claimed to have received "thousands" of supportive phone calls, and that children were offering him their allowance to keep the company going.[40] For all his promotional abilities, Bricklin's attempts to salvage his firm proved unconvincing.

Responding to Bricklin's media campaign, Hatfield told reporters, on returning from a government mission to Japan in mid-October (a conveniently timed escape at the height of the Bricklin outrage), that the project still had "superb potential, and that advice from the best qualified experts is that an annual production of 5,000 automobiles and a tight operating budget would be viable." But, he argued, the "main attraction" at this point was for an offshore company to get involved, giving such a firm eligibility under the auto pact, something on which "we understood we had an undertaking" from Ottawa "years ago," but that the federal government "never acted on it." Regardless, the premier stated, there would be no new money from New Brunswick if Malcolm was involved.[41]

Despite Hatfield's unwillingness to budge, Bricklin remained defiant to the end. In December, he wrote to the premier, lamenting that the province had "refuse[d] to include the management of Bricklin Canada Ltd. in any discussions pertaining to the future" of the firm since October. With no response to his entreaties, Bricklin told Hatfield that he had had no choice but to place GVI and its subsidiaries into US federal bankruptcy law's Chapter 11, and that "on Friday December 12th, 1975, I personally went bankrupt." He offered his resignation "with deep regret" and ended by telling Hatfield that "if there's anything I can ever do for the people of New Brunswick, please do not hesitate to call me." In a rather terse and perfunctory reply, Hatfield simply acknowledged receipt of Bricklin's resignation, and wrote that "I have directed that this matter be brought before the next shareholder's meeting of Bricklin Canada, Ltd."[42] The politics of fun, indeed.

In his final act as GVI chair, Bricklin sent out a characteristic press release from his adopted hometown, Scottsdale, "the West's Most Western Town," as he called it. Bricklin declared that, though he had "financially lost everything," he was committed to "stay in the saddle." His flurry of media appearances and public pleadings had not saved the company, nor had his nationalist appeal to the people, nor had calling upon his best promotional cowboy imagery. With no new investors, and the government as a final source of funding already tapped out, Malcolm could not pull off an Iacocca-like rescue for his firm.[43]

Bricklin's 1976 Arizona bankruptcy proceedings revealed the depth of GVI's troubled existence. As chair and majority shareholder, Bricklin listed personal debts of $32,365,100.03. The only assets he claimed in his bankruptcy statement were a rifle, a watch, skis, and personal effects with a value of $2,000. He owed American Express more than $11,000, Diner's Club over $2,000, and BankAmerica and Carte Blanche $1,000 each. Bricklin was forced to move from his posh ranch-style estate, operated by the Scottsdale Hilton, into a more modest address at 3800 East Lincoln Drive, Unit 15 (it was still a nice place).[44] Bricklin had personally guaranteed repayment of about $23 million in government loans. All told, in March 1976, G.S. Wheatley tabulated the total outlay for the project from all sources at $25.7 million, not including the $1.5 million that the province spent for the Simms plant. Meanwhile, the list of Bricklin's unsecured creditors ran to twenty-four pages.[45]

In 1976, the government quietly wound up BCL's operations. At the April GVI directors' meeting, the firm's shareholders (with Wheatley representing 1,529,996 shares) voted to remove Bricklin from the board.[46] At the final BCL board meeting in September, the directors passed motions reiterating the province's stance that "General Vehicle, Inc., was totally responsible for the marketing, warranty, and parts and service aspects of the Bricklin organization … [and] was also responsible for sole responsibility of the Bricklin vehicles as set out in the original equity arraignment" between the firm and the province.[47] This responsibility, presumably, included a lawsuit launched by one James Wilson, "with respect to injuries he received which were allegedly caused by a falling Bricklin door."[48]

By then, the firm's assets had all been sold off at auction, and the government-appointed receivers had sold the remaining SV1s sitting in the plant – including 287 mostly completed '75s and twelve '76s – to dealer Bill Byers of Columbus, Ohio, along with anything else that was left of the company.[49] According to Jack Siuta, president of Bricklin Owners International, there were, when the firm went under, about 800 Bricklins "on lots, museums or being held by collectors," with about 1,850 SV1s registered to owners in the United States and nine in different countries.[50] In 1979, the New Brunswick government still had two Bricklins in storage, one of which was intended to be put on permanent display in the New Brunswick Museum in Saint John, the other to be used a part of a travelling display by the province's Historical Resources Administration.[51]

Of course, GVI's demise didn't mean the end for Malcolm Bricklin. In fact, as a serial entrepreneur, Bricklin's bankruptcy (his second of several) represented just

Figure 7.3. Bricklin receivership auction poster, 1978.

another, albeit important, learning experience. Even if, as he admitted during the proceedings, the "possibility is I lose everything," he recognized that "the knowledge and experience I have gained, they won't take away."[52] And, in the case of the SV1, it had been a *bona fide* effort to coax a dream car into reality, even if it failed. Moreover, Bricklin's GVI bankruptcy marks yet another indication that, in an increasingly financialized world, the idea of personal bankruptcy was neither the end of a business career nor even much of a mark of shame. GVI's bankruptcy was a beginning, one that reflected Bricklin's own performative financialization and also the establishment of his personal brand. Despite his firm's ignominious end, Bricklin's name would retain its value, and GVI and the SV1's story would provide a stepping stone to further, even grander stages and entrepreneurial endeavours. Indeed, even with the demise of the dream of the SV1 and of GVI, bankruptcy would become, in post-70s, postmodern society, practically and performatively an entrepreneurial way of life for Malcolm Bricklin. As it would for so many notable others.

Demise, Part II, Denouncement and Deindustrialization

Beyond Malcolm Bricklin's and his firm's bankruptcies, GVI's failure also reflected two different aspects of an emerging, entwined political economy of demise, one of ideology, the other all too real. On the one hand, the quickly coagulating commentary surrounding Bricklin's spectacular demise denounced the ill-fated venture as a failure of government intervention in the economy, and the episode became part of a broader neoliberal discourse reshaping ideas around industrial policy. On the other hand, in the material, manufacturing world, the mid-1970s closure of an auto plant, even one as quixotic and unlikely as Bricklin's, represented a telling example in the developing narrative of North American deindustrialization. In this instance, the Bricklin plant's story and its fate pointed to the ongoing, uneven nature of this process across a deindustrialization continuum, but also to the emergence of a newer, leaner manufacturing condition. With Bricklin, one could see the beginnings of a post-1973 form of lean deindustrialization, one that revealed elements of the transition from Fordism to a third industrial revolution, and ultimately, in the distance, to a fourth: a decarbonized, digitized, robotic, industrial postmodernity.

The denouncement of the Bricklin project, and especially its government-backed structure, came fast and furious. Even during his September CBC interview (GVI was then still in receivership) Soles asked Bricklin whether his project – "this kind of enterprise" – had doomed similar efforts in Canada going forward. "It's doomed in Canada," Bricklin defiantly declared, "if the Canadians feel it's doomed." He lamented that "there's almost a feeling that anything the government gets involved in is not going to be successful. I almost feel that there's been a sigh of relief, that well, see 'we proved it, it's not successful.'" As if to emphasize the point, Soles drew a parallel between Bricklin's failure and another example of statist decline in the headlines, the financial crisis faced by a teetering New York City. "If you think you're having troubles," Soles challenged Bricklin, "you've got the whole city of New York right beside you, driving the same highway. If they can't find enough money, how do you feel hopeful that you can?" Bricklin optimistically replied that "I have the people of Canada behind me; New York doesn't."[53] Nonetheless, the insinuation stuck. Bricklin's demise was already being conflated with the inability or unwillingness of governments, including the administration of Gerald Ford in Washington (*New York Post*: "Ford to City: Drop Dead") to successfully manage or intervene in a rapidly fragmenting mid-1970s economic landscape.

In the months, years, and decades following the Bricklin's collapse, on television shows like *Take 30*, and in magazines, newspapers, scholarly reports, and the broader public discourse, the Bricklin incident was regularly featured as a shiny, plastic symbol of the shortcomings of statist economic policies. In 1976, *Maclean's* declared that "politically created industries" that are "uneconomic and require constant financial aid, just like Bricklin," had proved an "unmitigated disaster."[54] That same year, the *Globe and Mail* remarked that "government's panting pursuit of industry through grants, subsidies and whatever means might be at hand has been almost an article of faith." But this attitude "was changing." What seemed to have caused the change "was the spectacular collapse last fall of the Bricklin sportscar venture."[55]

A year later, Bricklin was again featured in *Maclean's*, as the most prominent of a number of "government subsidized failures" that had finally taught Atlantic provincial governments that the days of "the big project, often directed by someone from outside the province – and the $23 million Bricklin sting is the classic example – appear to be numbered."[56] In yet another 1977 article, *Maclean's* sniggered that, although Malcolm had "left the country $20 million poorer than he found it," his very name had contributed a new meaning to the English language: "Bricklin" now stood for "spectacular industrial failure at spectacular public expense."[57] Meanwhile, the *Wall Street Journal* notably featured Bricklin as a reason for the decision of governments in the Maritimes (a "northern Appalachia") to "pull back from costly schemes to attract industry."[58] A 1979 *Financial Post* article told readers that "the ghost of Bricklin Canada Ltd. still walks, pointing a skeletal finger at the perils of public investment," even if "these days it's a remarkably blithe spirit."[59]

By the 1980s, Bricklin had become something of an emblem of the failure of state intervention. Bricklin's prominence as a high-profile, high-risk automobile venture made it an easy target. In fact, between 1975 and 1977, fourteen government-assisted industries in New Brunswick had disappeared, costing the province nearly $50 million, while across the Martimes, there had a number of other government-backed failures, from stereo equipment to cruise ships.[60] Yet none of these failures gained the same notoriety or representational power as Bricklin. In his 1987 biography of Hatfield, Richard Starr wrote that "if the Bricklin car was the symbol during the [1974] election campaign of a better economic future, its failure was a harbinger for a string of other collapses, many of them enterprises backed with government dollars."[61]

For his part, Hatfield pointed out that the Bricklin's infamy far outstripped its actual cost. Even before the firm's collapse, in May 1975, he recognized that "sure, it is an expensive investment, but compared with other projects in the province it is quite average. Nobody took umbrage at our financing a plywood mill, but the Bricklin car caught everybody's fancy."[62] And, while Bricklin's failure resulted in "outcries of anguish in the national media and the punditry clucking at the principle of public investment," when these state investment policies did work, as they had with government support for a McCain Foods production facility that generated immense returns, few people complained.[63]

Nonetheless, given its high profile (if relatively low actual cost), academic studies also made Bricklin a shorthand in their mounting critique of the failures of state enterprise. Bricklin was prominently featured in Stanford Borins's and Lee Brown's 1986 book *Investments in Failure: Five Government Corporations That Cost the Canadian Taxpayer Billions*. Reflecting the increasingly critical tone taken towards the failures of state enterprise – of which Bricklin had become something of a poster child – the study cast "considerable doubt on the desirability" of government intervention. Over the course of their research, Borins and Lee "became increasingly indignant" and "expressed [their] anger in harsh and sardonic judgements about the individuals and management systems" responsible for the "decisions that wasted so many millions of dollars." The relatively modest Bricklin loss ($25 million to create 700 jobs; $19,200 each), was lumped in with Canadair ($1.4 billion; $78,000 a job), Deuterium of Canada ($425 million; $179,000 a job), Consolidated Computer ($71 million), and Churchill Forest Industries ($120 million). Bricklin was also the only case of an individual entrepreneur, or a consumer product, included in the study.[64]

Other political economy studies of the period also highlighted Bricklin in their analyses of the changing dynamics of business-government relations and of government regional development schemes gone awry, usually with a harsh judgment.[65] A notable contribution came from the historian John Reid. His summation of Seventies state intervention in the Maritimes placed the Bricklin in the centre of a narrative of decline: "Once again an attempt to produce employment by feeding subsidies to an outside entrepreneur had produced disruption in the lives of individuals, families, and communities, and had led only to eventual disillusionment."[66]

Eventually, and unsurprisingly, the Bricklin episode's identification with state failure had an impact on public policy, too, certainly in New Brunswick. A 1983 Science Council of Canada report concluded that the province's attempts to develop "an integrated industrial complex in Saint John" through the New Brunswick Development Corporation and Multiplex (the agency that had brought Bricklin to New Brunswick) was "largely abandoned due to a lack of success with either corporation and a number of other industrial development failures, most notably the Bricklin car assembly plant." In the Bricklin's wake, "the two corporations were disbanded."[67]

Meanwhile, Provincial Holding's Ltd. (PHL), New Brunswick's investment agency and Bricklin's official government shareholder, changed its tune as well, with a new emphasis on seeking to reduce the province's exposure as much as possible. G. Stephen Wheatley, a key player in the government's oversight and ownership of Bricklin, became the agency's leader, and times changed when it came to state ownership. In 1983, Wheatley declared that PHL "would rather have no investment" in private ventures. Instead, he told the *Financial Post*, "we try to get companies to find their capital elsewhere." In any event, since the Bricklin, the number of New Brunswick firms with loan guarantees had been steadily declining, as had the total amount outstanding. PHL, and the province, Wheatley stated, had become "staunchly free enterprise in its philosophy."[68]

By then, so, too, had much of the Canadian business and political firmament. As Canadians increasingly moved away from macroeconomic state intervention to embrace free market economic ideologies and policies starting in the 1970s, Bricklin's demise as a failure of public policy had become a sometimes hyperbolic article of faith. The 1980s and 1990s were decades of trade liberalization, deregulation, and state privatization, with the sale of many federal and provincial Crown corporations. In 1993, Thomas d'Aquino, the influential president of the Business Council on National Issues and a leading advocate of Canada-US free trade, cited Bricklin as one of two leading examples in the "long trail of unsuccessful ventures" connected to government initiatives. The other was the $100 million government-supported Westray mine in Nova Scotia, which closed following a 1992 explosion that killed twenty-nine miners.[69] A 2002 book, *Colossal Canadian Failures*, featured the Bricklin incident prominently and, of course, the government's role in the venture.[70] In 2012, almost four decades after its demise, the *Financial Post Magazine* lumped the Bricklin failure in with notorious private sector "Canadian Duds" such as the tectonic collapse of Research in Motion, the bailout of Dome Petroleum (a $6 *billion* debacle), and outright frauds like the Bre-X mining scandal, which featured criminality and suicide.[71]

In the twenty-first century, the Bricklin incident has largely retained its place in the collective consciousness, with the SV1 being branded as one of "the 50 worst cars of all time."[72] As a question of state enterprise, however, it's also clear that, in this instance, owing to its high profile, its timing, and the nature of its government ownership, the Bricklin had played a small but telling role in neoliberalism's emerging discourse, one that starting in the 1970s, around the time of GVI's failure, and saw any statist intervention as a misguided infringement on the sanctity of the free market. But Bricklin's demise had also played a small but telling role in the seismic real-world changes transforming the North American industrial economy of the Seventies, too.

As a post-embargo narrative of demise, the deindustrialization of North America's auto industry didn't start with the 1975 closure of the Bricklin factories and the layoff of the firm's seven hundred workers. Nor did it start with the wave of plant closures ordered by Lee Iacocca during Chrysler's near death in 1979–81. In the auto sector, and all other industries, for that matter, deindustrialization is an ongoing process, one that reshapes economic geographies, communities, and families every time a plant is closed or moved and workers lose their jobs.[73] Auto plants have been closing and/or moving, and workers have been losing their jobs, since the start of car manufacturing, the very onset of automobile industrial modernity. Indeed, since the advent of the first industrial revolution in the 1700s, industrialization, deindustrialization, *and* reindustrialization have existed and co-existed as sequential, overlapping, and simultaneous processes that ebb and flow over time. The warp and weft of this deindustrialization continuum is deeply influenced by the creative destruction wrought by entrepreneurs (especially automobile entrepreneurs) and the evolving position and culture of industrial firms, but also by changing production processes and technologies, state responses, class formation, and global and local economic and political events, among many factors.[74]

In fact, in the decades that witnessed the initial, spectacular growth and consolidation of the auto sector, the years between Henry Ford's 1903 start and his 1947 death, *hundreds* of North American auto factories and plants closed down, and thousands of workers, managers, and owners lost their livelihoods. From one-plant startups to established firms to electric and steam automobile manufacturers, the abandoned factories of defunct auto firms littered the early landscape of industrial modernity. Even during Detroit's postwar glory years, failures, relocations, and mergers resulted in the shuttering of plants across much of North America, especially those of the "independents," as they slowly succumbed to their industry's harsh competitive realities (Crossley, 1952; Packard, 1956; Studebaker, 1958, 1966). The last independent, American Motors Corporation, a result of the 1954 merger and restructuring of Hudson and Nash-Kelvinator, was itself swallowed by Iacocca's Chrysler in 1987.[75]

Beginning in the 1970s, however, auto sector deindustrialization took on a new and more pernicious meaning, as the Big Three and AMC started to close plants on a scale that brutally drove home their industry's economic power and the risk it represented. After decades of economic stability, the closure of auto factories employing hundreds and often thousands of workers came as a shock to the communities that had grown so dependent on these giant enterprises. Between 1978 and 1982, some 300,000 auto sector workers lost their jobs, many as a consequence of the Chrysler bailout. Along with auto assembly plants, supporting industries in steel, rubber, textiles, and a host of other manufacturing sectors across the United States and Canada, but especially in the Great Lakes region, saw factory closures. This was no longer solely a question of "the runaway factory," but permanent restructuring.[76]

The outright plant closures and demolitions, and the relocations southward (and northward) meant that a new economic geography was emerging in the 1970s and 1980s, one that resulted in a new term for the erosion and dislocation caused by deindustrialization: the rust belt. Historian Steven High has shown that, as ordinary North American people and their communities grappled with the dramatic post-1974 decline of manufacturing, the response to these closures from governments, unions, and workers differed on either side of the border, shaped by local as much as national identities, political cultures, and legal environments.[77] Along with the immediate impact on workers and their communities, the "half-life of deindustrialization" meant that the fallout from this process was felt across generations.[78]

The Bricklin episode can be read as a microcosm of the deindustrialization continuum, and a truncated version of this process within the auto sector and the broader industrial economy. From Bricklin and Hatfield's announcement of the venture to the plants' padlocking and the layoff of BCL's workers, this episode illustrated North American deindustrialization's important characteristics, particularly its impact on workers, and their response. Interestingly, and as a testament to the auto pact's benefits for Canadians, Bricklin's was the *only* auto assembly facility to close in Canada between 1966, when Studebaker closed its Hamilton, Ontario, facilities, and 1992, when AMC in Brampton, Ontario, was shuttered, a period during which the Canadian sector was simultaneously expanding its assembly capacity.[79] Meanwhile, across the border during the same timeframe, numerous American facilities closed their doors, including, notably, Chrysler's Dodge Main in Detroit (1980), Ford's Mahwah Assembly in New Jersey (1980), and GM's Fremont Assembly plant in California (1982).

In this broader context of North America's deindustrialization continuum, the September 1975 announcement that BCL's "controversial automobile plants were padlocked" was not a surprise for many of its workers. The venture's uncertainly and economic risk were captured by Judy Barrett, twenty-five, a light installer on the Saint John assembly line, who commented that, at Bricklin, "you never knew when you came in if this would be your last day."[80] After receiving their final paycheques in late September, Bricklin's workers were informed by the UAW that they were now technically laid off. While some had feared that the workers' cheques might bounce, the province stepped in to ensure that the $200,000 payroll was covered. But for hundreds of newly unemployed Bricklin workers, especially "for assembly workers without special skills, it's not a happy situation."[81]

By then, Bricklin's workers had already launched a wildcat strike in 1974, so it was unsurprising that their next step echoed much of the activist labour movement's response characteristic of the early part of the decade.[82] In October 1975, about two hundred of Bricklin's approximately seven hundred employees marched on government offices in Saint John, demanding that Hatfield *do* something (despite the fact that the New Brunswick government had already spent $23 million in taxpayer funds to create their jobs in the first place). During the protest, UAW officials even said that workers would be willing to invest $50 a month each towards saving the company, and that a UAW petition garnered 18,000 signatures in favour of keeping the plant open.[83] Malcolm, of course, was fully in support of his workers, despite some earlier misgivings regarding New Brunswick's work rules.

Despite these gestures, neither the union, nor Bricklin, nor the government was able or willing to keep the plant open, an outcome that was replicated across deindustrializing North America in the years to come. Workers who hoped that K.C. Irving would take over the company after it went into receivership included repairman Robert Horncastle Jr., who feared that "he and the other 700 Bricklin employees may soon join the province's 22,000 jobless."[84] While Saint John itself was doing alright, relatively speaking, in terms of (industrial) employment, the provincial outlook was changing fairly quickly, and not for the better: New Brunswick's unemployment rate jumped from 7.5 per cent in 1974 to 13.3 per cent in 1977.[85] Unemployment was rising all over North America, it seemed, in a decade beset by stagflation – a viscous combination of stagnant growth and high inflation that undermined industrialism and further eroded the credibility of Keynesian policymaking.[86]

Deindustrialization seemed to be happening outside of Saint John, too, including elsewhere in New Brunswick and the rest of the Maritimes. As a once-bustling extractive, manufacturing, and transportation region since the eighteenth century, the Maritimes had long been accustomed to the ebbs and flows of the deindustrialization continuum.[87] But since the early 1900s, the region's industrial fortunes had largely settled on the negative side of the scale, something that Hatfield was keenly aware of (hence, the Bricklin venture, among others). In the period after the 1960s, it wasn't just Bricklin that folded, though that was among the most infamous and high-profile examples of the region's ongoing industrial erosion. Across the Maritimes, there was a constant drumbeat of closures and layoffs, even as governments like Hatfield's pursued economic development projects in search of the brass ring of industrial modernity, sometimes simultaneously having to manage significant industrial closings and (less often) openings. In Saint John, which was slightly more industrial than much of the region (mostly because of the Irving oil, forestry, and shipbuilding operations), the impact of seven hundred lost jobs was less stark than it might have been elsewhere but still significant. Deindustrialization, "a wider socioeconomic, political, and cultural process with no fixed end point," according to High and Lachlan MacKinnon was, indeed, an uneven process.[88]

At the same time, Bricklin plant's closure reflected an emerging post-1973 "lean deindustrialization," a central aspect of industrial postmodernity. In its North American–wide, just-in-time, modularized, and outsourced production processes, Bricklin's operation had represented a midpoint between Fordism and a renewed lean manufacturing industrial era. But the firm's broader story also showed how (automobile) manufacturing and industry continued apace, albeit in fewer places and in a manner more geographically dispersed and much more efficient (with even greater technology, but fewer workers). As high industrial modernity's deindustrialization accelerated starting in the 1970s, it spread unevenly across North America, from "one-job towns" that were devastated by the closure of a sole employer to whole cities and regions that were decimated by tens of thousands of job losses.[89]

Nevertheless, even as traditional North American manufacturing regions deindustrialized and decentralized, they did so in a lean (manufacturing) form, one that included, in the case of the auto sector, a wave of reindustrialization from abroad.[90] From the 1970s to the 2010s, there was a significant decline in manufacturing employment in the United States, from a postwar peak of nearly twenty million workers in 1971 to approximately twelve million by the late 2010s. Directly within automotive manufacturing, there was an uneven yet steady decline, particularly for the Detroit Three, from nearly two million to approximately one million workers. Nonetheless, despite these dramatic changes, total automotive output remained largely consistent across this period, and the United States produced approximately the same number of vehicles in the 1970s as it did in the 1990s and the 2010s with fewer workers, even if there was a greater number of firms.[91]

In the auto sector, lean manufacturing and its corollary, lean deindustrialization, were the results of production and technological advances that, by the early 2000s, facilitated a transition to an electrified future, with restructuring *and* reindustrialization in the form of new assembly plants and battery facilities (and semiconductor plants), almost always supported by massive government subsidies (à la Bricklin). What ultimately emerged was a reindustrialized, roboticized, digitized, decarbonized, artificially intelligent fourth industrial revolution, led by auto entrepreneurs and firms and governments that were determined to pursue a new, electrified age of automobility.

Of course, since the 1970s, the other side of lean deindustrialization has been its corrosive impact. This has included the weakening of unions, as fewer workers manufacture more products; the ongoing capriciousness of capital in seeking cheaper locales with greater government support; the selective willingness of governments to provide financial support for some industries (e.g., automotive, semiconductors, and other technological industries) and their concurrent unwillingness to do much beyond managing closure in others (e.g., textiles, mines, mills); and the unrelenting dependence of society on technology.[92]

It's possible, then, to see Bricklin as a harbinger of neoliberal trends, including loosening national borders, deurbanizing and geographically dispersing manufacturing, and ending state ownership and intervention (beyond direct funding or temporary emergency nationalization), and as a microcosm of the range of the post-1973 deindustrialization continuum. Regardless of the accuracy of this interpretation, there's no question that people in New Brunswick had lost their jobs, and that the province's reputation took a tremendous beating. Much of that fell on the New Brunswick government, and especially the province's premier.

Demise, Part III. Hatfield, Drugs, Defeat, and Departure

Richard Hatfield may have escaped direct accountability for the Bricklin debacle, but the incident nonetheless played a key element in his own narrative of demise. In 1987, Dr. Everett Chalmers, one of Richard Hatfield's oldest hometown Tory supporters, remarked that, despite Hatfield's willingness to play along and make light of the fiasco after 1975, Bricklin "did something to Richard he never recovered from." Hatfield, Dr. Chalmers said, "got a big guilt complex from letting down the people of New Brunswick," and the Bricklin debacle haunted him for the rest of his career, despite his political survivability.[93]

Following his 1982 election victory, Hatfield's last term in office saw the premier's reputation for flamboyance degenerate into outright scandal around his alleged drug use and accusations of other illicit behaviours. These incidents, more than anything else, exposed Hatfield to criticisms about his lifestyle that he had been able to effectively sidestep up to that point in his political career. The accusations and allegations permanently destroyed the connections that he had built with

Figure 7.4. A dead end, cartoon by Josh Beutel, *Telegraph-Journal.*

the province's voters and led him to the worst electoral result in Canadian political history.

Since the 1960s, drug use in Canada had become a relatively common occurrence, a major element of the counterculture and for the baby boom generation. As historian Marcel Martel has shown, the 1960s and early 1970s witnessed a vigorous debate about drugs, their place in society, and their legal status, including the 1974 LeDain royal commission on the subject. Though the government did not move to end the prohibition of cannabis (and other drugs such as LSD), Canadian society was clearly starting to shift towards a more liberal approach to drug use.[94]

That shift in attitudes, however, did not necessarily apply to political leaders, at least not yet, and certainly not in New Brunswick. In 1984, during a visit by Queen Elizabeth II to commemorate the two-hundredth anniversary of New Brunswick's founding, just as Hatfield was about to board a plane with the monarch, the Royal Canadian Mounted Police (RCMP) discovered a small amount of marijuana in a pocket of his suitcase, causing a national scandal.[95] Hatfield claimed that the drugs had been planted in his luggage ("obviously, I do not know how it got there") and that he was effectively being framed by someone. Later, one former political operative claimed that the drugs had been placed in the premier's luggage by Paul Walsh, a journalist who was said to have been seeking revenge for having been romantically spurned by the premier.[96] Despite Hatfield's protestations, the case sparked a furor in New Brunswick and led to unsavoury headlines across Canada and beyond, and Hatfield faced trial in January 1985 for drug possession. The judge in the case acquitted the premier, and the RCMP started its own investigation of Hatfield's claim of a sabotage, but not before further allegations emerged regarding the premier's controversial lifestyle.[97]

Just two weeks after the premier was acquitted for drug possession, two young men, one of whom had been at Hatfield's trial, swore out affidavits to the Mounties that Hatfield had invited them to an all-night party at his home in 1981, where they saw the premier smoke marijuana and snort cocaine. Further, the pair claimed that Hatfield took them to Montreal on a government-chartered plane, where they continued their weekend-long party in a hotel room.[98] Hatfield steadfastly denied the allegations of drug use, saying that he was "unrevised and unrepentant" – using the tagline of former Conservative prime minister Arthur Meighen's biography. Nevertheless, he did admit to some of the salacious details of the incident:

> It is true that they [the men who had made the claims] were in my home together with others, some four years ago. However, they were strangers to me. Those who know me will confirm I am extremely gregarious. I meet and talk to people on the street, in the markets and the shops, in the restaurants and bars. I invite them to my house. I go to their houses. The door to my house is usually unlocked and frequently open. That is my way. I admit I am unconventional.[99]

Whether Hatfield used drugs remains unproven. Clearly, he had a very active social life in an era during which drug use was common. Malcolm Bricklin claimed that, during a round of golf on a trip to Acapulco they took together, Hatfield actively sought out drugs and successfully procured marijuana from staff at their resort. After that, Bricklin distinctly remembers the two of them navigating the course on a golf cart on which Hatfield had placed a small, fluttering Maple Leaf flag. He also recalled them having a conversation after the 1984 drug charges and laughing together about it.[100]

Regardless of whether the premier in fact used drugs, the charges, the accusations of drugs and partying, and his admissions about his "gregarious" and "unconventional" character changed perceptions of the premier and his behaviour dramatically after 1984. Libby Burnham, a long-time friend of Hatfield's, remarked that "the Hatfield I read about in the 1980s was not the Richard I knew. He was portrayed as flamboyant, eccentric[,] a playboy and a dilettante. It was as though the public Hatfield had consumed the private Richard and turned him into somebody else."[101] Even though he was found not guilty of the drug charges and gamely defended himself against other accusations, Hatfield's sometimes decadent private life had been exposed to the public, and he was unable to outpace the caricature that had been created to represent him.

In their 1991 revelatory biography of Hatfield, journalists Cormier and Michaud wrote that, following the allegations, "suddenly, aspects of Hatfield's life that had been accepted, even though they were outside the mainstream, became reprehensible – his bachelorhood, his trips to New York and Morocco, his doll collection." Even the way that the premier walked became a target for aspersions: "Someone had written in a magazine 'with his long, fine legs, Mr. Hatfield walks like a ballet dancer.' This would not be seen as a compliment in rural New Brunswick, where so many men consider hunting and softball part of manhood." The rumours of Hatfield's sexuality and his behaviour, according to Cormier and Michaud, had a significant impact on the 1987 campaign: "In New Brunswick, people do not talk about homosexuality; they ignore it … But the aspects of his life that many people found reprehensible followed him wherever he went like an official escort."[102]

In losing every single electoral seat, including his own, during the 1987 provincial election, Hatfield's fall was complete. The son of Hartland, the man who had come to personify so much about New Brunswick's people, its aspirations, and its foibles, was utterly repudiated. After being so unceremoniously dumped from the only job he'd ever really known, Hatfield was appointed a senator by Progressive Conservative prime minister Brian Mulroney. Sadly, in 1990, Hatfield was diagnosed with incurable brain cancer, and he died in 1991 at the age of sixty.

The Bricklin incident was only a small, if significant, part of Hatfield's lifetime in politics. He is remembered for championing French-English reproachment and national unity, his deep love for his province and its people, his relatively more conservative than progressive policies, and his unconventional yet always entertaining brand of politics. *Maclean's*, a magazine that featured him often, including on a famous cover, did not mention the Bricklin in its obituary of Hatfield, though it did address his "personal eccentricities" and many scandals.[103]

Interestingly, though he was homosexual and a publicly committed bachelor his whole life, in 2019, nearly three decades after Hatfield's death, a Florida man, John Hall, claimed to be his son. In a CBC story, Hall claimed that he had proof that his mother, Izetta "Toodie" McKeil, had given birth to him at the Evangeline Home for unwed mothers in Saint John in 1949. McKeil, he further claimed, was the daughter of a Hartland farmhand and a classmate of Richard's at Hartland High School in 1948. Toodie had given John up for adoption, and the Florida man's search for his father had led him to New Brunswick. Hall claimed that his birth mother remained friendly with Hatfield until they both died in 1991. Though there was no conclusive evidence of Hall's story, once more, long after he had passed on, Hatfield managed to surprise New Brunswickers and Canadians and remind them of his "exceptional presence." A rebirth, of sorts. And though there is a melancholy to Hatfield's story, Bricklin narratives of demise were not its only legacies.

Rebirth, Part I. Keeping the Dream Alive: Revivals, Commemoration, and Celebration

A few days after Bricklin's bankruptcy, Saint John maintenance worker Frank Richard lamented that "Malcolm Bricklin was a dreamer. He had one dream and that was all. And it almost came true."[104] Though Bricklin's dream of entrepreneurial success did not materialize with the SV1, his firm *had* existed, and he *had* succeeded in building three thousand undeniably stylish cars, no matter their mechanical shortcomings. As a material artefact, the SV1 has a special resonance in a world of automobility, one whose resilience has long outlasted GVI's short existence.[105] Bricklin's dream car has continued to live on as the tangible manifestation of a fantastical entrepreneurial idea, in the numerous attempts to revive the company after 1975, and through ongoing commemoration and celebration of the SV1 in the decades after the company's failure.

As a beacon of hope to every entrepreneur and auto enthusiast who has dreamed of launching their own sports car company, the idea of reviving SV1 production died hard. Almost as soon as the firm had been placed into receivership, speculation emerged of a miraculous rebirth of the car. At Hatfield's press conference following the government's decision, he teased about talks with unnamed Toronto investors interested in taking over the project, though he wouldn't discuss details.[106] Immediately after that press conference, Hatfield's Liberal nemesis John Turnbull suggested that he "get down on bended knee" to beg Saint John industrialist and the province's wealthiest man, K.C. Irving, to take over the company, a suggestion that, surprisingly, met with some interest, as long as the government significantly reduced its 67 per cent interest.[107] While nothing came of these last-minute stopgap attempts at revival, the government was soon fielding inquiries from a few interested parties.

The first of these was Aston Martin (est. 1913), the venerable British automaker perhaps most famous for its stylish cars in James Bond films. With the company

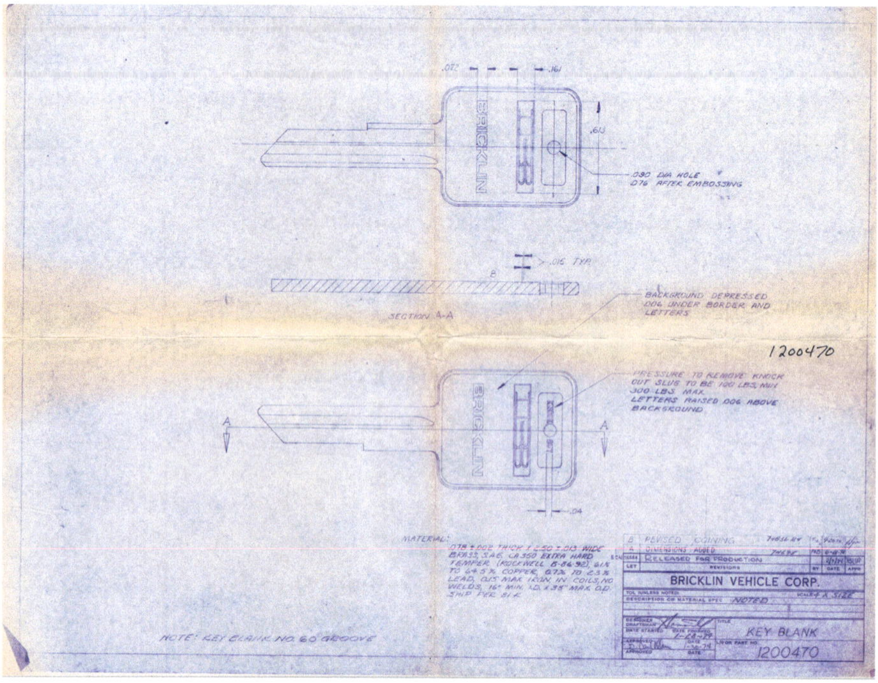

Figure 7.5. Design for a Bricklin embossed car key, 1974.

itself having gone bankrupt in 1974 (its fourth of seven), its leadership saw potential synergies in a Bricklin takeover, including the opportunity to take advantage of a ready-made plant and duty-free importation rights. In 1976, the New Brunswick government shipped two SV1s to the United Kingdom for an assessment by their potential suitors. Aston Martin evaluated the SV1 against GM's Corvettes and reported that it was feasible to see 4,000–5,000 Bricklins being sold annually at an even higher price than when the car ended production. Officials in New Brunswick considered this a legitimate proposal and indicated that the government "might be willing to consider lending more money to the project" if additional investors could be found. While Aston Martin was busy kicking the Bricklin's tires, Wespac, a Vancouver company, also expressed an interest in reviving the vehicle. Its head, C.E. Sawyer, had been a consultant for the New Brunswick government on the Bricklin enterprise and had seen GVI's problems up close, but he still felt that there was a possibility of making the SV1 work.[108]

Similarly, in early 1976, the Avanti Motor Company (1965–85, 1986–90), a Studebaker offshoot that produced small batches of their namesake cars, expressed serious interest. The Avanti had debuted in 1963 as a "halo" sportscar for Studebaker (1852–1967; autos, 1902–66), one of the last independent American

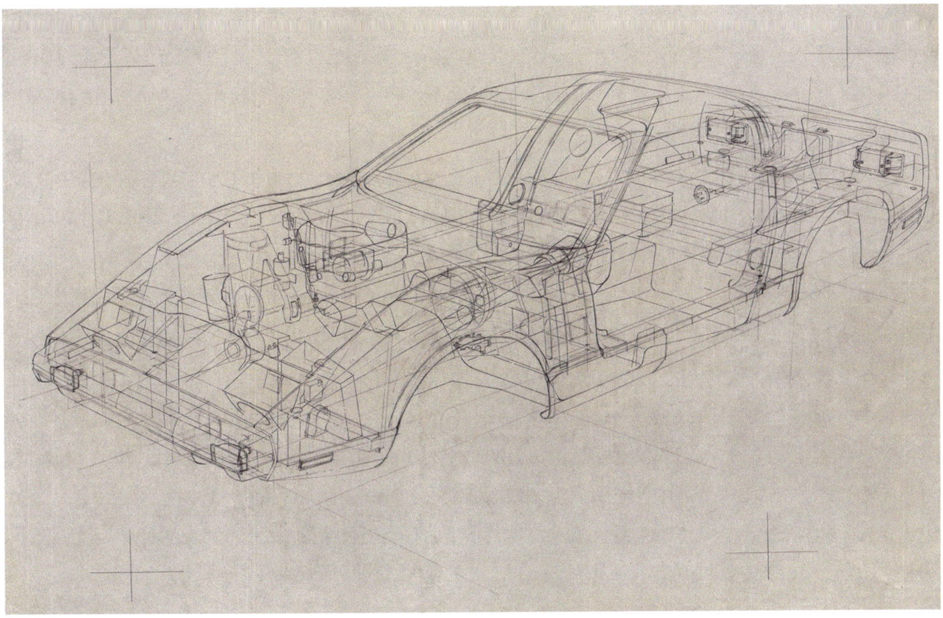

Figure 7.6. Bricklin schematics.

producers. Though the Avanti was heralded as "the Rolls Royce of the sportscar world," Studebaker got out of the car business in 1963 (continuing in Canada until 1966). Local Studebaker dealers in South Bend, Indiana, bought the Avanti rights and kept the car in production. By the mid-1970s, Avanti was hand-building about a hundred vehicles a year, and its owners were looking for a potential new plant that might return the brand to scaled manufacturing.[109] After Bricklin collapsed, Avanti executives visited the shuttered Saint John facility. Following some considerable back and forth, including the proposition that the New Brunswick government buy Avanti outright, nothing came of the venture, but it reflected the ongoing attention that Bricklin had generated from across the automotive sector.[110]

Two years later, New Brunswick fielded yet another proposal for a Bricklin revival. "Brickmar," a firm led by one Mr. W. Martin, who owned "a sizeable inventory of Bricklin parts and was active in the Bricklin owners' associations," approached the government in 1978 about the possibility of restarting production. In exchange for only $3.3 million in government money and all the Bricklin tooling and plants, Brickmar would produce 1,200–1,500 SV1s a year. New Brunswick officials ultimately felt that Martin's "enthusiasm probably outweighs the depth of his proposal," and passed on the approach.[111] In 1980, Hatfield replied to a California man who was looking to revive the Bricklin that the buildings were otherwise occupied and all the equipment had been sold, but that he could "submit a formal proposal outlining your plans."[112] A similar treatment was extended to another request in 1987, Hatfield's last year in office.[113] In the end, there were at least four significant efforts aimed at reviving the company.

All these attempts to resurrect the firm served to commemorate the fact that three thousand SV1s had actually been built and the project come so close to working. Just as importantly, they commemorated the fact that the SV1 had been built *by New Brunswickers* and in defiance of all the naysayers and critics. Hatfield put it best in 1978: although the outcome was "very disappointing because here was a product for which there was definitely a market, and still is," New Brunswickers had "proved we had the skill here to manufacture it."[114] In 1979, the *Financial Post*'s Robert Perry reported that busloads of New Brunswickers were going on tours of the remnants of Bricklin production facilities. Certainly, "the vestiges of Bricklin still have that degree of fascination," but far from being a lament for the SV1's demise, Perry realized that

> all these people aren't demonstrating a mere morbid curiosity, like bystanders at a horrible accident. They're saying *something*. And what they're saying goes like this:
>
> *We* did it. We built sports cars that people want. We have the heads and the hands to do that. We proved a lot to ourselves in that ordinary-looking little factory. And it's a shame we're not making sport cars right now. To those people, the Bricklin venture isn't a symbol of failure. Why, dammit, it's a badge of ability.[115]

This feeling – that, with the car's successful production, "the province's psyche gained *something*" – spilled into decades of commemoration for the SV1 as a historically and culturally significant event, as something worth remembering.[116] Indeed, in the decades after 1975, the SV1 and its maker have spawned songs, books, musicals, documentaries, and even celebratory stamps and coins issued by the Canadian government. As Bricklin once remarked to *Inc.* magazine, "the things that people see as failures are often the steps to success. I got my fame and power from the failure of the Bricklin. What did I get for the biggest failure of my life? I got a stamp and a $20 coin in Canada with my car's likeness on them."[117] Of course, Bricklin had gained much more than that.

Then there is the Safety Vehicle-1 itself. As a material artefact *that worked*, the Bricklin SV1 took on a life of its own after 1975. The Bricklin's residual appeal as a car was also helped by the fact that, as "compared against contemporary exoticars, virtually all of which cost two-to-four times as much, the Bricklin suffers very little in either design lapses or quality control," as one enthusiast wrote in *Special Interest*

Figure 7.7. Bricklin's spirit lives on: Canadian stamp, 1996 (left); commemorative $20 coin, 2003 (right).

Autos magazine in 1982 (though the latter point was questionable).[118] By the late 1980s, Terry Tanner, one of the original Bricklin engineers, had finally found fixes to virtually all the car's problems and had shared his knowledge with other Bricklin owners, who would drive long distances "in defiance of the belief that the car is unreliable." By then, with all the patches, aficionados could declare that the SV1 was a "fully reliable and durable automobile."[119]

Unsurprisingly, given the loyalty of many of its first customers and the SV1's unique place in the auto world, the Bricklin International Owners Club was formed in 1976, with chapters across eight states and provinces. As is common with many auto brand enthusiasts, a Bricklin culture has emerged since the 1970s, with SV1 auto shows and annual meetings called BIGs – Bricklin International get-togethers – all over North America. Despite its notorious reputation in the broader public, Bricklin owners *love* their SV1s. With at least a thousand cars still on the road in the twenty-first century, "Bricklineers" identify themselves by SV1 VIN, share Bricklin stories and tips, buy Bricklin merchandise ("Bricklinalia" – Bricklin-branded clothes, watches, posters, mugs, keychains, and belt buckles), get Bricklin tattoos, swap maintenance "Tech Tips," and even get married in Bricklins, as has happened on more than one occasion. The organization continued to publish the *Brickline* (four times a year) as late as the 2010s and maintains a website, one that keeps track of as many known Bricklins as possible.[120]

Ever the showman, Malcolm Bricklin also helped to keep the SV1 flame burning. He attended BIG meetings, contributed to articles in the *Brickline*, and regularly stayed in the news with his latest entrepreneurial adventures. During the September 11th terrorist attacks on New York City, Bricklin, on a flight to the United Kingdom, was forced to land in, of all places, Fredericton. It was the first

Figure 7.8. *Brickline*, January 1993 (left); *The Entrepreneur*, 2009 (right).

time he had been there since the 1970s, and his unexpected appearance generated newspaper stories. In 2011, the documentary *The Entrepreneur* was released, prominently featuring the SV1 in its promotional materials. And in 2011, just as theatre-loving Richard Hatfield had done so many times, Bricklin attended the premier of the musical *The Bricklin: An Automotive Fantasy* at the Fredericton Playhouse.[121] Long after the demise of the car company, the car and its spirit lived on.

Rebirth, Part II. Back (in)to the Future: The Bricklin SV1, the DeLorean DMC, and Other Influences

So similar are they in look and profile that the 1974–6 Bricklin SV1 is often mistaken for the 1981–3 DeLorean DMC-12. Indeed, the cars' commonalities extend far beyond their comparable style and shape. John Z. DeLorean (1925–2005) and his dream car share an entangled history with Malcolm Bricklin and *his* dream car, and the two firms "eerily similar rise and fall," according to the *New York Times*.[122] Yet, while Bricklin became infamous within the automotive world, DeLorean's car gained worldwide fame owing to the *Back to the Future* franchise (1985, 1989, 1990), a series of movies about a futuristic, time-travelling car with gull-wing doors, a special skin, and a disreputable past. Timing is everything, as they say.

Figure 7.9. Uncanny similarities: John and Christina DeLorean at the DMC Model 12 launch, New Orleans, 31 January 1977.

As we saw earlier, the two men knew one another. In 1972 and 1973, when Bricklin was designing and engineering the SV1, DeLorean, already a famous GM exec, appeared in Livonia a number of times to check out the project (as did a number of other Detroit heavyweights, including GM's Bunkie Knudsen), according to both Bricklin and Herb Grasse. After DeLorean's controversial departure from GM in 1973, Bricklin tried to hire him. Both were young, brash, connected to sexy sports cars: the *Detroit Free Press* once referred to the pair as "the Paul Newman and the Robert Redford of the auto industry."[123] Bricklin later claimed that DeLorean took Malcolm's prototype "Grey Ghost" as "the inspiration for his own car." There's no question about the similarities between the two vehicles: "Look at that car," Bricklin remarked in 2016 in reference to his SV1 prototype, "and you'll see it looks almost exactly like the DeLorean, including the color."[124] Even contemporaries, including the business journalist Rod McQueen, remarked that the DMC "bears remarkable resemblance to the ill-fated Bricklin."[125]

Among the obvious similarities between the two cars were the gull-wing doors, the futuristic body surfaces (although the DeLorean used stainless steel, not plastic), and their flamboyant yet flawed creators (the mainstream and tabloid press reported on both men's extravagant lifestyles). The DMC also made a virtue of safety, with a "lightweight steel spine and suspension, composite structure body," and airbags as standard equipment.[126] Moreover, the two men promoted their cars "in the same way," according to McQueen.[127] With a tagline "Live the Dream," the DeLorean DMC Model 12 had a splashy New Orleans launch on 31 January 1977, with a promised production date of 1979 (it was two years late). Like Bricklin's forecasts, DeLorean's promise of 30,000 DMC cars by its second year, 1981, was fantastical (it never came close). Instead of rural New Brunswick, DeLorean went to Northern Ireland to take advantage of a depressed Irish economy and a welcoming government seeking the panacea of industrial modernity. DeLorean production was backed by $40 million from private investors (including $500,000 from *Tonight Show* host Johnny Carson) and $104 million from the British government, to build cars in a plant in Dunmurry, near Belfast.[128] Both men purchased engines from major manufacturers to slot into their cars, although the DMC had a rear-mounted V-6 Renault engine compared to the eight-cylinder behemoths that powered the Bricklin.[129] Both cars were built on a wing and prayer, with the aim to sell to the American market. Both met with ignominy.

What explained the two cars' similarity, according to Bricklin, was the fact that he had told DeLorean about the type of features that would make a splash. The gull-wing doors, Bricklin claimed to have told DeLorean, were the only way to make a sports car stand out in the marketplace. Try to avoid costly stamping and painting, Bricklin had suggested; hence, the stainless-steel skin, which turned a vice into a virtue by simplifying production and focusing potential consumers' attention on the futuristic look and material, just like the SV1. Bricklin also claimed to have given DeLorean the tip that led him to Northern Ireland. The British had initially come to Bricklin during his Canadian production run with an offer to move, but he couldn't jump to Belfast because his deal with New Brunswick required him to stay until he was producing a thousand SV1s a month. But he had told DeLorean about the British offer and – voila! – the idea of DMC going to Northern Ireland happened.[130]

Even the two firms' collapse into seas of government-funded bankruptcy was similar.[131] Like Bricklin's, the DeLorean project, which ended up producing only nine thousand vehicles at a much higher cost than Bricklin's three thousand, became a symbol of the failure of state intervention, a sign of industrial decay, and a kind of cultural punch-line. DeLorean's infamous 1982 drug-trafficking arrest (he was charged but later acquitted of conspiring to smuggle $24 million of cocaine to fund the company) generated international headlines. By the mid-1980s, the DMC was as perhaps even more of an infamous flop than the SV1 had ever been.[132] In the *Back to the Future* movie, hero Marty McFly incredulously asks Doc Emmett Brown, "Wait a minute, Doc. Ah … Are you telling me you built a time machine … *out of a DeLorean*?" Justifying his choice of the notorious but futuristic DMC, Doc Brown explains, "the way I see it, if you're gonna build a time machine into a car, why not do it with some style? Besides, the stainless-steel construction made the flux dispersal – look out! [time-travelling car suddenly reappears]."

In the end, entwined as they were, DeLorean lamented that "Bricklin was thrown up at us approximately 31 million times." For his part, Bricklin remarked of the DMC that "DeLorean spent eight years doing what took us two years, spent $200 million or more doing it, and failed. He certainly had more credentials than us. Building a car company to build one car – I don't recommend it as a good investment."[133] Yet it does say something about the power of Bricklin's vision that the design, promotion, and manufacturing of the DMC so closely followed what Bricklin had done – less than a decade later. Back to the future, indeed.

The Bricklin's legacy in the auto industry didn't live on just through DeLorean, however. By the 1980s, some of the SV1's most notable concept, design, and production elements had become a part of the automobile landscape. The idea of a safety-first vehicle was not new in 1974, as firms such as Volvo had made safety a brand identifier starting as far back as the 1920s, and Ford had sold safety packages in the 1950s. But it was novel in terms of its emphasis for a new American vehicle firm in the 1970s, and certainly for a sports car. Yet, after the 1970s, safety became, to a very large degree, a standard selling feature of *all* cars (seat belts had been mandated in 1968; air bags in 1999; anti-lock brakes in 2004), reflecting the cultural shift that Bricklin's safety vehicle had anticipated. In 1972, Lee Iacocca had declared that "safety doesn't sell," but, by 1988, the Chrysler boss was featured in ads that publicly committed his firm to air bags, proclaiming "who says you can't teach an old dog new tricks?"[134] Today, safety is a fundamental part of every aspect of car marketing and design.

Along with safety, another conceptual contribution made by the SV1 was the fact that it was one of the earliest "crossover" vehicles. In this regard, the SV1 was not a crossover in terms of its design, but as an effort to combine two different category types of vehicles – sports cars and safety cars. However one describes it, Bricklin was developing this hybrid concept for his vehicle before the first "modern" SUVs appeared, starting with the 1979 AMC Eagle. In the 1990s and early 2000s, SUVs, CUVs, and other crossovers would become more popular than sedans.

In terms of Bricklin's design influence, plastic has become a central element of car design since the SV1. By 1980, the Big Three had shifted from chrome to plastic bumpers, a significant embrace of the material, if not as much as Bricklin's.[135]

Another indirect automotive descendant of Bricklin and the SV1 was General Motor's Saturn. Designed and launched as an entirely new GM division from the ground up in 1985 in an effort to meet consumer demands and, also, to push GM towards post-Fordist production techniques and labour relations, Saturn (1991–2010) was intended to be "a different kind of car company, a different kind of car." It, too, had some uncanny similarities with Bricklin's car. Marketed as a futuristic vehicle that leaned heavily on space-age imagery (it was named after the rockets of NASA's Apollo program, though few consumers made the connection), one of its most distinctive features was its use of plastic body panels. According to author Joe Sherman in *In the Rings of Saturn*, "a combination of steel and plastic would form Saturn's skin," like the Bricklin.[136]

More than a decade after Bricklin's demise, even the giant GM had problems with manufacturing plastic panelling on the Saturn S1, a testament to the difficulties the Bricklin operation (almost) overcame. According to former GM boss Bob Lutz, "the plastic panels were finicky. They took longer to produce than conventional stamped steel, and they grew and shrank when the temperature changed, requiring the cars to have wide, unappealing gaps around the doors, hood, and trunk for clearance."[137] Echoing the same problems Bricklin had faced, Lutz might as well have been complaining about the SV1. Saturn even tried marketing the plastic panelling with television ads showing wayward shopping carts bouncing harmlessly off the vehicles, in an unintended homage to Bricklin's hammer-on-plastic gimmick. By early in the new century, Saturn had reverted to steel for its body panels, but, by then, plastic was everywhere in car manufacture – another example of Bricklin's foresight, even if, for him, it had been necessitated by the desire to avoid an expensive paint shop. As another innovation, Bricklin's team had pioneered a type of protective "plastic spray coat would cover the acrylic and protect it while it was on the production line"; a version of that technique became standard in the industry for post-assembly vehicle shipping and storage.[138]

When it came to some of Bricklin's production techniques, auto manufacturers utilized versions of his approach in the years after the firm's collapse, especially in terms of simplifying complicated components such as engines by purchasing them from established suppliers. During the early years of the electric vehicle (EV) revolution, this was a common practice, and still is today. Tesla's Roadster (2008–) was the first new car in North America since the Bricklin to be manufactured in significant numbers by a start-up firm. It made its environmentally friendly chargeable batteries (an EV's "engine") a centrepiece of its marketing, but in the company's first few years, the car had batteries sourced from firms such as Panasonic. As another example, in 2012–15, Toyota Canada assembled 2,500 electric RAV4s at its

Woodstock, Ontario, plant for export back to California, paying Tesla $100 million to import its American-made batteries and drivetrain.[139] The practice echoed Bricklin's import of American-made AMC engines into Saint John to be put into his SV1s, which would be exported back to the United States.

And what of the SV1's most compelling feature – its gull-wing doors? While gull wings never became a common feature for Big Three production vehicles (Ford's 2016 Lincoln Navigator concept is a rare exception), Tesla's decision to include "falcon" wings on its Model X (2018–) speaks to their continuing attraction for futuristic carmakers. A significant reason why they have not become common is the extraordinary difficulty of manufacturing them well. This was something that Bricklin discovered fairly quickly, though he did get them to work eventually, with an air compressor system that solved the problem.[140] Nearly forty years after the SV1, Elon Musk faced persistent difficulties with the Model X's doors, though Tesla's issues revolved more around sensors and software than hinges and leaks.[141] Nonetheless, Tesla's decision to use gull-wing doors is only the most prominent connection linking Malcolm Bricklin's twentieth-century auto making and entrepreneurship to Elon Musk and the twenty-first century.

Rebirth, Part III. A Bridge to Industrial Postmodernity: Malcolm Bricklin, Elon Musk, and Tesla

Finally, the SV1 lives on through the entrepreneurial legacies passed on from Malcolm Bricklin to the most famous and successful automotive businessperson of the twenty-first century, Tesla's Elon Musk. As automobile entrepreneurs whose innovative, sexy, sports car firms were masterfully launched and promoted during periods of technological change, auto industry upheaval, and economic and social disruption in North America, the parallels are obvious and sometimes uncanny, even if Bricklin failed tremendously while Musk succeeded beyond his wildest dreams. Despite the vast dissimilarity in their firms' outcomes, in their origin stories, and especially in the parallels they share as archetypal entrepreneurial innovators and promoters, it's clear that Musk inherited quite a bit of Bricklin's stylistic and substantive strategies and methods, whether consciously or not. The similarity of their approaches is representative not only of the connection between Bricklin and Musk as automobile entrepreneurs but also as a transitional bridge from industrial modernity to industrial postmodernity.

Bricklin's and Musk's careers and personas parallel one another across the decades. Both portrayed themselves as anti-suit, anti-Detroit outsiders attempting to disrupt an auto industry that had grown stale and predictable. Bricklin was from

Philadelphia and Florida; Musk from South Africa by way of Canada. Both had peripatetic formative years and uneven educational experiences. Both styled themselves as self-made men who had achieved fortunes (both real and imagined) in other businesses, each of which reflected the economic tenor of their times (for Bricklin, hardware, scooters, importing Subarus; for Musk, digital technology, Paypal). Both have faced multiple legal entanglements over their entrepreneurial careers. Both were young men when their car ventures launched (Bricklin, thirty-five; Musk, thirty-three), and both very much epitomized and consciously utilized masculine expressions of their era's cultural moods, Bricklin as a Seventies sex symbol and Musk as a twenty-first-century tech symbol.[142]

As an entrepreneurial innovator, Musk largely followed a game plan laid out by Bricklin in the 1970s. Both led startup firms to launch sexy, stylish, innovative, two-seater roadsters; both firms attempted to take advantage of technological advances that reflected contemporary societal concerns.[143] In Bricklin's case, the innovation was plastic, and the concern was safety; in Tesla's, it was electric battery technology, digitization, and the environment. Both built their vehicles at existing plants that were geographically distant from traditional auto-making centres, and both firms received government support, directly in Bricklin's case (New Brunswick subsidies and ownership) and indirectly in Tesla's (a US Department of Energy loan and government carbon credits). Both even offered a choice of only five colours for their cars.

But it is as a promoter that Musk's efforts most closely echoed Bricklin's own style and method. Both men proved exceptionally good at generating awareness for themselves and their projects and products through their (often boastful) pronouncements, through attention-grabbing stunts and gimmicks, and by fanning their own fame through media savviness and a conscious cultivation of celebrity.[144]

Throughout their careers, both Bricklin and Musk made many fantastical announcements of products or production goals, quite a few of which never materialized. Bricklin, of course, confidently made numerous pronouncements about production targets for the SV1 that never came close to being achieved. He also amassed a long record of announcing new technologies, products, or whole ventures – from new engine technologies to new ways of selling cars to electric bikes to hydrogen fuel developments – that amounted to little or failed entirely.[145] Obviously, Musk's record is vastly better in terms of products that were successful, but he also has a history of overpromising. One example is Tesla's Cybertruck. Musk first unveiled the vehicle to the "jubilant cheers of brand loyalists" at a 2019 event (to coincide with the date and setting of the original *Blade Runner*, the 1982 science fiction film starring Harrison Ford) with a promised production date of 2021, later revised to 2022. In 2022, Musk appeared at yet another Cybertruck event, "wearing a black cowboy hat" and proclaiming "sorry for the delay. But you're going to [finally] have this next year, and it's really going to be great."[146] Additional delays meant that, as of mid-2023, Cybertruck production had yet to begin, attesting to the difficulties of launching a new vehicle. Based on his own experiences with the SV1, Bricklin could commiserate, though obviously on a dramatically different, and much more modest, scale. Meanwhile, some of Musk's other ventures, such as his 2013 Hyperloop announcement, have also been marked by delays or statements that do not cohere with reality.[147]

Similarly, when it comes to promotional stunts and attention-seeking behaviour, Bricklin and Musk are both accomplished showmen. As we saw earlier, Bricklin's history includes building himself an entire cowboy persona (including buying a working ranch) and stripping down in front of Chinese auto executives. On a much grander scale, Munk launched a Tesla into space. One uniquely comparable example stands out across the decades: hitting their vehicles with hammers. Bricklin's SV1 promotional act included hitting the car with a hammer to prove the plastic skin's durability, a stunt that was filmed as a potential television commercial. More than half a century later, Elon Musk also famously did the hammer bit at a promotional event for (again) his own prototype Cybertruck, though with somewhat less success.[148]

The stunts point to both entrepreneurs' media savviness and cultivation of celebrity in the service of fame, a critical ingredient of performative financialization. In Tesla's early days, Musk utilized media and celebrity connections to push the car's profile into the spotlight. In the '70s, Bricklin had Paul Newman and Bobby Unser pitch his car, appeared on *The Tonight Show* with Johnny Carson, and had the SV1 placed in the hit television show *Chico and the Man*. In 2009, by which point Tesla had sold only eight hundred Roadsters, early adopters included actors Arnold Schwarzenegger and podcaster Adam Carolla, and Musk appeared on the David Letterman show and had his car placed in the hit movie *Iron Man* (2008). Like Bricklin, Musk had a natural promotional gift of the gab: "We're fortunate because we are at the center of the confluence of a product with high sexual appeal that in a sense helps save the world."[149] Both men had a taste for the limelight and a thirst for recognition. As management scholar Sanford Borins wrote of Bricklin in 1986, he "seemed to have a tremendous need for instant gratification through fame, financial success, an its concomitant lifestyle … His satisfaction came from both selling and consequent instant recognition, in terms of fame and income."[150] He could have written something very similar about Musk.

Similarly, both entrepreneurs' promotional abilities generated an intensely loyal following, though, again, obviously the scale was different. Tesla's thousands of

Figure 7.10. Cracking the promotional code: Elon Musk and the Cybertruck, 21 November 2019.

fanatically loyal "fanboys" became well known as the firm grew successful. Even after Malcolm's bankruptcy, his star was not diminished among those few loyal Bricklin owners. In 1976, Jack Siuta, the Bricklin International Owners' first president, wrote in the *Brickline* that Malcolm Bricklin "was this most impressive man. He was an uncanny genius ... As he talked about the fall of his automotive empire, we felt so filled with consolation [and] regret we would have done almost anything for him – just for the asking ... Malcolm Bricklin could be president."[151] Truly, living the Bricklin dream.

Of course, despite the similarities in their entrepreneurial styles and strategies, there were profound and significant differences between the two men and the outcomes of their efforts. To a large degree, their fates were shaped by the timing of each man's appearance on the entrepreneurial automotive scene, and the technological possibilities that each was presented with. In the 1970s, the opportunities for technological innovation were much different and, in many ways, much more limited than those in the first two decades of this century. This can be seen most tangibly in the fact that Bricklin's moment marked the nadir of a long era of relative automotive technological atrophy, and the SV1 was the product of a motorized, pre-digitized automotive age. For his part, Musk entered the automotive sector at a moment of incredible innovation, and his Tesla Roadster could take advantage of an automotive landscape that was being completely transformed by advances in propulsion systems, materials, and digitization.

While both the SV1 and the Tesla Roadster were pitched as sexy roadsters, the Bricklin was meant for the generations of people who loved mechanical, gasoline-powered sports cars, quite a few of whom were collectors, mechanics, or tinkerers. It was the last "new" car that could be fixed by its owners, with little dependence upon digitization, a fact emphasized and celebrated by car expert Jay Leno in his assessment of the SV1 during a 2022 episode of his show *Jay Leno's Garage*.[152] And, although Bricklins did depend on battery power more than most '70s vehicles (even the doors were powered by the battery), its electronics proved problematic. The SV1 may have been innovative in its own high industrial way, but it was very much a fossil-fuelled, pre-digital car. By the time Tesla's Roadster was launched, the industrially postmodern digitized and electrified impact upon cars – including the way the car was designed, its battery-powered propulsion and electronics, and its dependence on software – had fundamentally changed the nature of automobiles.[153] In a very real way, the links between the Bricklin SV1 and the Tesla Roadster marked the passage between the two eras.

In the end, it bears repeating: even if the *outcomes* of the two ventures were immensely different, there are undeniable parallels, even across the chasm of time and technology, between the two men, their approaches, and their styles. The drastically divergent outcomes reflect not only each man's entrepreneurial abilities but also, and equally, the centrality of societal factors in shaping an entrepreneur's success. In a 2022 interview, Bricklin described flying to California to meet with Musk not long after the latter had gained control of Tesla. It would have been a fascinating conversation to listen to – a passing of the torch, so to speak.[154] Between the mid-twentieth and the early twenty-first centuries, they were the only two individuals who managed to build and bring new vehicles to market in North America, one unsuccessfully in the 1970s, the other much, much more successfully in the 2010s. Yet, despite his failure, Malcolm Bricklin was the only example of an entrepreneur in the postwar period who came close to achieving his own dream car, and so he and his automobile can lay some claim to being the spiritual precursor to Elon Musk and to industrial postmodernity's automotive rebirth beginning in the twenty-first century.

CONCLUSION

Malcolm Bricklin and His SV1: From Industrial Modernity to Industrial Postmodernity

***Dream Car* Song 14: "A Hell of a Ride," Allen Cole and Paul Ledoux, 2010**

Malcolm Bricklin was a man of his time, and a man ahead of his time. He was also a man very much at the end of his times, and at the transition between the industrial modern and the industrial postmodern.

Bricklin and his Safety Vehicle-1 represented a moment of recognition for North Americans that the endless, futuristic, material promise of industrial modernity was very much a dream (as it had always been for many). The realization that the convenience, speed, freedom, prosperity, and power of gasoline-powered automobility – the condition of modernity – was both a blessing and a curse, was becoming clear. For the first seven decades of the twentieth century, North American automobility had generated wealth and power for entrepreneurs and their corporations; had economically fuelled politicians, states, and their citizens; and had created society's car-dominated human and environmental landscape. The car, that talisman of the future and of technology, had reordered social relations, redefined risk, and become the ubiquitous, defining feature of a mobile, anonymous, ever-accelerating, capitalist, and liberal democratic North America.

But by the 1970s, things were changing. The automobile-fuelled society into which Bricklin had launched his venture in 1974 was undergoing seismic economic, political, social, and cultural shifts. From geopolitical eruptions to sexual revolutions to transformations in business philosophies and the role of the state, Bricklin likely did not recognize that a moment of profound change was upon him and the rest of society. He was simply attempting to follow in the footsteps of those creative destructors – the entrepreneurial innovators, promoters, and managers – who had set this world in motion by creating their own dream cars, no matter how tremendously difficult that task might be. Henry Ford had boasted that he had "invented the modern age." If building a car and a car company was the height of industrial modernity, then future-loving Malcolm Bricklin looked to be equal to the challenge. For a politician like Richard Hatfield, and his province, it seemed that he was.

In the end, the venture was not successful. But Bricklin's unique failure offers an equally unique opportunity. The story of Malcolm Bricklin, Richard Hatfield, and their fantastic car provides an indispensable vehicle for viewing and understanding the transformational changes that were reshaping society across the twentieth and early twenty-first centuries from the perspective of modernity's most important, active agent – automobility. The story of the SV1 allows us to see the world like a car.

Seeing like an SV1 – the way the car was conceptualized, how it was promoted and built, and why it failed – reveals much about the kaleidoscope of changes happening in North American society in the early 1970s, and the broader and deeper transition stretching from industrial modernity's late nineteenth-century beginnings to industrial post-modernity's emergence at the end of the twentieth and the beginning of the twenty-first century.

So, in the end, could the SV1 really have worked?

Malcolm came very close to pulling it off, after all. In November 1974, *Motor Trend*'s Steve Spence published a long article, "Adventures along the Yellow Bricklin Road," which, naturally, made a Wizard of Oz parable from Bricklin's automotive journey. Spence was sceptical about whether Bricklin could conquer the immense challenges inherent in launching a new auto company and a new car. But, after touring the Saint John plant and seeing SV1s being built, he thought that Malcolm had a chance: as Spence declared, "Yes, indeed, Malcolm Bricklin appears to have done it."[1]

And for all the criticism he and Hatfield faced, Bricklin's partners in the New Brunswick government also genuinely thought (and not just believed) that Malcolm could have done it. In January 1975, the consulting firm that New Brunswick had hired to assess Bricklin reported that it was "supportive of continuing the project" based on its assessment that "the start-up problems of this new automobile company can, in fact, be overcome."[2] In March, an internal government report made the case that, with the most recent infusion of $7.5 million of funds, "management has been strengthened somewhat, production planning and controls are being improved, and the parts situation appears to be improving." Though the report stated plainly that the company was "still in a start-up position with production not yet at a break even level," the venture seemed to be on a path towards viability.[3] In May, Hatfield himself understood that "there comes a time to make the decision whether the scheme is viable." "But," he also told reporters, "I feel that until we know whether a project can be successful in the market, or whether the high demand that experts forecast for it can become a fact, we should not close it down." Moreover, he recognized that Bricklin had achieved something very real: cars were being manufactured by "500 people working in two plants making union wages; it is not a fly by night outfit."[4]

Even as the SV1 faced mounting quality complaints, recalls, and questionable reviews, industry observers, consumers, and auto enthusiasts continued to believe in the Bricklin and that it could work. Malcolm's dream car really existed, even if it was flawed. A May 1975 *Motor Trend* article stated that the Bricklin was "an excellent concept with a firm beginning. The fit, finish and trim problems can all be ironed out … The Bricklin can be made into a nice little hustler."[5] As late as September 1975, as the company was being put into receivership, *Mechanix Illustrated* published "We Test the Amazing Bricklin," an article that hopefully overlooked the car's persistent problems and enthused that "we look for the '76 and '77 models to show even better craftsmanship and design development."[6] As for the SV1's quality issues, the firm was committed to solving the car's problems, and was making headway by the fall of 1975. Bricklin had hired machinist Frank Turner to fix the door problems, and a September 1975 *New York Times* article stated that "the water-leak problem has largely been overcome" for the 1975 models, and that the 1976 models would have a door clamp, sealing the car. And the hydraulic door mechanisms were being replaced with a "reed-air system that will open the doors in two seconds."[7] As a start up, the SV1 could still count on a little patience from many in the public, and some benefit of the doubt, too.

Moreover, despite all the SV1's well-known difficulties, market demand remained strong, and people still wanted the cars. In November 1974, *Motor Trend* reported that dealers were "in a state of frenzy" trying to get more Bricklins to sell. One dealer who had been in the business for more than four decades declared that having the Bricklin to sell was "the most exciting thing that's happened to

Figure C.1. Malcolm on the cover of the *Brickline*, 1977.

me since my son was born." He excitedly revealed that "people have been pouring into [his dealership] from 8 am until 10 at night. I've never seen anything like it. They ooh and aah and they push the buttons to the gull-wing doors, and they go nuts! Yesterday, I drove the car to my barber – about 10 miles from here – and two people, one guy in a Volks and another in a Mercedes, stopped me – they literally pulled me over to the curb!"[8] In June 1975, *Automation* magazine reported that Bricklins were "selling like bourbon at the Kentucky Derby" and that every SV1 was being "snapped up as soon as it hits a dealer's showroom," even if production "was another story."[9] Libby Burnham, a Hatfield campaign manager, recalled that "I had people phoning me, to lobby, to see if I could move them up on the list of people that were waiting to buy a Bricklin car. There was a lineup of people. There were hundreds waiting."[10] And despite all the public questions swirling about the venture in September 1975, that month Nova Scotia GM dealer L.J. Kiley wrote directly to Hatfield about acquiring a Bricklin dealership, just a few weeks before the firm was put into receivership.[11]

How long consumers would have continued to want the cars, given the Bricklin's ongoing quality problems, is another question. In the 1970s, quality was also an issue for Detroit's cars, an opening that Japanese manufacturers were exploiting to great effect. In the 1980s, Bricklin sold 160,000 low-quality Yugos before that vehicle's problems finally caught up with the car, and with Malcolm. Certainly, with all the SV1's difficulties, many dealers and customers were frustrated, and many deposits were returned. But there were just as many dealers and customers waiting for cars until the very end. Eventually, most of the SV1's problems were fixed following the firm's demise, though who knows how long is would have taken Malcolm to completely solve these problems on the production lines in Saint John and Minto.

Even after the firm had been put into receivership, Hatfield and his ministers still believed that the car could make it – but not without more money, which Bricklin had to find or which had to come from another investor. In October 1975, economic growth minister Lawrence Garvie told Bricklin that, as "both the Premier and I have previously stated, we are still convinced that this project can be viable given an infusion of additional financing and the adoption of a realistic operating budget." Garvie felt that if the firm cut its production goals down to 5,000–6,000 vehicles a year (something that Bricklin himself had accepted in August), then the province would continue its support, "provided that capital was forthcoming from other sources and that a realistic operating plan was developed."[12] Garvie also pointed out that Aston Martin had gone bankrupt and had been closed for six months in 1974 before reopening after finding new financing. In November 1975, Garvie told the legislature that Bricklin could have been reorganized to "run like the Lotus automobile operation."[13]

But Malcolm couldn't, or wouldn't, come up with a plan or the necessary outside funding to make this shift. According to Garvie, money wasn't the main issue: "had money been the only problem inhibiting the success of the venture, then the money would have been found."[14]

Why, ultimately, did the SV1 fail? The answer lies beyond all the managerial shortcomings, the engineering and production troubles, and the quality problems, many of which might have been overcome.

Fundamentally, Bricklin failed because Malcolm and his firm could not solve the puzzle of industrial modernity: the ability to mass manufacture quality automobiles to meet the demands of the market and thus make enough money to keep the operation going (and turn a profit). In other words, to successfully make real the dream of automobility. This was the titanically difficult problem that Henry Ford had solved in the 1910s (his solution, after all, had changed the world) but that Bricklin could not. Bricklin could make cars, but he could not make enough of them either well enough or fast enough to make enough money to keep production going. His operation could not satisfy what, by the 1970s, had become the foundational expectation of Fordist industrial modernity.

In a 1981 interview about the debacle, Bricklin admitted that, by the time they were manufacturing the cars, the challenges of production – despite BCL's ability to produce SV1s, such as they were – were simply too difficult to overcome, too costly to fix. Though he almost pulled it off, Bricklin should have realized that he did not have the managerial or technological capacity to oversee such a complex task at the level of financing he had secured. Nor did his firm, or the New Brunswick government for that matter, have the necessary technocratic scale, deep industrial knowledge (either Fordist or of emerging production systems), or – perhaps most importantly – the vast financial resources required to solve *the puzzle*. "The big problem," as Bricklin put it in 1977,

> was [that] I didn't have the faintest idea it would cost anywhere near what it did, and my credibility started dropping when I started asking for more money. They kept asking, "well, is that it?" and I'd say, "I don't know." It definitely wasn't what they wanted to hear. They wanted some end to it. I kept explaining that even General Motors goes out and raises money occasionally.[15]

Additional funding could certainly have helped solve the tremendous difficulty of car-making, though financing was not the sole factor in Bricklin's demise. The problem wasn't the car itself, which was admittedly a stylish vehicle, one that has aged rather well. Nor was it a matter of publicity or promotion or sales. As with the DeLorean a decade later, the challenge was not the demand side of the equation; it was the *supply*. The difficulty lay in the awesome effort, complexity, and cost required to make thousands of quality vehicles in a timely manner, something that in North America only a very few individuals, and a few remaining firms, had managed to achieve (though they all went bankrupt at least once – most recently in 2009, in GM and Chrysler's case). In the postwar period, not until the 2010s and 2020s did Elon Musk and Tesla successfully solve the puzzle again (and would, again, change the world): building a new car, with new technologies, to scale from startup, and selling enough of them to satisfy a fickle marketplace before the money runs out.

And if, indeed, a significant part of solving the puzzle in Bricklin's case was money, that meant it was also a very political problem, since Malcolm's money was coming from the government. His partner, New Brunswick, wouldn't cover the financial expense of overcoming the problem of industrial modernity because the *political* cost of continued support for the Bricklin was, ultimately, in Hatfield's view, greater than the economic cost. Without the help of the Canadian government, as Hatfield reminded everyone, New Brunswick did not have the resources of a Japan or a Germany or a Korea. It was a small province, with a modest government apparatus and limited financial resources. By itself, New Brunswick simply could not afford the cost of underwriting its own potential miracle on the Saint John River long enough to make the endeavour pay off.

The formula for solving the problem of industrial modernity (and its cost) did, in fact, exist, and Bricklin had tried to cut some corners by finding cheap labour and simplifying his production methods, not to mention getting New Brunswick to provide most of the funding. It had mostly worked: the car wasn't just a dream – three thousand of them existed. That dreamy outcome, however, was shaped by the reality that the SV1 simply cost so much more than anyone (should have) expected, and that the people who were financing the venture decided not to spend any more money. Hatfield could no longer justify the amount being asked for, with no clear idea on how long it would be before the province saw a return on their massive investment, if it did at all.

As a deeply politicized event, one made so by the project's tremendously risky nature and its exceedingly high profile, it wasn't just the politics of the financial cost that played a role in the Bricklin's demise. In Richard Hatfield's New Brunswick, politics was a local affair. In the years after 1975, Malcolm maintained that what ruined things "was just partisan politics!" In this, he provided two sometimes contradictory explanations. On the one hand, Bricklin did not blame Hatfield personally. It was "not the politician who backed us, Premier Hatfield," who was primarily at fault, even if he had put the firm into receivership. The problem, Malcolm declared, "was created by the opposition party … [that] knock everything that the people in power do – which is sort of a dumb thing to do, especially when it's creating jobs, and good publicity too."[16] No matter – he did not hold a grudge against New Brunswick: "They were not out to get me; they were just a political entity."[17] Ultimately, it was, in Malcolm's view, *politics* that did the Bricklin venture in, and politics that explains Hatfield's decision to end support for the project. "There's no way I can knock them," Bricklin said of Hatfield and the New Brunswick government: "It took tremendous courage to go as far as they did. I mean, we're dealing with people who really care about the car, make no mistake on that."[18]

On the other hand, Bricklin also felt that Hatfield ultimately understood that, if Bricklin succeeded, the car "would be bigger than Hatfield. And that was a problem." The way he saw it, "Hatfield's ego" was threatened enough that "he decided to end the project when the going got tough."[19] And it did get tough, since there was so much political pressure, with calls for Hatfield's resignation, and a boiling outrage from some in the media (a GVI exec maintained that "if this project fails, it will be the fault of a few reporters and some of the media [who] have set out to discredit the car from the outset").[20] Of course, in Hatfield's view, it simply came down to the fact that the promise Malcolm Bricklin had made in terms of what the project would cost had simply stopped being remotely close enough to the truth to be anything but politically damaging.

Understanding the dynamics of the Bricklin's failure is useful, but it also points to the deeper question of what it had all meant. Using the car to see beyond the issues solely around the firm's bad management, or provincial politics, or the tremendous amount of know-how, resources, and money required to successfully manufacture a car, is a better way of understanding the Bricklin and its significance. In 1977, John Porteous, the journalist who covered the story extensively for the *Financial Post*, wrote in his review of Fredericks's and Chambers's exposé, *Bricklin*, that the book had "done a good job of telling why the wonderful sports car failed." And yet, he also remarked, "what it cannot do is explain how so many people could be so ill advised. The answer to that question will likely never be told."[21]

Perhaps.

In the end, though the dream came close, it was still a dream. "Both men, Bricklin and Hatfield," according to Michael Enright, "were prisoners of their own dreams." Malcolm Bricklin, Enright wrote, "dreamed of a safe, snazzy sports car with his name on it, with off-the-shelf parts and a standard engine to keep costs down." If it had worked, he could have been the next Henry Ford or Walter Chrysler. For his part, Richard Hatfield "dreamed he could finally manage a Maritime province away from the image of wood hewers and water drawers."[22] Had the dream become a reality, Bricklin would have achieved a different kind of entrepreneurial immortality (success), and Hatfield might have had his own miracle on the Saint John River, and a different legacy. The irony of it all is that Hatfield, his government, and his province were simply doing what citizens elsewhere had been doing (though, rather more successfully) in their own quest for the dream of industrial modernity. Unfortunately for them, New Brunswick's quest to achieve industrial modernity came at the wrong time and was tied to the wrong guy. Within a few short years after the Bricklin debacle, governments across North America would normalize bailing out auto companies and investing directly in car plants – adding, retroactively, further insult to injury.

Ultimately, even if he had *almost* solved the problem of industrial modernity, Malcolm Bricklin, GVI, and his SV1 failed in 1975 because, along with the challenges of management, money, and politics, he had chosen to launch his automobile venture at a time of tremendous industrial, economic, and social change, and at a moment when society was fundamentally shifting in how functioned. And if the automobile was a central cause and consequence of this shift, seeing like an SV1 reveals how Malcolm Bricklin and his car were at the fulcrum of those changes.

If the Bricklin is a story of the 1970s as a decade of transition, then what, exactly, *had* changed during those years, and why and how had it changed? And what stayed the same?

Well, certainly Bricklin's and Hatfield's optimism, and their faith in a future of industrial possibility, had been drastically eroded. Until the early '70s, North American society had embraced a belief in the space age and jet age, a futurism that marked the postwar world, despite the Cold War and other challenges. Bricklin's failure, onrushing economic and political problems, and the diminished ideological horizons of the Seventies – a gloom that continued in some form for decades – represented the demise of this futuristic optimism.

Whether or not Bricklin, Hatfield, and the New Brunswick government were deluded in 1973 when they started their venture, it is unquestionable that their optimism for a future of high industrial modernity was very real and was gleaned from and based on the experiences of nations and firms, and politicians and entrepreneurs, from across the globe. The two men had faith in a technologically prosperous future, one driven by high industrial automobile modernity. Even with a high-risk venture like the Bricklin, and even for a small, rural province like New Brunswick, achieving auto production and all it entailed was a worthwhile aspirational goal, one that in 1973 seemed achievable. They had, in fact, achieved it, though they could not sustain it.

But, after the Bricklin's failure, and after the economic and political shocks of the early 1970s, it was clear that optimism about the future had been crushed by the blunt realities of a dramatically changed landscape. For Hatfield and Bricklin, the cost of the project, and the difficulties faced by the province and much of the rest of the continent, had not only changed the calculus and optimistic mood around the venture, but had even become part of a broader questioning of the very notion of a positive, optimistic, automobile-driven world. The zeitgeist of high industrial modernity had given way to a decade – and decades more – of a narrative of demise, of diminished expectations for ordinary people, and often their governments, too.[23]

Just as significantly, the faith in technology that had underpinned postwar optimism was also being called into question. From the early 1900s onwards, the car and its gasoline-powered internal combustion engine – the heart of industrial modernity – had been seen as a driving force for good, bestowing personal mobility, freedom, prosperity, and identity on millions of ordinary people. Automotive technology was nothing less than a form of magic. Cars allowed people to rearrange their everyday social interactions, to accelerate and expand their working, public, and private lives and networks, and to inhabit their most fantastically time-bending and geography-defying selves. Technology, and especially automobiles, had become the currency of high industrial modernity, and of society.

Yet, by the 1970s, the automobile as a technology, along with its associated impacts, was itself quickly coming to be seen as a problem to be solved. Along with the legal, social, cultural, racial, and gendered constraints and burdens it imposed, the gasoline-powered automobile increasingly led to pollution, economic instability, and unnecessary death. Even plastic, the SV1's signature material of technological modernity, was starting to shift in its meaning, from a beneficial, convenient "partner in modernity" to a problem (though plastic would continue its relentless conquest of the planet long after the demise of the SV1). Indeed, by the time Bricklin launched his car, it was becoming clear just how much the technology of automobility was costing society. Unsurprisingly, the externalities caused by the car's use had prompted a reaction, one that had deeply shaped the contours of the Bricklin venture, for good or for ill.

Whether it was the SV1's particular response – its safety features, its plastic skin, or its big engine – or, as the decade unfolded, the equally daunting issues around fuel economy and, especially, emissions, it was clear that the problem of the car's technology and its impact had became central to automobility's place in society, if not its viability. Bricklin's own emphasis on technological solutions for the safety problem illustrated the broader struggle to solve the problems of the car. It would take decades, and technological advancements well beyond Bricklin and the '70s, to "solve" the problems of the automobile, even if doing so only created a new set of problems. But there's also no question that some of the patterns of entrepreneurial innovation (and promotion) that would lead towards a third and fourth industrial revolution, and an electrified rebirth of automobile technology could be glimpsed, at a distance, from the vantage of the SV1.

Of course, the nature of the automobile business was changing, too. Once Bricklin decided to launch General Vehicle Incorporated and start producing the SV1, it became increasingly clear that, even though he utilized many of the existing practices and methods that the Big Three had employed for decades, the reasons for making cars, and the way cars were being made in North America, were undergoing profound transformations. From the philosophy underpinning the automobile business to its manufacturing and production methods, Bricklin's experience showed that the car business, and North American business itself, was becoming more financialized, more competitive, and much leaner. The tremendous difficulty of building a car in that early 1970s moment revealed Bricklin's adherence both to long-standing Big Three business and industry practices, and his willingness to embrace newfangled ideas about how to manufacture a car. Making the SV1 and its firm required an amalgam of past, present, and future approaches to building cars, and Bricklin sat at a telling juncture along that timeline.[24]

Profitability had always been a driving force in the auto sector, but in the '70s, and for a long time thereafter, it was increasingly the only important thing. When he hatched his dream car plan, Bricklin had himself expressed motives beyond simply making money as reasons for his SV1 (or at least those he claimed). Perhaps one of the most profound changes witnessed by the SV1 was the ideological shift in the auto sector, but also so much more broadly, that saw a full embrace of neoliberal nostrums in business and society. The demise of Bricklin was a small element of a wider denunciation of statist intervention, and of Keynes. By the 1980s, North America was fully in the market-driven, laissez-faire, free-trading, individualist grip of neoliberalism (save for some important exceptions, like the regulations imposed on auto makers as well as their periodic bailouts and financial support).

Meanwhile, the relentless focus on productivity and quality by the Japanese (which *led* to profitability, as Ford had first envisioned with his system) had, by the 1970s, already started to impact and reshape the performance of the Big Three in North America, though it would take decades for Detroit to internalize the lessons of these new processes and production systems. Then, especially starting in the early 2000s, additional motives beyond profitability and leaner and faster production – the drive for environmentally friendlier vehicles – would reshape the purpose and philosophy behind making cars and shift the direction of the auto business once more.

Correspondingly, there had also been changes to the role and nature of the entrepreneur, or at least in the shifting influence of the differing archetypal business leaders who shaped the auto industry. Bricklin's journey showed that, while innovators and promoters were still needed to launch a car company, managers – as organization men or newly emerging transaction men – had, by the early 1970s, come to dominate the auto industry and the broader scope of American business. Ironically, Bricklin's promotional abilities also reflected the increasingly financialized business world that was emerging. Performative financialization in the service of *selling*, but not *building*, had by the decade's end become the model for the (post) modern financialized business executive. In a post-1970 corporate world that increasingly emphasized the sanctity of the market – of shareholder value – it's not surprising that Bricklin's career moved away from the building of cars to other, even more performative ventures focused solely on selling.

Performance had always been a central element of politics, too. But the Seventies, and Bricklin's and Hatfield's experiences, were particularly telling in showing how much a media-saturated, celebrity- and fame-obsessed world had come to blur the lines between politics, entrepreneurship, and entertainment. The showman, and the politician, had existed and flourished as performers long before that decade, but "business as entertainment" and "politics as entertainment" – the show – became a central aspect of North America's political economy in a way that it had not been before. Bricklin's and Hatfield's experiences and careers showed just how much performance had become *the* defining aspect of politics and business, one that brought into question the fine line between what constituted a legitimate business pitch, a genuine campaign promise, and a grift.

As the SV1 had emerged during the sexual revolution, a significant element of performance, at least for Bricklin, was selling not just himself and his ideas, but also the sexuality of his car. Seeing like the SV1 provides insights into the changing sexual and social relations that the automobile had done so much to create across the twentieth century. After the Seventies, the SV1 illustrated how many aspects of automobile sexuality would change, as would many other broader aspects of gender and sexuality, from women's status in society to LGBTQ rights and abortion. But the Bricklin story also demonstrates that some things did not change as quickly as others. This was especially true for Richard Hatfield, whose flamboyant yet closeted gay existence was a testament both to the changes in North America's gendered and sexual dynamics but also the endurance of its underlying structures.

Perhaps the biggest change that the SV1 revealed was the broader transformation in the political economy of the North American automobile sector and its tremendous influence on society. From the time that Malcolm Bricklin got into the car business in the late 1960s to the last enquiries about resuscitating the failed Bricklin firm in the 1980s, the North American auto industry was fundamentally transformed. Until the early 1970s, the sector operated as a stable, successful, Big Three–dominated, domestically oriented industry that provided secure and well-paying union jobs clustered around the prosperous Great Lakes region, one that was framed by national borders and tariff walls. By the time GVI collapsed, the industry had become destabilized by self-inflicted wounds, offshore competition, and an incentive-maximizing, continentalized economic geography, one that upended decades-long patterns of investment, labour relations, and consumer buying habits. Bricklin's venture was a microcosm of many of these developments, and the SV1 acted as a symbol for changing views on government intervention and the emerging deindustrialization that corroded so much of the continent's economic base, both as a cause and consequence of this change.

In 1970s North America, seeing the world from behind the wheel of a 1975, Safety Suntan Bricklin Safety Vehicle-1 meant recognizing that the nature of industrial modernity was changing – was coming to an end. That world – a version of which Malcolm Bricklin and Richard Hatfield had tried to coax into existence in New Brunswick with their dream car – was no longer possible. Who knows if it ever would have been for a province like New Brunswick or with a venture like Bricklin's. Nonetheless, in the view from that SV1, it was also clear that a new form of automobility, and society, one that remained industrial but shed many of its pre-1970s "modern" elements, was simultaneously coming into view.

In 1970, the futurist Alvin Toffler had predicted some of these postmodern changes when he published *Future Shock*, a highly influential book that was written to "help us survive our *collision* with tomorrow." Toffler, a sociologist by training who had taught courses on "the sociology of the future," warned of the acceleration of change in what he called "super-technological" society. "Unless man quickly learns to control the rate of change in his personal affairs as well as in a society at large," he warned, "we are doomed to a massive adaptational breakdown." These changes, Toffler argued, were "bigger, deeper and more important than the industrial revolution." In many ways, Toffler was already writing about the disruptions of the third industrial revolution, the end of Keynesianism, the beginnings of neoliberalism, and deindustrialization. Ultimately, he was, like the SV1, seeing the shift towards an industrial postmodern society – the demise of the future that high industrial modernity had promised. Much of Toffler's book dealt with problems of modernity and, implicitly, all that the car had wrought to shape it: the speed of change; the ascendence of impermanence, consumerism, and disposability; the overwhelming influence of technology; and the environmental challenges, especially pollution, caused by the myriad of fossil-fuel burning internal combustion engines.[25]

Malcolm Bricklin and his SV1 were on their own collision course with the future. Bricklin unveiled his car at the very moment when the booms of the industrial modern were quickly giving way to the shocks of the early industrial postmodern, and when an automobile-driven future seemed to lose its way. Along with a deeper questioning of the viability of industrial modernity seen in Toffler's jeremiad, the automobile and its industry were already being critiqued directly in books with increasingly dystopian titles like *What's Good for GM* (1970), *Autokind vs. Mankind* (1971), *The Death of the Automobile* (1972), *Paradise Lost: The Decline of the Auto-Industrial Age* (1973), and *Automotive Nightmare* (1973).[26] With these and other critical treatments, "the adulatory view of the American automobile industry was shattered irrevocably in the early 1970s," as leading automotive historian James J. Flink put it.[27] All these books appeared just as Malcolm was launching his futuristic car project.

But what Toffler and these other doomsayers could not have known was that the disruptions of the early 1970s signified an end, but also a midpoint, and a new beginning.

The half century between the end of Model T production in 1927 and the Bricklin's appearance in 1974 marked the height of Fordist industrial modernity and its rapid demise. Fordism's end is a well-trodden scholarly debarkation point, one whose prominence permeates a broad range of approaches and analyses that reflect a view that the early '70s saw upheavals in the economy, labour, business, politics, international affairs, and social and cultural matters.[28] The Bricklin story confirms much of this narrative, and it also illuminates how so many aspects of North American society underwent dramatic change. Most prominently, the Bricklin case affirms the centrality of historical materialism as an essential element of industrial modernity, and the salience of the auto industry in its tremendous impact on the lives of people across North America, from ordinary workers to entrepreneurs and politicians. The end of Fordist practices could be seen most acutely in the widespread deindustrialization that appeared in North America during the decade, one of the most significant economic, political, social, and cultural processes of our time, and one that has impacted countless lives and whole cities and regions.

And yet, Bricklin's brief interlude as North America's first new auto manufacturer in three decades marks an important transition. Bricklin's operations represent a difficult moment of manufacturing's evolution between the practices of Ford's second industrial revolution, an ongoing third industrial revolution, and an emerging fourth. Thus, a form of Fordism continued to exist after the 1970s, though it both looked and acted different than it had in Henry's time. The North American auto sector became leaner and more globalized in its production and processes, and this shift had a tremendous impact upon workers in North America as the industry restructured (Chrysler), was revitalized by new entrants (Japanese and other foreign manufacturers), and reoriented its economic geography (northwards, then southwards).

The next half century following the Bricklin's demise saw the beginnings and full blossoming of industrial postmodernity. Although post-embargo deindustrialization had cut a destructive path across swaths of North America, industrialization did not end. Between the 1970s and the 2020s, industrialization, deindustrialization, and reindustrialization coexisted, an uneven and unfair process that decimated some towns and regions, sustained others, and revitalized still others. As the economic geography of North America was buffeted by changes in the auto and other industries with factory closures and relocations, manufacturing continued or emerged in new locales, producing new types of goods and utilizing new, far more advanced production processes and technologies. By the early 2000s, traditional Big Three automobile manufacturing's footprint had undoubtedly shrunk, but the continent's car-making capacity was also boosted by dozens of new plants from a constellation of nations outside of North America. At the same time, whole new industries that barely existed in the SV1's time emerged to reimagine manufacturing, creating unimaginably advanced technological products and utilizing the most advanced production processes, robotics, and supply chains yet created by humanity. As a corollary of lean manufacturing, many North American communities experienced a form of lean deindustrialization.

By the 2020s, the trends that had started in Bricklin's time had come into full bloom, and industrial postmodernity came fully into its own. Industrial postmodernity was a continuation of a form of Fordism, which conflated with third and fourth industrial revolution practices to create a new world of manufacturing, one based as much on semi-conductors and artificial intelligence as on automobility. In this new computerized, digitized, roboticized manufacturing world, industrial postmodernity also sought to move beyond its Fordist, carbonized legacy and to solve the problems it had inherited from industrial modernity's century of fossil fuel dependence. The automobile – its technology, its futurism, its society-shaping impact – had yet again played a pivotal role in the ongoing transformation to this brave new world.

Despite all its problems, the dream (of the) car retained its unquenchable desirability as the vehicle by which to change the world. If the early 1970s are the tectonic fault line in the seismic shift between Fordist, fossil-fuelled high modernity and leaner, greener, industrial postmodernity, then Bricklin's 1975 Safety Vehicle-1 can also be seen as automobility's indispensable representative midpoint vehicle, shining brightly between Ford's 1908 Model T and Tesla's 2017 Model 3.

EPILOGUE

Tesla Factory, Fremont, California, August 2018: Elon Musk, the Model 3, and "Production Hell"

***Dream Car* Song 15: "Highway to Hell," AC/DC, 1979**

Tesla Inc.'s spectacularly futuristic Fremont Factory sits near the edge of San Francisco Bay, in the heart of California's Silicon Valley, about a half hour's drive north from San Jose and an hour southeast from San Francisco. The sprawling, glittering factory, encompassing nearly two square kilometres, employing tens of thousands of people, utilizing thousands of robots, and housing the most advanced production processes in the world, was Tesla's first major manufacturing facility when it opened in 2010. Aside from the vehicles it produces, the plant is rightfully famous as the most visible, tangible, symbol of Tesla's "quest for a fantastic future."[1]

Less well known about Fremont is that its story also embodies industrial modernity's rise and demise and its rebirth as industrial postmodernity. Though Tesla's factory may epitomize the twenty-first century's fourth industrial revolution, Fremont has a much older history. In fact, the plant can trace its roots directly back to the dawn of automobile industrial modernity. Originally built in 1916 by the Chevrolet Motor Car Company (est. 1911) as Oakland Assembly (Durant and GM acquired Chevrolet in 1918), it was the first automobile manufacturing facility on the West Coast. Sometimes called "the Chevrolet Factory," for half a century thousands of workers assembled hundreds of thousands of Chevy products at the plant. During that time, Oakland utilized the latest Fordist production processes and played an

Figure E.1. Phases of car making in California: Oakland Assembly, 1916 (top left); Fremont, 1962 (top right); New United Motor Manufacturing Incorporated (NUMMI), 1984 (bottom left); Tesla, 2010 (bottom right).

integral role within Alfred Sloan's giant enterprise. In 1964, GM closed Oakland following the 1963 opening of its more modern Fremont Assembly facility (about forty-five minutes south), itself one of the last new factories built during Detroit's glory years. In the 1960s and early 1970s, Fremont did well, producing many more hundreds of thousands of Chevys in a facility that, despite labour difficulties, had union representation and paid good wages.[2]

In the early 1980s, however, Fremont was in trouble, as was GM and the rest of the American auto industry. Unable to compete with better and more efficiently produced foreign vehicles, especially from Japan, the facility was closed in 1982, during the depths of Detroit's post-1973 malaise. By the mid-1980s, GM realized that its survival depended on learning the Toyota production system (TPS), an essential aspect of the third industrial revolution, and a harbinger of Fordism's decline, though not its complete demise. In 1984, the facility reopened as New United Motor Manufacturing Incorporated (NUMMI), a joint venture between General Motors and Toyota, Japan's leading car manufacturer. Eventually, GM and Toyota together built identical but differently branded vehicles on the same line at NUMMI: for GM, the Pontiac Vibe (2003–8), and for Toyota, the better-selling Matrix (2003–8). Having learned its TPS lessons, GM in 2010 ended its joint venture with Toyota, and the plant was closed, seemingly yet another casualty of the process of automation, deindustrialization, and globalization.[3]

In the summer of 2018, nearly a decade after purchasing and modernizing the shuttered Fremont plant from Toyota, Elon Musk declared that Tesla had overcome its "production hell," as he called it, and had achieved the manufacturing milestone of assembling five thousand Model 3s a week at the factory. The Model 3, a battery-electric car boldly named as an homage to the Model T, aimed to replicate the mass-market success of Ford's car from a century before and promised to revolutionize and revitalize the automobile and its industry by providing inexpensive mobility without the problems associated with the internal combustion engine. By successfully mass manufacturing the Model 3, Tesla had accomplished its own Ford-like "miracle that God had wrought," and Musk had successfully achieved the American entrepreneurial dream that Malcolm Bricklin had so improbably sought four decades earlier. With Tesla's success, Musk had solved the problem of automobile industrial postmodernity – producing a quality electric battery–powered vehicle that avoided many of the problems of the internal combustion engine. Musk had undeniably changed the world with his own innovative dream car.[4]

The road to Tesla's titanic achievement had been extraordinarily difficult for Musk and his company. After gaining control of Tesla in 2004, Musk had taken years to start full-scale production, and, even then, progress towards his dream had come only very slowly, and very expensively. Between 2008 and 2012, Tesla managed to build about 2,400 production Roadsters, about 400 less than the number of SV1s that Bricklin had assembled in 1974–5. In 2013, Tesla built its 3,000th vehicle (a Model S), surpassing Bricklin's total output. In 2015, after numerous delays, Fremont began production of the Model X, the first vehicle since the Bricklin to feature gull-wing ("falcon") doors. In 2020, Tesla reached the production milestone of 1,000 Model Y vehicles a week, a monthly target that Bricklin had repeatedly promised in 1974 and 1975 yet never achieved (Bricklin Canada's best month was 429 SV1s). By 2022, Fremont was producing an astounding 1,700 vehicles *per day*: Musk had clearly solved the problem of mass automobile manufacturing. In 2018, fifteen years after its founding and ten years after starting production, Tesla finally turned a profit, something Bricklin never came close to accomplishing.[5] By then, Tesla had become famous for "selling the future," something Malcolm Bricklin had spent his whole career trying to do.[6]

Unquestionably, an incredulous reader will immediately dismiss any comparison between the Model 3 and the SV1, between the Tesla and Bricklin firms, or between Musk and Bricklin as entrepreneurs. After all, Tesla's electrified and digitized Roadster (built on a Lotus platform), its Model S, and all its successors, including the Model 3, are vehicles that represented many magnitudes of innovation beyond the relatively rudimentary SV1 safety sports car. Moreover, Tesla's rise had been powered by billions of dollars in private-sector money and sustained government support (mostly through carbon credits), the benefits of decades of technological and production advances since the 1970s, and immense and sustained publicity from a largely fawning media, not to mention the consumerist loyalty of those hundreds of thousands of Tesla "fanboys."

Considered one of the most controversial yet successful entrepreneurs and business leaders in modern history, and among the world's most influential, provocative, and wealthy people, Musk is often seen as a direct twenty-first-century successor to Henry Ford, himself regarded as the twentieth century's greatest visionary, disruptor, and entrepreneur. Their similarities do not end there. Both men experienced worldwide fame and, in the earlier part of their careers, a type of popular adulation that reflected the global impact of the far-reaching changes that each was responsible for. At the same time, both men's legacies are deeply sullied by poor labour relations, anti-Semitism, erratic behaviour, and actions that put in question their management of their firms, including the ownership of media outlets used to propagate hateful messages (the *Dearborn Independent*; Twitter, now X). Both men also took on quixotic and sometimes visionary projects often unrelated to their automotive enterprises (e.g., Fordlandia, Muscle Shoals; SpaceX), which were made possible by the vast fortunes that they accumulated.

Clearly, although Malcolm Bricklin is sometimes called a visionary, he is not in the same league as Ford or Musk. And yet, despite the decades of distance, generational differences, and profound social and technological changes separating each of them, Ford, Bricklin, and Musk are, in fact, intimately connected through a shared pursuit of their dream cars and through their roles in the story of industrial modernity's rise, decline, and rebirth as industrial postmodernity. Like Tesla's Fremont plant and its connections to automobile modernity's past, present, and future, the three men are bound together across history. With the Model T, Ford instigated mass automobile manufacturing. Though he failed, Bricklin's SV1 venture marked a transitional moment from Fordism to an industrial postmodernity. With his Model 3, Musk proved, beyond a shadow of a doubt, that EVs could be mass manufactured. In doing so, he recreated Ford's automobile-fuelled American dream in a manner that Bricklin could only, well, dream of, no matter how hard he might try.

Just as the SV1 signalled the end of an era that lasted from the early 1900s to the early 1970s, Musk's Model 3 signalled the end of an era that lasted from the 1970s to the 2020s, one that saw the decline of American Fordism, the emergence of neo-liberalism, and North America's shift towards a fourth industrial revolution, what the auto sector referred to as Industry 4.0. If Bricklin's venture represented Fordist industrial modernity's culmination and the start of its simultaneously sudden and slow demise, Tesla's success represented its final symbolic and literal end, and a full transition to industrial postmodernity, one that had taken nearly half a century.

But Tesla's electrifying success also represented a new, yet familiar, beginning. In this postmodern world, the dream of the car remained, even as the automobile and its processes were reshaped once more as society attempted to resolve the profound, existential problems that automobility had created. Once again, given its tremendous impact, for good or for ill, the automobile sat at the centre of society's most fundamental questions.

Acknowledgments

My family did not fully join automobile modernity until I was nine years old.

Until then, I had grown up thinking that mine was – I was sure – one of the only families in the world whose parents did not drive and did not own a car. It was easy to feel this way in suburban Agincourt, in Scarborough, a borough of Metropolitan Toronto, Ontario, in 1979. In the postwar period, Scarborough was a place that, like so much of the rest of North America, had been completely reshaped by automobility. Even as late as the 1950s, Agincourt had been a sleepy farming community on the edge of a provincial town. But when I was growing up in the 1970s, it had already become a fully integrated inner suburb of a booming, car-fuelled, highway-building metropolis and society.

Of course, there undoubtedly were other families, especially immigrant families like mine in this heavily multicultural part of Toronto, that did not drive or own a car. But as a kid, it didn't seem that way. It seemed like the *whole world* was immersed in automobility. In Agincourt, cars were everywhere: on the buzzing, mighty Highway 401, not far from our house; at the strip mall and in the big church parking lot across our busy street; in every driveway in front of every house of the curvilinear, suburban streets that surrounded our small, asphalt piece of the world.

In our townhouse complex, everyone except for us had a car, including my best friend Alkarim's family. They were from Pakistan, and his dad was a mechanic who gave me Pirelli tire decals that I peeled off to stick on my school binders. Four doors down was Phillip, a cool Jamaican teenager who would let me hang out with him every Sunday as he washed his red Camaro, listening to *The Rocky Horror Picture Show* soundtrack. Even though we shared the same decade, 1970s Agincourt was psychologically, if not geographically, a million miles away from Bricklin but also, in retrospect, culturally somehow right next door.

As a child living in the liminal space one step outside of the world of automobility, I was both completely fascinated by cars and, to be honest, somewhat stigmatized by the near-daily reminder that my parents did not drive or own a car. We mostly took the bus, or got rides from my father's brothers, two of whom lived nearby and both of whom drove. When I was nine, my father's eldest brother, Johnny, drove a Lincoln Continental Mark IV, something that I somehow intuitively knew marked him as a successful person, a big man about town. Or, perhaps, that is how I saw the way people perceived him. I realized that cars could *shape* people and their identities, shaped places like my neighbourhood, and even shaped how I understood the world.

Even after we joined automobility, I never forgot about the immensity of the car's everyday impact, and I remained deeply aware of the automobile's ubiquity, its necessity, its society-shaping power. My early detachment from automobility and necessitated observation of the car's influence probably explains why I see the condition of automobility the way I do, and it explains why I wrote *Dream Car* in the manner that I did. Automobility has always been more than a simple academic pursuit; the car was something that had, in its own formative power, pointedly forced me to understand the world in a particular way.

In the summer of 2021, when I asked my mother to confirm what year she first got her driver's licence (my father never drove), she replied, "Oh, that's a doozy of a question." After I mentioned that the word "doozy" became popularly associated with Duesenberg, a luxury brand of autos in the 1920s, we laughed at that reminder of automobility's sheer pervasiveness. In 1979, fourteen years after emigrating from Greece to Canada, my mother successfully took her driver's test and got a hand-me-down mid-70s, blue, wood-panelled, Ford County Squire station wagon from my uncle, and my family and I belatedly stepped into the world of automobility.

And, as it so happened, industrial modernity's transitional moment.

I first started work on this project in 2007, so there are many people whom I need to thank, given *Dream Car*'s long gestation and circuitous emergence. I would like to recognize the support of the Social Sciences and Humanities Research Council of Canada, and the Jackman Humanities Institute. Additional funding was provided by the L.R. Wilson/R.J. Currie Chair in Canadian Business History at the University of Toronto, and I am very grateful to the generous donors who have contributed to advance the study of business in history departments and of history in business schools. I would also like to thank my colleagues at the University of Toronto, in both the History Department and the Rotman School of Management, and at Trent University. Also, thank you to all my colleagues at the Canadian Business History Association and all the scholars in the Deindustrialization and the Politics of Our Time (DePOT) network.

Archivists and librarians are guardians of knowledge, history, and of truth, and I thank each and every archivist and librarian who has assisted in this book, including Dale Cogswell and Josh Green at the New Brunswick Public Archives, Kelly Dickinson and Tom Stillwell at the Legislative Assembly of New Brunswick, Carla Reczek at the North American Automotive History Collection at the Detroit Public Library, John Kyros at the General Motors Archives, and archivists at Library and Archives Canada. Thanks to Alexander Gates at the Canadian Automotive Museum in Oshawa, who was kind enough to lend out the Dr. Bigman collection, and Douglas Goold, who allowed me access to his private collection of automobile materials. Bill Jarvis provided helpful insights into auto ventures in the Maritimes. Thanks to John Leroux at the Beaverbrook Gallery for sharing some fantastic Bricklin images. I would also like to thank Ms. Barbara Jonas for providing valuable additional information on her brother Malcolm's long and amazing entrepreneurial career.

A deep and heartfelt thank you to my editor at the University of Toronto Press, Len Husband, who has been a wonderful professional colleague and great friend, despite my constant badgering. Thanks to Barbara Tessman for her close reading of the manuscript, and to Janice Evans for her work in making such a wonderful-looking book.

I'd like to thank those who assisted in the research of the book, many of whom have gone on to become first-class scholars, educators, and professionals in their own right, including James Onusko, Meaghan Beaton, Dwayne Collins, Jeremy Milloy, Blair Cullen, Stephanie Attley, and Orion Skoblo. Most especially, I would like to thank Han-Yi Huang, who provided tremendous help and scholarly advice – I could not have finished the book without her.

I'd also like to thank those who read and commented on earlier presentations and drafts of the book and those scholars and friends who have influenced my thinking about modernity, automobility, society, and history. Thank you to Keith Walden, Steve Penfold, Sarah Elvins, Finis Dunaway, Sean Mills, Brian Gettler, Greg Keenan, Donica Belisle, Ben Bradley, Matt Hayday, Jeremy Robbins, Steven High, Bruce Livesey, Don Nerbas, Jeff Garner, Laura Makadoro, Douglas Goold, Neville Britto, Greig Mordue, Laurence Mussio, Peter Neary, Bryan Palmer, Joan Sangster, Fred Burrill, Liz Kirkland, Emily Gann, Howard Green, Paul Barrett, Magda Fahrni, Ken Corts, Joe Martin, and Red Wilson. Thanks to the anonymous readers of the manuscript, whose comments improved the book. Daniel Wadhwani was kind enough to share notes from his wonderful 2023 Business History Conference Presidential Address in Detroit.

A special thought goes to Chris Armstrong. Chris shaped me, and my scholarship, more than he ever realized. Though he read the manuscript, we never had a chance to talk about it.

I gave conference presentations based on *Dream Car* at the Business History Conference, the Canadian Historical Association, and other venues across various years, including to the Montreal History Group, and at McMaster University, the University of Toronto, and Trent University. I published pieces on Bricklin in *Acadiensis* and *Business History Online*, parts of which appear in some form in the book. There are also two podcasts that I gave about the book: thank you to Ernest Granderson and Herb Emery. I published a blog post in 2016, "Procrastinating the Bricklin," which explained why I was taking so long to write the book, and why the delay was, in fact, improving the project. Thanks to all those anonymous reviewers, whose work is greatly appreciated, and also to David Frank, Don Wright, Gwendolyn Davies, Jan Wadlaw, and every other academic with whom I had a conversation about this topic, or who gave me a Bricklin and/or Hatfield "tip." And there are many others – thank you to all.

I'd also like to thank all the students who ever took the "Car in History" courses that I taught at Trent University and then at the University of Toronto. The many wonderful students across nearly two decades of that class taught me as much as I did them about the car and its impact, and this book has very much been shaped by all the valuable conversations we had in (and outside of) the class and by the excellent feedback I received from students who read early versions of *Dream Car*. This book is very much a product of the classroom, and has been written in style, structure, and content with students and teaching in mind.

Thank you to the countless people in my neighbourhood or at kids' sporting events over the years who have had to listen to me drone on and on about modernity and the Bricklin, and to my parents, Angela and Tassos, sisters Voula and Helen, in-laws Pat, John, Ian, Chris, and Nilla, and nieces and nephew who have also had to "put up with" the Bricklin over all these years. I will forever cherish the memory of being in Greece in 2022, where I wrote parts of chapter 6.

Most especially, I wish to thank my family. In some ways, my two amazing sons, Jack and Will, have grown up with this book, whether they realize it or not. My wife certainly realizes it, and she is probably even happier than I am to see it finally completed. I cannot say how much their, and especially her, support has meant through so many challenges and changes. Without Victoria, this book would not be here, nor would its author. I love her dearly.

Finally, I wish to thank Malcolm Bricklin, whom I interviewed in 2013 and in 2022. He was incredibly generous with his time, and the near full-day 2013 interview, held in various spots in New York City, including his son's subterranean table-tennis club, is truly a highlight of my career. Years later, I realized the irony of interviewing Malcolm Bricklin, the impresario of the automotive world, in Manhattan, the one place in North America where no one really needs a car (at one point we actually took the subway together). And yet, doing so made complete sense, as New York City, P.T. Barnum's city, is a city of dreams.

After all that has been written or said about him, I hope that this book has done justice to his fantastic career, his authentically larger-than-life personality, and his relentless optimism for the future.

***Dream Car* Bonus Track 1: "The Time Warp," *The Rocky Horror Picture Show,* 1975**

***Dream Car* Bonus Track 2: "New York, New York," Frank Sinatra, 1980**

***Dream Car* Bonus Track 3: "Fast Car," Tracy Chapman, 1988**

Abbreviations

ABC	American Broadcasting Company
AIDS	acquired immunodeficiency syndrome
AMC	American Motors Corporation
auto pact	Automotive Products Trade Agreement
AV	automated vehicle
BCL	Bricklin Canada Ltd.
BIG	Bricklin International get-together
Big Three	General Motors, Ford, and Chrysler
BMW	Bayerische Motoren Werke / Bavarian Motor Works
BVC	Bricklin Vehicle Corporation
Campaign GM	Campaign to Make General Motors Responsible
CAW	Canadian Auto Workers
CBC	Canadian Broadcasting Corporation
CES	Consumer Electronics Show
CR	*Consumer Reports*
CUV	compact utility vehicle / crossover utility vehicle
CVCC	compound vortex controlled combustion
Delco	Dayton Engineering Laboratories Company
DMC	Delorean Motor Company
DREE	Department of Regional Economic Expansion
EV	electric vehicle
FIRA	Foreign Investment Review Agency
GM	General Motors

GVI	General Vehicle Incorporated
HIV	human immunodeficiency virus
IBM	International Business Machines
ICE	internal combustion engine
IPO	initial public offering
ITC	information technology and communications
JIT	just-in-time delivery
LGBTQ	lesbian, gay, bisexual, transgender, queer/questioning
m-division	multidivisional corporate structure
MIP	modularity in production
MNE	multinational enterprises
MSRP	manufacturer's suggested retail price
NASA	National Aeronautics and Space Agency
NBC	National Broadcasting Company
NEP	new economic policy
NHTSA	National Highway Transportation and Safety Administration (US)
NUMMI	New United Motor Manufacturing Incorporated
OPEC	Organization of Petroleum Exporting Countries
PHL	Provincial Holdings Ltd. (New Brunswick)
PKD	partial knock-down
PSA	Peugeot Société Anonyme
RCA	Radio Corporation of America
RCMP	Royal Canadian Mounted Police
SUV	sport utility vehicle
SV1	Safety Vehicle-1 (the Bricklin)
TPS	Toyota production system
UA	universal automation
UAW	United Auto Workers
UN	United Nations
VIN	vehicle identification number
VW	Volkswagen

Notes about Sources

Two notes about the sources in this book.

First, on the story of Malcolm Bricklin and the SV1.

Over the many years that I worked on this book, I interviewed only one person, Malcolm Bricklin. This is not because I do not believe in the utility of oral history as a tool in the historians' toolkit. In fact, I am a firm advocate of the importance of oral histories and have used them on many occasions in other books and projects. The nature of this book, however, did not lend itself as easily to the utility of extensive oral interviews. Obviously, if Richard Hatfield had been alive, I would have interviewed him.

At the same time, Malcolm Bricklin and the Bricklin SV1 have been the subject of hundreds, if not thousands, of interviews, articles, and stories in various media over the decades. Anyone can go online and find videos, transcripts, articles, and podcasts that contain Bricklin's own words. Amazingly, over all the many times that he has been asked about his half-century career in the auto industry, he consistently tells the same stories. I would know, as I have likely looked at these materials more than most, and often with an historian's sceptical eye. Most of that online material is aimed at Bricklin aficionados, car obsessives and gearheads, automotive historians, or those interested in the curious, weird, and wonderful world of twentieth-century modernity.

Second, on the auto industry.

Along with the mass of material on Bricklin itself, there is an immense and ever-growing amount of scholarship, data, and information on the automobile, its industry, and its impact on the United States, Canada, North America, and the world. Even in 1975, Professor Lynwood Bryant of the Massachusetts Institute of Technology remarked that "if the academic study of cars were given space relative to their importance," the result would "fill at least forty percent" of American libraries.[1] In addition to archival and scholarly sources, the book utilizes music, films, popular culture, and many images that testify to the vastness of the car's influence on society. Indeed, so daunting is the scope and scale of the impact of automobility that using a single car, the Bricklin, as a vehicle to examine the automobile industry and its impact is probably the most sensible way of "seeing" automobility's tremendous influence on society.

Nonetheless, I happily admit that it is simply impossible to track down and confirm every single one of the multitudinous details and aspects of this "industry of industries." Any errors are my own.

Finally, in keeping with the book's open road thematic structure, the bibliography follows the same path: it is organized by chapter/subject, making it more useful as a reference tool for readers seeking sources on those particular aspects of automobility explored in the individual chapters of this book.

Notes

Preface

1 For example, a selection of Model T songs can be found at the Henry Ford Museum, at http://www.dalnet.lib.mi.us/henryford/docs/FordAndModelTSongsCollection_Accession163.pdf.

Prologue: On Stage, the Four Seasons Restaurant, New York City, 25 June 1974: Malcolm Bricklin, Richard Hatfield, and Their Fantastic Car

1 The "automotive P.T. Barnum" quote is from Danny Hakim, "Doubts Rising about a Venture to Import Chinese Cars," *New York Times*, 7 June 2005. The subject of thousands of newspaper and magazine articles during his half-century-long career, "Bricklin" yields tens of thousands of results in a Google search. Bricklin, his car, and his life have been the subject of three documentaries (one in French) as well as songs, books, poems, and a musical, *The Bricklin: An Automotive Fantasy*, which has been performed in Poland. Bricklin attended the musical's 2010 opening in Fredericton.

2 Tim Brooks and Earle Marsh, *The Complete Directory to Prime Time Network and Cable TV Shows, 1946–Present* (New York: Ballantine Books, 1999), 1251. A clip of the *Chico and the Man* episode featuring a Bricklin can be seen on YouTube at https://www.youtube.com/watch?v=UY1vrKLcLOk. The show had a rating of 28.5, meaning nearly 30 per cent of all American households watching television during that timeslot were tuned into *Chico and the Man*, a figure in the tens of millions of viewers.

3 The Kaiser-Frazer Corporation, which lasted from 1947 to 1953 and took advantage of the early postwar auto boom, was a notable exception, but it had been built on the remains of another auto firm, the Graham-Paige company, started in 1927; while Henry Kaiser was a leading industrialist, Joseph Frazer was a veteran of the auto sector, having worked at Packard, GM, and Chrysler. Kaiser-Frazer eventually became the Kaiser Jeep Corporation, which was sold to American Motors in 1969, which itself was then purchased by Chrysler in 1987. On Kaiser-Frazer, see Richard M. Langworth, *Kaiser-Frazer: The Last Onslaught on Detroit* (Kutztown, PA: Princeton Publishing, 1975).

4 John J. O'Connor, "Bricklin Safety Vehicle ('A Dream Come True') Will Debut in Northeast," *Advertising Age*, 1 July 1974; Ernst Holsendolph, "Acrylic 2-Seater Sells for $6,500," *New York Times*, 26 June 1974, 59. The 25 June 1974 event included a buffet with cocktails at 11:30 a.m., followed by the unveiling of the car at 12:30, and a press conference thereafter. National Automotive History Collection, Detroit Public Library, Bricklin Collection, Series I, Finance and Administrative Operations, box 3, Invitation, 25 June 1974.

Introduction: Industrial Modernity, Bricklin, and Industrial Postmodernity

1 Notably, it is the "industrial postmodern," not the "*post-industrial* modern," as industrialization, and automobile production, remain among the most salient features of the North American political economy despite widespread deindustrialization and disruptive change in the 1970s, symbolized by the Bricklin incident. In fact, one might remark that the automobile and its industry remain at the absolute centre of the twenty-first century's most compelling questions of identity, mobility, business, the economy, and, most especially, the environment. As agents of their own dramatic transformation and reinvention, the automotive industry and the automobile itself remain a constant in the shift from the industrial modern to the industrial postmodern. Humans' ongoing connection to the automobile and the car's perpetual sway over society continue to shape, and reshape, what it means to be modern. For views on this question, see, for example, David Harvey, *The Condition of Postmodernity: An Enquiry into the Origins of Cultural Change* (Cambridge, MA: Blackwell, 1990) and Barry Smart, *Postmodernity* (London: Routledge, 2016).

2 Jackie Webster, "The Little Car That Couldn't," *Maclean's*, 6 October 1975, 69.

3 Arthur R.M. Lower, *Canadians in the Making: A Social History of Canada* (Toronto: Longman, 1969), 424.

4 The 1981–2 DeLorean, which I discuss in more detail in chapter 7 and in the epilogue, was built in Belfast, Northern Ireland.

5 Across its various innumerable aspects, the auto industry has been one of the most studied and written about industries in history, while the car itself is at the centre of global political economy and popular culture. For a good critique of this dynamic, see Jim Conley and Arlene Tigar McLaren, *Car Troubles: Critical Studies of Automobility and Auto-Mobility* (New York: Routledge, 2009).

6 See, for example, Allen J. Matusow, *Nixon's Economy: Booms, Busts, Dollars and Votes* (Lawrence: University Press of Kansas, 1998); Daniel T. Rodgers, *Age of Fracture* (Cambridge, MA: Harvard University Press, 2011); Marc Levinson, *An Extraordinary Time: The End of the Postwar Boom and the Return of the Ordinary Economy* (New York: Basic Books, 2016); Jefferson Cowie, *Stayin' Alive: The 1970s and the Last Days of the Working Class* (New York: New Press, 2010); David Halberstam, *The Reckoning* (New York: William Morrow, 1986), 13; and Harvey, *Condition of Postmodernity*, vii.

7 For more on the 1965 Canada-US auto pact, see Dimitry Anastakis, *Auto Continent: Creating a Borderless North American Auto Industry, 1960–1971* (Toronto: University of Toronto Press, 2005).

8 Robert Bothwell, *Your Country, My Country: A Unified History of the United States and Canada* (Toronto: Oxford University Press, 2015); Stephen Azzi, *Reconcilable Differences: A History of Canada-US Relations* (Toronto: Oxford University Press, 2014); Doug Owram, *Born at the Right Time: A History of the Baby Boom Generation* (Toronto: University of Toronto Press, 1997).

9 Lower, *Canadians in the Making*, 426.

10 Multiple disciplines, including history, have differing definitions of "modernity," which is itself an interdisciplinary literary subfield with its own journal, *Modernism/Modernity*. The periodization, meaning, and specifics of the term are much debated. For a small sampling of some historical works that consider modernity, see, for example: Terry Smith, *Making the Modern: Industry, Art, and Design in America* (Chicago: University of Chicago Press, 1993); Brian Heaphy, *Late Modernity and Social Change: Reconstructing Social and Personal Life* (New York: Routledge, 2007); Couze Venn and Mike Featherstone, "Modernity," *Theory, Culture and Society* 23, 2–3 (2006): 457–65; Keith Walden, *Becoming Modern in Toronto: The Industrial Exhibition and the Shaping of a Late Victorian Culture* (Toronto: University of Toronto Press, 1997); Barry Buzan and George Lawson, *The Global Transformation: History, Modernity and the Making of International Relations* (Cambridge: Cambridge University Press, 2015); Glen Norcliffe, *The Ride to Modernity: The Bicycle in Canada, 1869–1900* (Toronto: University of Toronto Press, 2001); and Christopher Armstrong, *Making Toronto Modern: Architecture and Design, 1895–1975* (Montreal and Kingston: McGill-Queen's University Press, 2014). Works that look primarily at European modernity include Marshall Berman, *All That Is Solid Melts into Air: The Experience of Modernity* (New York: Simon & Schuster, 1982) and Modris Eksteins, *Rites of Spring: The Great War and the Birth of the Modern Age* (Toronto: Lester & Orpen Dennys, 1994).

11 Ian McKay, *The Quest of the Folk: Antimodernism and Cultural Selection in Twentieth-Century Nova Scotia* (Montreal and Kingston: McGill-Queen's University Press, 1994), x.

12 Walden, *Becoming Modern in Toronto*, 4.

13 John Urry, "The 'System' of Automobility," *Theory, Culture and Society* 21, 4–5 (2004): 25–6, emphases in original. Many other scholars have referred to the impact of the car on society as "Fordism." See Gijs Mom, *Atlantic Automobilism: Emergence and Persistence of the Car, 1895–1940* (New York: Berghahn, 2015). For another attempt to utilize the automobile to provide a technological synthesis of twentieth-century American history, see James Flink, *The Car Culture* (Cambridge, MA: MIT Press, 1975).

14 The "I invented the modern age" quote is from Douglas Brinkley, *Wheels for the World: Henry Ford, His Company, and a Century of Progress* (New York: Penguin Books, 2003), 181. Henry Ford has often been regarded as "the creator of the modern world … a man of the future, leading the world into the modern industrial era": Jeffrey Muldoon, "Henry Ford and His Legacy: An American Prometheus," in *The Palgrave Handbook of Management History*, edited by Bradley Bowden, Jeffrey Muldoon, Anthony M. Gould, and Adela J. McMurray (Cham, CH: Springer International Publishing, 2020), 522. See also, for example, Richard Snow, *I Invented the Modern Age: The Rise of Henry Ford* (New York: Scribner, 2014), and Ray Batchelor, *Henry Ford, Mass Production, Modernism, and Design* (Manchester: Manchester University Press, 1994).

15 David Harvey sees Fordism as occurring in the post-1945 period (see *Condition of Postmodernity*), whereas the framing described here has it beginning in the first decade of the 1900s.

16 This narrative structure also echoes that found in Vaclav Smil, *Made in the USA: The Rise and Retreat of American Manufacturing* (Cambridge, MA: MIT Press, 2013), which prominently features the auto sector, including the use of GM's story as an introductory tool for the book. It also borrows from Harvey, *The Condition of Postmodernity*. See also Daniel Bell, *The Coming of Post-Industrial Society: A Venture in Social Forecasting* (New York: Basic Books, 1973).

17 This conceptualization is, in part, inspired by and builds upon James Flink, "Three Stages of American Automobile Consciousness," *American Quarterly* 24, 4 (1972): 451–73; Rudi Volti,

"A Century of Automobility," *Technology and Culture* 37, 4 (1996): 663–85; and Volti, *Cars and Culture: The Life Story of a Technology* (Westport, CT: Greenwood Press, 2004). See also James Flink, *The Automobile Age* (Cambridge, MA: MIT Press, 1990) and Volti, *Society and Technological Change* (New York: Worth Publishers, 1988).

18 In fact, with the advent of automated vehicles (AVs) beginning in the 2020s, automobility has refashioned itself to be even more convenient and technologically advanced. Whether AVs lead to greater personal freedom, however, is still uncertain, given the expectation that driverless vehicles will remove our direct ability to control cars. For some of the complications of AVs, see, for example, P.A. Hancocka, Illah Nourbakhsh, and Jack Stewart, "On the Future of Transportation in an Era of Automated and Autonomous Vehicles," *Proceedings of the National Academy of Sciences* 116, 16 (2019): 7684–91.

19 James Scott, *Seeing Like a State: How Certain Schemes to Improve the Human Condition Have Failed* (New Haven, CT: Yale University Press, 1998). See also Peter J. Taylor, *Modernities: A Geohistorical Interpretation* (Minneapolis: University of Minnesota Press, 1999).

20 Owen Gutfreund, *Twentieth Century Sprawl: Highways and the Reshaping of the American Landscape* (New York: Oxford University Press, 2004) and Gutfreund, "Rebuilding New York in the Auto Age: Robert Moses and His Highways," in *Robert Moses and the Modern City: The Transformation of New York*, ed. Hilary Ballon and Kenneth T. Jackson (New York: W.W. Norton, 2007). On suburbanization, see Kenneth T. Jackson, *Crabgrass Frontier: The Suburbanization of the United States* (New York: Oxford University Press, 1985). Of course, by the 1960s, there was a reaction to this automotive rebuilding of North America.

21 In 1921, there were approximately 100 motor vehicles per 1,000 people in the United States; by 1960, that figure reached over 400; by 1967, 500; by 1975, 640; by 1985, 744; and by 2000, there were 800 vehicles for every 1,000 Americans. While Canadians did not adopt the automobile as zealously as did Americans, who remain the planet's greatest consumers of cars, they were usually only slightly behind. Oak Ridge National Laboratory, *Transportation Energy Data Book: Edition 35*, ORNL-6990, Oak Ridge, TN, September 2016, tables 3.5 and 3.6.

22 On the environment and the automobile in North America, see Tom McCarthy, *Auto Mania: Cars, Consumers, and the Environment* (New Haven, CT: Yale University Press, 2007), and particularly his chapter on Henry Ford's environmentalism. See also McCarthy, "The Coming Wonder? Foresight and Early Concerns about the Automobile," *Environmental History* 6, 1 (2001): 46–74. On other views of "seeing like a car," see Thomas Zeller, *Consuming Landscapes: What We See When We Drive and Why It Matters* (Baltimore: Johns Hopkins University Press, 2022) and Ben Bradley, *British Columbia by the Road: Car Culture and the Making of a Modern Landscape* (Vancouver: UBC Press, 2017). On a pre-car way of seeing the world, see J.I. Little, ed., *Fashioning the Canadian Landscape: Essays on Travel Writing, Tourism, and National Identity in the Pre-Automobile Era* (Toronto: University of Toronto Press, 2018).

23 The first industrial revolution, starting in the 1700s was defined by early factory steam production in basic goods like textiles and transportation, and by British-led nineteenth-century globalization; the second was defined by the American system of mass assembly production and global economic domination grounded in automobile industrial modernity; the third industrial revolution was another American-led production shift to digitization and automation, which launched industrial postmodernity. For some views of globalization, see the introduction in Andrew Smith and Dimitry Anastakis, eds., *Smart Globalization: The Canadian Business and Economic Experience* (Toronto: University of Toronto Press, 2014).

24 Or perhaps automobility and digitization become fused together, as can be seen in the automotive endeavours of Apple and Google, and the digitization endeavours of Tesla, GM, and others.

25 Geoffrey Hale, *Uneasy Partnership: The Politics of Business and Government in Canada* (Toronto: University of Toronto Press, 2018); William D. Coleman, *Business and Politics: A Study of Collective Action* (Montreal and Kingston: McGill-Queen's University Press, 1988). For another view of this dynamic, which uses Ford's five-dollar day as one of its examples, see Nathaniel Webb Smith, "The Market Process: Entrepreneurship, Intervention, and the Role of the State" (PhD diss., George Mason University, 2022).

26 For some views on the issue of memory and history, see, for example, Patrick Hutton, "Recent Scholarship on Memory and History," *History Teacher* 33, 4 (2000): 533–48 and Andrew Burke, *Hinterland Remixed: Media, Memory and the Canadian 1970s* (Montreal and Kingston: McGill-Queen's University Press, 2019).

27 These varying remembrances and interpretations of Bricklin will be examined in more detail throughout the book. For one view of how Bricklin is remembered as an artefact and element of cultural tourism, see Lee Jolliffe, "The Bricklin: From Automobile to Place Narrative," in *Automobile Heritage and Tourism*, ed. Michael V. Conlin and Lee Jolliffe (London: Routledge, 2016), 40–8.

28 On the Edsel and its place in consumer consciousness, see Thomas Dicke, "The Edsel: Forty Years as a Symbol of Failure," *Journal of Popular Culture* 43, 3 (2010): 486–502.

29 Still Pickens (H.A. Fredericks), "Introduction," in *How to Brickle: The New Brunswick Funny Book* (Saint John, NB: Omega Publications, 1977); Charlie Russell, "The Bricklin," as quoted in *How to Brickle*. Born in Miramichi, New Brunswick, Charlie Russell (1937–2011) was inducted in the Canadian Country Music Hall of Fame in 2003.

30 In 2010, the Toronto *Globe and Mail* published an article that stated that "the SV1 looked like an adolescent auto fantasy, but suffered from crippling design flaws and construction quality that conjured up a Soviet-era Lada." Peter Cheney, "The 12 Worst Cars Ever Built," *Globe and Mail,* 26 January 2010, https://www.theglobeandmail.com/globe-drive/culture/commuting/the-12-worst-cars-ever-built/article4392663/. See also Dan Neil, "The 50 Worst Cars of All Time," *Time Magazine,* 25 April 2017, https://time.com/4723114/50-worst-cars-of-all-time/.

31 CBC News, "Bricklin: The Musical Revs Up," 23 July 2010, https://www.cbc.ca/news/canada/new-brunswick/bricklin-the-musical-revs-up-1.902998; for a scholarly treatment of the musical, see Jennifer Andrews, "Reading the Bricklin: Narrating the Place of Dreaming in an Era of Self-Sufficiency," *Journal of New Brunswick Studies/Revue d'etudes sur le Nouveau-Brunswick* 4 (January 2013): 3.

32 By the early 2000s, even Bricklin himself had begun to be mocked, with one Toronto marketing publication writing, "If the North American auto industry was an episode of *Seinfeld*, then Malcolm Bricklin would be Kramer – called in on cue to deliver a pratfall that leaves viewers in hysterics." *Marketing* 110, 25 (2005): 6.

33 Glenn Howell, "A Short Drive in Bricklin's Bricklin," *Autoweek and Competition Press*, 16 November 1974, 10.

34 The launch had coverage in many newspapers in the United States and Canada. One example is Jon Everett, "Wraps Come Off N.B.'s Bricklin – New York Viewers Appear Impressed," *Saint John Telegraph Journal* (*TJ*), 26 June 1974.

35 On the Mustang and its launch, see Donald Farr, *Mustang: America's Original Pony Car* (New York: Motorbooks, 2017); Paul Ingrassia, *Engines of Change: A History of the American Dream in Fifteen Cars* (New York: Simon & Schuster, 2013); and Brinkley, *Wheels for the World*, 609–18.

36 Don Sherman, "Chevrolet Corvette Stingray vs. Bricklin SV1: America's Best Sports Car. Being 'Second' Doesn't Necessarily Mean Being 'Last,'" *Car and Driver*, 1 May 1975, 34–5, 41, 72.

37 John Dinkel, "America's New Sports Car: The Bricklin," *Road & Track*, September 1973, 98; Sherman, "Chevrolet Corvette Stingray," 35; Tom Benjamin, "Bricklin Gets Largely Favorable Reviews," *TJ*, 9 May 1975.
38 Bob Tripolsky, "We Test the Amazing Bricklin," *Mechanix Illustrated*, September 1975, 36–7.
39 Author's interview with Malcolm Bricklin, 6 October 2022.
40 On the utility of examining business failure, see Patrick Fridenson, "Business Failure and the Agenda of Business History," *Enterprise & Society* 5, 4 (2204): 562–82. See also Scott A. Sandage, *Born Losers: A History of Failure in America* (Cambridge, MA: Harvard University Press, 2005).
41 Among Chandler's most important works are *Strategy and Structure: Chapters in the History of the American Industrial Enterprise* (Cambridge, MA: MIT Press, 1962), *The Visible Hand: The Managerial Revolution in American Business* (Cambridge, MA: Belknap Press of Harvard University, 1977), and his edited volume *Managerial Innovation at General Motors* (New York: Arno Press, 1979). For a countervailing view of Chandler's work, see Robert F. Freeland, *The Struggle for Control of the Modern Corporation: Organizational Change at General Motors, 1924–1970* (Cambridge: Cambridge University Press, 2001).
42 The classic treatment is H.G.J. Aitken, "Defensive Expansionism: The State and Economic Growth in Canada," in *Approaches to Canadian Economic History*, ed. M.H. Watkins and W.T. Easterbrook (Montreal and Kingston: McGill-Queen's University Press, 1967).
43 There is an extensive literature on regional economic development in Canada, much of it, unsurprisingly, focused on Atlantic Canada. See, for example, Gerald Hodge, Heather M. Hall, and Ira M. Robinson, *Planning Canadian Regions,* 2nd ed. (Vancouver: UBC Press, 2017); Donald J. Savoie, *Looking for Bootstraps: Economic Development in the Maritimes* (Halifax: Nimbus Publishing, 2017); Savoie, *Regional Economic Development: Canada's Search for Solutions* (Toronto: University of Toronto Press, 1986); and James K. Bickerton, *Nova Scotia, Ottawa, and the Politics of Regional Development* (Toronto: University of Toronto Press, 1990).
44 Just a few examples include David Nasaw, *Andrew Carnegie* (New York: Penguin Books, 2007); Ron Chernow, *Titan: The Life of John D. Rockefeller, Sr.* (New York: Vintage Books, 2004); and David Cannadine, *Mellon: An American Life* (New York: Alfred A. Knopf, 2006).
45 Again, just a few examples include Robert Skidelsky, *John Maynard Keynes: 1883–1946: Economist, Philosopher, Statesman* (New York: Penguin Books, 2005); Richard Parker, *John Kenneth Galbraith: His Life, His Politics, His Economics* (Chicago: University of Chicago Press, 2006); and Thomas K. McCraw, *Prophets of Regulation* (Cambridge, MA: Belknap Press of Harvard University, 1984).
46 The "open road" idea was partially inspired by Ben Bradley's excellent and innovative *British Columbia by the Road.* Thanks also to Laura Makadoro for her insightful comments on the approach, suggesting that readers consider "what is lost if not all roads are taken," and that I should "run with the metaphor a bit more."
47 For but a few examples, see Barry Cadigan, "Malcolm Bricklin's Dream Machine," *Boston Globe*, 30 June 1974, A89; O'Connor, "Bricklin Safety Vehicle ('A Dream Come True') Will Debut in Northeast," *Advertising Age*, 1 July 1974; Michael Enright, "Wheeler-Dealer: How Mr. Bricklin Got His Dream Car and Mr. Hatfield Got the Bill," *Maclean's*, 17 November 1975, 54–6, 59; Rob Linke, "Malcolm Bricklin Dreams Big, Again," *TJ*, 4 May 2009, A1; and Malcolm Gunn, "Could Anything Have Saved Malcolm Bricklin's Dream?" *Prince George Citizen*, 24 December 2013, A36. Different figures have been cited for the final output produced by Bricklin, all around 2,900.
48 James Truslow Adams, *The Epic of America* (1931; New York: Routledge, 2017), 404, emphasis added. For other views, see, for example, Cal Jillson, *The American Dream: In History, Politics, Fiction* (Lawrence: University of Kansas Press, 2016).

49 Raymond Loewy, "Jukebox on Wheels," *Atlantic*, April 1955, 36; Carl Spielvogel, "Along the Highways and Byways of Finance," *New York Times*, 25 March, 1956, F3.

50 Charles L. Sanford, "'Women's Place in American Car Culture," *Michigan Quarterly Review* 19, 4 (1980): 532.

51 Pamela Walker Laird, *Advertising Progress: American Business and the Rise of Consumer Marketing* (Baltimore: Johns Hopkins University Press, 1998), 107.

52 Brinkley wrote that, even after he passed, "Henry Ford had long been a symbol of the American dream" (*Wheels for the World*, 519). In American culture, we see a constant connection between "dreams and cars" – between automobility and the possible – and there is a vast, interdisciplinary literature that connects the automobile to the American dream. A small sampling includes Bernard A. Weisberger, *Dream Maker: William Durant, Founder of General Motors* (Boston: Little, Brown, 1979); Ingrassia, *Engines of Change*; Earl Swift, *Auto Biography: A Classic Car, an Outlaw Motorhead, and 57 Years of the American Dream* (New York: It Books/HarperCollins, 2014); and Helene M. Lawson, *Ladies on the Lot: Women, Car Sales, and the Pursuit of the American Dream* (Lanham, MD: Rowman & Littlefield, 2000). For a much more critical view, see Catherine Lutz and Anne Lutz Fernandez, "Dream-Car: Myth Making, American Values and the Automobile," chap. 2 in *Carjacked: The Culture of the Automobile and Its Effect on Our Lives* (New York: Palgrave Macmillan, 2009). See also Cynthia Dettelbach, *In the Driver's Seat: The Automobile in American Literature and Popular Culture* (Westport, CT: Greenwood Publishing, 1976); Heon Stevenson, *Selling the Dream: Advertising the American Automobile* (London: Academy, 1995); and Jacob Anbinder, "Selling the World: Public Relations and the Global Expansion of General Motors, 1922–40," *Business History Review* 92, 3 (2018): 483–507.

Automotive work has often been connected to the American dream as well. See, for example, Ely Chinoy, *Automobile Workers and the American Dream* (Boston: Beacon Press, 1955); Michael Betzold and Richard Feldman, *End of the Line: Autoworkers and the American Dream* (New York: Weidenfield & Nicholson, 1988); and Greg Shotwell, *Autoworkers under the Gun: A Shop-Floor View of the End of the American Dream* (Chicago: Haymarket Books, 2011).

53 Walden, *Becoming Modern in Toronto*. This notion, was, however, limited largely to North American whites: mobility for racialized minorities was consciously curtailed. See Cotten Seiler, "'So That We as a Race Might Have Something Authentic to Travel By': African American Automobility and Cold War Liberalism," *American Quarterly* 58, 4 (2006): 1091–117.

54 I wish to thank Keith Walden for illuminating this central aspect of modernity and its connection to the automobile. On how mobility shapes modern identity, see also Eric Leed, *The Mind of the Traveler: From Gilgamesh to Global Tourism* (New York: Basic Books, 1991) and Cotten Seiler, *Republic of Drivers: A Cultural History of Automobility in America* (Chicago: University of Chicago Press, 2008).

55 In twentieth-century North America, this was just as essential for those with cars as it was for those without.

1. The Future (Technology)

1 In his *Grand Expectations*, James T. Patterson wrote that, in the three decades after 1945, Americans "developed ever-greater expectations about the capacity of the United States to create a better world abroad and a happier society at home. This optimism was not altogether new: most Americans, living in a land of opportunity, have always had great hopes for the future. But high expectations, rooted in vibrant economic growth, ascended as never before in the 1950s

and peaked in the 1960s." *Grand Expectations: The United States, 1945–1974* (New York: Oxford University Press, 1996), vii.

The term "1960s" is used primarily to refer to the chronological decade itself, while "the Sixties" refers to the period, which encompasses "the long 1960s," itself a periodization with varying definitions. See, for example, Dimitry Anastakis, *The Sixties: Passion, Politics and Style* (Montreal and Kingston: McGill-Queen's University Press, 2008), 3–17, and especially 14n3.

2 The embrace of futurism was not new, but it dramatically accelerated after 1945 for a host of reasons. The emergence of science fiction/speculative fiction writing as a major genre reflected this impulse; the World Science Fiction Convention held its first meeting in 1939. On different views of technology in American life, see, for example, David E. Nye, *American Technological Sublime* (Cambridge, MA: MIT Press, 1994) and Christopher Cumo, *Science and Technology in 20th-Century American Life* (Westport, CT: Greenwood Press, 2007).

3 See, for example, Matthew Wisnioski, *Engineers for Change: Competing Visions of Technology in 1960s America* (Cambridge, MA: MIT Press, 2012).

4 Jefferson Cowie, *Stayin' Alive: The 1970s and the Last Days of the Working Class* (New York: New Press, 2012); David Paul Kuhn, *The Hardhat Riot: New York City, and the Dawn of the White Working-Class Revolution* (New York: Oxford University Press, 2020).

5 See, for instance, Greg Donaghy, *Tolerant Allies: Canada and the United States, 1963–8* (Montreal and Kingston: McGill-Queen's University Press, 2003); Robert Bothwell, *Alliance and Illusion: Canada and the World, 1945–84* (Vancouver: UBC Press, 2007); and Stephen Azzi, *Reconcilable Differences: A History of Canada-US Relations* (Toronto: Oxford University Press, 2014).

6 There are many assessments of the baby boom generation, including Douglas Owram, *Born at the Right Time: The History of the Baby Boom Generation* (Toronto: University of Toronto Press, 1996); Bryan Palmer, *Canada's Sixties: The Ironies of Identity in a Rebellious Era* (Toronto: University of Toronto Press, 2008); and Victor Brooks, *Boomers: The Cold-War Generation Grows Up* (Chicago: Ivan R. Dee, 2009).

7 Yanek Mieczkowski, *Eisenhower's Sputnik Moment: The Race for Space and World Prestige* (Ithaca, NY: Cornell University Press, 2013).

8 The first Arrow was revealed to the public on 4 October 1957, the same date as the launch of Sputnik. In 1959, engineer Jim Chamberlin (1915–81), from Kamloops, BC, led a group of more than two dozen Canadians to NASA, and he became a key member of the space agency.

9 Even into the 1970s, when space exploration seemed to stall and the Apollo program was brought back down to earth by its costly realities, space continued to be a touchstone of North American culture, as cinematic blockbusters such as George Lucas's space opera *Star Wars* (1977) proved beyond a shadow of a doubt.

10 William Stadiem, *Jet Set: The People, the Planes, the Glamour, and the Romance in Aviation's Glory Years* (New York: Ballantine Books, 2014).

11 Jenifer Van Vleck, *Empire of the Air: Aviation and the American Ascendancy* (Cambridge, MA: Harvard University Press, 2013).

12 Ibid., 7.

13 Bret Joel Edwards, "A Bumpy Landing: Airports and the Making of Jet Age Canada" (PhD diss., University of Toronto, 2017).

14 This development, and some of its implications, will be considered in more detail in chapter 6, "Business (The State)."

15 Leslie Anne Ballard, Selma Sabanovic, Jasleen Kaur, and Stasa Milojevic, "George Charles Devol, Jr.," *IEEE Robotics and Automation Magazine*, September 2012, 114–19; Roberta C. Yafie, "Joe Engelberger: Father of Robotics," *American Metal Market* 107, 236 (1999): 2. See also

chapter 34, "Unimation," in Gerard O'Regan, *Pillars of Computing: A Compendium of Select, Pivotal Technology Firms* (Cham, CH: Springer International Publishing, 2015). The robotics industry's highest awards are named after Engelberger.

16 See the unpublished work of Salem Elzway, a PhD candidate at University of Michigan, "The Arm Race: A History of the Industrial Robot in Postwar America" (working title).

17 "Science: Father of Plastics," *Time Magazine*, 20 May 1940, 50; Joris Mercelis, *Beyond Bakelite: Leo Baekeland and the Business of Science and Invention* (Cambridge, MA: MIT Press, 2020).

18 Jeffrey L. Meikle, *American Plastic: A Cultural History* (New Brunswick, NJ: Rutgers University Press, 1995).

19 Susan Freinkel, *Plastic: A Toxic Love Story* (New York: Houghton Mifflin Harcourt, 2011), 8.

20 For views of automobility and the environment, see, for example, Tom McCarthy, *Auto Mania: Cars, Consumers and the Environment* (New Haven, CT: Yale University Press, 2007) and David A. Kirsch, *The Electric Vehicle and the Burden of History* (New Brunswick, NJ: Rutgers University Press, 2000). See also Ashlee Vance, *Elon Musk, Tesla, SpaceX and the Quest for a Fantastic Future* (New York: HarperCollins, 2015).

21 Henry Ford's ghost-written 1926 exposition on his work, his company, and the world, was titled *Today and Tomorrow* (New York: Doubleday, 1926).

22 On the great battle of the 1920s between GM and Ford, and the debate of styling versus production and management techniques in the evolution of the interwar auto industry, see David Gartman, *Auto Opium: A Social History of American Automobile Design* (London: Routledge, 1994), especially chap. 5, "The Depression and the Decade of Streamlining." For other views of GM's victory over Ford, one based on management and systems, see Richard S. Tedlow, "The Struggle for Dominance in the Automobile Market: The Early Years of Ford and General Motors," *Business and Economic History* 17 (1988): 49–62 and Arthur J. Khun, *GM Passes Ford: Designing the General Motors Performance-Control System* (University Park: Penn State University Press, 1990).

23 For another view of planned obsolescence, see Giles Slade, *Made to Break: Technology and Obsolescence in America* (Cambridge, MA: Harvard University Press, 2006), especially chap. 2, "The Annual Model Change."

24 David Gartman, "Harley Earl and the Art and Color Section: The Birth of Styling at Geneal Motors," *Design Issues* 10, 2 (1994): 3–26; William Knoedelseder, *Fins: Harley Earl, the Rise of General Motors, and the Glory Days of Detroit* (New York: Harper Business, 2018), 53; Stephen S. Bayley, *Harley Earl and the Dream Machine* (New York: Alfred A. Knopf, 1985); Harley Earl, "I Dream Automobiles," *Saturday Evening Post*, 227 (August 1954): 82.

25 On exhibitions and modernity, see Keith Walden, *Becoming Modern in Toronto: The Industrial Exhibition and the Shaping of Late Victorian Culture* (Toronto: University of Toronto Press, 1997).

26 On Motorama, see Bruce Berghoff, *The GM Motorama: Dream Cars of the Fifties* (Osceola, WI: Motorbooks International, 1995). On the public's reaction to the Model A, see Douglas Brinkley, *Wheels for the World: Henry Ford, His Company, and a Century of Progress* (New York: Penguin Books, 2003), 4–8.

27 Raymond Loewy, "Jukebox on Wheels," *Atlantic*, April 1955, 36–8.

28 On Virgil Exner, see Charles K. Hyde, *Riding the Roller Coaster: A History of the Chrysler Corporation* (Detroit: Wayne State University Press, 2003), 172–3. See also Steve Lethto, *Preston Tucker and His Battle to Build the Car of Tomorrow* (Chicago: Chicago Review Press, 2016).

29 Sally Clarke, "Managing Design: The Art and Colour Section at General Motors, 1927–1941," *Journal of Design History* 12, 1 (1999): 65–79; Knoedelseder, *Fins*; Heon Stevenson, *American Automobile Advertising, 1930–1980* (Jefferson, NC: McFarland & Company, 2008).

30 In 2018, Elon Musk launched a Tesla Roadster into space aboard his Falcon Heavy rocket. Gartman, *Auto Opium*, 202; Clayton Seams, "Here's Why So Many Astronauts Have Owned Corvettes," *Driving*, 14 April 2020, https://driving.ca/auto-news/entertainment/heres-why-so-many-astronauts-have-owned-chevrolet-corvettes.

31 Hyde, *Riding the Roller Coaster*, 202–5.

32 Gartman, *Auto Opium*, 159.

33 John Dinkel, "America's New Sports Car: The Bricklin," *Road & Track*, September 1973, 97.

34 The original Batmobile was sold for $4.2 million in 2013. Daniel Strohl, "RIP, Herb Grasse," *Hemmings*, 31 August 2021, https://www.hemmings.com/stories/2010/08/31/rip-herb-grasse; "Obituary: Herb Grasse, February 21, 1945 to August 24, 2010," *Sonora News*, 1 September 2010, http://sonorannews.com/archives/2010/100901/frontpage-Obit-Grasse.html; Randy Wyrick, "Every Picture Tells a Story," *Brickline* 41, 4 (2016): 10–15.

35 Grasse said that Malcolm Bricklin sent him a cheque for $30,000 to get started. "Ask Malcolm: Flying with the Grey Ghost," *Brickline* 41, 2 (2016): 21; Wick Humble, "1975 Bricklin SV1: Plastic Fantastic or Gull-Winged Turkey?" *Special Interest Autos* 68 (April 1982): 43–4.

36 Humble, "1975 Bricklin SV1," 40–51.

37 Bricklin used the "grey car" in his pitches to the banks and others in the period before a prototype was constructed. "1974 Design Review: Consumer Products," *Industrial Design* 21, 10 (1974): 52; G.T.F., "A Sportin' Chance for Safety," *Industrial Design* 21, 8 (1974): 32–5; "Obituary: Herb Grasse."

38 Don Sherman, "Chevrolet Corvette Stingray vs. Bricklin SV1: Americas Best Sports Car – Being 'Second' Doesn't Necessarily Mean Being 'Last,'" *Car and Driver*, 1 May 1975, 34–5, 41, 72. Another example is John J. O'Connor, "Bricklin Safety Vehicle ('A Dream Come True') Will Debut in Northeast," *Advertising Age*, 1 July 1974. Dinkel's "America's New Sports Car" also focused on the safety aspect as a new and innovative aspect of the car.

39 Author's interview with Malcolm Bricklin, 30 April 2013. In the documentary *The Bricklin: The Premier, the Promoter and Their Car* (dir. Dugald Maudsley, 2004), Bricklin remembered it as an electric cartoon vehicle with gull-wing doors.

40 On Ford's soybean/hemp plastic car, see Brinkley, *Wheels for the World*, 443, and "Popular Research Topics: Soybean Car," Henry Ford Museum, https://www.thehenryford.org/collections-and-research/digital-resources/popular-topics/soy-bean-car/. On the Renault 5s, see Jean-Louis Loubet, *Renault: Histoire d'une entreprise* (Boulogne-Billancourt, FR: ETAI, 2000), 176; Lawrence J. White, *The Automobile Industry since 1945* (1971; Cambridge, MA: Harvard University Press, 2014), 212.

41 Joseph J. Bohn, "Bricklin Views Plastic as 'Material of Future,'" *Automotive News*, 28 July 1975; G.T.F., "A Sportin' Chance for Safety," *Industrial Design* 21, 8 (1974): 34, 35; Bricklin Promotional Brochure, Public Archives of New Brunswick (PANB), Department of Commerce and Development, box 83, file 5321-1.

42 G.T.F., "A Sportin' Chance for Safety," 34, 35.

43 Paul Casey, "Bricklin's Bricklin," *Washington Post*, 16 February 1975, L7.

44 A clip, "Bricklin – 1974 Let's Make a Deal," can be seen on YouTube at https://www.youtube.com/watch?v=qcYf64aKDJo.

45 CP, "Ontario Science Centre Honors Malcolm Bricklin," *Moncton Transcript*, 30 July 1975. In this, as in so many other aspects of automaking, Bricklin happened upon a trend that would be common in the future. Since the EV revolution began in earnest in the 2010s, the Consumer Electronics Show (CES) has become an important venue for the latest car launches. For example, in 2022, GM's Mary Barra unveiled the company's Chevrolet Silverado EV truck at CES, one of a number of new auto products introduced at the show.

46 David J. Neuman, "… to Bumper," *Journal of Popular Culture* 8, 1 (1974): 183–4.

47 There is a vast literature on the social impact of the car. A very few examples include Peter D. Norton, *Fighting Traffic: The Dawn of the Motor Age in the American City* (Cambridge, MA: MIT Press, 2008); Dean Ruffilli, "The Car in Canadian Culture, 1898–1983" (PhD diss., University of Western Ontario, 2006); McCarthy, *Auto Mania*; Danielle Robinson, "Modernism at a Crossroad: The Spadina Expressway Controversy in Toronto, Ontario ca. 1960–71," *Canadian Historical Review* 92, 2 (2011): 295–322; and Stephen Davies, "'Reckless Walking Must Be Discouraged': The Automobile Revolution and the Shaping of Modern Urban Canada to 1930," *Urban History Review* 18, 2 (1989): 123–38.

48 Ford's efforts to save some of the past his car and processes had obliterated include famously preserving Midwestern square dances and songs and building a shrine to premodern America, Greenfield Village. See also, for instance, Ray Batchelor, *Henry Ford, Mass Production, Modernism, and Design* (New York: St. Martin's Press, 1994). For views on the coming of modernity to Canada, see G.B. Norcliffe, *Ride to Modernity: The Bicycle in Canada, 1869–1900* (Toronto: University of Toronto Press, 2001); see also Walden's *Becoming Modern in Toronto*.

49 The literature on Henry Ford, Fordism, and the impact of the automobile is immense. For a very small sample, see Allen Nevins, *Ford: The Times, the Man, the Company* (New York: Scribner, 1954); Allan Nevins, *Ford: Expansion and Challenge, 1915–1933* (New York: Scribner, 1957); Allan Nevins and Frank Ernest Hill, *Ford: Decline and Rebirth, 1933–1962* (New York: Scribner, 1962); Peter J. Ling, *American and the Automobile: Technology, Reform and Social Change, 1893–1923* (Manchester: Manchester University Press, 1990); James M. Rubenstein, *Making and Selling Cars: Innovation and Change in the US Automotive Industry* (Baltimore: Johns Hopkins University Press, 2001); Richard Bak, *Henry and Edsel: The Creation of the Ford Empire* (New York: Wiley, 2003); Stephen Watts, *The People's Tycoon: Henry Ford and the American Century* (New York: Vintage Books, 2005); and David Gartman, *From Autos to Architecture: Fordism and Architectural Aesthetics in the Twentieth Century* (New York: Princeton Architectural Press, 2009). On the impact of Ford in Canada, see David Roberts, *In the Shadow of Detroit: Gordon M. McGregor, Ford of Canada, and Motoropolis* (Detroit: Wayne State University Press, 2006). On Ford's wealth, see Brinkley, *Wheels for the World*, 264, 280.

50 On the growth of these enterprises and their impact on the market, see Rubenstein, *Making and Selling Cars*, and especially Alfred D. Chandler's classic *The Visible Hand: The Managerial Revolution in American Business* (Cambridge, MA: Belknap Press of Harvard University, 1977). For another view of the interplay between these giant corporations and the market, see Sally H. Clarke, *Trust and Power: Consumers, the Modern Corporation, and the Making of the United States Automobile Market* (New York: Cambridge University Press, 2007). On Ford's Canadian and international subsidiaries, see Dimitry Anastakis, "From Independence to Integration: The Corporate Evolution of the Ford Motor Company of Canada," *Business History Review* 78, 2 (2004): 213–53 and Mira Wilkins, *American Business Abroad: Ford on Six Continents* (1964; New York: Cambridge University Press, 2011).

51 Mom's *Atlantic Automobilism* is a deeply literary and discursive exploration of the spread of automobile modernity in Europe and the United States in the car's initial phases. As another example, see Samuele F.S. Pardini, "The Engines of History: The Automobile in American and Italian Literary Cultures, 1908–1943" (PhD diss., State University of New York at Buffalo, 2005).

52 See Mom, *Atlantic Automobilism*. For other views on industrial modernity and artistic expression, see, for example, William Solomon, "Slapstick Modernism: Charley Bowers and Industrial Modernity," *Modernist Cultures* 2, 2 (2006): 170–88; Cecilia Tichi, *Shifting Gears: Technology, Literature, Culture in Modernist America* (Chapel Hill: University of North Carolina

Press, 1987); and R.L. Rutsky, *High Tech: Art and Technology from the Machine Aesthetic to the Posthuman* (Minneapolis: University of Minnesota Press, 1999).

53 Earlier films, such as Fitz Lang's *Metropolis* (1927), had also provided a critique of industrialization.

54 On Brazil and the question of auto modernity, see Joel Wolfe, *Autos and Progress: The Brazilian Search for Modernity* (New York: Oxford University Press, 2010), 9–10; on Ford in Brazil, see Greg Grandin, *Fordlandia: The Rise and Fall of Henry Ford's Lost City* (New York: Macmillan, 2009).

55 Stephen Niblo, *Mexico in the 1940s: Modernity, Politics and Corruption* (Wilmington, DE: Rowman & Littlefield, 1999), 25–6.

56 Raymond G. Stokes, "Technology and the West German 'Wirtschaftswunder,'" *Technology and Culture* 32, 1 (1991): 1–22.

57 The VW Bug is the second-biggest-selling car of all time (after the Corolla), with 22 million vehicles produced around the world, ending only in 2003. Bernard Rieger, *The People's Car: A Global History of the Volkswagen Beetle* (Cambridge, MA: Harvard University Press, 2013).

58 Beverly Rae Kimes, *The Star and the Laurel: The Centennial History of Daimler, Mercedes, and Benz, 1886–1986* (Montvale, NJ: Mercedes-Benz of North America, 1986).

59 On Toyota and the Toyota Production System, see Jeffrey R. Bernstein, "Toyoda Automatic Looms and Toyota Automobiles," in *Creating Modern Capitalism: How Entrepreneurs, Companies and Countries Triumphed in Three Industrial Revolutions*, ed. Thomas K. McCraw (Cambridge, MA: Harvard University Press, 1995), 398–438, and James P. Womack, Daniel T. Jones, and Daniel Roos, *The Machine That Changed the World: The Story of Lean Production* (New York: Free Press, 2007).

60 Y. Togo and W. Wartman, *Against All Odds: The Story of the Toyota Motor Corporation and the Family That Created It* (New York: St. Martin's Press, 1993); Chalmers Johnson, *MITI and the Japanese Miracle: The Growth of Industrial Policy, 1925–1975* (Stanford, CA: Stanford University Press, 1982); Mark Metzler, *Capital as Will and Imagination: Schumpeter's Guide to the Postwar Japanese Miracle* (Ithaca, NY: Cornell University Press, 2013).

61 This approach, in South Korea and elsewhere, has been examined by development scholars such as Ha Joon Chang. See his *Kicking Away the Ladder: Development Strategy in Historical Perspective* (London: Anthem, 2002).

62 Donald Kirk, *Korean Dynasty: Hyundai and Chung Ju Yung* (London: Taylor and Francis, 2016); Seung-hun Chun, *The Economic Development of South Korea: From Poverty to a Modern Industrial State* (New York: Taylor and Francis, 2018).

63 Lewis H. Sidgelbaum, *Cars for Comrades: The Life of the Soviet Automobile* (Ithaca, NY: Cornell University Press, 2008); Stefan J. Link, *Forging Global Fordism: Nazi Germany, Soviet Russia, and the Contest over the Industrial Order* (Princeton, NJ: Princeton University Press, 2021).

64 Dimitry Anastakis, *Auto Pact: Creating a Borderless North American Auto Industry, 1960–1971* (Toronto: University of Toronto Press, 2005).

65 See, for example, Anthony M. Tremblay, *The Fiddlehead Moment: Pioneering an Alternative Canadian Modernism in New Brunswick* (Montreal and Kingston: McGill-Queen's University Press, 2019); Kurt Niergarth, *The Dignity of Every Human Being: New Brunswick Artists and Canadian Culture between the Great Depression and the Cold War* (Toronto: University of Toronto Press, 2015); and Joel Belliveau, "Acadian New Brunswick's Ambivalent Leap into the Canadian Liberal Order," in *Creating Postwar Canada: Community, Diversity, and Dissent, 1945–75*, ed. Magda Fahrni and Robert Rutherdale (Vancouver: UBC Press, 2008), 61–88.

66 John Leroux, “Make Way for Tomorrow: New Brunswick’s Visual and Cultural Modernity, 1930–1967” (PhD diss., University of New Brunswick, 2020).

67 On Beaverbrook, see Gregory P. Marchildon, *Profits and Politics: Beaverbrook and the Gilded Age of Canadian Finance* (Toronto: University of Toronto Press, 1996). On Dunn, see Duncan McDowall, *Steel at the Sault: Francis Hector Clergue, Sir James Dunn and the Algoma Steel Corporation, 1899–1956* (Toronto: University of Toronto Press, 1984). The two men were friends, and Dunn’s widow, Marcia Anastasia Christoforides, married Beaverbrook a year before his death.

68 In the ten years between 1961 and 1971, over 50,000 New Brunswickers left the province for other regions of Canada. *Historical Statistics of Canada*, table A339-349: Changes in the Population through Natural Increase and Migration, by Province, by Intercensal Intervals, 1931 to 1976, https://www150.statcan.gc.ca/n1/pub/11-516-x/sectiona/4147436-eng.htm#3.

69 On New Brunswick and its history, see Graham Wynn, *Timber Colony: A Historical Geography of Early Nineteenth Century New Brunswick* (Toronto: University of Toronto Press, 1981); G. Marquis, “Uneven Renaissance: Urban Development in Saint John, 1955–1976,” *Journal of New Brunswick Studies / Revue d’études sur le Nouveau-Brunswick* 1, 1 (2010): 91–112; and Tim Frink, *New Brunswick: A Short History* (Saint John, NB: Stonington Books, 1997).

70 The area’s other famous son was Andrew Bonar Law, born in 1858 in the village of Rexton, about twenty-five kilometres north of Bouctouche. Emigrating to the United Kingdom as a child, Bonar Law eventually became British prime minister in 1923, the first person born outside of the British Isles to do so.

71 For one complimentary view of K.C. and the family, see Donald Savoie, *“Thanks for the Business”: K.C. Irving, Arthur Irving, and the Story of Irving Oil* (Halifax: Nimbus Publishing, 2020). For another view, see Jacques Poitras, *Irving vs. Irving: Canada’s Feuding Billionaires and the Stories They Won’t Tell* (Toronto: Viking; 2014).

72 John DeMont, *Citizens Irving: K.C. Irving and His Legacy. The Story of Canada’s Wealthiest Family* (Toronto: Doubleday Canada, 1991).

73 As if to emphasize the Irving family’s feudalistic approach to the province, in 1972 K.C. moved his businesses to a trust held in Bermuda to avoid Canadian taxes.

74 For example, Stephen Dutcher, “’Looking Towards the Promised Land’: Modernity, Anti-Modernity and Co-operative Wholesaling in the Maritime Provinces, 1945–1961,” *Acadiensis* 34, 2 (2005): 46–73; James L. Kenny and Andrew Secord, “Public Power for Industry: A Re-Examination of the New Brunswick Case, 1940–1960,” *Acadiensis* 30, 1 (2001): 84–108; James L. Kenny, “A New Dependency: State, Local Capital, and the Development of New Brunswick’s Base Metal Industry, 1960–70,” *Canadian Historical Review* 78, 1 (1997): 1–39; R.A. Young, “‘And the People Will Sink into Despair’: Reconstruction in New Brunswick, 1942–52,” *Canadian Historical Review* 69, 2 (1988): 127–66; R.A. Young, “Planning for Power: The New Brunswick Electric Power Commission in the 1950s,” *Acadiensis* 12, 1 (1982): 73–99; Joshua John Dickison, “Making New Brunswickers Modern: Natural and Human Resource Development in Macquatac Regional Development Plan, 1965–1975” (MA thesis, University of New Brunswick, 2006); and James L. Kenny and Andrew G. Secord, “Engineering Modernity: Hydroelectric Development in New Brunswick, 1945–1970,” *Acadiensis* 39, 1 (2010): 3–26.

75 See, for example, Lachlan MacKinnon, “Importing the Clairtone Sound: Political Economy, Regionalism, and Deindustrialization in Pictou County,” *Labour/Le travail* 91 (Spring 2023): 147–168 and Garth Hopkins, *Clairtone: The Rise and Fall of a Business Empire* (Toronto: McClelland & Stewart, 1978).

76 On Volvo in Nova Scotia, see Dimitry Anastakis, "Building a 'New Nova Scotia': State Intervention, the Auto Industry, and the Case of Volvo in Halifax, 1963–1996," *Acadiensis* 34, 1 (2004): 3–30. On the CMI plant, see Peter Rasky, "They Sing Their Company Song: Canada and the New Japan," *Toronto Star*, 28 December, 1966. Nova Scotia held a 6 per cent share in the CMI firm, with $1.4 million in CMI debentures. R.S. Brookfield to Industrial Estates Limited Directors, "Re: CMI," 29 November, 1972, Nova Scotia Archives and Records Management (NSARM), RG 55, vol. 10, file IEL, Canadian Motor Industries, 1973–76; Dimitry Anastakis, *Autonomous State: The Struggle for a Canadian Car Industry from OPEC to Free Trade* (Toronto: University of Toronto Press, 2013), 258–60.

77 Anastakis, "Building a 'New Nova Scotia'"; Rasky, "They Sing Their Company Song"; Anastakis, *Autonomous State*. From 1972 to 1980, Irving Oil also built over a thousand Scot Trucks under the Atlantic Truck Company in Debert, Nova Scotia. Thanks to Bill Jarvis for bringing this to my attention.

78 Michel Lefévre, "Québec lasisse échapper un project quit aurait pu ressucited SOMA," *Le Devoir* (Montreal), 21 June 1973; author's interview with Malcolm Bricklin, 30 April 2013.

79 From 1962 to 1970, the Canadian dollar was pegged at 92.5 cents. In May 1970, the government of Pierre Trudeau allowed it to float; since Canadian and US dollars remained generally at par during the period between 1970s and 1976, I have not distinguished between them, and, unless otherwise specified, all figures are in Canadian dollars.

80 Larry Skorry, "Look Out Big Three! Here Comes the Canadian-Controlled Bricklin," *Canadian Machinery and Metalworking*, September 1973, 54–5. Initially, Bricklin told New Brunswick Multiplex officials in early 1973 that "at present the only location" for production being considered was in the United States, at the Checker Cab company's facilities. How serious that option was is unclear. Much of the early contact between Bricklin and Canadian officials emphasized Bricklin's and his team's role as "shareholders and executives of Subaru of America, a successful importer and distributor of Japanese vehicles." The Bricklin proposal also included Subaru America's annual report, where Bricklin was listed as a director, and which showed spectacular growth and profitability between 1971 and 1972. R.K. Fletcher (GM, Multiplex) to J.D. Love (Deputy Minister, DREE), 16 March 1973, PANB, box 501, file "Bricklin Canada.

81 Author's interview with Malcolm Bricklin, 30 April 2013.

82 Bricklin Canada Ltd., "A Submission to the Department of Regional Economic Expansion," 6 April 1973, PANB, box 2, file "Bricklin Canada." On Multiplex, see Greg Marquis, "Growth Fantasies: Setting the Urban Agenda in Saint John, New Brunswick, 1960–1976," *Acadiensis* 46, 1 (2017): 122–44.

83 R.K. Fletcher (general manager, Multiplex) to Milton Fry (manager, DREE), 9 April 1973, PANB, file 9, "Bricklin Canada Ltd.," box 301, File Bricklin Submission 559. See also Esther Crandall, "Bricklin Car Expected about July," *Globe and Mail*, 10 May 1974.

84 In 1971, Richard Nixon initially intended to include a unilateral termination of the auto pact in his package of "shocks," a measure that was averted only by the insistence of State Department officials who realized how disruptive such a move would be upon what had become an integrated North American auto sector. On the difficulties between Canada and the United States over the operation of the auto pact in the early 1970s, see Anastakis, *Autonomous State*, chap. 5.

85 Author's interview with Malcolm Bricklin, 30 April 2013.

86 Bricklin Canada Ltd. was incorporated on 26 June 1973. The agreement between GVI/Malcolm Bricklin and the New Brunswick government can be found in PANB, Office of Richard B. Hatfield, box 83, Bricklin, file 5600-B2, "Agreements-Financial, 1973." On Bricklin's arrangement with Hatfield, see Richard Starr, *Richard Hatfield: The Seventeen Year Saga* (Halifax:

Formac Publishing, 1987), 87; Lefévre, "Québec laisse échapper un projet"; "New Sports Car to Be Made Here," *Saint John Evening Times Globe*, 22 June 1973; Lyndon Watkins, "N.B. Car May Feature a Body of Glass Fibre," *Globe and Mail*, 23 June 1973, B23; and "DREE Gives a Boost to Bricklin," *Financial Times of Canada*, 6 May 1974.

87 "Statement by Premier Richard Hatfield Concerning the Bricklin Project," 2 December 1974, PANB, box 83, file 5321-14.

88 There are numerous examples of this perspective, including "We Test the Amazing Bricklin."

89 Hal Quinn, "Working Without a Net," *Maclean's*, 18 February 1985, 17.

90 "120-Member Staff Completes Vehicle," *Fredericton Daily Gleaner*, 7 August 1974.

91 Remarks by Mr. Harry A. Nason, Deputy Minister of Economic Growth, Public Accounts Committee Meeting, NB Legislative Assembly, 29 May 1975, PANB, box 83, file 5321-1.

92 Nova Scotia's Volvo operation in Halifax had had auto pact status since 1965, allowing it to export to the US market, as it usually spent enough money on Canadian-made parts and labour to qualify. But Ottawa also gave Volvo some breaks on hitting its requirements from time to time. On Volvo in Canada, see Anastakis, *Autonomous State*, 256–72 and Anastakis, "Building a 'New Nova Scotia.'"

93 "Statement by Premier Richard Hatfield Concerning the Bricklin Project," 2 December 1974, PANB, box 83, file 5321-14.

94 Sanford Borins with Lee Brown, *Investments in Failure: Five Government Corporations That Cost the Canadian Taxpayer Billions* (Toronto: Methuen, 1986), 46.

95 "Premier Predicts Success for Car," *Saint John Telegraph Journal*, 7 August 1974, emphasis added.

96 "Statement by Premier Richard Hatfield Concerning the Bricklin Project," 2 December 1974, PANB, box 83, file 5321-14.

2. Entrepreneur (Archetype)

1 E.B. White, "Farewell, My Lovely," *New Yorker*, 16 May 1936.

2 There are many works on these legendary business leaders and their role in American society. For a general view on the place of entrepreneurs in creating modern capitalism and consumption, see Nancy F. Koehn, *Brand New: How Entrepreneurs Earned Consumers' Trust from Wedgewood to Dell* (Cambridge, MA: Harvard University Press, 2001). On railroads and their impact in shaping American society, see Steven W. Usselman, *Regulating Railroad Innovation: Business, Technology, and Politics in America, 1840–1920* (New York: Cambridge University Press, 2003). For a good view of the historiographical debate about many of these businessmen and their image in American history, see Hal Bridges, "The Robber Baron Concept in American History," *Business History Review* 32, 1 (1958): 1–13.

3 Edward D. Kennedy, *The Automobile Industry: The Coming of Age of Capitalism's Favorite Child* (New York: Reynal and Hitchcock, 1941), 314; Sam Gindin, *The CAW: Birth and Transformation of a Union* (Toronto: Lorimer, 1995), 14; David L. Lewis, "Introduction: Special Issue on Cars," *Michigan Quarterly Review* 19, 4 (1980) and 20, 1 (1981): 435; Thomas K. McCraw and Richard S. Tedlow, "Henry Ford, Alfred Sloan, and the Three Phases of Marketing," in *Creating Modern Capitalism: How Entrepreneurs, Companies and Countries Triumphed in Three Industrial Revolutions*, ed. Thomas K. McCraw (Cambridge, MA: Harvard University Press, 1995), 266; David P. Billington, Jr., *Power, Speed, and Form: Engineers and the Making of the Twentieth Century* (Princeton, NJ: Princeton University Press, 2013), 79; Peter F. Drucker, *The Concept of the Corporation* (New York: Transaction Publishers 1983), 149.

4 J.A. Schumpeter, *The Theory of Economic Development* (Cambridge, MA: Harvard University Press, 1934) and *Capitalism, Socialism and Democracy* (New York: Harper and Brothers, 1942). On other views of entrepreneurship, see, for instance, José L. García-Ruiz and Pierangelo Toninellim, eds., *The Determinants of Entrepreneurship: Leadership, Culture, Institutions* (London: Routledge, 2015) and Geoffrey Jones and R.D. Wadhwani, "Entrepreneurship," in *Oxford Handbook of Business History*, ed. Geoffrey G. Jones and Jonathan Zeitlin (New York: Oxford University Press, 2008), 501–28.

5 On Tucker, see Charles T. Pearson, *The Indomitable Tin Goose: The True Story of Preston Tucker and His Car* (1960; New York: Motorbooks International, 1974). The Tucker case was portrayed in a 1988 feature film, *Tucker: The Man and His Dream*, directed by Francis Ford Coppola.

6 As it was in the rest of the world, of course, though it happened later elsewhere and with differing degrees of impact.

7 For only a very few examples of the impact of the automobile on various aspects of society, see Peter Norton, "Street Rivals: Jaywalking and the Invention of the Motor Age Street," *Technology and History* 48, 2 (2007): 331–59; Stephen Davies, "'Reckless Walking Must Be Discouraged': The Automobile Revolution and the Shaping of Modern Urban Canada to 1930," *Urban History Review* 18, 2 (1989): 123–38; Sarah A. Seo, *Policing the Open Road: How Cars Transformed American Freedom* (Cambridge, MA: Harvard University Press, 2019); and Clay McShane, *Down the Asphalt Path: The Automobile and the American City* (New York: Columbia University Press, 1994).

8 John A. Jakle, *Signs in America's Auto Age: Signatures of Landscape and Place* (Iowa City: University of Iowa Press, 2004); John A. Jakle and Keith A. Sculle, *The Gas Station in America* (Baltimore: Johns Hopkins University Press, 1994); John A. Jakle and Keith A. Sculle, *Supplanting America's Railroads: The Early Auto Age, 1900–1940* (Knoxville: University of Tennessee Press, 2017).

9 This revolution continues to reverberate into the twenty-first century, with the auto industry's role shifting business and society into an electrified, decarbonized future.

10 In his book *Made to Break: Technology and Obsolescence in America* (Cambridge, MA: Harvard University Press, 2005), Giles Slade utilizes the term "progressive obsolescence," an obsession with the "new" that made conspicuous consumers out of even middle- and working-class Americans, a dynamic that was largely created by the automobile industry. Progressive obsolescence was addressed by Roland Marchand in his *Advertising the American Dream: Making Way for Modernity, 1920–1940* (Berkeley: University of California Press, 1985), 156–60. On Sloan and the automobile industry's place in planned obsolescence, see David Farber, *Sloan Rules: Alfred P. Sloan and the Triumph of General Motors* (Chicago: University of Chicago Press, 2002) and Sally H. Clarke, *Trust and Power: Consumers, the Modern Corporation, and the Making of the United States Automobile Market* (Cambridge: Cambridge University Press, 2007).

11 Marchand, *Advertising the American Dream*, 4.

12 Tom McCarthy, *Auto Mania: Cars, Consumers and the Environment* (New Haven, CT: Yale University Press, 2009); Jack Doyle, *Taken for a Ride: Detroit's Big Three and the Politics of Pollution* (New York: Four Walls Eight Windows, 2000); Christopher Wells, *Car Country: An Environmental History* (Seattle: University of Washington Press, 2012).

13 For a view of the narrative role of the individual automobile entrepreneur and their agency "in an increasingly impersonal, globalized and corporatized world," see S. Borins and B. Hearst, "Cults of Personality: Fables of the Automobile Manufacturing Industry," chap. 3 in *Negotiating Business Narratives: Fables of the Information Technology, Automobile*

Manufacturing, and Financial Trading Industries (Cham, CH: Palgrave Macmillan/Springer, 2018), 23–36.

14 The idea of Detroit as "capital of the twenty-first century" comes from Stefan J. Link, *Forging Global Fordism: Nazi Germany, Soviet Russia, and the Contest over the Industrial Order* (Princeton, NJ: Princeton University Press, 2021), 1.

15 On Gay and entrepreneurship, see, for example, Arthur H. Cole, "An Approach to the Study of Entrepreneurship: A Tribute to Edwin F. Gay," *Journal of Economic History* 6, S1 (1946): 1–15.

16 Hugh Atiken, ed., *Explorations in Enterprise* (Cambridge, MA: Harvard University Press, 1965). Part 5 of the book is "Historical Varieties." Aitken studied Canadian-American economic relations and the state, along with technology history.

17 Daniel Wadhwani, "Gales, Streams, and Multipliers: Conceptual Metaphors and Theory Development in Business History," *Enterprise & Society* 21, 2 (2020): 320–33; Louis Galambos and Franco Amatori, "Entrepreneurial History in Motion: A Reply to R. Daniel Wadhwani's Comment," *Enterprise & Society* 21, 2 (2020): 340–2.

18 While he focused on innovation in *The Theory of Economic Development*, Schumpeter also further explored the "perennial gale of creative destruction" more closely than in *Capitalism, Socialism and Democracy*. Interestingly, neither book explicitly examines the auto sector or auto entrepreneurs. For some background on entrepreneurship and business studies, see Geoffrey Jones and R. Daniel Wadhwani, "Entrepreneurial Theory and the History of Globalization," *Business and Economic History On-Line* 5 (2007), https://thebhc.org/sites/default/files/joneswadhwani.pdf. By the 1940s, entrepreneurship studies were a central focus of business education, though, by the 1960s and 1970s, organizational studies had come to dominate explanations of business success, reflecting the scholarship and influence of Chandler and Sloan.

19 Daniel Wadhwani, notes from "Presidential Address," delivered at the Business History Conference, Detroit, 17 March 2023.

20 On the Model T, see Robert Casey, *The Model T: A Centennial History* (Baltimore: Johns Hopkins University Press, 2008); Jim Rasenberger, *America, 1908: The Dawn of Flight, the Race to the Pole, the Invention of the Model T, and the Making of a Modern Nation* (New York: Scribner, 2007); and Richard Snow, *I Invented the Modern Age: The Rise of Henry Ford* (New York: Scribner, 2013).

21 On the growth of the American production system, see David A. Hounshell's classic *From the American System to Mass Production, 1800–1932: The Development of Manufacturing Technology in the United States* (Baltimore: Johns Hopkins University Press, 1985). On sewing machines, see Frank P. Godfrey, *An International History of the Sewing Machine* (London: R. Hale, 1982); on telephony, see Robert MacDougall, *The People's Network: The Political Economy of the Telephone in the Gilded Age* (Philadelphia: University of Pennsylvania Press, 2014).

22 Donald F. Davis, *Conspicuous Production: Automobiles and Elites in Detroit, 1899–1933* (Philadelphia: Temple University Press, 1988).

23 On Chrysler, see Vincent Curcio's *Chrysler: The Life and Times of an Automotive Genius* (New York: Oxford University Press, 2005). On Chrysler's production innovations, see Michael Schwartz, "Markets, Networks, and the Rise of Chrysler in Old Detroit, 1920–1940," *Enterprise & Society* 1, 1 (2000): 63–99 and Carl Breer and Anthony J. Yanik, *The Birth of Chrysler Corporation and Its Engineering Legacy* (Warrendale, PA: SAE, 1994). Other automotive innovators could include Ransom Olds, Henry Leland (Cadillac), the Dodge Brothers, Louis Chevrolet, Charles Kettering, and even Preston Tucker (though, like Bricklin, he was a failure).

24 There is a vast literature on Henry Ford. Classic treatments include Frank Ernest Hill's three-volume, *Ford: The Times, the Man, the Company* (New York: Scribner, 1954), *Expansion and Challenge, 1915–1933* (New York: Scribner, 1957), and, with co-author Allan Nevins, *Decline and Rebirth, 1933–1962* (New York: Scribner, 1962). See also Mira Wilkins and Frank Ernest Hill, *American Business Abroad: Ford on Six Continents* (Detroit: Wayne State University Press, 1964). Recent reassessments include Stephen Watts, *The People's Tycoon: Henry Ford and the American Century* (New York: Vintage Books, 2005) and Douglas Brinkley, *Wheels for the World: Henry Ford, His Company and a Century of Progress* (New York: Penguin Books, 2003).

25 Charles E. Sorensen, with Samuel T. Williamson, *My Forty Years with Ford* (New York: W.W. Norton, 1956); Austin Weber, "The Man Behind the Moving Assembly Line: Henry Ford Took the Praise, but Charles Sorensen Did the Work," *Assembly* 46, 2 (2003): 62–7.

26 Henry Ford in collaboration with Samuel Crowther, "My Life and Work: Chapter IV Starting the Real Business," *McClure's Magazine* 54, 4 (1922): 26.

27 See Brinkley, *Wheels for the World*, 101–2 and Eva Holland, "Ford's Miracle Metal," *Business Week* (Industrial Edition), 2 September 2019, 35.

28 On the River Rouge plant, see Terry Smith, *Making the Modern: Industry, Art, and Design in America* (Chicago: University of Chicago Press, 1993) and see also Joshua B. Freeman, *Behemoth: A History of the Factory and the Making of the Modern World* (New York: W.W. Norton, 2018).

29 For an interesting perspective on the music inspired by Ford and his Model T, see "Car Tunes," an exhibit at the Henry Ford Museum, https://www.thehenryford.org/collections-and-research/digital-collections/sets/1721.

30 On some of the less savoury and more eclectic aspects of Ford's life and career, see, for example, Victoria Saker Woeste, *Henry Ford's War on Jews and the Legal Battle against Hate Speech* (Stanford, CA: Stanford University Press, 2012); Stephen Norwood, "Ford's Brass Knuckles: Harry Bennett, The Cult of Muscularity, and Anti-Labor Terror, 1920–1945," *Labor History* 37, 3 (1996): 365–91; Greg Grandin, *Fordlandia: The Rise and Fall of Henry Ford's Forgotten Jungle City* (New York: Metropolitan Books, 2009); and Barbara S. Kraft, *The Peace Ship: Henry Ford's Pacifist Adventure in the First World War* (New York: Macmillan, 1978). On Ford's place as the greatest entrepreneur, see, for example, Blaine Mcormick and Burton Folsom, Jr. "The Greatest American Entrepreneurs and Businesspeople in American History: A Replication of the 2001 Ranking," *Cogent: Business and Management* 7, 1 (2020): 1–13.

31 Brinkley, *Wheels for the World*, 521. Ford's sales chief, Norval Hawkins, "designed much of the company's distribution system, including procedures for selling cars." Walter Friedman, *Birth of a Salesman: The Transformation of Selling in America* (Cambridge, MA: Harvard University Press, 2009), 210.

32 John B. Rae, "The Fabulous Billy Durant," *Business History Review* 32, 3 (1958): 255–71; Bernard Weisberger, *The Dream Maker* (Boston: Little, Brown, 1979). See also William Pelfrey, *Billy, Alfred, and General Motors: The Story of Two Unique Men, a Legendary Company, and a Remarkable Time in American History* (New York: AMACOM, 2006).

33 Tesla Inc., is, of course, named after Nikola Tesla, the Serbian-American inventor, engineer, and electrical genius. The company was founded in July 2003 by Martin Eberhard and Marc Tarpenning, neither of whose names are easily marketable; nor, for that matter, is the name Musk, at least not for an automobile. In 1957, the *New York Times* noted that, "for all its leadership in modern industry, the motor [industry's] calling above all seems to have named the old tradition of product naming, when a manufacturer in pride gave his own name to the machine." "Topics of the *Times*," *New York Times*, 5 September 1957, 28.

34 For another view on Durant, see his daughter's memoir, Margery Durant, *My Father* (New York: Putnam, 1929).
35 In 1910, Briscoe launched the United States Motor Corporation, which collapsed two years later and was reorganized as the Maxwell Motor Car Company, which eventually became the nucleus of the Chrysler Corporation. Rae, "The Fabulous Billy Durant," 289.
36 On Tucker, see Alex Tremulis, "The 1946–48 Tucker: A Great Promise Unfulfilled," SAE Technical Paper Series 872001 (Whitevale, PA: SAE, 1987); Phil Egan, *Design and Destiny: The Making of the Tucker Automobile* (Orange, CA: On the Mark Publications, 1989); and Pearson, *The Indomitable Tin Goose*. On DeLorean, see below, chapter 7, "Demise." On Musk, see the epilogue.
37 Rae, "The Fabulous Billy Durant," 258–9. On the challenges of anticipating consumers' desires, see Clarke, *Trust and Power.*
38 See Dimitry Anastakis, *Auto Pact: Creating a Borderless North American Auto Industry, 1960–1971* (Toronto: University of Toronto Press, 2005), chap. 1, and Anastakis, "From Independence to Integration: The Corporate Evolution of the Ford Motor Company of Canada," *Business History Review* 78, 2 (2004): 213–53. On GM's machinations in 1918–21, see Alfred D. Chandler, *The Visible Hand: The Managerial Revolution in American Business* (Cambridge, MA: Belknap Press of Harvard University, 1977), 459–60.
39 On General Motors' history, see also Edward Cray, *Chrome Colossus: General Motors and Its Times* (New York: McGraw Hill, 1980); Timothy Jacobs, *A History of General Motors* (New York: Brompton Books, 1992); and Pelfrey, *Billy, Alfred, and General Motors.*
40 Chandler, *The Visible Hand*, 459; Julian Pettifer and Nigel Turner, *Automania: Man and the Motor Car* (London: Collins, 1984), 131. There is, amazingly, no feature film treatment of Durant's Horatio Alger–like rise and fall, nor even much of a literary legacy about this astonishing man and his story, particularly in comparison to Henry Ford.
41 On the m-division and its creation, see Chandler's classic *Strategy and Structure: Chapters in the History of the Industrial Enterprise* (New York: Beard Books, 1962). On Henry Ford II's reorganization of Ford, see David A. Houshnell, "Assets, Organizations, Strategies and Traditions: Organizational Capabilities and Constraints in the Remaking of the Ford Motor Company, 1946–1962," in *Learning by Doing in Markets, Firms and Countries*, ed. Naomi R. Lamoreaux, Daniel M.G. Raff, and Peter Temin (Chicago: University of Chicago Press, 1999).
42 Alfred P. Sloan, *Adventures of a White Collar Man* (New York: Doubleday, 1941); David Farber, *Sloan Rules: Alfred P. Sloan and the Triumph of General Motors* (Chicago: University of Chicago Press, 2002). See also McCraw and Tedlow, "Henry Ford, Alfred Sloan," 266–300. For a fascinating analysis of the early auto industry, see Clarke, *Trust and Power*.
43 Charles K. Hyde, *Arsenal of Democracy: The American Automobile Industry in World War II* (Detroit: Wayne State University Press, 2013); Walter Hayes, *Henry: A Life of Henry Ford II* (New York: Grove Weidenfeld, 1990); Victor Lasky, *Never Complain, Never Explain: The Story of Henry Ford II* (New York: R. Marek Publishers, 1981).
44 Hounshell, "Assets, Organizations, Strategies and Traditions"; Alan McKinlay and Ken Starkey, "After Henry: Continuity and Change in the Ford Motor Company," *Business History* 36 (1994): 184–205; the anecdote about the organizational chart is on 185.
45 On the Ford, IPO, see Brinkley, *Wheels for the World*, 572–3.
46 Drucker, *Concept of the Corporation*; Chandler, *Strategy and Structure*; Alfred P. Sloan, *My Years with General Motors* (Garden City, NY: Doubleday, 1964). On the metanarrative of Sloan's book and its complicated provenance and history, see Christopher McKenna, "Writing the Ghost-Writer Back In: Alfred Sloan, Alfred Chandler, John McDonald and the Intellectual Origins of

Corporate Strategy," *Management and Organizational History* 1, 2 (2006): 107–26 and John Kay, "The Concept of the Corporation," *Business History* 61, 7 (2019): 1129–43.

47 An example of the "organization man" in the public consciousness in this period is the bestselling Sloan Wilson novel *The Man in the Gray Flannel Suit* (New York: Simon & Schuster, 1955). Critiques of this image included William Whyte's *The Organization Man* (1956; Philadelphia: University of Pennsylvania Press, 2002). On the "Whiz Kids," see John A. Bryne, *The Whiz Kids: Ten Founding Fathers of American Business and the Legacy They Left Us* (New York: Doubleday Business, 1993).

48 On Musk's s management of Tesla as he battled to successfully scale up Model 3 output, see Len Sherman, "Tesla Survived Manufacturing Hell – Now Comes the Hard Part," *Forbes*, 20 December 2018, https://www.forbes.com/sites/lensherman/2018/12/20/tesla-survived-manufacturing-hell-now-comes-the-hard-part/?sh=2165149dfae2, and Tim Higgins and Susan Pulliam, "Elon Musk Races to Exit Tesla's 'Production Hell,'" *Wall Street Journal*, 27 June 2018, https://www.wsj.com/articles/elon-musk-races-to-exit-teslas-production-hell-1530149814.

49 More recently, the Ford Motor Company survived the Great Recession and automotive meltdown –which led both GM and Chrysler to bankruptcy – in part because of the efforts of Alan Mulally to save the company in the period between 2006 and 2014. See Bryce G. Hoffman, *American Icon: Alan Mulally and the Fight to Save Ford Motor Company* (New York: Penguin Random House, 2012).

50 Examples of lifecycle in business writing include Burkhard Schwenker and Klaus Spremann, *Management between Strategy and Finance* (Berlin: Springer, 2009), which includes an exploration of "the four seasons of business"; Burkhard Schwenker and Mario Müller-Dofel, *On Good Management: The Corporate Lifecycle. An Essay and Interviews with Franz Fehrenbach, Jürgen Hambrecht, Wolfgang Reitzle and Alexander Rittweger* (Wiesbaden: Springer Gabler, 2013); Anita McGahan and Joel A.C. Baum, eds., *Business Strategy over the Industry Life Cycle* (Bingley, UK: Emerald Group Publishing, 2009); and, in particular, Stephen Klepper, "Pre-Entry Experience and Firm Performance in the Evolution of the US Automobile Industry," *Advances in Strategic Management* 21 (2004): 289–315.

51 The quote from *Where Have All the Leaders Gone* is from the book's cover. Michael D. Fox, "Lee Iacocca: The Man, the Myth, the Corporation: Iacocca's Development as an American Western Mythical Hero and the Exploitation of This Condition in Chrysler Television Commercials, 1981–85" (MA thesis, Miami University, 1988); James V. Catano, "Entrepreneurial Masculinity: Re-tooling the Self-Made Man," *Journal of American & Comparative Cultures* 23, 2 (2000): 1–9; Albert Lewis Linel and Darlene E.R. Resling, *Lee Iacocca: A Play* (Baltimore: Learning Well, 1997); Jim Siress, "Lessons from the Great Leaders from Hannibal to Iacocca" (Shawnee Mission, KS, 1987). See also Bert Spector, "Flawed from the 'Get-Go': Lee Iacocca and the Origins of Transformational Leadership," *Leadership* 10, 3 (2014): 361–79.

52 On Iacocca's background and biography, see Lee Iacocca and William Novak, *Iacocca: An Autobiography* (New York: Bantam Books, 1984). The numerous biographies of Iacocca include David Abodaher, *Iacocca* (New York: Zebra Books, 1982) and Peter Wyden, *The Unknown Iacocca* (New York: William Morrow, 1987). More critical views of Iacocca can be found in Doron P. Levin, *Behind the Wheel at Chrysler: The Iacocca Legacy* (New York: Mariner Press, 1995).

53 On the Mustang, see Michael W.R. Davis, *Mustang and the Pony Car Revolution* (Charleston, SC: Arcadia Publishing, 2014) and Brinkley, *Wheels for the World*, 609–18.

54 On the minivan, see Paul Ingrassia, *Engines of Change: A History of the American Dream in Fifteen Cars* (New York: Simon & Schuster, 2012); Joseph E. Porac, José Antonio Rosa, Jelena Spanjol, and Michael Scott Saxon, "America's Family Vehicle: Path Creation in the US Minivan

Market," in *Path Dependence and Creation*, ed. Raghu Garud and Peter Karnoe (New York: Psychology Press, 2001), 213–42.

55 Hal Sperlich, who was the main force behind the minivan (and was also behind the K-Car), had been fired by Ford in 1976 and had joined Chrysler. At Chrysler, Sperlich had begun working on the K-Car in early 1978, before Iacocca had arrived. Robert Reich and John D. Donahue, *New Deals: The Chrysler Revival and the American System* (New York: Times Books, 1986), 39–40.

56 For more on these setbacks, see David Halberstam, *The Reckoning* (New York: William Morrow, 1986) and Dimitry Anastakis, *Autonomous State: The Struggle for a Canadian Car Industry from OPEC to Free Trade* (Toronto: University of Toronto Press, 2013), especially chap. 2.

57 Harry Anderson, "Can Chrysler Be Saved?" *Newsweek*, 13 August 1979, 52. For contemporaneous views on the Chrysler bailout, see Reich and Donahue, *New Deals*; Reginald Stuart, *Bailout: America's Billion Dollar Gamble on the "New" Chrysler Corporation* (South Bend, IN: And Books, 1980); Michael Moritz and Barrett Seaman, *Going for Broke: Lee Iacocca's Battle to Save Chrysler* (New York: Doubleday, 1983); and Steve Jefferys, *Management and Managed: Fifty Years of Crisis at Chrysler* (New York: Cambridge University Press, 1986). See also Charles K. Hyde, *Riding the Roller Coaster: A History of the Chrysler Corporation* (Detroit: Wayne State University Press, 2003).

58 Harry Anderson, "Can Chrysler Be Saved?" *Newsweek*, 13 August 1979, 52. "Statement by John Riccardo, Chairman of the Board, Chrysler Corporation," 31 July 1979, Walter Reuther Library (WRL), UAW-Chrysler Collection, box 11, file "Bailout."

59 In his book *Industrial Sunset: The Making of North America's Rust Belt* (Toronto: University of Toronto Press, 2004), historian Steven High writes, "By 1979, the automobile, the symbol of the American Dream, mass production and conspicuous consumption, had come to symbolize what was wrong with the old industrial heartland. Detroit and the auto industry were represented as one by the national media. Crisis in the auto industry and the near-bankruptcy of the Chrysler Corporation in 1979 were also projected onto the image of the Motor City itself" (25).

60 Before his death in 1987, Ford II said of Iacocca's firing, "I didn't want him around simply because I didn't want him to be chief executive of the Ford Motor Co … My standards are higher than that … There are lots of reasons I let (Iacocca) go. One of them is he's not really a good chief executive. Not from a broad viewpoint. Secondly, he's too conceited, too self-centered to be able to see the broad picture." David Phillips, "Lee Iacocca, Mustang Mastermind and Tireless Chrysler Savior, Dies at 94," *Automotive News Europe*, 2 July 2019, https://europe.autonews.com/automakers/lee-iacocca-mustang-mastermind-and-tireless-chrysler-savior-dies-94#:~:text=Iacocca%20told%20Automotive%20News%20in,before%20his%20death%20in%201987. An entire chapter of Iacocca's autobiography is devoted to hiring people from Ford Motor in the wake of his firing.

61 Denis Smith and Dominic Elliot, eds., *Key Readings in Crisis Management: Systems and Structures for Prevention and Recovery* (New York: Routledge, 2006).

62 Chrysler Corporation, "Analysis of Chrysler Corporation's Situation and Proposal for Government Assistance, September 15, 1979," 29, Bentley Historical Library (BHL), William Milliken Papers, box 713, file "Chrysler Corporation"; "400,000 Jobs Tied to Chrysler's Survival," *Toronto Star*, 12 September 1979.

63 "Statement of Lee Iacocca to Congress, 18 October, 1979," National Archives and Records Administration (NARA), RG 56, Subject Files Related to the Chrysler Corporation Bailout, 1979–1980, Office of the Assistant Secretary for Domestic Finance, box 5, File Chrysler Testimony of Others.

64 Tom Nicholson and James C. Jones, "Iacocca's 'Little Miracle,'" *Newsweek*, 3 August 1981, 64. Iacocca often pointed to the fact that American Motors had received loan guarantees, as had Lockheed in 1971 and the City of New York.
65 Anthony Whittingham, "A Giant's Fragile Kingdom," *Maclean's*, 20 August 1979.
66 The Chrysler bailout was, at its core, a deal to protect bankers from losses. It is noteworthy that the Treasury took the lead in the negotiations and that this was not seen by the administration as any type of industrial policy precedent, but a onetime financial transaction.
67 The battle over concessions, and the unwillingness of the Canadian side of the UAW to accept them, eventually led to the breakup of the international union and the creation of the Canadian Auto Workers (CAW), in 1985. See Anastakis, *Autonomous State*, chap. 6, "Schism." GM built a new plant on the Dodge Hamtramck site in 1985, manufacturing Cadillacs. The plant has since become "Factory Zero," with the first production the GMC Hummer EV rolling off the production line in 2021.
68 Lee Iacocca, *Where Have All the Leaders Gone?* (New York: Scribner, 2007), 169. Former CAW union head Buzz Hargrove tell the story of how, during one of Iacocca's speeches in Canada to CAW members as part of his campaign, he would dramatically declare that, if workers did not take concessions, it would mean "lights out" for the company – and how he arranged for the lights to be turned off at that very moment in his remarks, which Hargrove admitted was tremendously effective. Anastakis, *Autonomous State*, 220.
69 See, for example, "Does Chrysler Want to Stay in the Business Just to Build America's Gas Guzzlers?" *Newsweek*, 13 August 1979.
70 On Iacocca's impact as a communicator, see, for example, Judie Mosier Thorpe, "Lee Iacocca and the Generation of Myth in the Spokesman Advertising Campaign for Chrysler from 1980–1984," *Journal of American Culture* 11, 2 (1988): 41–5; George N. Dionisopoulos, "A Case Study in Print Media and Heroic Myth: Lee Iacocca, 1978–1985," *Southern Speech Communication Journal* 53, 3 (1988): 227–43. Two PhD dissertations have been written on Iacocca and his role as a communicator and spokesperson in turning Chrysler around: Jayne Margaret Megginson, "The Rhetoric of Lee Iacocca: The Man, the Myth, the Message" (Louisiana State University, 1986) and Judith Mosier Thorpe, "The Role of Persuasion for a Corporate Spokesman: An Analysis of the Arguments Lee Iacocca Presented on Behalf of Chrysler Corporation to the American Consumer and to Congress from 1979 to 1982" (Ohio State Univeristy, 1986).
71 Eduardo Porter, "Auto Bailout Seems Unlikely," *New York Times*, 14 April 2006.
72 Chrysler Corporation, "Status of Chrysler Corporation Negotiations to Complete the Requirements of the Loan Guarantee Act," 1 April 1980, WRL, UAW-Chrysler Collection, box 11, file "Bailout."; Extraordinary Costs from Disproportionate Burden Faced on Smaller Automobile Companies by Government Regulation," 23 June 1979, Chrysler, Howard Paster to Douglas Fraser, WRL, D. Fraser Papers, box 51, file 51-9.
73 Hyde, *Riding the Roller Coaster*, 255.
74 Clearly, there are some additional factors that help to explain Chrysler's turnaround beyond Iacocca's managerial and promotional wizardry. After suffering such a decline in the 1978–83 period, the industry experienced the benefits of a resurgence in consumer confidence, which, while not inevitable, was expected in the highly cyclical auto sector. This confidence was boosted by a more general economic turnaround that saw a decline in record-high interest rates, which benefited car sales significantly. Chrysler's new products were also appealing to consumers. Trade policies further helped fuel the Chrysler and Big Three rebound: the 1981 "voluntary" export restraints imposed by the administration of President Ronald Reagan upon Japan provided some relief for domestic carmakers.

75 Nicholson and Jones, "Iacocca's 'Little Miracle,'" 64.

76 The two books about Iacocca both reached the top of the bestseller lists and were reprinted numerous times. Examples of works that examine the "Iacocca management technique" include Maynard M. Gordon, *The Iacocca Management Technique: A Profile of the Chrysler Chairman's Unique Key to Business Success* (New York: Ballantine Books, 1985), and Rosemay Papa-Lewis and Louis Markert, "The Iacocca Management Technique: Make It Work for You," *NASSP Bulletin* 72 (1988): 98–9. In the 1980s, Iacocca and the Chrysler case became a staple of business and administrative courses at universities. Of course, many disagreed with this view and saw the bailout as an unholy attack on American free enterprise. See, for example, James K. Hickel, "The Chrysler Bail-Out Bust," *Backgrounder* (Washington, DC: Heritage Foundation) 276, 13 (1983): 1–7.

77 For a detailed assessment of this shift, see Dimitry Anastakis, "Industrial Sunrise? The Chrysler Bailout, the State, and the Re-industrialization of the Canadian Automotive Sector, 1975–1986," *Urban History Review* 35, 2 (2007): 37–50.

78 Micheleine Maynard, "Business: Yes, Assembly Lines Can Mix Apples and Oranges," *New York Times*, 17 August 2003.

79 Colin Beresford, "It's Official: Fiat Chrysler and PSA Group Are Now Stellantis," *Car and Driver*, 19 January 2021.

80 If there was a hero of that event, it was probably Barack Obama. On the 2008–9 bailout, see Steven Rattner, *Overhaul: An Insider's Account of the Obama Administration's Emergency Rescue of the Auto Industry* (New York: Houghton Mifflin, 2010) and Alex Taylor III, *Sixty to Zero: An Inside Look at the Collapse of General Motors – and the Detroit Auto Industry* (New Haven, CT: Yale University Press, 2010).

81 On the utility of examining business failure, see Patrick Fridenson, "Business Failure and the Agenda of Business History," *Enterprise & Society* 5 (December 2004): 562–82.

82 John Dinkel, "America's New Sports Car: The Bricklin," *Road & Track*, September 1973, 96.

83 "Malcolm Bricklin: 'A Promoter,'" *Fredericton Daily Gleaner*, 11 June 1975; "Bricklin Explains Resignation: Running a Company Not a Strong Point," *Moncton Transcript*, 11 June 1975.

84 "The Bricklin Is Born," *Road Test* 10, 8 (1974): 35, emphasis in original.

3. Risk (Safety)

1 For an important perspective on risk, and the difference between risk and uncertainty, see Ulrich Beck, *Risk Society: Towards a New Modernity* (New Delhi: Sage, 1992). See also Anthony Giddens, "Risk and Responsibility," *Modern Law Review* 62, 1 (1999): 1–10.

2 The sociologist Ulrich Beck has demarcated three epochs of risk: "pre-modern society" (the external hazards of natural disasters), "industrial society," (the man-made risk of accidents), and "risk society" (the self-jeopardy of man-made disasters). Most obviously, the automobile was the leading cause of risk in industrial society and of the man-made potential disasters of risk society, such as climate change. See Mads P. Sørensen and Allan Christiansen, *On Ulrich Beck: An Introduction to the Theory of Second Modernity and the Risk Society* (London: Routledge, 2013), 13–16. For other views of risk and modernity, see, for example Brian Heaphy, *Late Modernity and Social Change: Reconstructing Social and Personal Life* (New York: Routledge, 2007); Karin Zachmann, "Risk in Historical Perspective: Concepts, Contexts, and Conjunctions," in *Risk: A Multidisciplinary Introduction*, ed. Claudia Klüppelberg, Daniel Straub, and Isabell M. Welpe (Berlin: Springer, 2014), 3–35; and Arwen P. Mohun, *Risk: Negotiating Safety in American Society* (Baltimore: Johns Hopkins University Press, 2013). A significant aspect of industrial/

modern society was the establishment of insurance. As an indicator of the automobile's prevalence, auto insurance became compulsory in most jurisdictions in North America and required for drivers, and thus came to cover most of the population, unlike life insurance.

3 Between 1960 and 1975, the total passenger miles driven by Americans jumped from 1.27 trillion miles per year to 2.40 trillion miles. By 1990, that figure had reached 3.54 trillion miles, and by 2019, an astounding 5.57 trillion miles. See United States Bureau of Transportation Statistics, "Table 1-40, US Passenger Miles (Millions)," https://www.bts.gov/content/us-passenger-miles.

4 The significant literature on the politics of capital movement and deindustrialization includes Jefferson Cowie, *Capital Moves: RCA's 70-Year Quest for Cheap Labor* (Ithaca, NY: Cornell University Press, 1999); Steven High, *Industrial Sunset: The Making of North America's Rust Belt, 1969–1984* (Toronto: University of Toronto Press, 2003); and Bryan D. Palmer, *Capitalism Comes to the Backcountry: The Goodyear Invasion of Napanee* (Toronto: Between the Lines, 1994). Michael Moore's first broadly successful film, *Roger and Me* (1987), was an examination of the consequences of General Motors abandoning his (and Billy Durant's) hometown of Flint, Michigan.

5 For examples of the large literature on the car's impact on pedestrians and the battle over how this technology would shape society, see Peter D. Norton, *Fighting Traffic: The Dawn of the Motor Age in the American City* (Cambridge, MA: MIT Press, 2008); Norton, "Street Rivals: Jaywalking and the Invention of the Motor Age Street," *Technology and History* 48, 2 (2007): 331–59; and Jeremy Packer, *Mobility without Mayhem: Safety, Cars, and Citizenship* (Durham, NC: Duke University Press, 2008). See also Sarah A. Seo, *Policing the Open Road: How Cars Transformed American Freedom* (Cambridge, MA: Harvard University Press, 2019).

6 For some views on life expectancy, including the role of automobile safety, see Scott R. Kegler, Grant T. Baldwin, Rose A. Rudd, and Michael F. Ballesteros, "Increases in United States Life Expectancy through Reductions in Injury-Related Death," *Population Health Metrics* 15, 1 (2017): 150–4, and Steven H. Woolf and Heidi Schoomaker, "Life Expectancy and Mortality Rates in the United States, 1959–2017," *JAMA: The Journal of the American Medical Association* 322, 20 (2019): 1996–2016.

7 Tamara Myers, "Didactic Sudden Death: Children, Police, and Teaching Citizenship in the Age of Automobility," *Journal of the History of Childhood and Youth* 8, 3 (2015): 451–75. Bestselling author Danielle Steel's 1994 novel, *Accident* (New York: Dell Publishing, 1994), revolves around the consequences of a car accident on the Golden Gate Bridge.

8 This was certainly true in terms of the sheer number of fatalities on the road, though less so in the rate of the carnage in relation to population growth. In the United States, in 1899, the first year traffic fatality statistics were recorded, 26 people were killed in road fatalities. The figure reached a peak in 1972, with 54,589 deaths: "Motor Vehicle Traffic Fatalities and Fatality Rate, 1899–2003," https://web.archive.org/web/20110921222129/http://www.saferoads.org/federal/2004/TrafficFatalities1899-2003.pdf. In Canada, the number of fatalities from motor vehicle accidents was first tabulated in 1921, when the total number of deaths (drivers, passengers, pedestrians, and so on) was listed at 197. From the 1920s onwards, that number increased almost every year, eventually peaking in 1973 at 6,706: Historical Statistics of Canada, Table T271-284, "Motor Vehicle Traffic Accidents, 1921 to 1975," https://www150.statcan.gc.ca/n1/pub/11-516-x/sectiont/T271_284-eng.csv.

9 John B. Rae, *The American Automobile: A Brief History* (Chicago: University of Chicago Press, 1965), 95. Rae was instrumental in developing the fields of automotive history and

the history of technology, and all automotive historians are indebted to him, as James J. Flink wrote in "John Bell Rae (1911–1988)," *Technology and Culture* 30, 3 (July 1989): 718–22.

10 Peter Norton presents a persuasive periodization in his article "Four Paradigms: Traffic Safety in the Twentieth-Century United States," *Technology and Culture* 56, 2 (April 2015): 32. His paradigms are as follows:
1. 1900s–1920s: Safety First
2. 1920s–1960s: Control
3. 1960s–1980s: Crashworthiness
4. 1980s–present: Responsibility.

See also, Chris Dummitt, *The Manly Modern: Masculinity in Postwar Canada* (Vancouver: UBC Press, 2007).

11 On the growing critique of the automobile's place in society, see, for example, James Flink, "Three Stages of American Automobile Consciousness," *American Quarterly* 24, 4 (1972): 451–73 and Rudi Volti, "A Century of Automobility," *Technology and Culture* 37, 4 (1996): 663–85.

12 Again, there is a vast literature on many of these topics. On the revolt against highways, see, for example, Raymond Mohl, "Stop the Road: Freeway Revolts in American Cities," *Journal of Urban History* 30, 5 (2004): 674–706; on the highway beautification efforts of Lady Bird Johnson, Lewis L. Gould, ed., *Lady Bird Johnson: Our Environmental First Lady* (Lawrence: University Press of Kansas, 1999); on reactions to roadside culture and suburbanization, Clay McShane, *Down the Asphalt Path: The Automobile and the American City* (New York: Columbia University Press, 1994) and Steve Penfold, "'Are We to Go Literally to the Hot Dogs?' Parking Lots, Drive-ins, and the Critique of Progress in Toronto's Suburbs, 1965–1975," *Urban History Review* 33, 1 (2004): 8–23; on some of the issues that emerged from the question of air pollution, Dimitry Anastakis, "A 'War on Pollution'? Canadian Responses to the Automotive Emissions Problem, 1970–80," *Canadian Historical Review* 90, 1 (March 2009): 99–136; on the US Department of Justice and the auto industry, Glenn Yago, "What's Good for General Motors Is Good for General Motors," *In These Times* (Chicago) 3, 22 (1979): 12–14. Another book that considers the automobile backlash is Brian Ladd, *Autophobia: Love and Hate in the Automotive Age* (Chicago: University of Chicago Press, 2008).

13 This trend included a postwar generation of academics who had started to study it: since 1945, the automobile and its industry (the most significant influence within industrial modernity and its transition to industrial postmodernity) became, directly or indirectly, a matter of subject interest to leading scholars across a wide range of fields, particularly in business studies, entrepreneurship, multinational/organizations and their behaviour, and sociology, but also aspects of human geography, urbanization, climate change, the environment, technology, and engineering are related to or touch on the auto and the period before, during, and after Fordism.

14 An earlier critic of Detroit was John Keats in his book *The Insolent Chariots* (Philadelphia: Lippincott, 1958), while New York senator Daniel Patrick Moynihan was a key advocate of safety in this period. On safety and the automobile, see Packer, *Mobility without Mayhem*, and Joel Eastman, *Styling vs. Safety: The Development of Automotive Safety, 1900–1966* (Lanham, MD: University Press of America, 1984). Another early postwar critic of the car's impact on society was Lewis Mumford in *The Highway and the City* (Westport, CT: Praeger Publishing, 1958).

15 On Nader's background, see Justin Martin, *Nader: Crusader, Spoiler, Icon* (Cambridge, MA: Perseus Publishing, 2002) and Patricia Cronin Marcello, *Ralph Nader: A Biography* (Westport, CT: Greenwood Press, 2004).

16 On GM's smear campaign and its result, see Thomas Whiteside, *The Investigation of Ralph Nader: General Motors vs. One Determined Man* (New York: Arbor House, 1972).

17 In contemporary reviews, some of the book's conclusions as well as Nader's methodology were questioned for lacking a rigorous scientific approach. One reviewer criticized "the profusion of pseudo-scientific jargon" and noted that, "stripped of the rhetoric, the reader discovers that the most intriguing and difficult questions provoked by the book are nowhere discussed in it." James A. Henderson, Jr., "Review of *Unsafe at Any Speed*, by Ralph Nader," *Boston University Law Review* 46 (1966): 140. For another critical view of Nader and his impact, see Kenneth Whyte, *The Sack of Detroit: General Motors and the End of American Enterprise* (New York: Knopf, 2021).

18 The industry defended itself by claiming that drivers did not want the expensive and cumbersome safety features like seat belts offered as add-ons in the 1950s, or that poor highway engineering was the problem, or that, above all, the problem was driver error. See Jerry L. Mashaw and David L. Harfst, *The Struggle for Auto Safety* (Cambridge, MA: Harvard University Press, 1990); Walter Rugaber, "Critic of Auto Industry's Safety Standards Says He Was Trailed and Harassed; Charges Called Absurd," *New York Times*, 6 March 1966, 94; Morton Mintz, "GM's Goliath Bows to David," *Washington Post*, 27 March 1966, A-7; and Whiteside, *The Investigation of Ralph Nader*.

19 On the impact of *Unsafe at Any Speed* and the fallout from its publication, including GM's attempts to discredit Nader and the company's subsequent apology, see Hearings before the Subcommittee on Executive Reorganization of the Committee on Government Operations, United States Congress 89th Congress, Second Session: Traffic Safety: Examination and Review of Efficiency Economy, and Coordination of Public and Private Agencies Activities and the Role of the Federal Government, 22 March 1966, Part 4, *Congressional Record* (US Government Printing Office, Washington, DC,1966), starting on 1379.

20 Lizabeth Cohen, *A Consumers' Republic: The Politics of Mass Consumption in Postwar America* (New York: Knopf, 2003), 354–5.

21 This was even more true for Transport Canada, the Canadian regulatory agency that was created to echo US regulation. Canadian regulators often did not even test vehicles but simply relied upon NHTSA's findings. Since the Canadian industry was effectively integrated into that of the US, this made sense on most issues, though there were some significant cross-border differences. Perhaps the greatest divergence between the two regulatory regimes on either side of the border concerned emissions; at one point in the 1970s and 1980s, North America actually had *three* regulatory regimes for emissions – one for California, one for the rest of the United States, and one for Canada, with the Canadian regime being the least strict. For more on this, see Anastakis, "A 'War on Pollution'?"

22 Jameson M. Wetmore, "Delegating to the Automobile: Experimenting with Automotive Restraints in the 1970s," *Technology and Culture* 56, 2 (April, 2015): 440–63; Eastman, *Styling v. Safety*; Amy Beth Gangloff, "Medicalizing the Automobile: Public Health, Safety, and American Culture, 1920–1967" (PhD diss., Stony Brook University, 2006).

23 Cohen, *A Consumer's Republic.*

24 Jil Mcintosh, "From 'Most Unsafe Car' to Safety Leader: Malcolm Bricklin Played a Little-Known Role," *National Post*, 2 June 2017, DT5.

25 "The Subaru 360 (Not Acceptable)," *Consumer Reports*, April 1969, 220–2; author's interview with Malcolm Bricklin, April 13 2013.

26 Donald F. Davis, *Conspicuous Production: Automobiles and Elites in Detroit, 1899–1933* (Philadelphia: Temple University Press; 1988); Steven W. Usselman, Sally Clarke, and Naomi

Lamoreaux, *The Challenge of Remaining Innovative: Lessons from Twentieth Century American Business* (Stanford, CA: Stanford Business Books, 2009).

27 James J. Flink, "Innovation in Automotive Technology: After a Long Interval of Stagnation, Automotive Technology May Be Entering a Period of Renewed Creativity," *American Scientist* 73, 2 (1985): 151–61.

28 Lawrence J. White, *The Automobile Industry since 1945* (1971; Cambridge, MA: Harvard University Press, 2014), 258. Catalytic converters came into widespread use in 1973 following GM's decision to offer them on its vehicles. The 1962–3 Chevrolet Corvair Monza and the Oldsmobile Jetfire were the first turbo-powered passenger cars. On the idea of battery electric vehicles, White's study concluded that "it will take a major breakthrough, not just the 'normal' marginal improvements over time, to bring electrical power packages to the point at which they are roughly competitive with internal combustion engines." White, *The Automobile Industry*, 235.

29 See, for example, Thomas E. Bonsall, *More Than They Promised: The Studebaker Story* (Stanford.CA: Stanford University Press, 2022), which chronicles the firm's postwar successes in the late 1940s and early 1950s in chapter 7, "Studebaker Amnia Vincit," and James Ward, *The Fall of the Packard Motor Car Company* (Stanford, CA: Stanford University Press, 1995).

30 Ralph Nader, *Unsafe at Any Speed: The Designed-In Dangers of the American Automobile* (New York: Grossman Publishers, 1965); Robert L. Shook, *Honda: An American Success Story* (New York: Prentice Hall, 1988), 23 and 37.

31 Even its name, the Civic, was a soothing antidote for the upheaval of the period. On Soichiro Honda and the CVCC engine, see John Rothfeder, *Driving Honda: Inside the World's Most Innovative Car Company* (New York: Portfolio, 2014), 62.

32 See, for example, the Ford Company's historical page on its 1950s safety efforts, "Ford Pioneers Auto Safety," https://corporate.ford.com/articles/history/ford-pioneers-auto-safety.html.

33 Dimitry Anastakis, *Autonomous State: The Struggle for a Canadian Car Industry from OPEC to Free Trade* (Toronto: University of Toronto Press, 2013), 59.

34 Paul C. Judge, "Selling Autos by Selling Safety: Car Makers Now Stress the Safety Features," *New York Times*, 26 January 1990, D1.

35 Stan Luger, *Corporate Power, American Democracy, and the Automobile Industry* (New York: Cambridge University Press, 2000), 63.

36 As cited in Rob Sass, "Smoking Permitted Only by the Engine," *New York Times*, 20 March 2011, AU6. Wetmore, "Delegating to the Automobile," 453; Luger, *Corporate Power*, 122n24.

37 Ernst Holsendolph, "Acrylic 2-Seater Sells for $6,500," *New York Times*, 26 June 1974, 59.

38 "Bricklin Vehicle Corp. and General Vehicle, Inc. (Prospectus), September, 1972," National Automotive History Collection (NAHC), Detroit Public Library (DPL), MS57, Bricklin Canada, Ltd., accession 57, series I, box 1; John Dinkel, "America's New Sports Car: The Bricklin," *Road & Track*, September 1973, 97.

39 "Confidential Overview of Bricklin Mexico S.A., February 1975," NAHC, DPL, MS57, Bricklin Canada, Ltd., accession 57, series I, box 1, file 8, p. 5.

40 See, for example, The Cato Institute, "Regulation: Bumpers to Bumpers in Court," *Regulation: AEI Journal on Government and Society* 9, 2 (1985): 11.

41 Holsendolph, "Acrylic 2-Seater."

42 Malcolm Gunn, "Could Anything Have Saved Malcolm Bricklin's Dream?" *Prince George Citizen*, 24 December 2013, A36.

43 Don Sherman, "Chevrolet Corvette Stingray vs. Bricklin SV1: America's Best Sports Car: Being 'Second' Doesn't Necessarily Mean Being 'Last,'" *Car and Driver*, 1 May 1975, 72. Another example is John J. O'Connor, "Bricklin Safety Vehicle ('A Dream Come True') Will Debut in

Northeast," *Advertising Age*, 1 July 1974. Dinkel's article in *Road & Track* also focused on the safety aspect as a new and innovative aspect of the car.

44 Phil Casey, "Bricklin's Bricklin," *Washington Post*, 16 February 1975, L7.

45 "Bricklin Vehicle Corp. and General Vehicle, Inc. (Prospectus), September, 1972," NAHC, DPL, MS57, Bricklin Canada, Ltd., accession 57, series I, box 1, p. 7.

46 Leah Young, "Small Auto Firm Win Big Honors," *Journal of Commerce*, 3 April 1975; "Foreign Sports Cars Get Best Stop-and-Go Test Ratings," *Vancouver Sun*, 12 May 1976, 25.

47 Ronald C. Makowski to Bricklin, 2 May 1975 and Irving S. Soble to Bricklin, 16 June 1975, NAHC, DPL, Bricklin Canada, series II, box 4, file 9.

48 Bricklin/GVI "Stock Prospectus," n.d., 7, NAHC, DPL, MS57, accension 57, series I, box 1, Bricklin Canada, Ltd.

49 "Confidential Overview of Bricklin Mexico S.A., February 1975," NAHC, DPL, MS57, Bricklin Canada, Ltd., accession 57, series I, box 1, file 8, p. 5.

50 "February Newsletter: Public Relations & Advertising Activities, Andy Copp," n.d., Public Archives of New Brunswick (PANB), Department of Commerce and Development, file 5600-B12, Public Relations, vol. II, box 83, "Bricklin 1974–78."

51 "People," *Maclean's*, 9 February 1976, 44.

52 B. Tripolsky, "Bricklin Comes Back with a Rotary Engine," *Mechanix Illustrated*, January 1977; E. Willis, T. Bartrand, and J. Beard, "Engineering Study on the Rotary-Vee Engine Concept," SAE Technical Paper 890332 (1989), 77–94; S. Bailey and J. Caton, "A Review and Thermodynamic Analysis of a Rotary-Vee Internal Combustion Engine," SAE Technical Paper 950453 (1995), 4–14.

53 Rob Linke, "Malcolm Bricklin Dreams Big, Again," *Saint John Telegraph-Journal* (*TJ*), 4 May 2009, A1; "Electrovaya in Venture with Malcolm Bricklin's Visionary Vehicles," *Canadian Press*, 14 January 2008.

54 The EV3 can be seen at Visionary Vehicles, https://www.vvcars.com/.

55 The *Fortune 500* database of American's largest corporations from 1955 to 2005 can be viewed at https://money.cnn.com/magazines/fortune/fortune500_archive/full/1955/1.html.

56 White, *The Automobile Industry*, 250.

57 *DesRosiers Automotive Yearbook 2000* (Richmond Hill, ON: DesRosiers Automotive Consultants, 2000), 112.

58 On the size of the US auto industry in this period, see Thomas Klier and James Rubenstein, *Who Really Made Your Car? Restructuring and Geographic Change in the Auto Industry* (Kalamazoo, MI: W.E. Upjohn Institute, 2008). On roadside culture, see the extensive and impressive work of John A. Jakle and Keith A. Sculle, including *The Gas Station in America* (Baltimore: Johns Hopkins University Press, 1994) and *Supplanting America's Railroads: The Early Auto Age, 1900–1940* (Knoxville: University of Tennessee Press, 2017). On the power and influence of the US auto sector, see, for example, the various works of Charles Hyde, including *Arsenal of Democracy: The American Automobile Industry in World War II* (Detroit: Wayne State University Press, 2013) and *Riding the Roller Coaster: A History of the Chrysler Corporation* (Detroit: Wayne State University Press, 2003); David R. Farber, *Sloan Rules: Alfred P. Sloan and the Triumph of General Motors* (Chicago: University of Chicago Press, 2002); Steven Watts, *The People's Tycoon: Henry Ford and the American Century* (New York: Vintage Books, 2005); and Richard Bak, *Henry and Edsel: The Creation of the Ford Empire* (New York: Wiley, 2003).

59 See, for instance, Ted McClelland, *Midnight in Vehicle City: General Motors, Flint and the Strike that Created the Middle Class* (Boston: Beacon Press; 2021) and David Stebenne, *Promised Land: How the Rise of the Middle Class Transformed America, 1929–1968* (New York: Scribner, 2020).

60 On the UAW and its history in this period, see Nelson Lichtenstein, *The Most Dangerous Man in Detroit: Walter Reuther and the Fate of American Labor* (New York: Basic Books, 1995) and John Barnard, *American Vanguard: The United Auto Workers during the Reuther Years, 1935–1970* (Detroit: Wayne State University Press, 2004).
61 On John Kenneth Galbraith, see James Ronald Stanfield and Jacqueline Bloom Stanfield, *John Kenneth Galbraith* (London: Palgrave Macmillan, 2011).
62 On productivity in this period, see James M. Rubenstein, *Making and Selling Cars: Innovation and Change in the US Automotive Industry* (Baltimore: Johns Hopkins University Press, 2001), 34–7; see also the seminal book by Daniel Roos, Daniel T. Jones, and James P. Womack, *The Machine That Changed the World* (New York: Free Press, 1990).
63 Sam Gindin, *The Canadian Auto Workers: The Birth and Transformation of a Union* (Toronto: Lorimer, 1995); Lichtenstein, *The Most Dangerous Man.*
64 High, *Industrial Sunset*; Jefferson Cowie, *Stayin' Alive: The 1970s and the Last Days of the Working Class* (New York: New Press, 2010).
65 Andrea Hiott, *Thinking Small: The Long Strange Trip of the Volkswagen Beetle* (New York: Ballantine Books, 2012); Bernhard Rieger, *The People's Car: A Global History of the Volkswagen Beetle* (Cambridge, MA: Harvard University Press, 2013); Thomas Frank, *The Conquest of Cool: Business Culture, Counterculture and the Rise of Hip Consumerism* (Chicago: University of Chicago Press, 1998).
66 The Canadian government managed to avoid the worst of the Nixon shocks by pleading for exemptions on the surcharge, which it received, and luckily avoiding the abrogation of the auto pact. On the Nixon shocks, see Douglas A. Irwin, "The Nixon Shock after Forty Years: The Import Surcharge Revisited," *World Trade Review* 12, 1 (2013): 29–56 and Bruce Muirhead, "From Special Relationship to Third Option: Canada, the US, and the Nixon Shock," *American Review of Canadian Studies* 34, 3 (2004): 439–46.
67 For an interesting overview of the Canadian political economy of dependence, see Paul Kellogg, *Escape from the Staple Trap: Canadian Political Economy after Left Nationalism* (Toronto: University of Toronto Press, 2015).
68 Jefferson Cowie, *Capital Moves: RCA's Seventy-Year Quest for Cheap Labor* (Ithaca, NY: Cornell University Press, 1999).
69 Gus Tyler, "Labor's Multinational Pains," *Foreign Policy* 12 (Autumn 1973): 113–32; on "runaway plants" in the United States, see Andy Battle, "Runaway: A History of Postwar New York in Four Factories" (PhD diss., City University of New York, 2019).
70 See United States International Trade Commission, *Automotive Trade Statistics 1964–80* (Washington, DC: United States International Trade Commission, 1981), 2, https://www.usitc.gov/publications/332/pub1203.pdf.
71 On Studebaker, and its Canadian facility, see Donald T. Critchlow, *Studebaker: The Life and Death of an American Corporation* (Bloomington: Indiana University Press, 1996); Bonsall, *More Than They Promised.*
72 Dimitry Anastakis, *Auto Pact: Creating a Borderless North American Auto Industry, 1960–1971* (Toronto: University of Toronto Press, 2005).
73 Anastakis, *Autonomous State.*
74 Rae, *The American Automobile,* 212; Statistics Canada, Cat. nos. 65-004 and 65-007, cited in James G. Dykes, *Background on the Automotive Products Trade Agreement* (Toronto: Motor Vehicle Manufacturer's Association, 1985), n.p.
75 Anastakis, *Autonomous State*, 193–208.
76 White, *The Automobile Industry*, 62. Chapter 5 of White's book is "Entry into the Automobile Industry."

77 Sally Clarke, "Managing Design: The Art and Colour Section at General Motors, 1927–1941," *Journal of Design History* 12, 1 (1999): 65–79. See also Clarke's excellent book, *Trust and Power: Consumers, the Modern Corporation, and the Making of the United States Automobile Market* (Cambridge: Cambridge University Press, 2007).
78 Peter Carlson, "The Flop Heard Round the World: That Name. That Grille. Ford Had High Expectations, but When the Edsel Debuted in 1957, It Became America's Most-Hyped Failure," *Washington Post*, 4 September 2007; Thomas E. Bonsall, *Disaster in Dearborn: The Story of the Edsel* (Stanford, CA: Stanford General Books, 2002); Gayle C. Warnock, *The Edsel Affair: … What Went Wrong? A Narrative* (Paradise Valley, AZ: Pro West, 1980).
79 Douglas Brinkley, *Wheels for the World: Henry Ford, His Company, and a Century of Progress* (New York: Penguin Books, 2003), 577; Joseph C. Ingraham, "Edsel Cars Offer Style Innovation: Ford Motor Company Reveals the Edsel, Newest Member of Family," *New York Times*, 27 August 1957, 29; Joseph C. Ingraham, "Edsel Is First New Car to Be Offered by One of the Big Three since 1938," *New York Times*, 8 September 1957, X37.
80 Thanks to Magda Fahrni for her feedback in illuminating this important aspect of the chapter and for providing suggestions on some key language in the paragraph. For more on risk, see her excellent "Glimpsing Working-Class Childhood through the Laurier Palace Fire of 1927: The Ordinary, the Tragic, and the Historian's Gaze," *Journal of the History of Childhood and Youth* 8, 3 (2015): 426–50, especially 435.
81 Alden Nowlan, "Hatfield Country: Where a Politician Can Be Culturally Immersed without Drowning," *Maclean's*, November 1971, 80.
82 "Bricklin 'Risky' but Could Pay Off," *Saint John Evening Times Globe*, 5 September 1974.
83 "120-Member Staff Completes Vehicle," *Fredericton Daily Gleaner*, 7 August 1974.
84 Claude Bourque, originally in *L'Evangeline* (Moncton), translated and republished as "The Bricklin: Is Now the Time to Have Faith in It?" *TJ*, 12 August 1974.
85 "Don't Look for Failure" (editorial), *Moncton Times*, 19 August 1974.
86 "A Lot Is Riding on It for Premier Hatfield," *Saint John Evening Times Globe*, 17 June 1974.
87 Steve Spence, "Adventures on the 'Yellow Bricklin Road,'" *Motor Trend*, November 1974, 64.

4. Showman (Politician)

1 Fame, and its historical evolution, is the subject of many scholarly explorations, including Joshua Gamson, *Claims to Fame: Celebrity in Contemporary America* (Berkeley: University of California Press 1994); Susan J. Douglas and Andrea McDonnell, *Celebrity: A History of Fame* (New York: New York University Press 2019); and Fred Inglis, *A Short History of Celebrity* (Princeton, NJ: Princeton University Press, 2010). On the "democratic theatre and the natural performer," see Leo Braudy, *The Frenzy of Renown: Fame and Its History* (New York: Oxford University Press, 1986).
2 Though nowadays, the auto sector vies, and overlaps, with the information technology and communications (ITC) sector.
3 Danny Hakim, "Doubts Rising about a Venture to Import Chinese Cars," *New York Times*, 7 June 2005. Like any good showman, Bricklin himself played up the Barnum association. See, for example, David Kiley, "A Bit of P.T. Barnum in Me," *Bloomberg Businessweek*, 1 October 2005, 1.
4 Basem Wasef, "Malcolm Bricklin Gets Heated in 'The Entrepreneur': Brash Automotive Exec Is the Subject of a New Documentary," *Rolling Stone*, 6 August 2013; Spurlock was executive producer of *The Entrepreneur* (Jonathan Bricklin, 2013); Richard Truett, "Malcolm Bricklin's Latest Venture Involves Three-Wheeled EVs, Space Pod Simulators and High-End Art," *Autoweek*,

15 May 2017; Dahl, "Would You Buy a Chinese Car from This Man?" Inc., 1 July 2005, https://www.inc.com/magazine/20050701/disruptor-bricklin.html.

5 Michael Enright, "Wheeler-Dealer: How Mr. Bricklin Got His Dream Car and Mr. Hatfield Got the Bill," *Maclean's*, 17 November 1975, 55.

6 H.A. Fredericks and Allan Chambers, *Bricklin* (Potters Bark, UK: Brunswick Press, 1977), 6–7; Ruth Smith, "Central Florida Women: Twirp Twirl," *Orlando Sentinel*, 2 March 1955, 14; "Engagements," *Orlando Sentinel*, 19 April 1959, 11-E; "Wedding Bells Ring Out for August Brides," *Orlando Sentinel*, 31 August 1959, 8-A; Enright, "Wheeler-Dealer," 55–6.

7 As quoted in Fredericks and Chambers, *Bricklin*, 6–7.

8 In 1963, Bricklin, described by the *Orlando Sentinel* as "quite an energetic young man," expanded Handyman into Handyman Properties Inc. to "lease land and buildings" to the chain. "A New Corporation," *Orlando Sentinel*, 28 November 1963, 106. On histories of franchising, see Thomas S. Dicke, F*ranchising in America: The Development of a Business Method, 1840–1980* (Chapel Hill: University of North Carolina Press, 1992) and Steve Penfold, *The Donut: A Canadian History* (Toronto: University of Toronto Press, 2008).

9 "Handyman Founder Sells Out," *Orlando Sentinel*, 25 October 1964, 8-D.

10 Fredericks and Chambers, *Bricklin*, 7–11; Phil Casey, "Bricklin's Bricklin," *Washington Post*, 16 February 1975, L7.

11 "Handyman, Inc. 4 Men Sued: Investor Seeks $1.2 Million Damages," *Orlando Sentinel*, 17 December 1964, 17; Fredericks and Chambers, *Bricklin*, 6. Bricklin contests this interpretation. Author's interview with Malcolm Bricklin, 6 October 2022.

12 Fredericks and Chambers, *Bricklin*, 11.

13 Andrea Rapini, *The History of the Vespa: An Italian Miracle* (New York: Routledge, 2019).

14 For Bricklin's account of the Lambretta story, see Craig Fitzgerald, "How MTV's DNA, the NYC Police, and a Forged Contract Led to Subaru of America," *Hagerty Media*, 15 June 2021, https://www.hagerty.com/media/automotive-history/how-the-dna-of-mtv-the-nyc-police-and-a-forged-contract-led-to-subaru-of-america/.

15 Randall Rothenberg, *Where the Suckers Moon: An Advertising Story* (New York: Knopf, 1994), 42; Fredericks and Chambers, *Bricklin*, 11.

16 Jil Mcintosh, "From 'Most Unsafe Car' to Safety Leader; Malcolm Bricklin Played a Little-Known Role," *National Post*, 2 June 2017, DT5; Rothenberg, *Where the Suckers Moon*, 44.

17 Rothenberg, *Where the Suckers Moon*, 44. See, for example, Walter Friedman, *Birth of a Salesman: The Transformation of Selling in America* (Cambridge, MA: Harvard University Press, 2009), chap. 5, "The Pyramid Plan"; Jessica Burch, "Crisis or Opportunity? Amway and an Unfamiliar Story of Economic Growth in the 1970s," in *After the Boom: Continuity and Change in the Western Industrialized World after 1970*, ed. Sebastian Voight (Toronto: University of Toronto Press, 2020), 37.

18 "Robert M. Lienert, "Finding Happiness on $20 Million," *Automotive News*, May 1974, 6; Earl Emmons, "The New Subaru Is 'Cheap and Ugly,'" *Tampa Tribune Times*, 12 January 1969, 10-D; "950-Pound Japanese Car to Make American Debut," *New York Times*, 10 May 1968, 68; "'Bug' Folks May Say 'Gnats' to Japanese Auto Import," *Chicago Tribune*, 17 May 1968, C8; Rothenberg, *Where the Suckers Moon*, 44.

19 "Subaru Co. to Move to Pennsauken," *Camden (NJ) Courier-Post*, 10 March 1969, 19; Jason Vuic, *The Yugo: The Rise and Fall of the Worst Car in History* (New York: Hill and Wang, 2010), 24. Bricklin was not interviewed or consulted for Vuic's book and disagreed vehemently with much of its interpretation of the Yugo episode and his career.

20 John McDonnell, "Report Blasts Japan's Minicar," *Chicago Tribune*, 4 April 1969, C6; Vuic, *The Yugo*, 7; Jay Apt, "Personalities in Business: Bricklin to Turn Dream into Subaru Showplace," *Camden (NJ) Courier-Post*, 27 October 1969, 17.

21 Dan Fisher, "Subaru Hopes to Hitch Star to New Image," *Los Angeles Times*, 23 June 1969, B10; "Ethics Body Studies Role of Fineman," *Camden (NJ) Courier-Post*, 30 August 1969, 9.

22 Rothenberg, *Where the Suckers Moon*, 51. Bricklin contests this characterization of his departure from Subaru, though he does not deny the gun story (he claims this was done as a joke, and not to scare off unwelcome guests). Author's interview with Malcolm Bricklin, 6 October 2022.

23 Bricklin disputed this characterization of the events. Bill Vance, "Lemon Squeezer: Charismatic Salesman Malcolm Bricklin Moved from One Failed Scheme to Another," *Kamloops Daily News*, 21 February 2002, B6; Michael Gunn, "Subaru 360," Washington (PA) *Observer-Reporter*, 25 October 2007, D1, https://news.google.com/newspapers?nid=2519&dat=20071025&id=GzJkAAAAIBAJ&sjid=_ycMAAAAIBAJ&pg=369,49498564. Author's interview with Malcolm Bricklin, 6 October 2022. Lamm stayed with Subaru of America until 1990.

24 John Lamm, "The Bricklin SV1 Sports Car!" *Motor Trend*, July 1974, 89.

25 By 1974, journalists would write that "the 360 is long gone – done in by charges the tiny vehicle was unsafe for American highways –but Subaru has become successful in this country with larger, and more expensive models." Dan Fisher "Move Over, GM – Malcolm Bricklin and Mom Are Here: First Real Competitor since the Kaiser-Frazer 'Handyman' Turns His Talents to Car Making," *Los Angeles Times*, 23 June 1974, E1.

26 Frederick and Chambers, *Bricklin*, 15; Greg Conderacci and Nick Thomas, "If Publicity Spells Success, the Bricklin Will Surpass Chevy: Lavish Galas, Fashion Models Greet New Auto's Debut; Complaint? Tell It to Mom," *Wall Street Journal*, 30 December 1974, 1.

27 "Public Relations' Updates" (various months), Public Archives of New Brunswick (PANB), Department of Commerce and Development, box 83, folder 5600-B12, "Public Relations," vol. II, Bricklin 1974–78.

28 Philip H. Dougherty, "Advertising: New Bricklin Auto," *New York Times*, 17 June 1974, 50.

29 A Bricklin newspaper advertisement for dealers can be found in PANB, Department of Commerce, Companies Files, box 501, file "Bricklin Canada Limited"; Fredericks and Chambers, *Bricklin*, 31.

30 Wheatley also wrote that "in general, however, the show confirmed the marketability of the car and leaves productionability the main risk." G.S. Wheatley, "Trip Report, New York– Detroit–Las Vegas, January 30, 1974," PANB, Department of Commerce and Development, Bricklin Canada Limited, box 556, vol. 6, files 43-1670, July 1973–May 1974; Fredericks and Chambers, *Bricklin*, 38; author's interview with Malcolm Bricklin, 13 April 2013; Dougherty, "Advertising: New Bricklin Auto," 50.

31 Fredericks and Chambers, *Bricklin*, 30.

32 Bob Clift (former Bricklin chassis designer and test engineer), "The Birth of the First Bricklin," *Brickline* 18, 2 (July 1993): 9.

33 Casey, "Bricklin's Bricklin," L7; "Confidential Review of Bricklin Mexico, S.A., February, 1975," National Automotive History Collection (NAHC), Detroit Public Library (DPL), series I, box 1, file 8.

34 Steve Spence, "Adventures along the 'Yellow Bricklin Road,'" *Motor Trend*, November 1974, 34.

35 "Malcolm Bricklin and His Magic Car," *People*, 27 May 1974; "Eyecatchers: Don Quixote of Detroit," *Time*, 27 May 1974; "A Promoter Cranks Up a New Car," *Business Week*, 27 April 1974, 44.

36 Author's interview with Malcolm Bricklin, 30 April 2013. See also "National '75 Auto Shows Feature Bricklin SV1," *Brickline* 1, 2 (1975): 1; "Public Relations' Updates" (various months),

PANB, Department of Commerce, box 83, folder 5600-B12, "Public Relations," vol. II, Bricklin 1971 70.

37 Spence, "Adventures along the 'Yellow Bricklin Road,'" 62; Conderacci and Thomas, "If Publicity Spells Success," 36.

38 Bricklin generated quite a bit of media attention for this event. See, for example, Peter Moon, "A Car Is Born: Hatfield Helps Unveil the Bricklin in New York Ceremony," *Globe and Mail*, 26 June 1974, 11 and Ernst Holsendolph, "Acrylic 2-Seater Sells for $6,500," *New York Times*, 26 June 1974, 59: see also Fredericks and Chambers, *Bricklin*, 1; "Invitation, 25 June 1974," NAHC, DPL, Bricklin Papers, series II, box 4, file 9.

39 Fredericks and Chambers, *Bricklin*, 5; Moon, "A Car Is Born," 11. Fredericks and Chambers also write that "the technician who drove one of the cars from Saint John to New York had not dared to travel over 35 miles an hour for fear he would lose the shock absorbers," 2. In later interviews, Bricklin flatly rejected the Fredericks and Chambers claims as untrue.

40 Michael D. Jonas (Bricklin General Counsel) to Dale Carter (City Manager, Scottsdale), 22 November, 1974, NAHC, Bricklin Papers, box 4, file 9, series II.

41 Press Release, "Mother Bricklin," n.d., ibid.

42 "'Squeaky Clean' Boy Wonder," *Financial Post*, 21 February 1976, 3.

43 Between the SV1 and the Yugo, Bricklin had also taken over distribution of the Fiat X1/9 and 124 Spider after Fiat pulled out of the US market. On VW in America, see Bernard Rieger, *The People's Car: A Global History of the Volkswagen Beetle* (Cambridge, MA: Harvard University Press, 2012) and Thomas Frank's *The Conquest of Cool: Business Culture, Counterculture and the Rise of Hip Consumerism* (Chicago: University of Chicago Press, 1998). Honda's American odyssey is treated in Robert L. Shook, *Honda: An American Success Story* (New York: Prentice Hall, 1988).

44 Vuic, *The Yugo*, 90; author's interview with Malcolm Bricklin, 6 October 2022.

45 Greg Keenan, "Malcolm Bricklin Wants to Sell You Another Car," *Globe and Mail*, 4 January 2005, A1.

46 Marc Clark, "A Galloping Success for a Korean Pony," *Maclean's*, 9 December 1985, 32; David Halberstam, *The Reckoning* (New York: William Morrow, 1986), 699.

47 Vuic, *The Yugo*, 5; Brock Yates, "Detroit Lucks Out Again," *Washington Post*, 15 March 1987, W61; author's interview with Malcolm Bricklin, 30 April 2013. In *The Entrepreneur*, Jonathan Bricklin stated that, in the mid-eighties "the Yugo was making my father half a million dollars a month for 24 straight months until he sold the company for $20 million."

48 Warren Brown, "Yugo Distributor Seeks Chapter 11 Protection," *Washington Post*, 31 January 1989, C1.

49 On the Yugo's demise and Bricklin's bankruptcy, see Vuic, *The Yugo*, 177–85; "Kravis Acquires Ranch," *New York Times*, 22 April 1991, D7; "Roundup: Courts," *Washington Post*, 23 August 1991, B02; and Andy Holloway, "Malcolm Bricklin: 'When You're Succeeding, You Tend to Get the Feeling You Know More Than You Know,'" *Canadian Business*, 17 February 2003, 28–9. Author's interview with Malcolm Bricklin, 6 October 2022. Charles M. Thomas and Helen Kahn, "Bricklin Ordered to Pay $17 Million to Backers," *Automotive News* 5398 (1991): 2.

50 Peter C. Newman, "1991: It Was Easier to Laugh Than to Cry," *Maclean's*, 23 December 1991, 43.

51 "Bricklin Unplugged," *Maclean's*, 20 November 1997, 71.

52 "Opening Notes: Bricklin Wheels out His Latest Vehicle," *Maclean's*, 14 August 1995, 10; "A Bricklin for the Nineties," *Maclean's*, 26 February 1996, 42; Martha Groves, "Bricklin Back in the Race, Now Peddling an Electric Bicycle," *Los Angeles Times*, 12 July 1996; "Business Notes: Bricklin Unplugged," *Maclean's*, 20 October 1997, 71; Chris Kraul, "Real Visionary Has Come

Up Flat … Again," *Los Angeles Times*, 21 June 1997. Author's interview with Malcolm Bricklin, 6 October 2022.

53 See the film *The Entrepreneur* and a discussion of the meeting in Dahl, "Would You Buy a Chinese Car from This Man?" *Inc.*, 1 July 2005, 68, https://www.inc.com/magazine/20050701/disruptor-bricklin.html. Author's interview with Malcolm Bricklin, 6 October 2022.

54 On the development of the Chinese auto sector, see Nicola Meier, *China: The New Developmental State? An Empirical Analysis of the Automotive Industry* (Bern, CH: Peter Lang International Academic Publishers, 2018).

55 Author's interview with Malcolm Bricklin, 6 October 2022; Keenan, "Malcolm Bricklin Wants to Sell," A1; Dahl, "Would You Buy a Chinese Car" 68.

56 "Bad News for the Big 3: $13K a Pop," *Maclean's*, 14 January 2008, 44.

57 Dahl, "Would You Buy a Chinese Car" 68.

58 "Entrepreneur Bricklin Sues Chery over Failed Deal," *Reuters*, 21 July 2008, https://www.reuters.com/article/sppage023-n21419445-oisbi/entrepreneur-bricklin-sues-chery-over-failed-deal-idINN2141944520080721.

59 Gail Kachadourian, "Bricklin, Chery End Joint-Venture Plans," *Automotive News* 81, 6231 (2006): 3; Christie Schweinsberg, "Malcolm Bricklin, Visionary Vehicles Switch to Plan B," *Ward's Dealer Business* 41, no. 1 (2007). 16; Alysha Webb, "Sour Chery: Bricklin Suit Claims Corruption," *Automotive News*, 21 July 2008.

60 In 2013, Bricklin was awarded a $2 million payout for his former employee's fraud against him during the deal. Joseph Lichterman, "Auto Entrepreneur Bricklin Wins $2 Million for Fraud," *Reuters*, 15 July 2013, https://www.reuters.com/article/us-autos-detroit-bricklinidUSBRE96E0SV20130715.

61 Ann Hornaday, "The Entrepreneur," *Washington Post*, 6 September 2003, WW29.

62 "Exclusive: Tesla Readies Export of Model Y to Canada from China," *Reuters*, 24 April 2023, https://www.reuters.com/business/autos-transportation/tesla-readies-export-model-y-canada-china-source-memo-2023-04-24/. Vietnamese EV manufacturer VinFast had already started exporting to the United States in 2022. BYD began originally as a battery maker in 1995 and has since become a giant technology conglomerate headquartered in Shenzhen, Guangdong Province.

63 Sandra Gwyn, "Hanging Out with Hatfield: The Happiest Premier, If Not the Best," *Saturday Night*, January–February 1979, at 34.

64 "Aristocrat and Country Squire," *Financial Post*, 4 June 1977, 27.

65 One 1971 description of Hatfield: "What is he really like? Vital statistics: he is 39, unmarried, and handsome. He is of our time in every sense – likes movies such as 'The Strawberry Statement' and was an early patron of 'Hair.' He enjoys trying new things as they come along; not long ago, for instance, he injured his back in a snowmobile accident. He is a connoisseur of good food and travel. For some reason, the style of Moroccans appeals to him and he has already paid two visits to that country. But to know the man, is to know that 'politics is his life.'" "Canada Profile No. 2: Richard Hatfield," *Canada and the World*, February 1971, 20.

66 Chris Wood, "Hatfield's Politics of Fun," *Maclean's*, 26 October 1987, 22.

67 Della Margaret Maude Stanley, *Louis Robichaud: A Decade of Power* (Halifax: Nimbus Publishing, 1991), 42–5; "Fredericton: Somebody's Got to Go," *Maclean's*, 21 March 1977, 4; Gerry Childs, "So Say the 'Three Musketeers,'" *Atlantic Advocate*, January 1971, 19, 22, 25, 28.

68 Gwyn, "Hanging Out with Hatfield," 41.

69 Michel Cormier and Achille Michaud, *Richard Hatfield: Power and Disobedience*, trans. Daphne Ponder (Fredericton: Goose Lane, 1992), 22; Richard Starr, *Richard Hatfield: The Seventeen-Year Saga* (Halifax: Formac Publishing, 1987), 52–3.

70 Allan Fotheringham, "A Very Political Mistress," *Maclean's*, 2 November 1987, 64.
71 Alden Nowlan, "Hatfield Country: Where a Politician Can Be Culturally Immersed without Drowning," *Maclean's*, November 1971, 80.
72 Later, Leon Stern won a $2.75 million breach-of-contract suit against Bricklin in a Philadelphia court, one that came to light only during the bankruptcy proceedings. "'Squeaky Clean' Boy Wonder," 3.
73 "Jonathan Livingston Bricklin: Cowboy's Plant Needs $8 million," *Financial Times*, 2 December 1974.
74 Chambers and Fredericks, *Bricklin*, 60; Jackie Webster, "The Little Car That Couldn't," *Maclean's*, 6 October 1975, 69.
75 Bruce Little, "The Bricklin … Bucking the Odds," *Windsor Star*, 17 August 1974.
76 Still Pickens [H.A. Fredericks], "Introduction," in *How to Brickle: The New Brunswick Funny Book* (Saint John, NB: Unipress, 1977), n.p.
77 Allan Fotheringham, "In Praise of Richard Hatfield," *Maclean's*, 13 May 1991, 68. Fotheringham had related the same story, almost word for word, in an earlier column in *Maclean's* ("A Very Political Mistress," 64).
78 Wood, "Hatfield's Politics of Fun," 22. For another view on the premier, see Greg Marquis, "The Hatfield Era in New Brunswick: The 'Politics of Fun'?" *Acadiensis Blog*, 3 May 2022, https://acadiensis.wordpress.com/2022/05/03/the-hatfield-era-in-new-brunswick-the-politics-of-fun/.
79 John Porteous, "Richard Hatfield: A Very Private Premier from the Proper Side of the Tracks," *Impetus*, June 1975, 13.
80 Ibid., 10.
81 New Brunswick, Synoptic Report of the Legislative Assembly of New Brunswick (*Hansard*), vol. 7, 9 December 1975, 2663–4; "'Squeaky Clean' Boy Wonder," 3.
82 "Car Conks, but Political Fight Is just Revving Up," *Financial Post*, 21 February 1976, 3; Legislative Assembly Debates, 9 December, 1975.
83 Allan Chambers, "Hatfield Rejects Call to Resign," *Fredericton Daily Gleaner*, 29 September 1975, 1; Frederick and Chambers, *Bricklin*, 122–3.
84 See, for example, New Brunswick, *Hansard*, vol. 7, 5 December 1975, 2626.
85 John Porteous, "Bricklin Workers Still Believe in 'Dream Car,'" *Financial Post*, 4 October 1975, 14.
86 Pickens, "Introduction," in *How to Brickle*; Still Pickens [H.A. Fredericks], "Introduction," in *Bricklemanship: The New Brunswick Grief Book* (Fredericton: Omega Publications, 1978).
87 Gwyn, "Hanging Out with Hatfield," 41.
88 Ibid.
89 David Folster, "A Rabbit with Elephantiasis," *Maclean's*, 5 March 1979, 22–3; David Folster, "Closing in for the Kill?" *Maclean's*, 8 September 1980, 24.
90 David Folster, "New Brunswick: Slimming down a Durable Tory," *Maclean's*, 7 July 1980, 30.
91 Starr, *Richard Hatfield*, 114–15; "Fredericton: Somebody's Got to Go," 4; Dorothy Dearborn, "Spring Election Unlikely after New Brunswick Resignations," *Financial Post*, 4 February 1978, 14.
92 Dorothy Dearborn, "Close Finish Likely in N.B. Election," *Financial Post*, 21 October 1978, 45.
93 Philip Mathais, "Richard Hatfield Faces Toughest Test Yet," *Financial Post*, 23 August 1978, 23.
94 From the *Saint John Telegraph-Journal* (*TJ*), 22 October 1978, as quoted in Starr, *Richard Hatfield*, 123.
95 Gwyn, "Hanging Out with Hatfield," 33.
96 Michael Clugston, "Acadia Returns the Favour," *Maclean's*, 3 October 1982, 22.

97 For one view on the pitch, see Fabien Guimtrandy and Thierry Burger-Helmchen, "The Pitch: Some Face-to-Face Minutes to Build Trust," *Administrative Sciences* 12, 47 (2022). See also Matthew S. Wood, David J. Scheaf, and Sean M. Dwyer, "Fake It 'Til You Make It: Hazards of a Cultural Norm in Entrepreneurship," *Business Horizons* 65, 5 (September–October, 2022): 681–96.

98 Winifred Morgan, *The Trickster Figure in American Literature* (New York: Palgrave Macmillan, 2013); Mac Linscott Ricketts, "The North American Indian Trickster," *History of Religions* 5 (Winter 1966): 327–50.

99 Karen Halttunen, *Confidence Men and Painted Women: A Study of Middle-Class Culture in America, 1830–1870* (New Haven, CT: Yale University Press, 1982); Irving Wallace, *The Fabulous Showman: The Life and Times of P.T. Barnum* (New York: Alfred A. Knopf, 1959), 3–4.

100 Halttunen, *Confidence Men and Painted Women*, chap. 1; Wallace, *The Fabulous Showman*, 120; Buford Adams, *E Pluribus Barnum: The Great Showman and the Making of Popular Culture* (Minneapolis: University of Minnesota Press, 1997), 1–2.

101 Brooks Atkinson, "Theatre Review: The Music Man," *New York Times*, 20 December 1957, 31.

102 For a small sample on these charismatics, see Kenneth D. Ackerman, *Boss Tweed: The Rise and Fall of the Corrupt Pol Who Conceived the Soul of Modern New York* (New York: Carroll & Graf Publishers, 2005); Richard D. White, *Kingfish: The Reign of Huey P. Long* (New York: Random House, 2006); Donald I. Warren, *Radio Priest: Charles Coughlin, the Father of Hate Radio* (New York: Free Press, 1996); David Elliott, *Bible Bill: A Biography of William Aberhart* (Edmonton: Reidmore Books, 1987); Alanna Nash, *The Colonel: The Extraordinary Story of Colonel Tom Parker and Elvis Presley* (New York: Simon & Schuster, 2003); Andrew Finstuen, Grant Wacker, and Anne Blue Wills, eds., *Billy Graham: American Pilgrim* (New York: Oxford University Press, 2017). The Graham book is divided into three sections, "Religion," "Politics," and "Culture." For another view of conmen in history, see Jane Savage Railey, *A Century of Swindles: Ponzi Schemes, Con Men, and Fraudsters* (Guiford, CT: Lyons Press, 2021). A more recent example of the politician/entertainer as conman is Maggie Haberman, *Confidence Man: The Making of Donald Trump and the Breaking of America* (New York: Penguin, 2022).

103 Edward J. Balleisen, *Fraud: An American History from Barnum to Madoff* (Princeton, NJ: Princeton University Press, 2017), 5. For another view, see Kurt Andersen, *Fantasyland: How America Went Haywire: A 500-Year History* (New York: Random House, 2017).

104 There is a vast literature on business practices and techniques such as salesmanship and promotion and their intersection with legal and illegal activities, particularly in financial services. See, for a small sampling, Friedman, *Birth of a Salesman*; Nicholas Lemann, *Transaction Man: The Rise of the Deal and the Decline of the American Dream* (New York: Farrar, Straus and Giroux, 2019); Christopher Armstrong, *Blue Skies and Boiler Rooms: Buying and Selling Securities in Canada, 1870–1940* (Toronto: University of Toronto Press, 1997).

105 Newman had also famously starred as poolshark "Fast Eddie" Felson in 1961's *The Hustler*. In 1979, the *Detroit Free Press* called Bricklin and John DeLorean "the Paul Newman and Robert Redford of the auto industry": Glenna McWhirter, "DeLorean, Bricklin Spin New Dreams," *Detroit Free Press*, 29 July 1979.

106 The historiography on Barnum is vast. In addition to the book by Harris and the other works cited above, see R. Werner, *Barnum* (New York: Harcourt, Brace, 1923); Philip Kunhardt and Peter W. Kunhardt, *P.T. Barnum: America's Greatest Showman* (New York: Knopf, 1995); and Timothy J. Lukes, *Politics and Beauty in America: The Liberal Aesthetics of P.T. Barnum, John Muir, and Harley Earl* (New York: Palgrave Macmillan, 2016).

107 As stated in *The Entrepreneur*. The film can be accessed on a variety of platforms.
108 "'Squeaky Clean' Boy Wonder," 3.
109 Hatfield, as quoted in Dugald Maudsley, dir., *The Bricklin: The Premier, the Promoter and Their Car* (episode, Turning Points of History, 2004).
110 "The Godfather" (editorial), *TJ*, 3 January 1975.
111 "'Squeaky Clean' Boy Wonder," 3.
112 The pursuit of this ideal included building a paean to the past at bucolic Greenfield Village, encouraging the rescue of quickly fading Midwestern square dancing, and constructing a "perfect" company town on the banks of the Amazon. On the first two examples, see Stephen Watts, *The People's Tycoon: Henry Ford and the American Century* (New York: A.A. Knopf, 2005), 421. On Fordlandia, his Brazilian company town, see Greg Grandin, *Fordlandia: The Rise and Fall of Henry Ford's Forgotten Jungle City* (New York: Metropolitan Books, 2009).
113 He had "always wanted to be a cowboy since [he] was a kid." Bricklin, as quoted in Maudsley, dir., *The Bricklin*.
114 Barbara Wilkins, "To the Top: Malcolm Bricklin and His Magic Car," *People*, 27 May 1974, 24–6.
115 "Eyecatchers: Don Quixote of Detroit,"42.
116 Lemann, *Transaction Man*.
117 The auto industry plays a central role in Tedlow's argument, with chapters on GM, Iacocca, and Elon Musk. See Richard S. Tedlow, *The Emergence of Charismatic Business Leadership* (New York: Rosetta Books, 2021).
118 As quoted in Rob Linke, "Malcolm Bricklin Dreams Big, Again," *TJ*, 4 May 2009, A1; Alex Taylor III, "This Year's Model: Malcolm Bricklin, Who Brought You the Yugo and the Subaru, Is Betting That Cars from China Will Rock the US," *Fortune*, 12 June 2006, 41.
119 "Malcolm Bricklin to Address Society of Automotive Analysts on Future of Auto Industry," *PR Newswire* (New York), 22 February 2005, 1.
120 Dahl, "Would You Buy a Chinese Car," 68.
121 See, for example, Malcolm Bricklin, "Guest Column: Plugged-in Approach Needs New, Switched-on Manufacturers," *Financial Times* (London), 6 March 2007, 1.
122 Linke, "Malcolm Bricklin Dreams Big," A1.
123 Lamm, "The Bricklin SV1 Sports Car!" 89–90.
124 C.E. Sawyer (Wespac Development Planning Corporation) to H. Nason, 28 April 1975, PANB, box 83, file 5600-B-14, "Reports of the Bricklin Project," 2.
125 Starr, *Richard Hatfield*, 88.
126 Nancy Southam, ed., *Remembering Richard: An Informal Portrait of Richard Hatfield by His Friends, Family and Colleagues* (Halifax: Formac, 1993), 26–7.
127 Ibid.
128 *Woodstock Bugle*, 7 April 1976, from Neil V. Rosenberg, "Goodtime Charlie and the Bricklin: A Satirical Song in Context," *Journal of the Canadian Oral History Association* 3, 1 (1978): 36. Russell became a member of the Bricklin International Owners Club in 1992, Vehicle Idenification Number 2792. Charlie Russell, "Not Another Edsel, No Siree!!!!!" *Brickline* 18, 2 (1993): 12–13.
129 Porteus, "Richard Hatfield," 8–10.
130 "Richard Hatfield: The Globe-Trotter and Bon Vivant Who's Been in Power for 11 Years," *Chatelaine*, September 1981, 105, emphasis in original.
131 Bricklin, as quoted in Maudsley, dir., *The Bricklin*.
132 John Kenneth Galbraith, *The Great Crash, 1929* (1955; Boston: Houghton Mifflin, 1997), 132–3.

133 J.L. Granatstein, *Yankee Go Home? Canadians and Anti-Americanism* (Toronto: HarperCollins, 1996).

134 See Stephen Azzi, *Walter Gordon and the Rise of Canadian Nationalism* (Montreal and Kingston: McGill-Queen's University Press, 1999) and Kari Levitt, *Silent Surrender: The Multinational Corporation in Canada* (Montreal and Kingston: McGill-Queen's University Press, 1970); on FIRA, Greg Donaghy, *Tolerant Allies: Canada and the United States, 1963–68* (Montreal and Kingston: McGill-Queen's University Press, 2003) and Robert Bothwell, *Alliance and Illusion: Canada and the World, 1945–84* (Vancouver: UBC Press, 2007).

135 Granatstein, *Yankee Go Home*; Stephen Azzi, *Reconcilable Differences: A History of Canada-US Relations* (Toronto: Oxford University Press, 2015); Robert Bothwell, *Your Country, My Country: A Unified History of the United States and Canada* (Toronto: Oxford University Press, 2015).

136 Cormier and Michaud, *Richard Hatfield*, 85.

137 Bricklin, as quoted in Maudsley, dir., *The Bricklin*; "Bricklin Trying to Make Break-Even Point Monthly," *Sherbrooke Record*, 4 July 1975, 2.

138 The poem can be found in "Bricklin Booster," letter to the *Saint John Times Globe*, 26 May 1975, PANB, Office of Richard Hatfield, box 83, file 5600-B-13, "Bricklin, Public Opinion and Responses." It was also quoted in the Bricklin workers' newsletter: see *Brickline* 1, 3 (1975): 5.

5. Sex (Gender)

1 Bricklin foresaw a total market potential of nearly 600,000 vehicles in the "sport" and "safety" categories, of which he aimed to have 30,000 sales by the firm's third year. "Bricklin Vehicle Corporation, and General Vehicle Inc.," Prospectus, n.d., National Automotive History Collection (NAHC), Detroit Public Library (DPL), file 1, box 1, series I, Bricklin Papers, exhibit B.

2 Author's interview with Malcolm Bricklin, 30 April 2013.

3 Douglas Brinkley, *Wheels for the World: Henry Ford, His Company, and a Century of Progress* (New York: Penguin Books, 2003).

4 Both the US and Canadian populations became majority urban after 1920, according to each country's census. Ellen K. Rothman, *Hands and Hearts: A History of Courtship in America* (Cambridge, MA: Harvard University Press, 1987).

5 Beth Bailey, "From Front Porch to Back Seat: A History of the Date," *Magazine of History* 18, 4 (2004): 23–6; Bailey, *From Front Porch to Back Seat: Courtship in Twentieth-Century America* (Baltimore: John Hopkins University Press, 1989).

6 David L. Lewis, "Sex and the Automobile: From Rumble Seats to Rockin' Vans," *Michigan Quarterly Review* 19, 4 (1980): 518, republished in David L. Lewis and Laurence Goldstein, eds., *The Automobile and American Culture* (Ann Arbor: University of Michigan Press, 1980).

7 Though race and the car are not a focus of this book, the field has a large literature. A small sample includes Gretchen Sorin, *Driving while Black: African American Travel and the Road to Civil Rights* (New York: Liveright Publishing, 2020); Cotten Seiler, *Republic of Drivers: A Cultural History of Automobility in America* (Chicago: University of Chicago Press, 2009); and Elizabeth Esch, *The Color Line and the Assembly Line: Managing Race in the Ford Empire* (Oakland: University of California Press, 2018).

8 Seiler, *Republic of Drivers*. Figures are from the Historical Statistics of the United States and Statistics Canada (various); see also Stephen Davies, "'Reckless Walking Must Be Discouraged':

The Automobile Revolution and the Shaping of Modern Urban Canada to 1930," *Urban History Review* 10, 2 (1989): 123–38.

9 "Nearly 40 percent of the nation's reluctant males are driven to pop the question while riding, wheeling or parking in a car," according to a 1967 *Motor Trend* survey of 1,100 marriages: James Joseph, "Sex and the Single Car," *Motor Trend*, April 1967, 45; Laurie Essig, *Love, Inc.: Dating Apps, the Big White Wedding, and Chasing the Happily Neverafter* (Berkeley: University of California Press, 2019), 143; Karen Dubinsky, *The Second Greatest Disappointment: Honeymooning and Tourism at Niagara Falls* (New Brunswick, NJ: Rutgers University Press, 1999). On motels, see John A. Jakle, Keith A. Sculle, and Jefferson S. Rogers, *The Motel in America* (Baltimore: Johns Hopkins University Press, 1996).

10 The relationship was also documented extensively in photographic form, a rare and amazing record for historians of New Brunswick and queer history. See Meredith J. Bratt and Dusty Green, *Len and Cub: A Queer History* (Fredericton: Goose Lane Editions, 2022).

11 "Automobiles with Sex Appeal," *Literary Digest*, 2 March, 1929, 64.

12 As quoted in Lewis, "Sex and the Automobile," 518.

13 Quoted in Clay McShane, *The Automobile: A Chronology of Its Antecedents, Development, and Impact* (London: Routledge, 2013), 58.

14 Mark Laver, "Autoeroticism: Sex, Cars, and Jazz," in *Jazz Sells: Music, Marketing, and Meaning* (London: Routledge, 2005), 91; Helen Lynd and Robert Lynd, *Middletown: A Study of Modern American Culture* (1929; San Diego: Harcourt Brace Javanovich, 1959), 114; James A. Wren, Jeffrey I. Godshall, Michael J. Kollins, James K. Wagner, and Anthony J. Yanik, "The Automobile: The Unwanted Child," SAE Technical Paper Series 98, 4 (1987): 416–45; James Flink, *The Automobile Age* (Cambridge, MA: MIT Press, 1990), 159, 160; Peter Ling, "The Making of the American Dream: Sex and the Automobile in the Jazz Age," *History Today* 39, 11 (1989): 18–24.

15 For more on the impact of the car, see John Heitmann, *The Automobile and American Life* (Jefferson, NC: McFarland, 2009).

16 Lawrence B. Finer, "Trends in Premarital Sex in the United States, 1954–2003," *Public Health Reports* 122, 1 (2007): 73–8; Gary S. Cross, *Machines of Youth: America's Car Obsession* (Chicago: University of Chicago Press, 2018), especially chap. 4, "Cruising and Parking: The Peer Culture of Teen Automobility, 1950–70," Lewis, "Sex and the Automobile," 525. "Blueberry Hill" was written in 1940.

17 Scott Patrick Moyers, "Going Nowhere Fast: The Car, the Highway and American Identity in Vladimir Nabokov's 'Lolita' and Robert Frank's 'The Americans'" (MA thesis, College of William and Mary, 1997).

18 Tom Wolfe, *The Kandy-Kolored Tangerine-Flake Streamline Baby* (1963; New York: Picador, 2009), 78, emphasis added. Kenneth Charles Blaisdell, "Keepers of the Flame: A Search for a Values in the Magazines of the Car-Culture (Automobiles)" (PhD diss., Rensselaer Polytechnic Institute, 1984).

19 Roland Marchand, *Advertising the American Dream: Making Way for Modernity, 1920–1940* (Berkeley: University of California Press, 1985), 22.

20 David Gartman, *Auto Opium: A Social History of American Automobile Design* (London: Routledge, 1994), 173. See also "Automobiles with Sex Appeal," 64.

21 There is a vast literature on Elvis. On his sexuality, see, for example, April Long, "Elvis: The Sex God," *Vox*, 1 August 1997: 62; Sharon Cowan, "The Elvis We Deserve: The Social Regulation of Sex/Gender and Sexuality through Cultural Representations of 'The King,'" *Law, Culture and the Humanities* 6, 2 (2010): 221–44. The "hoochy-koochy" quote is from Jack Gould, "TV: New

Phenomenon Elvis Presley Rises to Fame as Vocalist Who Is Virtuoso of Hootchy-Kootchy," *New York Times*, 26 November 1956, 36.

22 Lewis, "Sex and the Automobile," 526

23 J.G. Ballard, *Crash* (London: Johnathan Cape, 1973), made into an equally controversial 1996 film by David Cronenberg.

24 Charles Sanford, "'Woman's Place' in American Car Culture," *Michigan Quarterly Review* 19, 4 (1980): 532–47.

25 For a small sample, see Georgine Clarsen, "Gender and Mobility: Historicizing the Terms," in *Mobility in History: The State of the Art in the History of Transport, Traffic, and Mobility*, ed. Gijs Mom, Gordon Pirie, and Laurent Tissot (Neuchâtel, CH: Editions Alphil – Presses Universitaires Suisses, 2009); Virginia Scharf, *Taking the Wheel: Women and the Coming of the Motor Age* (New York: Free Press, 1991); Katherine J. Parkin, *Women at the Wheel: A Century of Buying, Driving, and Fixing Cars* (Philadelphia: University of Pennsylvania Press, 2017); Georgine Clarsen, *Eat My Dust: Early Women Motorists* (Baltimore: Johns Hopkins University Press, 2008); Maude-Emmanuelle Lambert, "Québécoises et Ontariennes en voiture! L'expérience culturelle et spatiale de l'automobile au féminin (1910–1945)," *Revue d'histoire de l'Amérique française* 63, 2–3 (2009–10): 305–30.

26 Margaret Walsh, "Gendering Mobility: Women, Work and Automobility in the United States," *History* 93, 3 (2008): 380; Bailey, *From Front Porch to Back Seat*; Stephen Bayley, *Sex, Drink, and Fast Cars: The Creation and Consumption of Images* (Boston: Faber and Faber, 1986); Heon Stevenson, *Selling the Dream: Advertising the American Automobile, 1930–1980* (London: Academy, 1995).

27 Kat Eschner, "Before She Was an Etiquette Authority, Emily Post Was a Road Warrior," *Smithsonian Magazine*, 11 September 2017, https://www.smithsonianmag.com/smart-news /she-was-etiquette-authority-emily-post-was-road-warrior-180964806/.

28 Richard M. Clark, "Dick Humbird and the Devil Wagon of Doom: Cars, Carnivores, and Feminine Carnality in This Side of Paradise," *F. Scott Fitzgerald Review* 11, 1 (2013): 34.

29 McShane, *The Automobile*, 55.

30 On Filumena Lassandro, see Dimitry Anastakis, *Death in the Peaceable Kingdom: Canadian History through Murder, Execution, Assassination and Suicide from Confederation to the War on Terror* (Toronto: University of Toronto Press, 2015), 119–28.

31 Jane Nicholas, *The Modern Girl: Feminine Modernities, the Body, and Commodities in the 1920s* (Toronto: University of Toronto Press, 2014), 184–5.

32 Walsh, "Gendering Mobility," 381; Laura L. Behling, "'The Woman at the Wheel': Marketing Ideal Womanhood, 1915–1934," *Journal of American Culture* 20, 3 (1997): 13–14.

33 Parkin, *Women at the Wheel*, x; Walsh, "Gendering Mobility"; Elaine Tyler May, *Homeward Bound: American Families in the Cold War Era* (1988; New York: Basic Books, 2018); Ruth Roach Pearson, *"They're Still Women After All": The Second World War and Canadian Womanhood* (Toronto: McClelland & Stewart, 1986).

34 Not until the 1980s did car manufacturers directly target auto categories to women's tastes. Walsh, "Gendering Mobility," 380, 388; Margaret Walsh, "Gender and Automobility: Selling Cars to American Women after the Second World War," *Journal of Macromarketing* 31, 1 (2011): 57–72; "Somewhere West of Laramie: Women in the Driver's Seat," *Chatelaine*, November 1986, 4; Victoria Vantoch, *The Jet Sex Airline Stewardesses and the Making of an American Icon* (Philadelphia: University of Pennsylvania Press, 2013).

35 See Parkin, "Cars as Female," in *Women at the Wheel*, 147–53; Karal Ann Marling, "America's Love Affair with the Automobile in the Television Age," in *Autopia: Cars and Culture*, ed. Peter Wollen and Joe Kerr (London: Reaktion Books, 2002), 356. See also H. Karmasin, "Ernest

Dichter's Studies on Automobile Marketing," in *Ernest Dichter and Motivation Research*, ed S. Schwarzkopf and R. Gries (London: Palgrave Macmillan, 2010), 109–125.

36 Charles K. Hyde, *Storied Independent Automakers: Nash, Hudson, and American Motors* (Detroit: Wayne State University Press, 2009).

37 Frank A. Salamone, *Popular Culture in the Fifties* (New York: University Press of America, 2001), 55; Blaisdell, "Keepers of the Flame," 128; Jerry W. Passon, *The Corvette in Literature and Culture: Symbolic Dimensions of America's Sports Car* (Jefferson, NC: McFarland, 2011).

38 Gartman, *Auto Opium*, 174.

39 Randy Leffingwell and Darwin Holmstrom, *The Muscle Car: History of American Performance Cars* (St. Paul, MN: Crestline, 2007); William Mckinney, "The Classic Muscle Car Era" (MA thesis, Clemson University, 2009).

40 Elaine Tyler May, *America and the Pill: A History of Promise, Peril, and Liberation* (New York: Basic Books, 2010); Carl Djerassi, *This Man's Pill: Reflections on the 50th Birthday of the Pill* (New York: Oxford University Press, 2001).

41 Margaret Walsh, "At Home at the Wheel? The Woman and Her Automobile in the 1950s," *Third Eccles Centre Plenary Lectures Given at the American Studies Annual Conference, 2006* (London, 2007).

42 See, for example, S.L. Bottles, *Los Angeles and the Automobile: The Making of a Modern City* (Berkeley: University of California Press, 1987) and Dean Ruffilli, "The Car in Canadian Culture, 1898–1983" (PhD diss., University of Western Ontario, 2006).

43 Chris Dummitt, *The Manly Modern: Masculinity in Postwar Canada* (Vancouver: UBC Press, 2007), especially chap. 5, "On the Road" and (though the author has brought into question his own work) his "A Crash Course in Manhood: Men, Cars, and Risk in Postwar Vancouver," in *The Sixties: Passion, Politics and Style*, ed. Dimitry Anastakis (Montreal and Kingston: McGill-Queen's University Press, 2009), 71–98.

44 The 1970 Dodge Charger 500 Commercial can be seen at https://www.youtube.com/watch?v=R5IM5YaCVlI&t=55s.

45 Margery Krevsky, *Sirens of Chrome: The Enduring Allure of Auto Show Models* (Pontiac, MI: Momentum Books, 2008).

46 There is a gigantic trove of books about American muscle cars, sports cars, and racing.

47 Ken Purdy, "The Complete Sports Car Stable," *Playboy*, April 1957, 23; "*Playboy*'s Sports Car Jacket," *Playboy*, May 1960, 45; Jeff Perez, "Playboy Was Named after a Car Company, and Its Legacy Reflects That," Motor1.com, 28 September 2017, https://www.motor1.com/features/181911/hugh-hefner-playboy-automotive-legacy/; the GTO quote is from Parkin, *Women at the Wheel*, 148.

48 Elizabeth Fraterrigo, *Playboy and the Making of the Good Life in Modern America* (New York: Oxford University Press, 2011), 65, 67.

49 "Safety Fast," *Playboy*, September 1974, 158–9.

50 Darren Dahl, "Would You Buy a Chinese Car from this Man?" *Inc.*, 1 July 2005, https://www.inc.com/magazine/20050701/disruptor-bricklin.html.

51 Brock Yates, "America's Other Sports Car," *Car and Driver*, July 1974, 31–3; Bricklin Promotional Brochure, Public Archivers of New Brunswick (PANB), Department of Commerce and Development, box 83, file 5321-1.

52 Michael Enright, "Wheeler-Dealer: How Mr. Bricklin Got His Dream Car and Mr. Hatfield Got the Bill," *Maclean's*, 17 November 1975, 55.

53 "Remarks by Harry A. Nason, Deputy Minister of Economic Growth, Public Accounts Committee Meeting, NB Legislative Assembly, 29 May 1975," PANB, Department of Commerce and Development, box 83, file 5321-1.

54 Hal Quinn, "Working without a Net," *Maclean's*, 18 February 1985, 17.
55 Don Sherman, "Chevrolet Corvette Stingray vs. Bricklin SV1: Americas Best Sports Car: Being 'Second' Doesn't' Necessarily Mean Being 'Last,'" *Car and Driver*, 1 May 1975, 41.
56 Ron Wakefield, "Bricklin SV1," *Road & Track*, April 1975, 72; Yates, "America's Other Sports Car," 31–3; Bricklin Promotional Brochure, PANB, Department of Commerce and Development, box 83, file 5321-1.
57 "Safety Fast," 158.
58 Judith Brannen, "The Maritime Singer Six: New Brunswick Had Its Own Car 124 Years before the Bricklin," *Atlantic Advocate*, May 1975, 12.
59 Dugald Maudsley, dir., *The Bricklin: The Premier, The Promoter and Their Car* (episode, *Turning Points of History*, 2004); Andy Holloway, "Malcolm Bricklin: 'When You're Succeeding, You Tend to Get the Feeling You Know More Than You Know,'" *Canadian Business*, 17 February 2003.
60 Author's interview with Malcolm Bricklin, 6 April 2013.
61 Enright, "Wheeler-Dealer," 55.
62 Richard Starr, *Richard Hatfield: The Seventeen-Year Saga* (Halifax: Formac Publishing, 1987), 85.
63 Ron Wakefield, "Bricklin on the Bricklin," *Road & Track*, April 1975, 70.
64 David Allyn, *Make Love Not War: The Sexual Revolution, an Unfettered History* (New York: Routledge, 2016), 232; "A Look Back at Burt Reynolds' Iconic Nude Photoshoot in *Cosmopolitan*," *Cosmopolitan*, 8 September 2018, https://www.cosmopolitan.com/entertainment/news/a48108/burt-reynolds-cosmo-classic/; Chadwick Lee Roberts, "Consuming Liberation: *Playgirl* and the Strategic Rhetoric of Sex Magazines for Women, 1972–1985" (PhD diss., Bowling Green State University, 2011).
65 Michel Cormier and Achille Michaud, *Richard Hatfield: Power and Disobedience*, trans. Daphne Ponder (Fredericton: Goose Lane, 1992), 85.
66 Fredericks, as quoted in Maudsley, dir., *The Bricklin*; the *Columbus Dispatch* would later refer to Bricklin as "the urban cowboy from Philadelphia": "Malcolm Bricklin" *Columbus Dispatch*, 19 June 2015, https://www.dispatch.com/story/news/2015/06/19/malcolm-bricklin/23670862007/.
67 Grasse, as quoted in Maudsley, dir., *The Bricklin*.
68 Marchand, *Advertising the American Dream*, 33, 161; Julian Pettifer and Nigel Turner, *Automania: Man and the Motor Car* (London: Collins, 1984), 130. Considered one of the most important, and famous, campaigns in advertising history, the Jordan ads have been discussed in numerous books and articles. See, in addition to Marchand's book, John B. Rae, *The American Automobile: A Brief History* (Chicago: University of Chicago Press, 1965), 48.
69 Ad for the Playboy, *Saturday Evening Post*, 23 June 1923.
70 In "Unlocking the Locked Step of Law and Morality," *Globe and Mail*, 12 December 1967, the editorialist wrote that "the state has no right or duty to creep into the bedrooms of the nation."
71 Doug Owram, *Born at the Right Time: A History of the Baby Boom Generation* (Toronto: University of Toronto Press, 1997), particularly chap. 10, "Sexual Revolutions and Revolutions of the Sexes, 1965–1793"; Allyn, *Make Love Not War*; Dimitry Anastakis, *Re-Creation, Fragmentation and Resilience: A Brief History of Canada since 1945* (Toronto: Oxford University Press, 2018), chap. 3, "Family Snapshot: Images and Realities of Ordinary Life."
72 Allyn, *Make Love Not War*, chap. 20, "Sexual Freedom on Demand"; Elana Levine, *Wallowing in Sex: The New Sexual Culture of 1970s American Television* (Chapel Hill, NC: Duke University Press, 2007).
73 Lewis, "Sex and the Automobile," 527; Keith Hammonds, "Drive-Ins, Like Cheap Gas, Fade into Yesteryear," *New York Times*, 30 May 1982, S4, 4; Virginia Matthews, "Sex That Didn't Sell: A Supermodel's Striptease for Citroen got a Reaction from Everyone but Car Buyers," *Marketing*

Magazine (Toronto), 10 May 1999, 24. While Claudia Schiffer protested that the director had "made the campaign dramatic and sexy as well as tasteful," the ad was roundly criticized.

74 Parkin, *Women at the Wheel*, 174–5. In her chapter "Masculinity as a Vehicle," Elizabeth C. Hirschman explores the gendered meanings of Harley-Davidson motorcycles, the Ford F-150 truck, and the Ford Mustang, "the surviving member of the 1960s phenomenon of the 'muscle car'": *Branding Masculinity: Tracing the Cultural Foundations of Brand Meaning* (New York: Routledge, 2016), 41. In the early twenty-first century, Chrysler launched a series of ads that returned to an emphasis on muscle-car masculinity and American nationalism. Thanks to one of the anonymous reviewers for pointing this out.

75 Author's interview with Malcolm Bricklin, 30 April 2013.

76 Conor Flavey, "Foregrounds: Mapping Gay, Lesbian and Bisexual History in Fredericton, 1969–1992" (MA thesis, University of New Brunswick, 2015), 35.

77 "For a time, Hatfield's marriage plans – or lack of them – were a matter of some concern. One reporter even brought the subject up on election night, presumably because someone felt that a premier has to have a spouse. In the spring of 1972 when Trudeau gave up bachelorhood, it prompted questions in the Legislature about Hatfield's domestic plans." Starr, *Richard Hatfield*, 51. For another view of Hatfield, see John Porteus, "Richard Hatfield: A Very Private Premier from the Proper Side of the Tracks," *Impetus*, June 1975, 8–10.

78 Janet Cawley, "Politician Pays Price for Life on the Edge," *Chicago Tribune*, 25 March 1985, https://www.chicagotribune.com/news/ct-xpm-1985-03-25-8501160769-story.html.

79 Norm Atkins, as related in Nancy Southam, ed., *Remembering Richard: An Informal Portrait of Richard Hatfield by His Friends, Family and Colleagues* (Halifax: Formac, 1993), 114.

80 On Studio 54, see Anthony Haden-Guest, *The Last Party: Studio 54, Disco, and the Culture of the Night* (New York: William Morrow, 1997).

81 He claimed in one interview in 1980 with Joan Sutton of the *Toronto Star* that he had thought of getting married twice, both times before he was thirty. Starr, *Richard Hatfield*, 51. None of the biographies of Hatfield mention any romantic relationships with women.

82 Journalist Bill Fox recalled that "throughout his political career there was speculation about Hatfield's bachelor status. It was an earlier time, both in terms of public attitudes and in terms of journalistic genre. Reporters were content to respect Hatfield's right to a private life – an attitude that might find less favour with the 'gotcha' journalism of today." Bill Fox, in Southam, ed., *Remembering Richard*, 134.

83 Michael Valpy, "The Outing of Richard Hatfield," *Globe and Mail*, 21 July 1994, A2.

84 Allan Fotheringham, "In Praise of Richard Hatfield," *Maclean's*, 13 May 1991, 68. For a view on how the media and society's treatment of politicians' privacy changed over the course of the twentieth century in Canada, see Christopher Dummitt, *Unbuttoned: A History of Mackenzie King's Private Life* (Montreal and Kingston: McGill-Queen's University Press, 2017).

85 Cawley, "Politician Pays Price for Life on the Edge." As an aside, the author Sandra Gwyn, in discussing Hatfield's doll collection, once wrote that "when his collection of dolls became famous, all those snide, nudge-and-wink stories missed the point entirely." According to Gwyn, the point about the dolls wasn't what they said about his sexuality, but his personality and collecting sensibility: Gwyn, in Southam, ed., *Remembering Richard*, 91.

86 Dalton Camp, in Southam, ed., *Remembering Richard*, 12; Sandra Gwynn, "Hanging Out with Hatfield: The Happiest Premier, If Not the Best," *Saturday Night*, January–February 1979, 34.

87 Starr, *Richard Hatfield*, 161.

88 "Richard Hatfield: The Globe-Trotter and Bon Vivant Who's Been in Power for 11 Years," *Chatelaine*, September 1981, 59, 105, 110.

89 Gerald Regan in Southam, ed., *Remembering Richard*, 16–7.

90 David Adams Richards, in Southam, ed., *Remembering Richard*, 120.

91 Cormier and Michaud, *Richard Hatfield*, 282.

92 Valpy, "The Outing of Richard Hatfield," A2; "Gays 'Sad' about Hatfield's Silence," *Globe and Mail*, 14 July 1994, A4.

93 Valpy, "The Outing." During the Kingsclear Youth Training Centre sexual and physical abuse inquiry in 1994, Hatfield was also named, though his supporters dismissed the allegations as "outright lies." John DeMont with Brenda Bouw, "'A Sordid Soap Opera': A New Brunswick Inquiry into Sexual Abuse Reveals a Shameful Legacy," *Maclean's*, 18 July 1994, 14.

94 Gary Mason, "Is B.C. Ready for an Openly Gay Party Leader?" *Globe and Mail*, 22 January 2011, A10.

95 On the Klippert case, and postwar changes in attitudes towards sexuality, see Anastakis, *Re-Creation, Fragmentation and Resilience*, chap. 3.

96 See, for example, Michael E. Graydon, "'We Had Become a Community': Gays of Ottawa (go) and the Birth of Community, 1971–7," *Canadian Historical Review* 99, 1 (2018): 594–622.

97 Which is not to say that there was not a gay community in the province, one that was often facilitated by automobility. See, for example, the story of Leonard "Len" Keith and Joseph "Cub" Coates, and how access to a Model T created the mobility and privacy to explore same-sex relations in rural New Brunswick. Meredith J. Batt and Dusty Green, *Len and Cub: A Queer History* (Fredericton: Goose Lane, 2022), 66–9.

98 Joanna Everitt, "Mobilization on the Periphery: LGBT Activism and Success in Atlantic Canada," in *Queer Mobilizations: Social Movement Activism and Canadian Public Policy*, ed. Manon Tremblay (Vancouver: UBC Press, 2015), 125–42; V.J. Korinek, "'The Most Openly Gay Person for at Least a Thousand Miles': Doug Wilson and the Politicization of a Province, 1975–1983," *Canadian Historical Review* 84, 4 (December 2003): 517–50; V.J. Korinek, "'We're the Girls of the Pansy Parade': Historicizing Winnipeg's Queer Subcultures, 1930s–1970," *Histoire sociale/Social History* 45, 89 (May 2012): 117–55.

99 Flavey, "Foregrounds."

100 Tom Warner, *Never Going Back: A History of Queer Activism in Canada* (Toronto: University of Toronto Press, 2002).

101 P. Girard, "Sexual Orientation as a Human Rights Issue in Canada, 1969–1985," *Dalhousie Law Journal* 10 (1986): 267–81.

102 There is little scholarly material on New Brunswick's human rights history. On the Canadian history, see Dominique Clément, *Canada's Rights Revolution: Social Movements and Social Change, 1937–82* (Vancouver: UBC Press, 2008).

103 Valpy, "The Outing of Richard Hatfield," A2; "Gays 'Sad' about Hatfield's Silence," A4.

104 Flavey, "Foregrounds," 116–17.

105 Christabelle Sethna and Steve Hewitt, "Clandestine Operations: The Vancouver Women's Caucus, the Abortion Caravan, and the RCMP," *Canadian Historical Review* 90, 3 (2009): 463–95.

106 Beth Palmer, "'Lonely, Tragic, but Legally Necessary Pilgrimages': Transnational Abortion Travel in the 1970s," *Canadian Historical Review* 92, 4 (2011): 637–65; Christabelle Sethna, Beth Palmer, Katrina Ackerman, and Nancy Janovicek, "Choice, Interrupted: Travel and Inequality of Access to Abortion Services since the 1960s," *Labour / Le travail* 71 (Spring 2013): 29–48.

107 F.L. Morton, *Morgentaler v. Borowski: Abortion, the Charter and the Courts* (Toronto: McClelland & Stewart, 1992); Martine Perrault and Linda Cardinal, "Le droit au choix et le choix du droit: L'expérience de l'Ontario Coalition for Abortion Clinics et le jugement

Morgentaler," *Canadian Journal of Political Science / Revue canadienne de science politique* 29, 2 (1996): 243–67.

108 Katrina Ackerman, "'Not in the Atlantic Provinces': The Abortion Debate in New Brunswick, 1980–1987," *Acadiensis* 41, 1 (2012): 75–101; Lianne McTavish, "Abortion in New Brunswick," *Acadiensis* 44, 2 (2015): 107–30.

6. Business (The State)

1 Dimitry Anastakis, "The New Big Three," chap. 2 in *Autonomous State: The Struggle for a Canadian Car Industry from OPEC to Free Trade* (Toronto: University of Toronto Press, 2013); Joseph Kraft, "The Downsizing Decision," *New Yorker*, 27 April 1980, https://www.newyorker.com/magazine/1980/05/05/the-downsizing-decision.

2 On Chrysler's near demise, see Dimitry Anastakis, "The Last Automotive Entrepreneur? Lee Iacocca Saves Chrysler, 1978–1986," Business and Economic History Online, 2007, https://thebhc.org/last-automotive-entrepreneur-lee-iacocca-saves-chrysler-1978-1986-0.

3 David A. Hounshell, *From the American System to Mass Production, 1800–1932* (Baltimore: Johns Hopkins University Press, 1984), 11.

4 Alfred P. Sloan, *My Years with General Motors* (1964; Garden City, NY: Doubleday, 1990), 64, emphasis added. See also John Macdonald, *A Ghost's Memoir: The Making of Alfred P. Sloan's "My Years with General Motors"* (Cambridge, MA: MIT Press, 2002).

5 Lech Gąsiorkiewicz and Jan Monkiewicz, eds., *Innovation in Financial Services: Balancing Public and Private Interests* (New York: Routledge, 2001). Daniel Bell, *New York Review*, 30 April 1964, cited as Sloan quote in W.D. Baasal, *Preliminary Chemical Engineering Plant Design* (Dordrecht, NL: Springer Dordrecht, 1990), 406; J. Rowe, "Why the Engineers Left the Shop Floor," *Washington Monthly*, June 1984; Samuel Evan Milner, *Robbing Peter to Pay Paul: Power, Profits, and Productivity in Modern America* (New Haven, CT: Yale University Press, 2021).

6 For an excellent analysis of this process, see James M. Rubenstein, *Making and Selling Cars: Innovation and Change in the US Automotive Industry* (Baltimore: Johns Hopkins University Press, 2001).

7 On the Chrysler bailout, see Anastakis, *Autonomous State*, chap. 5.

8 On the auto pact and its impact, see Anastakis, *Auto Pact: Creating a Borderless North American Auto Industry, 1960–1971* (Toronto: University of Toronto Press, 2005) and Anastakis, *Autonomous State*.

9 There are many books on the Model T and its impact. One example is Robert Casey, *The Model T: A Centennial History* (Baltimore: Johns Hopkins University Press, 2008).

10 As quoted in Vincent Curcio, *Henry Ford* (New York: Oxford University Press, 2013), 105, emphasis added.

11 On the five-dollar day, see, for example, Stephen Meyer, *The Five Dollar Day: Labor Management and Social Control at the Ford Motor Company, 1908–1921* (Albany: SUNY Press, 1981). On Ford and the Great Migration, see Heather Barrow, *Henry Ford's Plan for the American Suburb: Dearborn and Detroit* (Ithaca, NY: Cornell University Press, 2021), particularly chap. 5, "The Lives of Automobile Workers."

12 For another view on this matter, see John Betton and Thomas J. Hench, "'Any Color as Long as It's Black': Henry Ford and the Ethics of Business," *Journal of Genocide Research* 4, 4 (2000): 533–41. On his fight over the Selden patent, see Wiliam Greenleaf, with an introduction by David L. Lewis, *Monopoly on Wheels: Henry Ford and the Selden Patent* (1961; Detroit: Wayne State University Press, 2011). On the battle with the Dodge brothers, see Charles K. Hyde, *The*

Dodge Brothers: The Men, the Motor Cars, and the Legacy (Detroit: Wayne State University Press, 2005). On the reaction to the five-dollar day, see Stefan J. Link, *Forging Global Fordism* (Princeton, NJ: Princeton University Press, 2020), 41.

13 See, for example, Jacob Anbinder, "Selling the World: Public Relations and the Global Expansion of General Motors, 1922–40," *Business History Review* 92, 3 (2018): 483–507.

14 Including, through the foundations established by each man, philanthropy, education, historical preservation, and other forms of corporate power.

15 *Hearings before the Committee on Armed Services, United States Senate*, "Nominees Designate – Charles E. Wilson to be Secretary of Defense … Tuesday January 15, 1953" (Washington, DC: US Government Printing Office, 1953), 26.

16 The famous misquote has a history of its own. See, for example, John Steele Gordon, "The Ordeal of Engine Charlie," *American Heritage* 46, 1 (1995), https://www.americanheritage.com/ordeal-engine-charlie. See also Ellen Terrell, "When a Quote Is Not (Exactly) a Quote: General Motors," *Inside Adams: Science, Technology and Business*, Library of Congress Blogs, 22 April 2016, https://blogs.loc.gov/inside_adams/2016/04/when-a-quote-is-not-exactly-a-quote-general-motors/. For another view, see Richard S. Tedlow, *The Emergence of Charismatic Business Leadership* (New York: Rosetta Books, 2021), chap. 3. The Wilson misquote is also featured in Vaclav Smil, *Made in the USA: The Rise and Retreat of American Manufacturing* (Cambridge, MA: MIT Press, 2013), ix.

17 Edward S. Herman, *Corporate Control, Corporate Power* (New York: Cambridge University Press, 1981), 265–7; Donald E. Schwartz, "The Public-Interest Proxy Contest: Reflections on Campaign GM," *Michigan Law Review* 69, 3 (January 1971): 419–538; Eileen Shanahan, "G.M. Urged to Respond to Public Need," *New York Times*, 22 February 1970, 49; Herbert Mitgang, "G.M. Challenged on 'Responsibility,'" *New York Times*, 17 May 1970, 129.

18 Milton Friedman, "The Social Responsibility of Business Is to Increase Its Profits," *New York Times Magazine*, 13 September 1970, SM17.

19 On the article, its impact, and responses, see, for example, Sean McAleer, "Friedman's Stockholder Theory of Corporate Moral Responsibility," *Teaching Business Ethics* 7 (2003): 437–51; Thomas Carson, "Friedman's Theory of Corporate Social Responsibility," *Business and Professional Ethics Journal* 12, 1 (1993): 3–32; Glenn Feldman, "Putting Uncle Milton to Bed: Reexamining Milton Friedman's Essay on the Social Responsibility of Business," *Labor Studies Journal* 32, 2 (2007): 125–41; and "Greed Is Good. Except When It's Bad," *New York Times*, 13 September 2020, https://www.nytimes.com/2020/09/13/business/dealbook/milton-friedman-essay-anniversary.html. The "staple" remark is from McAleer, "Friedman's Stockholder Theory," 437.

20 Marilyn Bender, "Catching the Conscience of the Corporation: Activists Losing Votes but Gaining Recognition," *New York Times*, 5 May 1972, 57; Schwartz, "Public-Interest Proxy Contest," 430. See also Donald E. Schwartz, "Proxy Power and Social Goals: How Campaign GM Succeeded," *Saint John's Law Review* 4, 45 (May 1971), 764–71; General Motors, *1971 Annual Report* (Detroit: GM Corporation, 1971), 9.

21 Hillel Levin, *John DeLorean: The Maverick Mogul* (London: Orbis Publishing, 1983), 72–5; see also J. Patrick Wright and John Z. DeLorean, *On a Clear Day You Can See General Motors: John Z. DeLorean's Look Inside the Automotive Giant* (London: Sidgwick & Jackson, 1979).

22 On the ascendence of the financial men, see Robert Freeland, *The Struggle for the Modern Corporation: Organizational Change at General Motors, 1924–1970* (New York: Cambridge University Press, 2011), especially 285–6.

23 Jerry M. Flint, "Man in Business," *New York Times*, 12 December 1971, F5.

24 As with the Charles Wilson misquote, the provenance of Murphy's alleged statement is difficult to discern, yet it has been credited to him numerous times. See, for example, Maria Aluchna,

"Corporate Governance Theories: A Synthesis," in *Transforming Governance: New Values, New Systems in the New Business Environment* ed. Maria Aluchna and Güler Aras (London: Routledge, 2015), 16; Andrzej Sopoćko, "The Central Bank Feeding the Budget: The Heresy That Must Become Routine," in *Innovation in Financial Services: Balancing Public and Private Interests* ed. Lech Gąsiorkiewicz and Jan Monkiewicz (London: Routledge, 2021), 104. The sentence "The point is that General Motors is not in business to make cars, but to make money" was written by Daniel Bell in a 1964 response to economist Harry Johnson about the former's review of *My Years with General Motors* in the *New York Review*, 30 April, 1964.

25 Jerry M. Flint, "Ford Says Company Profit Is its Social Responsibility," *New York Times*, 12 May 1972, 55.

26 See, for example, Youn Ki, "Large Industrial Firms and the Rise of Finance in Late Twentieth-Century America," *Enterprise & Society* 19, 4 (2018): 903–45; Milner, *Robbing Peter to Pay Paul*; and Rana Foroohar, *Makers and Takers: The Rise of Finance and the Fall of American Business* (New York: Crown Publishing Group, 2016). Foroohar's second chapter, "The Fall of Business," and includes sections entitled "Bean Counters vs Car Guys" and "Robert McNamara, and the Financialization of Industry." See also Mark S. Mizruchi, *The Fracturing of the American Corporate Elite* (Cambridge, MA: Harvard University Press, 2013) and Per Hansen, "From Finance Capitalism to Financialization: A Cultural and Narrative Perspective on 150 Years of Financial History," *Enterprise & Society* 15, 4 (2014): 605–42.

27 See, for example, Nicholas Lemann, *Transaction Man: The Rise of the Deal and the Decline of the American Dream* (New York: Farrar, Straus and Giroux, 2019).

28 Seymour Melman, *Profits without Production* (New York: Alfred Knopf, 1983), xii.

29 Ibid., xvii.

30 David Halberstam, *The Reckoning* (New York: William Morrow, 1986), 45; Eric Rolfe Greenberg, "David Halberstam, *The Reckoning* (review)," *Management Review* 76, 1 (1987): 63.

31 Steve Spence, "Adventures along the 'Yellow Bricklin Road,'" *Motor Trend*, November 1974, 62, emphasis in original.

32 Bob Clift, "Speaking of Engineering: BVC Final Report, Western Cooling Trip, May 1973, 28 June, 1973," reproduced in *Brickline* 20, 3 (1995): 4–5.

33 For an excellent overview, see Rubenstein, *Making and Selling Cars.*

34 On Kaiser, see Richard M. Langworth, *Kaiser-Frazer: The Last Onslaught on Detroit* (New York: Automobile Quarterly, 1975); on Tucker, see Charles T. Pearson, *The Indomitable Tin Goose: The True Story of Preston Tucker and His Car* (New York: Motorbooks International Publishers, 1974) and Phillip S. Egan, *Design and Destiny: The Making of the Tucker Automobile* (Orange, CA: On the Mark Publications, 1989). "A Promoter Cranks Up a New Car," *Business Week*, 27 April 1974, 44.

35 The classic statement on the emergence of the m-division is Alfred D. Chandler's *Strategy and Structure: Chapters in the History of American Industrial Enterprise* (Cambridge, MA: MIT Press, 1962). Bricklin's organizational chart can be found in "Provincial Holdings Ltd., Bricklin Canada, General," Public Archives of New Brunswick (PANB), Bricklin Collection, vol. 23, box 384.

36 H.A. Fredericks and Allan Chambers, *Bricklin* (Potters Bark, UK: Brunswick Press, 1977), 14.

37 Clifford E. Sawyer, a management consultant hired by New Brunswick to advise the firm (and who became a director), told Bricklin that he "had no idea of the original logic concerned with the selection of Scottsdale as a key location," and in August 1975 he recommended moving the headquarters to Detroit (Livonia). G.E. Sawyer to Malcolm Bricklin, 18 August 1975, PANB, box 514, file "Correspondence/Malcolm Bricklin," no. I; "Confidential Review of Bricklin Mexico, S.A., February, 1975," National Automotive History Collection (NAHC), Detroit Public Library (DPL), series I, box 1, file 8.

38 Author's interview with Malcolm Bricklin, 13 April 2013.
39 Walter Friedman, *Birth of a Salesman* (Cambridge, MA: Harvard University Press, 2004), 218.
40 See, for example, "Minutes of the Meeting of the Board of Directors of Bricklin Canada Ltd.," 22 April 1975, PANB, box 514, file April 21 1975, no. I.
41 "Government of New Brunswick, Department of Economic Growth: A Report – The Bricklin Project," 28 May 1975, NAHC, DPL, series I, box 1, file 10, 20.
42 Ibid.
43 Bricklin/GVI, "Stock Prospectus," n.d., NAHC, DPL, accension 57, series I, box 1, MS57, Bricklin Canada Limited, 11–12.
44 PANB, box 83, file "Bricklin."
45 "Bricklin 'Risky' but Could Pay Off," *Saint John Evening Times Globe*, 5 September 1974.
46 Bruce Wennerstrom, "Motoring World: Yes, There Really Is a Bricklin," *Autoweek and Competition Press*, 5 October 1974, 9.
47 "Remarks by Harry A. Nason ...," Public Accounts Committee Meeting, New Brunswick Legislative Assembly, 29 May 1975, 2, PANB, box 83, file 5600-B1, "Bricklin, General; "Bricklin/GVI, "Stock Prospectus," n.d., NAHC, DPL, accension 57, series I, box 1, MS57, Bricklin Canada Limited, 11–12.
48 Darren Dahl, "Would You Buy a Chinese Car from This Man?" *Inc.*, 1 July 2005, https://www.inc.com/magazine/20050701/disruptor-bricklin.html.
49 Author's interview with Malcolm Bricklin, 30 April 2013. DeLorean is covered in more detail in chapter 7.
50 "Top Bricklin Appointment Supported by Government," *Moncton Times*, 15 January 1975.
51 C.E. Sawyer (Wespac Development Planning Corporation), "Note to File," 13 September 1975, PANB, box 83, file 5600-B-14, "Reports of the Bricklin Project," 3.
52 Ibid.
53 Sanford Borins with Lee Brown, *Investments in Failure: Five Government Corporations That Cost the Canadian Taxpayer Billions* (Toronto: Methuen, 1986), 44; H.A. Fredericks, as quoted in Dugald Maudsley, dir., *The Bricklin: The Premier, the Promoter and Their Car* (episode of *Turning Points of History*, 2004).
54 Press Release, n.d, NAHC, DPL, file 2, Press Kits and Press Releases, box 5.
55 "Province Has Majority of Bricklin Directors," *Fredericton Daily Gleaner*, 20 March 1975.
56 Wick Humble, "1975 Bricklin SV: Plastic Fantastic or Gull-Winged Turkey?" *Special Interest Autos*, April 1982, 44.
57 On the close relationship between Ford and Bennett, see Stephen Watts, *The People's Tycoon: Henry Ford and the American Century* (New York: Vintage Books, 2006), 451. See also Stephen Norwood, "Ford's Brass Knuckles: Harry Bennett, The Cult of Muscularity, and Anti-Labor Terror, 1920–1945," *Labor History* 37, 3 (1996): 365–91.
58 Dahl, "Would You Buy a Chinese Car?"
59 Friedman, *Birth of a Salesman*, 10.
60 Friedman's excellent *Birth of a Salesman* begins with an epigraph about auto dealers and the First World Salesmanship Congress in 1916, held in Detroit, with Henry Ford in attendance. The book prominently features automobile salesmanship, including at 209–24. See also Sally Clarke, *Trust and Power: Consumers, the Modern Corporation, and the Making of the United States Automobile Market* (Cambridge: Cambridge University Press, 2007), chap. 6.
61 Roger Worth, "Bricklin's Plunge Leaves Skid Marks $30 Million Long," *Financial Post*, 21 February 1976, 3.

62 There is a large literature on Highland Park and the assembly line. A small sample includes Marc Greuther, "Present at the Creation: Ford Highland Park Plant, 23 March 1914, 9:20 A.M.," *Technology and Culture* 45, 1 (2004): 120–2; April Key Jacques, "Inside the Crystal Palace: A History of Henry Ford's Highland Park Plant" (MA thesis, University of Michigan, 2008); and David E. Nye, *America's Assembly Line* (Cambridge, MA: MIT Press, 2013). For a view that challenges the "myth" of Ford's assembly line, see Karel Williams, Colin Haslam, John Williams, Andy Adcroft, and Sukhdev Johal, "The Myth of the Line: Ford's Production of the Model T at Highland Park, 1909–16," *Business History* 35, 3 (1993): 66–87.

63 John Porteous, "Brooklyn Goes Public – in PR," *Financial Post*, 28 June 1975, C6. On factories, see Joshua Benjamin Freeman, *Behemoth: A History of the Factory and the Making of the Modern World* (New York: W.W. Norton, 2018).

64 This was a great irony, in that Henry Ford had initially been obsessed with rooting out wastefulness. See Tom McCarthy, "Henry Ford: Take-Back, Waste Reduction, and Recycling at the Rouge," *Progress in Industrial Ecology* 3, 4 (2006): 302–28.

65 James P. Womack, David Jones, and Daniel Roos, *The Machine That Changed the World: The Story of Lean Production* (New York: Free Press, 1990). See also Masaaki Imai, *Kaizen: The Key to Japan's Competitive Success* (New York: McGraw-Hill, 1986).

66 Bricklin Promotional Brochure, PANB, Department of Commerce and Development, box 83, file 5321-1.

67 Donald E. Hegland, "Building the Bricklin – A Sports Car Is Born," *Automation: The Production Engineering Magazine*, June 1975, 44. Barry Barton, another American brought in from AMC who started as head of production scheduling at Saint John in April of 1975, remarked that "it's nice to have one homogenous product to work with and it becomes a production planner's dream." GS Wheatley, "Trip Report, Minto, NB," 10 April 1975, PANB, Department of Economic Growth, box 556, file 43-1725, vol. 9, February–April 1975.

68 For a view of modularization and its different elements, see Akira Takeishi and Takahiro Fujimoto, "Modularization in the Car Industry: Interlinked Multiple Hierarchies of Product, Production, and Supplier Systems," in *The Business of Systems Integration*, ed. Andrea Prencipe, Andrew Davies, and Michael Hobday (London: Oxford, 2003), 254–78; J. Pandremenos, J. Paralikas, K. Salonitis, G. Chryssolouris, "Modularity Concepts for the Automotive Industry: A Critical Review," *CIRP Journal of Manufacturing Science and Technology* 1, 3 (2009): 148–52.

69 Rubenstein, *Making and Selling Cars*, 98; Michael Schwartz, "Markets, Networks, and the Rise of Chrysler in Old Detroit, 1920–1940," *Enterprise & Society* 1, 1 (2000): 63–99.

70 Dimitry Anastakis, "Building a 'New Nova Scotia': State Intervention, the Auto Industry, and the Case of Volvo in Halifax, 1963–1996," *Acadiensis* 34, 1 (2004): 3–30.

71 Jesse LeCavalier, *The Rule of Logistics: Walmart and the Architecture of Fulfillment* (Minneapolis: University of Minnesota Press, 2016).

72 Mohammed A. Omar, *The Automotive Body Manufacturing Systems and Processes* (Chichester, UK: John Wiley & Sons, 2011).

73 On the complexities of stamping and painting, see Rubenstein, *Making and Selling Cars*, 101–2; on Henry Ford's famous statement about car colours, see Douglas Brinkley, *Wheels for the World: Henry Ford, His Company, and a Century of Progress* (New York: Penguin Books, 2003), 181–2. Author's interview with Malcolm Bricklin, 30 April 2013.

74 On the celebration, see Jackie Webster, "Spotlight on N.B.," *Atlantic Advocate*, October 1974, 36.

75 For one view of Saint John, see Bonnie Huskins and Michael Boudreau, "Irresponsibility, Obligation, and the Manly Modern: Tensions in Working-Class Masculinities in Postwar Saint John, New Brunswick," *Labour / Le travail* 78 (Fall 2016): 165–96.
76 G.S. Wheatley to H.A. Nason, "Bricklin Canada Ltd." 27 December 1974, PANB, box 83, file 5321-2, "Bricklin, Financial."
77 Department of Economic Growth, "Memorandum to Cabinet: Advance of Funds to PHL, $1,000,000," 6 November 1974, PANB, box 83, file 5600-B-2, "Bricklin, Financial Agreements," vol. I, 1974.
78 See, for example, Freeman, *Behemoth*, 237, which addresses GM's decentralization strategies.
79 Terry Tanner, as quoted in Maudsley, dir., *The Bricklin*.
80 "Confidential: Bricklin Canada Ltd., Briefing Report," 14 March 1975, PANB, box 83, file 5600-B-14, "Reports of the Bricklin Project," 9.
81 G.S. Wheatley to File, "Trip Report: Detroit–New York, November 27–30, 1973," 6 December 1973, PANB, box 83, file 5600-B1, "Bricklin, General."
82 "Bricklin SV1 Road Test," *Road & Track*, April 1975, 83.
83 Robert Ankli and Fred Frederickson, "The Influence of American Manufacturers on the Canadian Automobile Industry," *Business and Economic History* 10 (1981): 110.
84 R.H. Coase, "The Acquisition of Fisher Body by General Motors," *Journal of Law and Economics* 43, 1 (2000): 15–32.
85 Society of Automotive Engineers, *A History of the Automotive Internal Combustion Engine* (Warrendale, PA: Society of Automotive Engineers, 1976).
86 "Minutes of the Meeting of the Board of Directors of Bricklin Canada Ltd.," 22 April 1975, PANB, box 514, file "April 21 1975," no. I.
87 Author's interview with Malcolm Bricklin, 13 April 2013.
88 John Dinkel, "America's New Sports Car: The Bricklin," *Road Track*, September 1973, 98.
89 Author's interview with Malcolm Bricklin, 13 April 2013.
90 "Malcolm Bricklin Tells His Story," *Take 30*, September 1975, CBC Archive, https://www.cbc.ca/player/play/1503839243.
91 Hegland, "Building the Bricklin," 46.
92 Fredericks and Chambers, *Bricklin*, 54.
93 G.S. Wheatley to H.A. Nason, "Bricklin Canada Ltd.," 27 December 1974, PANB, box 83, file 5321-2, "Bricklin, Financial"; Department of Economic Growth, Memorandum to Cabinet, 8 November 1974, PANB, box 83, file 5006 B-12, "Bricklin Canada Limited."
94 Robert M. Lienert, "Finding Happiness on $20 Million," *Automotive News*, 6–13 May 1974.
95 Lawrence J. White, *The Automobile Industry since 1945* (1971; Cambridge, MA: Harvard University Press, 2014), 28, emphasis added.
96 Anastakis, *Auto Pact*, 125.
97 See the excellent Elgin Country Archives online exhibit "The St. Thomas Ford Assembly Plant, 1965–2011," at https://www.elgincounty.ca/ElginCounty/CulturalServices/Archives/st_thomas_ford_exhibit/index.html.
98 Hegland, "Building the Bricklin," 44.
99 Ibid.; author's interview with Malcolm Bricklin, 13 April 2013; John Porteous, "Bricklin Workers Still Believe in 'Dream Car,'" *Financial Post*, 4 October 1975, 14.
100 Hegland, "Building the Bricklin," 47–8.
101 "Minutes of the Meeting of the Board of Directors of Bricklin Canada Ltd.," 22 May 1975, PANB, box 514, file May 27 1975, no. I, 5.

102 G.S. Wheatley to File, "Trip Report: Detroit–New York, November 27–30, 1973," 6 December, 1973, PANB, box 83, file 5600-B1, "Bricklin, General"; Hegland, "Building the Bricklin," 45; Joseph J. Bohn, "Bricklin Views Plastic as 'Material of Future,'" *Automotive News*, 28 July 1975.

103 Terry Tanner, "Tech Tips: Hood," *Brickline* 16, 3 (1991): 20.

104 Hegland, "Building the Bricklin," 48.

105 G.S. Wheatley, "Trip Report, Minto, NB," 29 April 1975, PANB, Department of Economic Growth, box 556, file 43-1725, vol. 9, February–April 1975; Spence, "Adventures along the 'Yellow Bricklin Road,'" 91.

106 Humble, "1975 Bricklin SV" 47; Hegland, "Building the Bricklin," 48; Michel Cormier and Achille Michaud, *Richard Hatfield: Power and Disobedience*, trans. Daphne Ponder (Fredericton: Goose Lane, 1992), 65; Randy Poulos, "Bricklin: An Estimated Build History," *Brickline* 8, 1 (1983): 18.

107 Author's interview with Malcolm Bricklin, 13 April 2013; C.E. Sawyer (Wespac Development Planning Corporation) to H. Nason, 28 April 1975, PANB, box 83, file 5600-B-14, "Reports of the Bricklin Project," 3; Sawyer, "Note to File," 13 September 1975, PANB, box 83, file 5600-B-14, "Reports of the Bricklin Project," 2.

108 *Brickline* 1, 3 (1975): 1; "Bricklin Trying to Make Break-Even Point Monthly," *Sherbrooke Record*, 4 July 1975, 2.

109 "Confidential: Bricklin Canada Ltd., Briefing Report," 14 March 1975, PANB, box 83, file 5600-B-14, "Reports of the Bricklin Project," 12; *New York Times* News Service, "Bricklin Incurable Optimist," *Calgary Herald*, 22 September 1975, 27; C.E. Sawyer (Wespac Development Planning Corporation) "Note to File," 13 September 1975, PANB, box 83, file 5600-B-14, "Reports of the Bricklin Project," 9; G.S. Wheatley, "Trip Report: Minto NB," 20 January 1975, PANB, box 556, file 43-1758, vol. 8.

110 Hegland, "Building the Bricklin," 49.

111 "Press Release: Premier Richard Hatfield, September 15, 1975," PANB, box 83, file 5600-B-14, "Statements by Premier and Economic Growth Minister"; Department of Economic Growth, "Memorandum to Cabinet: Advance of Funds to Provincial Holdings Ltd.," 8 November 1974, PANB, box 83, file 5600-B-2, "Bricklin, Financial Agreements," vol. I, 1974.

112 R. Stenning (NB Multiplex Corporation Ltd.) to Clifford N. Taylor (Bricklin), 20 December 1973, PANB file 9, Bricklin Canada Ltd., box 301, File Bricklin Submission No. 559.

113 "We Know Bricklin Isn't Ford: UAW Negotiators," *Saint John Times Globe*, 14 August 1974; Spence, "Adventures along the 'Yellow Bricklin Road,'" 64; Collective Labour Agreement between Bricklin Canada Ltd. and International Union, United Automobile, Aerospace and Agricultural Implement Workers of America (UAW) Local 1890, 1November 1974, agreement in PANB, box 548.

114 G.S. Wheatley, "Trip Report, Minto, NB," 29 April 1975, 1, PANB, Department of Economic Growth, box 556, file 43-1725, vol. 9, February–April 1975; Porteous, "Bricklin Workers Still Believe in 'Dream Car,'" 14; Hegland, "Building the Bricklin," 47; Porteous, "Bricklin Goes Public," C6.

115 Hegland, "Building the Bricklin," 47.

116 See the dozens of plant visit reports filed by G.S. Wheatley over the course of BCL's existence, especially in PANB, box 556, file 43-1758, vols. 7–9, various dates.

117 Spence, "Adventures along the 'Yellow Bricklin Road,'" 65.

118 Porteous, "Bricklin Workers Still Believe in 'Dream Car,'" 14.

119 Dahl, "Would You Buy a Chinese Car?"

120 Porteous, "Bricklin Goes Public," C6.

121 "Bricklin, Union to Talk in Bid to End Lockout," *Saint John Telegraph-Journal* (*TJ*), 10 January 1975; "Workers at Saint John Bricklin Plant End Two-Day Walkout," *Fredericton Daily Gleaner*, 13 January 1975, 1.
122 Bricklin, as quoted in Maudsley, dir., *The Bricklin*.
123 "BLC Pride and Quality Teams Chosen," *Brickline* 1, 2 (1975): 4.
124 C.E. Sawyer (Wespac Development Planning Corporation) to H. Nason, 28 April 1975, PANB, box 83, file 5600-B-14, "Reports of the Bricklin Project," 2.
125 See Steven High's important work *Industrial Sunset: The Making of North America's Rust Belt* (Toronto: University of Toronto Press, 2003).
126 For views on the Japanese and European auto manufacturers in North America, including their impact on rural communities, see Michele M. Hoyman, *Power Steering: Global Automakers and the Transformation of Rural Communities* (Lawrence: University Press of Kansas, 1997); Ernest J. Yanarella, *The Politics of Industrial Recruitment: Japanese Automobile Investment and Economic Development in the American States* (New York: Praeger, 1990); and Robert Perrucci, *Japanese Auto Transplants in the Heartland: Corporatism and Community* (New York: Routledge, 1994). On GM in Tennessee, see Joe Sherman, *In the Rings of Saturn* (New York: Oxford University Press, 1994).
127 In the late nineteenth and early twentieth century, through the practice of "bonusing," municipal governments would provide funding to build plants. See Ankli and Frederickson, "The Influence of American Manufacturers," 105.
128 J.P. Francis (acting deputy minister, DREE) to Joseph M. Rose (Bricklin), 25 April 1974, and J.B. Heppell to G. Stephenson Wheatley, 3 May 1974, PANB, Department of Commerce and Development, box 569, vol. 26, file "Companies, Bricklin."
129 Gregory Skwira, "Mexico Expansion Eyed: Bricklin Seeking Baja Loan," *Detroit Free Press*, 17 July 1975, 24; "Minutes of the Meeting of the Board of Directors of Bricklin Canada Ltd.," 22 May 1975, PANB, box 514, file "May 22 1975," no. I; "Confidential Review of Bricklin Mexico, S.A., February, 1975," NAHC, DPL series I, box 1, file 8, the backlog quote is on p. 8; "$20 Million Bricklin Plant for Mexico?" *TJ*, 24 May 1975; Edison Steward, "State in Mexico Offers $20 Million" *Saint John Times Globe*, 22 April 1975.
130 Kenneth P. Thomas, *Capital beyond Borders: States and Firms in the Auto Industry, 1960–94* (New York: Saint Martin's Press, 1996); see also his *Competing for Capital: Europe and North America in a Global Era* (Washington, DC: Georgetown University Press, 2000), 33–7, and *Investment Incentives and the Global Competition for Capital* (London: Palgrave Macmillan, 2011), 58 ("a way of life").
131 Paul H. Weaver, *The Suicidal Corporation: How Big Business Fails America* (New York: Touchstone Books, 1988), 34; for a fascinating insiders account of the decision about where to locate, see 33–9. See also Anastakis, *Autonomous State*, 105–7.
132 On the emergence of this dynamic, see A.J. Jacobs, *The New Domestic Automakers in the United States and Canada: History, Impacts and Prospects* (Lanham, MD: Lexington Books, 2016); Thomas, *Capital beyond Borders*. David Leyton-Brown, "The Mug's Game: Automotive Investment Incentives in Canada and the United States," *International Journal* 35, 1 (1979–80), 170–84; and John Holmes, "From Three Industries to One: Towards and Integrated North American Automobile Industry," in *Driving Continentally: National Policies and the North American Auto Industry*, ed. Maureen Appel Molot (Ottawa: Carleton University Press, 1993).
133 The classic expression of this acceptance is found in H.G.J. Aitken, "Defensive Expansionism: The State and Economic Growth in Canada," in *Approaches to Canadian Economic History*, ed. W.T. Easterbrook and M.H. Watkins, rev. ed. (Montreal and Kingston: McGill-Queen's University Press, 2000).

134 Bricklin was sometimes characterized as a Canadian-owned firm. See, for instance, Larry Skory, "Look Out Big Three! Here Comes the Canadian-Controlled Bricklin," *Canadian Machinery and Metalworking*, September 1973, 54.

135 The federal government made auto pact status conditional on meeting a 50 peer cent Canadian content requirement and manufacturing at least 10,000 vehicles a year, which was similar to what was expected from Volvo. A. Gillespie to M. Bricklin, 6 June 1973 and "Statement by Premier Richard Hatfield Concerning the Bricklin Project," 2 December 1974, PANB, box 83, file 5600-B1, "Bricklin, General."

136 As a further irony, the federal government never granted Bricklin auto pact status, since the company never hit the 10,000 vehicles a year production target required by Ottawa. Bricklin may have also seen auto pact status as a way to use GVI to import duty-free from offshore, which would have been attractive to someone who had already imported Subarus. An early Bricklin prospectus stated that "by manufacturing in Canada, the company will also be able to import European or Japanese cars duty-free, through a Canadian port of entry, through provisions of a Department of National Revenue memorandum." GVI, "Bricklin of Canada: Submission to the Department of Regional Economic Expansion," April 6 1973, PANB, box 2, file "Bricklin."

137 Touche Ross & Co. to the Board of Directors, "Bricklin Vehicle Corporation," 15 September 1972, NAHC, DPL, series I, box 1, file 2.

138 Touche Ross & Co., "Bricklin Canada Ltd., Report and Financial Statement," 30 June 1974, PANB, box 2, file 1.

139 "Statement by Premier Richard Hatfield Concerning the Bricklin Project," 2 December 1974, PANB, box 83, file "Statements."

140 In President Obama's statement explaining the government buyout, he "recognized the importance of a viable auto industry to the well-being of families and communities across our industrial Midwest and across the United States. In the midst of a deep recession and financial crisis, the collapse of these companies would have been devastating for countless Americans, and done enormous damage to our economy – beyond the auto industry. It was also clear that if GM and Chrysler remade and retooled themselves for the 21st century, it would be good for American workers, good for American manufacturing, and good for America's economy." The complete statement, published 1 June 2009, can be read at MarketWatch, http://www.marketwatch.com/story/full-text-of-president-obamas-statement-on-gm. See also Tavia Grant and Greg Keenan, "GM Files for Bankruptcy Protection," *Globe and Mail*, 1 June, 2009.

141 G.S. Wheatley to File, "Trip Report: Detroit–New York, November 27–30, 1973," 6 December 1973, PANB, box 83, file 5600-B1, "Bricklin, General."

142 Lienert, "Finding Happiness on $20 Million"; Phil Casey, "Bricklin's Bricklin," *Washington Post*, 16 February 1975, L7.

143 Casey, "Bricklin's Bricklin," L7.

144 As quoted in Maudsley, dir., *The Bricklin*.

145 Diana Fong, "From Yugoslavia to Montvale," *New York Times*, 25 August 1985, A2.

146 Borins with Brown, *Investments in Failure*, 45.

147 Sloan's first biography was called *Adventures of a White Collar Man* (New York: Doubleday, Doran & Company, 1941).

7. Demise (Rebirth)

1 "Bricklin Canada, Ltd., Financial Proposal," National Automotive History Collection (NAHC), Detroit Public Library (DPL), series IV, file 1, box 13.

2 H.A. Fredericks and Allan Chambers, *Bricklin* (Potters Bark, UK: Brunswick Press, 1977), 116–19; John Peters, "Honey Pot Finally Dry: Bricklin into Receivership," *Saint John Telegraph-Journal* (*TJ*), 26 September 1976.

3 Interoffice Memo, Draft response to Ronald Duguay from Richard Hatfield, G. Stephenson Wheatley, 24 March 1987, Public Archives of New Brunswick (PANB), box 2, file 43-1194, "Bricklin."

4 "DREE Gives a Boost to Bricklin," *Financial Times of Canada,* 6 May 1974; "Bricklin 'Risky' but Could Pay Off," *Saint John Evening Times Globe*, 5 September 1974.

5 David Halberstam, *The Reckoning* (New York: William Morrow, 1986), 333.

6 E.B. Merchant, "$1,120,000 Loan Authorized: More Cash For Bricklin," *TJ*, 24 April 1974, 1.

7 D. Jenning to P.S. Creaghan, "Bricklin Canada Ltd.," October 4 1974, PANB, Department of Economic Growth, box 556, file 43-1725, vol. 7, January–October 1974.

8 "Statement by Premier Richard Hatfield Concerning the Bricklin Project, Monday, December 2, 1974," PANB, box 83, file 5600-B-14, "Statement by Premier and Economic Growth Minister."

9 Department of Economic Growth, "Memorandum to Cabinet: Advance of Funds to PHL, $1,000,000," 6 November 1974, and "Memorandum to Cabinet: Advance of Funds to Provincial Holdings Ltd.," 8 November 1974, PANB, box 83, file 5600-B-2, "Bricklin, Financial Agreements," vol. I, 1974; "Directors, October 2nd 1974," PANB, Department of Commerce and Development, box 567 (42745), file, "Bricklin Canada Ltd., Directors Meetings," Bricklin Books.

10 "Statement by Premier Richard Hatfield Concerning the Bricklin Project, Monday, December 2, 1974," PANB, box 83, file 5600-B-14, "Statement by Premier and Economic Growth Minister."

11 Allan Chambers, "Hatfield Announces New Bricklin Loan," *Fredericton Daily Gleaner*, 3 December 1974, 1; "Bricklin Auto Venture to Get $2.5 Million More," *Fredericton Daily Gleaner*, 13 December 1974, 1; G.S. Wheatley to H.A. Nason, "Bricklin Canada Ltd.," 27 December 1974, PANB, box 83, file 5321-2, "Bricklin, Financial."

12 Roger Worth, "New Brunswick Doubles Its Stake in Bricklin," *Financial Post*, 8 February 1975, 30; "Press Release: Premier Richard, January 30, 1975," PANB, box 83, file 5600-B-14, "Statements by Premier and Economic Growth Minister."

13 "Confidential: Bricklin Canada Ltd., Briefing Report," 14 March 1975 PANB, box 83, file 5600-B-14, "Reports of the Bricklin Project," 10; E.B. Merchant, "Added $7,120,000 Promised Bricklin," *TJ*, 1 May 1975, 2.

14 "Press Release: Premier Richard, September 15, 1975" PANB, box 83, file 5600-B-14, "Statements by Premier and Economic Growth Minister."

15 "Memorandum to Cabinet, Department of Economic Growth," 22 August 1975, PANB, Department of Commerce and Development, box 568, vol. 12, File "Companies, Bricklin Canada, General Correspondence, December 1975–August 1976."

16 Richard Starr, *Richard Hatfield: The Seventeen-Year Saga* (Halifax: Formac Publishing, 1987), 95.

17 "Minutes of Meeting Held on March 18, 1975 in the Conference Room of Bricklin Canada Ltd., Grandview Industrial Park, Saint John, N.B." and "Minutes Held in Livonia," 27 May 1975, NAHC, DPL, I, box 1, file 12 General Vehicle Corporate Minutes,; "Minutes of the Meeting of the Board of Directors of Bricklin Canada Ltd.," 22 April 1975, PANB, box 514, file "April 21 1975," no. I; Wick Humble, "1975 Bricklin SV: Plastic Fantastic or Gull-Winged Turkey?" *Special Interest Autos*, April 1982, 49.

18 "Minutes of Meeting Held on March 18, 1975 in the Conference Room of Bricklin Canada Ltd., Grandview Industrial Park, Saint John, N.B." and "Minutes Held in Livonia," 27 May 1975, NAHC, DPL, I, box 1, file 12 General Vehicle Corporate Minutes; "Minutes of the Meeting of the Board of Directors of Bricklin Canada Ltd.," 22 April 1975, PANB, box 514, file "April 21 1975," no. I.

19 Humble, "1975 Bricklin SV," 45.
20 Fredericks and Chambers, *Bricklin*, 3–4; Humble, "1975 Bricklin SV," 49.
21 "Government of New Brunswick, Department of Economic Growth: A Report – The Bricklin Project," 28 May 1975, NAHC, DPL, series I, box 1, file 10, 23.
22 Bricklin Technical Service Bulletin No. 13, "Safety Recall Campaign 75-0155, Improper Seating, Roadwheel," Canadian Automotive Museum (CAM), Dr. Sandy Bigman Bricklin Papers, box T6A2, file 2020.01.02; "GVI Recalls 965 Bricklins," *Bricklin Dealer News* 1, 1 (1975), reprinted in *Brickline* 20, 4 (1997): 13.
23 See, for example, "Minutes of the Meeting of the Board of Directors of Bricklin Canada Ltd.," 24 June 1975, PANB, box 514, file "June 24 1975," no. I; C.E. Sawyer (Wespac Development Planning Corporation) "Note to File," 12 September 1975, PANB, box 83, file 5600-B-14, "Reports of the Bricklin Project," 6.
24 "Malcolm Bricklin Addresses Dealers," *Bricklin Dealer News* 1, 1 (1975), reprinted in *Brickline* 20, 4 (1997): 11.
25 "Bricklin Price Boosted," *Brickline* 1, 2 (1975): 3.
26 "1976 Bricklin Safety Vehicle-1 Manufacturer's Suggested Retail Price," CAM, Bigman Bricklin Papers, box T6A5, file, 01.129.
27 Canadian Press, "Dealers Await Missing Parts: Bricklin Car Shipments Slow," *Calgary Herald*, 31 March 1975, 24.
28 C.E. Sawyer (Wespac Development Planning Corporation) "Note to File," 12 September 1975, PANB, box 83, file 5600-B-14, "Reports of the Bricklin Project," 6.
29 C.E. Sawyer (Wespac Development Planning Corporation) "Note to File," 19 August 1975, PANB, Department of Commerce and Development, box 513, Companies Files, C.E. Sawyer Records.
30 Ralph M. Henry to G. Stephenson Wheatley, 15 September 1975, PANB, Department of Economic Growth, box 556, File 43-1868, Vol. 12, September–November 1975; Bricklin Canada Ltd., "Financial Proposal," 17 September 1975, PANB, box 83, file 5600-B-2, "Bricklin, Financial Arrangements."
31 Roger Worth, "Bricklin Repair Bill $30 a Person," *Financial Post*, 21 February 1976, 1, 3–4.
32 "Minutes of a Reconvened Meeting of the Board of Directors … Wednesday, the 24th of September, 1975," PANB, Department of Commerce, Tabled Documents, file "September 23, 1975"; "Vows of Silence for Hatfield, Bricklin," *TJ*, 25 September 1972, 2. Author's interview with Malcolm Bricklin, 5 October 2022. The very next day, on 25 September, Hatfield coldly informed BCL's trustees, the Royal Trust Company, that "events of default have occurred," and that should BCL "fail to make payment on demand, we hereby authorize and direct you to take whatever steps necessary" to have the company put into receivership. Government of New Brunswick (Richard Hatfield) to Peter W. Carrodus, Royal Trust Company, 25 September 1975, PANB, box 83, file 5600-B-2, "Bricklin, Financial Arrangements."
33 "Statement by Premier Richard Hatfield Concerning the Bricklin Project," 26 September 1975, NAHC, DPL, series IV, file 1, box 13; John Porteous, "Bricklin Workers Still Believe in 'Dream Car,'" *Financial Post*, 4 October 1975, 14.
34 "Malcolm Bricklin Tells His Story," *Take 30*, September 1975, CBC Archive, https://www.cbc.ca/player/play/1503839243; Michael Enright, "Wheeler-Dealer: How Mr. Bricklin Got His Dream Car and Mr. Hatfield Got the Bill," *Maclean's*, 17 November 1975, 54.
35 "Malcolm Bricklin Tells His Story." In May 1975, Bricklin told the BCL board that he had met with representatives of the investment firm Pitfield, MacKay, Ross & Company "concerning the possibility of a public offering" of 51 per cent of the company to Canadians for $50 million, giving the firm a valuation of $100 million. "Minutes of the Meeting of the

Board of Directors of Bricklin Canada Ltd.," 22 May 1975, PANB, box 514, file "May 22 1975," no. I.

36 "Malcolm Bricklin Tells His Story."
37 B.J. Walker to Hon. L. Garvie, H.A. Nason, 7 October 1975, PANB, Department of Economic Growth, box 556, file 43-1868, vol. 12, September–November, 1975.
38 "Press Release," n.d., PANB, box 514, file "Bricklin Safety Vehicle"; NAHC, DPL, "Background Notes," series II box 4, file 11, no. I.
39 "The Day the Ignition Failed," *Financial Post*, 21 February 1976, 3.
40 "Bricklin Calls Shutdown 'a Temporary Setback,'" *TJ*, 27 September 1975, 1.
41 "Statement by Premier Richard Hatfield, News Conference, Friday, October 17, 1975," PANB, box 83, file 5600-B-14, "Statement by Premier and Economic Growth Minister."
42 M. Bricklin to R. Hatfield, 15 December 1975 and R. Hatfield to M. Bricklin, 6 February 1976, PANB, box 83, file 5600-B1, "Bricklin, General"; "Press Release, 15 December, 1975," PANB, box 514, file "Bricklin Safety Vehicle Background Notes," series II, box 4, file 11, no. I.
43 "Press Release," n.d., PANB, box 514, file "Bricklin Safety Vehicle Background Notes," series II, box 4, file 11, no. I.
44 "'Squeaky Clean' Boy Wonder," *Financial Post*, 21 February 1976, 3.
45 G. Stephenson Wheatley, "Bricklin Canada Ltd. Information Summary (Confidential), March 3, 1976," 7, PANB, Department of Economic Growth, box 556, file 43-1725, vol. 9, February–April, 1975; Roger Worth, "Bricklin's Plunge Leaves Skid Marks $30 Million Long," *Financial Post*, 21 February 1976, 3.
46 "Minutes of the Meeting of the Board of the Directors of Bricklin Canada Limited," 23 April 1976, PANB, box 2.
47 "Minutes of the Meeting of the Board of Directors of Bricklin Canada Limited," 29 September 1976, PANB, box 2.
48 G.S. Wheatley to Gilbert Graham, 19 August 1976, PANB, box 2.
49 Humble, "1975 Bricklin SV," 49.
50 Bricklin International, *BI News*, 2 (December 1975): 1, Canadian Automotive Museum (CAM), Sandy Bigman Bricklin Papers, box T6A2, file 2020.01.39.
51 Gerald S. Merrithew to Harold N. Fanjoy, 23 November 1979, PANB, box 2.
52 "Follow Up on the News: The Bricklin Dream," *New York Times*, 2 November 1975, 39.
53 "Malcolm Bricklin Tells His Story." On New York's fiscal crisis in the Seventies, see Kim Phillips-Fein, *Fear City: New York's Fiscal Crisis and the Rise of Austerity Politics* (New York: Metropolitan Books, 2017).
54 Peter Bremelow, "The Heart's in the Right Place, but the Head's Another Matter," *Maclean's*, 12 July 1976, 47.
55 David Folster, "Faith in Industry is Flagging," *Globe and Mail*, 3 July 1976, 8.
56 Lyndon Watkins, "Business: Are the Martimes Finally Getting Wise to Corporate Welfare Bums?" *Maclean's*, 13 June 1977, 62–3.
57 "If at First You Don't Succeed, Consider Malcolm Bricklin," *Maclean's*, 26 December 1977, 9.
58 Frederick Rose, "Northern Appalachia: Canada's Depressed Maritimes Pull Back from Costly Schemes to Attract Industry," *Wall Street Journal*, 9 November 1977, 48.
59 Robert L. Perry, "They Don't Speak Ill of Bricklin," *Financial Post*, 24 November 1979, 6.
60 See, for example, Lachlan MacKinnon, "Importing the Clairtone Sound: Political Economy, Regionalism, and Deindustrialization in Pictou County," *Labour/Le travail* 91 (Spring 2023): 147–68.
61 Starr, *Richard Hatfield*, 98.

62 "New Brunswick Can Say No to Foreign Investment," *Canadian Business*, May 1975, 29.

63 On the New Brunswick government providing government loan guarantees to McCain, see Tony Stoffman and Daniel Van Leersum, *From the Ground Up: The First Fifty Years of McCain Foods* (McCain Foods, 2007), 7–8; Perry, "They Don't Speak Ill of Bricklin," 6.

64 Sanford Borins with Lee Brown, *Investments in Failure: Five Government Corporations That Cost the Canadian Taxpayer Billions* (Toronto: Methuen, 1986), 1–2, 143.

65 See, for example, Allan Tupper, *Public Money in the Private Sector* (Kingston: Institute of Intergovernmental Relations, 1982), 4, 49–51; Donald J. Savoie, *Regional and Economic Development: Canada's Search for Solutions* (Toronto: University of Toronto Press, 1986), 176, 211; Stephen Brooks and Andrew Stritch, *Business and Government in Canada* (Scarborough, ON: Prentice-Hall Canada, 1991), 193.

66 John Reid, "The 1970s: The Sharpening of the Skeptical Edge," in *The Atlantic Provinces in Confederation*, ed. E.R. Forbes and D.A. Muise (Toronto: University of Toronto Press, 1993), 469.

67 Michael Jenkin, *The Challenge of Diversity: Industrial Policy in the Canadian Federation* (Ottawa: Science Council of Canada, 1983), 62.

68 Chris Wood, "Government a Reluctant Investor," *Financial Post*, 11 June 1983, 7.

69 Nancy Wook with Luke Fisher and Brian Bergman, "Taking Care of Business: Should Governments Bankroll the Private Sector?" *Maclean's*, 6 September 1993, 17.

70 Randy Richmond and Tom Villemaire, *Colossal Canadian Failures* (Toronto: Dundurn, 2002), 89–94.

71 "Canadian Duds," *Financial Post Magazine*, February 2012, 10. Another 1992 piece compared Bricklin to the then-unbuilt Confederation Bridge: "The doubters, inured to tarnished dreams in Atlantic Canada, just shrug. People in this part of the country, used to promises of sporty Bricklin cars, bumper cucumber crops and floods of offshore oil riches, will believe in the bridge – dubbed Span of Green Gables –when they're driving over it." Elaine Flaherty, "Prince Edward Island Was Promised Continuous Transportation …" CanWest News, 29 September 1993, 1.

72 "The only Bricklin I ever sat in caught on fire and burned to the axles. This is notably ironic, since the car's creator – the smooth-talking Malcolm Bricklin – didn't include an ashtray or lighter in the car, to discourage smoking. Despite its hand-removing, 100-lb. gull-wing doors, the SV1 was supposed to exemplify the safer car of the future; the name stands for 'Safety Vehicle 1.' The bodies were made of brightly colored, dent-resistant plastic, like PlaySkool furniture. Another safety feature: incredible, crust-of-the-Earth-cooling slowness. All those resin panels and compressible bumpers added hundreds of pounds that the emissions-limited V8s couldn't handle. This thing couldn't outrun the Rose Bowl Parade. Less than 3,000 of the wedgy coupes were built, but Malcolm Bricklin was far from through, as we'll see." Dan Neil, "The 50 Worst Cars of All Time," *Time Magazine*, 25 April 2017, https://time.com/4723114/50-worst-cars-of-all-time/.

73 For examples of the vibrant literature on deindustrialization, see, Barry Bluestone and Bennett Harrison, *The Deindustrialization of America: Plant Closings, Community Abandonment, and the Dismantling of Basic Industry* (New York: Basic Books, 1982); Steven P. Dandeaneau, *A Town Abandoned: Fling, Michigan, Confronts Deindustrialization* (Albany: SUNY Press, 1996); David Sobel and Susan Meurer, *Working at Inglis: The Life and Death of a Canadian Factory* (Toronto: Lorimer, 1997); Jefferson Cowie and Joseph Heathcott, *Beyond the Ruins: The Meanings of Deindustrialization* (Ithaca, NY: ILR Press, 2003); Guian A. McKee, *The Problem of Jobs: Liberalism, Race, and Deindustrialization in Philadelphia* (Chicago: University of Chicago

Press, 2010); David Koistinen, *Confronting Decline: The Political Economy of Deindustrialization in Twentieth-Century New England* (Gainesville: University Press of Florida, 2016); and Lachlan Mackinnon, *Closing Sysco: Industrial Decline in Atlantic Canada's Steel City* (Toronto: University of Toronto Press, 2020).

74 Fred Burrill and Dimitry Anastakis, "Explaining Industrial Closures," presented at the Deindustrialization and the Politics of Our Time (DePOT) annual conference, 23 June 2023, Sydney, NS. For a view of reindustrialization, see Dimitry Anastakis, "Industrial Sunrise? The Chrysler Bailout, the State, and the Re-industrialization of the Canadian Automotive Sector, 1975–1986," *Urban History Review / Revue d'histoire urbaine* 35, 2 (2007): 37–50.

75 Charles K. Hyde, *Storied Independent Automakers: Nash, Hudson, and American Motors* (Detroit: Wayne State University Press, 2009); Patrick R. Foster, *American Motors: The Last Independent* (Iola, WI : Krause Publications, 1993).

76 Steven High, *Industrial Sunset: The Making of North America's Rust Belt, 1969–1984* (Toronto: University of Toronto Press, 2003), 6, 94–6. Astoundingly, from the 1960s to the early 1980s, over 100,000 plants closed in the United States, leading to an estimated 22.3 million job losses (ibid., 93).

77 Ibid., 9–13.

78 Sherry Lee Linkon, *The Half-Life of Deindustrialization: Working-Class Writing about Economic Restructuring* (Ann Arbor: University of Michigan Press, 2018).

79 See Anastakis, "Industrial Sunrise?"

80 Proteus, "Bricklin Workers Still Believe in 'Dream Car,'" 14.

81 "Bricklin Plant Layoffs Extended Second Week," *Fredericton Daily Gleaner*, 22 September 1975, 5; Proteus, "Bricklin Workers Still Believe in 'Dream Car,'" 14.

82 Jefferson Cowie, *Stayin' Alive: The 1970s and the Last Days of the Working Class* (New York: New Press, 2010).

83 Canadian Press, "Bricklin Wants Second Chance," *Calgary Herald*, 8 October 1975, 3.

84 Jackie Webster, "The Little Car That Couldn't," *Maclean's*, 6 October 1975, 69.

85 Conference Board of Canada, *The Provincial Economies, 1961–1979 Data* (Ottawa, ON: Conference Board of Canada, 1980), tables 23.5 and 23.6, "Key Economic Indicators: New Brunswick," 207–11.

86 Michael Bruno, *Economics of Worldwide Stagflation* (Oxford: Basil Blackwell, 1985). For the European response to stagflation, see Jordi Catalan Vidal, "The Stagflation Crisis and the European Automotive Industry, 1973–85," *Business History* 59, 1 (2017): 4–34.

87 T.W. Acheson, "The National Policy and the Industrialization of the Maritimes, 1880–1910," *Acadiensis* 1, 2 (1972): 3–28; J.G. Reid and J.H. Reid, "The Multiple Deindustrializations of Canada's Maritime Provinces and the Evaluation of Heritage-Related Urban Regeneration," *London Journal of Canadian Studies* 31,1 (2016): 89–112; L. Anders Sandberg, "The Deindustrialization of Pictou County, Nova Scotia: Capital, Labour and the Process of Regional Decline, 1881–1921" (PhD diss., McGill University, 1985).

88 Lachlan MacKinnon and Steven High, "Deindustrialization in Canada: New Perspectives," *Labour/Le travail* 91 (Spring 2023): 13; see also, for example, MacKinnon, *Closing Sysco*.

89 Steven High, *One Job Town: Work, Belonging, and Betrayal in Northern Ontario* (Toronto: University of Toronto Press, 2018); Steven High, *Deindustrializing Montreal: Entangled Histories of Race, Residence, Class* (Montreal and Kingston: McGill-Queen's University Press, 2022).

90 A.J. Jacobs, *The New Domestic Automakers in the United States and Canada: History, Impacts and Prospects* (Lanham, MD: Lexington Books, 2016); Dimitry Anastakis, *Autonomous*

State: The Struggle for a Canadian Car Industry from OPEC to Free Trade, chap. 7, "Transplant"; James M. Rubenstein, *Making and Selling Cars: Innovation and Change in the US Automotive Industry* (Baltimore: Johns Hopkins University Press, 2001), chap. 6, "… to Reskilling Labor."

91 The US auto industry produced about 11 million vehicles in the years 1971, 1979, 1987, 1993, 2001, 2007, 2014, and 2017. DesRosiers Automotive Consultants, *DesRosiers Annual Yearbook 2018* (Richmond Hill, ON: DesRosiers Automotive Consultants, 2019), 103.

92 Dimitry Anastakis "Lean Deindustrialization: Fighting the Good Fight in Ontario's Auto Sector," *Our Times: Canada's Independent Labour Magazine* (Spring 2023), 35–6.

93 As quoted in Starr, *Richard Hatfield*, 97.

94 Marcel Martel, *Not This Time: Canadians, Public Policy and the Marijuana Question* (Toronto: University of Toronto Press, 2006); Edgar-André Montigny, *The Real Dope: Social, Legal, and Historical Perspectives on the Regulation of Drugs in Canada* (Toronto: University of Toronto Press, 2017).

95 Christopher Wood, "A Matter of Marijuana," *Maclean's*, 5 December 1984, 16.

96 This accusation was floated by Donald F. Ripley in his book *Bagman: A Life in Nova Scotia Politics* (Toronto: Key Porter Books, 1993).

97 Hatfield and the RCMP had a long and stormy relationship in New Brunswick, going back to the mid-1970s investigation of a kickback scheme in which a number of Tory bagmen were accused, but ultimately found not guilty, of fundraising irregularities.

98 Robert Miller, "Richard Hatfield under Fire," *Maclean's*, 18 February 1985, 12–15.

99 Janet Cawley, "Politician Pays Price for Life on the Edge," *Chicago Tribune*, 25 March 1985 https://www.chicagotribune.com/news/ct-xpm-1985-03-25-8501160769-story.html).

100 Author's interview with Malcolm Bricklin, 30 April 2013.

101 Libby Burnham, as related in Nancy Southam, ed., *Remembering Richard: An Informal Portrait of Richard Hatfield by His Friends, Family and Colleagues* (Halifax: Formac, 1993), 144.

102 Michel Cormier and Achille Michaud, *Richard Hatfield: Power and Disobedience*, trans. Daphne Ponder (Fredericton: Goose Lane, 1992), 282.

103 John DeMont with E. Kaye Fulton, "A Passionate Canadian: Richard Hatfield Succumbs to Cancer at 60," *Maclean's*, 6 May 1991, 18.

104 Porteous, "Bricklin Workers Still Believe in 'Dream Car,'" 14.

105 There is a significant literature on the automobile in material culture history. For example, Mimi Sheller, "Automotive Emotions," *Theory, Culture and Society* 21, 4–5 (2004): 221–42.

106 Enright, "Wheeler-Dealer," 55.

107 Webster, "The Little Car That Couldn't," 69.

108 "Encore for Bricklin?" *Financial Post*, 22 May 1976; Various correspondence, PANB, Department of Commerce and Development, box 569, vol. 33, file 43-1082, "Companies, Wespac." John Porteous, "Bricklin Rebounding?" *Financial Post*, 24 July 1976, 2.

109 Donald T. Critchlow, *Studebaker: The Life and Death of an American Corporation* (Bloomington: Indiana University Press, 1996).

110 N.D. Altman to Lawrence Garvie, 7 January 1976, PANB, Department of Commerce and Development, box 569, file 43-1542, "Companies, Avanti Motor Corporation, January 1976."

111 G. Stephenson Wheatley to G.S. Merrithew, 9 January 1978, PANB, Department of Commerce and Development, box 569, vol. 32, file 43-1081, "Companies, Brickmar."

112 Richard Hatfield to G. Petrolekas, 14 December 1980 PANB, box 2.

113 Interoffice memo, draft response to Ronald Duguay from Richard Hatfield, G. Stephenson Wheatley, 24 March 1987, PANB, box 2, file 43-1194, "Bricklin."

114 Michael Fox, "Why Hatfield Believes Banks Don't Do Enough to Help the Economy of Atlantic Provinces," *Financial Post*, 13 May 1978, 6.

115 Perry, "They Don't Speak Ill of Bricklin," 6, emphasis in original. Today, the Bricklin plant on Grandview Avenue in Saint John houses a fire-hydrant manufacturing firm, which moved in in 1980.

116 See, for example, Lee Joliffe, "The Bricklin: From Automobile to Place Narrative," in *Automobile Heritage and Tourism*, ed. Michael V. Conlin and Lee Jolliffe (New York: Routledge, 2017), 40–8 and Jennifer Andrews, "The Bricklin: Narrating the Place of Dreaming in an Era of Self-Sufficiency," *Journal of New Brunswick Studies* 4 (2013): 31–46.

117 Darren Dahl, "Would You Buy a Chinese Car from This Man?" *Inc.*, 1 July 2005, https://www.inc.com/magazine/20050701/disruptor-bricklin.html.

118 Humble, "1975 Bricklin SV," 51.

119 Richard Truett, "Believers Breathe New Life into Bricklin's Dream," *Orlando Sentinel*, 10 August 1989, G1, 21.

120 June Stark (VIN 2200), "Bricklin Wedding Story," *Brickline* 34, 4 (2009): 4; Jerry Blackett, "My Lover for Sports Cars – VIN 30," *Brickline* 21, 2 (1996): 24. The *Brickline* can be found at CAM, Sandy Bigman Bricklin Papers, box T6A5, file, 01.138. The Bricklin International Owners Club is at http://www.bricklin.org/.

121 "Entrepreneur Reflects on Gull-Winged Car; Malcolm Bricklin Says Politics, Not Quality, Killed the Car," *Saint John Times-Transcript*, 23 July 2011, A9; "Bricklin Roars onto Silver Screen," CBC News, 19 October 2004, https://www.cbc.ca/news/canada/new-brunswick/bricklin-roars-onto-silver-screen-1.466118; Jennifer Pritchett, "New Brunswickers Opened Homes, Hearts; Planes Diverted to Moncton After Attacks," *Fredericton Daily Gleaner*, 10 September 2011, A1.

122 Rob Sass, "Smoking Permitted Only by the Engine," *New York Times*, 20 March 2011, AU6.

123 Glanna McWhirther, "DeLorean, Bricklin Spin New Dreams," *Detroit Free Press*, 29 July 1976, 54–5.

124 "Ask Malcolm: Flying with the Grey Ghost," *Brickline* 41, 2 (2016): 21.

125 Roderick McQueen, "On a Gull-Wing and a Prayer," *Maclean's*, 16 July 1979, 38–9.

126 Ibid.

127 Roderick McQueen,"Preview: Car Trouble," *Maclean's*, 16 October 1978, 21.

128 DeLorean and his car have generated a large scholarly and popular output, including books, documentaries, and innumerable magazine and online articles. See, for example, Chris Hegedus, exec. prod., *Myth and Mogul: John DeLorean* (Netflix, 2021); Alex Pappademas, "Demon Underneath: John DeLorean and the Invention of the Future," *Epic Magazine*, 11 December 2018, https://theoutline.com/post/6776/john-delorean-rise-and-fall-big-money-the-fbi-celebrities-and-cocaine.

129 Ivan Fallon and James Strodes, *DeLorean: The Rise and Fall of a Dream-Maker* (London: Hamish Hamilton, 1983): 68–9; McQueen, "On a Gull-Wing and a Prayer," 38–9.

130 Author's interview with Malcolm Bricklin, 6 April 2013. In 2022, Bricklin repeated the same assertion. On DeLorean, see Ivan Fallon and James Strodes, *Dream Maker: The Rise and Fall of John Z. DeLorean* (New York: Putman, 1985).

131 Graham Brownlow, "Back to the Failure: An Analytic Narrative of the DeLorean Debacle," *Business History* 57, 1 (2015): 155–80.

132 Fallon and Strodes, *Dream Maker.*

133 Andy Holloway, "Malcolm Bricklin: 'When You're Succeeding, You Tend to Get the Feeling You Know More Than You Know,'" *Canadian Business*, 17 February 2003, 28–9.

134 Paul C. Judge, "Selling Autos by Selling Safety: Car Makers Now Stress the Safety Features," *New York Times*, 26 January 1990, D1.
135 The embrace of plastic caused Houdaille, a major parts-manufacturing conglomerate, to shed its chrome bumper business in the 1970s as part of its restructuring. Max Holland, *When the Machine Stopped: A Cautionary Tale of Industrial America* (Cambridge, MA: Harvard University Press, 1989); Mark Reutter, "A Terrible Takeover Tale: How KKR and Houdaille Teamed Up and Ruined a Company," *Business and Society Review*, 1 June 1989, 43–6.
136 Paul A. Eisenstein, "GM's Saturn Drives the Hopes of Plastics Industry," *Chicago Tribune*, 25 November 1990, https://www.chicagotribune.com/news/ct-xpm-1990-11-25-9004070697-story.html; Joe Sherman, *In the Rings of Saturn* (New York: Oxford University Press, 1944), 92.
137 Bob Lutz, *Car Guys vs. Bean Counters: The Battle for the Soul of American Business* (New York: Portfolio, 2011), 47. See also Doug Smock, "Finally We Get Some Truth on Plastic Body Panels," *DesignNews*, 28 June 2011, https://www.designnews.com/materials-assembly/finally-we-get-some-truth-plastic-body-panels.
138 G.S. Wheately, "Trip Report, Saint John," 9 September 1975, 2, PANB, Department of Economic Growth, box 556, file 43-1868, vol. 12, September–November 1975.
139 See "Toyota Announces Decision to Build RAV4 Electric Vehicle at Toyota's Woodstock, Ontario Production Facility," 5 August 2011, http://media.toyota.ca/releases/toyota-announces-decision-to-build-rav4-electric-vehicle-at-toyotas-woodstock-ontario-production-facility.
140 "Air Door with Electric Air Compressor Installation," CAM, Dr. Sandy Bigman Bricklin Papers, box T6A5, file 01.165.
141 "Richard Truett, "Perfect Gull-Wing Door Remains a Fantasy; Safety Issues Dog Tesla's Model X," *Automotive News*, 5 September 2016, 3.
142 For views on Musk's early life and career, see Ashlee Vance, *Elon Musk: Tesla, SpaceX, and the Quest for a Fantastic Future* (New York: Ecco/HarperCollins, 2015) and Jimmy Soni, *The Founders: The Story of PayPal and the Entrepreneurs Who Shaped Silicon Valley* (New York: Simon & Schuster, 2022).
143 Tesla had been founded by Markin Eberhard and Marc Tarpenning in 2003; Musk became an investor the next year.
144 For one view of this dynamic, see S. Borins and B. Hearst, "Cults of Personality: Fables of the Automobile Manufacturing Industry," in *Negotiating Business Narratives: Fables of the Information Technology, Automobile Manufacturing, and Financial Trading Industries* (Cham, CH: Palgrave Macmillan/Springer, 2018), 23–36.
145 For example, J. Donald Williamson, "Bricklin SV? Turner Rotary Engine Promoted by Bricklin," *Automotive News*, 9 August 1976. Author's interviews with Malcolm Bricklin, 13 April 2013 and 6 October 2022.
146 Jack Ewing, "Musk Says Tesla Will Sell Its Cybertruck Next Year," *New York Times*, 9 April 2022, B3. The "jubilant" quote is from "Cybertruck Has Musk Charged," *Australian*, 23 November 2019, 3.
147 Grace Kay, "Elon Musk's Boring Company Says It Will Begin Testing Its Hyperloop, Nearly 9 Years after the Futuristic Transportation System Was First Proposed," *Business Insider*, 26 April 2022.
148 John Dinkel, "America's New Sports Car: The Bricklin," *Road & Track*, September 1973, 97. For a view of Musk's truck-smashing incident, see Greg Kumparak, "Elon Musk Says Sledgehammering Cybertruck Led to the Onstage Window Failure," *Techcrunch.com*, 25 November 2019, https://techcrunch.com/2019/11/25/elon-musk-says-sledgehammering-cybertruck-led-to-the-onstage-window-failure/. Henry Ford had also done something similar as a demonstration in 1940, hitting a soybean/plastic trunk with an ax.

149 Jean Halliday, "Tesla Motors," *Advertising Age*, 16 November 2009, 17.

150 Borins and Brown, *Investments in Failure*, 45.

151 Jack Siuta, "Malcolm Bricklin – An Impression" (editorial), *Brickline* 1, 6 (1976): 26.

152 The famous comedian gave the SV1 a positive review and called the venture a "noble failure." See "Jay Leno's Garage: Jeff Dunham's Under Appreciated 1975 Bricklin SV1," April 2022, YouTube, https://www.youtube.com/watch?v=OSP80Xr_O58.

153 For another view of Tesla, see Edward Niedermeyer, *Ludicrous: The Unvarnished Story of Tesla Motors* (Dallas: BenBella Books, 2019).

154 Bricklin's recollection was that the two had a discussion about some of the latter's approaches, including a disagreement over Tesla's lack of dealerships (Bricklin said that he told Musk that he would run into customer service trouble eventually if he did not have a way to service the cars through dealerships). Author's interview with Malcolm Bricklin, 6 October 2022.

Conclusion: Malcolm Bricklin and His SV1: From Industrial Modernity to Industrial Postmodernity

1 Steve Spence, "Adventures along the 'Yellow Bricklin Road,'" *Motor Trend*, November 1974, 66.

2 "Press Release: Premier Richard, January 30, 1975," Public Archives of New Brunswisk (PANB), box 83, file 5600-B-14, "Statements by Premier and Economic Growth Minister."

3 "Bricklin Canada Ltd., Briefing Report," 14 March 1975, PANB, box 83, file 5600-B-14, "Reports of the Bricklin Project."

4 "New Brunswick Can Say No to Foreign Investment," *Canadian Business*, May 1975, 29.

5 Jim Brokaw, "Road Test Comparison: Corvette and Bricklin," *Motor Trend*, May 1975, 96.

6 Bob Tripolsky, "We Test the Amazing Bricklin," *Mechanix Illustrated*, September 1975, 36–7.

7 "Bricklin Incurable Optimist," *Calgary Herald*, 22 September 1975, 27; Tom Swan, "Wheretofore Are Thou, Malcolm?" *Road Test*, April 1977, 72.

8 Spence, "Adventures along the 'Yellow Bricklin Road,'" 64–5.

9 Donald E. Hegland, "Building the Bricklin – A Sports Car Is Born," *Automation: The Production Engineering Magazine*, June 1975, 44.

10 Libby Burnham, as quoted in Dugald Maudsley, dir., *The Bricklin: The Premier, the Promoter and their Car* (episode of *Turning Points of History*, 2004).

11 L.J. Kiley to R. Hatfield, 11 September 1975, PANB, box 83, file 5600-B1, "Bricklin, General."

12 Garvie to Bricklin, Telex, 10 October 1975, PANB, box 83, file 5600-B1, "Bricklin, General."

13 The 1974 bankruptcy was Aston-Martin's fifth; it would experience two more, one in 1981 and another in 2007. "Statement by Honourable Lawrence Garvie, Q.C., Minister of Economic Growth to the Legislative Assembly, 18 November, 1975," PANB, Department of Economic Growth, box 556, file 43-1868, vol. 12, September–November, 1975.

14 Ibid.

15 Swan, "Wheretofore Are Thou, Malcolm?" 72.

16 Wick Humble, "A Conversation with Malcolm Bricklin," *Special Interest Autos*, April 1982, 46–7.

17 J. Donald Williamson, "Bricklin SV-? Turner Rotary Engine Promoted by Bricklin," *Automotive News*, 9 August 1976.

18 Michael Enright, "Wheeler-Dealer: How Mr. Bricklin Got His Dream Car and Mr. Hatfield Got the Bill," *Maclean's*, 17 November 1975, 55.

19 Author's interviews with Malcolm Bricklin, 13 April 2013 and 4 October 2022. In both interviews, nine years apart, Bricklin made almost the exact same remarks.

20 John Porteous, "Brooklyn Goes Public – in PR," *Financial Post*, 28 June 1975, C6.

21 John Porteous, "The Road to Oblivion," review of *Bricklin*, *Financial Post*, 13 August 1977, 11.

22 Enright, "Wheeler-Dealer," 55.

23 Paul Krugman, *The Age of Diminished Expectations*, 3rd ed. (Cambridge, MA: MIT Press, 1997).

24 Christoph Roser, *"Faster, Better, Cheaper" in the History of Manufacturing: From the Stone Age to Lean Manufacturing and Beyond* (Boca Raton, FL: CRC Press, 2017).

25 Alvin Toffler, *Future Shock* (New York: Random House, 1970), 4. Along with Toffler, there were a number of works that examined the end of Fordist domination in the early 1970s and considered the shape of society in its wake, often with pessimism. See Daniel Bell, *The Coming of Post-Industrial Society: A Venture in Social Forecasting* (New York: Basic Books, 1976) and Theodore Roszak, *Where the Wasteland Ends: Politics and Transcendence in Post-Industrial Society* (New York: Doubleday, 1972).

26 Edward Ayres, *What's Good for GM* (Nashville: Aurora Publishers, 1970); Kenneth Scheider, *Autokind vs. Mankind: An Analysis of Tyranny, a Proposal for Rebellion, a Plan for Reconstruction* (New York: Norton, 1971); Alisdair Aird, *Automotive Nightmare* (New York: Hutchinson, 1973); John Jerome, *The Death of the Automobile: The Fatal Effect of the Golden Era, 1955–1970* (New York: Norton, 1972); Emma Rothschild, *Paradise Lost: The Decline of the Auto-Industrial Age* (New York: Vintage Books, 1973). See also Lawrence J. White, *The Automobile Industry since 1945* (Cambridge, MA: Harvard University Press, 1971).

27 James J. Flink, "*The Car Culture* Revisited: Some Comments on the Recent Historiography of Automotive History," in *The Automobile and American Culture*, ed. David L. Lewis and Laurence Goldstein (Ann Arbor: University of Michigan Press, 1980), 411.

28 On Fordism and its end, see, for example, Steven Tolliday and Jonathan Zeitlin, eds., *Between Fordism and Flexibility: The Automobile Industry and Its Workers* (New York: St. Martin's Press, 1992); Ash Amin, ed., *Post-Fordism: A Reader* (Oxford: Blackwell, 2008); and Andrea Wigfield, *Post-Fordism, Gender and Work* (London: Routledge, 2018).

Epilogue: Tesla Factory, Fremont, California, August 2018: Elon Musk, the Model 3, and "Production Hell"

1 Ashlee Vance, *Elon Musk: Tesla, SpaceX, and the Quest for a Fantastic Future* (New York: HarperCollins, 2017); Richard Munson, *Tesla: Inventor of the Modern* (New York: W.W. Norton, 2018). For a view of labour relations at Tesla Fremont, see Timothy J. Minchin, "'The Factory of the Future': Historical Continuity and Labor Rights at Tesla," *Labor History* 62, 4 (2021): 434–53.

2 On Oakland, see Chris Rhomberg, *No There There: Race, Class, and Political Community in Oakland* (Berkeley: University of California Press, 2004).

3 On NUMMI and Tesla's histories at Fremont, see Yuji Muranaga and Takeo Nakajima, "Mixing the Best of Toyota and GM: NUMMI to Greet 25th Anniversary," *Japan Spotlight: Economy, Culture and History* 27, 3 (2008): 17; John Shook, "How to Change a Culture: Lessons from NUMMI," *MIT Sloan Management Review* 51, 2 (2010): 63–8.

4 Hamza Shaban, "Elon Musk: Tesla Has Moved from 'Production Hell' to 'Delivery Logistics Hell,'" *Washington Post*, 17 September 2018, https://www.washingtonpost.com/technology/2018/09/17/elon-musk-tesla-has-moved-production-hell-delivery-logistics-hell/.

5 Tesla did not turn a profit solely on its auto business (without subsidies and credits) until 2021. On Tesla and its production history, see Greg Perkins and Johann Peter Murmann, "What Does the Success of Tesla Mean for the Future Dynamics in the Global Automobile Sector?" *Management and Organization Review* 14, 3 (2018): 471–80. In 2023, Tesla was surpassed as the world's largest EV manufacturer by the Chinese firm BYD, which stands for "Build Your Dreams."

6 Enrique Dans, "The Secret of Tesla's Success Is Not Selling Cars: It's Being Able to Anticipate the Future," *Forbes*, 9 September 2019, https://www.forbes.com/sites/enriquedans/2019/09/09/the-secret-of-teslas-success-is-not-selling-cars-its-being-able-to-anticipate-thefuture/?sh=5708027a4973.

Notes about Sources

1 Quoted by Charles L. Sanford in "Women's Place in American Car Culture," *Michigan Historical Review* 19, 4 (1980): 532.

Bibliography

As *Dream Car* provides a survey of many aspects of automobility's impact and evolution, the bibliography is organized by chapter, making it more useful to a reader seeking information and sources on specific themes addressed in the book. Archival sources, government publications, newspapers, periodical, journal, and magazine sources, along with annual reports and interviews are included at the end of the bibliography.

Prologue and Introduction

Theses

Smith, Nathaniel Webb. "The Market Process: Entrepreneurship, Intervention, and the Role of the State." PhD diss., George Mason University, 2022.

Scholarly Books and Articles

Adams, James Truslow. *The Epic of America*. 1931; New York: Routledge, 2017.

Aitken, H.G.J. "Defensive Expansionism: The State and Economic Growth in Canada." In *Approaches to Canadian Economic History*, edited by M.H. Watkins and W.T. Easterbrook, 183–221. Montreal and Kingston: McGill-Queen's University Press, 1967.

Anastakis, Dimitry. *Auto Continent: Creating a Borderless North American Auto Industry, 1960–1971*. Toronto: University of Toronto Press, 2005.

Anbinder, Jacob. "Selling the World: Public Relations and the Global Expansion of General Motors, 1922–40." *Business History Review* 92, 3 (2018): 483–507.

Andrews, Jennifer. "Reading the Bricklin: Narrating the Place of Dreaming in an Era of Self-Sufficiency." *Journal of New Brunswick Studies/Revue d'etudes sur le Nouveau-Brunswick* 4 (January 2013): 31–46.

Armstrong, Christopher. *Making Toronto Modern: Architecture and Design, 1895–1975*. Montreal and Kingston: McGill-Queen's University Press, 2014.

Azzi, Stephen. *Reconcilable Differences: A History of Canada-US Relations*. Toronto: Oxford University Press, 2014.
Batchelor, Ray. *Henry Ford, Mass Production, Modernism, and Design*. Manchester: Manchester University Press, 1994.
Berman, Marshall. *All That Is Solid Melts into Air: The Experience of Modernity*. New York: Simon & Schuster, 1982.
Betzold, Michael, and Richard Feldman. *End of the Line: Autoworkers and the American Dream*. New York: Weidenfield & Nicholson, 1988.
Bickerton, James K. *Nova Scotia, Ottawa, and the Politics of Regional Development*. Toronto: University of Toronto Press, 1990.
Bothwell, Robert. *Your Country, My Country: A Unified History of the United States and Canada*. Toronto: Oxford University Press, 2015.
Bradley, Ben. *British Columbia by the Road: Car Culture and the Making of a Modern Landscape*. Vancouver: UBC Press, 2017.
Brinkley, Douglas. *Wheels for the Word: Henry Ford, His Company, and a Century of Progress*. New York: Penguin Books, 2003.
Brooks, Tim, and Earle March. *The Complete Directory to Prime Time Network and Cable TV Shows, 1946–Present*. New York: Ballantine Books, 1999.
Burke, Andrew. *Hinterland Remixed: Media, Memory and the Canadian 1970s*. Montreal and Kingston: McGill-Queen's University Press, 2019.
Buzan, Barry, and George Lawson. *The Global Transformation: History, Modernity and the Making of International Relations*. Cambridge: Cambridge University Press, 2015.
Cannadine, David. *Mellon: An American Life*. New York: Alfred A. Knopf, 2006.
Chandler, Alfred. *Managerial Innovation at General Motors*. New York: Arno Press, 1979.
– *Strategy and Structure: Chapters in the History of the American Industrial Enterprise*. Cambridge, MA: MIT Press, 1962.
– *The Visible Hand: The Managerial Revolution in American Business*. Cambridge, MA: Belknap Press of Harvard University, 1977.
Chernow, Ron. *Titan: The Life of John D. Rockefeller, Sr*. New York: Vintage, 2004.
Chinoy, Ely. *Automobile Workers and the American Dream*. Boston: Beacon Press, 1955.
Coleman, William D. *Business and Politics: A Study of Collective Action*. Montreal and Kingston: McGill-Queen's University Press, 1988.
Conley, Jim, and Arlene Tigar McLaren. *Car Troubles: Critical Studies of Automobility and Auto-Mobility*. New York: Routledge, 2009.
Cowie, Jefferson. *Stayin' Alive: The 1970s and the Last Days of the Working Class*. New York: New Press, 2010.
Davis, Michael W.R. *Mustang and the Pony Car Revolution*. Charleston, SC: Arcadia Publishing, 2014.
Dettelbach, Cynthia G. *In the Driver's Seat: The Automobile in American Literature and Popular Culture*. Westport, CT: Greenwood, 1976.
Dicke, Thomas S. *Franchising in America: The Development of a Business Method, 1840–1980*. Chapel Hill: University of North Carolina Press, 1992.
Eksteins, Modris. *Rites of Spring: The Great War and the Birth of the Modern Age*. Toronto: Lester & Orpen Dennys, 1994.
Fischer-Tiné, Harald, Stefan Huebner, and Ian Tyrrell, eds. *Spreading Protestant Modernity: Global Perspectives on the Social Work of the YMCA and YWCA, 1889–1970*. Honolulu: University of Hawaii Press, 2020.
Flink, James J. *The Automobile Age*. Cambridge, MA: MIT Press, 1990.
– *The Car Culture*. Cambridge, MA: MIT Press, 1975.

– “Three Stages of American Automobile Consciousness.” *American Quarterly* 24, 4 (1972): 451–73.

Freeland, Robert F. *Struggle for Control of the Modern Corporation: Organizational Change at General Motors, 1924–1970*. Cambridge: Cambridge University Press, 2001.

Fridenson, Patrick. “Business Failure and the Agenda of Business History.” *Enterprise & Society* 5 (December 2004): 562–82.

Gutfreund, Owen. “Rebuilding New York in the Auto Age: Robert Moses and His Highways.” In *Robert Moses and the Modern City: The Transformation of New York*, edited by Hilary Ballon and Kenneth T. Jackson, 86–93. New York: W.W. Norton, 2007.

– *Twentieth Century Sprawl: Highways and the Reshaping of the American Landscape*. New York: Oxford University Press, 2004.

Halberstam, David. *The Reckoning*. New York: William Morrow and Company, 1986.

Hale, Geoffrey. *Uneasy Partnership: The Politics of Business and Government in Canada*. Toronto: University of Toronto Press, 2018.

Hancocka, P.A., Illah Nourbakhsh, and Jack Stewart. “On the Future of Transportation in an Era of Automated and Autonomous Vehicles.” *Proceedings of the National Academy of Sciences* 116, 16 (2019): 7684–91.

Harvey, David. *The Condition of Postmodernity: An Enquiry into the Origins of Cultural Change*. Cambridge, MA: Blackwell, 1990.

Hodge, Gerald, Heather M. Halls, and Ira M. Robinson. *Planning Canadian Regions*, 2nd ed. Vancouver: UBC Press, 2017.

Hutton, Patrick. “Recent Scholarship on Memory and History.” *History Teacher* 33, 4 (2000): 533–48.

Ingrassia, Paul. *Engines of Change: A History of the American Dream in Fifteen Cars*. New York: Simon & Schuster, 2013.

Jackson, Kenneth T. *Crabgrass Frontier: The Suburbanization of the United Statesi*New York: Oxford University Press, 1985.

Jillson, Cal. *The American Dream: In History, Politics, Fiction*. Lawrence: University of Kansas Press, 2016.

Jolliffe, Lee. “The Bricklin: From Automobile to Place Narrative.” In *Automobile Heritage and Tourism*, edited by Michael V. Conlin and Lee Jolliffe, 40–8. London: Routledge, 2016.

Laird, Palmela Waler. *Advertising Progress: American Business and the Rise of Consumer Marketing*. Baltimore: Johns Hopkins University Press, 1998.

Langworth, Richard M. *Kaiser-Frazer: The Last Onslaught on Detroit*. Kutztown, PA: Princeton Publishing, 1975.

Lawson, Helene M. *Ladies on the Lot: Women, Car Sales, and the Pursuit of the American Dream*. Lanham, MD: Rowan & Littlefield, 2000.

Leed, Eric. *The Mind of the Traveler: From Gilgamesh to Global Tourism*. New York: Basic Books, 1991.

Levison, Marc. *An Extraordinary Time: The End of the Postwar Boom and the Return of the Ordinary Economy*. New York: Basic Books, 2016.

Little, J.I., ed. *Fashioning the Canadian Landscape: Essays on Travel Writing, Tourism, and National Identity in the Pre-Automobile Era*. Toronto: University of Toronto Press, 2018.

Lower, Arthur R.M. *Canadians in the Making: A Social History of Canada*. Toronto: Longman, 1969.

Lutz, Catherine, and Anne Lutz Fernandez. “Dream-Car: Myth Making, American Values, and the Automobile.” In *Carjacked: The Culture of the Automobile and Its Effect on Our Lives*, 13–38. New York: Palgrave Macmillan, 2009.

Matusow, Allen J. *Nixon’s Economy: Booms, Busts, Dollars and Votes*. Lawrence: University of Kansas Press, 1998.

McCarthy, Tom. *Auto Mania: Cars, Consumers and the Environment*. New Haven, CT: Yale University Press, 2009.

– "The Coming Wonder? Foresight and Early Concerns about the Automobile." *Environmental History* 6, 1 (2001): 46–74.

McCraw, Thomas K. *Prophets of Regulation*. Cambridge, MA: Belknap Press of Harvard University, 1984.

McKay, Ian. *The Quest of the Folk: Antimodernism and Natural Selection in Twentieth-Century Nova Scotia*. Montreal and Kingston: McGill-Queen's University Press, 1994.

Mom, Gijs. *Atlantic Automobilism: Emergence and Persistence of the Car, 1895–1940*. New York: Berghahn, 2015.

Muldoon, Jeffrey. "Henry Ford and His Legacy: An American Prometheus." In *The Palgrave Handbook of Management History*, edited by Bradley Bowden, Jeffrey Muldoon, Anthony M. Gould, and Adela J. McMurray, 522–44. Cham, CH: Springer International Publishing, 2020.

Nasaw, David. *Andrew Carnegie*. New York: Penguin Books, 2007.

Norcliffe, G.B. *Ride to Modernity: The Bicycle in Canada, 1869–1900*. Toronto: University of Toronto Press, 2001.

Oak Ridge National Laboratory. *Transportation Energy Data Book: Edition 35*, ORNL-6990. Oak Ridge, TN, September 2016.

Owram, Doug. *Born at the Right Time: A History of the Baby Boom Generation*. Toronto: University of Toronto Press, 1997.

Parker, Richard. *John Kenneth Galbraith: His Life, His Politics, His Economics*. Chicago: University of Chicago Press, 2006.

Pickens, Still [H.A. Fredericks]. "Introduction." In *How to Brickle: The New Brunswick Funny Book*. Saint John, NB: Unipress, 1977.

Rodgers, Daniel T. *Age of Fracture*. Cambridge, MA: Harvard University Press, 2011.

Savoie, Donald J. *Looking for Bootstraps: Economic Development in the Maritimes*. Halifax: Nimbus Publishing, 2017.

– *Regional Economic Development: Canada's Search for Solutions*. Toronto: University of Toronto Press, 1986.

Scott, James. *Seeing Like a State: How Certain Schemes to Improve the Human Condition Have Failed*. New Haven, CT: Yale University Press, 1998.

Seiler, Cotten. *Republic of Drivers: A Cultural History of Automobility in America*. Chicago: University of Chicago Press, 2008.

– "'So That We as a Race Might Have Something Authentic to Travel By': African American Automobility and Cold War Liberalism." *American Quarterly* 58, 4 (2006): 1091–17.

Shotwell, Greg. *Autoworkers under the Gun: A Shop-Floor View of the End of the American Dream*. Chicago: Haymarket Books, 2011.

Skidelsky, Robert. *John Maynard Keynes, 1883–1946: Economist, Philosopher, Statesman*. New York: Penguin Books, 2005.

Smart, Barry. *Postmodernity*. London: Routledge, 2016.

Smil, Vaclav. *Made in the USA: The Rise and Retreat of American Manufacturing*. Cambridge, MA: MIT Press, 2013.

Smith, Andrew, and Dimitry Anastakis, eds. *Smart Globalization: The Canadian Business and Economic Experience*. Toronto: University of Toronto Press, 2014.

Smith, Terry. *Making the Modern: Industry, Art, and Design in America*. Chicago: University of Chicago Press, 1993.

Snow, Richard. *I Invented the Modern Age: The Rise of Henry Ford*. New York: Scribner, 2014.

Stevenson, Heon. *Selling the Dream: Advertising the American Automobile*. London: Academy, 1995.

Swift, Earl. *Auto Biography: A Classic Car, an Outlaw Motorhead, and 57 Years of the American Dream*. New York: It Books/HarperCollins, 2014.
Taylor, Peter J. *Modernities: A Geohistorical Interpretation*. Minneapolis: University of Minnesota Press, 1999.
Urry, John. "The 'System' of Automobility." *Theory, Culture and Society* 21, 4–5 (2004): 25–39.
Venn, Couze, and Mike Featherstone. "Modernity." *Theory, Culture and Society* 23, 2–3 (2006): 457–65.
Volti, Rudi. *Cars and Culture: The Life Story of a Technology*. Westport, CT: Greenwood Press, 2004.
– "A Century of Automobility." *Technology and Culture* 37, 4 (1996): 663–85.
– *Society and Technological Change*. New York: Worth Publishers, 1988.
Walden, Keith. *Becoming Modern in Toronto: The Industrial Exhibition and the Shaping of a Late Victorian Culture*. Toronto: University of Toronto Press, 1997.
Weisberger, Bernard A. *Dream Maker: William Durant, Founder of General Motors*. Boston: Little, Brown, 1979.
Zeller, Thomas. *Consuming Landscapes: What We See When We Drive and Why It Matters*. Baltimore: Johns Hopkins University Press, 2022.

Online Sources and Other Digital Media

"Car Tunes." Henry Ford Museum. https://www.thehenryford.org/collections-and-research/digital-collections/sets/1721.
"*Chico and the Man* Clip." YouTube. https://www.youtube.com/watch?v=UY1vrKLcLOk.
"Ford and Model T Songs Collection, 1910–1939, Accession 163." Henry Ford Museum. http://www.dalnet.lib.mi.us/henryford/docs/FordAndModelTSongsCollection_Accession163.pdf.

Chapter 1. The Future (Technology)

Theses and Unpublished Papers

Dickison, Joshua John. "Making New Brunswickers Modern: Natural and Human Resource Development in Macquatac Regional Development Plan, 1965–1975." MA thesis, University of New Brunswick, 2006.
Edwards, Bret Joel. "A Bumpy Landing: Airports and the Making of Jet Age Canada." PhD diss., University of Toronto, 2017.
Elzway, Salem. "The Arm Race: A History of the Industrial Robot in Postwar America." Unpublished paper, University of Michigan.
Leroux, John. "Make Way for Tomorrow: New Brunswick's Visual and Cultural Modernity, 1930–1967." PhD diss., University of New Brunswick, 2020.
Pardini, Samuele F.S. "The Engines of History: The Automobile in American and Italian Literary Cultures, 1908–1943." PhD diss., State University of New York at Buffalo, 2005.
Ruffilli, Dean. "The Car in Canadian Culture, 1898–1983." PhD diss., University of Western Ontario, 2006.

Scholarly Books and Articles

Anastakis, Dimitry. *Auto Pact: Creating a Borderless North American Auto Industry, 1960–1971*. Toronto: University of Toronto Press, 2005.

– "Building a 'New Nova Scotia': State Intervention, the Auto Industry, and the Case of Volvo in Halifax, 1963–1996." *Acadiensis* 34, 1 (2004): 3–30.
– "From Independence to Integration: The Corporate Evolution of the Ford Motor Company of Canada." *Business History Review* 78, 2 (2004): 213–53.
–, ed. *The Sixties: Passion, Politics and Style*. Montreal and Kingston: McGill-Queen's University Press, 2009.
Azzi, Stephen. *Reconcilable Differences: A History of Canada-US Relations*. Toronto: Oxford University Press, 2014.
Bak, Richard. *Henry and Edsel: The Creation of the Ford Empire*. New York: Wiley, 2003.
Ballard, Leslie Anne, Selma Sabanovic, Jasleen Kaur, and Stasa Milojevic. "George Charles Devol, Jr." *IEEE Robotics and Automation Magazine*, September 2012, 114–19.
Batchelor, Ray. *Henry Ford, Mass Production, Modernism, and Design*. Manchester: Manchester University Press, 1994.
Bayley, Stephen. *Sex, Drink, and Fast Cars: The Creation and Consumption of Images*. Boston: Faber and Faber, 1986.
Belliveau, Joel. "Acadian New Brunswick's Ambivalent Leap into the Canadian Liberal Order." In *Creating Postwar Canada: Community, Diversity, and Dissent, 1945–75*, edited by Magda Fahrni and Robert Rutherdale, 61–88. Vancouver: UBC Press, 2008.
Berghoff, Bruce. *The GM Motorama: Dream Cars of the Fifties*. Osceola, WI: Motorbooks International, 1995.
Bernstein, Jeffrey R. "Toyoda Automatic Looms and Toyota Automobiles." In *Creating Modern Capitalism: How Entrepreneurs, Companies and Countries Triumphed in Three Industrial Revolutions*, edited by Thomas K. McCraw, 398–438. Cambridge, MA: Harvard University Press, 1995.
Borins, Sanford, with Lee Brown. *Investments in Failure: Five Government Corporations That Cost the Canadian Taxpayer Billions*. Toronto: Methuen, 1986.
Bothwell, Robert. *Alliance and Illusion: Canada and the World, 1945- 84*. Vancouver: UBC Press, 2007.
Brinkley, Douglas. *Wheels for the World: Henry Ford, His Company, and a Century of Progress*. New York: Penguin Books, 2003.
Brooks, Victor. *Boomers: The Cold-War Generation Grows Up*. Chicago: Ivan R. Dee, 2009.
Chandler, Alfred. *The Visible Hand: The Managerial Revolution in American Business*. Cambridge, MA: Belknap Press of Harvard University, 1977.
Chang, Ha Joon. *Kicking Away the Ladder: Development Strategy in Historical Perspective*. London: Anthem, 2002.
Chun, Seung-hun. *The Economic Development of South Korea: From Poverty to a Modern Industrial State*. New York: Taylor and Francis, 2018.
Clarke, Sally. "Managing Design: The Art and Colour Section at General Motors, 1927–1941." *Journal of Design History* 12, 1 (1999): 65–79.
– *Trust and Power: Consumers, the Modern Corporation, and the Making of the United States Automobile Market*. Cambridge: Cambridge University Press, 2007.
Cowie, Jefferson. *Stayin' Alive: The 1970s and the Last Days of the Working Class*. New York: New Press, 2010.
Cumo, Christopher. *Science and Technology in 20th-Century American Life*. Westport, CT: Greenwood Press, 2007.
Davies, Stephen. "'Reckless Walking Must Be Discouraged': The Automobile Revolution and the Shaping of Modern Urban Canada to 1930." *Urban History Review* 18, 2 (1989): 123–38.

DeMont, John. *Citizens Irving: K.C. Irving and His Legacy – The Story of Canada's Wealthiest Family.* Toronto: Doubleday Canada, 1991.

Donaghy, Greg. *Tolerant Allies: Canada and the United States, 1963–68.* Montreal and Kingston: McGill-Queen's University Press, 2003.

Dutcher, Stephen. "'Looking towards the Promised Land': Modernity, Anti-Modernity and Co-operative Wholesaling in the Maritime Provinces, 1945–1961." *Acadiensis* 34, 2 (2005): 46–73.

Ford, Henry. *Today and Tomorrow.* New York: Doubleday, 1926.

Frink, Tim. *New Brunswick: A Short History.* Saint John, NB: Stonington Books, 1997.

G.T.F. "A Sportin' Chance for Safety." *Industrial Design* 21, 8 (1974): 32–5.

Gartman, David. *Auto Opium: A Social History of American Automobile Design.* London: Routledge, 1994.

– *From Autos to Architecture: Fordism and Architectural Aesthetics in the Twentieth Century.* New York: Princeton Architectural Press, 2009.

– "Harley Earl and the Art and Color Section: The Birth of Styling at General Motors." *Design Issues* 10, 2 (1994): 3–26.

Grandin, Greg. *Fordlandia: The Rise and Fall of Henry Ford's Forgotten Jungle City.* New York: Metropolitan Books, 2009.

Hopkins, Garth. *Clairtone: The Rise and Fall of a Business Empire.* Toronto: McClelland & Stewart, 1978.

Hyde, Charles K. *Riding the Roller Coaster: A History of the Chrysler Corporation.* Detroit: Wayne State University Press, 2003.

Johnson, Chalmers. *MITI and the Japanese Miracle: The Growth of Industrial Policy, 1925–1975.* Stanford, CA: Stanford University Press, 1982.

Kenny, James L. "A New Dependency: State, Local Capital, and the Development of New Brunswick's Base Metal Industry, 1960–70." *Canadian Historical Review* 78, 1 (1997): 1–39.

–, and Andrew G. Secord. "Engineering Modernity: Hydroelectric Development in New Brunswick, 1945–1970." *Acadiensis* 39, 1 (2010): 3–26.

Khun, Arthur J. *GM Passes Ford: Designing the General Motors Performance-Control System.* University Park: Penn State University Press, 1990.

Kimes, Beverly Rae. *The Star and the Laurel: The Centennial History of Daimler, Mercedes, and Benz, 1886–1986.* Montvale, NJ: Mercedes-Benz of North America, 1986.

Kirk, Donald. *Korean Dynasty: Hyundai and Chung Ju Yung.* London: Taylor and Francis, 2016.

Kirsch, David A. *The Electric Vehicle and the Burden of History.* New Brunswick, NJ: Rutgers University Press, 2000.

Knoedelseder, William. *Fins: Harley Earl, the Rise of General Motors, and the Glory Days of Detroit.* New York: Harper Business, 2018.

Kuhn, David Paul. *The Hardhat Riot: New York City and the Dawn of the White Working-Class Revolution.* New York: Oxford University Press, 2020.

Lethto, Steve. *Preston Tucker and His Battle to Build the Car of Tomorrow.* Chicago: Chicago Review Press, 2016.

Ling, Peter J. *American and the Automobile: Technology, Reform and Social Change, 1893–1923.* Manchester: Manchester University Press, 1990.

Link, Stefan J. *Forging Global Fordism: Nazi Germany, Soviet Russia, and the Contest Over the Industrial Order.* Princeton, NJ: Princeton University Press, 2020.

Loubet, Jean-Louis. *Renault: Histoire d'une entreprise.* Boulogne-Billancourt, FR: ETAI, 2000.

MacKinnon, Lachlan. "Importing the Clairtone Sound: Political Economy, Regionalism, and Deindustrialization in Pictou County." *Labour/Le travail* 91 (Spring 2023): 147–68.

Marchildon, Gregory P. *Profits and Politics: Beaverbrook and the Gilded Age of Canadian Finance*. Toronto: University of Toronto Press. 1996.

Marquis, Greg. "Growth Fantasies: Setting the Urban Agenda in Saint John, New Brunswick, 1960–1976." *Acadiensis* 46, 1 (2017): 122–44.

McCarthy, Tom. *Auto Mania: Cars, Consumers and the Environment*. New Haven, CT: Yale University Press, 2009.

McDowall, Duncan. *Steel at the Sault: Francis Hector Clergue, Sir James Dunn and the Algoma Steel Corporation, 1899–1956*. Toronto: University of Toronto Press, 1984.

Meikle, Jeffrey L. *American Plastic: A Cultural History*. New Brunswick, NJ: Rutgers University Press. 1995.

Mercelis, Joris. *Beyond Bakelite: Leo Baekeland and the Business of Science and Invention*. Cambridge, MA: MIT Press, 2020.

Metzler, Mark. *Capital as Will and Imagination: Schumpeter's Guide to the Postwar Japanese Miracle*. Ithaca, NY: Cornell University Press, 2013.

Mieczkowski, Yanek. *Eisenhower's Sputnik Moment: The Race for Space and World Prestige*. Ithaca, NY: Cornell University Press, 2013.

Neuman, David J. "… to Bumper." *Journal of Popular Culture* 8, 1 (1974): 183–4.

Nevins, Allan. *Ford: Expansion and Challenge, 1915–1933*. New York: Scribner, 1957.

– *Ford: The Times, the Man, the Company*. New York: Scribner, 1954.

–, and Frank Ernest Hill. *Ford: Decline and Rebirth, 1933–1962*. New York: Scribner, 1962.

Niblo, Stephen. *Mexico in the 1940s: Modernity, Politics and Corruption*. Wilmington, DE: Rowman & Littlefield, 1999.

Niergarth, Kurt. *The Dignity of Every Human Being: New Brunswick Artists and Canadian Culture between the Great Depression and the Cold War*. Toronto: University of Toronto Press, 2015.

Norcliffe, G.B. *Ride to Modernity: The Bicycle in Canada, 1869–1900*. Toronto: University of Toronto Press, 2001.

Norton, Peter D. *Fighting Traffic: The Dawn of the Motor Age in the American City*. Cambridge, MA: MIT Press, 2008.

Nye, David E. *American Technological Sublime*. Cambridge, MA: MIT Press, 1994.

O'Regan, Gerald. "Unimation." In *Pillars of Computing: A Compendium of Select, Pivotal Technology Firms*, 219–23. Cham, CH: Springer International Publishing, 2015.

Owram, Doug. *Born at the Right Time: A History of the Baby Boom Generation*. Toronto: University of Toronto Press, 1997.

Palmer, Bryan. *Canada's Sixties: The Ironies of Identity in a Rebellious Era*. Toronto: University of Toronto Press, 2008.

Patterson, James T. *Grand Expectations: The United States, 1945–1974*. New York: Oxford University Press, 1996.

Poitras, Jacques. *Irving vs. Irving: Canada's Feuding Billionaires and the Stories They Won't Tell*. Toronto: Viking; 2014.

Rieger, Bernard. *The People's Car: A Global History of the Volkswagen Beetle*. Cambridge, MA: Harvard University Press, 2013.

Roberts, David. *In the Shadow of Detroit: Gordon M. McGregor, Ford of Canada, and Motoropolis*. Detroit: Wayne State University Press, 2006.

Robinson, Danielle. "Modernism at a Crossroad: The Spadina Expressway Controversy in Toronto, Ontario ca. 1960–71." *Canadian Historical Review* 92, 2 (2011): 295–322.

Rubenstein, James M. *Making and Selling Cars: Innovation and Change in the US Automotive Industry*. Baltimore: Johns Hopkins University Press, 2001.

Rutsky, R.L. *High Tech: Art and Technology from the Machine Aesthetic to the Posthuman.* Minneapolis: University of Minnesota Press, 1999.

Savoie, Donald. *"Thanks for the Business": K.C. Irving, Arthur Irving, and the Story of Irving Oil.* Halifax: Nimbus Publishing, 2020.

Sidgelbaum, Lewis H. *Cars for Comrades: The Life of the Soviet Automobile.* Ithaca, NY: Cornell University Press, 2008.

Slade, Giles. *Made to Break: Technology and Obsolescence in America.* Cambridge, MA: Harvard University Press, 2006.

Solomon, William. "Slapstick Modernism: Charley Bowers and Industrial Modernity." *Modernist Cultures* 2, 2 (2006): 170–88.

Stadiem, William. *Jet Set: The People, The Planes, The Glamour, and the Romance in Aviation's Glory Years.* New York: Ballantine Books, 2014.

Stevenson, Heon. *American Automobile Advertising, 1930–1980.* Jefferson, NC: McFarland & Company, 2008.

Stokes, Raymond G. "Technology and the West German 'Wirtschaftswunder.'" *Technology and Culture* 32, 1 (1991): 1–22.

Tedlow, Richard S. "The Struggle for Dominance in the Automobile Market: The Early Years of Ford and General Motors." *Business and Economic History* 17 (1988): 49–62.

Tichi, Cecilia. *Shifting Gears: Technology, Literature, Culture in Modernist America.* Chapel Hill: University of North Carolina Press, 1987.

Togo, Y., and W. Wartman. *Against All Odds: The Story of the Toyota Motor Corporation and the Family his Created It.* New York: St. Martin's Press, 1993.

Tremblay, Anthony M. *The Fiddlehead Moment: Pioneering an Alternative Canadian Modernism in New Brunswick.* Montreal and Kingston: McGill-Queen's University Press, 2019.

Vance, Ashlee. *Elon Musk, Tesla, SpaceX and the Quest for a Fantastic Future.* New York: HarperCollins, 2015.

Van Vleck, Jenifer. *Empire of the Air: Aviation and the American Ascendancy.* Cambridge, MA: Harvard University Press, 2013.

Walden, Keith. *Becoming Modern in Toronto: The Industrial Exhibition and the Shaping of a Late Victorian Culture.* Toronto: University of Toronto Press, 1997.

Watts, Stephen. *The People's Tycoon: Henry Ford and the American Century.* New York: A.A. Knopf, 2005.

White, Lawrence J. *The Automobile Industry since 1945.* 1971; Cambridge, MA: Harvard University Press, 2014.

Wilkins, Mira, and Frank Ernest Hill. *American Business Abroad: Ford on Six Continents.* Detroit: Wayne State University Press, 1964.

Wisnioski, Mathew. *Engineers for Change: Competing Visions of Technology in 1960s America.* Cambridge, MA: MIT Press, 2012.

Wolfe, Joel. *Autos and Progress: The Brazilian Search for Modernity.* Oxford: Oxford University Press, 2010.

Womack, James P., David T. Jones, and Daniel Roos. *The Machine That Changed the World: The Story of Lean Production.* New York: Free Press, 2007.

Wynn, Graham. *Timber Colony: A Historical Geography of Early Nineteenth Century New Brunswick.* Toronto: University of Toronto Press, 1981.

Yafie, Roberta C. "Joe Engelberger: Father of Robotics." *American Metal Market* 107, 236 (1999): 2.

Young, R.A. "'And the People Will Sink into Despair': Reconstruction in New Brunswick, 1942–52." *Canadian Historical Review* 69, 2 (1988): 127–66.

Online Sources and Other Digital Media

"1974 *Let's Make a Deal* Clip." YouTube. https://www.youtube.com/watch?v=qcYf64aKDJo.
Lang, Fritz, dir. *Metropolis.* 1927; Parufamet, film.
Lucas, George, dir. *Star Wars.* 1977; 20th Century Fox, film.
"Popular Research Topics: Soybean Car." Henry Ford Museum. https://www.thehenryford.org/collections-and-research/digital-resources/popular-topics/soy-bean-car/.

Chapter 2. Entrepreneur (Archetype)

Theses and Unpublished Papers

Fox, Michael D. "Lee Iacocca, the Man, the Myth, the Corporation: Iacocca's Development as an American Western Mythical Hero and the Exploitation of his Condition in Chrysler Television Commercials, 1981–85." MA thesis, Miami University, 1988.
Megginson, Jayne Margaret. "The Rhetoric of Lee Iacocca: The Man, the Myth, the Message." PhD diss., Louisiana State University, 1986.
Thorpe, Judith Mosier. "The Role of Persuasion for a Corporate Spokesman: An Analysis of the Arguments Lee Iacocca Presented on Behalf of Chrysler Corporation to the American Consumer and to Congress from 1979 to 1982." PhD diss., Ohio State University, 1986.
Wadhwani, R. Daniel. Presidential address delivered at the Business History Conference, 17 March 2023, Detroit.

Scholarly Books and Articles

Abodaher, David. *Iacocca.* New York: Zebra, 1982.
Anastakis, Dimitry. *Autonomous State: The Struggle for a Canadian Car Industry from OPEC to Free Trade.* Toronto: University of Toronto Press, 2013.
– *Auto Pact: Creating a Borderless North American Auto Industry, 1960–1971.* Toronto: University of Toronto Press, 2005.
– "Industrial Sunrise? The Chrysler Bailout, the State, and the Re-industrialization of the Canadian Automotive Sector, 1975–1986." *Urban History Review/ Revue d'histoire urbaine* 35, 2 (2007): 37–50.
Billington, David P., and David P. Billington Jr. *Power, Speed, and Form: Engineers and the Making of the Twentieth Century.* Princeton, NJ: Princeton University Press, 2013.
Borins, S., and B. Hearst. "Cults of Personality: Fables of the Automobile Manufacturing Industry." In *Negotiating Business Narratives: Fables of the Information Technology, Automobile Manufacturing, and Financial Trading Industries*, 23–36. Cham, CH: Palgrave Macmillan/ Springer, 2018.
Breer, Carl, and Anthony J. Yanik. *The Birth of Chrysler Corporation and Its Engineering Legacy.* Warrendale, PA: SAE, 1994.
Bridges, Hal. "The Robber Baron Concept in American History." *Business History Review* 32, 1 (1958): 1–13.
Brinkley, Douglas. *Wheels for the World: Henry Ford, His Company, and a Century of Progress.* New York: Penguin Books, 2003.
Bryne, John A. *The Whiz Kids: Ten Founding Fathers of American Business and the Legacy They Left Us.* New York: Doubleday Business, 1993.
Casey, Robert. *The Model T: A Centennial History.* Baltimore: Johns Hopkins University Press, 2008.

Catano, James V. "Entrepreneurial Masculinity: Re-tooling the Self-Made Man." *Journal of American and Comparative Cultures* 23, 2 (2000): 1–9.

Chandler, Alfred. *Strategy and Structure: Chapters in the History of the American Industrial Enterprise.* Cambridge, MA: MIT Press, 1962.

– *The Visible Hand: The Managerial Revolution in American Business.* Cambridge, MA: Belknap Press of Harvard University, 1977.

Clarke, Sally H. *Trust and Power: Consumers, the Modern Corporation, and the Making of the United States Automobile Market.* Cambridge: Cambridge University Press, 2007.

Cole, Arthur H. "An Approach to the Study of Entrepreneurship: A Tribute to Edwin F. Gay." *Journal of Economic History* 6 (S1) (1946): 1–15.

Cray, Edward. *Chrome Colossus: General Motors and Its Times.* New York: McGraw-Hill, 1980.

Curcio, Vincent. *Chrysler: The Life and Times of an Automotive Genius.* New York: Oxford University Press, 2005.

Davies, Stephen. "'Reckless Walking Must Be Discouraged': The Automobile Revolution and the Shaping of Modern Urban Canada to 1930." *Urban History Review* 18, 2 (1989): 123–38.

Davis, Donald F. *Conspicuous Production: Automobiles and Elites in Detroit, 1899–1933.* Philadelphia: Temple University Press, 1988.

Davis, Michael W.R. *Mustang and the Pony Car Revolution.* Charleston, SC: Arcadia Publishing, 2014.

Dionisopoulos, George N. "A Case Study in Print Media and Heroic Myth: Less Iacocca, 1978–1985." *Southern Speech Communication Journal* 53, 3 (1988): 227–43.

Doyle, Jack. *Taken for a Ride: Detroit's Big Three and the Politics of Pollution.* New York: Four Walls Eight Windows, 2000.

Drucker, Peter F. *Concept of the Corporation.* 1946; New York: John Day, 1983.

Durant, Margery. *My Father.* New York: Putnam, 1929.

Farber, David. *Sloan Rules: Alfred P. Sloan and the Triumph of General Motors.* Chicago: University of Chicago Press, 2002.

Freeman, Joshua Benjamin. *Behemoth: A History of the Factory and the Making of the Modern World.* New York: W.W. Norton, 2018.

Fridenson, Patrick. "Business Failure and the Agenda of Business History." *Enterprise & Society* 5 (December 2004): 562–82.

Friedman, Walter. *Birth of a Salesman: The Transformation of Selling in America.* Cambridge, MA: Harvard University Press, 2009.

Galambos, Louis, and Franco Amatori. "Entrepreneurial History in Motion: A Reply to R. Daniel Wadhwani's Comment." *Enterprise & Society* 21, 2 (2020): 340–2.

García-Ruiz, José L., and Pierangelo Toninellim, eds. *The Determinants of Entrepreneurship: Leadership, Culture, Institutions.* London: Routledge, 2015.

Gindin, Sam. *The CAW: Birth and Transformation of a Union.* Toronto: Lorimer, 1995.

Godfrey, Frank P. *An International History of the Sewing Machine.* London: R. Hale, 1982.

Grandin, Greg. *Fordlandia: The Rise and Fall of Henry Ford's Forgotten Jungle City.* New York: Metropolitan Books, 2009.

Halberstam, David. *The Reckoning.* New York: William Morrow, 1986.

Hayes, Walter. *Henry: A Life of Henry Ford II.* New York: Grove Weidenfeld, 1990.

Hickel, James K. "The Chrysler Bail-Out Bust." *Backgrounder*, no. 276 (13 July 1983): 1–7.

High, Steven. *Industrial Sunset: The Making of North America's Rust Belt, 1969–1984.* Toronto: University of Toronto Press, 2003.

Hoffman, Bryce G. *American Icon: Alan Mulally and the Fight to Save Ford Motor Company.* New York: Penguin Random House, 2012.

Hounshell, David A. "Assets, Organizations, Strategies and Traditions: Organizational Capabilities and Constraints in the Remaking of the Ford Motor Company, 1946–1962." In *Learning by Doing in Markets Firms and Countries*, edited by Naomi R. Lamoreaux, Daniel M.G. Raff, and Peter Temin, 185–208. Chicago: University of Chicago Press, 1999.

– *From the American System to Mass Production, 1800–1932: The Development of Manufacturing Technology in the United States*. Baltimore: Johns Hopkins University Press, 1985.

Hugh Atiken, ed. *Explorations in Enterprise*. Cambridge, MA: Harvard University Press, 1965.

Hyde, Charles K. *Arsenal of Democracy: The American Automobile Industry in World War II*. Detroit: Wayne State University Press, 2013.

– *Riding the Roller Coaster: A History of the Chrysler Corporation*. Detroit: Wayne State University Press, 2003.

Iacocca, Lee, and William Novak. *Iacocca: An Autobiography*. New York: Bantam, 1984.

Ingrassia, Paul. *Engines of Change: A History of the American Dream in Fifteen Cars*. New York: Simon & Schuster, 2013.

Jacobs, Timothy. *A History of General Motors*. New York: Brompton Books, 1992.

Jakle, John A. *Signs in America's Auto Age: Signatures of Landscape and Place*. Iowa City: University of Iowa Press, 2004.

Jakle, John A., and Keith A. Sculle. *The Gas Station in America*. Baltimore: Johns Hopkins University Press, 1994.

– *Supplanting America's Railroads: The Early Auto Age, 1900–1940*. Knoxville: University of Tennessee Press, 2017.

Jefferys, Steve. *Management and Managed: Fifty Years of Crisis at Chrysler*. New York: Cambridge University Press, 1986.

Jones, G., and R.D. Wadhwani. "Entrepreneurship." In *Oxford Handbook of Business History*, edited by Geoffrey G. Jones and Jonathan Zeitlin, 501–28. New York: Oxford University Press, 2008.

Jones, Geoffrey, and R. Daniel Wadhwani. "Entrepreneurial Theory and the History of Globalization." *Business and Economic History On-Line*, vol. 5 (2007).

Kennedy, Edward D. *The Automobile Industry: The Coming of Age of Capitalism's Favorite Child*. New York: Reynal and Hitchcock, 1941.

Klepper, Steven. "Pre-Entry Experience and Firm Performance in the Evolution of the US Automobile Industry." *Advances in Strategic Management* 21 (December 2004): 289–315.

Koehn, Nancy F. *Brand New: How Entrepreneurs Earned Consumers' Trust from Wedgewood to Dell*. Cambridge, MA: Harvard University Press, 2001.

Kraft, Barbara S. *The Peace Ship: Henry Ford's Pacifist Adventure in the First World War*. New York: Macmillan, 1978.

Levin, Doron P. *Behind the Wheel at Chrysler: The Iacocca Legacy*. New York: Mariner Books, 1995.

Lewis, David L. "Introduction: Special Issue on Cars." *Michigan Quarterly Review* 19, 4 (1980) and 20, 1 (1981): 435.

Linel, Albert Lewis, and Darlene E.R. Resling. *Lee Iacocca: A Play*. Baltimore: Learning Well, 1997.

Link, Stefan J. *Forging Global Fordism: Nazi Germany, Soviet Russia, and the Contest Over the Industrial Order*. Princeton, NJ: Princeton University Press, 2020.

MacDougall, Robert. *The People's Network: The Political Economy of the Telephone in the Gilded Age*. Philadelphia: University of Pennsylvania Press, 2014.

Marchand, Roland. *Advertising the American Dream: Making Way for Modernity, 1920–1940*. Berkeley: University of California Press, 1985.

McCarthy, Tom. *Auto Mania: Cars, Consumers and the Environment*. New Haven, CT: Yale University Press, 2009.

McCraw, Thomas K., and Richard S. Tedlow. "Henry Ford, Alfred Sloan, and the Three Phases of Marketing." In *Creating Modern Capitalism: How Entrepreneurs, Companies and Countries Triumphed in Three Industrial Revolutions*, edited by Thomas K. McCraw, 266–300. Cambridge, MA: Harvard University Press, 1995.

McGahan, Anita, and Joel A.C. Baum, eds. *Business Strategy over the Industry Life Cycle*. Bingley, UK: Emerald Group Publishing, 2009.

McKinlay, Alan, and Ken Starkey. "After Henry: Continuity and Change in the Ford Motor Company." *Business History* 36 (1994): 184–205.

McCormick, Blaine, and Burton W. Folsom. "The Greatest American Entrepreneurs and Businesspeople in American History: A Replication of the 2001 Ranking." *Cogent: Business and Management* 7, 1 (2020): 1–13.

McShane, Clay. *Down the Asphalt Path: The Automobile and the American City*. New York: Columbia University Press, 1994.

Moritz, Michael, and Barrett Seaman. *Going for Broke: Lee Iacocca's Battle to Save Chrysler*. New York: Doubleday, 1983.

Nevins, Allan, and Frank Ernest Hill. *Ford: Decline and Rebirth, 1933–1962*. New York: Scribner, 1962.

Norton, Peter D. "Street Rivals: Jaywalking and the Invention of the Motor Age Street." *Technology and History* 48, 2 (2007): 331–59.

Norwood, Stephen. "Ford's Brass Knuckles: Harry Bennett, The Cult of Muscularity, and Anti-Labor Terror, 1920–1945." *Labor History* 37, no. 3 (1996): 365–91.

Pearson, Charles T. *The Indomitable Tin Goose: The True Story of Preston Tucker and His Car*. 1960; New York: Motorbooks International, 1974.

Pelfrey, William. *Billy, Alfred, and General Motors: The Story of Two Unique Men, a Legendary Company, and a Remarkable Time in American History*. New York: AMACOM, 2006.

Pettifer, Julian, and Nigel Turner. *Automania: Man and the Motor Car*. London: Collins, 1984.

Porac, Joseph E., José Antonio Rosa, Jelena Spanjol, and Michael Scott Saxon. "America's Family Vehicle: Path Creation in the US Minivan Market." In *Path Dependence and Creation*, edited by Raghu Garud and Peter Karnoe, 213–42. New York: Psychology Press, 2001.

Rae, John B. "The Fabulous Billy Durant." *Business History Review* 32, 3 (1958): 255–71.

Rasenberger, Jim. *America, 1908: The Dawn of Flight, the Race to the Pole, the Invention of the Model T, and the Making of a Modern Nation*. New York: Scribner 2007.

Rattner, Steven. *Overhaul: An Insider's Account of the Obama Administration's Emergency Rescue of the Auto Industry*. New York: Houghton Mifflin, 2010.

Reich, Robert, and John D. Donahue. *New Deals: The Chrysler Revival and the American System*. New York: Times Books, 1986.

Seo, Sarah A. *Policing the Open Road: How Cars Transformed American Freedom*. Cambridge, MA: Harvard University Press, 2019.

Schumpeter, J.A. *Capitalism, Socialism and Democracy*. New York: Harpers and Sons, 1942.

– *The Theory of Economic Development*. Cambridge, MA: Harvard University Press, 1934.

Schwartz, Michael. "Markets, Networks, and the Rise of Chrysler in Old Detroit, 1920–1940." *Enterprise & Society* 1, 1 (2000): 63–99.

Schwenker, Burkhard, and Klaus Spremann. *Management Between Strategy and Finance*. Berlin: Springer Gabler, 2009.

Schwenker, Burkhard, and Mario Müller-Dofel. *On Good Management the Corporate Lifecycle: An Essay and Interviews with Franz Fehrenbach, Jürgen Hambrecht, Wolfgang Reitzle and Alexander Rittweger*. Wiesbaden: Springer Gabler, 2013.

Slade, Giles. *Made to Break: Technology and Obsolescence in America*. Cambridge, MA: Harvard University Press, 2006.

Sloan, Alfred P. *Adventures of a White-Collar Man*. New York: Doubleday, 1941.
Smith, Denis, and Dominic Elliot, eds. *Key Readings in Crisis Management: Systems and Structures for Prevention and Recovery*. New York: Routledge, 2006.
Smith, Terry. *Making the Modern: Industry, Art, and Design in America*. Chicago: University of Chicago Press, 1993.
Snow, Richard. *I Invented the Modern Age: The Rise of Henry Ford*. New York: Scribner, 2014.
Sørensen, Charles E., with Samuel T. Williamson. *My Forty Years with Ford*. New York: W.W. Norton, 1956.
Spector, Bert. "Flawed from the 'Get-Go': Lee Iacocca and the Origins of Transformational Leadership." *Leadership* 10, 3 (2014): 361–79.
Stuart, Reginald. *Bailout: America's Billion Dollar Gamble on the "New" Chrysler Corporation*. South Bend, IN: And Books, 1980.
Taylor, Alex, III. *Sixty to Zero: An Inside Look at the Collapse of General Motors and the Detroit Auto Industry*. New Haven, CT: Yale University Press, 2010.
Thorpe, Judie Mosier. "Lee Iacocca and the Generation of Myth in the Spokesman Advertising Campaign for Chrysler from 1980–1984." *Journal of American Culture* 11, 2 (1988): 41–5.
Tremulis, Alex. "The 1946–48 Tucker: A Great Promise Unfulfilled." SAE Technical Paper Series 872001. Whitevale, PA: SAE, 1987.
Usselman, Steven W. *Regulating Railroad Innovation: Business, Technology, and Politics in America, 1840–1920*. New York: Cambridge University Press, 2003.
Wadhwani, Daniel. "Gales, Streams, and Multipliers: Conceptual Metaphors and Theory Development in Business History." *Enterprise & Society* 21, 2 (2020): 320–33.
Watts, Stephen. *The People's Tycoon: Henry Ford and the American Century*. New York: A.A. Knopf, 2005.
Weisberger, Bernard. *The Dream Maker*. Boston: Little, Brown, 1979.
Wells, Christopher. *Car Country: An Environmental History*. Seattle: University of Washington Press, 2012.
Whyte, William. *The Organization Man*. Philadelphia: University of Pennsylvania Press, 2002.
Wilkins, Mira, and Frank Ernest Hill. *American Business Abroad: Ford on Six Continents*. Detroit: Wayne State University Press, 1964.
Wilson, Sloan. *The Man in the Gray Flannel Suit*. New York: Simon & Schuster, 1955.
Woeste, Victoria Saker. *Henry Ford's War on Jews and the Legal Battle against Hate Speech*. Stanford, CA: Stanford University Press, 2012.
Wyden, Peter. *The Unknown Iacocca*. New York: William Morrow, 1987.

Online Sources and Other Digital Media

"Car Tunes." Henry Ford Museum. https://www.thehenryford.org/collections-and-research/digital-collections/sets/1721.
Coppola, Francis Ford, dir. *Tucker: The Man and His Dream*. 1988; Paramount Pictures, film.
"'Whiz Kids' Brought Financial Expertise and Modern Management to Ford Motor Company." Ford Motor Company. https://ophelia.sdsu.edu:8443/ford/09-05-2011/about-ford/heritage/people/whizkids/659-whiz-kids.html.

Chapter 3. Risk (Safety)

Theses

Battle, Andy. "Runaway: A History of Postwar New York in Four Factories." PhD diss., City University of New York, 2019.

Gangloff, Amy Beth. "Medicalizing the Automobile: Public Health, Safety, and American Culture, 1920–1967." PhD diss., Stony Brook University, 2006.

Scholarly Books and Articles

Anastakis, Dimitry. *Autonomous State: The Struggle for a Canadian Car Industry from OPEC to Free Trade*. Toronto: University of Toronto Press, 2013.

– *Auto Pact: Creating a Borderless North American Auto Industry, 1960–1971*. Toronto: University of Toronto Press, 2005.

– "A 'War on Pollution'? Canadian Responses to the Automotive Emissions Problem, 1970–80." *Canadian Historical Review* 90, 1 (2009): 99–136.

Bak, Richard. *Henry and Edsel: The Creation of the Ford Empire*. New York: Wiley, 2003.

Barnard, John. *American Vanguard: The United Auto Workers during the Reuther Years, 1935–1970*. Detroit: Wayne State University Press, 2004.

Beck, Ulrich. *Risk Society: Towards a New Modernity*. New Delhi: Sage, 1992.

Bonsall, Thomas E. *More Than They Promised: The Studebaker Story*. Stanford, CA: Stanford University Press, 2022.

– *Disaster in Dearborn: The Story of the Edsel*. Stanford, CA: Stanford General Books, 2002.

Brinkley, Douglas. *Wheels for the World: Henry Ford, His Company, and a Century of Progress*. New York: Penguin Books, 2003.

Clarke, Sally. "Managing Design: The Art and Colour Section at General Motors, 1927–1941." *Journal of Design History* 12, 1 (1999): 65–79.

Clarke, Sally H., Naomi R. Lamoreaux, and Steven W. Usselman. *The Challenge of Remaining Innovative: Insights from Twentieth-Century American Business*. Stanford, CA: Stanford Business Books, 2009.

Cohen, Lizabeth. *A Consumers' Republic: The Politics of Mass Consumption in Postwar America*. New York: Knopf, 2003.

Cowie, Jefferson. *Capital Moves: RCA's 70-Year Quest for Cheap Labor*. Ithaca, NY: Cornell University Press, 1999.

– *Stayin' Alive: The 1970s and the Last Days of the Working Class*. New York: New Press, 2010.

Critchlow, Donald T. *Studebaker: The Life and Death of an American Corporation*. Bloomington: Indiana University Press, 1996.

Davis, Donald F. *Conspicuous Production: Automobiles and Elites in Detroit, 1899–1933*. Philadelphia: Temple University Press, 1988.

Dummitt, Christopher. *The Manly Modern: Masculinity in Postwar Canada*. Vancouver: UBC Press, 2007.

Dykes, James G. *Background on the Automotive Products Trade Agreement*. Toronto: MVMA, 1985.

Eastman, Joel. *Styling vs. Safety: The Development of Automotive Safety, 1900–1966*. Lanham, MD: University Press of America, 1984.

Farber, David. *Sloan Rules: Alfred P. Sloan and the Triumph of General Motors*. Chicago: University of Chicago Press, 2002.

Flink, James J. "Innovation in Automotive Technology: After a Long Interval of Stagnation, Automotive Technology May Be Entering a Period of Renewed Creativity." *American Scientist* 73, 2 (1985): 151–61.

– "John Bell Rae (1911–1988)." *Technology and Culture* 30, 3 (1989): 718–22.

– "Three Stages of American Automobile Consciousness." *American Quarterly* 24, 4 (1972): 451–73.

Frank, Thomas. *The Conquest of Cool: Business Culture, Counterculture and the Rise of Hip Consumerism*. Chicago: University of Chicago Press, 1998.

Giddens, Anthony. "Risk and Responsibility." *Modern Law Review* 62, no. 1 (1999): 1–10.

Gindin, Sam. *The Canadian Auto Workers: The Birth and Transformation of a Union*. Toronto: Lorimer, 1995.

Gould, Lewis L., ed. *Lady Bird Johnson: Our Environmental First Lady*. Lawrence: University Press of Kansas, 1999.

Heaphy, Brian. *Late Modernity and Social Change: Reconstructing Social and Personal Life*. New York: Routledge, 2007.

Henderson Jr., James A. "Review of *Unsafe at Any Speed*, by Ralph Nader." *Boston University Law Review* 46 (1966): 135–41.

High, Steven. *Industrial Sunset: The Making of North America's Rust Belt, 1969–1984*. Toronto: University of Toronto Press, 2003.

Hiott, Andrea. *Thinking Small: The Long Strange Trip of the Volkswagen Beetle*. New York: Ballantine Books, 2012.

Hyde, Charles K. *Arsenal of Democracy: The American Automobile Industry in World War II*. Detroit: Wayne State University Press, 2013.

– *The Dodge Brothers: The Men, the Motor Cars, and the Legacy*. Detroit: Wayne State University Press, 2005.

– *Riding the Roller Coaster: A History of the Chrysler Corporation*. Detroit: Wayne State University Press, 2003.

– *Storied Independent Automakers: Nash, Hudson, and American Motors*. Detroit: Wayne State University Press, 2009.

Irwin, Douglas A. "The Nixon Shock after Forty Years: The Import Surcharge Revisited." *World Trade Review* 12, 1 (2013): 29–56.

Jakle, John A., and Keith A. Sculle. *The Gas Station in America*. Baltimore: Johns Hopkins University Press, 1994.

–, and Jefferson S. Rogers. *The Motel in America*. Baltimore: Johns Hopkins University Press, 1996.

Keats, John. *The Insolent Chariots*. Philadelphia: Lippincott, 1958.

Kegler, Scott R., Grant T. Baldwin, Rose A. Rudd, and Michael F. Ballesteros. "Increases in United States Life Expectancy through Reductions in Injury-Related Death." *Population Health Metrics* 15, 1 (2017): 150–4.

Kellogg, Paul. *Escape from the Staple Trap: Canadian Political Economy after Left Nationalism*. Toronto: University of Toronto Press, 2015.

Klier, Thomas, and James Rubenstein. *Who Really Made Your Car? Restructuring and Geographic Change in the Auto Industry*. Kalamazoo, MI: W.E. Upjohn Institute, 2008.

Ladd, Brian. *Autophobia: Love and Hate in the Automotive Age*. Chicago: University of Chicago Press, 2008.

Lichtenstein, Nelson. *The Most Dangerous Man in Detroit: Walter Reuther and the Fate of American Labor*. New York: Basic Books, 1995.

Luger, Stan. *Corporate Power, American Democracy, and the Automobile Industry*. New York: Cambridge University Press, 2000.

Marcello, Patricia Cronin. *Ralph Nader: A Biography*. Westport, CT: Greenwood Press, 2004.

Martin, Justin. *Nader: Crusader, Spoiler, Icon*. Cambridge, MA: Perseus Publishing, 2002.

Mashaw, Jerry L., and David L. Harfst. *The Struggle for Auto Safety*. Cambridge, MA: Harvard University Press, 1990.

McShane, Clay. *Down the Asphalt Path: The Automobile and the American City*. New York: Columbia University Press, 1994.

Mohl, Raymond. "Stop the Road: Freeway Revolts in American Cities." *Journal of Urban History* 30, 5 (2004): 674–706.

Mohun, Arwen P. *Risk: Negotiating Safety in American Society*. Baltimore: Johns Hopkins University Press, 2013.

Muirhead, Bruce. "From Special Relationship to Third Option: Canada, the US, and the Nixon Shock." *American Review of Canadian Studies* 34, 3 (2004): 439–46.

Mumford, Lewis. *The Highway and the City*. Westport, CT: Praeger, 1958.

Myers, Tamara. "Didactic Sudden Death: Children, Police, and Teaching Citizenship in the Age of Automobility." *Journal of the History of Childhood and Youth* 8, 3 (2015): 451–75.

Nader, Ralph. *Unsafe at Any Speed: The Designed-In Dangers of the American Automobile*. New York: Grossman Publishers, 1965.

Norton, Peter D. *Fighting Traffic: The Dawn of the Motor Age in the American City*. Cambridge, MA: MIT Press, 2008.

– "Four Paradigms: Traffic Safety in the Twentieth-Century United States." *Technology and Culture* 56, 2 (2007): 319–34.

– "Street Rivals: Jaywalking and the Invention of the Motor Age Street." *Technology and History* 48, 2 (2007): 331–59.

Packer, Jeremy. *Mobility Without Mayhem: Safety, Cars, and Citizenship*. Durham, NC: Duke University Press, 2008.

Palmer, Bryan. *Capitalism Comes to the Backcountry: The Goodyear Invasion of Napanee*. Toronto: Between the Lines, 1994.

Penfold, Steve. "'Are We to Go Literally to the Hot Dogs?' Parking Lots, Drive-ins, and the Critique of Progress in Toronto's Suburbs, 1965–1975." *Urban History Review* 33, 1 (2004): 8–23.

Rae, John B. *The American Automobile: A Brief History*. Chicago: University of Chicago Press, 1965.

Rothfeder, John. *Driving Honda: Inside the World's Most Innovative Car Company*. New York: Portfolio, 2014.

Roos, Daniel, Daniel T. Jones, and James P. Womack. *The Machine That Changed the World*. New York: Free Press, 1990.

Rubenstein, James M. *Making and Selling Cars: Innovation and Change in the US Automotive Industry*. Baltimore: Johns Hopkins University Press, 2001.

Seo, Sarah A. *Policing the Open Road: How Cars Transformed American Freedom*. Cambridge, MA: Harvard University Press, 2019.

Sørensen, Mads P., and Allan Christiansen. *On Ulrich Beck: An Introduction to the Theory of Second Modernity and the Risk Society*. London: Routledge, 2013.

Stanfield, James Ronald, and Jacqueline Bloom Stanfield. *John Kenneth Galbraith*. London: Palgrave Macmillan, 2011.

Stebenne, David. *Promised Land: How the Rise of the Middle Class Transformed America, 1929–1968*. New York: Scribner, 2020.

Steel, Danielle. *Accident*. New York: Dell, 1994

Tyler, Gus. "Labor's Multinational Pains." *Foreign Policy* 12 (Autumn 1973): 113–32.

Volti, Rudi. "A Century of Automobility." *Technology and Culture* 37, 4 (1996): 663–85.

Ward, James. *The Fall of the Packard Motor Car Company.* Stanford, CA: Stanford University Press; 1995.

Warnock, Gayle C. *The Edsel Affair: … What Went Wrong? A Narrative*. Paradise Valley, AZ: Pro West, 1980.

Watts, Stephen. *The People's Tycoon: Henry Ford and the American Century*. New York: A.A. Knopf, 2005.

Wetmore, Jameson M. "Delegating to the Automobile: Experimenting with Automotive Restraints in the 1970s." *Technology and Culture* 56, 2 (2015): 440–63.

White, Lawrence J. *The Automobile Industry since 1945*. 1971; Cambridge, MA: Harvard University Press, 2014.
Whiteside, Thomas. *The Investigation of Ralph Nader: General Motors vs. One Determined Man*. New York: Arbor House, 1972.
Whyte, Kenneth. *The Sack of Detroit: General Motors and the End of American Enterprise*. New York: Knopf, 2021.
Woolf, Steven H., and Heidi Schoomaker. "Life Expectancy and Mortality Rates in the United States, 1959–2017." *JAMA: The Journal of the American Medical Association* 322, 20 (2019): 1996–2016.
Yago, Glenn. "What's Good for General Motors Is Good for General Motors." *In These Times* (Chicago) 3, 22 (1979): 12–14.
Zachmann, Karin. "Risk in Historical Perspective: Concepts, Contexts, and Conjunctions." In *Risk: A Multidisciplinary Introduction*, edited by Claudia Klüppelberg, Daniel Straub, and Isabell M. Welpe, 3–35. Berlin: Springer, 2014.

Online Sources and Other Digital Media

"Ford Pioneers Auto Safety." Ford Motor Company. https://corporate.ford.com/articles/history/ford-pioneers-auto-safety.html.
"Meet the Bricklin 3EV: Redefining the Price of Fabulous." Visionary Vehicles. https://www.vvcars.com/.
Moore, Michael, dir. *Roger and Me*. 1989; Warner Bros., documentary.

Chapter 4. Showman (Politician)

Scholarly Books and Articles

Ackerman, Kenneth D. *Boss Tweed: The Rise and Fall of the Corrupt Pol Who Conceived the Soul of Modern New York*. New York: Carroll & Graf Publishers, 2005.
Adams, Buford. *E Pluribus Barnum: The Great Showman and the Making of Popular Culture*. Minneapolis: University of Minnesota Press, 1997.
Andersen, Kur. *Fantasyland: How America Went Haywire: A 500-Year History*. New York: Random House, 2017.
Armstrong, Christopher. *Blue Skies and Boiler Rooms: Buying and Selling Securities in Canada, 1870–1940*. Toronto: University of Toronto Press, 1997.
Azzi, Stephen. *Walter Gordon and the Rise of Canadian Nationalism*. Montreal and Kingston: McGill-Queen's University Press, 1999.
Balleisen, Edward J. *Fraud: An American History from Barnum to Madoff*. Princeton, NJ: Princeton University Press, 2017.
Bothwell, Robert. *Alliance and Illusion: Canada and the World, 1945–84*. Vancouver: UBC Press, 2007.
– *Your Country, My Country: A Unified History of the United States and Canada*. Toronto: Oxford University Press, 2015.
Braudy, Leo. *The Frenzy of Renown: Fame and Its History*. New York: Oxford University Press, 1986.
Burch, Jessica. "Crisis or Opportunity? Amway and an Unfamiliar Story of Economic Growth in the 1970s." In *Since the Boom: Continuity and Change in the Western Industrialized World after 1970*, edited by Sebastian Voight, 35–55. Toronto: University of Toronto Press, 2020.
Cormier, Michel, and Achille Michaud. *Richard Hatfield: Power and Disobedience*. Translated by Daphne Ponder. Fredericton: Goose Lane, 1992.

Dicke, Thomas S. *Franchising in America: The Development of a Business Method, 1840–1980*. Chapel Hill: University of North Carolina Press, 1992.

Donaghy, Greg. *Tolerant Allies: Canada and the United States, 1963–68*. Montreal and Kingston: McGill-Queen's University Press, 2003.

Douglas, Susan J., and Andrea McDonnell. *Celebrity: A History of Fame*. New York: New York University Press 2019.

Elliott, David. *Bible Bill: A Biography of William Aberhart*. Edmonton: Reidmore Books, 1987.

Finstuen, Andrew, Grant Wacker, and Anne Blue Wills, eds. *Billy Graham: American Pilgrim*. New York: Oxford University Press, 2017.

Frank, Thomas. *The Conquest of Cool: Business Culture, Counterculture and the Rise of Hip Consumerism*. Chicago: University of Chicago Press, 1998.

Fredericks, H.A., and Allan Chambers. *Bricklin*. Potters Bark, UK: Brunswick Press, 1977.

Friedman, Walter. *Birth of a Salesman: The Transformation of Selling in America*. Cambridge, MA: Harvard University Press, 2009.

Galbraith, John Kenneth. *The Great Crash, 1929*. 1955; Boston: Houghton Mifflin, 1997.

Gamson, Joshua. *Claims to Fame: Celebrity in Contemporary America*. Berkeley: University of California Press 1994.

Grandin, Greg. *Fordlandia: The Rise and Fall of Henry Ford's Forgotten Jungle City*. New York: Metropolitan Books, 2009.

Granatstein, J.L. *Yankee Go Home? Canadians and Anti-Americanism*. Toronto: HarperCollins Canada, 1997.

Haberman, Maggie. *Confidence Man: The Making of Donald Trump and the Breaking of America*. New York: Penguin Press, 2022.

Halttunen, Karen. *Confidence Men and Painted Women: A Study of Middle-Class Culture in America, 1830–1870*. New Haven, CT: Yale University Press, 1982.

Kunhardt, Philip, and Peter W. Kunhardt. *P.T. Barnum: America's Greatest Showman*. New York: Knopf, 1995.

Lemann, Nicholas. *Transaction Man: The Rise of the Deal and the Decline of the American Dream*. New York: Farrar, Straus and Giroux, 2019.

Lukes, Timothy J. *Politics and Beauty in America: The Liberal Aesthetics of P.T. Barnum, John Muir, and Harley Earl*. New York: Palgrave Macmillan, 2016.

Meier, Nicola. *China: The New Developmental State? An Empirical Analysis of the Automotive Industry*. Bern, CH: Peter Lang International Academic Publishers, 2018.

Morgan, Winifred. *The Trickster Figure in American Literature*. New York: Palgrave Macmillan, 2013.

Nash, Alanna. *The Colonel: The Extraordinary Story of Colonel Tom Parker and Elvis Presley*. New York: Simon & Schuster, 2003.

Penfold, Steve. *The Donut: A Canadian History*. Toronto: University of Toronto Press, 2008.

Pickens, Still [H.A. Fredericks]. "Introduction." In *How to Brickle: The New Brunswick Funny Book*. Saint John, NB: Unipress, 1977.

Railey, Jane Savage. *A Century of Swindles: Ponzi Schemes, Con Men, and Fraudsters*. Essex, CT: Lyons Press, 2021.

Rapini, Andrea. *The History of the Vespa: An Italian Miracle*. New York: Routledge, 2019.

Ricketts, Mac Linscott. "The North American Indian Trickster." *History of Religions* 5 (Winter 1966): 327–50.

Rosenberg, Neil V. "Goodtime Charlie and the Bricklin: A Satirical Song in Context." *Journal of the Canadian Oral History Association* 3, 1 (1978): 27–46.

Rothenberg, Randall. *Where the Suckers Moon: An Advertising Story*. New York: Knopf, 1994.

Shook, Robert L. *Honda: An American Success Story*. New York: Prentice Hall Direct, 1988.
Southam, Nancy, as told by Dalton Camp. *Remembering Richard: An Informal Portrait of Richard Hatfield by His Friends, Family and Colleagues*. Halifax: Formac Publishing, 1993.
Starr, Richard. *Richard Hatfield: The Seventeen-Year Saga*. Halifax: Formac Publishing, 1987.
Tedlow, Richard S. "The Struggle for Dominance in the Automobile Market: The Early Years of Ford and General Motors." *Business and Economic History* 17 (1988): 49–62.
Vuic, Jason. *The Yugo: The Rise and Fall of the Worst Car in History*. New York: Hill and Wang, 2010.
Wallace, Irving. *The Fabulous Showman: The Life and Times of P.T. Barnum*. New York: Alfred A. Knopf, 1959.
Warren, Donald I. *Radio Priest: Charles Coughlin, the Father of Hate Radio*. New York: Free Press, 1996.
Werner, R. *Barnum*. New York: Harcourt, Brace, 1923.
White, Richard D. *Kingfish: The Reign of Huey P. Long*. New York: Random House, 2006.
Wood, Mathew S., David J. Scheaf, and Sean M. Dwyer. "Fake It 'Till You Make It: Hazards of a Cultural Norm in Entrepreneurship." *Business Horizons* 65, 5 (2022): 681–96.

Online Sources and Other Digital Media

Bricklin, Jonathan, dir. *The Entrepreneur*. 2013; documentary.
"The Bricklin International Owner Club." Bricklin International. http://www.bricklin.org/.
Dahl, Darren. "Would You Buy a Chinese Car from this Man?" Inc., 1 July 2005. https://www.inc.com/magazine/20050701/disruptor-bricklin.html.
"Entrepreneur Bricklin Sues Chevy Over Failed Deal." *Reuters*, 21 July 2008. https://www.reuters.com/article/sppage023-n21419445-oisbi/entrepreneur-bricklin-sues-chery-over-failed-deal-idINN2141944520080721.
Lichterman, Joseph. "Auto Entrepreneur Bricklin Wins $2 Million for Fraud." *Reuters*, 15 July 2013. https://www.reuters.com/article/us-autos-detroit-bricklinidUSBRE96E0SV20130715.
Marquis, Greg. "The Hatfield Era in New Brunswick: The 'Politics of Fun'?" *Acadiensis Blog*, 3 May 2022. https://acadiensis.wordpress.com/2022/05/03/the-hatfield-era-in-new-brunswick-the-politics-of-fun/.
Maudsley, Dugald, dir. *The Bricklin: The Premier, the Promoter and Their Car.* Episode, Turning Points in History, 2004.
"Tesla Readies Export of Model Y to Canada from China." *Reuters*, 24 April 2023. https://www.reuters.com/business/autos-transportation/tesla-readies-export-model-y-canada-china-source-memo-2023-04-24/.

Chapter 5. Sex (Gender)

Theses

Blaisdell, Kenneth Charles. "Keepers of the Flame: A Search for a Values in the Magazines of the Car-Culture (Automobiles)." PhD diss., Rensselaer Polytechnic Institute, 1984.
Flavey, Conor. "Foregrounds: Mapping Gay, Lesbian and Bisexual History in Fredericton, 1969–1992." MA thesis, University of New Brunswick, 2015.
Mckinney, William. "The Classic Muscle Car Era." MA thesis, Clemson University, 2009.
Moyers, Scott Patrick. "Going Nowhere Fast: The Car, the Highway and American Identity in Vladimir Nabokov's 'Lolita' and Robert Frank's 'The Americans.'" MA thesis, College of William and Mary, 1997.
Roberts, Chadwick Lee. "Consuming Liberation: *Playgirl* and the Strategic Rhetoric of Sex Magazines for Women, 1972–1985." PhD diss., Bowling Green State University, 2011.
Ruffilli, Dean. "The Car in Canadian Culture, 1989–1983." PhD diss., University of Western Ontario, 2006.

Scholarly Books and Articles

Ackerman, Katrina. "'Not in the Atlantic Provinces': The Abortion Debate in New Brunswick, 1980–1987." *Acadiensis* 41, 1 (2012): 75–101.

Allyn, David. *Make Love Not War: The Sexual Revolution, an Unfettered History.* New York: Routledge, 2016.

Anastakis, Dimitry. *Death in the Peaceable Kingdom: Canadian History through Murder, Execution, Assassination and Suicide from Confederation to the War on Terror.* Toronto: University of Toronto Press, 2015.

– *Re-Creation, Fragmentation, and Resilience: A Brief History of Canada Since 1945.* Toronto: Oxford University Press, 2018.

–, ed. *The Sixties: Passion, Politics, and Style.* Montreal and Kingston: McGill-Queen's University Press, 2009.

Baily, Beth L. "From Front Porch to Back Seat: A History of the Date." *Magazine of History* 18, 4 (2004): 23–6.

– *From Front Porch to Back Seat: Courtship in Twentieth-Century America.* Baltimore: Johns Hopkins University Press, 1994.

Ballard, J.G. *Crash.* London: Johnathan Cape, 1973.

Batt, Meredith J., and Dusty Green. *Len and Cub: A Queer History.* Fredericton: Goose Lane, 2022.

Bottles, S.L. *Los Angeles and the Automobile: The Making of a Modern City.* Berkeley: University of California Press, 1987.

Clark, Richard M. "Dick Humbird and the Devil Wagon of Doom: Cars, Carnivores, and Feminine Carnality in This Side of Paradise." *F. Scott Fitzgerald Review* 11, 1 (2013): 32–53.

Clarsen, Georgine. *Eat My Dust: Early Women Motorists.* Baltimore: Johns Hopkins University Press, 2008.

– "Gender and Mobility: Historicizing the Terms." In *Mobility in History: The State of the Art in the History of Transport, Traffic, and Mobility*, edited by Gijs Mom, Gordon Pirie, and Laurent Tissot, 123–8. Neuchâtel: Editions Alphil – Presses universitaires suisses, 2009.

Cormier, Michel, and Achille Michaud. *Richard Hatfield: Power and Disobedience.* Translated by Daphne Ponder. Fredericton: Goose Lane, 1992.

Cowan, Sharon. "The Elvis We Deserve: The Social Regulation of Sex/Gender and Sexuality through Cultural Representations of 'The King.'" *Law, Culture and the Humanities* 6, 2 (2010): 221–44.

Cross, Gary S. *Machines of Youth: America's Car Obsession.* Chicago: University of Chicago Press, 2018.

Djerassi, Carl. *This Man's Pill: Reflections on the 50th Birthday of the Pill.* New York: Oxford University Press, 2001.

Dubinsky, Karen. *The Second Greatest Disappointment: Honeymooning and Tourism at Niagara Falls.* New Brunswick, NJ: Rutgers University Press, 1999.

Dummitt, Christopher. *The Manly Modern: Masculinity in Postwar Canada.* Vancouver: UBC Press, 2007.

– *Unbuttoned: A History of Mackenzie King's Private Life.* Montreal and Kingston: McGill-Queen's University Press, 2017.

Esch, Elizabeth. *The Color Line and the Assembly Line: Managing Race in the Ford Empire.* Oakland, CA: University of California Press, 2018.

Essig, Laurie. *Love, Inc.: Dating Apps, the Big White Wedding, and Chasing the Happily Neverafter.* Berkeley, CA: University of California Press, 2019.

Everitt, Joanna. "Mobilization on the Periphery: LGBT Activism and Success in Atlantic Canada." In *Queer Mobilizations: Social Movement Activism and Canadian Public Policy*, edited by Manon Tremblay, 125–42. Vancouver: UBC Press, 2015.

Finer, Lawrence B. "Trends in Premarital Sex in the United States, 1954–2003." *Public Health Reports* 122, 1 (2007): 73–8.

Flink, James J. *The Automobile Age*. Cambridge, MA: MIT Press, 1990.

Fraterrigo, Elizabeth. *Playboy and the Making of the Good Life in Modern America*. New York: Oxford University Press, 2011.

Gartman, David. *Auto Opium: A Social History of American Automobile Design*. London: Routledge, 1994.

Girard, P. "Sexual Orientation as a Human Rights Issue in Canada 1969–1985." *Dalhousie Law Journal* 10 (1986): 267–81.

Graydon, Michael E. "'We Had Become a Community': Gays of Ottawa (go) and the Birth of Community, 1971–7." *Canadian Historical Review* 99, 1 (2018): 594–622.

Haden-Guest, Anthony. *The Last Party: Studio 54, Disco, and the Culture of the Night*. New York: William Morrow, 1997.

Heitmann, John. *The Automobile and American Life*. Jefferson, NC: McFarland, 2009.

Hirschman, Elizabeth. *Branding Masculinity: Tracing the Cultural Foundations of Brand Meaning*. New York: Routledge, 2016.

Hyde, Charles K. *Storied Independent Automakers: Nash, Hudson, and American Motors*. Detroit: Wayne State University Press, 2009.

Jakle, John A., Keith A. Sculle, and Jefferson S. Rogers. *The Motel in America*. Baltimore: Johns Hopkins University Press, 1996.

Karmasin, H. "Ernest Dichter's Studies on Automobile Marketing." In *Ernest Dichter and Motivation Research*, edited by S. Schwarzkopf and R. Gries, 109–125. London: Palgrave Macmillan, 2010.

Korinek, V.J. "'The Most Openly Gay Person for at Least a Thousand Miles': Doug Wilson and the Politicization of a Province, 1975–1983." *Canadian Historical Review* 84, 4 (2003): 517–50.

– "'We're the Girls of the Pansy Parade': Historicizing Winnipeg's Queer Subcultures, 1930s-1970." *Histoire sociale/Social History* 45, 89 (2012): 117–55.

Krevsky, Margery. *Sirens of Chrome: The Enduring Allure of Auto Show Models*. Pontiac, MI: Momentum Books, 2008.

Lambert, Maude-Emmanuelle. "Québécoises et Ontariennes en voiture! L'expérience culturelle et spatiale de l'automobile au féminin (1910–1945)." *Revue d'histoire de l'Amérique française* 63, 2–3 (2009–10): 305–30.

Laver, Mark. "Autoeroticism: Sex, Cars, and Jazz." In *Jazz Sells: Music, Marketing, and Meaning*, 84–137. London: Routledge, 2005.

Leffingwell, Randy, and Darwin Holmstrom, *The Muscle Car: History of American Performance Cars*. St. Paul, MN: Crestline, 2007.

Lewis, David L. "Sex and the Automobile: From Rumble Seats to Rockin' Vans." *Michigan Quarterly Review* 19, 4 (1980): 518–28.

Ling, Peter. "The Making of the American Dream: Sex and the Automobile in the Jazz Age." *History Today* 39, 11 (1989): 18–24.

Lynd, Helen, and Robert Lynd. *Middletown: A Study of Modern American Culture*. San Diego: Harcourt Brace Jovanovich, 1959.

Marchand, Roland. *Advertising the American Dream: Making Way for Modernity, 1920–1940*. Berkeley: University of California Press, 1985.

Marling, Karal Ann. "America's Love Affair with the Automobile in the Television Age." In *Autopia: Cars and Culture*, edited by Peter Wollen and Joe Kerr, 354–62. London: Reaktion Books, 2002.

May, Elaine Tyler. *America and the Pill: A History of Promise, Peril, and Liberation*. New York: Basic Books, 2010.
McShane, Clay. *The Automobile: A Chronology of Its Antecedents, Development, and Impact*. London: Routledge, 2013.
McTavish, Lianne. "Abortion in New Brunswick." *Acadiensis* 44, 2 (2015): 107–30.
Morton, F.L. *Morgentaler v. Borowski: Abortion, the Charter and the Courts*. Toronto: McClelland & Stewart, 1992.
Nicholas, Jane. *The Modern Girl: Feminine Modernities, the Body, and Commodities in the 1920s*. Toronto: University of Toronto Press, 2014.
Owram, Doug. *Born at the Right Time: A History of the Baby Boom Generation*. Toronto: University of Toronto Press, 1997.
Palmer, Beth. "'Lonely, Tragic, but Legally Necessary Pilgrimages': Transnational Abortion Travel in the 1970s." *Canadian Historical Review* 92, 4 (2011): 637–65.
Parkin, Katherine J. *Women at the Wheel: A Century of Buying, Driving, and Fixing Cars*. Philadelphia: University of Pennsylvania Press, 2017.
Passon, Jerry W. *The Corvette in Literature and Culture: Symbolic Dimensions of America's Sports Car*. Jefferson, NC: McFarland, 2011.
Pearson, Ruth Roach. *"They're Still Women After All": The Second World War and Canadian Womanhood*. Toronto: McClelland & Stewart, 1986.
Perrault, Martine, and Linda Cardinal. "Le droit au choix et le choix du droit: L'expérience de l'Ontario Coalition for Abortion Clinics et le jugement Morgentaler." *Canadian Journal of Political Science / Revue canadienne de science politique* 29, 2 (1996): 243–67.
Pettifer, Julian, and Nigel Turner. *Automania: Man and the Motor Car*. London: Collins, 1984.
Rothman, Ellen K. *Hands and Hearts: A History of Courtship in America*. Cambridge, MA: Harvard University Press, 1987.
Salamone, Frank A. *Popular Culture in the Fifties*. New York: University Press of America, 2001.
Sandford, Charles L. "'Women's Place' in American Car Culture." In *The Automobile and American Culture*, edited by David L. Lewis and Laurence Goldstein, 137–52. Ann Arbor: University of Michigan Press, 1980.
Scharf, Virginia. *Taking the Wheel: Women and the Coming of the Motor Age*. New York: Free Press, 1991.
Seiler, Cotten. *Republic of Drivers: A Cultural History of Automobility in America*. Chicago: University of Chicago Press, 2008.
Sethna, Christabelle, and Steve Hewitt. "Clandestine Operations: The Vancouver Women's Caucus, the Abortion Caravan, and the RCMP." *Canadian Historical Review* 90, 3 (2009): 463–95.
Sethna, Christabelle, Beth Palmer, Katrina Ackerman, and Nancy Janovicek. "Choice, Interrupted: Travel and Inequality of Access to Abortion Services since the 1960s." *Labour / Le travail* 71 (Spring 2013): 29–48.
Sorin, Gretchen. *Driving While Black: African American Travel and the Road to Civil Rights*. New York: Liveright Publishing, 2020.
Southam, Nancy, as told by Dalton Camp. *Remembering Richard: An Informal Portrait of Richard Hatfield by His Friends, Family and Colleagues*. Halifax: Formac Publishing, 1993.
Starr, Richard. *Richard Hatfield: The Seventeen-Year Saga*. Halifax: Formac Publishing, 1987.
Stevenson, Heon. *Selling the Dream: Advertising the American Automobile*. London: Academy, 1995.
Tremblay, Anthony M. *The Fiddlehead Moment: Pioneering an Alternative Canadian Modernism in New Brunswick*. Montreal and Kingston: McGill-Queen's University Press, 2019.
Vantoch, Victoria. *The Jet Sex Airline Stewardesses and the Making of an American Icon*. Philadelphia: University of Pennsylvania Press 2013.

Walsh, Margaret. "At Home at the Wheel? The Woman and Her Automobile in the 1950s." *Third Eccles Centre Plenary Lectures, Given at the American Studies Annual Conference, 2006* (London, 2007).
– "Gender and Automobility: Selling Cars to American Women after the Second World War." *Journal of Macromarketing* 31, 1 (2011): 57–72.
– "Gendering Mobility: Women, Work and Automobility in the United States." *History* 93, 3 (2008): 376–95.
Warner, Tom. *Never Going Back: A History of Queer Activism in Canada.* Toronto: University of Toronto Press, 2002.
Wolfe, Tom. *The Kandy-Kolored Tangerine-Flake Streamline Baby.* 1963; New York: Picador, 2009.
Wren, James, et al. "The Automobile: The Unwanted Child." SAE Technical Paper, 1989.

Online Sources and Other Digital Media

Cronenberg, David, dir. *Crash.* 1996; Alliance Communications, Recorded Picture Company, Columbia TriStar Film Distributors International, film.
Dahl, Darren. "Would You Buy a Chinese Car from this Man?" Inc., 1 July 2005. https://www.inc.com/magazine/20050701/disruptor-bricklin.html.
"Dodge Charger 500 Commercial (1970)." YouTube. Last accessed last accessed 25 October, 2022. https://www.youtube.com/watch?v=R5IM5YaCVlI&t=55s.
Eschner, Kat. "Before She Was an Etiquette Authority, Emily Post Was a Road Warrior." *Smithsonian Magazine*, 11 September, 2017. https://www.smithsonianmag.com/smart-news/she-was-etiquette-authority-emily-post-was-road-warrior-180964806/.
Maudsley, Dugald, dir. *The Bricklin: The Premier, the Promoter and Their Car.* Episode, *Turning Points of History*, 2004.

Chapter 6. Business (The State)

Theses

Jacques, April Key. "Inside the Crystal Palace: A History of Henry Ford's Highland Park Plant." MA thesis, University of Michigan, 2008.

Scholarly Books and Articles

Aitken, H.G.J. "Defensive Expansionism: The State and Economic Growth in Canada." In *Approaches to Canadian Economic History*, edited by M.H. Watkins and W.T. Easterbrook, 183–221. Montreal and Kingston: McGill-Queen's University Press, 1967.
Aluchna, Maria. "Corporate Governance Theories: A Synthesis." In *Transforming Governance: New Values, New Systems in the New Business Environment*, edited by Maria Aluchna and Güler Aras, 7–40. London: Routledge, 2015.
Anastakis, Dimitry. *Autonomous State: The Struggle for a Canadian Car Industry from OPEC to Free Trade.* Toronto: University of Toronto Press, 2013.
– *Auto Pact: Creating a Borderless North American Auto Industry, 1960–1971.* Toronto: University of Toronto Press, 2005.
– "Building a 'New Nova Scotia': State Intervention, the Auto Industry, and the Case of Volvo in Halifax, 1963–1996." *Acadiensis* 34, 1 (2004): 3–30.

– "The Last Automotive Entrepreneur? Lee Iacocca Saves Chrysler, 1978–1986." Business History Conference, Wilmington, DE, 2007.
Anbinder, Jacob. "Selling the World: Public Relations and the Global Expansion of General Motors, 1922–40." *Business History Review* 92, 3 (2018): 483–507.
Ankli, Robert, and Fred Frederickson. "The Influence of American Manufacturers on the Canadian Automobile Industry." *Business and Economic History* 10 (1981): 101–13.
Barrow, Heather. *Henry Ford's Plan for the American Suburb: Dearborn and Detroit.* Ithaca, NY: Cornell University Press, 2021.
Betton, John, and Thomas J. Hench. "'Any Color as Long as It's Black': Henry Ford and the Ethics of Business." *Journal of Genocide Research* 4, 4 (2000): 533–41.
Borins, Sanford, with Lee Brown. *Investments in Failure: Five Government Corporations That Cost the Canadian Taxpayer Billions.* Toronto: Methuen, 1986.
Brinkley, Douglas. *Wheels for the World: Henry Ford, His Company, and a Century of Progress.* New York: Penguin Books, 2003.
Carson, Thomas. "Friedman's Theory of Corporate Social Responsibility." *Business and Professional Ethics Journal* 12, 1 (1993): 3–32.
Casey, Robert. *The Model T: A Centennial History.* Baltimore: Johns Hopkins University Press, 2008.
Chandler, Alfred. *Strategy and Structure: Chapters in the History of the American Industrial Enterprise.* Cambridge, MA: MIT Press, 1962.
Clarke, Sally H. *Trust and Power: Consumers, the Modern Corporation, and the Making of the United States Automobile Market.* Cambridge: Cambridge University Press, 2007.
Curcio, Vincent. *Henry Ford.* New York: Oxford University Press, 2013.
Egan, Phillip S. *Design and Destiny: The Making of the Tucker Automobile.* Orange, CA: On the Mark Publications, 1989.
Feldman, Glenn. "Putting Uncle Milton to Bed: Reexamining Milton Friedman's Essay on the Social Responsibility of Business." *Labor Studies Journal* 32, 2 (2007): 125–41.
Foroohar, Rana. *Makers and Takers: The Rise of Finance and the Fall of American Business.* New York: Crown Publishing Group, 2016.
Fredericks, H.A., and Allan Chambers. *Bricklin.* Potters Bark, UK: Brunswick Press, 1977.
Freeland, Robert F. *Struggle for Control of the Modern Corporation: Organizational Change at General Motors, 1924–1970.* Cambridge: Cambridge University Press, 2001.
Freeman, Joshua Benjamin. *Behemoth: A History of the Factory and the Making of the Modern World.* New York: W.W. Norton, 2018.
Friedman, Walter. *Birth of a Salesman: The Transformation of Selling in America.* Cambridge, MA: Harvard University Press, 2009.
Gąsiorkiewicz, Lech, and Jan Monkiewicz, eds. *Innovation in Financial Services: Balancing Public and Private Interests.* New York: Routledge, 2001.
Greenleaf, Wiliam. *Monopoly on Wheels: Henry Ford and the Selden Patent.* 1961; Detroit: Wayne State University Press, 2011.
Halberstam, David. *The Reckoning.* New York: William Morrow, 1986.
Hansen, Per H. "From Finance Capitalism to Financialization: A Cultural and Narrative Perspective on 150 Years of Financial History." *Enterprise & Society* 15, 4 (2014): 605–42.
Herman, Edward S. *Corporate Control, Corporate Power.* New York: Cambridge University Press, 1981.
High, Steven. *Industrial Sunset: The Making of North America's Rust Belt, 1969–1984.* Toronto: University of Toronto Press, 2003.
Holmes, John. "From Three Industries to One: Towards an Integrated North American Automobile Industry." In *Driving Continentally: National Policies and the North American Auto Industry,* edited by Maureen Appel Molot, 23–61. Ottawa: Carleton University Press, 1993.

Hounshell, David A. *From the American System to Mass Production, 1800–1932: The Development of Manufacturing Technology in the United States*. Baltimore: Johns Hopkins University Press, 1985.
Hoyman, Michele M. *Power Steering: Global Automakers and the Transformation of Rural Communities*. Lawrence: University Press of Kansas, 1997.
Huskins, Bonnie, and Michael Boudreau. "Irresponsibility, Obligation, and the Manly Modern: Tensions in Working-class Masculinities in Postwar Saint John, New Brunswick." In *Labour / Le travail* 78 (Fall 2016): 165–96.
Hyde, Charles K. *The Dodge Brothers: The Men, the Motor Cars, and the Legacy*. Detroit: Wayne State University Press, 2005.
Imai, Masaaki. *Kaizen: The Key to Japan's Competitive Success*. New York: McGraw-Hill, 1986.
Jacobs, A.J. *The New Domestic Automakers in the United States and Canada: History, Impacts and Prospects*. Lanham, MD: Lexington Books, 2016.
Ki, Youn. "Large Industrial Firms and the Rise of Finance in Late Twentieth- Century America." *Enterprise & Society* 19, 4 (2018): 903–45.
Langworth, Richard M. *Kaiser-Frazer: The Last Onslaught on Detroit*. Kutztown, PA: Princeton Publishing, 1975.
LeCavalier, Jesse. *The Rule of Logistics: Walmart and the Architecture of Fulfillment*. Minneapolis: University of Minnesota Press, 2016.
Lemann, Nicholas. *Transaction Man: The Rise of the Deal and the Decline of the American Dream*. New York: Farrar, Straus and Giroux, 2019.
Levin, Hillel. *John DeLorean: The Maverick Mogul*. London: Orbis Publishing, 1983.
Link, Stefan J. *Forging Global Fordism: Nazi Germany, Soviet Russia, and the Contest Over the Industrial Order*. Princeton, NJ: Princeton University Press, 2020.
Macdonald, John. *A Ghost's Memoir: The Making of Alfred P. Sloan's "My Years with General Motors."* Cambridge, MA: MIT Press, 2002.
McAleer, Sean. "Friedman's Stockholder Theory of Corporate Moral Responsibility." *Teaching Business Ethics* 7 (2003): 437–51.
McCarthy, Tom. "Henry Ford: Take-Back, Waste Reduction, and Recycling at the Rouge." *Progress in Industrial Ecology* 3. 4 (2006): 302–28.
Melman, Seymour. *Profits without Production*. New York: Alfred Knopf, 1983.
Meyer, Stephen. *The Five Dollar Day: Labor Management and Social Control at the Ford Motor Company, 1908–1921*. Albany: SUNY Press, 1981.
Milner, Samuel Evan. *Robbing Peter to Pay Paul: Power, Profits, and Productivity in Modern America*. New Haven, CT: Yale University Press, 2021.
Mizruchi, Mark S. *The Fracturing of the American Corporate Elite*. Cambridge, MA: Harvard University Press, 2013.
Norwood, Stephen. "Ford's Brass Knuckles: Harry Bennett, The Cult of Muscularity, and Anti-Labor Terror, 1920–1945." *Labor History* 37, 3 (1996): 365–91.
Nye, David E. *America's Assembly Line*. Cambridge, MA: MIT Press, 2013.
Omar, Mohammed A. *The Automotive Body Manufacturing Systems and Processes*. New York: John Wiley & Sons, 2011.
Pandremenos, J., J. Paralikas, K. Salonitis, and G. Chryssolouris. "Modularity Concepts for the Automotive Industry: A Critical Review." *CIRP Journal of Manufacturing Science and Technology* 1, 3 (2009): 148–52.
Pearson, Charles T. *The Indomitable Tin Goose: The True Story of Preston Tucker and His Car*. 1960; New York: Motorbooks International, 1974.
Perrucci, Robert. *Japanese Auto Transplants in the Heartland: Corporatism and Community*. New York: Routledge, 1994.

Rubenstein, James M. *Making and Selling Cars: Innovation and Change in the US Automotive Industry*. Baltimore: Johns Hopkins University Press, 2001.

Schwartz, Donald E. "Proxy Power and Social Goals: How Campaign GM Succeeded." *Saint John's Law Review* 4, 45 (1971): 764–71.

– "The Public-Interest Proxy Contest: Reflections on Campaign GM." *Michigan Law Review* 69, 3 (1971): 419–538.

Sherman, Joe. *In the Rings of Saturn*. New York: Oxford University Press 1994.

Sloan, Alfred P. *Adventures of a White-Collar Man*. New York: Doubleday, 1941.

– *My Years with General Motors*. Garden City, NY: Doubleday, 1964.

Smil, Vaclav. *Made in the USA: The Rise and Retreat of American Manufacturing*. Cambridge, MA: MIT Press, 2013.

Society of Automotive Engineers. *A History of the Automotive Internal Combustion Engine*. Warrendale, PA: Society of Automotive Engineers, 1976.

Sopoćko, Andrzej. "The Central Bank Feeding the Budget: The Heresy That Must Become Routine." In *Innovation in Financial Services: Balancing Public and Private Interests*, edited by Lech Gąsiorkiewicz and Jan Monkiewicz, 97–112. New York: Routledge, 2001.

Takeishi, Akira, and Takahiro Fujimoto. "Modularization in the Car Industry: Interlinked Multiple Hierarchies of Product, Production, and Supplier Systems." In *The Business of Systems Integration*, edited by Andrea Prencipe, Andrew Davies, and Michael Hobday, 254–78. London: Oxford University Press, 2003.

Tedlow, Richard S. *The Emergence of Charismatic Business Leadership*. New York: Rosetta Books, 2021.

Thomas, Kenneth P. *Capital Beyond Borders: States and Firms in the Auto Industry, 1960–1994*. New York: St Martin's Press, 1996.

– *Competing for Capital: Europe and North America in a Global Era*. Washington, DC: Georgetown University Press, 2000.

– *Investment Incentives and the Global Competition for Capital*. London: Palgrave Macmillan, 2011.

Watts, Stephen. *The People's Tycoon: Henry Ford and the American Century*. New York: A.A. Knopf, 2005.

Weaver, Paul H. *The Suicidal Corporation: How Big Business Fails America*. New York, 1988.

White, Lawrence J. *The Automobile Industry since 1945*. 1971; Cambridge, MA: Harvard University Press, 2014.

Williams, Karel, Colin Haslam, John Williams, Andy Adcroft, and Sukhdev Johal. "The Myth of the Line: Ford's Production of the Model T at Highland Park, 1909–16." *Business History* 35, 3 (1993): 66–87.

Womack, James P., David T. Jones, and Daniel Roos. *The Machine That Changed the World: The Story of Lean Production*. New York: Free Press, 2007.

Wright, J. Patrick, and John Z. DeLorean. *On a Clear Day You Can See General Motors: John Z. DeLorean's Look Inside the Automotive Giant*. London: Sidgwick & Jackson, 1979.

Yanarella, Ernest J. *The Politics of Industrial Recruitment: Japanese Automobile Investment and Economic Development in the American States*. New York: Praeger 1990.

Online Sources and Other Digital Media

Dahl, Darren. "Would You Buy a Chinese Car from This Man?" Inc., 1 July 2005. https://www.inc.com/magazine/20050701/disruptor-bricklin.html.

Gordon, John Steele. "The Ordeal of Engine Charlie." *American Heritage* 46, 1 (1995). https://www.americanheritage.com/ordeal-engine-charlie.

Maudsley, Dugald, dir. *The Bricklin: The Premier, the Promoter and Their Car.* Episode, *Turning Points of History*, 2004.

"The St. Thomas Ford Assembly Plant, 1965–2011." Elgin County Culture Services Archives, Elgin County. https://www.elgincounty.ca/ElginCounty/CulturalServices/Archives/st_thomas_ford_exhibit/index.html.

Terrell, Ellen. "When a Quote Is Not (Exactly) a Quote: General Motors." *Inside Adams: Science, Technology & Business Blog*, Library of Congress. https://blogs.loc.gov/inside_adams/2016/04/when-a-quote-is-not-exactly-a-quote-general-motors/.

Chapter 7. Demise (Rebirth)

Theses and Unpublished Papers

Burrill, Fred, and Dimitry Anastakis. "Explaining Industrial Closures." Paper presented at the Deindustrialization and the Politics of Our Time (DePOT) annual conference, 23 June 2023, Sydney, NS.

Sandberg, Anders L. "The Deindustrialization of Pictou County, Nova Scotia: Capital, Labour and the Process of Regional Decline, 1881–1921." PhD diss., McGill University, 1985.

Scholarly Books and Articles

Acheson, T.W. "The National Policy and the Industrialization of the Maritimes, 1880–1910." *Acadiensis* 1, 2 (1972): 4–34.

Anastakis, Dimitry. *Autonomous State: The Struggle for a Canadian Car Industry from OPEC to Free Trade.* Toronto: University of Toronto Press, 2013.

– "Industrial Sunrise? The Chrysler Bailout, the State, and the Re-industrialization of the Canadian Automotive Sector, 1975–1986." *Urban History Review/ Revue d'histoire urbaine* 35, 2 (2007): 37–50.

Andrews, Jennifer. "Reading the Bricklin: Narrating the Place of Dreaming in an Era of Self-sufficiency." *Journal of New Brunswick Studies/Revue d'etudes sur le Nouveau-Brunswick* 4 (January 2013): 31–46.

Borins, S., and B. Hearst. "Cults of Personality: Fables of the Automobile Manufacturing Industry." In *Negotiating Business Narratives: Fables of the Information Technology, Automobile Manufacturing, and Financial Trading Industries*, 23–36. Cham, CH: Palgrave Macmillan /Springer, 2018.

Borins, Sanford, with Lee Brown. *Investments in Failure: Five Government Corporations That Cost the Canadian Taxpayer Billions.* Toronto: Methuen, 1986.

Bruno, Michael. *Economies of Worldwide Stagflation.* Oxford: Basil Blackwell, 1985.

Cormier, Michel, and Achille Michaud. *Richard Hatfield: Power and Disobedience.* Translated by Daphne Ponder. Fredericton: Goose Lane, 1992.

Cowie, Jefferson, and Joseph Heathcott. *Beyond the Ruins: The Meanings of Deindustrialization.* Ithaca, NY: ILR Press, 2003.

– *Stayin' Alive: The 1970s and the Last Days of the Working Class.* New York: New Press, 2010.

Critchlow, Donald T. *Studebaker: The Life and Death of an American Corporation.* Bloomington: Indiana University Press, 1996.

Dandeaneau, Steven P. *A Town Abandoned: Flint, Michigan, Confronts Deindustrialization.* Albany: SUNY Press, 1996.

DeMont, John. *Citizens Irving: K.C. Irving and His Legacy: The Story of Canada's Wealthiest Family.* Toronto: Doubleday Canada, 1991.

Fallon, Ivan, and James Srodes. *DeLorean: The Rise and Fall of a Dream-Maker*. London: Hamish Hamilton, 1983.

Foster, Patrick R. *American Motors: The Last Independent*. Iola, WI: Krause Publications, 1993.

Fredericks, H.A., and Allan Chambers. *Bricklin*. Potters Bark, UK: Brunswick Press, 1977.

Halberstam, David. *The Reckoning*. New York: William Morrow, 1986.

High, Steven. *Deindustrializing Montreal: Entangled Histories of Race, Residence, Class*. Montreal and Kingston: McGill-Queen's University Press, 2022.

– *Industrial Sunset: The Making of North America's Rust Belt, 1969–1984*. Toronto: University of Toronto Press, 2003.

– *One Job Town: Work, Belonging, and Betrayal in Northern Ontario*. Toronto: University of Toronto Press, 2018.

Holland, Max. *When the Machine Stopped; A Cautionary Tale of Industrial America*. Cambridge, MA: Harvard University Press, 1989.

Hyde, Charles K. *Storied Independent Automakers: Nash, Hudson, and American Motors*. Detroit: Wayne State University Press, 2009.

Jacobs, A.J. *The New Domestic Automakers in the United States and Canada: History, Impacts and Prospects*. Lanham, MD: Lexington Books, 2016.

Jenkin, Michael. *The Challenge of Diversity: Industrial Policy in the Canadian Federation*. Ottawa: Science Council of Canada, 1983.

Jolliffe, Lee. "The Bricklin: From Automobile to Place Narrative." In *Automobile Heritage and Tourism*, edited by Michael V. Conlin and Lee Jolliffe, 40–8. London: Routledge, 2016.

Koistinen, David. *Confronting Decline: The Political Economy of Deindustrialization in Twentieth-Century New England*. Gainesville: University Press of Florida, 2016.

Linkon, Sherry Lee. *The Half-Life of Deindustrialization: Working-Class Writing about Economic Restructuring*. Ann Arbor: University of Michigan Press, 2018.

Lutz, Bob. *Car Guys vs. Bean Counters: The Battle for the Soul of American Business*. New York: Portfolio, 2011.

MacKinnon, Lachlan. *Closing Sysco: Industrial Decline in Atlantic Canada's Steel City*. Toronto: University of Toronto Press, 2020.

–, and Steven High. "Deindustrialization in Canada: New Perspectives." *Labour/Le travail* 91 (Spring 2023): 13–30.

Martel, Marcel. *Not This Time: Canadians, Public Policy and the Marijuana Question*. Toronto: University of Toronto Press, 2006.

McKee, Guian A. *The Problem of Jobs: Liberalism, Race, and Deindustrialization in Philadelphia*. Chicago: University of Chicago Press, 2010.

Montigny, Edgar-André. *The Real Dope: Social, Legal, and Historical Perspectives on the Regulation of Drugs in Canada*. Toronto: University of Toronto Press, 2017.

Niedermeyer, Edward. *Ludicrious: The Unvarnised Story of Tesla Motors*. Dallas: BenBella Books, 2009.

Reid, J.G., and J.H. Reid. "The Multiple Deindustrializations of Canada's Maritime Provinces and the Evaluation of Heritage-Related Urban Regeneration." *London Journal of Canadian Studies* 31, 1 (2016): 89–112.

Reid, John. "The 1970s: The Sharpening of the Sceptical Edge." In *The Atlantic Provinces in Confederation*, edited by E.R. Forbes and D.A. Muise, 460–504. Toronto: University of Toronto Press, 1993.

Richmond, Randy, and Tom Villemaire. *Colossal Canadian Failures*. Toronto: Dundurn, 2002.

Ripley, Donald F. *Bagman: A Life in Nova Scotia Politics*. Toronto: Key Porter Books, 1993.

Rubenstein, James M. *Making and Selling Cars: Innovation and Change in the US Automotive Industry*. Baltimore: Johns Hopkins University Press, 2001.

Savoie, Donald J. *Regional Economic Development: Canada's Search for Solutions*. Toronto: University of Toronto Press, 1986.
Sheller, Mimi. "Automotive Emotions." *Theory, Culture and Society* 21, 4–5 (2004): 221–42.
Sobel, David, and Susan Meurer. *Working at Inglis: The Life and Death of a Canadian Factory*. Albany: SUNY Press, 1997.
Soni, Jimmy. *The Founders: The Story of PayPal and the Entrepreneurs Who Shaped Silicon Valley*. New York: Simon & Schuster, 2022.
Southam, Nancy, as told by Dalton Camp. *Remembering Richard: An Informal Portrait of Richard Hatfield by His Friends, Family and Colleagues*. Halifax: Formac Publishing, 1993.
Starr, Richard. *Richard Hatfield: The Seventeen-Year Saga*. Halifax: Formac Publishing, 1987.
Tupper, Allan. *Public Money in the Private Sector*. Kingston, ON: Institute of Intergovernmental Relations, 1982.
Vidal, Jordi Catalan. "The Stagflation Crisis and the European Automotive Industry, 1973–85." *Business History*, 59: 1 (2017): 4–34.

Online Sources and Other Digital Media

Dahl, Darren. "Would You Buy a Chinese Car from this Man?." Inc., 1 July 2005. https://www.inc.com/magazine/20050701/disruptor-bricklin.html.
Hegedus, Chris, executive producer. *Myth and Mogul: John DeLorean*. 2021; Netflix, documentary series.
"Jay Leno's Garage: Jeff Dunham's Under Appreciated 1975 Bricklin SV1." YouTube. https://www.youtube.com/watch?v=OSP80Xr_O58.

Conclusion and Epilogue

Scholarly Books and Articles

Aird, Alisdair. *Automotive Nightmare*. New York: Hutchinson, 1973.
Amin, Ash, ed. *Post-Fordism: A Reader*. Oxford: Blackwell, 2008.
Ayres, Edward. *What's Good for GM*. Nashville: Aurora Publishers, 1970.
Bell, Daniel. *The Coming of Post-Industrial Society: A Venture in Social Forecasting*. New York: Basic Books, 1976.
Flink, James J. "*The Car Culture* Revisited: Some Comments on the Recent Historiography of Automotive History." In *The Automobile and American Culture*, edited by David L. Lewis and Laurence Goldstein, 405–18. Ann Arbor: University of Michigan Press, 1980.
Jerome, John. *The Death of the Automobile: The Fatal Effect of the Golden Era, 1955–1970*. New York: Norton, 1972.
Krugman, Paul. *The Age of Diminished Expectations*, 3rd ed. Cambridge, MA: MIT Press, 1997.
Lewis, David L., and Laurence Goldstein, eds. *The Automobile and American Culture*. Ann Arbor: University of Michigan Press, 1980.
Minchin, Timothy J. "'The Factory of the Future': Historical Continuity and Labor Rights at Tesla." *Labor History* 62, 4 (2021): 434–53.
Munson, Richard. *Tesla: Inventor of the Modern*. New York: W.W. Norton, 2018.
Muranaga, Yuji, and Takeo Nakajima. "Mixing the Best of Toyota & GM: NUMMI to Greet 25th Anniversary." *Japan Spotlight: Economy, Culture and History* 27, 3 (2008): 17–19.
Perkins, Greg, and Johann Peter Murmann. "What Does the Success of Tesla Mean for the Future Dynamics in the Global Automobile Sector?" *Management and Organization Review* 14, 3 (2018): 471–80.

Rhomberg, Chris. *No There There: Race, Class, and Political Community in Oakland*. Berkeley: University of California Press, 2004.
Roser, Christopher. *"Faster, Better, Cheaper" in the History of Manufacturing: From the Stone Age to Lean Manufacturing and Beyond*. Boca Raton, FL: CRC Press, Taylor & Francis Group, 2017.
Roszak, Theodore. *Where the Wasteland Ends: Politics and Transcendence in Post-Industrial Society*. New York: Doubleday, 1972.
Rothschild, Emma. *Paradise Lost: The Decline of the Auto-Industrial Age*. New York: Random House, 1973.
Sandford, Charles L. "'Women's Place' in American Car Culture." In *The Automobile and American Culture*, edited by David L. Lewis and Laurence Goldstein, 137–52. Ann Arbor: University of Michigan Press, 1980.
Scheider, Kenneth. *Autokind vs. Mankind: An Analysis of Tyranny, a Proposal for Rebellion, a Plan for Reconstruction*. New York: Norton, 1971.
Shook, John. "How to Change a Culture: Lessons from NUMMI." *MIT Sloan Management Review* 51, 2 (2010): 63–8.
Toffler, Alvin. *Future Shock*. New York: Random House, 1970.
Tolliday, Steven, and Jonathan Zeitlin, eds. *Between Fordism and Flexibility: The Automobile Industry and Its Workers*. New York: St. Martin's Press 1992.
Vance, Ashlee. *Elon Musk, Tesla, SpaceX and the Quest for a Fantastic Future*. New York: HarperCollins, 2015.
White, Lawrence J. *The Automobile Industry since 1945*. 1971; Cambridge, MA: Harvard University Press, 2014.
Wigfield, Andrea. *Post-Fordism, Gender, and Work*. London: Routledge, 2018.

Online Sources and Other Digital Media

Maudsley, Dugald, dir. *The Bricklin: The Premier, the Promoter and Their Car*. Episode, *Turning Points of History*, 2004.

Archival Sources

Bentley Historical Library, Ann Arbor, MI: William Milliken Papers
Canadian Automotive Museum, Oshawa, ON: Dr. Sandy Bigman Collection
Library and Archives Canada, Ottawa, ON: Department of Industry
National Archives and Records Administration, College Park, MD: Records of the Department of the Treasury
National Automotive History Collection, Detroit MI: Bricklin Corporate Records
Public Archives of New Brunswick, Fredericton, NB: Office of Richard Hatfield, Department of Commerce and Development, and Department of Economic Development and Tourism
Walter Reuther Library, Detroit, MI: Douglas Fraser Papers and UAW-Chrysler Collection

Government Publications

Hearings Before the Committee on Armed Services, United States Senate. "Nominees Designate – Charles E. Wilson to Be Secretary of Defense … Tuesday January 15, 1953." Washington, DC: US Government Printing Office, 1953.
Hearings Before the Subcommittee on Executive Reorganization of the Committee on Government Operations. United States Congress 89th Congress, 2nd Session. "Traffic Safety: Examination and

Review of Efficiency Economy, and Coordination of Public and Private Agencies Activities and the Role of the Federal Government." 22 March 1966, Part 4, *Congressional Record.* Washington, DC: US Government Printing Office, 1966.
Historical Statistics of Canada. Various.
Historical Statistics of the United States. Various.
Statistics Canada. Various.
Synoptic Report of the Proceedings of the Legislative Assembly of New Brunswick (*Hansard*). Fredericton. Various years.
United States Bureau of Transportation Statistics. Table 1-40, US Highway Passenger Miles. https://www.bts.gov/content/us-passenger-miles.
United States International Trade Commission, *Automotive Trade Statistics 1964–80.* Washington, DC: United States International Trade Commission, 1981. https://www.usitc.gov/publications/332/pub1203.pdf.

Newspapers, Periodicals, and Trade Journals

Advertising Age
Atlantic Advocate
Australian
Automation: The Production Engineering Magazine
Automotive News
Autoweek & Competition Press
Bloomberg Business Week
Boston Globe
Brickline
Business Insider
Business Week
Calgary Herald
Camden (NJ) Courier-Post
Canada and the World
Canadian Business
Canadian Machinery and Metalworking
Canadian Press
CanWest News
Car and Driver
Chatelaine
Chicago Tribune
Columbus Dispatch
Consumer Reports
Cosmopolitan
DesignNews
Detroit Free Press
Driving
Epic Magazine
Financial Post
Financial Post Magazine
Financial Times

Financial Times of Canada
Forbes
Fortune
Fortune 500
Fredericton Daily Gleaner
Globe and Mail
Hagerty Media
Hemmings
Impetus
Industrial Design
Journal of Commerce
Kamloops Daily News
Le Devoir (Montreal)
L'Evangeline
Literary Digest
Los Angeles Times
Maclean's
Marketing Magazine (Toronto)
McClure's Magazine
Mechanix Illustrated
Moncton Times
Moncton Transcript
Motor Trend
National Post
Newsweek
New Yorker
New York Review
New York Times
Orlando Sentinel
People
Playboy
Prince George Citizen
PR Newswire
Reuters
Road & Track
Road Test
Rolling Stone
Saint John Evening Times
Saint John Evening Times Globe
Saint John Telegraph-Journal
Saint John Times Globe
Saturday Evening Post
Saturday Night
Sherbrooke Record
Sonora News
Special Interest Autos
Tampa Tribune Times

Techcrunch
Time Magazine
Toronto Star
Vancouver Sun
Vox
Wall Street Journal
Ward's Dealer Business
Washington Monthly
Washington (PA) Observer-Reporter
Washington Post
Windsor Star

Annual Reports

DesRosiers Automotive Yearbook. Richmond Hill, ON: DesRosiers Automotive Consultants, various years.

General Motors. *Annual Report*. Detroit: GM Corporation, various years.

Interviews

Malcolm Bricklin, interviews with the author, 6 April 2013 and 5 October 2022.

Illustrations and Credits

1.14 Bricklin behind the podium, Saint John plant opening, August 1974. Source: Provincial Archives of New Brunswick, P228/55.
2.1 Henry Ford, 1921. Source: From the Collections of The Henry Ford, gift of Ford Motor Company, 84.1.1660.P.O.3015.
2.2 William Crapo Durant, c. 1915–20. Source: Library of Congress, George Grantham Bain Collection, LC-DIG-ggbain-21075.
2.3 Alfred P. Sloan, 1937. Source: Sloan: Library of Congress, Harris & Ewing Collection, photograph by Harris & Ewing, LC-DIG-hec-22048.
2.4 Lee Iacocca, 1970s. Source: *New York Times.*
2.5 Lee Iacocca on the cover of *Time*, 1964, 1983, and 1985. Source: *Time* magazine.
2.6 Bricklin, Las Vegas, 1974. Source: Detroit Public Library, National Automotive History Collection, Bricklin, file 14-1-08, MS57.
3.1 General Motors' Corvair de luxe 700 ad, 1960.
3.2 Ralph Nader testifying before Congress, 1966. Source: *New York Times.*
3.3 Ralph Nader on the cover of *Time*, 12 December 1969. Source: *Time* magazine.
3.4 Advertisement for a 1978 Civic. Source: Honda.
3.5 Bricklin safety specs. Source: Detroit Public Library, National Automotive History Collection, Bricklin Canada Ltd., file 14-3-16; 14-3-17, MS57.
3.6 Bricklin advertising. Source: Provincial Archives of New Brunswick, Bricklin promotional brochure, file 5321-1, box 83.
3.7 SV1 panels, 1974. Source: Detroit Public Library, National Automotive History Collection, Bricklin Canada Ltd., file 15-7-17, MS57.
3.8 Bricklin at the launch of his safety car, 6 August 1974. Source: Provincial Archives of New Brunswick, P228-58.
4.1 Bricklin, c. 1974. Source: Provincial Archives of New Brunswick, RS417-76-12-i.
4.2 Lambretta scooters, New York City, 1970s. Source: Getty Images/Walter Leporati.
4.3 Subaru 360 ad, 1969.
4.4 An SV1 under guard, February 1974. Source: Detroit Public Library, National Automotive History Collection, Bricklin Canada Ltd., file 15-6-29, MS57.
4.5 Bricklin with Paul Newman and Bobby Unser, February 1974. Source: Detroit Public Library, National Automotive History Collection, Bricklin Canada Ltd., file 4-1-01, MS57.
4.6 Bricklin with Senator Barry Goldwater, c. 1975. Source: Detroit Public Library, National Automotive History Collection, Bricklin Canada Ltd., file 14-2-01.
4.7 Bricklin with *Auto News*'s Wally Scott, c. 1975. Source: Detroit Public Library, National Automotive History Collection, Bricklin Canada Ltd., file 14-1-13.
4.8 A Bricklin as the pace car at the Arizona 150/Bricklin 150, 1974. Source: Detroit Public Library, National Automotive History Collection, Bricklin Canada Ltd., file 14-2-1, MS57.
4.9 SV1 under wraps, New York City, June 1974. Source: Detroit Public Library, National Automotive History Collection, Bricklin Canada Ltd., file 15-6-09, MS57.
4.10 Albert Bricklin and Richard Hatfield, New York City, June 1974. Source: Detroit Public Library, National Automotive History Collection, Bricklin Canada Ltd., file 14-2-13, MS57.
4.11 The stylish, nonconformist auto entrepreneur. Source: Detroit Public Library, National Automotive History Collection, Bricklin Canada Ltd., file 14-2-17, MS57.
4.12 At the Tavern on the Green, Central Park. Source: Detroit Public Library, National Automotive History Collection, Bricklin Canada Ltd., file 15-6-13, MS57.
4.13 SV1 tilted on a spit. Source: Detroit Public Library, National Automotive History Collection, Bricklin Canada Ltd., file 15-6-01, MS57.

Index

The letter f following a page number indicates a figure.